P. A. Stolypin

P. A. Stolypin

The Search for Stability in Late Imperial Russia

Abraham Ascher

Stanford University Press
Stanford, California
2001

Stanford University Press
Stanford, California
© 2001 by the Board of Trustees of the
Leland Stanford Junior University
Printed in the United States of America

Library of Congress Cataloging-in-Publication Data

Ascher, Abraham.
  P. A. Stolypin : the search for stability in late imperial Russia /
Abraham Ascher.
    p. cm.
  Includes bibliographical references and index.
  ISBN 0-8047- 3977-3 (alk. paper)
   1. Stolypin, Petr Arkadevich, 1862–1911. 2. Statesmen—Russia—
Biography. 3. Russia—Politics and government—1904–1914. I. Title.
DK254.S595 A9   2001
947.08'3'092—dc21
[B]   00-063520

This book is printed on acid-free, archival-quality paper.

Original printing 2001

Last figure below indicates year of this printing:
10   09   08   07   06   05   04   03   02   01

Typeset by John Feneron in 9.5/12.5 Trump Mediaeval

To my family

Acknowledgments

In writing this book I have received support and help from many institutions and individuals, and I should like to express my appreciation to them. Financial support from the National Endowment of the Humanities, the Institute for Advanced Studies at the Hebrew University of Jerusalem, the American Council of Learned Societies, the Earhart Foundation, and the Research Foundation of the City University of New York enabled me to take time off from teaching and made possible research trips to archives in Europe. I was cordially received in various archives, all of which made available documents relevant to my subject: the Bakhmetev Archive at Columbia University, the Russian State Archive in St. Petersburg, the State Archives in Helsinki, the Public Record Office in London, the Haus-Hof-und-Staatsarchiv in Vienna, and the Politisches Archiv des Auswärtigen Amts in Bonn. The State Archive in the Russian Federation in Moscow graciously permitted the photocopying of numerous documents on my topic. Librarians at Columbia University, the Slavonic Library of Helsinki University, the library of the Graduate School of the City University, and the New York Public Library responded graciously to all my requests for books, pamphlets, and newspapers. Mr. Edward Kasinec and his staff at the New York Public Library not only provided me with the material I asked for but also on occasion came up with additional sources.

Sage Publications gave me permission to reprint large parts of my article, "Prime Minister P. A. Stolypin and his 'Jewish' Advisor," which appeared in the *Journal of Contemporary History* 30, no. 3 (July 1995), pp. 513–32. I should also point out that for my discussion of Stolypin's role in the turbulent events from 1905 to 1907 I have drawn heavily on my previous work on the Revolution of 1905 published by Stanford University Press, though I have added a fair amount of new material that I found in my necessarily more extensive research on Stolypin.

I am grateful to friends who read the manuscript and gave me the benefit of their thoughtful criticisms: Paul Avrich, Julian Franklin, Guenter Lewy, Allen McConnell, Marc Raeff, and Daniel Orlovsky. As

in the past, Stanford University Press has encouraged me in this project, and their editors, John Feneron and Martin Hanft, were extremely
helpful in improving the manuscript. I also want to thank my family,
and especially my wife, Anna S. Ascher, for their encouragement and
forbearance during the many years I devoted to the writing of the
book.

The shortcomings of the book are, of course, my responsibility.

A.A.

Contents

(14 pages of photographs follow page 260)

A Note to the Reader

During Stolypin's lifetime, Russia was still using the Julian calendar, which was then thirteen days behind the Gregorian calendar used in the West. I have given all dates in the text according to the Russian calendar; I have also used the Russian date alone in the notes for issues of newspapers and other periodicals, which were often dated in both forms on their covers.

The transliteration of Russian names inevitably poses a problem, and I have opted to use the forms most commonly known for the handful of people the reader is likely to be familiar with already: Tsar Nicholas, Count Witte, Tolstoy. Otherwise I follow the Library of Congress transliteration system, modified to eliminate soft and hard signs. The list below is designed to define certain terms and offices mentioned in the text.

Chief procurator of the Most Holy Synod: the chief administrator of the Russian Orthodox Church, with direct access to the tsar.

City governor: the chief authority in larger cities such as St. Petersburg, Moscow, Odessa, and Sevastopol; his powers were equivalent to those of a governor.

Dvorianstvo: nobility.

Gendarmes: members of a special police force under the direct authority of the Ministry of Internal Affairs.

Governor: the chief authority in the provinces; responsible to the minister of internal affairs.

Governor-general: the chief authority in a few important provinces (notably St. Petersburg and Moscow) and in the borderlands; his rank was equivalent to that of a minister, and he had direct access to the tsar.

Guberniia: a province.

Kulak (a "fist"): a well-to-do peasant who owned a fairly large farm, who could afford to hire some laborers, and who often lent money to other peasants.

Okhrana: security police.

State Council: an appointed body of dignitaries, established in 1810, that advised the tsar on legislation.

Uezd: a county, including a city or town and several rural districts (volosti).

Volost: a district in rural regions.

Zemtsy (sing. zemets): individuals active in zemstvo affairs.

European Russia in 1905

Introduction

No Russian statesman has ever enjoyed so meteoric a rise to the heights of power and endured as rapid and humiliating a fall as Petr Arkadevich Stolypin, prime minister and minister of internal affairs from 1906 to 1911. Nor has any other statesman ever been the object, at one and the same time, of as much uncritical adulation and unrestrained vilification. These divergent assessments have not been confined to his policies, which sought to stem the revolutionary tide of 1905 and bring about fundamental changes in Russian society and politics. There has also been much controversy about Stolypin's personality. Many of his contemporaries disdained him as a man who lusted for power, as a cold-hearted politician without scruples in pursuing his career. Allegedly lacking a vision for Russia, he merely implemented the plans and directives of the tsar or ambitious politicians in St. Petersburg. Others, however, admired him as a noble, fearless man, a leader of uncommon intelligence, selflessly devoted to public service and to the well-being of Russia.[1]

In large measure, the different assessments of Stolypin were rooted in the circumstances of his rise to power. When Stolypin joined the government and assumed the critical post of minister of internal affairs at the relatively young age of forty-four, he was a person without national stature, his administrative and political experience having been limited to service in the provinces. His most important post had been the governorship of Saratov, where he gained a reputation as a forceful administrator adroit in containing widespread unrest. Firmly committed to maintaining law and order, he also advocated reform, particularly in the countryside, where he believed that the peasants should be encouraged to abandon the commune, which he considered largely responsible for their poverty. But beyond a small circle of senior officials in St. Petersburg, Stolypin was virtually unknown. When he arrived in the capital in April of 1906, very few even within the political elite suspected that he might emerge as the dominant figure in the government, overshadowing men with decades of experience at the pinnacle of power. Nor did anyone expect him to possess the qualities necessary to cope with the political distemper widespread after the upheavals of 1905. His rapid rise to eminence did not endear him to senior officials who had been replaced or who had never succeeded in reaching the highest positions of government.

Within weeks of his arrival in St. Petersburg, Stolypin applied the full force of governmental authority to stamp out unrest, a policy bound to provoke criticism. The left lost no time reviling him as an unprincipled and ruthless politician who would bend every effort to maintain autocratic rule in Russia. Within short order, leaders of various sectors of Russian liberalism became almost as passionate in denouncing him. But moderates, conservatives, and reactionaries initially praised the new minister as a visionary and charismatic leader who would succeed in stabilizing the country, which had teetered on the edge of chaos during the revolutionary turbulence of 1905. Abroad, in most Western countries, politicians and journalists viewed him as a remarkable statesman, with talents comparable to those of the legendary Bismarck, a man destined to revitalize Russia and restore its prestige after the ignominious defeat by the Japanese in 1904 and 1905. It was a comparison that Stolypin did not discourage. Long before he moved to St. Petersburg he frequently suggested that his views on social and economic questions were modeled on those of Bismarck. And, ironically, just as German conservatives had distrusted Bismarck, a growing number of rightists in Russia lost confidence in Stolypin soon after he became prime minister. The extremists on the right turned against Stolypin because they feared that he planned to restore order not merely by resorting to the whip but also by introducing reforms that would fundamentally alter the prevailing social and economic system. If the reactionaries were not quite as vociferous as the left in castigating Stolypin, their barbs were more effective in weakening him politically because they enjoyed access to the tsar and his entourage at court. Early in 1911 a sizable number of moderates also turned against Stolypin because of his willful behavior, leaving him with the support of only the conservatives, who represented a minority, albeit a significant minority, of the political class. By the time he was assassinated in September of that year—the eighteenth attempt on his life—the tsar's confidence in him had plunged. The prime minister now appeared to be a spent force, incapable of continuing to guide the ship of state.

The voluminous journalistic, polemical, or scholarly writings on Stolypin that have appeared over the past eighty years or so reflect all these divergent evaluations of his role as head of the Russian government. In the Soviet Union, historians invariably echoed Lenin, who attacked Stolypin with special venom because he saw in him an astute statesman whose dual program of repression and reform might well have succeeded in undermining the revolutionary cause. Lenin denounced the prime minister as the "hangman-in-chief," or simply as a hangman, tyrant, reactionary, or "pogrom maker."[2] Soviet scholars made no attempt to write a full-scale biography of Stolypin but produced, instead, elaborately documented works to substantiate Lenin's charges.

Among Soviet academics, A. Ia. Avrekh, the most prolific historian of the Stolypin era, set the tone. He examined numerous aspects of the prime minister's tenure in office and invariably concluded that the man's sole concern was to preserve the old order. Stolypin, in Avrekh's view, constantly maneuvered between political groups, manipulated party leaders, and resorted to the most pernicious repression, all to consolidate the autocratic regime. But these efforts, no matter how ingenious, could not succeed. The situation in Russia was revolutionary, Avrekh insisted, and no strategy, tactic, or policy that the government adopted could forestall the inevitable collapse of tsarism and the triumph of socialism. Avrekh's assessment of Stolypin, accepted as dogma by almost all Soviet historians, thus served a political purpose, to buttress the Soviet leaders' claim of legitimacy for their political system.[3]

Views of Stolypin in the West have been more diversified and nuanced. Although many scholars emphasize the harshness of his police measures and contend that his goal of revitalizing the monarchical order was almost certainly unattainable, they do not deny that he was moved by a grand vision for Russia, the establishment of domestic tranquillity and the modernization of the empire.[4] And there is a corps of scholars and writers, several of them émigrés from Russia, who have portrayed Stolypin in a distinctly favorable light. They have stressed his heroic qualities, his reformist zeal, his passion for justice, and his "straightforward" patriotism. Leonid Strakhovsky, a professor of history at the University of Toronto, referred to him as "a true guardian of the constitutional regime." And almost without exception the admirers of Stolypin have seen him as the "only statesman who could have prevented revolution."[5] The warmest praise was heaped upon Stolypin by Aleksandr Solzhenitsyn, who, in his *August 1914*, devoted some seventy-four pages to the prime minister's career and personality and another seventy to the circumstances surrounding his assassination. Stolypin, according to Solzhenitsyn, "had a constant anxious awareness of all Russia as though it were there in his breast. Unsleeping compassion, a love that nothing could alter. But though his love was all gentleness and tenderness, when anything threatened the things that mattered to him he was as unyielding as an oak. All his life was like that." Stolypin's "actions were never at any time governed by self-interest."[6] The crudest and most unconvincing adulation of Stolypin was written by a Russian émigré in 1928, a certain F. M. Goriachkin who, in a tirade against the revolutionaries who took over Russia in 1917, hailed the prime minister for having been the "First Russian Fascist," in effect a forerunner of Mussolini.[7]

During the declining years of the Soviet Union, when intellectuals tried to grapple with the question of when Russia took a wrong turn into Communist despotism, interest in Stolypin exploded and the country was overspread by an avalanche of publications on the Stolypin era: newspaper articles, scholarly debates in learned journals, reprints of memoirs, documents (especially those bearing on the assassination), speeches by Stolypin, as well as assessments of his years in office long unavailable in the Soviet Union. Activists who admired Stolypin hurled the same words at defenders of Communism that Stolypin had hurled at revolutionaries in the Duma in the spring of 1907: "They need great upheavals; we need a great Russia."

Most recently, on July 8, 2000, President Vladimir Putin gave what has been described as a "state of the state" address to the Federal Assembly of Russia, in which he made an explicit reference to Stolypin. The thrust of Putin's speech was that Russia must be modernized through fundamental reform if it is to "survive as a nation, as a civilization." He declared himself to be in favor of a thorough democratization of the country and stressed two major goals that Stolypin had pursued, political stability and a stable economy. In elaborating on his program, Putin proposed several initiatives undertaken by Stolypin over ninety years ago, most notably the establishment of "the legal foundation for private property rights where they have not so far been established. This primarily concerns land [and] real estate." In addition, Putin hearkened back to Stolypin in insisting that Russia must have an "effective state" capable both of guaranteeing "human rights" and of serving as the driving force in enacting a wide range of reforms of the country's political, economic, and social institutions. His ultimate goal, Putin announced, was the creation of a "civil society" that would become "the government's equal partner." But Putin warned that this would be difficult because the Russian people had little experience in dealing with "the false conflicts between the values of personal freedom and the state's interests." It was at this point that he invoked Stolypin's name: "So far, we have not always succeeded in combining patriotic responsibility for the country's future with what Stolypin once described as civil freedoms." President Putin correctly diagnosed Stolypin's most intractable problem as prime minister, the formation of a "strong state" in which the people's right to exercise their civil liberties and political rights would be guaranteed. But Putin was misguided in suggesting that in Stolypin's time there was a "false conflict" between these two goals. The conflict between them was real, and recent news accounts from Russia suggest that it continues to be one of the more troublesome issues that the political leadership of the country will have to confront.[8]

Generally, the arguments about Stolypin over the past decade have not been fundamentally different from those of the previous eighty years, but there has been a dramatic shift in the dominant attitude. Much more so than ever before, Stolypin has been heralded as a farsighted statesman whose policies were precisely the ones Russia needed to develop into a prosperous, stable, and powerful country. For example, in a scholarly article published in 1994, A. I. Glagolev criticized Soviet historians for mentioning Stolypin only in "an abusive context" and contended that the prime minister ranks with such outstanding reformers as Peter the Great, M. M. Speransky, N. S. Mordvinov, E. F. Kankrin, and P. O. Kiselev, among others.[9] In addition, in recent years Stolypin has been widely hailed in the former Soviet Union as a man who, had he lived longer and had he continued to lead the government, could have prevented the agony of revolution. Russian scholars and journalists have paid special attention to Stolypin's agrarian program, the premise of which was the conversion of Russia's peasantry into owners of private property. The absence in Imperial Russia of a large class of people with their own property, it is now frequently argued, explains the failure of the rule of law and democratic institutions to take root. Some writers have been carried away by their enthusiasm for Stolypin and have claimed that the standard of living in Russia was higher in 1913 than in the 1980s.[10]

The adulation of Stolypin reached a high point during a two-day conference on October 16 and 17, 1997, at Omsk in honor of his 135th birthday. Organized by the Administration of the Omsk District (oblast), the Omsk State University, the Center of Russian Culture, and the Omsk branch of the United Institute of History, Philology and Philosophy, the conference featured more than thirty papers on the "reformist activities of P. A. Stolypin." Although the participants acknowledged that many of Stolypin's proposals were not implemented during his lifetime, there was a consensus that he was "one of the most important politicians and statesmen" in Russian history and that the "ideas of the great reformer have not lost their relevance for contemporary Russia." The conference passed a series of resolutions that called for further studies of Stolypin's "reformist activities" and urged the authorities in Omsk to propose to the government in Moscow that it consider ways of memorializing "the great Russian reformer." In the meantime, the city of Omsk should name one of its streets for the former prime minister.[11]

My own interest in Stolypin did not grow out of this contemporary fascination with his reform proposals, at least not on a conscious level. When I worked on my history of the Revolution of 1905 I realized that although the many studies of Stolypin contain much important information, they do not do justice to the complexities of his personality and policies. There are only two comprehensive biographies of Stolypin. The study by Mary Schaeffer Conroy, based on extensive research, is an essential starting point for scholars interested in the Stolypin period, but it appeared in 1976, before the archives in the Soviet Union were readily accessible to Western scholars. The second, by Ludwik Bazylow, is in Polish, which I do not read.[12] Bazylow did consult the relevant archives in Leningrad and Moscow, and insofar as I could judge from his use of sources it is an impressive work of scholarship that sheds much light on Stolypin's administration when he was prime minister and on the political parties represented in the Third Duma. Although Bazylow is sympathetic to Leninist interpretations of the Stolypin era, he appears to have avoided the crude simplifications often encountered in Soviet historical works of the 1970s. That is confirmed by reviews of his book.[13] But Bazylow chose not to pay attention to the handwritten correspondence in the archives, which contains interesting information on Stolypin's personality as well as on his role as governor of Saratov from 1903 to 1906. Nor did Bazylow consult the archives in Helsinki or Western Europe, which also have a fair amount of material by and on Stolypin.

One reason for the failure of Soviet historians to undertake a full-scale biography was no doubt their inclination to minimize the role of individuals in shaping the course of history; they tended, instead, to emphasize the primacy of social groups and the role of various impersonal factors. I do not share that outlook. My own reading of history has persuaded me that however important these factors may be, strong individuals have often intervened in the historical process and have produced results that appeared to contemporaries to be highly improbable. And there is little doubt in my mind that by force of personality Stolypin succeeded in reestablishing governmental authority in the years 1906 and 1907 and in implementing the agrarian reforms, the most far-reaching reforms in Russia since the emancipation of the peasants in 1861. He also placed on the political agenda a series of reform proposals that touched on virtually all aspects of Russian society and were designed to reshape the country in a fundamental way.

Whether Stolypin's achievements were desirable or progressive, a favorite concern of Soviet scholars, is a legitimate question for historians, but it is not the only one or even the most critical one. For five pivotal years in Late Imperial Russia, Stolypin was, next to the tsar, the dominant figure in the political arena, and he played the major role in seeking to shore up a crumbling edifice. In 1911, when an assassin's bullet ended his life, Russia, though far from free of acute social and political strife, was considerably less turbulent than in 1906. For that reason alone Stolypin deserves to be studied in depth. The student of Russian history is justifiably curious about the personality, policies, strategies, and tactics of the leader who succeeded where others had failed.

Ideological preconceptions have not, however, been the only deterrent to the writing of a full-scale biography of Stolypin. The archival material on the prime minister is skimpy, making it extremely difficult for the biographer to locate the kind of personal information he needs to present a convincing portrait. Shortly after Stolypin's death a commission of seven officials collected a wide range of papers from Stolypin's office in the Elagin Palace, his apartment in St. Petersburg, and from his estate in Kolnoberzhe, Kovno Province. Most of the official documents were stored in the state archives in the capital, and some of the more personal items, such as letters by and to Stolypin, were handed over to his family. A few important items were published in *Krasnyi arkhiv* during the 1920s and many more in the documentary collection on the Revolution of 1905–7 that was published in the years from 1955 to 1965,[14] but much of the material in the hands of the state and the family was somehow lost. In 1961 the documents that remained were assembled in Leningrad and are now stored in the *Rossiiskii gosudarstvennyi istoricheskii arkhiv* (Russian State Historical Archive, or RGIA) in St. Petersburg. I refer to these as the Stolypin Archive.[15] In addition, there are some documents relevant to Stolypin's political activities in the *Gosudarstvennyi Arkhiv Rossiiskoi Federatsii* (State Archive of the Russian Federation, or GARF) in Moscow. Finally, two state archives in Helsinki contain a large number of documents bearing on Stolypin's policy toward Finland, a highly contentious issue during his period as prime minister.

Unfortunately, in none of these collections are there any unpublished documents on the earliest period of Stolypin's life and career. Moreover, only a portion of Stolypin's personal correspondence has survived. But it would be a mistake to conclude that the material is insufficient for a reasonably comprehensive biography. For one thing, there are some 230 letters from Stolypin to his wife, the vast majority of them written between 1903 and 1906, a critical period in Stolypin's career and in the history of Russia. For the most part, these letters are highly personal, interesting because they provide details of the extraordinarily close relationship between Stolypin and his wife and family. But a fair number of the letters touch on major political events and shed new light on his attitude toward the revolutionary turbulence in Saratov in 1905 and 1906 when he was governor of the province. The letters also contain some vivid descriptions of his meetings with leading political figures in St. Petersburg and, most important, of his meetings with Tsar Nicholas II. And a letter by Stolypin to his wife on August 28, 1911, four days before his assassination, indicates that his mood at that difficult time in his career was more self-confident than has been assumed. In addition, the archive contains copies of various documents he drafted as governor of Grodno in 1902, as well as notes that Stolypin jotted down to clarify his own thinking on some major issues. These notes are extremely valuable not only in revealing how Stolypin reached decisions on complex matters but also in providing new insights on what motivated him in adopting one or another decision.

Moreover, the archives of the German and British foreign ministries have numerous lengthy and informative reports from ambassadors stationed in St. Petersburg that were especially rich in information on Stolypin.[16] The reports are not simply stodgy accounts by bureaucrats on developments in Russia. Stolypin liked to cultivate goodwill among foreigners and often spoke candidly to foreign diplomats about his aspirations, program, conflicts with the Duma, and the political manipulations at the tsarist court. The single most informative source on Stolypin's personal affairs is the volume of reminiscences of his daughter, Maria Petrovna von Bock. Von Bock was devoted to her father, and her memoirs frequently strike a hagiographical note. But I have not found any outright inaccuracies in her work; indeed, on several controversial issues, such as her father's relationship with the tsar and the imperial family, her accounts are corroborated by ambassadorial reports and by memoirs of the prime minister's contemporaries.

Not to be overlooked in any attempt to understand Stolypin's role as a statesman are his speeches in the Duma and State Council. Eloquent, detailed, and precise, they not only yield important information on his policies but also help us to understand his personality: his self-assuredness and determination to press forward with his program. Finally, there is the daily and periodical press, which after the Revolution of 1905 was free to publish almost anything the editors considered newsworthy. Journalists succeeded in obtaining both hard information and gossip from senior officials, Duma deputies, and members of the State Council, and much of the time their accounts of how decisions on major issues were reached at the top echelons of government and of intrigues at all levels of authority are remarkably revealing and accurate.

The Stolypin who emerges from an examination of the extant documents is quite different from the cold-hearted, ruthless ogre often encountered in scholarly works. Indeed, no one-sided characterization of his personality and conduct can possibly provide an accurate portrayal of the man because it misses an essential feature, the complex, even divergent, impulses that motivated his conduct. A few examples will suffice. It is true that he did not shrink from the use of force to stamp out unrest and that at times he resorted to force more extensively than could possibly be justified, but he was not bloodthirsty. In fact, he lamented the use of force and preferred nonviolent means to curb the opposition. Nor was he a man without principles, prepared to advance his own career at all costs. Almost from the moment he became interested in public affairs as a young man in his twenties he concluded that Russia must adopt major reforms to develop into a prosperous, stable, and powerful country. By the time he assumed national office in 1906 he had developed a fairly sophisticated vision for Russia that he sought to implement as prime minister. Although deeply committed to Russian nationalism and to the strengthening of the Russian state, he was not a narrow-minded, intolerant bigot. He remained faithful to the end of his life to the principle of monarchical rule and occasionally he himself acted willfully, yet he did not consider it advisable to abolish the elected legislature as an institution or to deprive it of all authority. Even though many of the doctrines and tactics of the extremists on the right appalled him, he occasionally sought their support and even assisted them financially. Like all successful politicians, he could be pragmatic when it suited his purposes.

Moreover, despite his public demeanor as an unfeeling man, he was capable of expressing deep emotions, an aspect of his personality that emerges forcefully in his correspondence with his wife, which has never before been closely examined. On one matter he was unyielding, his determination to do his duty to his monarch, country, and family. His devotion to "duty," a word that appears frequently in his private letters, is not surprising in view of his profound religiosity. The word "God" also appears frequently in those letters, and there can be no doubt about the authenticity of his faith or about the depth of his devotion to Russian Orthodoxy.

In depicting Stolypin as a far more complicated—and interesting—man than the standard description of him in much of the scholarly literature, my aim is not to glorify him. When I began this study I had no idea what my portrait of him would look like. In fact, some of the material I found in what remained of his archive in St. Petersburg astonished me, and I studied it with special care. I do not intend to ignore his blemishes, but at the same time I do not believe it would be appropriate to ignore the evidence in the documents, published and unpublished, that reveal him to have been less single-minded—and hence more human—than I had been led to believe.

My study of the sources on Stolypin have also made me more conscious than I had been of the pivotal role of Stolypin in both domestic as well as foreign affairs during the years from 1906 to 1911. This may seem obvious and banal, but it should be noted that according to the Fundamental Laws of 1906 the prime minister was not slated to play a dominant role in all affairs of state. Foreign and military affairs were to remain under the direct control of the tsar. Formally, the establishment of a united government, a major goal of Count Witte while he was prime minister from October 1905 till April 1906 and subsequently of Stolypin, was not fully achieved. The ministers of war and of foreign affairs reported directly to the tsar and could bypass the prime minister and the cabinet on issues relating to their respective departments. But we now know that in fact Stolypin did not confine himself to purely domestic issues, where he was clearly the dominant voice. He also insisted on making his mark—with a fair amount of success, it should be noted—in foreign and military affairs. Stolypin was unbending in his determination to keep Russia out of foreign entanglements that could embroil the country in war. Weakened by the debacle in the conflict with Japan in 1904–5 and by the domestic strife of the Revolution of 1905, the country could not, in Stolypin's view, contemplate an assertive policy in the international sphere. The prime minister prevailed on this issue in the highest councils of the government and, in fact, according to a recent, authoritative study of the subject, Russian policy continued to "bear the imprint of Stolypin's outlook in foreign affairs" for three years after his assassination, until early in 1914.[17]

This aspect of his influence on national politics is rarely touched upon in the passionate debates over the significance for Russian history of Stolypin's assassination. But the absence of a powerful figure in the cabinet firmly committed to a pacific foreign policy certainly had a major bearing on the government's decisions in the summer of 1914. Some dignitaries, most notably the former minister of internal affairs, P. N. Durnovo, continued to urge the tsar to stay on the sidelines in the event of a European conflagration, and their reasoning was similar to Stolypin's. But without a strong voice in the cabinet and at court they had no chance of prevailing.

A biographical study of Stolypin also demonstrates, once again, that the bureaucracy and the nobility of Imperial Russia were far from monolithic. At first glance, there was little in Stolypin's upbringing or social background to suggest that he would favor economic, social, and political changes abhorred by most members of his social milieu and many of his acquaintances. He was born into a family of nobles with deep roots in Russian history; he enjoyed the advantages of wealth, privilege, and education; and he moved steadily and easily up the ladder of the bureaucracy. Yet at an early stage in his life, when he was in his early thirties, he had concluded that if Russia was to be a strong and prosperous country it would have to be thoroughly modernized. This is not to suggest that Stolypin was a constitutionalist in our sense of the word, much less a liberal. He never abandoned his devotion to the monarchy and remained convinced that the tsar must continue to play a vital role in the empire.

Stolypin can best be described as an authoritarian reformer, or as a pragmatic conservative, but by itself that does not make him unique among Russian statesmen. He was, as one of his closest advisers, S. E. Kryzhanovskii, put it, a "new phenomenon" on the Russian scene because he was the first political leader to seek support not only from the traditional center of power, the monarchy, but also from the public at large. He recognized that unless the masses in Russia were transformed into full citizens who participated at some level in the political process, the fires of revolution would not be put out and lasting tranquillity would not be achieved. Even though he drastically and illegally changed the parliamentary system of 1906 and on several occasions resorted to extraparliamentary methods to introduce change, he always insisted that an elected body must remain and must participate meaningfully in the business of government. That conviction, as much as anything else, marked him off from the extremists of the right and from the tsar.

In the end, it was the extremist opposition to Stolypin and the failure

of Tsar Nicholas to support his policies that undermined many of his reform proposals and weakened him as a government leader, though no
one can say with certainty what his political fate would have been had
he not been assassinated. Despite his loyalty to the monarchy, his success in emasculating the liberal and left opposition, and his fervor after
1909 in championing the nationalist cause within the empire, Stolypin
could not retain the support of those he was trying to save. There is an
element of Greek tragedy in all this. The tsar, his entourage, and the ultraconservatives could not bring themselves to yield a portion of their
privileges and prerogatives in return for a reduced, though still significant, role in a changed Russia. It is not at all certain that had they been
more farsighted and willing to make concessions that Stolypin's policies
would have succeeded in modernizing and stabilizing the empire. But
from the standpoint of the guardians of the old order there does not seem
to have been a more promising alternative. Which is why a study of
Stolypin is so instructive about the fate of the Russian Empire.

1

The Early Years

Petr Arkadevich Stolypin was born in 1862 into an aristocratic and wealthy family with a long and distinguished history of service to the Russian monarchy. The name can be traced all the way to the late sixteenth century, when a Gregory Stolypin was inscribed on a list of nobles in the chronicles, the Church records of major events in Russian history. In the mid-seventeenth century one of Gregory's descendants participated in a war between Russia and Poland and a century later another descendant died fighting against Pugachev's rebellion, the largest jacquerie in the eighteenth century before the French Revolution. But the Stolypins did not achieve national stature until the early nineteenth century, when Arkadii Alekseevich, our Stolypin's grandfather, a close friend of the statesman Michael M. Speransky, was appointed senator and chief procurator of one of the Senate's departments.* Stolypin's father, a professional soldier, fought in the Crimean War and the Russo-Turkish War in 1877 and rose to the rank of lieutenant general. He served for a time as adjutant to Tsar Alexander II and from 1877 to 1878 was governor-general of Eastern Rumelia; during the last six years of his life (1892–99) he occupied the post of commandant of the Kremlin.

Petr Arkadevich's mother, Natalia Mikhailovna, came from an equally illustrious family. She was the daughter of Prince Mikhail Dmitrievich Gorchakov, who, during his long career in government service, had been viceroy of Poland and commander in chief in the Crimea. Her uncle, Alexander Mikhailovich Gorchakov, was for twenty-six years (from 1856 to 1882) the minister of foreign affairs.[1]

Both of Stolypin's parents were highly cultivated people who socialized with some notable men of letters. His mother, an intelligent and well-educated person, had a passion for literature and had made the ac-

---

*Created by Peter I in 1711 to serve as a temporary government during his absence from the capital, the Senate evolved in the nineteenth century into a supreme court and administrative supervisory agency. Senators were appointed by the tsar.

quaintance of Gogol and Lermontov.[2] His father, Arkadii Dmitrievich, was an accomplished musician who owned a Stradivarius, which he played with a fair degree of skill and on which he composed several scores. He was also an amateur sculptor who counted among his friends Count Lev Tolstoy, whom he met in 1855 in the army during a military sortie in the Crimean War. Over the succeeding few decades, the Stolypin family occasionally visited Tolstoy at his home in Iasnaia Poliana, and Tolstoy met all the Stolypin children. But eventually the two families drifted apart. General Stolypin scorned Tolstoy's spiritualism and what he considered to be the writer's romantic view of the peasants with whom Tolstoy sought to cultivate close ties. By the same token, Tolstoy disapproved of the general's intimacy with court circles after he had assumed the post of commandant of the Kremlin. Nevertheless, Tolstoy's failure to attend the general's funeral in 1899 deeply hurt the Stolypin family.[3] But Tolstoy's personal relationship with the Stolypins helps explain why he felt free in 1907 to send a personal plea to the prime minister to abandon his repressive policies.

Not much is known about Stolypin's childhood and adolescence. He spent his earliest years on the family estate in Srednikovo near Moscow, but when he was still a young child his parents settled in Kovno province, a region in the northwestern part of the empire in which the peasants were predominantly Lithuanian and the landlords largely Polish. He received a solid and traditional education. He picked up a fair amount of English from his English governess, and his German and French tutors gave him a good grounding in their respective tongues. In his correspondence with his wife he would write in all those languages, especially when he expressed his affection for her; often the language was stylistically and grammatically rather quaint and, at times even amusing, but its meaning was always clear. The family estate at Kolnoberzhe, Kovno province, had a library with some ten thousand books, and the young Stolypin read widely in literature and art. He was especially fond of Turgenev's novels and the poetry of A. K. Tolstoy and A. N. Apukhtin. Apukhtin, a writer who achieved a degree of prominence in the 1880s, was an occasional visitor at the estate, and Stolypin remained on friendly terms with him.

The second of three sons, Stolypin seems to have been brought up in a household that was close-knit and affectionate. The one major tragedy was the death of his older brother, killed in a duel about which we have no details. According to some reports, Petr Stolypin also fought a duel with the man who had killed his brother and suffered a wound in his right arm, which remained partially paralyzed for the rest of his life. But according to more credible accounts, Stolypin's arm withered as a result of a mysterious ailment while he was a teenager. Several operations failed to correct the deformity, and for the rest of his life Stolypin wrote with some difficulty. He would hold the pen in his right hand and guide it with his left.[4] The deformity made it impossible for him to follow in the footsteps of his father and those of his older brother, both of whom had pursued a military career. He also had to give up his favorite hobby, drawing.

Stolypin did not inherit his father's musical gifts or his penchant for what might be called good living, but physically, intellectually, and temperamentally he very much resembled the older man. Even as a youngster Stolypin was tall and cut an impressive figure; he was also bright and showed a lively interest in contemporary affairs. He seems at all times to have shared his father's conservative outlook; there is no evidence that he ever rebelled against the social order or that he was even tempted by radicalism or liberalism, as was his younger brother, Alexander, who had a brush with the police for his involvement with a group critical of tsarism. It seems plausible, as the journalist A. S. Izgoev suggested in 1912, that one essential feature of Stolypin's political outlook was shaped by the "drama" of Tsar Alexander II's assassination in 1881 by terrorists who belonged to the revolutionary organization *Narodnaia volia* (The People's Will). The murder appalled Stolypin, who could not conceive of Russia without a strong monarch as head of state. He always harbored a deep and instinctive distrust of the Russian intelligentsia, who, he believed, had engineered the assassination and would never abandon its hostility toward the monarchy.[5]

In his personal habits, however, Petr Stolypin differed markedly from his father. He never smoked, he drank liquor only on special occasions and then in very small quantities, and he played cards only rarely, when he was stuck in small towns during his travels and had nothing else to do. His father seems to have been addicted to the card table and was unusually successful as a gambler. He won the estate at Kolnoberzhe, for many years the favorite residence of the Stolypins, in a high-stakes card game.[6]

The younger Stolypin was a serious person, thoroughly, perhaps even obsessively, devoted to his work and his career. He was also a profoundly religious man who regularly attended church services and meticulously observed the rituals of Russian Orthodoxy. The frivolous side of life held little interest for him. In his many public utterances, for example, there is virtually no trace of levity. He had a way with words, he could express himself cleverly, and his extemporaneous remarks were often eloquent, even brilliant. But he rarely displayed wit or even a light touch.

In 1881 Stolypin enrolled in the University of St. Petersburg, where he studied natural sciences and wrote a thesis on the tobacco industry in southern Russia, a subject befitting his practical bent. He worked diligently at his studies, and his efforts were duly rewarded. During his final examination he was grilled very intensively, especially by D. I. Mendeleev, the inventor of the periodic table, who delved into subjects on which no one had lectured because they were rather obscure and still under research. But Stolypin was never nonplused and, to the examiners' surprise, answered all the questions correctly. Suddenly Mendeleev stopped, exclaiming: "My God, what am I doing? Well, enough. Five, five [the highest grade], splendid."[7]

While still a student at the university Stolypin wooed Olga Borisovna Neidgardt, who had been affianced to his older brother. Because of his youth—he had not yet reached his twenty-second birthday—Stolypin feared that Olga Borisovna's father would object to the marriage, and it was with much trepidation that he asked Boris Aleksandrovich for his daughter's hand. Neidgardt smiled as he responded in French: "La jeunesse est un defaut duquel on se corrige chaque jour." ("Youth is a defect which corrects itself every day.")[8]

Stolypin's daughter, who reported this bon mot, added that Neidgardt knew full well "that he would not find a better husband for her." Be that as it may, the marriage was certainly an extraordinarily happy one. Olga Borisovna, brought up in a noble family distinguished for its service to the state, was an attractive and highly competent person, deeply devoted to her husband, five daughters, and son. She seems never to have complained about her husband's onerous work schedule and never tried to dissuade him from pursuing his career despite the dangers he faced from terrorist attacks as he moved up the bureaucratic ladder. By the same token, Stolypin's attachment to her was very strong: he consulted her not only about family affairs but also about professional matters and never lost his affection or respect for her. There is not the slightest hint of serious marital problems. When Stolypin was away from home, which happened with some frequency once he occupied senior administrative posts, he sent his wife letters or postcards almost daily, and gave her details about all his activities: how he had slept, when he got out of bed, what and when he had eaten, whom he was seeing, which members of the family he had visited, what subjects he had discussed with officials and friends. In short, during his travels he continued the daily conversations he would have with her when he was at home.

In the correspondence he frequently expressed his love and longing for her with great tenderness and at times with a certain playfulness, an aspect of his personality unknown to the public. No one outside of his own family ever indicated that Stolypin displayed warmth toward others or that he ever became emotional about personal matters. The first extant item that provides a glimpse into Stolypin's affectionate relationship with his wife is a postcard of September 13, 1899, in a curious mix of Russian, English, and French that began as follows: "My beloved, il est 10 heures and I want to kiss you befor to goo to bed.[sic!]" After some general comments in Russian about his business activities, he reverted to the two foreign languages she also knew: "Je suis satisfait" and ended with the following words: "I kant [sic!] live without you, my darling."[9] On another occasion that same year, 1899, he told his wife that "I think that it is rare that after 15 years of marriage [a couple] would love each other as passionately and strongly as you and I. For me, you and the children are everything and without you I would somehow feel that the ground has been cut from under my feet. It is distressing to be away from you."[10] Five years later he wrote the following card to her in broken French: "Your dear face and your silhouette on the avenue . . . are always before my eyes. I have left behind in Kolnoberzhe all that is dear to me . . . . May the Good Lord watch over you. I am already thinking of my return [and] it seems to me that before long I will [return]—what joy it will give me to be at complete rest with all those I love. I hope that you are all in good health. I cover you with kisses."[11] Often, his letters contained rather direct references to a strong physical relationship with his wife. After a long separation from her in the spring of 1904, he wrote: "Angel my comforter, there was no letter [from you], I want to kiss you tenderly, tenderly, I am not bored but simply long for you, do you love me? Yes?"[12] On July 16 of that year he ended a letter to his wife with the following words: "Olia, how I want you. I love you, my angel."[13]

At times, there was also a marked strain of morbidity in their correspondence, reflecting a fear that some terrible catastrophe might befall them. "Don't torture yourself," he wrote on August 13, 1903, "with dark thoughts and premonitions. There is a God and by turning to Him all dark thoughts will be dispelled. One must live properly and all will be well."[14] But he had his own, unexplained fears about his family. "I tremble when I think of you and pray for the safety of my treasure [wife and children]," he wrote in August 1899.[15] After a visit to an acquaintance, General Gazenkampf, who was depressed because his wife had just died, Stolypin wrote: "Darling, don't die! I want to live with you and kiss you."[16] Stolypin turned for comfort to God not only in his moments of apprehension. He made it a practice to attend church services on his official travels, as he faithfully informed his wife. Often he ended his letters to her with the words "My love for Christ and you is boundless."[17]

However demanding his work schedule, Stolypin made every effort to be attentive to his family. If they were not entertaining guests, he and his wife would read to each other before retiring for the night, always at precisely 11:00 o'clock. "In this way, they read almost all of the historical novels of [K] Waliszewski, then Tolstoy's *Resurrection* when it was printed in *Niva*, and many other pieces of Russian, French, and English literature."[18] Stolypin also made a point of maintaining a close relationship with his children. His oldest daughter, Maria von Bock, recalled that the "most wonderful time was in the evening," when he retired to his study but was available to his children. Maria would enter the study, "climb up on the soft ottoman, be hugged, and [listen to] the wonderful tales which he told." She found the stories interesting even in later years, when he related them to the younger children. For Maria, Stolypin was "the endlessly loving, always beloved father." She never forgot that although he could not be at home for her sixteenth birthday he made sure to leave a present for her with the following note: "All we ask is that you give us as much joy in the future as you have in the past sixteen years."[19] She could never understand her friends who asked her if she feared her father, who "was so stern in appearance. Fear Papa? For me, this was impossible from the very day of my birth to his end. To love him, to respect him, to be afraid that I might distress him, yes. But to fear to go to him? This never entered my mind."[20]

After completing his university studies in 1885, Stolypin moved to St. Petersburg, where he worked for two years in the Ministry of Internal Affairs and then for two years in the Statistics Department of the Ministry of Agriculture. It was essentially routine work, although Stolypin did learn a great deal about agrarian conditions in the Russian Empire, a subject that would become a central concern for him seventeen years later when he was prime minister. One of his projects was to survey the literature on Russian agriculture, and in 1887 the department published a volume he had prepared listing books and articles that had appeared on the subject prior to 1886. The volume provides a good indication of the issues in agriculture that especially interested him: private peasant farming, various projects on the sale of land by communes with the aid of the Peasant Bank, and the question of overcrowding in some regions of the countryside.[21]

In 1889, Stolypin decided to return to his home in Kovno province, where he owned three residences, one in the city itself and two in the countryside. It was customary for the family to spend about five months in the city of Kovno and to make the long trip to Kolnoberzhe, the preferred home, shortly after Easter. Except for brief summer vacations in Switzerland, the Stolypins spent the remaining seven months at Kolnoberzhe. Even though the living quarters were still somewhat antiquated—the estate did not have its own up-to-date bathing facilities—the Stolypins felt very much at home. Each year when the family showed up, the employees made a point of rolling out the welcome mat. The gate to the estate would be draped with greenery and banners, and all the workers would line up for a formal welcome, men on one side and women on the other. Stolypin disliked such ceremonies, but his annual request to the steward not to stage them went unheeded. The steward considered it inappropriate to welcome the master of the estate without due respect.[22]

By the late 1890s the Stolypins had inherited another six estates. Located in the provinces of Nizhnii Novgorod, Saratov, Penza, Moscow, Kazan, and at the border of Kovno and Germany, the estates ranged in size from 140 desiatiny (about 378 acres) in Moscow to 4,845 desiatiny in Kazan. All in all, the Stolypins owned close to 7,500 desiatiny of land. Once a year Stolypin made the rounds of the family estates, checking on the administrative efficiency and profitability of each one. His annual trip to the estate near the German border was especially instructive for him. Because there were no decent roads leading up to the estate in Kovno, Stolypin would pass through parts of Prussia to reach his destination. During these trips "abroad" he came to admire greatly the efficiency of German farmers and made a point of studying their work habits and productivity. His later advocacy of agrarian reform in Russia was very much influenced by his observations in Prussia.[23]

The precise value of the family estates is unknown, but there is no doubt that Stolypin was a man of substantial means. In 1902 he sold his estate in Saratov, about 1,000 desiatiny, to seven peasants for 112,500 rubles, a very large sum of money at the time. We also know that when the Stolypins traveled from the city of Kovno to Kolnoberzhe the party consisted of twenty people, which means that the family employed a personal staff of no fewer than thirteen (servants, governesses, and drivers). Still, the Stolypins managed their finances very carefully, more in keeping with bourgeois frugality than the free spending habits generally associated with the Russian nobility. On his trips to his estates Stolypin often reported to his wife on specific and relatively minor expenditures, rarely missing an opportunity to complain about what he regarded as exorbitant prices. In a letter from Saratov on August 13, 1903, he told his wife that dinner at a restaurant had been much too expensive. "Yesterday I dined with two people and the cost of the food was 9 r[ubles] 45 k[opeks]. And dinner consisted of 4 courses and pastries. Stewed fruit of apples and prunes."[24] At the same time, his wife maintained a detailed record of all her daily expenses in Kolnoberzhe and of the monthly family income. Each evening the cook provided her with the bills that had accumulated that day and Madame Stolypin would duly record each figure. The weighty books she used for her accounts, many of them preserved in the Stolypin Archive, are similar to the logs of accountants and reveal how many kopecks she spent on bread, butter, sugar, vegetables, etc. For the month of March 1902, for example, the income in Kolnoberzhe amounted to 496 rubles and 37 and a half kopecks, and expenditures came to 408 rubles and 69 kopecks. For the entire year of 1899, the expenses for running the household came to 14,267 rubles and 67 kopecks, further evidence of the comfortable circumstances of the Stolypins—at the time the average annual income of workers in Moscow was 300 rubles and the top 25 percent of civil servants earned between 2,000 and 5,000 rubles a year. By 1902 the annual expenses rose to 23,837 rubles and by 1906 (when they had moved to St. Petersburg and Stolypin had joined the government as a minister) to 32,752 rubles.[25]

Madame Stolypin also kept detailed records of income and expenses for the other family estates.[26] She was accurate "to the point of pedantry," but much to her chagrin she was a "very poor mathematician." She was frequently unable to add the figures correctly and in frustration appealed for help. "With a smile, . . . [Stolypin] would sit down at the account book, examine the figures, correct them, and then go back to his work."[27] In urging Russian peasants to husband their resources carefully, Stolypin was advocating a practice he himself strictly followed in his personal affairs.

Although Kolnoberzhe was neither the largest nor the most beautiful of the Stolypin estates, it remained the family's summer residence. The children especially enjoyed living there, and Stolypin himself also retained fond memories of his childhood years on the estate. The Stolypins enjoyed the natural beauty of the countryside, the clean air, the fresh vegetables, and the tranquillity, all of which contrasted starkly to the atmosphere in Kovno. Socializing with like-minded people was easy, as several prominent families lived on nearby estates: Count E. I. Totleben, the hero of Sevastopol; General Kardashevskii; and P. A. Miller, the future assistant minister of trade and commerce, to mention only a few. Also, friends from Kovno would regularly visit the Stolypins in Kolnoberzhe, spending several days at a time at the estate.

Despite his wealth, however, Stolypin was more interested in work than in socializing. Upon his return to Kovno province in 1889, he accepted election by the local nobility as district marshal of the nobility, a post established in the eighteenth century under Catherine II for the administration of the local regions of the empire. Although the government in the course of the nineteenth century redefined the post in various ways, it remained a significant pillar in the administrative structure of the state, serving both the interests of the nobility and the autocracy. The district marshals were in effect the administrative heads of a local region of a province known in Russian as the *uezd* (district), roughly comparable to an American county. They chaired several local committees, among them the Council of Arbiters of the Peace, that dealt with such issues as the land settlements after the emancipation of the serfs in 1861, and with peasant affairs generally. They also chaired the boards that administered the drafting of men into the army, bureaus and committees concerned with supervising taverns, and commissions that decided on financial compensation for individuals whose property was seized by right of eminent domain. (In districts where zemstvos, local organs of self-government, existed, which was not the case in Kovno, the district marshal of the nobility also presided over the local assemblies of the zemstvos.)[28]

Stolypin discharged his duties as district marshal conscientiously and effectively and in the process received a good education in local government. In chairing the local committee of arbiters he became acquainted with the intricacies of land disputes, the functioning of the legal system, and the hardships peasants encountered in earning their livelihood. One of his more notable initiatives was to promote the building of a public meeting house (*narodnyi dom*) at which workers and other ordinary people could attend theatrical performances, public balls, and, eventually, films. In the tearoom, reading materials of various kinds were available for workers and peasants. A few rooms in the building were set aside for overnight guests. Stolypin and his wife, both of whom took great satisfaction in the success of the meeting house, frequently attended public events there.[29] Another special interest of Stolypin's in the 1880s was the creation of an Agricultural Society, which fostered education on agrarian issues and helped establish a cooperative for the purchase of agricultural machinery for use by peasants and for the sale of their products. The society continued to function until 1940.[30]

Though important, the work as a district marshal of the nobility did not amount to a full-time occupation. Stolypin could still supervise the cultivation of his own lands, which he did with great passion. "Everything," his daughter recalled, "took second place to worries about sowing, mowing, planting in the forests, and working in the orchard."[31] Even after he became governor of Grodno he would spend his vacations at Kolnoberzhe and would devote a fair amount of time to "household management." When a neighbor teased him about his work and told him that "you are not the governor in this matter!" Stolypin shot back: "Not the governor, but a landowner, which is more important and more necessary."[32] Within ten years or so of his settling down in Kovno, the estate in Kolnoberzhe was transformed into a model farm that produced impressive quantities of wheat, rye, barley, oats, peas, and potatoes. Still, Stolypin's experience in running a farm convinced him that Kovno was not really suited for large-scale agriculture. Because the soil was not very fertile, farmers had to resort heavily to the use of chemicals to stimulate productivity. As a result, agricultural products in Kovno tended to be relatively expensive and thus at a clear disadvantage in competition with products from the southern provinces. Stolypin concluded that farmers in Kovno should gradually shift to animal husbandry, an idea he ardently promoted a few years later when he occupied a higher administrative post in the province.[33]

Agriculture was not the only subject on which Stolypin's views took shape during his years in Kovno. His particular brand of nationalism evolved as a result of his long stay in a western province of the empire, a multinational area with a population slightly in excess of 1.5 million. Even though Kovno had been annexed by Russia in 1795, the Great Russians still made up only a small minority, slightly less than 5 percent according to the census of 1897. The vast majority, about 68 percent, was Lithuanian and the second largest group was Jewish, somewhat over 13.5 percent. The Poles, who represented slightly over 7 percent of the population, were widely resented, not only because the Lithuanians and Russians considered them to be an alien group culturally but also because some 75 percent of the privately held land was in their hands. In other western border regions, the Polish minorities also owned a disproportionate amount of the privately held lands.[34] Stolypin came to view this distribution of ethnic groups and of land ownership as a potential danger for Russia because it kept the ethnic Russians in a position of inferiority in an area bordering on the powerful states of Germany and Austria-Hungary. Although he occasionally made disparaging remarks about the Poles, whom he suspected of wanting to spread Catholicism, he never advocated the uprooting of their culture or that of other minorities. His primary concern was national security and political stability, not cultural or religious uniformity.

In fact, Stolypin's long residence among a variety of ethnic groups seems to have made him quite tolerant of minorities, a trait not generally associated with Russian nationalists. His benevolent attitude toward the Jews in the 1880s and 1890s is a case in point and merits notice because it led him to initiate some important reforms when he was prime minister. Numbering some five million people, the Jews were widely viewed as a group marked by "inner vices," as an alien and corrosive element that could not be assimilated into Russian society. For decades a wide range of disabilities were imposed on them: most notably, they were forced to reside, with few exceptions, in the Pale of Settlement in the western regions of the empire. In addition, they were subjected to special taxes, excluded from many professions, and their attendance at schools and universities was constrained by rigid quotas.[35] Stolypin's view of the Jews was quite distinctive, as is clear from comments by his daughter, Maria. For one thing, her father harbored no ill will toward them; on the contrary, he considered them to be "not only necessary, but very convenient and pleasant." They performed important functions, since they "were thatchers or house painters, tenant farmers and grain buyers." Maria also recalled the local store owner in Kovno, a certain Shapiro, who "had everything and if he did not have what you wanted for a religious ceremony or such, he was prepared to take the first train to Vilna or to Berlin." Although the Stolypins were too thrifty to patronize Shapiro's store with any frequency, they did employ a Jewish orchestra for performances at special dinners they hosted at their home. On those occasions Stolypin "loved to perform the Hebrew dance 'maiufess' with the musicians . . . [who] executed the tune with special fervor."[36] By itself, Stolypin's benevolent attitude toward Jews and his occasional contacts with them may not appear to be very significant, but in Late Imperial Russia not many members of the nobility and bureaucracy were as open-minded.

In 1899, Stolypin was appointed marshal of the nobility of Kovno province, which meant that he now occupied the second highest position in the region's hierarchy (next to that of the governor). Many of the functions he performed in the new position were similar to those he had performed as district marshal, but the scope of his responsibilities was much larger. With considerable enthusiasm, Stolypin quickly took an interest in broad issues affecting the entire province. Most notably, he began a study of economic trends in Kovno to enable him to devise practical measures to improve the competitiveness of local farms.

His first concern was to deal with a serious underlying problem in the province's economy: grain farmers were being driven out of business because farmers in the interior provinces of the empire, where the soil was more fertile, could produce grain at substantially lower cost. Even after transportation costs were taken into account, the imported grain was less expensive than the local product. Stolypin concluded that if the agricultural sector of Kovno were to survive it would have to turn to other products such as milk and, more important, cattle.

In 1901 he issued a comprehensive, seventeen-page report on the local economy in which he warned that nothing less than the future well-being of the province was at stake. One of the distinctive features of the report was its thoroughness, which was to become a hallmark of all of Stolypin's reports and speeches. Before publicly committing himself on an issue he would read very widely, paying special attention to government studies and documents, to which he would frequently refer to invest his utterances with an aura of authority. His command over the minutest details and his focus on practical approaches to problems added to the cogency of his arguments.

Cattle-raising in Kovno could succeed, he argued in his report of 1901, only if foreign markets, especially in Germany, were opened up for farmers. Trade agreements with Germany would expire in two years, in 1903, and it was not too early to take measures to maximize the chances for Kovno's farmers in obtaining a large share of the market in that burgeoning country, which Stolypin believed to be "colossal." Stolypin also believed that local landowners could become the chief suppliers of meat for the large military establishment in Kovno. For some reason, the military market had been lost by Kovno landlords in 1900.

Stolypin warned, however, that Kovno faced major obstacles. For one thing, sanitary conditions in local slaughterhouses (as well as in those of the rest of the country) were woefully inadequate, and he warned that unless these were improved it would not be possible to export cattle or meat to Germany, which for over a decade had refused to import Russian meat for fear that it might be contaminated. The root problem, according to Stolypin, was that Russia did not have an adequate supply of veterinarians who could inspect the cattle, a serious matter since cattle were often afflicted with an epizootic disease. In the entire empire there were only four veterinarian institutes, capable of training some two

hundred people a year. This was far too small a number; as a consequence, many inspectors at slaughterhouses were unqualified. In an attempt to dramatize the seriousness of the shortage of trained inspectors
Stolypin related the travails of the town of Telshakh, Kovno province:
the management of the local slaughterhouse spent a total of eighteen
months looking for a qualified veterinarian. Finally a well-trained person was employed, but he became ill and died within two weeks. The
search had to begin all over again.

Stolypin concluded his report with an appeal to the nobles of Kovno
to select a commission to study his proposals, decide which ones were
feasible, and then design plans to implement them. The most urgent
matter, in his view, was the upcoming negotiations with Germany over
trade agreements. The government in St. Petersburg should be urged to
press for the maintenance of low import duties and the abolition of restrictions by Germany on all imports of cattle, swine, and meat from the
province of Kovno.[37]

Another issue that Stolypin took up as provincial marshal of the nobility was the establishment of insurance schemes for workers, both in
industry and in agriculture. His views on the subject are spelled out in a
lengthy handwritten statement preserved in his archive and most
probably composed early in 1902. It seems likely that Stolypin drafted
the statement to sort out his thoughts, which he did from time to time
when he was contemplating a legislative or executive initiative on a particularly sensitive subject. There is no evidence of his having made the
statement public in 1902; conceivably, he shelved the project when he
left Kovno in the spring of 1902 for a higher administrative position. But
it is clear from his comments that the Kovno Assembly of Nobles had
already discussed the question of workers' insurance in general terms
and that he prepared the report to encourage favorable action. Be that as
it may, the statement deserves scrutiny because it indicates the drift of
his thinking at a relatively early stage in his public career and because
some four years later as prime minister he included a proposal for workers' insurance in the first communiqué outlining the program of his
newly formed government.

Once again, Stolypin read widely before formulating his views. He
studied governmental policy on workers' insurance in Germany, Switzerland, Austria, Great Britain, France, Italy, Belgium, Norway, and the
United States and compared the various approaches. He discussed,
among other things, the categories of workers included in the insurance
scheme, how much the workers were required to contribute, what benefits they could expect, and the solvency of the insurance funds. He paid

special attention to the workings of the insurance scheme in Saxony and Würtemberg, two German states from which he obtained an abundance of statistical information. Stolypin's tone in dealing with all this rather dry material makes it clear that he found the government's intervention in behalf of workers appealing. Indeed, in the very second sentence of the statement Stolypin revealed that for him workers' insurance was not simply a humanitarian undertaking but served a significant political purpose: in introducing workers' insurance, he noted, "Bismarck promoted the idea of state socialism, which directed the labor movement into a calmer course." In 1902, when Stolypin drafted his statement, labor unrest in Russia had already emerged as a serious issue and had engaged the attention of the minister of internal affairs and of other senior governmental officials. A perennial debate among them was whether the official response to labor unrest should be repression, economic concessions, or a combination of the two. In his first direct comment on working class conditions in Russia, Stolypin clearly came out on the side of concessions. He retained that position in later years, though he then also favored repressive measures.

In the last section of the report he urged the Assembly of the Nobility to resolve two basic questions: Should the province of Kovno adopt workers' insurance and, if so, what kind should be established? To help the nobles reach a decision, he offered to make available the factual material he had collected. In his next-to-last comment Stolypin stressed that it was in the nobles' and in the province's economic interest to provide protection for workers; a failure by the authorities in Kovno to do so would prompt laborers to move to areas where "material conditions were not as wretched."[38]

Stolypin's last major initiative in Kovno had to do with a particularly complicated matter, the introduction of zemstvos in the western province. When these organs of self-government were created in 1864 in the Russian Empire they were deliberately withheld from the provinces of the Polish-Russian borderlands (Kovno, Vilna, Grodno, Volhynia, Podolia, Kiev, Minsk, Mogilev, Vitebsk) for fear that in that region they would be dominated by groups hostile to the government. The Polish rebellion had been harshly suppressed only a year earlier, and the authorities in St. Petersburg believed that the Poles, still seething over their defeat but economically powerful, would succeed in having a large number of their candidates elected to the zemstvos. But the absence of zemstvos in so large an area was clearly an anomaly, and in 1901–2 senior officials in the Department of Internal Affairs tried to find a way of establishing self-government in the region without jeopardizing the authority of the central government. In the end, the minister of internal affairs, D. S. Sipiagin, proposed what he considered to be a "simplified" system of zemstvos in the western provinces: "councilors" who would serve in the organs of self-government would not be elected as they were elsewhere but would be appointed by provincial governors. But Sipiagin's project was widely derided as an unacceptable "parody" of the very idea of zemstvos, which were designed to give the people a say in running their affairs. Before he could reconsider the project he was killed by a terrorist. His successor, V. K. Plehve, wanted his own reform project and consequently called on various officials in St. Petersburg and the provinces for advice, among them Stolypin.

Stolypin's report, drafted in 1902, anticipates many of the changes in local self-government in the western provinces that he would propose years later as prime minister and that embroiled him in his most painful political brouhaha. If his many years in the western regions of the empire made him tolerant of the culture of minorities, it also made him apprehensive about the ability of the local Russian population to maintain its cultural identity. As he pointed out in his report to Plehve, he approached the projected zemstvo reform not from the standpoint of its administrative feasibility or propriety but rather from the standpoint of its likely impact "on the entire structure of local life." Thus, he did not object to the introduction of zemstvos in the western provinces but warned against establishing them on the same principles as those in the rest of the empire, where the zemstvo boards were elected. If elections were held, the Poles would surely become the dominant force in many boards. It was not, he said, that he suspected the Poles of disloyalty. On the contrary, most of them, in his view, were thoroughly conservative, unlikely to resort to antigovernment actions. The real problem in the western provinces was the possible eruption of conflict between Poles and Russians over cultural issues, a conflict that would inevitably involve Belorussian and Lithuanian peasants and to some extent also the Jews. Stolypin feared that periodic elections to zemstvos would sharpen the cultural struggles and produce an "unhealthy atmosphere." Extremists would most likely be elected, and they would take measures that would "inoculate" the population against Russian cultural values. Stolypin apparently assumed that zemstvos under the influence of Poles would seek to strengthen Catholicism at the expense of Russian Orthodoxy. "We must take into account," he warned, "a certain impulsiveness and frivolous passion of the Polish character."

The appointment of zemstvo boards by the central government had already been ruled out as contrary to the principle of self-government, and Stolypin agreed with that decision. But if elections similar to those held in the interior of Russia were also to be avoided, some procedure would have to be found to involve the local populations in the disbursements of funds. He considered it essential that local committees with the authority to collect taxes for local needs be accountable to the people in their districts. Stolypin proposed the adoption of procedures that the minister of justice in 1884, D. N. Nabokov, had introduced for the selection of juries. Fearful of what he regarded as irresponsible conduct of juries,* Nabokov had devised a scheme to weed out untrustworthy individuals. Civil servants were charged with choosing committees, half of them officials such as marshals of the nobility, justices of the peace, and police officials, who in turn picked lists of potential jurors. To further ensure the selection of acceptable jurors, a *numerus clausus* was established limiting the number of Jews who could serve on juries, and no Jew was allowed to serve in trials involving "crimes against religion."[39] The one feature of the procedure that Stolypin wished to change was the restrictions on Jews, which seemed to him unjustified given the large number of Jews in the western provinces. Since Plehve was known to be a fervent anti-Semite, Stolypin's view on Jewish participation in the procedure for selecting zemstvo members, voiced in a report to the minister of internal affairs, struck one recent historian as verging on "impudence." Plehve did not adopt Stolypin's recommendations, but he also seems not to have taken offense.[40]

In fact, in May 1902, Plehve appointed Stolypin governor of Grodno, a province in the northwestern region of European Russia, apparently on the recommendation of Count Aleksander Tyshkevich (Tyszkiewicz), a member of the State Council. According to Prince A. D. Obolenskii, Tyshkevich had been much impressed by Stolypin's work as marshal of the nobility in Kovno, especially by his role in the Agricultural Society and his dealings with the Poles, a large minority that liked and respected him.[41] For Plehve, Stolypin was an ideal candidate for promotion: he was an intelligent and educated man, and he was also a nobleman who knew how to assert his authority.[42] Stolypin's family was not pleased at the prospect of leaving Kovno. When Plehve summoned Stolypin from his vacation spot in Elster, Germany, late in 1902, "we pretended to ourselves," Stolypin's daughter recalled, "that the interview did not concern a new appointment." Indeed, Stolypin's summons to St. Petersburg was very puzzling to the family, since "any sort of 'careerism' was alien

---

*The most notable case was a jury's acquittal in 1878 of Vera Zasulich, who had shot and wounded the police chief of St. Petersburg, General Trepov.

to my father's nature." The puzzle was solved three days later when a telegram arrived from Stolypin informing his family that he had been named governor of Grodno. "Papa told us that he would not return to Elster but would go straight to Grodno."[43] The speed with which Stolypin accepted the post and began his new duties hardly betokened reluctance to accept the promotion or indifference to advancing his career. It was part of the Stolypin mystique, carefully cultivated by him and his family, that he moved up the bureaucratic ladder simply out of a sense of duty to the tsar and the empire. That mystique served him well and helps to explain his rapid rise to the leadership of the government. In fact, there is a fair amount of evidence, to be noted in the next chapter, that he rarely missed an opportunity to advance his career, but he was so discreet and sophisticated in doing so that he succeeded in hiding his ambitions even from his closest relatives.

Grodno was, to be sure, a relatively small province; yet for a man barely forty years old Stolypin's move to the leadership of that region was a signal achievement. He was the youngest governor in the entire empire.

In its diversity of population Grodno bore some striking similarities to Kovno. Of its roughly 1,500,000 inhabitants, about 54 percent were Russians (mainly Belorussian), slightly over 20 percent Poles, and some 18 percent Jews. Although agriculture was the single largest sector of the economy, less than half the population made its living on the land. The relatively large number of industrial establishments employed over 22 percent of the workforce. The military services, which had an unusually large presence in the province, employed almost 19 percent of the population, either as uniformed men or as workers. More than half of the privately held land (about 53 percent) was in the hands of Poles.[44]

Stolypin remained in Grodno for only ten months, but during that short time he made some major proposals on Russia's most critical domestic issue, the agrarian question. He did this as chairman of two conferences—one on July 16, and the other on November 26, 27, 28, and 29, 1902—of the Grodno Provincial Committee on the Needs of Agriculture, attended by twenty-five to thirty local dignitaries and landlords. In his lengthy opening remarks on July 16, Stolypin touched on a wide range of issues and suggested various projects to improve Grodno's economy, most of which received a full airing at the November meetings. It is no exaggeration to say that had Stolypin's proposals been implemented, Grodno would have undergone major economic and social changes.

First and foremost, he called for measures to encourage peasants to become independent farmers living on their own *khutory*, consolidated individual farmsteads outside the villages (where peasants lived with their families). To increase the number of such farmsteads several specific steps needed to be taken. For one thing, the so-called system of "interconnected land tenure" (*shnurovoe zemlepolzovaniie*) would have to be eliminated. Under this system, every peasant household worked lands divided into strips located in various parts of the village; the purpose was to provide each peasant with some land of differing quality, but the serious drawback was that much time was wasted walking from one strip to another. Moreover, the system encouraged the retention of the three-field rotation, also a drag on productivity. But Stolypin insisted that more than the abolition of strip-farming was necessary to improve farming in Grodno. Time and again during his various interventions in the discussions he urged the abolition of the system of "servitude," a reference to two age-old rights of peasants in Grodno and other provinces in the southwestern parts of the empire: to send their cattle for pasturing on lands owned by landlords and to fell trees in the forests, also owned by landlords. The exercise of these rights by the peasants had led to endless lawsuits and highly destructive exploitation of forests and pastures. Stolypin considered the "servitudes" and strip farming so harmful to agriculture that he repeatedly warned that if they were not abolished there could be no hope for a "serious improvement of agriculture." The authorities, Stolypin suggested, should take immediate legal steps to eliminate the practices and not wait until the peasants come to be persuaded of their own "free will" that they were a detriment to efficient farming. If peasants took the initiative, Stolypin suggested, the process might not be peaceful.[45]

Stolypin proposed several other measures to improve the province's economy. He urged the reorganization of the credit system so that loans could be advanced more expeditiously to farmers and the establishment of schools to disseminate information on the most up-to-date methods in agriculture. To overcome the primitive state of animal husbandry, farmers should be taught how to clear swamps, the breeding ground for many diseases. He repeated a point he had stressed as marshal of the nobility in Kovno, that Germany had closed its borders to Russian cattle out of fear that Russia was exporting diseased meat.

Stolypin did not limit himself to purely economic issues. He also urged the construction of fireproof buildings to prevent the numerous fires that were ravaging the houses of many peasants. He advocated the adoption of new steps by the authorities to counter widespread lawlessness; here he had in mind measures to prevent land seizures, horse-stealing, and thievery from fields and gardens. He also wanted internal and foreign trade to be more rigorously regulated so as to prevent trade in grain of low quality, a practice that had hurt local farmers. Stolypin believed that committees on the local level were in the best position to come up with specific proposals to handle these matters, and he asked that such committees send their suggestions to the Provincial Committee no later than October 15, 1902.[46]

After Stolypin had delivered his speech, he urged the assembled dignitaries to give careful consideration to his proposals, but in keeping with Plehve's instruction, he admonished them not to take up "general questions"—that is, matters that touched on national politics.[47] The discussions were lively, and one of the liveliest did involve an issue of national import, the establishment of a wide range of schools to educate large numbers of youngsters. In elaborating on this point, Stolypin insisted that "without knowledge . . . farming will not enjoy success." He therefore called for the creation of elementary schools as well as schools of agriculture and, more specifically, of agronomy. In addition, local authorities should sponsor lectures on the most efficient methods of farming and should issue publications on the subject. Stolypin acknowledged that his educational reforms would be expensive. He estimated that the building of just one school would cost 300,000 rubles; since each of the nine districts in Grodno would need a school, the total financial outlay would come to 2.7 million rubles, a sum that the provincial authorities could not afford. Stolypin suggested that the government in St. Petersburg provide the necessary funds.[48]

Not everyone at the meeting was persuaded by Stolypin's argument. Prince A. K. Sviatopolk-Chetvertinskii warned that educating the masses was a dangerous undertaking. Most people, he asserted, must devote themselves to physical labor, for which education was unnecessary. Indeed, in his view it should be confined to the "well-to-do classes." The moral and political views of the masses were such that if they were educated they would inevitably "strive for a coup d'état, for social revolution and anarchy." To support his point, he cited Western Europe as an instructive example. The masses there had become literate and as a consequence they had adopted radical doctrines and had developed into a force capable of challenging the existing authorities. "It may be," Sviatopolk-Chetvertinskii concluded, "that my point of view is out of date, that the danger [I foresee] and the views [I express] are more applicable to the last century, but this is my conviction, which I have the courage to maintain."[49]

No sooner had Prince Chetvertinskii made this remark than Stolypin took the floor to refute him with a short speech in which he demonstrated how far removed he was from the reactionary wing of the Russian nobility. "We should not fear literacy and enlightenment," he pleaded. In fact, nowhere had the education of the masses led to anarchy. To buttress his assertion, Stolypin compared conditions in Germany with those in Italy. In the latter country anarchism was a strong movement, but the educational system was weak. By contrast, Germany had produced a system of public education that was the envy of many advanced countries, and yet no state could boast of a more tranquil and loyal citizenry; there was no danger of revolution. Turning his attention to Russia, he insisted that the "[d]issemination of knowledge about agriculture depends on public education, [and] without it an agrarian country cannot exist and will, bit by bit, come to ruin." Then he advanced a distinctly political argument in support of his position: by promoting education among farmers, "you will give security to the agricultural class, the most conservative in every country." That was the best protection against socialism, a doctrine that attracted the masses only when they were destitute and without opportunities to better their lot.[50]

The Provincial Committee on the Needs of Agriculture supported many of Stolypin's proposals, but he did not stay long enough in Grodno to press for their implementation. After only ten months in the province he was offered the governorship of Saratov, a much more prestigious and challenging post. Moreover, in Grodno Stolypin was subordinate to a governor-general seated in Vilno, who exercised authority over the provinces of Vilno, Kovno, and Grodno. He had no differences with the governor-general, the liberal Prince P. D. Sviatopolk-Mirskii, but he was inclined to "operate independently," and that he could not do in Grodno.[51]

In an interview in 1909, when he had been prime minister for three years and his government had introduced most of his reform proposals in the Duma, Stolypin said that his views on the agrarian question had been formed during his years in Kovno from 1889 to 1902. He was right, though he could have gone further and could have indicated that by the time he left Grodno for Saratov in 1903 he held firm views on a wide range of issues. By 1903 he had also advocated, among other things, fundamental reform of the educational system, the introduction of a system of social insurance for workers, the strengthening of the legal order, and the establishment of zemstvos of a special kind in the western provinces. This amounted to a comprehensive program of restructuring essential institutions. What he had not yet done was to express himself publicly on specifically political issues. That was because he had not yet been tested in this sphere. In Kovno and in Grodno in the 1890s and early part of the twentieth century there was no serious political challenge to the existing authorities. We do know, of course, that Stolypin was a firm supporter of the monarchical order; once he faced political challenges (in his next post), he made that clear.

In light of his numerous initiatives as a marshal of the nobility and as a governor, it is hard to credit the assertion that his career in the provinces was "entirely ordinary, in no way distinguishable from the careers of other bureaucrats" who became governors.[52] Much more than the vast majority of imperial officials at the time, Stolypin was an activist who viewed government as an instrument for producing change and who proposed many projects to improve conditions in the districts or provinces under his jurisdiction. He remained an activist throughout the remainder of his life, and the policies he pursued after he left Grodno were essentially consistent with views he had formed in the 1890s. What is remarkable is that during the early phase of his career as a public figure no one seems to have sensed that he was a powerful personality with the potential to leave a mark on national affairs matched by few other statesmen in Imperial Russia.

2

Governor of Saratov

In moving to Saratov, Stolypin assumed one of the most demanding provincial posts in the empire, challenging in ways he could not have anticipated. A resident for most of his life in the western borderlands, he was only generally familiar with conditions in the heartland of Russia. Although he had inherited an estate in Saratov province, he had not spent much time there and in 1902 had actually sold the property. His half-brother, Dmitrii, a resident of Saratov and a political moderate with some experience in public affairs, had introduced him to several local noblemen, but there is no evidence of a close relationship between Stolypin and the Saratov gentry. During his initial period in the province, Stolypin relied on Dmitrii in orienting himself to his new surroundings, but beyond that he was on his own in settling down in a region very different from Grodno and Kovno. As his daughter noted, "Everything . . . was alien, unfamiliar. The pure Russian speech of the peasants, their foreign appearance, known to me only from pictures, was strange. From the railway car we saw the endless, immense regions, [and] fields, [and], from a distance, the [local] churches in the villages. It was all foreign, familiar only from books."[1]

Located in the eastern part of the central Russian plateau on the Volga River, Saratov in 1903 was home to roughly 2.5 million people, about 90 percent of whom were peasants. Ethnically, the population was predominantly Slavic, though in some districts there were sizable pockets of indigenous Mordvinians, Tatars, Chuvash, and Kalmyks. Also, in the Kamyshin district some 40 percent of the population was German, descended from the German settlers of the eighteenth century. The major agricultural product of Saratov was grain, produced in the northern part of the province blessed with rich, black soil. By the early twentieth century Saratov had become the leading producer of flour in the empire and an important center of transportation. But a majority of the peasants still lived in communes, which militated against efficient farming.* Al-

*For a discussion of the commune system, see below, pp. 57–58, 85, 154–56.

so the implementation of the decree emancipating the peasants in 1861 led to a reduction of peasant landholdings of about 38 percent. It has been estimated that well over half of the peasants worked a mere six desiatiny (about fifteen acres), not enough to permit anything other than a hand-to-mouth existence. Very few peasants belonged to the category of middle income farmers. On the other hand, a relatively small number of large landowners, 893 in all, owned estates of five hundred or more desiatiny for a total of some two million desiatiny. Periodic droughts in the region only added to the woes of the people.[2]

Industry had penetrated the province, and about 10,000 of the 200,000 residents of the capital city, also named Saratov, belonged to the working class. In the other regions of the province there were small pockets of industry. The conditions under which workers lived were wretched. In the capital, as Stolypin's daughter recalled, "everything . . . spelled despondency and anguish for me. The streets were laid out as if with a ruler, with small, sad houses along each side, completely bare of vegetation except for several emaciated lindens around the cathedral. Shady characters lived in those houses and there were so many [drunkards]. . . . [My] God, how I hated it!"[3]

For Stolypin, Saratov was also a challenging assignment because of its history of social and political turbulence. One reason for the province's volatility seems to have been the steady influx of religious dissenters and discontented peasants from central Russia. By the late nineteenth century the province was also a center to which the government exiled criminals and other "unreliable elements." More important, the zemstvos in the province and the city duma in the capital were unusually vocal on a wide range of public issues, the result in large measure of the long-standing cooperation between liberals among the land-owning class and radicals within the intelligentsia. But political activism was not limited to liberals and radicals. Militant conservatives also turned Saratov into a center of agitation. On top of all that, a very poor harvest in 1905 provoked widespread unrest in the countryside. Saratov was now one of the more turbulent regions of the empire.[4]

Within weeks of his arrival in March 1903, Stolypin gave notice that he planned to be an activist governor. In mid-August, when his family was still in Kolnoberzhe, he wrote his wife that he had little to tell her about himself because "aside from work there is nothing. The theater opened, but I was not there. It is tedious to be still feeling one's way. I have to reform the police and take control of everything." His schedule was extremely demanding: on August 20 he planned to attend a conference of district police chiefs to resolve various questions and induct new police constables, after which he intended to complete some "urgent" work on provincial reform; he planned to spend a week, toward the end of the month, touring districts of the province that he had not yet visited. He maintained his hectic schedule even after his family joined him in Saratov in the fall. "He took half an hour of rest after dinner, during which he and Mama walked back and forth along the hall [of their house], and later, a half hour after evening tea. That was all. The rest of the time, he worked."[5] The relatively leisurely pace of his life in Kovno and Grodno had come to a sudden end.

So had the political tranquillity to which Stolypin had become accustomed. A month after taking office in Saratov he faced a serious problem in Balashov district, an area that would be a center of intense conflict for the next three years. In this, his first encounter with political dissidence, Stolypin initially took some rash actions that revealed his lack of experience in the political arena. But at the same time he displayed certain traits—firmness coupled with flexibility—that would increasingly become the hallmark of his conduct in high office.[6]

It all began unexpectedly in April 1903 with the suicide of a schoolteacher named Stepurin in the town of Makarovo. Policemen examining the dead man's papers found a "clear allusion" to a plot by the town's teachers to stage political assassinations, though the targets were not identified. Without conducting his own examination of the evidence, Stolypin immediately followed the advice of the police that he dismiss three teachers implicated in the plot. Within a few weeks, Stolypin ordered the dismissal of several additional teachers suspected of belonging to the conspiracy and directed the inspector of schools to be more vigilant in supervising his employees.

Within society in Balashov, Stolypin's moves against the teachers aroused much indignation, all the more so since one of the persons incarcerated, Spuv, belonged to a locally prominent family and was the sister of a land captain and zemstvo deputy. S. A. Unkovskii, the newly appointed marshal of the nobility, a man of liberal views, asked the governor for permission to convoke a meeting of the district gentry assembly to discuss Spuv's dismissal. Stolypin refused, claiming that Spuv's guilt was beyond doubt. The governor offered new evidence, the testimony of Pyzina, a teacher who had also been arrested but had since then repented. As stated in Stolypin's report to the minister of internal affairs, Pyzina had exposed "the guilt of several individuals."[7] Unkovskii was not impressed, and in October 1903 he organized a formal protest by the zemstvo assembly against the dismissals.

The liberals in the assembly accused Stolypin of dismissing the teachers in order to placate conservative clergymen in Saratov who had spread false charges against them in an attempt to weaken schools not under the authority of the Church. The assembly also unanimously adopted a resolution to be sent to the bishop of Saratov informing him that twenty priests in Balashov district were engaged in "slanderous activity"—that is, in circulating denunciations of innocent teachers. The assembly added a warning that the priests would be dismissed from their parishes if they did not stop their campaign of vilification. Finally, the resolution directed school authorities not to employ any new teachers without the express approval of the executive board of the local zemstvo in Balashov.

The controversy over the teachers was not the only cause of bad blood between the Balashov zemstvo and Stolypin. The governor was also offended by the decision of the zemstvo to accord special honor to a prominent physician, Vladimir Chenykaev, by hanging his portrait on a wall in his hospital in Turki, Saratov province. In and of itself, it seemed to be a trivial matter, but for over a decade Chenykaev had been something of a legend in antigovernment circles. The authorities, on the other hand, looked upon him as a dangerous troublemaker. In the years from 1892 to 1895 he had been the key figure in a group that agitated against the government and against religion and urged peasants to refuse to pay taxes. Chenykaev barely escaped conviction at the time, but within a few years he was again in trouble with the police on suspicion of agitating against the government.[8] Then, early in 1902 he was arrested for conducting political propaganda at his hospital. Before he went to trial, the Balashov zemstvo assembly unanimously elected him to the Investigating Committee of the zemstvo. The deputies justified their vote in favor of Chenykaev on the grounds that they were certain he would be released for lack of evidence. But the authorities in St. Petersburg, blaming outside agitators such as the doctors for the agrarian disorders of that year in various parts of the empire, were not inclined to be lenient even toward Chenykaev, who had requested release because of illness. At the insistence of the Department of Police, the doctor was exiled to Vologda for three years.[9]

In honoring Chenykaev and in supporting the dismissed teachers, the Balashov zemstvo was clearly thumbing its nose at the authorities. Stolypin, convinced that he had acted with considerable restraint, was puzzled and could not understand why the zemstvo activists were hostile to him. "None of the [dismissed teachers]," he told Plehve in a report explaining his handling of the affair, "was deprived of the right to continue working; but I considered their further employment in the

Balashov district intolerable."[10] He made a special point of defending the imprisonment of Spuv. Because of her family connections, deep convictions and strong personality, she exercised "great influence over her colleagues" and thus posed a real danger if she remained in Makarovo.[11]

Actually, Stolypin could easily have nullified the Balashov zemstvo's resolutions in support of the dismissed teachers and in honor of Chenykaev. As governor, he had the authority to veto measures that had not been submitted to him before consideration by the zemstvo, and the deputies in Balashov had failed to notify Stolypin of their intentions. Apparently, Stolypin simply did not know that he had that power. Nevertheless, he was not prepared to accept the zemstvo's actions without expressing his strong disapproval.

He summoned the marshal of the nobility, Unkovskii, to his office and demanded answers to four provocative questions: On what basis did he, Unkovskii, a government official, assert at the zemstvo meeting that the teachers were innocent of all charges? What evidence did he have for the claim that the clergy was spreading slanderous charges against the teachers? What was the basis for his contention that twenty priests had conducted themselves in an unseemly manner and had circulated slanderous charges about the teachers? Why did the marshal of the nobility permit the zemstvo assembly to vote on "illegal motions"? Unfazed, Unkovskii answered all the queries. That Stolypin did not prohibit the dismissed teachers from obtaining work in other regions of the province suggested, he argued, that the charges against them were unfounded. Unkovskii also asserted that it was generally known that the priests were trying to undermine the zemstvo schools. The incident as to Chenykaev's portrait, he insisted, was not in any way intended as a political gesture by the zemstvo. When Unkovskii also accused Stolypin of bias against the zemstvo, the governor shot back by asking whether "the zemstvo assembly was openly declaring war against the administration or whether the assembly had unintentionally made a series of mistakes."[12] Unkovskii did not answer the question directly. He simply noted that the zemstvo in Balashov was liberal and if Stolypin considered that to be an "antigovernment" position, then he, Unkovskii, would have to resign and take his case to the people who had elected him marshal of the nobility.

Stolypin assured Unkovskii that he did not necessarily regard "the liberal point of view as an antigovernment" position and did not accept his offer to resign. The governor explained what appeared to be a conciliatory stand to Plehve: "It seemed to me to be a great mistake to play into the hands of the leadership of the Balashov opposition and to turn

Unkovskii into a victim of the government." Stolypin did not delude himself into believing that his conflicts with the zemstvo were over. He expected further "heated" and unpleasant discussions with liberal activists.[13]

He was right. He soon faced an avalanche of criticism as various conferences in the province (for example, of insurance agents and of doctors) expressed distress over what they regarded as arbitrary conduct. Even conservatives such as Count D. S. Olsufev, chairman of the provincial zemstvo board, signed a telegram praising Dr. Chenykaev and supporting his efforts to secure release from police custody. Now Stolypin called Olsufev on the carpet and demanded an explanation for having signed the telegram, but nothing could mollify him. Olsufev was to pay dearly for a relatively mild protest to the authorities. On November 18, 1903, Plehve sent Stolypin a strictly confidential memorandum stating that in view of Olsufev's support of Chenykaev he would not be appointed to any position in the Ministry of Internal Affairs.[14] Olsufev had set his heart on appointment to a vice-governorship. In despair, he resigned from the zemstvo board and suffered what seems to have been deep emotional distress.

In this first confrontation with the political opposition, Stolypin did not acquit himself with distinction. He acted impetuously; he had not mastered the regulations governing the zemstvos; and he appeared to have little understanding of the burgeoning liberal movement in Russia. Yet in some respects he displayed sound political instincts. He did not brand all opposition to the authorities as seditious, a fairly common tendency among defenders of the autocracy. And he realized the importance of not turning opponents of Tsarism into martyrs by resorting to excessively harsh measures.

Faithful to that principle, in later years he would occasionally meet with political opponents to discuss their differences without rancor and sometimes even with humor, as was recalled by the professional revolutionary S. V. Anikin, a leader of the Trudoviks (moderate socialists) in the First Duma in 1906. Stolypin had directed public institutions in Saratov not to employ him, and when a local zemstvo in Petrovsk district nevertheless offered him a post the governor vetoed the appointment. Anikin then sought a meeting with the governor, who "was so gracious that he received me in his luxurious office in Saratov." In the course of the meeting, Stolypin indicated that he was disturbed by Anakin's view that all the land should be given to the peasants. Anikin replied that he did indeed believe that "peasants should have all the land." To which Stolypin responded: "You may say this to me, Stolypin,

but not to the peasants." Stolypin did not change his mind about per-
mitting the employment of Anikin, but he nevertheless succeeded in
making a favorable personal impression on the revolutionary.[15]

Stolypin learned an important lesson from his first political challenge. Never again would he be unaware of his prerogatives, such as not
knowing that he could veto measures passed by a zemstvo. He now took
pains to study the details of the constitutional arrangements—in the
provinces and later in the capital—and used his prerogatives to the
maximum. He seems also to have realized early on in his career as a political leader that the struggle against the opposition would have to be
waged on several levels, that reliance on force alone would be self-
defeating. He opted for a more sophisticated strategy, and he would have
ample opportunity during the next two years in Saratov to test its effectiveness. His future career depended upon its success.

Stolypin also understood that to solidify his position as governor and
to advance in his career it would be necessary to cultivate good relations
with individuals in senior positions of authority in the capital. Early in
March 1904, he spent about a week in St. Petersburg and, much to his
satisfaction, discovered that his work in Saratov had not gone unnoticed. "Today," he wrote his wife on March 2, "I sat for one and a half
hours in Plehve's reception room and one and a half minutes in his office, . . . [and] he said that he wants to hear from me in [more] detail and
set aside a special time [for another meeting]. He asked me with a smile
what my general impressions were of my sinecure in Saratov province.
He went on to add that it was one of the most difficult and neglected
provinces." On leaving Plehve's office, he visited the seventy-year-old
Count I. I. Vorontsov-Dashkov, who had occupied several senior posts
in the civil service and was then chairing the Executive Committee of
the Red Cross. There were serious shortages in the theater of war—the
war with Japan had broken out a month earlier—and the committee
tried to find ways of quickly shipping tea, sugar, tobacco, and candles to
the front. Stolypin sent his wife a telegram on this matter with instructions to have Saratov newspapers publicize the shortages and ask readers
to donate goods. The last sentence in Stolypin's letter indicated that he
was not shy about seeking important contacts: "I have requested that I
be presented to the Sovereign (probably on Monday) and to both Em-
presses."[16] Six days later, on March 8, his request was granted and his
audience with the tsar went splendidly. Nicholas "was affectionate and
loquacious: he talked about the province, the patriotism that had been
awakened [by the war], asked about Sasha [Stolypin's son]. He ended

with an expression of confidence that all would go well with me in the province."[17] Stolypin could hardly have been more pleased.

During his week's stay in St. Petersburg Stolypin made several additional connections with dignitaries. He visited, among others, A. A. Makarov, a senior official in the Department of Police, Count N. D. Obolenskii, a member of the tsar's entourage at court, and dined at the house of B. V. Stürmer, former governor of Iaroslavl and now director of the Department of General Affairs in the Ministry of Internal Affairs. On March 6, Stolypin spent another half-hour with Plehve, "who agreed with all my ideas, so I am very satisfied." At the homes of the dignitaries he picked up all sorts of gossip and rumors, among them that he had been considered for a very difficult assignment, the governorship of Ekaterinoslav, a center of intense industrial unrest at the time. "Thank God," he told his wife, "I was not called upon."[18] Stolypin may not have wanted that particular post, but he had every reason to feel honored by his reception in the upper reaches of St. Petersburg society; only forty-two years old, he was already regarded as an energetic governor who could be counted upon to deal firmly with challenges to authority.

Stolypin's message to his wife about the Red Cross is one of the few references we have of his involvement in the war effort. It is strange that a senior official who was deeply patriotic left no detailed statement of his attitude toward the war. Stolypin's daughter tells us that when hostilities began, she could not understand the "lack of patriotic sentiment" in Saratov, particularly surprising to her since she had just read Tolstoy's *War and Peace*, which she viewed as a glorification of the Russian people for resisting the French invader. She asked her father for an explanation; he replied as follows: "How is it possible for the peasant to go gladly to war, defending leased land in regions previously unknown to him? This is a grievous and troublesome war, unredeemed by any impulse to make sacrifices."[19] Stolypin, of course, was right: the basic cause of the war was the imprudent policies of expansionism in the Far East pursued by various senior officials and influential men at court, several of them reckless adventurers pure and simple.[20] Stolypin seems to have realized this and therefore kept his own counsel on the diplomatic maneuvers that had led to the war. But he loved Russia, and the country's military defeats pained him. On May 20, 1905, when he learned of the disastrous defeat of the Russian navy in the Straits of Tsushima, he wrote to his wife: "How sad is the defeat of [Vice Admiral Z. P.] Rozhdestvenskii—this is the end of everything! Can you believe it, there are Russians who rejoice over it."[21] When he heard that the war had finally ended, in June 1905, he was relieved and overjoyed. "Papa's whole face changed," his daughter recalled, "illuminated by joy. He removed his cap, crossed himself, and, kissing Mama, said 'What happiness!'"[22] The debacle of the war profoundly influenced his thinking about Russia's role in international affairs: when he led the government after 1906 he always insisted on a nonbelligerent, basically cautious foreign policy.

Whatever his private views, he enthusiastically supported the war effort in public and did his utmost to further the work of the Red Cross. On one occasion, when a group of Red Cross workers left Saratov in 1904 for the front, he made a powerful speech invoking Russian patriotism that, according to his daughter, moved the entire audience to tears. "More than the inspired and passionately delivered words of my father, his face spoke and our eyes heard more than was actually said aloud. Tears flowed hotly. Many sobbed audibly. We forgot that Russian soldiers were being risked for land that was not Russian, that the fields where they were destined to find death were far removed from our homes. Those whom we honored that day were going to aid and support our soldiers. One eternal truth shone brightly, that each son of Russia had an obligation to serve his Tsar, to arise in defense of the Homeland from all encroachments on her majesty and honor." The speech was greeted with "a singular . . . and prolonged 'hurrah'"; for the first time Stolypin became conscious of his oratorical abilities. When his wife complimented him on having delivered a magnificent speech, he replied: "Truly? It even seemed to me that I did not speak so poorly this time. And I do not understand it. I have always considered myself such a stammerer, and I had not intended to make a big speech."[23] The confession is surprising given his later reputation as a powerful orator.

Two months after his return to Saratov from St. Petersburg, in mid-May of 1904, Stolypin discovered that his relief at not having to cope with violent unrest in Ekaterinoslav did not spare him from such an ordeal. He was forced to deal with an outburst of violence in Saratov, the first such challenge in his career. It took place in the Atkarsk district in the northwestern part of the province. His letters to his wife on the incident, though brief, are revealing about his general attitude toward disorders in the countryside. He did not yet consider them a serious problem and thought that "one day we will be done with them, [since] the peasants there are usually calm." He found it "boring for one's work to be constantly interrupted by such events." His real interest was to administer Saratov province, not to put down rebellious peasants. And if he had to do it, "I hope to avoid corporal punishment."

As soon as Stolypin learned that peasants in the Atkarsk district had "willfully seized products from food stores" he went to the region and began to talk to the ringleaders in hopes of persuading them to call off the rampage. "I simply lost my voice from reprimanding [the people] at meetings." Fearful for his safety, "my young Cossacks immediately were seized with a certain trembling." But Stolypin's strategy, to be used frequently in future confrontations, worked: the "rebellion" was put down quickly without bloodshed. As Stolypin reported to his wife on May 20: "Everything ended happily. . . . Thank God, I succeeded in avoiding arrests [and] floggings."[24] Plehve, delighted with the outcome, sent Stolypin a "secret letter" on June 16 in which "he thanked me in extremely complimentary language for the speed and energy with which order was restored in the Atkarsk district."[25]

Throughout 1904, Stolypin traveled extensively in Saratov familiarizing himself with local conditions, and unexpectedly he gained further experience in handling unrest. In mid-June, he went to the Tsaritsyn district on the southern tip of the province, and as soon as he arrived in the city of Tsaritsyn he was told of an ongoing incident in the local prison. A large number of prisoners persisted in singing revolutionary songs, which the local authorities considered an intolerable form of protest. As Stolypin tells it, the warden "lost his head and was afraid to let me into the prison." He was also afraid to punish any of the prisoners. "It seems," Stolypin concluded, "that the warden is a coward." Stolypin took charge, and on each of the next two days he spent several hours discussing political issues with the prisoners. In the end, they promised not to sing any more and to observe the rules of the prison. Only two prisoners were "slapped" into a cell, and then calm was fully restored. In the meantime, a procurator and the provincial inspector of prisons had rushed to the scene from Saratov, but their services were not needed. "Fear has a hundred eyes," Stolypin told his wife.[26] He concluded that if men in positions of responsibility magnified dangers out of all proportion they could not deal with crises rationally.

Stolypin's handling of the boisterous prisoners in Tsaritsyn was probably the first time that he resorted to what one of his earliest biographers dubbed the tactic of siege, which Stolypin much preferred to the tactic of storming the opposition.[27] Instead of using force immediately to put down a challenge to authority, he tried to talk troublemakers into abandoning unruly or lawless behavior. In one way or another, the tactic of siege became central to all of Stolypin's dealings with the opposition in Saratov and to a large extent later on when he was prime minister.

While touring in the Tsaritsyn district Stolypin recorded impressions that make clear that despite his loyalty and emotional attachment to the old order in Russia, especially its political system, he believed that his country had much to learn from Western Europe. On June 15, he wrote his wife about two "oases" he had visited in the southern tip of the province. The first was a French steel plant in Tsaritsyn itself, one of the largest industrial establishments in all of Russia. Part of the workforce and many of the foremen were French, but Russians worked amicably side by side with the foreigners. Russians were being trained for skilled work so that in time they would be able to replace the Frenchmen. Even then, in 1904, half the engineers, including the assistant director, were Russian. The workers were well treated; schools and hospitals had been built for them, and they, in turn, had not staged any strikes and had not participated in any disorders. All this greatly appealed to Stolypin as a model for factories owned by Russians. He also hoped that Russian workers would learn from their French colleagues the importance of saving some of their income and placing it in savings banks.

The second "oasis" that impressed Stolypin was the village of Sarepta, one of the German colonies established on the Volga in the eighteenth century. Stolypin referred to Sarepta as "an old Westphalian corner fully transferred to our steppe." He was enchanted by the hamlet with paved roads, stone houses with modern plumbing, numerous gardens, and vineyards. The *volost* (smallest administrative district) elder, the clerk, and the *volost* judge had all been educated in Europe. "One could not find fault with the order that prevailed in the district." Stolypin was particularly impressed by the fact that all official business with him was conducted in Russian. Moreover, when the local amateur orchestra began to play, "all the Germans began to sing loudly 'God Save the Tsar.'" It is not surprising that Stolypin was enchanted by a village such as Sarepta: it was efficiently run, its residents retained their ethnic customs, and yet they were thoroughly loyal to the Russian state.

Much to Stolypin's amazement, it took him only ten minutes to travel from Sarepta to an exotic Kalmyk village (*aul*), where he was shown local gods preserved in boxes, yurts (nomad's tents), and where he saw young children smoking pipes. "What an immense country, Russia!" Stolypin exclaimed.[28]

Nothing pleased Stolypin more in his frequent travels than public expressions of love for the tsar, even if that occasionally added to his administrative burdens, as it did late in June 1904, when he learned that he would have to leave Saratov for Kuznetsk for a week to make preparations for a brief visit by Nicholas to that town. Full of excitement,

Stolypin told his wife that he had been asked to accompany the tsar during his entire stay in Saratov province, which was to last almost a full day. One of his most difficult problems was to decide who would meet the sovereign: "Everyone" in this city of Old Believers, he wrote his wife, "wants to see the Tsar, and I am besieged [with requests]. Although only a deputation can be admitted, how can one refuse people who have never seen the Sovereign in person?" Stolypin ordered the local authorities to spruce up the streets and to build a pavilion for dignitaries to receive Nicholas. His one concern was the weather; a downpour, frequent at that time of the year, could "spoil everything."[29]

The enthusiastic reception accorded to Nicholas by the people of Kuznetsk was duly recorded by Stolypin, who was ecstatic at the success of the event. "Everything turned out excellently," he told his wife, "but how much anxiety and preparation went into these 10 minutes." The governor had to make certain that the railways ran on schedule on the day of the tsar's visit, that the pavilion was completed, that some four hundred children representing all the local schools were lined up with flags on the platform at the railway station, and that the right dignitaries were selected to address the tsar. The *volost* elder uttered the following words: "Your Majesty, accept the bread and salt from your peasants; don't be concerned, Little Father Tsar, we are all for you." The presentation of the children to the tsar was a great success; at Stolypin's request, the monarch spoke to many of them and after the event told Stolypin that the meeting with them had been "excellent." Nicholas also made a point of mingling with the peasants; he recognized one of them and recalled that they had once met, several years earlier, when he was still "without a beard. The peasants were delighted." The peasants lined up for several miles along the route taken by the tsar's carriage, and the sovereign "greeted them from the window." It was evident, Stolypin exulted, that "the vast majority of the people love the tsar and are selflessly devoted to him."[30]

Most thrilling of all for Stolypin was the invitation he received to join the tsar in his train in Saratov on his return trip to St. Petersburg. "He received me in one of his cabinets and I have never seen him so loquacious—he charmed me with his tenderness. He asked me about the peasants, about the agrarian question, about the difficulties of administering [the province]. He turned to me, for example, thus: 'Answer me, Stolypin, with complete candor.' He was very satisfied with his tour and said: 'When I see the people and this power, I feel the strength of Russia.'" The tsar ended his comments to Stolypin with the following words: "'You remember that when I sent you to Saratov province I told you that I give you this province "to restore its health" and now I say—continue to act in this way, firmly, judiciously, and calmly, as you have until now.' Then he promised very earnestly that he would come to Saratov province [again], to Balashov district (!!)." The audience with the tsar, Stolypin told his wife on July 2, was an event he would always remember, since it was so "unexpected."[31]

Stolypin's ecstasy was short-lived. On July 15, he learned that Plehve had been assassinated, an event that in many ways was a turning point in the evolution of the public mood in 1904. The elimination of the most dynamic figure in the government both exposed the depth of despair over the state of affairs in the country and opened up new possibilities for popular agitation against the war and the government. Appointed to head the Ministry of Internal Affairs in April 1902, Plehve had come to symbolize the capriciousness and intransigence of the autocratic regime.

The tsar regretted the loss of a "friend and an irreplaceable Minister of Internal Affairs," and the conservative newspaper *Novoe vremia* lauded him as one of "the most steadfast and staunchest supporters of order . . . [against] the enemies of Russia." The assassination was such a vile crime, according to the paper, that it should receive a "moral rebuff from all reasonable [and] steadfast friends of order and legality."[32]

That this did not happen startled Count Aloys Lexa von Aehrenthal, the Austro-Hungarian ambassador to St. Petersburg and a knowledgeable observer of conditions in Russia. "The most striking aspect of the present situation," Aehrenthal told his superiors in Vienna, "is the total indifference of society to an event that constituted a heavy blow to the principles of government. One could hardly have expected sympathy for a minister who because of his authoritarian bent must have made many enemies. But . . . a certain degree of human compassion, or at least concern and anxiety with respect to the immediate future, would be natural. Not a trace of this is to be found. Up to now I have found only totally indifferent people or people so cynical that they say that no other outcome was to be expected."

Even conservatives and loyal servants of the tsar expressed no regret over Plehve's murder. Aehrenthal was "genuinely surprised" that "barely 24 hours after the terroristic act, Count Lamsdorff [the minister of foreign affairs], with startling candor, critically analyzed Plehve's activities in the tone of a man filled with a sense of moral relief at the disappearance of an inconvenient and uncongenial colleague." Witte, long at odds with Plehve, expressed similar sentiments, as did "most of Plehve's colleagues," even those who occupied high positions in the

Ministry of Internal Affairs. It was evident to Aehrenthal that the assassination was "in the last resort . . . directed at the person of the Tsar" and amounted to an attack on the entire system of government. "It can be said," the ambassador concluded, "that practically all strata of the educated population of Russia regard the government's struggle against the revolutionary opposition with total apathy, if not with *Schadenfreude* [malicious joy]."[33] Aehrenthal had put his finger on a critical fact: the fragility of the autocracy's popular support, a precondition for the eruption of a political storm.

Stolypin also sensed the significance of Plehve's assassination, which explains his shock and dismay on learning the news. "At first I did not believe it . . . [but then] at 6 in the evening I received confirmation." His next statement, "The poor Sovereign!" suggests that he immediately realized that Plehve's murder signified more than the removal of a despised minister; it was in fact an assault on the autocracy.[34] A day later he confessed that he was thoroughly "confused," all the more so because Saratov had been struck by an epidemic of cholera. He had planned to go to St. Petersburg for a few days and then accompany his mother-in-law to Vienna to consult a doctor about her loss of hearing. Plehve had granted him permission to absent himself from Saratov for a total of ten days, but now he doubted the wisdom of leaving without new approval from the Ministry of Internal Affairs.[35] In the end, he decided to make the trip, but he confessed that he was "not entirely composed" because he did not know who the next minister of internal affairs would be and feared that his new superior might not approve his traveling to Vienna. In fact, Stolypin was apprehensive not simply about his travel plans but about his professional future. "In general," he wrote his wife on July 18, 1904, "the question of the new minister is very important for me. What kind of policies [will he pursue] and will he have the confidence in me personally [that has been bestowed upon me] till now? An anxious time."[36]

At first, the journey was relaxing and had a "calming effect on his nerves." He wrote on one of his stops, Chulpanovka, that he had no access to newspapers and was totally ignorant of latest developments; given the alarming events in the capital, he did not mind in the slightest.[37] But once he reached St. Petersburg on his way to Austria his mood turned sour again. The people in the capital appeared to him to be thoroughly despondent. "Today [I heard] ominous rumors that Admiral [V. K.] Vitgoft was killed and that the entire squadron at Port Arthur was sent out and destroyed. Good Lord, what a difficult time for Russia externally as well as internally. The only bright spot is the birth of an heir." As a devoted monarchist he was cheered by this event, but at the same time Stolypin was full of foreboding: "What awaits this infant and what will be his fate and the fate of Russia?"[38]

As was his wont, Stolypin made the rounds of leading figures in St. Petersburg, but this time with less success than on previous visits. His visits to Stürmer and to A. A. Lopukhin, the director of police, went well enough for him personally, but the other officials he saw were anxious and dejected. Everyone speculated about who would be appointed in Plehve's place—each day a new name emerged as a likely candidate— and everyone spoke about the immediate future with a sense of foreboding. Abroad, Russia was being militarily humiliated by Japan, and at home the terrorists did their work with seeming impunity. "God, what a misfortune," Stolypin exclaimed. Highly sensitive to Russia's standing in the world, he did not look forward to his trip to Vienna. "For me, the journey to Vienna is a misfortune, especially since I will be ashamed to look at the faces of the Germans; it will be offensive to me to take into my hands the foreign newspapers. And what a mood I'm in!"[39] Stolypin regarded any humiliation of his country a personal affront to himself.

One meeting in St. Petersburg went badly and deserves to be recounted because it helps to explain his greatest political and personal defeat, suffered in 1911, near the end of his career. It was his encounter with P. N. Durnovo, a senior official with a distinctly dubious reputation. Durnovo had joined the civil service in 1872 and within twelve years had advanced to the position of director of the Department of Police in St. Petersburg. A loyal supporter of Plehve (at the time the head of the police in the Department of Internal Affairs), he appeared to be destined to rise even higher on the bureaucratic ladder. In 1893, however, Durnovo's career suffered a setback when his exploits as a womanizer led to a scandal. He had befriended a lady of easy virtue who was also the frequent companion of an ambassador representing either Brazil or Spain. Suspecting his paramour of betrayal, Durnovo ordered his agents to pilfer a batch of her love letters. The lady complained to the ambassador, who indignantly reported the theft to Emperor Alexander III. Aghast at the impropriety by one of his officials, Alexander issued an unambiguous order: "Get that swine out of here within twenty-four hours." Durnovo's career appeared to be finished, but soon after Alexander's death he managed to obtain new government appointments, first to the Governing Senate and then to the Ministry of Internal Affairs.[40]

According to Stolypin, Durnovo greeted him in an "extremely unfriendly" manner and told him that in view of the cholera epidemic in

Saratov he ought not to be away from the province. As Stolypin was about to leave, after a long discussion of administrative affairs, he told Durnovo that he had been struck by his "unfriendly manner." Durnovo "began to laugh and said: don't pay any attention to it." Stolypin expressed his dismay in a brief comment to his wife: "Sont cela bel e bon, mais je n'y suis pas habitue." (That is all well and good, but I am not accustomed to this.) It was the beginning of a long and bitter enmity between the two men, explicable only as personal rivalry or simply as mutual dislike. Politically, the two men shared many views, though there were some important differences between them on how to deal with unrest.

One reason for Stolypin's visit to Durnovo had been to secure permission from the Ministry of Internal Affairs to accompany his mother-in-law to Vienna to see a medical specialist. In the absence of a head of the ministry—Plehve's successor had not yet been appointed—no senior official was prepared to take it upon himself to approve Stolypin's request. As Stolypin put it, everyone is "afraid to take a step," a telling commentary on the workings of the tsarist bureaucracy. The decision was left up to the tsar himself, and Durnovo agreed to make the request at the time he presented an official report to Nicholas. The tsar gave his approval.[41]

Stolypin's letters to his wife from Vienna contained the usual details about his daily activities and expenses. He rented two rooms at a daily cost of eighteen krons, or seven rubles and twenty kopecks. The hotel was quiet, but at a cost of two rubles and twenty kopecks dinner was too expensive. He accompanied his mother-in-law to several specialists, one of whom massaged her ears with a vibrator and that seemed to improve her hearing somewhat. All in all, the prognosis was that she would need these treatments for two months to effect a substantial improvement. Stolypin remained in Vienna for about a week.[42]

After his return to Russia in mid-August 1904, Stolypin enjoyed two months of relative calm, which was unexpectedly interrupted by the so-called banquet campaign, an outburst of public discontent that marked the beginning of a nationwide assault on the autocracy that lasted two and a half years. The sponsor of the campaign, the liberal Union of Liberation,* had initially urged supporters to hold the first banquets on February 19, 1904, to celebrate the anniversary of the emancipation of

---

*An underground organization that called for the liquidation of the autocracy, the establishment of a constitutional form of government, self-determination for the nationalities of the empire, and economic as well as social reforms.

the serfs. Modeled on the famous banquets in Paris in 1847–48, the events were intended to unite "the bulk of the country's intelligentsia around the constitutional banner." But the wave of patriotism after the outbreak of the war made it advisable to postpone a demonstration of opposition to the government. By the fall, however, the public mood had changed, and now the Union advised supporters around the country to organize banquets in honor of the fortieth anniversary of the judicial reforms. Such banquets with a clearly political focus were not normally allowed, and liberals had to negotiate at length with the government, which in the end relented, on the understanding that all the gatherings would be "private."

The rash of political meetings—some thirty-eight in twenty-six cities—was unprecedented. Never before had so many citizens, most of them from the educated classes, joined forces to give vent to their profound unhappiness with the state of affairs. The banquets adopted various kinds of resolutions, but to one degree or another all contributed to mobilizing support for the demands of liberal activists.

In Saratov province, liberals together with radicals (including Social Democrats) organized several banquets. In addition, between November 1904 and early January 1905 a number of mass meetings, sometimes attracting as many as a thousand people, were held at various hotels. The demands were everywhere more or less the same: the resolutions called for civil liberties, amnesty for political prisoners, and a democratically elected constituent assembly. The ferment was national in scale, but in few regions was it as intense as in Saratov, where banquets continued to be held until the eve of Bloody Sunday. The last one in Saratov attracted fifteen hundred people.[43]

The events of Bloody Sunday, on January 9, 1905, proved to be decisive in transforming what had been a peaceful campaign by relatively small sectors of society for fundamental reform into a national offensive against the old order that eventually enlisted the support of huge numbers of workers, peasants, and national minorities. Ironically, even the procession of workers on that fateful Sunday had been intended as a peaceful affair. It was organized by Father Gapon, a mercurial and enigmatic figure. The workers and their families, numbering somewhere between 50,000 and 100,000, marched on the Winter Palace with a petition that amounted to a desperate plea to the tsar, still referred to as "the father," to treat his subjects not as slaves but as human beings, and to institute reforms to lighten their burden because such were the dictates of compassion. In calling for a constituent assembly elected on the basis of a democratic suffrage, civil liberties for all citizens, the right to establish trade unions, and an eight-hour working day, Gapon clearly aligned his followers with the political opposition that had turned increasingly vocal and militant in 1904. It should be noted, however, that the petition did not demand the abolition of the monarchy or the introduction of socialism. Nor did it contain threats of violence.

Nevertheless, the government, out of fear, meanness, or simple stupidity, decided to disperse the procession, by force if necessary. When the marchers did not heed the officers' orders to disperse, soldiers began to shoot indiscriminately into the crowds, killing 130 and seriously wounding close to 300. The fury of the people in the streets was uncontrollable, as was the anger of citizens throughout the empire. Indeed, the massacre electrified public opinion in virtually every region of the country. The U.S. consul in Odessa did not exaggerate when he wrote to the State Department that "[a]ll classes condemn the authorities and more particularly the Emperor. The present ruler has lost absolutely the affection of the Russian people, and whatever the future may have in store for the dynasty, the present Czar will never again be safe in the midst of his people."[44]

The news about Bloody Sunday reached Saratov province within a day, on January 10, and provoked great agitation. Within two days, on January 12, strikes erupted in a series of factories, railways, and other establishments in the provincial capital, and although estimates of the number of workers and white collar employees who left their jobs vary, ranging from two thousand to seventy-five hundred, there is no doubt that it was the most extensive work stoppage ever in that region of the country. On the same day, a crowd of workers and sympathizers marched toward the center of the city, but a force of policemen and Cossacks stood in their path. When some marchers sought to break through the police line, they were dispersed by Cossacks who made liberal use of their whips. During the next two days activists, among them Social Democrats, distributed some ten thousand leaflets appealing for support. By the 14th the strike had spread to some smaller enterprises; employees of the city government and provincial and district zemstvos also left their jobs. One day later a large number of students at various schools stopped attending class.

In large measure, the strikers' demands in Saratov echoed those voiced by liberals during the banquet campaign. But the strikers now put forward some demands of their own; they still demanded a constitutional order, but they also called for an end to the war with Japan, the introduction of an eight-hour day, the right to celebrate May 1 without loss of pay, elimination of overtime, increased pay, improvement in sanitary conditions at places of work, elimination of searches and fines at factories, and a promise not to punish workers who had laid down their tools nor to dock them for days lost during the strike. At one large meeting attended by some two thousand people, many of whom (perhaps eight hundred) were allegedly armed with "revolvers, sporting guns, daggers, Finnish knives, and iron canes," speakers called for an armed uprising aimed at the overthrow of the autocracy. Within a few days, three-quarters of the factories in the Saratov region were closed down and the strike movement had spread to other towns in Saratov province: in Tsaritsyn, forty-five hundred went on strike, and in Kuznets, three hundred followed suit. All told, ninety-six hundred men and women left their jobs in Saratov province.[45]

Stolypin wasted no time in taking firm measures to stop the strikes. On January 12, he issued an announcement informing workers that, according to Point 1 of Article 105 of the Industrial Regulations, any worker who missed more than three days of work risked having his contract annulled and being dismissed immediately. Stolypin also prohibited gatherings of workers in streets or public places and warned that the slightest attempt to disturb the peace would be stopped by force. In order to avoid any "unfortunate incidents," people lingering in public spaces should not hesitate to honor requests from the police to disperse.[46]

The first wave of strikes in Saratov began to peter out on January 17 and ended completely on January 20. Employers had made some concessions, mainly in the form of higher wages, but according to the chief of the Saratov Gendarme Administration, D. M. Pomerantsev, many workers were also moved to end the strike because they had concluded that their leaders were more interested in troublemaking than in gaining better conditions for employees. It may also be that the police had succeeded in intimidating strikers. Pomerantsev claimed that no fewer than forty-seven people had been arrested for disorderly conduct and had received prison sentences ranging from two weeks to three months.[47]

Strikes and street demonstrations were not the only reactions in Saratov to Bloody Sunday. Within days of the massacre the Provincial Zemstvo Assembly met and seriously considered passing a resolution demanding a constitution for Russia. Such a step would have been unthinkable had M. F. Melnikov, the provincial marshal of the nobility, chaired the meeting, but he did not attend because of illness. His replacement, Prince E. E. Ukhtomskii, the district marshal of the nobility, was a fervent liberal, and he urged the Assembly to adopt the radical measure. On hearing of the zemtsi's plans, Stolypin issued a warning that it would be illegal for them even to discuss general political questions. The zemtsi retreated and closed the meeting without voting on the resolution. But in an act of defiance Count A. D. Nesselrode then took it upon himself to organize an unofficial meeting of the zemtsi, who approved the eleven points adopted by the zemstvo congress in November 1904, shortly before the inauguration of the banquet campaign.[48] It amounted to a call for a constitution. N. N. Lvov's proposal that the resolution together with the eleven points be presented to Stolypin was denounced as much too moderate, indeed as "reactionary." Count Nesselrode argued that if there was to be any visit to the governor it should be by a delegation of zemtsi together "with the people," which would have been a rather bold move. After Stolypin threatened to deal harshly with such a delegation the zemtsi decided to drop the plan. Nesselrode immediately went abroad, apparently to avoid further conflicts with the governor.[49]

On January 29, Stolypin sent a detailed report to A. G. Bulygin, the minister of internal affairs, on his efforts to contain unrest in Saratov over the preceding three weeks. The report is noteworthy for three reasons: it reveals Stolypin's strategy in dealing with massive unrest; it presents his analysis of the causes of the disorders; and it suggests that he had been deeply fearful that he might not be able to prevail. He did not say in so many words that the opposition would succeed in undermining his authority, but a central theme of his report, repeated several times, was that he lacked the force necessary to cope with the demonstrators and strikers.

Early in the report he pointed out that as soon as the strikes began he took stock of the strikers in the province and the troops at his disposal. Initially, about six thousand factory workers and railway employees had left their jobs. His military force consisted of thirty-five hundred men; of these only about two thousand owned uniforms and only a few of them were equipped with revolvers. The governor also could call on eighty Cossacks and forty mounted police. In other words, close to one-half of the available troops, all of them mobilized as recently as December 1904, had not yet been fitted out with uniforms and had not yet received the training necessary to turn them into a disciplined force. Stolypin was relieved that the new recruits were outside the city of Saratov at the time of unrest; their use in controlling crowds could easily have resulted in disaster.[50]

Stolypin's complaint that he lacked the wherewithal to deal with the mounting unrest was a constant refrain in the reports of local officials. The truth is that despite Russia's deserved reputation as a repressive police state, the police were notably inefficient, primarily because the gov-

ernment was niggardly in its appropriations for the security forces. Salaries were extremely low, conditions of work were deplorable, and there
were far too few officers, fewer, in fact, than the government's own
guidelines. In the rural regions of the empire, where some ninety million people lived, the Ministry of Internal Affairs could dispose of only
1,582 constables and 6,874 sergeants. As a result, corruption and other
forms of dishonesty on the part of policemen were perennial problems.
Under the best of circumstances, the authorities faced enormous difficulties in dealing with criminality and the maintenance of order. In periods of intense unrest, these tasks often overwhelmed conscientious officials, of whom there were not that many to start with.[51] For Stolypin,
the lack of adequate and reliable security forces proved to be a major
handicap.

He believed that the ideal way to handle masses of demonstrators
was to deploy a large number of policemen and soldiers at a few strategic
locations so as to intimidate the crowds into dispersing and thus to
avoid armed conflict. Hours after the strike erupted, the governor met
with the military commanders in Saratov and they all agreed not to di-
vide their forces into small units but to concentrate on the protection of
the railways, the state liquor stores, the theater, the banks, and the wa-
terworks. But, as Stolypin noted, he did not have enough troops "to protect all the factories . . . [several of which] were located 4 to 6 versts from
the city; if . . . [I had deployed small] groups of soldiers [and they] had
been crushed by a crowd, then this would have had an intoxicating effect on it [the crowd]." The morale of the marchers and demonstrators
would have been boosted, encouraging them to undertake ever more
daring actions. To the governor's delight, the tactic worked perfectly: at
railway workshops and the railway depot, the crowd was so surprised by
the sight of armed soldiers that it did not advance and soon split into
separate groups. The governor also sent a telegram, signed by all the senior officers, to St. Petersburg requesting an additional Cossack regiment
to help him with the policing of Saratov.

Stolypin maintained close contact with the commanding officer,
General A. I. Petrov, and other senior officers, meeting with them every
evening to decide which establishments were to be protected by troops
the next day. Stolypin was especially proud of his decision, against the
advice of city officials, to keep the theater open. Obviously, his motive
was to send a message to the strikers that he would do his utmost to
keep the city functioning normally. "I insisted," Stolypin wrote to Bulygin, "that performances continue and I personally attended [the thea-

ter]." He did so even though "I received letters threatening me and my family."

Stolypin also sought to set an example of fearlessness by personally leading troops in a particularly threatening situation. When a group of demonstrators gathered at a grove near the railway depot he twice appeared with fifty artillerymen, a show of force that by itself prompted the demonstrators to disperse. But these triumphs proved to be short-lived. A day or so later, on January 16, some three thousand people, many of them carrying weapons of various kinds, appeared at the grove. The governor had hoped to forestall such new meetings by maintaining a military presence in the area, but, once again, he could not act as he wished because he did not have enough troops.

Stolypin decided to bide his time until he could bring up reinforcements. In the meantime, a delegation from the city duma and provincial zemstvo appeared and asked him not to use force against the people in the grove and in general to act as gently as possible. One of the duma notables declared that the government would not be weakened by a workers' march and mass meeting even if revolutionary songs were sung. Another suggested that city council representatives be allowed to serve as intermediaries in negotiating with the workers. "I answered," Stolypin reported to the Ministry of Internal Affairs, "that my response would be brief: 'I have taken an oath.' The city council member answered that he too had taken an oath. I reminded [the delegation] that it was my duty to preserve order by all measures, that I would more willingly shed my own blood than that of a stranger, but that in the event of resistance by the crowd or any kind of violence on its part I would resort to the most extreme measures: that there is no revolution here and would not be, and that I would prevent not only a procession but even a simple gathering of the people." Stolypin reported with no small measure of satisfaction that the organizers of the meeting understood his position. The crowd in the grove dispersed as soon as it became evident that the governor had succeeded in bringing to the scene a substantial military force.

Stolypin insisted that only by resorting to strong measures could he foil the opposition's attempt to sow panic and incite the crowds into ever more daring actions against the authorities. There was no doubt in his mind that he faced not a workers' but a revolutionary movement. "The workers," he wrote, "left work partly because they were coerced, partly out of curiosity, and partly from a desire to achieve [economic] gains. They had not themselves prepared any demands. The lists of demands that they brandished were supplied to them by revolutionary circles, but the workers often tore off the first points of the lists, consisting of political demands (constituent assembly, end of the war, and an end to all legal proceedings for political crimes) and, turning to the factory director, often said: '[Go] directly to point four'" (which dealt with economic issues).[52]

A curious mix of toughness and even bravado coupled with self-promotion and pessimism pervaded the entire report to the minister of internal affairs. Stolypin boasted of his success in containing the unrest with a show of force and personal courage. At the same time, he stressed that he had achieved his successes with a minimum actual use of force. His public vow to arrest anyone who "engaged in unrest in the streets or in [public] institutions" had sufficed to persuade most citizens to remain off the streets.

He conceded in his report that he also did not shrink from making threats he knew to be legally dubious. In an attempt to halt the strikes at public institutions (the railways, schools, hospitals, etc.) he decided to resort to an extreme measure, that, he admitted, "exceeded [his] authority." He warned the zemstvo chairmen and the mayors of cities that workers in their jurisdictions who left their jobs would be dismissed and could be re-employed "only with . . . [the governor's] agreement." This bold step, Stolypin boasted, was "completely successful." To be sure, some people questioned the governor's right to order the dismissal of strikers, but nevertheless the employees quickly returned to their jobs.

All in all, the agitators had not succeeded in provoking general panic in Saratov, an outcome for which Stolypin took credit. True, there were "rumors," which he neither confirmed nor denied, that the Cossacks had beaten workers with whips; and he conceded that by the end of the month ninety-four people (among them two journalists and six employees of various public institutions) had been taken into custody. But he did not think that this in any way diminished his claim to have routed the opposition without resort to significant force.

One other feature of this report deserves to be noted. Stolypin insisted that the workers were merely the pawns of the revolutionaries.[53] This was, however, not his characteristic position on the growing upheaval in Russia. Indeed, at about the time he wrote the report to Bulygin, Stolypin also prepared a much longer, and immeasurably more nuanced "Most Loyal Report on the Province of Saratov for the Year 1904." Addressed directly to the tsar, it was the first time that he took up issues of a national dimension. Stolypin began with strong criticism of zemstvo activists and in particular of the Third Element (the technical experts employed by the zemstvos). The latter, he contended, rejected all attempts at gradual change. He spoke scornfully of the zemstvo employees' "contempt and complete ignorance of other classes and their attitude toward, and often direct disregard of, the vital interests of the country. They have a passion for a rupture, and instinctively prefer a revolutionary course to reform by legal means." And yet, in light of "our military failures" and "governmental weakness" the zemstvo activists and the Third Element in Saratov were gaining in strength, especially among students, medical personnel, and lawyers. It seemed to Stolypin that "[we] are experiencing a state crisis, accompanied, naturally, by destructive occurrences and events of a chaotic character."

Stolypin went on to warn, however, that it would be a grave mistake to ignore the supporters of the zemstvo activists and Third Element. The authorities faced a dilemma: "It is impossible to lean on them [that is, the activists] for support since they are hostile [to us], but to apply only repression against them would only strengthen them." On the other hand, the "party," as Stolypin referred to them, could in fact be useful to the authorities if it were restrained by "others who stand amongst the people." He elaborated on this only briefly, pointing out that one "must await and support the birth of a landowners' party that is rooted in the people and that, opposed to the theorists, might render harmless the 'third element.'"[54] These tantalizingly vague statements have been interpreted, with considerable plausibility, as a reference to the formation of a political movement of moderate noble landlords who would counteract the Third Element.[55] Stolypin certainly favored such a moderate "party" and took various steps to encourage its formation.[56]

However, the basic thrust of the "Most Loyal Report" of 1905 was different. Stolypin's central concern was to impress upon the tsar the necessity of fundamental reforms in the countryside, which, he emphasized, would have a moderating effect on the peasantry and therefore on the entire political landscape. He was suggesting that a moderate peasantry could serve as an effective counterweight to the radical Third Element.

Before spelling out his recommendations, Stolypin reviewed the economic situation in Saratov. Except for disturbing news from the Far East and growing agitation by radicals, the year had passed quietly and the harvest had been reasonably good. Still, Stolypin detected signs of "deep disorder in peasant life." The reason for this was the widespread poverty and even hunger among the peasantry, which he attributed to the antiquated methods of farming that "paralyze the personal initiative and spontaneity of the peasant and doom him to wretched vegetation."[57] In his view, one institution bore the blame for hampering economic growth in the countryside. That was the commune, to which the peasant was fiercely attached, in part because he had a passion for equality in land allotments that the commune system guaranteed and in part because he simply did not understand that better arrangements were possible. Under the prevailing system of land distribution, which provided for periodic repartitions of the land to take into account the changes in family size, the peasant enjoyed no proprietary rights in the land he worked and therefore had little incentive to amass funds to purchase land or the tools to improve productivity. Yet the peasants did yearn for more land, a yearning they sought to satisfy periodically by illegally seizing the lands of large landowners.

The only way to counter the deleterious effects of the commune, in Stolypin's view, was to eliminate it as an institution and transform the peasants into owners of land. The result would be growing respect for public order, since "the small owner represents the nucleus on which rests the stable order of the state." The peasants, Stolypin assured the tsar, could potentially serve as a pillar of stability because, aside from land reform, they had little interest in the kind of political changes that revolutionaries were advocating.[58] In short, Stolypin thought of the peasants as a counterpoise to the militant zemstvo activists and the Third Element. Stolypin here was voicing an old idea, formulated most eloquently in seventeenth-century England by General Ireton in the Putney debates, that the owner of property is most likely to be a responsible and law-abiding citizen because he has a stake in society. Of course, the idea that the commune should be abolished to stimulate prosperity was not new; for decades various committees had advocated it and S. Iu. Witte, the forceful minister of finance from 1892 to 1903, was the most recent proponent of the idea. But no one before Stolypin stressed the need to utilize to the maximum the authority of the state's administrative machinery to bring about the breakup.[59] In particular, he urged active involvement of the Peasant Bank in promoting the development of private farming. This would be especially desirable now that "Your Imperial Highness has graciously begun to listen to the voice of the people which is to be expressed by a State Duma," a reference to the discussion in official circles at the time about the establishment of a representative institution. From the context it appears that Stolypin supported such an institution, though he did not specifically say so.[60]

Much as he argued in favor of the abolition of the commune as a prerequisite for political stability, Stolypin held that such a reform would not by itself immediately halt the unrest sweeping the country. He believed that local authorities must be given additional powers to deal with disorder. Specifically, he requested that governors be granted greater latitude in imposing "punishments for infringement of order by administrative means."[61] But the burden of restoring order should not rest solely on the shoulders of governors, who were likely to become the target of the "most bitter attacks," which would place them in an "entirely unbearable" position. He urged the formation of special administrative courts so that the task of meting out punishments would be carried out by a "collective body."[62] These last points, stressing a firm policy toward unrest, were surely music to Tsar Nicholas's ears. When he read the report he wrote the following on his copy: "The ideas expressed here deserve attention."[63] Stolypin had now gone far in establishing his reputation in St. Petersburg as a decisive, imaginative, and effective administrator.

That his approach to the turmoil was beginning to resonate with the elite of St. Petersburg became evident to Stolypin early in March 1905 during one of his brief trips to the capital. He had traveled via Moscow, a somber city still under the pall of the assassination of Grand Duke Sergei Aleksandrovich a few weeks earlier. By contrast, in the capital the sun shone brightly, there was much traffic in the streets "as if no threat were hanging over Russia." Stolypin had other reasons to be cheerful in the capital. With some excitement, he wrote his wife that he had learned from I. G. Knoll, the vice-governor of Saratov, then also in St. Petersburg, "that in Petersburg many people are talking about my activities, that everywhere he hears talk about me." Other acquaintances also told him that "many in Petersburg talk about the governor of Saratov." Stolypin reacted with appropriate modesty: "All this inspires me with melancholy," as if to suggest anxiety about moving up the bureaucratic ladder. Yet he was delighted to learn that V. N. Kokovtsov, the minister of finance, expressed interest in meeting him. Stolypin arranged for what appears to have been simply a courtesy call, not unimportant for an ambitious young governor.[64]

The intensification of social and political conflict in Saratov throughout 1905 was almost tailor-made for someone with his gifts. Many provincial governors, who faced conditions similar to those in Saratov, could think of no better policy than to remain in their mansions and give free rein to the police and the military to cope with the turbulence. Stolypin, on the other hand, implemented his policy of active engagement wherever trouble arose. It was a risky approach to the upheaval because it exposed him not only to personal defeats but also to personal danger. As it turned out, Stolypin won many of the skirmishes and thus enhanced his reputation for extraordinary personal courage. Of course, he was well aware of the impact on public opinion of his dramatic exploits, although he sought to convey the impression that he was merely following a cardinal principle of politics. "Nervousness," he once said to an editor, "is pardonable in ladies; in politics there must be no nerves."[65]

Although the accounts of his heroism are far too numerous to be repeated, a few deserve mention, if for no other reason than that they shed light on Stolypin's personality. They are also important because his fearlessness and his confrontational style help explain his effectiveness as governor and later on as prime minister. Even many of his opponents acknowledged that he was a leader who commanded respect because he did not ask others to do what he would not do himself. In large measure, these exploits endowed him with charisma, that rare attribute to which all leaders aspire.

When he heard sometime in 1905 (there is no exact date for this incident) that a huge crowd had gathered in a large square in Saratov, he immediately went there without bothering to take along a police escort and confidently marched toward the "enraged people." As soon as his presence was noted, several men hurled shouts and threats at him. One "sturdy chap" came up to him with a club in his hands, but to everyone's surprise Stolypin did not flinch. He took off his greatcoat and threw it to the young man: "Hold it!" Taken aback, the man dutifully picked up the coat, letting the club drop to the ground. Then the governor turned to the crowd and firmly ordered the people to disperse. "And everyone dispersed." "There are people," according to the author of this account, "who without studying the matter possess the power to command."[66]

On another occasion, during a tour of the countryside in Saratov in mid-1905, someone fired two shots at Stolypin. According to his daughter, "Papa actually saw the fleeing criminals. Papa threw himself after them but was restrained by his assistant, Prince Obolenskii, who held Papa's arm."[67] Some weeks later, as he was addressing a rebellious crowd, a man suddenly aimed a revolver at him. The governor opened his coat and challenged the would-be assassin by shouting "Shoot!" The revolutionary dropped his arm and "the revolver slipped from his grasp."[68] It is worth noting that Stolypin did not confine his bold moves to unrest on the left. During one of his travels in the province of Saratov, he encountered a group of "reactionary hooligans" throwing bricks at liberals and Jews. Without hesitation, he cried out: "Is this the way you show your loyalty to your Sovereign?"[69]

One additional detailed account of how Stolypin handled a serious flare-up in February 1905 in Mordovskii Karai, Balashov district, deserves attention because it demonstrates, at one and the same time, his bravery, toughness, tenacity, and harshness in a particularly striking way. The authenticity of the account is beyond doubt; the author, the journalist A. A. Argunov, was a man of the left, without any wish to embellish Stolypin's feats or to glorify him in any way.

The troubles in Mordovskii Karai began with claims by local peasants that the landlord, N. N. Lvov, a man with impeccably liberal credentials, had in his possession a document proving that part of the forest on his estate belonged to them. For ten years efforts had been made to locate the "official document" and many legal battles had been fought in the courts, but no such paper was found. Early in 1905 the peasants lost patience and began a campaign to force Lvov to hand over the land they claimed to be theirs. Some disorders had broken out, and Stolypin, fearing that the agitation would spill over into widespread violence, agreed to appear at a meeting on February 17 of three thousand people, old and young, male and female. The *starshina* [elder], named Serdobintsev, greeted the governor with the traditional bread and salt, but Stolypin "unceremoniously" refused the offer and immediately challenged the crowd: "I am the representative of our Tsar! I came to stop unrest here. Why do you chop down the trees that belong to Lvov?" The peasants replied in a friendly tone that "[t]he forest belongs to us" and asked Stolypin to produce the "plan" of Lvov's estate, which, they continued to insist, would prove the legitimacy of their claim.

By this time, the exchange between the peasants and the governor had become so noisy that Stolypin called an end to the meeting and asked the crowd to select fifteen people with whom he would continue the discussions. The crowd immediately turned down the request and simply reiterated the demand for the document. Stolypin left in a huff, spent half an hour in the office of the district administration, and returned with a list of forty-five names of people who, he claimed, had instigated the campaign to cut down trees in the disputed forest. He asked all forty-five to step forward, but only three did so. Angrily, Stolypin ordered the police officer, a certain Sakharov, to "find all of them!" Together with four village constables and twenty Cossacks, Sakharov did his best but could locate only eight additional "ringleaders." Stolypin now ordered four companies of soldiers to push back the crowd and make arrests. Defiantly, the peasants exclaimed that they would not give up any of their comrades and challenged the governor to "take the entire village."

The crowd now pressed forward against the soldiers lined up in front of them. Stolypin ordered the soldiers to advance toward the peasants, making a clash imminent. On the advice of one peasant, the crowd started to take into their hands whatever they could find—pickets, logs, and stones—to repel the Cossacks. Having done so, the peasants went on the offensive, forcing the troops to retreat. One soldier was severely wounded and the rest retreated. Stolypin and his forces had suffered a humiliating defeat.

Nevertheless, Stolypin, after he had gone to the *volost* administration building, tried to calm the peasants who had followed him by engaging them in a conversation about the conflict. His hope, as he had put it in a letter to his wife, was to "bring them to their knees" by "nagging" them.[70] But they were in a rage and replied to him with "abuse and threats." "Beat the Cossacks," shouted the peasants, several of whom also threatened to beat the governor. At that moment he was alone, without any police or Cossack protection, and yet he made no attempt to escape. "He tried," according to Argunov, "to defeat the peasants with his courage and the threat of retribution." Stepping down from the porch of the administration building, Stolypin admonished the angry crowd: "I am only one [person] among you. You can kill me but you should know that you would kill me but not the governor: tomorrow a governor will take my place and will present himself to you." In an instant the crowd fell silent, though a few peasants in the back continued to shout "Beat him up!" Realizing that his efforts were in vain, Stolypin jumped on his horse and galloped away, curses ringing in his ears and stones and logs falling around him.

The police now released the alleged instigators of the unrest, and the peasants decided to settle accounts with the *starshina*, Serdobintsev, whom they accused of having handed the ringleaders over to Stolypin. Serdobintsev tried, unsuccessfully, to flee from the village. The peasants gave him a terrible beating and then spent a day celebrating their victory. "Hurrah!" they shouted, "[we] defeated the Cossacks. We do not betray our comrades!" But they had misjudged Stolypin, who did not readily accept defeat.

One day after the peasants' celebration, Stolypin appeared with six Cossacks and two police constables looking for a suitable building to quarter troops. They found one in the town of Viazovka, not far from Mordovskii Karai, and a few days later thirty Cossacks, a sizable company of infantrymen, and several pieces of artillery arrived at the building. The governor had a list of ringleaders and immediately ordered his men to arrest the suspects. There was much "wailing and crying" by the wives and children of forty-four peasants taken into custody, but no one dared to stand in the way of the soldiers. Elated by his victory, Stolypin ordered the ringing of church bells to summon the people to prayer. A large crowd gathered in the village square and expressed "loyalty" to the authorities. Stolypin, in turn, expressed satisfaction over the outcome and boasted that the "official document" concerning Lvov's estate had been erased from the memory of the peasants.[71]

The governor's victory attracted favorable comment in St. Petersburg. On March 14, A. S. Ermolov, the minister of agriculture, informed the tsar that "thanks to the energetic actions of the governor of Saratov, Stolypin," the felling of trees on Lvov's estate was quickly stopped and "did not spread beyond the boundaries of a very small area."[72] Similar praise was heaped upon Stolypin for another success in suppressing agrarian unrest a few months later by D. F. Trepov, the assistant minister of internal affairs, who had emerged as the tsar's principal adviser on how to deal with the growing unrest. On August 6, Trepov lauded Stolypin in a report to Nicholas for leading a company of Cossacks in person to an area where disorders had erupted and restoring order. With his troops, Trepov noted, Stolypin had forced peasants to return to landlords grain they had seized. In addition, Stolypin's troops had conducted searches of peasants' households, and anyone found to have quantities of supplies larger than he could explain "convincingly" was arrested. In one action alone, seventy-five peasants were taken into custody; thirty of the "most guilty" were kept in jail for one to three months, and others were freed after two weeks. Stolypin also initiated a judicial inquiry into the causes of the disorders.[73] The tsar, delighted with Stolypin's successes, sent him a special telegram commending him for his "exemplary action."[74]

Stolypin faced his most serious crisis in Saratov in the summer of 1905, when a doctors' strike, the climax of an intense conflict between the zemtsi and the administration, brought medical services in the province to a halt. Stolypin viewed the strike as the consequence of the utterly unreasonable conduct of one group of doctors. He made this clear in a letter to his wife, in which he stated that there were two tendencies among the doctors, one progressive and the other destructive. His quarrel was only with the latter, and he found it difficult to believe that the doctors as a group really wanted to join forces with "the elements of destruction and violence." But if they did, he would not be deterred by the numerous threats leveled at him: "I will do my duty and preserve order and tranquillity, which society requires for the introduction of reform. . . . I hope that God will help me to overcome this difficulty."[75]

In fact, the roots of the fierce conflict between the doctors of Balashov and the governor's office were rather more complicated. Soon after the outbreak of the Russo-Japanese War a sizable number of physicians and other medical personnel had been drafted, putting those who remained in Saratov under enormous pressure. By April 1905, over one-third of the medical positions in Balashov district remained unfilled, posing a serious danger to public health, especially since there were signs of an impending cholera epidemic. At the same time, the zemstvo employees in Saratov, including many medical professionals, leaned toward radicalism, and by the spring of 1905 their mood had turned militant. On May 29–31, for example, a meeting of teachers in Saratov publicly demanded the overthrow of the government and the nationalization of the land. According to the *Okhrana* chief in Saratov, teachers at the end of the meeting "quite openly remarked that after such discussions they would act dishonorably if they did not begin strenuous propaganda among the *narod*." In fact, about two hundred teachers did go to the countryside to bring their political message to the peasants.[76] All these developments only reinforced Stolypin's conviction that the Third Element was responsible for inculcating villagers with revolutionary ideas. It also reinforced his inclination to dismiss suspicious zemstvo employees without bothering to conduct thorough investigations of charges against them. In the spring of 1905 he ordered the discharge of six medical employees suspected of having engaged in radical activities.

Another source of tension between doctors and the governor's office was the so-called "black agitation," which referred to the campaign of vilification of zemstvo employees by priests and policemen. The campaign was believed to have been inspired by the archbishop of Saratov, Germogen, a full-blooded reactionary. In February and March of 1905, the provincial zemstvo, fearful that the "black agitation" would provoke peasants into violence against zemstvo employees (some incidents had already occurred) warned Stolypin that he would face a strike if he did not restrain Germogen and his followers.[77]

Stolypin was in no mood to conciliate the zemstvo activists. Late in May 1905 he accused the Saratov Sanitary Society and its Balashov branch of having engaged in radical activities and shut them both down. Shortly thereafter the fears of the zemtsi about the impact of the right-wing agitation against them appeared to be confirmed. In June, a group of peasants threw a schoolteacher (A. K. Menshov) suspected of radicalism off his bicycle and beat him unconscious. The police took Menshov into custody and made no effort to treat his wounds. By chance, two doctors stumbled on Menshov, took care of him, and then informed their colleagues about the incident. This brought the conflict between the local doctors and the governor's office to a head. Twenty-two representatives of the Union of Medical Personnel of the Balashov District warned the district zemstvo assembly that they would go on strike on July 15 unless the authorities took measures to curb the rightists. Two weeks later, when the strike was in full swing, the Balashov Medical Union raised the ante: it demanded that the six employees dismissed on Stolypin's orders be reinstated.

Liberal deputies in the zemstvo sympathized with the doctors but refused to support a strike, not only because such an action would be illegal but also because the liberals did not wish to deprive the people of sorely needed medical services, already far from adequate. In Balashov the local zemtsi actually urged the doctors not to strike, but at the same time they dispatched a delegation of four men to Saratov to appeal to Stolypin "on the doctors' behalf" to change his policies. Stolypin was adamant: he refused to rehire the six employees, and to strengthen his hand he asked St. Petersburg to send him a contingent of doctors and medical assistants to replace the strikers. Stolypin knew that his provocative plan to use scabs would fail for the simple reason that the government had no doctors to spare. But the tone of a letter to his wife suggests that he was in such a rage over the doctors' opposition to him that his judgments were shaped more by emotion than reason. Stolypin revealed that in a conversation with Sumarokov, a member of the zemstvo board, he had denounced the doctors unsparingly: "It is vile," Stolypin had said, "to resort to lies and to slander the governor in order to provoke a strike and incite the population." In reply, Sumarokov, according to Stolypin, "babbled on that this was not directed at me, that [they] acted appropriately toward me, but that the government plays a double game and that it is necessary to fight against it, and the doctors have chosen this method [the strike], as a means of struggle."[78]

Stolypin would not budge because he was absolutely convinced that he was in the right and that he enjoyed popular support on the issue. "I will not lose self-control," he wrote his wife on June 30, "and rely on God. In this matter, I am right and believe that a majority of the sensible people condemn the doctors, and [I believe] that they will fail. I believe that even the population is turning against them [doctors] and that they will not succeed in winning them over to the revolution. I have asked for another regiment of Cossacks and have not lost hope of maintaining order."[79] Stolypin's self-righteousness and rigidity left little room for compromise with the physicians.

During the first two weeks of July, as relations between Stolypin and the zemstvo activists deteriorated, his mood was full of foreboding. The burden of administering Saratov was in itself overwhelming, but now he was also being called upon to assume chores in other parts of the country. He had been asked to serve as an honorary member of the Council of the Moscow Orphanage, an appointment that provoked dismay in Saratov. "From all sides demands are made on me," he told his wife on July 4, "and, I must say, there is regret about my apparent departure [from Saratov]. That is how people understand my appointment as honorary trustee. Oh, if only it were calm! I myself do not understand why I was appointed to the Moscow Orphanage! Here in the province the sick children from these orphanages are hired out for work in the forests—that is probably the reason [for my appointment]."[80] In a rare display of despair, Stolypin confessed to his wife on July 13 that he was close to being overwhelmed by the prolonged struggle. "God, so much pressure all the time, and how difficult it will be to set things right. . . . Am terribly tired, it is 12 o'clock and my eyes stick together."[81]

Most troubling to Stolypin was a new outburst of militancy and boldness by the opposition in Saratov. While traveling on official business early in July in the Petrovsk district he unexpectedly received a package containing a series of startlingly radical resolutions adopted by a meeting of the local Council on the Economy and approved by the Chairman of the Zemstvo Board and by many members of the Provincial Zemstvo Board. The resolutions proposed the appropriation of all privately owned lands and their distribution to the peasants and the abolition of the standing army; they also urged activists to mobilize the people against the nobility, and expressed support for the Peasants' Union, which advocated the convocation of a constituent assembly. Most alarmingly, the council advised the people to study warfare so as to prepare themselves for a military struggle with the government. In his report on the council's meeting to the Ministry of Internal Affairs, Stolypin noted that he immediately sent a telegram to the procurator of the Saratov District Court (D. D. Mikulin) and the commander of the gendarmerie (General T. V. Pomerantsev), directing them to undertake an investigation of the Council on the Economy. The commander warned Stolypin that the citizens attending the council's meeting probably were not violating the law, but he agreed to do the governor's bidding anyway. Stolypin, for his part, acknowledged that no one could be certain of the investigation's outcome, but he was nevertheless convinced that the chairman of the Zemstvo Board and the members of the board who had attached their signatures to the resolutions should be dismissed. In his view, government action was necessary because "the population is confused by clandestine and overt propaganda, which until now had been effective only among the immoral lower classes of the population, who have been terrorized by some activists."[82]

In private, Stolypin voiced even greater outrage and favored even more drastic measures. On July 12 he wrote his wife that he feared that the council's actions and the conduct of the zemstvo activists "will be an all-Russian scandal" and thought that it might be necessary to arrest the entire zemstvo board.[83] Over the next few days, Stolypin was inundated by a steady stream of alarming news. On July 14 a group of local activists who had just returned from Moscow told him that they had completely lost confidence in the government and that they considered it pointless to appeal to the authorities for reforms. Only an appeal to the people to take matters into their own hands seemed to offer any hope of improving conditions. Two of the zemstvo activists, S. A. Kotliarevskii and N. V. Davydov, insisted that "there is no government, that Bulygin's project [for a duma] is idiotic, and that there is no way out of this situation." For Stolypin, "all this . . . [was] sad and ghastly." He concluded that he must try to persuade the zemstvo deputies to moderate their views and planned to deliver a candid speech to them, but he was afraid that he would not have the time to prepare himself adequately for the talk "since every day and evening I am hampered by urgent matters and telegrams about disorders and arson from different parts of the province."[84]

Within a period of about two weeks early in the summer of 1905, some forty estates in Saratov had been set ablaze by arsonists. Stolypin reported to the Ministry of Internal Affairs that "panic is on the rise among landlords, who are abandoning and selling their estates." To be sure, often villagers were terrorized by gangs of peasants into staging attacks on landlords' properties. But the governor also acknowledged that the wretched conditions in the countryside drove people to despair, and he urged the authorities in St. Petersburg to provide additional land to the "most needy" peasants, many of whom, according to Stolypin, retained their "love" for the tsar. In fact, when he talked to crowds of ordinary people during his efforts to calm them he was often accused of deliberately failing to carry out the good intentions of the monarch. Peasants openly charged him with concealing a tsarist "rescript" promising generous relief to them. The land question, Stolypin insisted, was now the most critical issue and should be quickly addressed by the government.[85]

Stolypin's letters and postcards to his wife during his frequent visits to trouble spots throughout Saratov province reveal a man torn between great anguish over the growing unrest, not only in the region under his authority but throughout the country, and his determination not to appear overly alarmist. He kept Olga Borisovna informed of political developments, but he rarely described them in detail and went out of his way to allay her anxieties. On July 6, for example, he wrote her the following soothing words in a mix of two foreign languages: "Ne t'inquiette pas, pour le moment tous est tranquil. Tu said, que je ne te trompais pas. Aujourd'hui pas de lettres [from you]. I bless and love you, my darling. I kiss the children."[86]

The tranquillity to which Stolypin referred was merely a temporary respite. For some three months the doctors' strike dominated Saratov politics, provoking enormous tensions in society and several rather ugly incidents. As Stolypin had foreseen, the strikers encountered widespread hostility. For one thing, the Balashov district zemstvo and the Saratov zemstvo provincial assembly refused to support the strike, producing something of a rift in opposition circles. In addition, many people were furious at the doctors for refusing them medical services, and one group of irate citizens went so far as to attack and seriously wound a physician. On the other hand, in mid-July a terrorist fired a revolver at the governor as he was traveling through the village of Turki. The assassin missed his target, but a few days later, on July 21, Stolypin suffered a wound during a melee that can only be described as a pogrom. The details of what happened that day at a meeting of doctors at the Central Hotel in Balashov are still somewhat hazy, but there is little dispute about the general course of events, which created such an uproar that the governor felt obliged to publish his own account of the incident.

The ruckus began when a crowd of peasants and petty bourgeois (meshchane) estimated at two thousand gathered outside the Central Hotel to protest the doctors' decision to strike. The crowd became incensed on hearing what appeared to be revolutionary songs emanating from rooms occupied by doctors. But according to one eyewitness, the people in the street were mistaken. He claimed that some doctors were indeed singing, but the songs were not political at all; one of them, for example, was the popular "Sunrise and Sunset." But then some inflammatory reports reached the crowd about antigovernment activities in another nearby location. A portrait of the tsar had allegedly been slashed in the zemstvo building where the local board was meeting under the chairmanship of N. N. Lvov, the well-known liberal. Also, cries of "Down with the Autocracy" and "Beat the Police" could be heard in the street outside that building. Lvov had actually come to Balashov to persuade the doctors not to strike, but the crowd either did not know that or did not care. Very quickly, the crowd turned into a mob, cursing the members of the zemstvo and throwing stones and bricks at the hotel. A shouting match ensued between agitated doctors and policemen, who made no energetic efforts to control the mob. Lvov appeared in the street, tried to calm everyone, and offered the protection of his own room to some of the doctors, their wives, and doctors' assistants. One young lady, he recalled, was so distraught that she fell onto his bed and began to weep.

Lvov did not succeed in calming the unruly crowd, which made its way into the courtyard of the hotel, posing an immediate danger to the doctors. At that point Stolypin unexpectedly appeared on the scene with a squadron of Cossacks. Stolypin spoke to the crowd in an effort to restore order and then entered the hotel. The governor told Lvov and the doctors that he had learned that the doctors had sung revolutionary songs in their rooms. Anyone guilty of such misconduct, he insisted, would have to be punished. At his request, policemen began to draw up a list of all the people in the hotel. Then he returned to the street, where he was greeted with the singing of "God Save the Tsar." He ordered the crowd to move to one side and Cossacks took up positions near the exit of the hotel to provide safe passage for the doctors. Stolypin now returned to the hotel and promised the besieged doctors that anyone who wanted to leave could do so with "complete safety." Lvov recalled Stolypin's words: "Not one hair on your heads will be touched!"

Lvov took his suitcase and, together with two ladies to whom he offered a ride, hailed a cab. As soon as the cab began to move, one person appeared at the window with a mailed fist. Then stones were thrown at Lvov, and one struck him in the leg; another stone hit one of the ladies. Lvov noticed that Stolypin jumped from his carriage and sought to restrain the crowd, without much success. According to credible accounts, a few Cossacks used their *nagaikas* (whips) to restrain the mob, but most made no such effort and in fact allowed the people in the street to attack the carriage and several doctors trying to make their escape; some Cossacks even joined in these attacks. Stolypin, standing on his carriage, threatened the crowd and the rampaging Cossacks with his fists, but that did not stop anyone. The chief of the Saratov Provincial Gendarmes reported that the crowd's rage was simply uncontrollable.

The doctors "should be hanged," the rioters yelled. "They have taken thousands [of rubles] from us. Some of them have shot at your Excellency. All of them have sucked our blood."[87] In the words of Lvov, who was bleeding from the blow he had received, "This was something wild and disgusting." On reaching the railway station, Lvov spoke to Stolypin about the ghastly violence: Stolypin responded by showing the zemstvo activists his own bloodied finger on his right hand. A stone had also struck Stolypin.

After the departure of the doctors from Balashov, there was more violence. Unruly gangs destroyed the homes of two zemstvo deputies and beat up two doctors. Another residence escaped that fate only because soldiers protected it. Although Stolypin had tried to stop the rampage by ordering Cossacks to patrol the streets throughout the night and by personally appearing at a residence that was being threatened, he was widely accused of not having been forceful enough in containing the mob and the Cossacks.[88]

A. Nikonov, a barrister who wrote an account of the incident, stated flatly that "[t]he events were not provoked by spontaneous, outraged feelings of patriotism, but by the direct instigation of the police under [General] Sakharov with the connivance of the governor himself, who did not even order the crowd to disperse but limited himself to securing from individuals in the crowd a promise not to resort to force on the condition that a list would be made of the names of the people meeting [in the building] and that they would be punished." According to Nikonov, the unrest ended only after dark had set in and the mob had finished its grisly work.[89] The barrister's account was not balanced. It distorted the role of the authorities, but in the tense atmosphere of 1905 it seemed plausible to many people in Saratov.

Realizing that the reaction to the outburst of violence in Balashov reflected poorly on his administration, Stolypin took the unusual step of explaining his conduct in a liberal publication widely read by the intelligentsia. In a communiqué to the legal journal *Pravo* he referred to the nasty brawl as an "unfortunate incident" that had resulted from the people's anger at the doctors for having gone out on strike and for having sung "unlawful songs." He indicated that he understood the people's rage, but he also insisted that he could not condone their actions. He had done his utmost, he explained, to calm the crowd by promising to file legal charges against the doctors in the hotel who had been guilty of misconduct, but once the doctors left the hotel the crowd could not be restrained. Although he conceded that some Cossacks had joined the mob, he took pains to claim that the blows delivered by them had not inflicted serious harm on anyone. In short, Stolypin tried to be measured and even-handed in apportioning blame for the ruckus and at the same time make clear his condemnation of the mob's behavior. "Whatever the cause of these incidents of mob law," he wrote, "it was an illegal and wild incident of arbitrariness that I could not tolerate." He promised an investigation and vowed to prosecute everyone guilty of illegal conduct.[90]

The tsar, however, viewed the incident differently, as is evident from his reaction to a report on the violence in Balashov drafted by General Trepov on August 6. Trepov's report basically followed the account given by Stolypin in *Pravo*; and in his conclusion the assistant minister of internal affairs, himself a notorious hard-liner, remarked that "unfortunately" some Cossacks had unnecessarily used their *nagaikas*. The tsar did not share Trepov's regret about the Cossacks' resort to force. Nicholas wrote the following words next to the report: "Very well done."[91] The tsar also sent a telegram to the people of Balashov commending them for their "patriotic display" and for taking it upon themselves to punish the insurrectionists.[92]

Not surprisingly, the events outside the hotel in Balashov stimulated sympathy for the doctors, who, in turn, became more militant. On July 22 the staff of the Balashov district executive committee joined the strike, and early in August delegates to a meeting of the Saratov Medical Union called on zemstvo supporters to arm themselves and urged the members of the zemstvo assembly to vote funds for the acquisition of weapons.[93] Stolypin reacted in kind. On August 25, after an investigation of the pogrom on July 21, the governor issued a ukase ordering the police to arrest thirty-six doctors and medical assistants for their participation in meetings preceding the outbreak of unrest at the Balashov Central Hotel. The ukase also ordered the arrest of twenty-two people who had taken part in the attacks on the physicians. It turned out that three doctors on Stolypin's list had in fact not been in Balashov on July 21. Liberals were outraged, not only by the mistake but also by Stolypin's decision to arrest more physicians than *pogromshchiki*. In protest, the Saratov Medical Union decided on September 6 to resign in all districts of Saratov if the ukase of August 25 were implemented. Actually, the provisions of the ukase were for some inexplicable reason never enforced; but the strike continued nevertheless. It did not end until mid-October, when Stolypin granted clemency to the thirty-six doctors and medical assistants he had listed in his ukase.[94]

It was probably no accident that Stolypin's nod to leniency came at roughly the same time that Tsar Nicholas granted the October Manifesto in response to a national strike that had brought the government to its knees. As so often during the Revolution of 1905, events had developed in an unplanned, unorganized, and unpredictable manner. Although a few opposition leaders had broached the idea of a general strike, no one sensed that the urban labor movement might be on the verge of its greatest show of strength and its most notable triumph. Indeed, the leaders of all the radical movements were taken by surprise, as was the government. Not until vast numbers of workers had laid down their tools did leaders of revolutionary parties appreciate the significance of the strike movement and become active in it. In short, the general strike of October 1905 was a classic example of a momentous historical event that developed spontaneously.

The initiative was taken in Moscow, a center of labor unrest, in the fall of 1905, in response to a call for a general strike, to start on October 4, by the Central Bureau of the All-Russian Union of Railroad Employees and Workers. Within four days the strike had invaded many branches of the economy, and by October 16, Moscow was an eerie city. "Neither gas nor electric lights work," *Russkie vedomosti* reported; "the movement of trams, either horse-drawn or electrical, has not resumed. The telegraph system, telephones, and post offices do not work. A majority of the stores are closed, and the entrances and windows are boarded up with gates and shutters. The main business in stores is food items, conducted while the windows are blocked up by wooden shutters. The water lines have begun to work; in various parts of the city water is available [only] at certain times, from the morning until 1:30 P.M." Fearing a catastrophe, the city council deputy A. I. Guchkov declared that "the present strike can be explained only as a psychosis that has seized our society."[95]

The disease was highly contagious. Virtually every urban center in the empire was affected by it. It has been estimated that more than two million workers and other employees joined the general strike. The empire was paralyzed. Deprived of virtually all services, people believed that they were "experiencing the predicament of Robinson Crusoe."[96]

Saratov was not spared the labor unrest. The troubles in the city began on October 3 with a protest movement among students over a relatively minor incident at the city's Technical School. The students were upset because one of their number had been expelled for some minor infraction of rules and demanded his reinstatement. The school was shut down, and very quickly students at other schools joined public demonstrations. In the evening of October 8, a crowd of students from different schools met at the Lipki Garden and sang revolutionary songs. At two

high schools students asked the directors of their schools for permission
to hold requiem services for Prince S. N. Trubetskoi, the liberal rector of
Moscow University who had unexpectedly died at the age of forty-three.
The requests, rather innocuous, were denied, which only prompted the
students to become bolder in seeking to organize public meetings of protest. On October 9, by which time news of the strike in Moscow had
reached Saratov, telegraph operators and employees of the transportation office left their jobs, closing down all transportation in the city. The
strike spread quickly, and by October 13 the city was paralyzed, in the
grip of a general strike. Of the forty-eight hundred workers in industrial
establishments monitored by the Factory Inspectorate, thirty-seven
hundred laid down their tools.[97]

Although the strike in Saratov was, on the whole, peaceful, there
were numerous meetings at which speakers called not only for economic concessions (higher wages, an eight-hour day, improved sanitary
conditions, legislation to protect women and children in the workplace)
but also for such fundamental political changes as the introduction of a
constitutional order and universal suffrage. At times, speakers urged
their listeners to organize "militia units" that would destroy government institutions and banks. Collections were regularly made at rallies
for the purchase of weapons and the distribution of revolutionary literature. On October 12, a doctor Gordon appealed to a crowd of five thousand to wage a relentless struggle "to the death" against the autocracy
and demanded the "destruction of the entire House of Romanov" and
the establishment of a "democratic-republican system" of government.
At another meeting, political activists proposed that the "Central Strike
Committee" assume the role of a "Provisional Revolutionary Government." At yet another mass gathering, the crowd supported the formation of a detachment of a hundred people to launch an attack on the provincial prison to free all political prisoners.

The general strike spread quickly throughout the province of Saratov. In the city of Balashov, for example, six establishments with 533
workers closed down, a large proportion of the factories in this relatively
small urban center (with a population of about 17,500 people). Thirty-
three leaders of the strike movement were arrested, and there were a few
clashes between demonstrators and the authorities, but the most serious outbursts of violence did not occur until after the general strike had
ended on October 17, and then the instigators were right-wing opponents of the strike.[98]

Stolypin was not in Saratov during most of the general strike. He was
traveling along the Volga, apparently returning from a vacation in Kol-

noberzhe. But the vice-governor, I. G. Knoll, managed to get reports to him by special courier on developments in Saratov. The news of the unrest alarmed Stolypin, in part because he feared that Knoll would not follow the nuanced policy that he favored during periods of crisis. "I cannot conceal from myself the present difficulties of the situation in Saratov," he wrote his wife on October 15. "I fear that Knoll will be too zealous and will embitter our radicals. At this time we must proceed with a great deal of caution and we must take into account the public mood— at the beginning of a revolution it is necessary to act, at one at the same time, with firmness and with a view to inspire confidence in all strata who have not yet gone over to the side of the government's opponents. I also found this difficult after I had been slandered in the [conflict in] Balashov, but I rely on God's help. . . . I believe that at the present time the only way of operating is, on the one hand, to act with calm benevolence, and on the other, with force that is carefully organized."[99] Stolypin's mode of handling unrest was rather sophisticated; only individuals with the appropriate temperament could adopt it, and the governor worried that his subordinate did not have the requisite skills and patience. Indeed, at times even Stolypin himself fell short and applied more force than necessary to settle a political or economic conflict.

As he proceeded along the Volga, the news from Saratov continued to be alarming. On October 12, Knoll informed him by telegram that "[t]he situation is more menacing. The entire garrison is unprepared."[100] Two days later, the vice-governor told Stolypin that he had dispersed several meetings at which speakers advocated armed attacks on such governmental institutions as the local treasury and weapons depots. Stolypin immediately sent a telegram to the minister of internal affairs asking that additional troops be sent to Saratov from Astrakhan.

By this time, in mid-October, he was also beginning to worry about not being with his family during such trying days. In Nizhnii he had been told that regular traffic would not be restored until January and consequently he and his family would not be reunited for another two months. Even worse, Stolypin feared that communications between him and his wife would be interrupted, an eventuality that he considered to be "ghastly." But he refused to succumb to despair. On October 15 he wrote his wife that even though he could not be sure when they would see each other again, "I firmly trust God. He will help us, protect us and lead us out of the difficult situation."[101] A day later he wrote in the same vein: "I rely on God. I know how you behave in such moments! I know how you sacrifice for the children at these times when you are far from me. But we will both do our duty and the Lord God will save us."[102]

Stolypin feared that in carrying out his duty he might on occasion have to take actions he did not relish. His only hope, Stolypin told his wife, was that God would "protect me from having to spill blood. Let Him send down to me the intelligence, calm, and courage to lead out of crisis *painlessly* that part of the country that has been entrusted to me at this historic moment."[103] That Stolypin was a deeply religious man and that he had an unshakable commitment to performing his duty is evident in many of his public utterances. But his qualms about spilling blood were expressed most clearly and forcefully in his correspondence with his wife. Publicly, he sought to convey an image of resolute toughness.

By the time Stolypin returned to Saratov, on October 20, the political landscape was being transformed in the empire as a whole and in Saratov. Moreover, a new wave of turbulence, unprecedented in scope and intensity, roiled one region after another. Both developments resulted directly from the national crisis engendered by the general strike.

For several days in mid-October the government in St. Petersburg had been paralyzed in attempting to prevent a total collapse of the country. "Nobody knows," the German ambassador to Russia wrote on October 15, "who is to give orders. The ministers attack one another." Until October 12, the government took no measures at all to cope with the strike. That day the tsar, in a fit of despair, ordered General Trepov to deal vigorously with the unrest. Trepov immediately sent a directive to police chiefs in all provinces with a sizable revolutionary movement to "act in the most drastic manner" to prevent any disorders, "not stopping at the direct application of force." A day later Trepov ordered the governor-general of Moscow to prevent all public meetings that had not been sanctioned. The police must disperse illegal meetings "with all means, including the overt use of force." On October 14, Trepov issued a proclamation to the people of St. Petersburg that has since become notorious. Printed on the first page of the daily newspapers and posted on walls and fences in the capital, the proclamation began by promising that lives and property would be protected. The police and the army, it continued, had been ordered to put down all disturbances with the "most decisive measures." If crowds refused to disperse, policemen and soldiers were "not to use blanks and not to spare bullets." It was his duty, Trepov contended, to warn people about the "painful consequences" that would result from participation in street disorders.

Given the tense atmosphere in the streets, it is hard to imagine a government action less calculated to restore calm than Trepov's provocative proclamation. On the very day it was distributed, some forty thousand people defiantly streamed into the streets near the university. In addition, every auditorium in the university buildings was filled to capacity with adherents from various labor unions. To everyone's surprise, "at the time of the meetings," one eyewitness reported, "nowhere near the university could the army or police be seen; everyone was expecting them [in view of Trepov's proclamation]."

Why the police and the army ignored Trepov is not clear. Conceivably, his subordinates realized that any action to disperse the crowd would have led to a bloodshed even more terrible than the one on Bloody Sunday. They may also have doubted that success in scattering the crowds would guarantee an end to the strike. Whatever the reason, the continuation of the strike prompted several senior advisers to conclude that political reform was necessary to bring the crisis to an end. The main spokesman of the "reformers" was S. Iu. Witte, who had returned from the peace negotiations in Portsmouth with a greatly enhanced reputation as a statesman and political leader. Witte still believed that a progressive autocracy with far-sighted leadership was the best form of government for the country, but he recognized that in view of the revolutionary assault on authority it was now impossible to re-establish the old order. He therefore hoped to salvage as much as possible of that order by means of political concessions to the opposition.[104]

After much agonizing and endless delay, the tsar accepted Witte's recommendation on October 17 to issue the "October Manifesto," and appointed him prime minister. In the manifesto, Nicholas committed himself to granting the population of the empire "the unshakable foundations of civic freedom based on the principles of real personal inviolability, freedom of conscience, speech, assembly, and union." He would permit the election of a representative body, a Duma; classes previously excluded from the political process would be permitted to participate in the voting. Moreover, and most important, the tsar declared that no law would be enacted without the approval of the State Duma. This meant that Nicholas was no longer an autocratic ruler in the sense that his word, and his word alone, was law. However much he and his advisers might later try to circumvent this interpretation of the manifesto, it was clear beyond doubt that in committing himself to the "unbreakable rule that no law can become effective without the approval of the [elected] State Duma," Nicholas had renounced his prerogative to rule as an absolute monarch. The tsar's action marked a decisive departure from a system of rule that had prevailed in Russia for centuries.

It was not only the tsar's legal authority, however, that changed as a result of the turbulence in 1905. The country also underwent changes that no one would have believed possible a year earlier. The press not only expanded with astonishing speed—between 1900 and 1914 the number of newspapers increased tenfold—but it would print virtually any news it considered important. Political movements across the entire political spectrum, including the revolutionaries, now published and distributed newspapers as well as periodicals. These political movements, representing right-wing extremists, middle-class liberals, peasants and socialists, participated in elections for local institutions of self-government and for the national duma. Workers established a wide range of associations such as trade unions, clubs, cultural societies, consumer cooperatives, and production cartels. This is not to suggest that the authorities no longer sought to limit the press's freedom to publish or to rein in the various associations. Repression remained a weapon to which the government resorted with regularity after 1905. Still, there can be no doubt that slowly, painfully, against all odds, the Russian people were creating institutions free of government control and thus appeared to be taking the first steps on the road to creating a civil society, a prerequisite for a genuine constitutional order.

These changes, however, did not proceed smoothly. No sooner had the Manifesto been issued than massive unrest erupted throughout the empire, so serious that one can speak of an unraveling of the social and political order. Precisely at the moment when the autocracy was at its weakest, when it had been compelled to grant its first major concession, the defenders of the old order unleashed their most intense and ferocious attacks on the advocates of change. This took the form of a rash of pogroms in many sectors of the country. Although Jews were the principal focus of the pogroms, they were not the only ones to come under attack. The rampaging mobs also targeted the intelligentsia and students—anyone, in fact, who was presumed to have participated in the movement to extract the Manifesto from the tsar or who simply joined it. All told, 690 anti-Jewish pogroms occurred, primarily in the southwestern provinces; 876 people were killed and between 7,000 and 8,000 injured. In a few cities the Jews lost property estimated at more than a million rubles. Altogether, the damage to property during the pogroms has been calculated at sixty-two million rubles.[105]

The failure of Witte's government to stem the mob violence was only one symptom of its impotence. For a few weeks, it also could not cope with a new wave of disturbances in the countryside and a rash of mutinies in the army and navy. The unrest among military units was so widespread that the minister of war, General Rediger, thought that the country, which had just experienced a vast outburst of popular violence in the cities and in the villages, was threatened with "total ruin."

A pogrom lasting two days (October 19–20) broke out in Saratov while Stolypin was still en route home from Kolnoberzhe. Vice-governor Knoll assumed a stance of benevolent neutrality toward the attacks on Jews and on the local Social Democratic paper by "petty merchants, workers, salesmen, cabbies and even members of the intelligentsia." About 10 people were murdered and 124 incurred injuries (66 of which were serious); in addition, the *pogromshchiki* looted 168 apartments and shops as well as the local synagogue.[106] As soon as Stolypin returned to the city, he ordered a halt to the violence, and "in the course of ten minutes the pogroms were stopped."[107] Although that claim of his effectiveness, made by the liberal newspaper *Russkie vedomosti*, is something of an exaggeration, it is true that the governor "immediately" took charge of the operation to halt the violence. "Seeing the governor's energetic efforts," one report noted, "the police officers and the army units also took part in the suppression [of the pogrom] and by 4 PM the pogrom stopped completely."[108]

Commentators on the left have charged that Stolypin deliberately absented himself from the city at the time of the pogrom and that he "tacitly approved of the rightist offensive."[109] The charge is baseless. As already noted, he was out of town throughout the October strike and tried his best to get back as quickly as possible. More to the point, Stolypin did not sanction popular violence of any kind. An authentic conservative, he feared that mobs on a rampage were a threat not only to their targets but to order in general, which he was determined to uphold. He made his position clear in an announcement eight days after he had quelled the pogrom: "[E]very infringement of the rights of an individual or his property, regardless of his nationality or religion, will be suppressed with the application of military force."[110]

Stolypin was actually baffled by the outbreak of violence against Jews in Saratov. In a private conversation at the time with Ia. Teitel, the only Jew who then served as a judge in the Russian Empire, the governor noted that there was no antagonism between Christians and Jews in the province, which he attributed to the fact that the Jews in Saratov did not make their living as "usurers, shop-keepers, [or] exploiters." He let Teitel know that he planned to take the "most energetic measures" to put down the disorders. In response to Teitel's suggestion that the authorities contribute small sums of money to help the families ravaged by the pogrom, Stolypin expressed sympathy for the idea but did not think it would be wise for him to use public funds to help Jews. "The lower classes, he said, are still agitated and one must [therefore] act cautiously."[111]

In Saratov, peasant unrest was by far the most serious and most persistent form of violence from below. From October to December 1905, the authorities registered 509 incidents in the countryside, 440 of them in four districts, Serdobsk, Balashov, Atkarsk, and Saratov. Within a span of eighteen days, from October 16 to November 4, enraged peasants set fire to forty estates in the Balashov district alone; in Petrovsk district, twenty-nine estates were destroyed. In general, the agrarian unrest in Saratov followed a predictable pattern: a crowd of peasants appeared at an estate, disarmed the employees, took the keys to the buildings, seized the cattle and crops as well as other possessions, and then burned down the buildings. Liquor stores were also a target of roving gangs of peasants, who emptied the shops of their goods and cash.[112] Another sign of deep discontent among the peasants was the rapid increase in the membership of the All-Russian Peasants' Union, an organization with a radical economic and political program. Formed in July 1905, it had a membership of some ten thousand in Saratov province by the fall of that year.

The agrarian unrest was so widespread that Stolypin found it impossible to invoke his favored tactics, which were designed to nip in the bud any mass discontent before it flared up in violence. In late April 1905 he developed a strategy based on the one he had used in curbing urban unrest. First and foremost, he intended to remain in constant touch with zemstvo leaders and police officials, who were charged with monitoring the mood of peasants in their districts. If the officials on the spot learned of sharp conflicts between peasants and landlords, they were to summon the parties in the dispute to their offices and seek to promote an amicable settlement. If that failed and there was a danger of violence, the governor, in agreement with senior military officers, would dispatch sizable military forces to the region in the hope of discouraging illegal action by the peasants.[113] This was a plausible strategy in the spring of 1905, when the peasant movement was still in its early stages. By late October, however, the agrarian movement had gone too far for efforts at mediation or intimidation to be effective.

On October 20, Stolypin wrote to the Ministry of Internal Affairs that he now had to rely primarily on "decisive measures," and he warned that unless the army in Saratov was reinforced the maintenance of order would be impossible. Trepov agreed to send additional troops from Penza and other locations. By this time, the governor had at his disposal thirty-four companies of infantry, three Cossack regiments, thirteen Cossack companies, two squadrons of dragoons, and one brigade of reserves. To strengthen his hand in dealing with disorders, he secured permission from the Ministry of Internal Affairs to place the province under Reinforced Security, which gave him enhanced authority to impose fines, keep citizens in jail for up to three months, and dismiss local government and zemstvo employees. The troops dealt harshly with the unruly peasants, often arresting large numbers of them in regions struck by unrest.[114]

Toward the end of 1905, Stolypin also took it upon himself to send troops to neighboring Samara province to quell a peasant disturbance that local officials could not suppress and that he apparently feared would spill over to his province. The intervention in another province was illegal, but that did not prevent the tsar from sending Stolypin a special telegram of thanks on January 4, 1906: "To Saratov Governor Stolypin. Informed through the Minister of Internal Affairs of the exemplary action shown by you in dispatching troops on your own initiative to suppress disorders within the borders of Novouzensk county, Samara province, and long esteeming your loyal service, I declare to you my sincere gratitude. Nicholas."[115]

It is worth noting that although Stolypin increasingly relied on the army to put down unrest, his orders to the troops never reached the level of ruthlessness characteristic of the directives issued by the minister of internal affairs, Durnovo, or of several generals in the field. On January 6, 1906, Durnovo had learned that unrest had broken out in the small town of Kagarluka in Kiev province. He feared that the local police would not be able to protect nearby landed estates, and therefore issued the following instructions to the governor-general of Kiev, V. A. Sukhomlinov: "I earnestly request, in this and similar cases, that you order the use of armed force without the slightest leniency and that insurgents be annihilated and their homes burned in the event of resistance. It is necessary once and for all to stop, with the most severe measures, the spreading willfulness that threatens to destroy the entire state. Under the present circumstances, the restoration of the authority of the government is possible only by these means." Arrests (Stolypin's favored measure of repression), Durnovo asserted, were useless, for it was impossible to bring hundreds of people to justice in small, remote regions of the empire. "The army must be inspired with such orders [as Durnovo had issued]."[116]

On October 28, Stolypin reported to St. Petersburg that "[in] the province of Saratov the situation is still very alarming, but order has been fully maintained."[117] Privately, however, Stolypin was considerably less sanguine. In a letter of October 31, 1905, to his wife he voiced deep anxieties about events in the countryside: "My Olinka: It seems that the horrors of our revolution surpass the horrors of the French [revolution]. Yesterday in the Petrovsk district at the time of a pogrom directed at the estate of Aplacheev the Cossacks (50 men) dispersed a crowd of many thousands. 20 were killed, many were wounded. . . . And in Malinovka peasants beat to death 43 people convicted in front of the church for desecrating a saint. The leader of the gang [of peasants] was in a full-dress uniform taken from a colonel, a local landlord. [The landlord] . . . was also put to death, but three members of the intelligentsia were placed under custody till the arrival of higher authorities. The local peasants are divided into two parties warring against each other. Life no longer counts for anything. I am pleased with the arrival of [General-Adjutant V. V.] Sakharov [sent to Saratov to quell unrest]—all this bloodshed will not be my responsibility. And there will be much shedding of blood. . . . May God give me the strength to survive all this."[118]

Troubled though he was by the rampant violence, Stolypin was not inclined to turn down a promotion that would put him in a position of having to resort to force on a much wider scale than in Saratov. The very day Sakharov arrived in Saratov—he stayed at the governor's residence—Stolypin wrote his wife with considerable satisfaction that the general had told him that he would be appointed to the cabinet being formed by the new prime minister, Witte. "And you, Dutya [a term of endearment for his wife] are already unhappy. Thank God, no one has offered me anything." The last sentence, suggesting relief, did not convey his true sentiments. The newspapers, he told his wife, were writing about his appointment. *Rus*, for example, had reported that because of events in Balashov, where he was reputed to have scored a great victory against the opposition, people thought that the matter of his appointment was already a settled matter. Nowhere in the letter did he suggest that he would turn down a senior post in St. Petersburg.[119] The newspaper accounts were not far off the mark. Stolypin's name had come up for consideration for appointment as minister of internal affairs, but his candidacy did not receive much support at court, apparently because he was not well known.[120]

The month of November 1905, a period of almost constant turbulence throughout the country, continued to be stormy in Saratov. To Stolypin, the agrarian unrest now appeared to be a real war, another "Pugachevshchina," a reference to the bloody upheaval in the countryside in the 1770s, and he acknowledged that "things are going badly." In five districts of the province "a complete revolt" had broken out, leaving virtually no farmstead intact. "Every day a few are killed and wounded." The capital, Saratov, had remained relatively peaceful, but he could venture into the villages "only with the army, of course—now any other way is not sensible." Once again, he expressed relief that General Sakharov, in charge of pacifying the countryside, freed him from the responsibility of spilling blood. Even though he worked seventeen hours a day (from 8 A.M. until 1 A.M.), when he went to bed, thoroughly exhausted, he still left piles of official papers on his desk untouched. Nevertheless, not a day passed without his writing to his wife, always ending with his usual expressions of love: "My darling, my dear . . . I want to kiss you."[121] Only on November 20, a month after Stolypin had initially reported that order was being maintained in the province, did a semblance of calm actually return to the Saratov countryside, though even then strikes still continued in some industries and in some schools.[122] Nor had the violence ended entirely in Saratov. In fact, the Stolypins learned to their dismay that on November 27 a terrorist act had been perpetrated in their own home while they were out of town. That day a young woman pretending to have a petition for General Sakharov was permitted to enter the governor's residence, where the general was then living. When the woman set foot in the general's study, she shot him point blank and killed him on the spot.[123]

In any case, the relative calm in Saratov that Stolypin had detected on November 20 proved to be short-lived. A new storm erupted in several regions of the country and, in particular, in Moscow, where a fierce rebellion broke out on December 8. There is no clear evidence of a direct link between the events in Moscow and Saratov, but Bolsheviks played a critical role in both cities, and the course of the uprising in Moscow definitely influenced developments in Saratov. Late in November, representatives of socialist parties in Saratov formed a local Soviet of Workers' Deputies. According to G. M. Derenkovskii, a Soviet historian, that soviet adopted a Menshevik strategy—that is, it did not set a date for an uprising, as did the soviet in Moscow. Despite pressure from Bolsheviks, the Saratov soviet on December 8 limited itself to a call for a general strike without mentioning armed action. Derenkovskii attributes the moderation of the Saratov soviet to the severe police repression imposed by local authorities—that is, by Stolypin. In fact, even the initial response to the strike call was rather tepid, but it is true that it became weaker after the police arrested twenty-five leaders of the strike movement during the night of December 9–10. Leaders still at large went underground, which hampered their efforts to direct the strike.[124]

When news of the Moscow insurrection, which initially seemed to be succeeding, reached Saratov in the second week of December, activists in the province took heart.[125] They redoubled their efforts, and by December 15 some five thousand workers were on strike, a sizable number but smaller than the strike movement in October. On December 16, about two thousand people marched to the jail to free political prisoners, only to be stopped by a large force of Cossacks and infantrymen. Violence flared up, and, according to some reports, the soldiers killed seven people and wounded nineteen. Stolypin claimed in his official report that the firing had been started by the marchers and that the Cossacks fired back only after one of their men and his horse had been wounded. The governor also reported a smaller number of killed, three rather than seven; at the same time he claimed that twenty-three, not nineteen, had been wounded.

A day after the clash, the police succeeded in arresting most leaders of the Social Democrats and made additional arrests late in December and early in January. Also, the police took into custody seven leaders of the All-Russian Peasants' Union. In the meantime, on December 19 the strike had begun to peter out; though serious, the disturbances in Saratov in December clearly did not amount to an "armed uprising," a point that Stolypin was eager to stress in his report to his superiors in the Ministry of Internal Affairs. To drive home this point, Stolypin went out of his way to deny that artillery had been used in Saratov to end the strike and to control the demonstrators. In a not very subtle way he seemed to be disassociating himself from the army's conduct in Moscow, where artillery had been used to deadly effect in defeating the insurgents and had aroused deep anger.[126]

For some four months after the failure of the December strike Stolypin concentrated on restoring order in Saratov and on mobilizing public support for his policies. More than ever, he believed that the mailed fist alone would not suffice to curb the opposition. He hoped to rally landowners and nobles behind the constituted authorities, and it soon became apparent that he might succeed. Only six days after the issuance of the October Manifesto, when violence from below had intensified greatly in the cities and the countryside, Stolypin informed the assistant minister of internal affairs that "even the most extreme urban zemstvo circles recognize the dangers" and had begun "to display full confidence [and] solidarity with me"; they went so far as to "ask for energetic measures" to restore order. Stolypin found the change in their mood "striking."[127] For the next three months, the move to the right of Saratov liberals continued at a rapid pace. At the Saratov provincial zemstvo assembly, meeting from January 22 to February 7, 1906, the liberals were "totally demolished" by reinvigorated conservatives.[128]

Stolypin, however, did not intend to rely only on conservative nobles and zemstvo activists to mobilize support for his policies. He launched what can be called a public relations campaign to overcome the friction that had divided the citizens of Saratov. Together with the elected mayor of Saratov and the chairman of the provincial zemstvo executive board, he signed an appeal to the people early in November 1905 calling on everyone to return to work and await the Duma's approval of the "fundamental rights of civil freedom" that the tsar himself had promised. In January 1906, the governor's office organized the distribution of about thirty thousand leaflets urging the peasants to keep calm and show "confidence" in the "reforms undertaken for the renewal of Russia."[129]

It would be a mistake to dismiss Stolypin's stress on reform as merely a publicity stunt designed to pacify the people in his province. In a memorandum to the Ministry of Internal Affairs of January 11, 1906, marked "secret," the governor offered an analysis of the recent agrarian unrest similar to the one he had sent to the tsar.* But his language now was more direct and his demand for reform more forceful. Again, he argued that the immediate cause of the disorders was revolutionary propaganda from "zemstvo agents" who had won the sympathy of "very broad strata of society." He also censured lower officials who were so confused by political reforms, especially the October Manifesto, that they had become paralyzed and had failed to act resolutely to stem the unrest. The press had contributed to the confusion by adopting an unprecedented tone of hostility toward all authority. Finally, not only many police officers but also leaders of zemstvos had concluded that "all is permitted and that in fact authority had been abolished." Even the army could not always be relied upon to maintain order.

Nevertheless, Stolypin insisted that "the weakness and confusion of the authorities only made possible the peasant movement but did not create it." He warned that however diligently officials labored to stamp out unrest, they would not succeed in maintaining order permanently so

*Discussed above, pp. 57–58.

long as poverty remained widespread in the countryside. "Half-starving [and] without savings, illiterate peasants readily listen to the promises of agitators and are favorably disposed toward wild, destructive outbursts." And the poverty was not simply or primarily the consequence of a land shortage. "I cannot but note that in many places of unrest there were peasants with adequate allotments who engaged in violence and peasants with small holdings who did not engage in unrest." The root problem, Stolypin contended, was the commune, which discouraged initiative and hard work, corrupted the peasantry, and remained the main threat to social peace. The only solution of the agrarian crisis was for the government to take steps to increase greatly the "class of small landowners, this basic cell of the state, which by nature is organically opposed to every notion of destruction."[130] Stolypin's missive to the Ministry of Internal Affairs amounted to a succinct summary of his views on the turbulence that had shaken the Russian Empire to its foundations in the fall and winter of 1905–6. He continued to insist, as he had since his earliest days in public life, that the authorities must commit themselves to dealing not only with the manifestations of discontent but also with its underlying causes.

Stolypin's views on the agrarian situation may seem sensible and even obvious, but in 1906 not many senior officials agreed with him. In a report late in January of that year to the tsar, the minister of internal affairs, Durnovo, summarized the opinions of seventeen governors of provinces particularly hard hit by peasant unrest and devoted one long paragraph to Stolypin's position because it differed markedly from that of the other governors. All seventeen focused on the revolutionary agitation by zemstvo activists, teachers, doctors, and doctors' assistants, as the critical immediate cause of the disorders in the countryside. In some localities, according to the governors, priests too had urged peasants to take matters into their own hands, as had the liberal press. The governors also claimed that peasants had interpreted the October Manifesto as a document that gave them the right to pillage. The failure of local authorities to act firmly when the unrest began had had the effect of encouraging further disorders, although the shortage of policemen and military force often inhibited the authorities from taking energetic action at the first sign of unrest. To contain the turbulence, most governors called for more repression, for speedier judicial proceedings against the unruly peasants, and for tougher measures against agitators. Durnovo then pointed out that the governor of Saratov was unique in advocating a "radical reform," the abolition of the commune. The minister referred to Stolypin's report of January 11 discussed above, which insisted that the only way to prevent future upheavals in the country-side was to create a class of petty proprietors who "by nature oppose every destructive theory." A note attached to Durnovo's report indicated that it was read by the tsar on February 4.[131]

In the meantime, Prime Minister Witte carried out Nicholas's promise to hold an election for a Duma. The electoral law promulgated on December 11 vastly increased the number of voters envisaged in August, when the government announced the election of the so-called Bulygin Duma. Somewhere between 20 and 25 million citizens could cast ballots, but even now the suffrage was not universal, equal, or direct. Eligibility depended on the ownership of property or the payment of taxes, and the population was divided into four curiae: landowners, peasants, town dwellers, and workers. Each curia chose electors who then made the final selection of Duma deputies. As planned, electoral power was distributed unequally: peasants represented 42.3 percent of the electors, landowners 32.7 percent, town dwellers 22.5 percent, and workers 2.5 percent. This worked out to one elector for every two thousand landowners, four thousand urban dwellers, thirty thousand peasants, and ninety thousand workers. Women, some 7 million agricultural workers, 3.5 million servants, 2 million day laborers, 1 million construction workers, 1 million employees in commerce, and a few smaller groups were not represented at all.

On the whole, despite government attempts to influence the electoral process, the election proceeded smoothly and fairly. Numerous parties, ranging from extremists on the right to the moderate left (Trudoviks or Laborites) participated. The Social Democrats (Bolsheviks and Mensheviks) as well as the Socialist Revolutionaries officially boycotted the elections, claiming that regardless of the composition of the Duma it would serve the cause of the counterrevolution. Although the boycott was quite effective, in some localities people ignored it and elected SDs and SRs. All in all, the results, a stunning defeat for the government, demonstrated that Witte and his supporters still did not grasp the depth of disaffection among the vast majority of Russians. The prime minister had counted on peasant support for the tsar and for that reason had agreed to give them so large a share of the total number of electors. As it turned out, none of the parties to the right of the Kadets (Constitutional Democrats), who were committed to a British style constitutional order, did well. The Octobrists, satisfied with the concessions granted by the October Manifesto, gained only 13 seats, and the extreme right did not have a single seat in the Duma; on the other hand, voters returned 185 Kadets (with adherents) as deputies, 112 Nonpartisans (virtually all of them hostile to the old order), 17 Socialists (SD, SR, Polish Socialist Party), and 94 who composed the "Other Left" (including Trudoviks—who stood somewhere between the Kadets and the moderate socialists).[132]

Russkie vedomosti, a liberal paper close to the Kadets, was not far off the mark in its analysis of the significance of the election, though it proved to be far too optimistic in predicting the quick demise of the autocracy. "Russia is experiencing a great moment," an editorial announced on March 22. "A powerful force of national self-consciousness has arisen and has firmly pushed aside what was obsolete into the irrevocable past. The bureaucracy is in its last days; its most desperate efforts do not and will not help it to retain the power that has slipped out of its grasp. All vital and conscious elements of the Russian people must exert themselves finally to break the last vestiges of the hated system."

Even before all the results of the election had trickled in, the Ministry of Internal Affairs sensed that the Duma would pose a serious challenge to monarchical rule. In response to a confidential memorandum to twenty-seven governors by Durnovo asking for their assessment of the elections, a substantial number of the provincial administrators blamed the defeat on popular discontent with long-standing official policies, discontent that the Kadets had exploited effectively. Stolypin, in a separate report to the Ministry of Internal Affairs, left no doubt that in his mind the people strongly supported their antigovernment deputies. On April 20, seven days before the opening of the Duma, he wrote to Durnovo that a day earlier, when the deputies in his province were scheduled to leave for St. Petersburg, a crowd of ten thousand inhabitants of the city, "among them many workers and students," filled the entire railway station and began to sing the *Marseillaise*. To prevent any "undesirable incidents" during the sendoff, Stolypin ordered that the train be dispatched ahead of schedule. Only after the people had encountered mounted patrols and had left the station did they stop singing.[133] The only remedy for the latest expression of antigovernment sentiment that Durnovo could think of was to let conservatives know that if the Duma veered too far to the left, it would have to be dissolved.[134]

Before it met, however, the tsar decided on a change of government. He had never been comfortable with Witte, an incredibly arrogant man who, the ultraconservatives claimed, was not only unprincipled in vacillating between support for liberal causes and support for the autocracy but was also bent on enhancing his own dictatorial power at the expense of Nicholas's authority. The senior advisers at court also concluded that Durnovo was so unpopular because of his repressive policies that it was

unthinkable to have him appear in the Duma as a government spokesman. In the end the court entourage decided on a thorough shakeup, and
on April 24 the tsar announced the selection of a new government
whose one distinguishing feature appeared to many to be its lack of distinction.

The prime minister, I. L. Goremykin, was so obviously a nonentity
that public opinion was taken by surprise at his appointment, and virtually no one could be found to say a good word about him. Six weeks earlier, when diplomats in St. Petersburg speculated about Witte's likely
successor, Goremykin's name was not even mentioned. A sixty-seven-
year-old bureaucrat, Goremykin was a colorless man without firm convictions or any strcng urge to exercise leadership. A. V. Gerasimov, head
of the St. Petersburg *Okhrana* and a staunch conservative, dismissed
Goremykin as "an indolent person who is not at all interested in politics. He asked for only one thing, that he be bothered as little as possible."[135] Clearly, he was not a suitable head of government under the new
and difficult conditions prevailing in Russia in 1906.

Except for V. N. Kokovtsov, who agreed after considerable hesitation
to accept the post of minister of finance, P. Kh. Schwanebach was the
only person in the government with experience in national domestic affairs, and he was more interested in gaining support for ultra right-wing
causes and intrigues than in running the Office of the State·Comptroller.
Witte scornfully dismissed him as a man whose only merit lay in the
fact "that he had fallen in with a Montenegrin princess."[136] The critical
question was the appointment of a minister of internal affairs, for he
would be responsible for the maintenance of order. Very few senior officials believed that the unrest had been completely stamped out or that
revolutionary agitation had ended.

On April 22, seven days before the Duma was scheduled to hold its
first session, Stolypin was summoned to St. Petersburg. We have no record of his thoughts as he journeyed to the capital, but in view of the
speculation in the newspapers six months earlier about his possible
promotion, it can safely be assumed that he expected to be offered a ministerial post. Certainly, the letter he wrote his wife on April 26 suggests
no surprise, only exultation. It also contained what must be one of the
most emotional and moving accounts of an interview with Tsar Nicholas II: "Olia, my invaluable treasure. Yesterday my fate was decided! I
am the minister of internal affairs in a bloodstained, shaken country
that represents one sixth of the world, and this at one of the most difficult historical moments, which occurs once in a thousand years. The
human resources here are small, [and therefore] it is necessary to have

faith in God, strong reliance on Him to support, [and] to teach me. God, help me. I feel that He will not abandon me, I feel calm because He will not abandon me." But Stolypin also stressed that his wife's love and confidence would be indispensable for his success. "You will be my support [and] help, my adored one, my eternal love. All the treasures of love that you have given me have sustained my faith in the goodness of human beings until my forty-fourth year. You are pure, my beloved. You are my guardian angel."

Having expressed his delight over his new appointment, Stolypin described how the tsar persuaded him to accept the post of minister of internal affairs. On April 25 he was "ordered" to appear at the palace in Tsarskoe Selo at 6:00 in the evening. He traveled together with Goremykin, the incoming prime minister, who saw the tsar first by himself. At the conclusion of that interview, Stolypin entered the monarch's chamber and immediately expressed, as he put it hours later, "all my apprehensions, telling Him that the task is beyond my strength, that to select the governor of Saratov on the eve of the Duma and for him to resist the firm and organized opposition in the Duma—that is to doom the ministry to failure. I told Him that there is a need for a person who will have influence over the Duma and authority within the Duma and who will be able to preserve order. The Sovereign retorted that He did not want a ministry based on a fortuitous majority; all that He said to me had already been considered from all angles. I asked Him if He had thought about the fact that my name alone would provoke a storm in the Duma, to which He replied that this too had entered his mind." Stolypin then spelled out his program, which he had already discussed with Goremykin, who had approved it with minor changes.

At the end of his conversation with the tsar, Stolypin made a final plea: "I implored Him to spare me from the horror of the new situation, ... I confessed to Him [my doubts] and bared my entire soul, with the proviso that if He, as Sovereign, orders me then I would be obliged to accept and would give up my life for Him; I would await His verdict. He remained quiet for one second and said: 'I order you, I do this quite deliberately, and understand your selflessness [in accepting]; I bless you—this is for the good of Russia.' Saying this, He seized me with both arms and shook me warmly. I said, 'I will obey You,' and kissed the hand of the Tsar. He and Goremykin and probably I had tears in our eyes. The die is cast: the future will tell whether I will be able to cope with the circumstances."[137]

If Stolypin's account of his meeting with the tsar can be taken as accurate, and it probably can since it was for his wife's eyes only, the new minister of internal affairs began his tenure brilliantly. He was properly modest and even turned down the offer of appointment initially, though it is clear that he hankered for the post. It was in his interest to hesitate in accepting, not simply because that was considered to be polite. He knew that he faced enormous difficulties. Not only would most of the Duma deputies fiercely oppose him as a matter of principle because of his strong measures against liberals and radicals in Saratov. His proposals for reform would also provoke the opposition of ultraconservatives, many of whom were influential at court. If Stolypin was to prevail, he would need the unstinting support of Nicholas, not known as a reliable supporter of his ministers or as a man with many firm political principles. By spelling out his program and by securing the tsar's acceptance of it, Stolypin sought to assure himself of the strongest possible political base from which to implement his policies. And by securing from the tsar an expression of firm personal support, Stolypin believed that he had solidified that political base. During the initial period of his tenure in the government, as will be seen below, that tie to Nicholas—personal and emotional, as well as political—proved to be invaluable to Stolypin. It made possible the more notable achievements that Stolypin could ultimately claim as his legacy for Russia.

The interview also, however, revealed a political weakness of Stolypin that ultimately turned out to be fateful for him: his utter dependence on the tsar. The subservience of ministers to the sovereign was, of course, an essential feature of the autocratic system of rule in Imperial Russia. It was also the single most divisive issue in the political conflicts of the early twentieth century and a topic to which any study of Stolypin must return time and again. For Stolypin, the issue was a matter of deepest concern because as minister of internal affairs and later on as prime minister he was acutely aware of his obligations to the monarch and of his reliance on him in implementing his policies. But as a minister at a time when there was an elected legislature with certain clearly defined prerogatives, he could not disregard the reality that the principle of autocracy, proclaimed for some four centuries as the dominant factor in Russian history, had been undermined and, moreover, that it was no longer accepted as valid by substantial sectors of society. On the other hand neither the tsar nor the conservatives, who still wielded a great deal of political influence, had reconciled themselves to the extinction of the autocratic system.

There was some disagreement among the proponents of autocracy as to its precise meaning, but all tended to subscribe to the definition in the first article of the "Fundamental Laws" of 1832: "The Emperor of all the

Russias is a sovereign with autocratic and unlimited powers. To obey the commands not merely from fear but according to the dictates of one's conscience is ordained by God himself."[138] Apparently, the inclusion of the two words "autocratic" and "unlimited," which mean the same thing, was designed to emphasize that the emperor's powers were boundless. In theory, the tsar could do as he wished. He set policy, he established the laws of the land, and he was responsible for their enactment.

Of course, even before the Revolution of 1905 the tsar's reach was not as broad as the principle of autocracy implied. The ruler's attempt to impose his will on the vast empire of some 129 million people could not possibly succeed fully even though he had at his disposal a bureaucracy that served at his pleasure and whose authority extended to the lowest level of local affairs. The critical point is that all servants of the state were ultimately accountable to him and on issues about which he cared deeply he was the final arbiter. A revealing incident in September 1905, during one of the more turbulent phases of the revolution, indicates the scope of the tsar's authority. In an endeavor to calm student unrest, the rector of Moscow University, Prince S. N. Trubetskoi, asked the minister of education for permission to add sixty-two Jews to the previously established quota of admission (3 percent of the student body). No doubt aware of the tsar's keen interest in the "Jewish question," the minister sent the following reply to Trubetskoi: "The University's petition . . . will be submitted by me this week in my report to His Imperial Majesty for an opinion."[139] Even on what would normally be regarded a trivial matter the minister did not feel free to take action on his own.

The "Fundamental Laws of 1906," which were drafted by the government to codify the new political arrangements following the issuance of the October Manifesto, recognized the legislative authority of the Duma but also set aside extensive prerogatives for the tsar. To be sure, the authors of the document agreed not to refer to the tsar's "unlimited" powers, but they nevertheless included the following, only slightly less sweeping words: "To the all-Russian Emperor belongs the Supreme Autocratic power." Indeed, the tsar's powers remained very extensive, much broader than those of any monarch at the time in Central or Western Europe. The Russian emperor retained a veto power over all legislative measures, controlled the administration of the empire, determined foreign policy, commanded the military forces, and had the right to impose martial law or states of emergency on regions beset by unrest. Moreover, the tsar alone could pardon convicts, commute penalties handed out by courts, and issue a "general forgiveness" to criminals.

The tsar also remained the "Head of the Church," which he administered through the Most Holy Ruling Synod. And he retained the authority to dissolve the Duma at his discretion; the only condition was that the ukase of dissolution must indicate when new elections would be held and when the new Duma would be convoked. Finally, Nicholas possessed a power most directly relevant to Stolypin's acceptance of a ministerial post: he alone appointed and discharged all ministers.[140]

Nicholas staunchly defended the autocratic system of rule, and any challenge to it, real or imagined, provoked his ire. He venerated the memory of his father, Alexander III, who had been an imposing personality and who had governed with an iron fist, and believed that it was his "sacred mission" to follow in his footsteps. Like his father, he must be uncompromising in upholding the principle of autocracy, the only political idea for which he could muster any passion. Nicholas was also much influenced by K. P. Pobedonostsev, the reactionary procurator of the Most Holy Synod after 1880, who contended that stability could be maintained in Russia only if society remained hierarchically organized and the masses unquestioningly obeyed the existing authorities.[141]

But, ironically, Nicholas was not endowed with the requisite qualifications to lead a large and powerful nation. Although moderately intelligent, he had not received the necessary training or experience for leadership, he showed little interest in studying affairs of state, and he lacked the personal drive and ambition to instill a sense of purpose and direction in the ministers and bureaucracy. Nicholas's private letters and diary reveal him to have been a man of personal charm with strong religious convictions and deep affection for his wife and family, but also a man strangely indifferent to the world about him. He took pains to record how he spent evenings with his family and to describe his various sporting interests, going so far as to note the number of birds he had bagged in his hunts. He could be deeply moved by such events as the loss of his favorite dog, Iman. "I must confess," he wrote in his diary on October 22, 1902, "the whole day after it happened I never stopped crying—I shall miss him dreadfully when I go for walks. He was such an intelligent, kind, and loyal dog!"[142] Yet the great events of his rule—the wars with Japan and the Central Powers, the demands of the liberals for a constitution, the industrial strikes, the violence of 1905, the breakdown of public order that year—received scant attention from him.

Nicholas was also a narrow-minded, prejudiced man, incapable of tolerating people who did not fit his conception of the true Russian. He disliked the national minorities, especially the Jews, and showed little sympathy for proposals to improve their status within the empire. Nor could he abide the intelligentsia. When Prince P. D. Sviatopolk-Mirskii, then governor-general of Vilna, Grodno, and Kovno, accompanied the tsar on a provincial tour someone at a banquet mentioned the word "intelligentsia," provoking Nicholas to declare: "How repulsive I find that word." He added, wistfully, that the Academy of Sciences ought to expunge the word from the Russian dictionary. Nicholas had persuaded himself that all groups of the population except for the intelligentsia were completely devoted to him.[143]

For a man with Stolypin's temperament and commitment to reform to serve a ruler with values and interests so different from his own was bound to be difficult. He could implement his policies only with the approval of the tsar; if he ever lost the confidence of the tsar he would cease to be effective. Stolypin's obeisance to the tsar during the interview made that abundantly clear. But then Stolypin never abandoned his faith in monarchical rule, so this was a liability he accepted as a matter of principle. In fact, in the letter of April 26, discussed above, Stolypin indicated that he might remain minister of internal affairs for only "three to four months," long enough to "withstand the impending shock, [and] somehow initiate the possibility of working together with the people's representatives [i.e., Duma] and thus render a service to the country." He even went so far as to speculate that he might fail very quickly and would not remain in office for more than two months, in which case he would still be remembered as "the first constitutional Minister of Internal Affairs in Russia."[144] This statement should not be interpreted as support on his part for a parliamentary system of government under which ministers were responsible to the legislature. What he meant was that he would be the first minister of internal affairs at a moment unique in Russian history, since an elected legislative body now participated in the political process as promised in the October Manifesto.

Be that as it may, Stolypin threw himself into his work with great energy and enthusiasm. Three days after his appointment, he was working eighteen hours a day, meeting with many senior officials of his department and with governors, often till well after midnight. More mundane chores also kept him busy. He ordered an entirely new wardrobe, and he looked for a residence in the city and a dacha in the outskirts. He was especially pleased that his relations with Goremykin were very friendly, and he was confident that the prime minister would not hamper him in carrying out his policies or interfere in the work of his department. His principal concern at the time was the Duma, then in a "terrible mood [and] embittered" because the Fundamental Laws, giving equal powers with the Duma to an unelected upper chamber, had been promulgated before the formation of the new cabinet and the meeting of the legislature. There would be, he predicted correctly, "major brawls" over this, since the new arrangement clearly and sharply reduced the power of the Duma. Interestingly, Stolypin did not pass judgment on the Fundamental Laws, but he voiced apprehensions about the conduct of the Duma because a majority of the deputies were "very extreme." On the other hand, he praised the tsar's opening address to the Duma, which the ruler himself had composed. "One would have to be made of stone not to be deeply moved. It was not a speech, but an ardent prayer."[145] In fact, the monarch's brief address consisted of little more than broad generalities bound to leave the deputies unmoved. It did nothing to close the vast gap between the opposition, now enjoying a popular mandate, and the forces of the old order.[146]

In April 1906 no one expected Stolypin to emerge as the leader of the government within three months and as the most powerful voice of the establishment. Although he had occupied important posts in the bureaucracy, he had never held a senior position in the capital, and he knew little about the workings of the central administration. Not surprisingly, in the writings of many commentators in 1906, and of virtually all historians since then, there is a note of perplexity about his appointment as minister of internal affairs. As the State Councilor A. A. Polovtsev wrote in his diary on April 25, 1906, everyone praises Stolypin, but "no one can say anything about him."[147] The historian P. N. Zyrianov, writing in 1992, argued that the political class in 1906 was actually critical of Stolypin, contending that the governor of Saratov was too young, too inexperienced, and too little known in the capital for appointment to such a prominent and powerful a position. Zyrianov conceded that he did not really understand why the tsar chose him for the most critical post in the government. Zyrianov echoed the views of Avrekh, who at the end of a lifetime of studying the Stolypin era still believed that the circumstances surrounding the governor's promotion remained puzzling. Avrekh suggested that Stolypin's brother, Alexander, may have been right in suggesting that the tsar, impressed by the governor's success in suppressing agrarian unrest in Saratov, took the initiative in selecting Stolypin for the ministerial post.[148] In a study published some twenty years ago, Mary Schaeffer Conroy speculated that Stolypin's brother-in-law, D. B. Neidgardt, a former city governor of Odessa and scion of a powerful family, used his influence at court to advance Stolypin's career. Even more important, according to another speculation, may have been the intervention of General Trepov, a close advisor to the tsar and an admirer of Stolypin's performance as governor of Saratov.[149]

Whatever the merits of these speculations, they overlook two important factors in Stolypin's rise to eminence, luck and his bold initiatives in establishing contact with dignitaries in the capital. It was sheer good fortune that in June 1904, Tsar Nicholas decided on a goodwill tour of Kuznetsk, Saratov province, and asked him not only to oversee the necessary preparations but also to join him for a personal meeting on the imperial train, during which Stolypin made a favorable impression on the tsar. It was, in fact, the governor's second meeting with the monarch that year, and that in itself was unusual. Generally, governors made the most strenuous efforts to establish direct personal contact with dignitaries in St. Petersburg and in particular with the minister of internal affairs, to discuss their policies and to secure support for them. Although officials were prepared to consider proposals of the governors, they were reluctant to schedule meetings with the senior staff. There were simply too many such requests and normally governors could at best expect to see the minister of internal affairs once a year for no more than twenty minutes.[150] But Stolypin received permission to make two trips to St. Petersburg in 1904, and on his first he saw the minister of internal affairs, Plehve, for thirty minutes and also succeeded in obtaining a brief audience with the tsar. By the time of his second visit Plehve had been assassinated, but Stolypin still managed to visit several senior officials. Stolypin may not have been well known at court, but by late 1904 he had made the acquaintance of a fair number of very influential people in the capital.

However, there were other reasons for Stolypin's rapid rise to eminence. He was a conscientious and highly capable administrator, and, despite the claims of his political opponents and many historians, ever since the 1890s at the latest Stolypin had a vision for the transformation of Russia that gained in depth and scope with almost each passing year. In Saratov he had developed a sophisticated strategy for handling revolutionary turbulence that fused persuasion with repression in a way that set him apart from virtually all other officials and conservatives. He had prepared several long reports on the condition of Russia and on reforms he considered necessary, all of which reached the desks of leading officials and, more important, the desk of the tsar himself. Indeed, it is a tribute to his adroitness that he succeeded in impressing men in the highest circles of power, and yet almost every dignitary and every journalist thought of him as an unassuming person, a good provincial bureaucrat but not much more than that. Stolypin was a clever and thoughtful man, not only in statecraft but also in building a reputation as an energetic and imaginative leader. It would be rash to suggest that he was destined to reach the heights of power in Imperial Russia, but it would be even more rash to contend that his promotion in 1906 was entirely fortuitous. He possessed the rare talent of being able, at one and the same time, to pursue his ambitions resolutely yet retain an aura of modesty. For an aspiring statesman, that talent is invaluable.

3

Fighting the Revolution,
April-August 1906

By all accounts, during the first few weeks of Stolypin's tenure as minister of internal affairs, he maintained a low profile and rarely took part in the cabinet's deliberations. No one could be certain whether he was timid or simply reluctant to speak out until he felt sure of his ground. Having spent virtually his entire career as an official in the provinces, he was unfamiliar with the operation of the central government in St. Petersburg, and consequently he may well have been insecure about committing himself on issues involving complicated political and procedural matters. In an interview late in 1906, he admitted as much. He had been a governor for only a short time, he noted, and the experience had not yet turned him into a "bureaucrat. I was a stranger in the bureaucratic world of Petersburg . . . [and] I had no connections at Court." Moreover, he considered himself "merely a public figure: I lived mainly on estates and was an ordinary Marshal of the Nobility."[1] In saying this, Stolypin was excessively modest, but in his first weeks in the capital he did betray an uncharacteristic reluctance to take charge. V. I. Gurko, the assistant minister of internal affairs, detected a certain provincialism and inexperience in Stolypin's approach to his duties. When subordinates sought his advice on specific issues, he often said that "in Saratov" or "in Grodno" we did "thus and so." Much of the time the various departments in his ministry "were left to their own devices," a serious matter, since Stolypin often appointed people of limited ability to high posts.[2] He was not the best judge of men and, in any case, the pool of talent was small.

However, Stolypin's quiet demeanor should not be mistaken as lassitude. He worked hard at learning the ways of the capital and his own department, though Gurko, full of resentment because of his forced resignation for misappropriating funds, suggested that from the moment Stolypin assumed leadership of the Ministry of Internal Affairs, he focused primarily on personal advancement. He "decided to become head

of the government. He pursued this course subtly and intelligently, out-
witting even that sly Ulysses, Goremykin." Gurko provided no hard
evidence to substantiate his assertion, but Stolypin was certainly ambitious enough to covet the post of prime minister. However, even Gurko
granted that Stolypin was not motivated by ambition alone. Stolypin
quickly sensed that Goremykin was too lazy to administer the country's
affairs at so critical a juncture. Equally important, he realized, soon after
settling into his new post, that the effective execution by the minister of
internal affairs of "internal policy" depended "upon the united activities of all the ministers and, therefore, could be achieved only by having
the Minister of Interior become head of the government." Apparently,
some of Stolypin's relatives and a few Duma deputies agreed with him
and encouraged him to seek the highest post in the cabinet.[3]

In truth, Goremykin was a disaster as prime minister, not only in the
eyes of liberals and moderates but also of conservatives. A fervent monarchist, he decided to treat the Duma with the utmost contempt. After
his one speech in the legislature on May 13, in which he made some
general recommendations for reform, he let it be known that henceforth
he would ignore the chamber; he would not bother to attend its sessions
and would urge his ministers to stay away. If government officials were
summoned by deputies to answer queries, the ministers, Goremykin
advised, should send subordinates to speak on their behalf. In short,
Goremykin planned to act "as if [the deputies] did not exist." In early
May, only days after the Duma had convened, he asked S. E. Kryzhanovskii, an assistant minister of internal affairs, to prepare a plan to
change the electoral law so that more "satisfactory" results could be ensured by a new election. For Goremykin, it was now simply a matter of
time before the legislature would be dissolved.[4] Even so staunch a conservative as Gurko believed that the prime minister acted irresponsibly.
In ignoring the Duma, he was sending a message to the country that the
"new constitution" enacted by the October Manifesto would not be
taken seriously and could be withdrawn "tomorrow."[5]

Stolypin kept his own counsel, but he clearly did not share the prime
minister's attitude toward the Duma. He was the only minister who
regularly attended debates in the legislature; the others followed Goremykin's directive and sent lower-ranking officials. The government,
moreover, did not bother to introduce any significant legislative proposals. It was not until May 15 that it submitted the first two proposals for
the Duma's consideration, both of them trivial: one called for the establishment of a local school, and the other for the building of a steam
laundry and a greenhouse for the University of Iuriev (Tartu).

Even if Stolypin kept his eye on the prime ministership from the moment he arrived in the capital, he did not neglect his work as head of the Ministry of Internal Affairs, which exercised authority over the provincial administration and the police and which had been subjected to intense criticism for its handling of unrest in 1905 and early 1906. In a shrewd move designed to curry favor with the press, he invited the journalist S. N. Syromiatnikov to his office on May 19, barely three weeks after assuming his new post, for the first of many talks about current events. The two men had been classmates at the University of St. Petersburg but had not known each other. Stolypin had read Syromiatnikov's articles in *Slovo* during the revolutionary upheaval of 1905 and was impressed with them, especially with their conservative point of view. The admiration quickly became mutual; Syromiatnikov was impressed by Stolypin's open-mindedness, his willingness to listen to points of view different from his own. The two men established a close relationship that lasted throughout Stolypin's period in office.[6] The friendship with Syromiatnikov was only the first of numerous efforts by Stolypin to cultivate the press.

On a more substantive level, within two weeks as head of the Ministry of Internal Affairs Stolypin launched several initiatives in what he regarded as his priority, the restoration of governmental authority. He began to bombard governors, military commanders, and the minister of war with telegrams and letters on the dangers of revolutionary agitation in various parts of the empire and with directives on how to cope with them. On May 9 he sent a circular to all governors emphasizing the heavy responsibility that lay on their shoulders in combating the rising lawlessness. Local officials must see to the "preservation of order, property, and life," an essential precondition for the reform of state institutions to which the monarch had committed himself.[7] About three weeks later, on May 29, when a new wave of peasant unrest had erupted, Stolypin sent a telegram marked "secret" to all governors-general and governors directing them to adopt firm measures against this latest challenge to authority. He repeated his admonition to officials that the prevention of such "rebellious manifestations" must be one of the "most important concerns" of administrative authorities. In all instances of unrest, officials must act "in a most decisive manner, without any hesitation" to restore order and to prevent the spread of disturbances. They must develop precise plans in conjunction with local military officers and issue appropriate instructions. "I am confident that under conditions of timely, firm, and astute directives the available police and military forces suffice for the maintenance of order."[8] It is remarkable how quickly Stolypin's perspective changed; as governor, he had regularly complained about the insufficiency of the armed force at this disposal.

As minister of internal affairs, however, his concerns were necessarily broader than they had been in Saratov. His study of *Okhrana* reports alarmed him deeply and convinced him that the revolutionary threat to the state was even more serious than he had believed. On June 2, he informed Rediger, the minister of war, that he had learned that in Kronstadt, an important naval fortress that guarded the approaches to St. Petersburg at the head of the Gulf of Finland, a military-revolutionary organization of Social Democrats and Socialist Revolutionaries was successfully conducting propaganda among military units. Some 50 percent of the men in the lower ranks acknowledged that they were "conscious"—that is, that they supported the revolutionary cause. Among sailors the agitators had been even more successful: some 80 percent considered themselves to be "conscious." At almost daily meetings orators called on the men to proceed to Peterhof with arms in their hands to pressure the tsar to accede to all demands of the State Duma. The lower-ranking men were in such a militant mood, Stolypin told Rediger, that they were prepared to take action even before the conflict between the Duma and the government reached the breaking point. Revolutionaries actually tried to restrain the sailors because the moment was not yet propitious for an armed uprising.[9] On the very day that Stolypin sent this letter to Rediger, V. F. von der Launits, the city governor of Petersburg, reported on "huge meetings" taking place in Kronstadt and warned that the revolutionaries were planning an "outburst" that "will serve as a signal for a general revolt in Petersburg."[10]

On June 10, Stolypin sent another circular to all governors-general and governors spelling out in more detail than ever before the measures to be taken in the event of "general unrest," which he expected to break out in the near future. The circular is noteworthy for two reasons: it reveals the careful attention Stolypin paid to the maintenance of order during the initial period of his tenure in office, and it indicates that however harsh his approach, he did not follow the example of his predecessor Durnovo, who ordered the indiscriminate shooting of rebels. Stolypin directed local officials to conduct extensive searches, to arrest the leaders of revolutionary groups, as well as unruly railwaymen, agitators in the army, and civilian custodians of weapons and bombs. The arrests should follow "formal inquiries," but if that turned out to be impossible then officials should resort to administrative expulsions or to the filing of charges against individuals in "Special Conferences," which, according to a statue of 1881, had the right in regions placed under the emergency rules known as "Reinforced Security" to expel from their areas of residence for one to five years anyone suspected of revolutionary activities. The "Special Conferences" consisted of five men: two from the Ministry of Internal Affairs, two from the Ministry of Justice, and an assistant minister who served as chairman. The conference's decisions required confirmation by the minister of internal affairs.

Stolypin also urged the governors to take special measures to protect government and railway buildings and railway junctions, telegraph offices, banks, prisons, and weapons depots. Any telegraph offices that fell into the hands of rebels should be closed immediately. The press should be curbed and printing plants closed down if necessary. Convinced that the country faced a new upsurge of violence, the new minister of internal affairs did not want his subordinates to be uncertain about how to deal with it. At the same time, he directed them not to make any public reference to his circular, so as to prevent "panic."[11]

In the meantime, relations between the government and the Duma deteriorated rapidly. Three days before the legislature held its first meeting, there were signs of a serious rift. Deputies were stunned by the government's issuance on April 24 of the so-called "Fundamental Laws of 1906," which had been secretly drafted and which in several ways undermined the thrust of the October Manifesto. Not only did it assign vast power to the tsar;* it also reaffirmed the ukase of February 20, 1906, which transformed the State Council into an upper chamber with powers equal to those of the Duma. Half of the 198 members of the council were to be appointed by the tsar and the other half were to be elected by relatively small, elite social groups. Moreover, the Fundamental Laws stipulated that if the legislature failed to adopt a budget "at the beginning of the fiscal period," the previous budget would remain in force, a provision that provided the government with a strong hand in negotiations over fiscal matters.

The list of civil rights accorded to Russian subjects in the Fundamental Laws touched on important areas, but the restrictions left the government with considerable latitude in defining their scope. The document provided for due process, the inviolability of private property, freedom of assembly, freedom of expression ("within the limits fixed by law"), freedom of association ("for purposes not contrary to laws"), and freedom of religion, although "the conditions under which [the people]

*See above, pp. 91–92.

may avail themselves of this freedom are determined by law."[12] When the Duma was in recess, the government could, under Article 87, rule by decree, which became a dead letter if it were not passed by both houses of the legislature within two months after they reconvened. It should also be noted that the Fundamental Laws differed from all other laws in that they alone could be revised only on the tsar's initiative. The constitution of 1906, a term frequently used to describe the Fundamental Laws, marked a liberalization of the political order that had existed at the beginning of the Revolution of 1905, but it was a far cry from the aspirations of Russian liberals. Some liberals, in fact, believed that in issuing them the government had inflicted a fatal blow to the revolution. Only the opposition's victory in the Duma elections kept alive the liberals' hope that the gains of the revolution could still be consolidated.

From the moment the Duma met, however, that hope began to fade very quickly. There were alarming signs that it would not be able to coexist with the government and that an open clash might jeopardize all the gains of 1905. Dominated by the opposition, the legislature on May 5 adopted an "Answer to the Throne" (that is, a response to the tsar's very general speech welcoming the deputies) that amounted to a demand for political changes of the most fundamental kind, changes that would have transformed the country's political system into a constitutional monarchy with paramount authority vested in the Duma. The "Answer" also called for amnesty for all political prisoners, the abolition of the emergency regulations of 1881, the introduction of universal and equal suffrage and free education, and agrarian reforms that would include the compulsory alienation of private land.

This demand for far-reaching change came at a time when the tsar, whose grasp of political realities was never strong, had persuaded himself that most of the people remained loyal to him and that he would therefore be able to weather the storm without having to live up to the commitments he had made in the October Manifesto. Thus, when the president of the Duma, S. A. Muromtsev, sought to present the "Answer" in person to the monarch, Nicholas refused to receive him. To add insult to injury, the court did not even communicate directly with President Muromtsev. The prime minister informed Muromtsev of the tsar's decision and asked that the document be sent to him for transmittal to Nicholas. For the Kadets, the constitutionalists who dominated the proceedings in the Duma, this rebuff was no trivial matter. They had sought to follow the custom of the British parliament of delivering to the monarch a reply to the address from the throne and thus to underscore their intention to introduce Western constitutional practices in

Russia. Stunned by the government's callous treatment of Muromtsev, they and virtually all Duma deputies denounced the government for "defying us." As one journalist noted, "[T]he higher authorities here are destined to take no single step which is not fatal."[13]

Within the government, resentment against the Duma rose sharply. Seven of the sixteen ministers urged the cabinet to issue a declaration denouncing the Duma even before it had concluded its deliberations of the "Answer to the Throne." On the advice of Rediger, cooler heads prevailed, but Goremykin's speech of May 13, in which he in effect rejected as unacceptable all the reforms proposed in the "Answer," provoked the deputies into throwing down another gauntlet. Almost unanimously, the chamber voted in favor of a resolution declaring complete lack of confidence in the government and demanding its immediate resignation and replacement by a cabinet enjoying the confidence of the State Duma.

A day after this vote, every member of the Council of Ministers agreed, at a formal meeting, that cooperation with the Duma was now impossible and that the legislature would have to be dissolved. The only question was the timing. According to a reliable source, A. P. Izvolskii, the minister of foreign affairs, and Stolypin were alone in urging patience. Izvolskii feared that a dissolution at that time would alienate public opinion in Europe and damage Russia's international standing. Stolypin conceded that forceful action against the Duma was unavoidable, but he preferred to stand fast for now. He and Izvolskii wanted to wait until passions died down; perhaps the Duma might yet come to its senses and engage in constructive work. All the other ministers insisted that the deputies were deliberately stirring up the opposition, possibly to the point of revolution, so that they would be able to take power. Goremykin apparently did not reveal his own views on disbanding the legislature. He merely asked that the deliberations be kept confidential, and that all the ministers be prepared for an emergency.[14] His admonition was widely ignored; newspapers carried numerous articles, many of them well founded, about discussions within the government and at court on whether and when to do away with the legislature.

Every hardening of the government's attitude toward the Duma was reciprocated by a new display of distemper by the deputies. On May 24, Gurko, then the assistant minister of internal affairs, appeared in the chamber at Stolypin's request to speak on the agrarian question. Before Gurko uttered a single word, he was greeted by catcalls: "Resign! Resign!" The president of the Duma politely called for decorum, a request that provoked further shouts of "Resign! Will the [minister] leave soon?" When Gurko began to speak, there was so much noise that he could not be heard. He offered to "try to speak louder" and somehow managed to deliver his speech. As soon as Muromtsev introduced the minister of agriculture, A. S. Stishinskii, as the next speaker, the shouting from the floor burst out once more. The Trudoviks were the main offenders. The president's warning that "we can do our work only if order is maintained" had no effect on them. Nor could the Trudoviks be swayed from their tactic by private pleas from leading Kadets, who still wanted to prove that the Duma could conduct its business in an orderly manner. For the next six weeks whenever government officials sought to address the legislature, they were met by angry shouts urging them to resign.[15]

Probably the most valuable work of the Duma was to conduct interpellations, which were inquiries into wrongdoing by government officials. The minister of a department suspected of misconduct was expected to appear in person in the chamber to answer the deputies' queries. Even though the Duma could do little to force officials to mend their ways, the unfavorable publicity could prompt malefactors to think twice about acting illegally. More important, perhaps, the interpellation, widely reported in the press, brought to public notice the arbitrariness and corruptness of the bureaucracy. In the course of its nine-week existence, the Duma voted in favor of over four hundred interpellations, which comes to almost six a day. Not surprisingly, the court and the government despised the entire procedure.

It was during one of the more turbulent interpellations that Stolypin made his debut in the Duma. He immediately demonstrated that he was an orator and debater of extraordinary skills. Tall, handsome, self-assured, he impressed his audience as a fearless man, in command of the relevant facts and convinced that his views were correct. He did not fear to confront directly anyone who challenged his authority and excelled at hurling telling barbs at his opponents. He was, in fact, an unusually talented polemicist and phrase-maker, and he seemed to enjoy tangling with the obstreperous Duma deputies. Never flustered, he knew how to strike a pose of defiance and reveled in letting the deputies know that their hostility did not trouble him in the least and that their attacks on him would not sway him from pursuing policies he considered best for Russia. There was more than a touch of arrogance in his demeanor, which must have been especially annoying for the deputies because his ringing voice enabled him to make himself heard despite the frequent shouts and hisses.

Stolypin appeared in the Duma on June 8 to respond to an interpellation about a certain A. P. Shcherbakov, who, it was charged, had been unjustly tried under provisions of martial law, apparently for disorderly conduct. Stolypin indicated that he had not yet had an opportunity to examine the case and could therefore not answer any questions on the matter. But the debate in the Duma quickly turned to another, far more explosive issue, the pogrom in Bialystok early in June, during which at least eighty-two Jews and six non-Jews had been killed and 169 shops and houses had been plundered. On the third day of the attacks Stolypin sent a telegram to all governors and city governors reminding them of their duty to suppress pogroms, whether directed at landlords or at Jews, "with the most decisive measures." Inaction or official connivance with the marauders, he warned, would have the "most serious consequence."[16] Newspapers had in fact carried many articles indicating that local officials and respected citizens in Bialystok had either inflamed the population against the Jews or actually participated in the looting.

The most dramatic moment in the Duma debates came when Prince S. D. Urusov, assistant minister of internal affairs for a few months in late 1905 and early 1906 and now a deputy and a member of the Kadet Party, delivered a speech accusing the government of having played a decisive role in fomenting pogroms throughout 1905 and in the early months of 1906. Urusov also referred to the revelation that had come to light the preceding February, that a certain Captain M. S. Komissarov had been in charge of a printing press, located in an out-of-the-way room in the Department of Police in St. Petersburg, that was used to produce anti-Jewish proclamations. When someone stumbled on the press and asked Komissarov what kind of work he did, he replied: "We can arrange any massacre you like; a massacre of ten or a massacre of ten thousand." "I can add," Urusov continued, "that in Kiev a massacre of ten thousand had been arranged to take place on February 3, [1906], but it was successfully averted." He warned that even a government responsible to the Duma could not prevent outbreaks of mass violence unless it purged the entire administration of the "dark forces" that would stop at nothing to maintain the old order. "Herein lies a great danger, and this danger will not disappear so long as in the direction of affairs and in the fortunes of our country we continue to feel the influence of men who have the education of policemen and sergeants, and are *pogromshchiki* on principle." The deputies greeted the speech with "endless and thunderous applause."[17]

Even before these startling revelations, Stolypin felt called upon to defend his department and especially the police. He could not, he insisted, be expected to answer all charges of illegal conduct by his department prior to his assumption of office, though he conceded that some policemen had engaged in political agitation and had attended meetings of extremist parties. For his part, he assured the deputies that he would not tolerate illegal conduct or violence of any kind. "These actions are wrong and the ministry is obliged to take the most energetic measures to see to it that they are not repeated, and I guarantee that they will not be repeated." But then he pointed out that the leaflets mentioned by Urusov had not been nearly as lethal as the revelations about them suggested. In Vilno, for example, they were destroyed as soon as officials in St. Petersburg learned about their distribution. This was true of several other towns, according to Stolypin.

He also made some observations clearly designed to impart a benign gloss on past conduct of the police, if not exactly to vindicate it. True, mistakes had been made by policemen and officials, but he insisted that most officials had faithfully carried out their obligations. In the course of seven months, from October 1905 to April 1906, almost three hundred policemen had lost their lives in the line of duty and close to four hundred had been injured. It seemed to some in the legislative chamber that in citing these statistics, Stolypin was appealing to the deputies to be indulgent toward policemen who had sympathized with the *pogromshchiki*. The deputies, however, were not impressed by Stolypin's remarks and interrupted him with derisive laughter and shouts of "Enough!" and with so much noise that at one point the president called for order in the chamber.

Nor were the deputies impressed by Stolypin's more general point about the role of the government, which sounded like a lesson in political science: "One must not forget that governmental inaction leads to anarchy, that government is not an instrument designed for inaction or ingratiation. Government is an instrument of authority that rests on laws, from which it is clear that a minister should and will demand from his bureaucrats circumspection, caution, and justice, but [also] firm execution of [their] duty and of the law."[18] One can hardly quarrel with Stolypin's views on the role of government, but in emphasizing this particular point during a debate of official malfeasance, which contributed to the massacre of dozens of innocent citizens, he gave the impression of gross insensitivity.

Predictably, not many deputies were persuaded that he would take appropriate measures to prevent such outrages in the future. When, after Urusov's speech, he repeated his vow not to tolerate illegal conduct by officials, the stenographic report indicated that he was greeted with "noise, shouts: and the Bialystok pogrom?!" He then rejected the argument put forth by the deputy M. M. Vinaver that he regarded the question of the pogroms and their prevention from too narrow a legal standpoint. Stolypin could not understand this criticism. Was Vinaver suggesting that he ought to change Russia's legal system? His duty, he insisted, was "firmly and fairly to maintain order in Russia." At this point the deputies once again shouted and whistled, prompting Stolypin to adopt a defiant tone, which soon became his trademark: "This noise impedes me, but it cannot trouble me or confuse me. This is my role, and I have no right to seize legislative power; I cannot change the law. You will change the law and will work to do so (*Noise, shouts: 'resign!'*)." Stolypin then left the chamber, which was in such an uproar that President Muromtsev announced: "Under these conditions the meeting cannot continue. I am resorting to the President's prerogatives, and am ordering a one-hour recess of the meeting (*applause*)."[19]

Stolypin spoke on two other occasions in the First Duma, once very briefly on a procedural issue and the second time to assure the chamber of the government's genuine interest in providing relief to citizens threatened by famine. In the spring of 1906 a drought ravaged 127 districts in the empire, and hundreds of thousands of people faced food shortages. The Duma, charging the government with failing to take adequate steps to care for the needy, adopted an interpellation, to which Stolypin responded on June 12. Stolypin denied the charge, discussed the government's previous efforts in providing grain to needy people, and promised to introduce a funding bill to support additional relief efforts. But even on this issue, on which everyone agreed that quick action was called for, the deliberations degenerated into a nasty squabble. Enraged at the deputies' accusations, Stolypin declared that "I say again to those persons who, stepping up to this tribune from the left, announce that they are not filled with self-deception and self-importance; I say in response to their slanders, their threats, their . . . (*noise, shouts: Enough!*), their threat to seize executive power (*noise, shouts: Enough!*), that the Minister of Internal Affairs, the bearer of legal authority, will not answer them (*noise, shouts: Enough! Bialystok! Pogromshchik! Enough! Away with him!*)."[20] In the end, after more wrangling, the Duma and the government agreed on a bill providing fifteen million rubles for famine relief, the only time the deputies were able to pass legislation that was actually implemented by the government.

For the next three weeks, Stolypin rarely showed up at the Duma, no doubt because he now knew that the legislature would soon be dissolved. But on July 4 he appeared in the ministerial gallery and carefully followed the debate that day on the vexing agrarian issue. It was the single most contentious issue in the many controversies between the government and the Duma, and the one over which the Goremykin government came to grief. Still it is a mistake to contend that the various debates over amnesty, capital punishment, the emergency regulations, and, above all, ministerial responsibility merely served as a cover for the only significant struggle between the people and the defenders of the old order, the struggle over the disposition of the gentry's land.[21] An overwhelming majority of the deputies in the Duma felt deeply about civil liberties and human rights—the very first subject they took up, after all, was amnesty—and the sessions devoted to capital punishment and the government's handling of the pogroms produced some of the bitterest clashes between deputies and government officials. Moreover, it is arguable that the Kadets placed greater weight on transforming the legislature into a body with sovereign powers than on instituting specific reforms, including agrarian reforms. In their view, once the Duma became the dominant factor in the Russian state major reforms would be quickly enacted. By the same token, there is little evidence to suggest that Tsar Nicholas and his senior advisers were any less concerned about retaining the upper hand politically than they were about protecting the property rights of the gentry. There is no reason to assume that if the Duma and the government had feuded only over human rights and political power, the conflict between them would have been markedly less acrid.

Nonetheless, the Duma did devote far more time to the agrarian issue than to any other, and conflict over it was the immediate cause of the final rupture between the tsarist authorities and the legislature. The sticking point was that every proposal introduced in the Duma on the agrarian issue provided, in one form or another, for some compulsory alienation of private lands. Under no circumstances would the government agree to any such measure. When Stolypin sat in the ministerial gallery on July 4, the deputies were discussing precisely such a measure, and in the process they delivered some militant speeches, to which the minister of internal affairs listened very attentively. He was gathering material for a report to the tsar on the legislature, which was debating a so-called "Appeal to the People." In the "Appeal," the deputies assured the people that the Duma was working on an agrarian bill calling for some expropriation of private property. It ended with a statement that on the surface appeared to be moderate but struck the authorities as a veiled incitement to unrest: "The State Duma hopes that the population will calmly and peacefully await the completion of the work on the promulgation of such a law." The wording seemed to imply that if the

Duma's proposal did not become law, the people need no longer restrain themselves.[22] Through some last-minute maneuvers by the Kadet leadership, which did not want to provoke the government, the "Appeal" was neither adopted nor rejected. But that did not impress hard-line conservatives, who viewed the proceedings as a further vindication of their charge that the legislature was nothing but a nest of revolutionism.

It is difficult to determine exactly when Stolypin became a firm advocate of the Duma's dissolution. He had all along been reluctant to urge such a drastic step, but in mid-June he had concluded that the country "was passing through a severe crisis," though he did not believe that it was "on the brink of a precipice or would be mastered by the revolutionary forces." Yet it was clear to him that the government could not possibly accept the demands of the Kadets: complete amnesty would free the "most dangerous elements of society" and would encourage others to commit similar crimes; the expropriation of private lands would be "unjust and would be economically ruinous"; the death penalty could not be abolished at a time when police officers and others were regularly being assassinated throughout the country. Although he granted that much could be said in favor of enacting the principle of "equality of rights for all," the "backward state of education" and the prevailing ethnic hatreds made it essential that the authorities proceed cautiously and slowly. In outlining his positions to the British ambassador to St. Petersburg, Sir Arthur Nicolson, Stolypin insisted that the government was not reactionary and "knew full well that they must advance on the lines of progress. His own ideal was the British Constitution, but it was impossible to cast Russia at once into that mould. In some years she might possibly reach that goal, but sudden and impetuous changes would work ruin." Indeed, he was convinced that if power were handed over to the Kadets, "disorder would [soon] reign universally. The new [Kadet] Government would have to adopt repressive measures, and in but very few weeks the outcry against them would be louder than against the present Government."[23]

If Nicolson's report can be credited, Stolypin's ultimate vision for Russia in 1906 was far more progressive than has generally been assumed. On the other hand, he made it abundantly clear on many occasions that he was a constitutionalist but not a supporter of parliamentary government—that is, he believed that the monarch in Russia should govern the country according to a set of rules, the so-called Fundamental Laws, but he did not believe in the political pre-eminence of elected representatives. It may well be that Stolypin was carried away during the conversation with the British ambassador by a desire to please his interlocutor. Or perhaps the translation of Stolypin's words was imperfect; his spoken English was not fluent. In any case, Stolypin's comments amounted to a wholesale rejection of the Kadet program, which called for the immediate introduction of parliamentary government. Under the circumstances, there was virtually no chance that common ground would be found between the government and the Duma.

And yet for about two weeks, beginning approximately in mid-June, senior officials at court and several ministers, including Stolypin, undertook last-ditch efforts to prevent a showdown with the Duma. The efforts took the form of feverish negotiations with liberals and Octobrists about the formation of a new government to include some individuals from the opposition. Everyone insisted on secrecy, but few of the participants could resist the temptation to talk to one or two associates. The result was a deluge of rumors, implausible assertions about clandestine meetings, not to mention endless behind-the-scene intrigues. To what extent the tsar was informed about these maneuvers and gave his approval to the quest for an accord with the liberals is not clear. There is no doubt that he knew about some of the negotiations, and it is certain that he himself entered into a discussion with one leading member of the Union of October 17. Most likely, he encouraged the negotiations to see where they would lead. Subjected to a barrage of contradictory advice, unable to choose among alternate policies, Nicholas probably decided to exhaust all possibilities. At the very least, he would be able to delay a final decision on how to deal with the Duma. Shilly-shallying on key issues was certainly in keeping with his conduct of affairs of state.

D. F. Trepov, the commandant of the court and a very close confidant of the tsar, made the first move, apparently acting on his own authority without consulting the leading ministers or anyone else. Through an intermediary, he approached P. N. Miliukov, the leader of the Constitutional Democrats (Kadets), who agreed to meet with Trepov so long as it was clear that no binding agreements would be reached. The two men met secretly at the Cuba Restaurant. Without wasting words, Trepov suggested that Miliukov join what he called a "ministry of confidence." Miliukov did not reject the idea, but insisted that the point was not to select individuals for high posts but to agree on policies. Before Kadets could join a government, the court would have to indicate willingness to adopt the kind of changes liberals favored. In all, Miliukov listed seven of the most essential demands in the Kadet program, among which were ministerial responsibility, expropriation of privately owned land, and amnesty for political prisoners. This did not faze Trepov, who seemed prepared to accept the establishment of a government composed of members of the Duma majority as well as five other points of the Kadet program. He balked only at the demand that amnesty be granted to political prisoners. "The Tsar," he said, "will never pardon assassins of the Tsar."

It is still not clear why Trepov undertook the initiative and why he was so forthcoming in the meeting with Miliukov. When news of the restaurant meeting reached the court, the tsar's advisers concluded that Trepov must have lost touch with reality. His own brother, A. F. Trepov, was appalled by the meeting and tried to talk the commandant into dropping the negotiations with Miliukov. But to all the arguments against the formation of a Kadet ministry, D. F. Trepov offered only one response: "All is lost, and we must save the Emperor and the dynasty from an inevitable catastrophe."

There is evidence to suggest that at least for a short while the tsar took the commandant's proposal for a ministry of confidence seriously. But as soon as Nicholas came under pressure from opponents to the scheme (from Kokovtsov in particular), he abandoned the idea. Goremykin did not even bother to take up the matter with the tsar because he was certain that Nicholas would never agree to a Kadet ministry. Nor did Goremykin discuss Trepov's maneuvers with Stolypin because he suspected the minister of internal affairs of having played a role in the commandant's intrigues.[24]

Be that as it may, Stolypin held another series of discussions with liberals over the formation of a new government. These were initiated by Izvolskii, the foreign minister and the most liberal member of the government, who was deeply distressed over the deterioration in the relations between the Duma and the government. He secured permission from Nicholas to approach the liberals and to include Stolypin in the discussions. While Izvolskii, supported by A. S. Ermolov, a moderate, a former minister of agriculture and now a member of the State Council, established contact with leading members of the Duma and with state councilors, Stolypin conducted "parallel conferences" with liberals. Every night he and Izvolskii "compared notes."[25]

One of the more interesting meetings took place late one night at Stolypin's residence on Aptekarskii Island between the minister of internal affairs and Miliukov, with Izvolskii in attendance. Miliukov adopted a moderate and conciliatory stance: he assured his host that the Kadets would not insist on heading the Ministries of War, Navy, and Court, since it was the "monarch's prerogative" to make appointments to those posts. When Stolypin asked, with a touch of irony in his voice, whether a Kadet minister of internal affairs would be able to carry out the necessary police functions, to which the liberals were "unaccustomed," Miliukov answered, also assuming a tone of irony, that the Kadets were well aware of the "elementary functions of the authorities," though they would surely make changes in the way those functions were executed. To calm Stolypin's apprehensions, Miliukov "added that the conduct of the Kadets in the government should not be judged on the basis of their role in the opposition."

According to Miliukov, the question of whether all the other posts in the new government should go to Kadets or to representatives of various groups, including the bureaucracy, was simply not discussed. Stolypin, however, assumed that Miliukov would insist on a "purely Kadet" ministry, not an unreasonable assumption, given Miliukov's utterances on the composition of a ministry of confidence. Indeed, in an interview published on July 1 in *Russkie vedomosti*, he was unambiguous about the kind of government the Kadets would be prepared to join: "Only a ministry composed exclusively of adherents of our party. We will not join any sort of coalition government."[26] In any case Stolypin, unwilling to countenance a purely Kadet ministry, decided to turn elsewhere. He approached Muromtsev, but that initiative was unproductive, apparently because the president of the Duma was not sufficiently influential among the Kadets to enter into a binding agreement with the minister of internal affairs.[27]

Some time after the interview with Stolypin, Miliukov claimed that he never took Stolypin's overture seriously because he was convinced that the court and the prime minister were determined to dissolve the Duma at all costs. In fact, in mid-June Stolypin still preferred a more nuanced course because he wanted to avoid taking an action that would be seen as purely repressive. No doubt he was now bent on dissolving the Duma, but he wished to do so only after the formation of a new government composed of moderate bureaucrats and moderate liberals, who would promise to introduce reform and to maintain order. He therefore turned to D. N. Shipov, a highly respected leader of the Octobrists, with a request that he head a new government, whose first act would be to disband the Duma. In many ways, the approach to Shipov made sense. He was sufficiently conservative to be acceptable to the court and at the same time his integrity and long involvement in the zemstvo movement might have gained him at least the grudging acceptance of many Kadets. Certainly, if any person could have bridged the gap between the tsarist authorities and society, it was Shipov. Hence, many members of the State Council and the State Duma assumed that his appointment was a fait accompli. Shipov was startled to discover this because he was unalterably opposed to the Duma's dissolution and did not even want to meet with Stolypin to discuss the formation of a new government.[28]

On the morning of June 17, Shipov received a telegram from Peterhof inviting him to an audience with the tsar. A loyal monarchist, he could not refuse such an invitation. He now decided to see Stolypin after all, not to discuss the minister's proposal that he head the government but to find out why he was being summoned. At the meeting, also attended by Izvolskii, Stolypin emphasized that the Duma was not capable of constructive work and had to be dissolved. In no uncertain terms, Shipov replied that he considered such an action "wrong and . . . from a political standpoint, criminal"; he would not be a party to it. Disappointed and displeased, Stolypin nevertheless spoke at length on the need for a coalition government led by Shipov. Shipov remained adamant, pointing out that the kind of coalition government Stolypin had in mind would never enlist the cooperation of the Duma. He insisted that only a government led and dominated by Kadets would be effective, and that Muromtsev, the president of the Duma, would be a good choice as prime minister. It was not a suggestion acceptable to Stolypin. As Shipov left he told his host of his upcoming audience with the tsar, about which the minister had apparently not been informed. They agreed to remain in touch.[29]

At his meeting with the tsar, Shipov candidly expressed his view that there were no constitutional grounds for dismissing the Duma. Such an action would inevitably raise the question of whether the government still took the October Manifesto seriously. He also predicted that a new election would produce a Duma to the left of the present one. And he repeated what he had already told Stolypin, that a coalition government would be effective only if the Kadets joined it, but that it seemed obvious that they would not agree to do so. As he ended the interview, Nicholas thanked Shipov for his advice: "I am very glad that you spoke candidly; I noticed that you spoke without holding back, and am very grateful to you."[30]

According to Izvolskii, until July 5 the court had been inclined to invite the Kadets into the government and had even taken seriously Shipov's advice that Muromtsev be asked to head a new government. But that day several events had strengthened the hand of the reactionaries, making it easier for Stolypin to move against the Duma. Admiral G. P. Chukhnin had been assassinated in Sevastopol, and Major General A. A. Kozlov had met a similar fate in St. Petersburg. Most important of all, the Duma had taken up the "Appeal to the People," widely viewed by officials as a disguised threat by the opposition parties to mobilize mass action against the authorities. Infuriated, the government and the court made an irrevocable decision to dissolve the legislature.

The tsar's advisers remained divided on the issue to the very last moment. D. F. Trepov, for many months an uncompromising hardliner, opposed dissolution on the grounds that it would provoke new and dangerous violence from below. Count V. B. Frederiks, the minister of court and highly influential with the tsar, sided with Trepov. Frederiks was in a state of panic at the very idea of disbanding the Duma and tried to convince Stolypin that such a measure would have the "most fateful consequences—including the collapse of the monarchy." Frederiks argued that the Duma was loyal to the tsar, and that if the monarch personally expressed his displeasure with its behavior and coupled that with threats of firm measures, the legislature would change course and resume its work in a quiet and constructive way. The foreign minister, Izvolskii, also remained an opponent of dissolution and urged that further attempts be made to reach a compromise with the Duma. Within the cabinet he was the most ardent proponent of a conciliatory approach to parliamentary rule, motivated in part by the fact that Russia was then drawing closer to France and Great Britain, two countries that would be distressed by forceful action against the legislature.[31]

But powerful individuals and groups lobbied furiously in favor of dissolution. The United Nobility, a right-wing organization that enjoyed easy entree to the tsarist court, campaigned so intensely against the Duma that it became, in the words of one historian, "the prime instigator" of the legislature's "untimely demise."[32] Prince A. A. Shirinskii-Shikhmatov, the chief procurator of the most holy synod, and P. Kh. Schwanebach, the state comptroller, as well as Gurko pressured Goremykin to exert influence on the tsar in favor of dissolution, but the prime minister hardly needed to be prodded. He despised the legislature and "secretly . . . painstakingly" prepared the ground for action against it. Stolypin apparently remained uneasy about so drastic a measure, but by July 5, when the tsar made the decision in favor of dissolution he was convinced that there was no alternative. He now had concluded that the radicals in the Duma were inciting the population and felt that "as Minister of the Interior . . . the reins were slipping out of his hands, & that if the state of things . . . continued much longer he could not be responsible for the maintenance of order."[33] On the day Stolypin reached this conclusion Goremykin asked the tsar to be relieved of his post and recommended that Stolypin be named to succeed him. The tsar readily agreed.

According to one account, Stolypin was distinctly unenthusiastic when the tsar informed him of his decision to appoint him the next prime minister. Izvolskii thought that Stolypin had doubts about his suitability for the post but felt he could not refuse, especially since Nicholas made his usual emotional defense of his prerogatives. "I am obligated before God," he told Stolypin, "before my country, and before myself to fight, and would rather perish than hand over without any resistance all power to those who stretch out their hands for it."[34] Stolypin may simply have been assuming his favorite stance of modesty, but in addition he would not have wished to appear to be too eager to assume the new post because he wanted to press for the tsar's approval to dismiss Stishinskii and Shirinskii-Shikhmatov, two rabid reactionaries who were unalterably opposed to the very idea of popular representation. Stolypin sought to broaden the appeal of his government, at least among the more moderate groups within the opposition, by replacing them with members of the Duma and State Council. Nicholas agreed to Stolypin's requests.[35]

Two days after the tsar had reached his decisions on the Duma and the new government, the full cabinet voted in favor of dissolution. Only Goremykin, Stolypin, and Schwanebach had been informed of the tsar's intentions. In right-wing circles it was rumored that Goremykin was surprised at his dismissal.[36] But a day after the cabinet's vote, Goremykin arrived in high spirits at another cabinet meeting held at night at his house. "Ca y est! Congratulate me, gentlemen, for having received the greatest favor the Tsar could confer on me: I have been released from the post of Chairman of the Ministers' Council, and my successor is P. A. Stolypin, who, of course, retains the post of Minister of the Interior." He announced that the Duma would be dissolved on Sunday, July 9.[37]

Stolypin joined the group only after Goremykin had made his announcements and gave an account of various meetings he had held with members of the court entourage and the tsar about the impending dissolution of the legislature. Baron Frederiks was "greatly agitated" and had told Stolypin of his plan to have the tsar make a personal appeal to the Duma to moderate its policies and thus forestall its dissolution. Stolypin dismissed the idea, arguing that it would be "dangerous," even "fatal," to have the tsar enter into a direct conflict with the Duma. To which Frederiks answered that many of the tsar's advisers believed that "the whole trouble lay in the choice of ministers." Stolypin also confirmed that he had tried to impress upon the tsar that he lacked the experience to assume the leadership of the government and that he was "unfamiliar with the crosscurrents of St. Petersburg society," but Nicholas had cut him off. "No. Peter Arkadevich, here is the icon before which I often pray. Let us make the sign of the Cross and let us ask the Lord to help us both in this difficult, perhaps historic, moment." The tsar then "made the sign of the Cross over Stolypin, embraced and kissed him." Before leaving, Stolypin spelled out the details of how and when the dissolution would be enacted.[38]

The government feared resistance to the dissolution and at one meeting was briefed by the director of the Department of Police, M. I. Trusevich, on measures to prevent unrest. Stolypin, still not fully comfortable as head of the Ministry of Internal Affairs, "remained mum" during the discussions of purely police matters. He focused on placing the final touches on the tsar's manifesto announcing the action against the Duma. Also, after directing ministers to go about their business to deflect any suspicions, he informed Muromtsev that he would appear at the Duma on Monday, July 10, to respond to an interpellation on the Bialystok pogrom. And when Muromtsev, at the urging of his colleagues requested an audience with the tsar to head off dissolution, Stolypin informed him that he would be received on July 9.[39] All the deceptions worked.

That is surprising, because the military and other preparations undertaken by the government were so extensive and not at all disguised. More than twenty-two thousand troops, composed of forty artillery battalions, cavalry guards, and four companies armed with machine guns, were massed in St. Petersburg. All the railway stations were occupied by armed guards, and on July 7 a patrol boat and a cruiser could be seen on the Neva River. Also on that day, the police in St. Petersburg began to close down radical newspapers and to arrest leading Social Democrats and Socialist Revolutionaries.[40]

The massive display of force, not only in the capital but also in many cities throughout the empire, succeeded in keeping demonstrations of support for the Duma to a minimum. Some 185 deputies, mainly Kadets, did meet in Vyborg, about seventy miles from St. Petersburg, and issued a manifesto that amounted to a militant call to action against a government measure that most Duma representatives acknowledged to have been legal. The manifesto urged the people to protest the dissolution by refusing to pay taxes or to serve in the military. Although it infuriated Stolypin and conservatives generally, the manifesto did not evoke widespread civil disobedience or even a large protest movement. Exhausted from a year and a half of turbulence and confronted in the cities by the threat of unemployment, the masses in 1906 were much more reluctant than they had been in 1905 to defy the authorities. Moreover,

an effective campaign of passive resistance requires extensive preparation. For some reason, the Kadets did virtually nothing to prepare the
ground for an organized response to the dissolution. They simply assumed that the masses were still in a militant and activist mood.[41]

Within two days of assuming the office of prime minister, Stolypin
initiated a campaign to broaden support for his government and policies.
The campaign took many forms and lasted throughout his period as a
national leader. Stolypin understood, long before any other political
leader in Russia, that the era when a small group at court could conduct
the nation's business without paying attention to the rest of society had
passed. That is not to suggest that Stolypin favored democratic rule. Not
at all. But he did believe in opening up the system of rule to larger elements of society, or at least to take those elements into his confidence.

The prime minister's first move was an overture to moderates who
had gone out of their way to shun any activity that could be construed as
illegal. They were all men who had distinguished themselves in public
service: A. I. Guchkov, Count P. A. Geiden, Shipov, N. N. Lvov, G. E.
Lvov, A. F. Koni (a distinguished jurist), and M. A. Stakhovich. Stolypin
made no attempt to enlist the support of the Kadets because after the
Vyborg Manifesto he considered them to be too radical. His initiative
was a risky undertaking. If the negotiations yielded no results, the prestige of his government would inevitably suffer a blow at the very moment it was trying to organize itself.

Surprisingly, Stolypin made his first approach to Shipov, who only
two weeks earlier had made clear his aversion to the dissolution of the
Duma and to the prime minister's policies. Still, Shipov did not reject
the overture, and on July 15 he and Prince G. E. Lvov visited Stolypin,
who immediately made a direct appeal to the two men: "I turn to both of
you with the request that you join the ministry I am forming and help
realize the constitutional principles in the Manifesto of October 17." It
was a polite beginning to a conversation that quickly degenerated into a
nasty quarrel. The two men indicated that before they could respond to
Stolypin's offer, they would want to know the specifics of the prime
minister's program. They pointed out that they favored a speedy convocation of a new Duma and the immediate abolition of capital punishment. Irritated, Stolypin declared that this was no time for words or programs; it was a time for action. He saw no urgency in convoking a
Duma; he was well aware of the kind of reforms Russia needed. To
which Shipov replied caustically that all of Stolypin's predecessors—he
mentioned D. A. Tolstoy, D. S. Sipiagin, V. K. Plehve, as well as Witte—
were also familiar with Russia's needs, but they had not introduced ap-

propriate reforms. He then predicted that Stolypin's policies would end
the same way as his predecessors', in failure and repression. The prime
minister shot back angrily: "What right have you to speak like this?"
"You have invited us to join your cabinet," Shipov responded, "and I am
obliged to express my views candidly." Realizing that there was no
meeting of minds, Shipov and Lvov told Stolypin that further discussions were futile and left.[42]

Criticized by several moderates for having rebuffed the prime minister, Shipov and Lvov reopened contact with Stolypin and tried to obtain
clarification from him on his program. On July 17 they sent him a letter
outlining their views on the policies the new government should follow.
If the prime minister agreed with them, they or other members of the
opposition would be able to join the government. They listed the following seven points: at least seven of the thirteen ministers, including the
minister of internal affairs, must be from society and not from the bureaucracy; the government must guarantee that civil liberties would be
respected; it must commit itself to the abolition of all emergency measures as well as to speedy elections for a new Duma; and it must submit
legislation to that Duma providing for the compulsory alienation of
land, the abolition of capital punishment, and amnesty for political
prisoners. In his reply, Stolypin did not yield an inch. He expressed
"sincere regrets" at the two men's refusal to take up his offer and then
made it clear that he intended to proceed with his reform program before
the Duma met. Shipov and Lvov were now convinced that they had
made the right decision in refusing to join Stolypin's cabinet.[43] In the
end Geiden, who had tried to persuade Stolypin to be more forthcoming
in meeting the moderates' demands, agreed that the two men had acted
wisely. "It is clear," he told Shipov, "that you were invited to play the
role of hired boys for women of easy virtue."[44]

In the meantime Stolypin, fearful of failure, followed Guchkov's advice that he try to enlist Koni and Geiden. Geiden could not resist the
temptation of occupying a high position and immediately expressed interest in the post of state comptroller, which Stolypin dangled in front of
him, but Koni, despite intense pressure, was extremely reluctant even to
discuss joining the cabinet. He agreed to accompany Geiden on a visit to
Stolypin, who again refused to adopt the program formulated by the
moderates he had seen previously. Under the circumstances, Koni
would not enter the government, and the offer to Geiden was withdrawn.[45]

Complicated negotiations continued at various levels, but only one
other round of discussions deserves attention because it sheds light on

the tsar's role in these maneuvers. Stolypin approached Guchkov and N. N. Lvov, offering the former the post of minister of trade and industry and the latter the post of minister of agriculture. Both men accepted in principle, but they too wanted the government to adopt a common program, and they asked that additional men from society be included in the cabinet. Stolypin agreed to appoint other moderates but again rejected the idea of defining a program in advance. Clearly, he wanted to be free to determine the direction of the new government and did not want to be bound by promises to any minister. Still, he continued to hope that he would succeed in enlisting the services of Guchkov and Lvov and therefore suggested that they meet with the tsar. They could not refuse.

The audience with Nicholas was in every way a fiasco. Guchkov told the tsar that he still believed it was necessary for the government to adopt a program, and he also told him that although he personally did not like Jews, he believed that at least some of the restrictions imposed on them should be lifted. Nicholas would hear of no concessions to the Jews; such a step would give the appearance of weakness on the part of the government and would, in any case, lead to massive pogroms. The two men left with the impression that the tsar was "totally unaware of the situation in the country and of the mood of the people and society" and concluded that participating in the government would be "fruitless" because they would be "impotent."[46] The tsar's impression of the two men was equally unflattering. In a note to Stolypin he declared that after meeting with them for an hour, he was convinced that neither one was suitable for a post in the cabinet. Moreover it seemed to him altogether undesirable to bring into the government an "entire group of people with a program." All the same, he said, there was no reason to lose heart.[47]

By July 20, only ten days after the discussions had begun, it was clear that Stolypin's overtures to society would end as all previous such overtures had ended, in failure. The moderates insisted on certain concessions that the prime minister would not make, and given the passions aroused by the dissolution of the Duma, they could hardly be expected to show more flexibility. Had they done so, their standing in society would have plummeted. An English observer in St. Petersburg, basing himself on information from Stolypin, contended that "However much ... [the moderates] might desire to get a Ministerial portfolio, they felt that in joining a coalition Ministry containing a bureaucratic element, they would be denounced as traitors by their friends who were left out in the cold, and who hoped to see the Government capitulate unconditionally and efface itself completely. There was still a possibility that sooner or later the Govt. would be compelled to capitulate in this way, and then those who had joined it would be permanently boycotted by the victors."[48] On the other hand, the tsar and Stolypin continued to recoil from any concessions that would appear to undermine autocratic government, and as long as that was the case, no compromise with society was possible. It is odd that Stolypin had not realized this all along. He seems genuinely to have believed that an agreement with the moderates was essential and feasible, and he initiated the negotiations in good faith. As so often during his tenure as prime minister, Stolypin was prepared to cooperate with members of the opposition, but only if they did his bidding. He never did understand the true meaning of compromise.

Stolypin considered his failure to broaden his government a serious blow to his overall political strategy. "Stolypin," Guchkov recalled, "was very depressed by our refusal. I remember that at this time he gave a very pessimistic characterization of the Tsar and his circle, and I answered that if Russia, the dynasty, and the Tsar himself were to be saved, it would have to be done without the Tsar, without regard to his wishes, predilections, and whims."[49] This was a remarkable exchange between two men utterly devoted to the monarchical principle. Over the next five years Stolypin would come to appreciate the wisdom of Guchkov's advice about the tsar, but by conviction and temperament he was incapable of acting on that advice.

Stolypin's depression soon gave way to bitterness over the conduct of the moderates. In late July the prime minister conceded that it would have been much easier for him to pacify the country had he succeeded in attracting to his government men from the outside who were highly regarded and enjoyed the trust of society. He attributed his failure to do so to the "party doctrinairism" (*Parteidoktrinarismus*) of the moderates.[50] On August 12 he told Kokovtsov that the men with whom he had negotiated were adept at criticizing the authorities but flinched at assuming the responsibilities of governing. "They strive for power as power," he told the minister of finance, "and even more for the applause of their supporters; but to share a common responsibility—that is an entirely different matter."[51] It does not seem to have occurred to Stolypin that he was guilty of the same kind of intransigence.

Stolypin's failure to secure the support of moderates prompted much speculation about his fate and the fate of the country. On July 21, *Russkie vedomosti* reported that the tsar had rejected Stolypin's nominees for cabinet posts, and that as a result his own position was shaky; rumors circulated in the capital that the court had already decided to replace him with a dictator.[52] Two days later the paper repeated the rumor and in an editorial warned that "the government and the people were again poised against each other, prepared for new clashes." It predicted that the struggle would assume the most intense form: there would be strikes, disturbances, armed conflicts, and assassinations.[53] A general strike had in fact been called for July 21, giving credence to this bleak assessment of future developments.

Despite Stolypin's personal drive and diligence, which by themselves made his cabinet vastly more competent and energetic than Goremykin's, the new government did not appear to the opposition to be much of an improvement over its predecessor. True, Stolypin had forced the resignation of two of the most outspoken reactionaries, Prince A. A. Shirinskii-Shikhmatov and A. S. Stishinskii, and had replaced them with two men known to be moderates with Octobrist sympathies: P. P. Izvolskii, the brother of the foreign minister, as procurator of the Most Holy Synod and Prince B. A. Vasilchikov as minister of agriculture. D. A. Filosofov, the new minister of trade and commerce, apparently was also mildly moderate in his political views. But all the other men appointed by Goremykin remained at their posts; only two of them—Izvolskii, the minister of foreign affairs, and P. M. Kauffmann, the minister of education—were moderates. P. Kh. Schwanebach, an unreconstructed reactionary and probably the most effective intriguer on the extreme right, continued to serve as state comptroller. He was not on good terms with Stolypin and did his best to undermine him at court, where, it was generally known, he "wield[ed] considerable influence."[54] Within the cabinet, Schwanebach could count on the support of the minister of justice, I. G. Shcheglovitov, a man who was "not disposed to err on the side of leniency."[55] The critical point was that the government was still drawn from the bureaucracy, and so could not command the trust of society.

To repair that deficiency, Stolypin stepped up his efforts to secure popular approval for his policies. He dipped into his discretionary fund and provided S. E. Kryzhanovskii, since April 1906 the omnipresent assistant minister of internal affairs, with about three million rubles a year for confidential disbursements to some thirty newspapers and to political movements such as the Octobrists and for a while to the right-wing Union of the Russian People. The main beneficiary was the newspaper *Rossiia*, which had been called the semiofficial mouthpiece of the government but which in fact served as Stolypin's organ for the dissemination of his views. "Stolypin was not only the ruling spirit of our newspaper, he was also a very vigorous political writer, a great polemicist, many of whose articles were published [anonymously] only when they had been considerably toned down," wrote Syromiatnikov, one of the editors.[56] The prime minister arranged for the appointment of I. Ia. Gurliand as the second editor, and thus two of his closest collaborators saw to it that the paper hewed to the official line. The two editors also sent special circulars to governors informing them of forthcoming articles they considered especially important.[57]

Syromiatnikov apparently was a full-time editor, but Gurliand, a colorful man with an extraordinary career, held a high post in the Ministry of Internal Affairs and was one of Stolypin's most influential advisers on domestic affairs. According to Gurliand's wife, the two men understood each other so well they could finish each other's sentences.[58]

Gurliand is a distinctly Jewish name, which makes it puzzling that he occupied such a high position in Stolypin's inner circle. In Imperial Russia, Jews could not reach the pinnacles of political power; they could not even attain the rank of full professor in the academy, which is where Gurliand pursued a successful career before entering government service. Fortunately, the Russian State Historical Archive in St. Petersburg has a file on Gurliand that contains information enabling us to solve the riddle.

He was indeed born a Jew. One of the first documents in Gurliand's file is his birth certificate, which states that on August 8, 1868, Iliia Iakovlevich was circumcised "in accordance with the law of Moses." The certificate was signed by the Berdichev Rabbi.[59] Gurliand's father had completed studies at the rabbinical seminary in Vilna and for ten years served as a rabbi in a town in Poltava province. In the mid-1870s he moved to Kharkov, where he worked as a notary and published several popular works on various issues relating to legal questions. Iliia Iakovlevich's uncle, Chaim Jonah (1843–90), was also a rabbi who achieved a degree of eminence. He served as inspector of the Jewish teachers' seminary in Zhitomir and in the 1880s as rabbi of Odessa. He also published a seven-volume work on the Jews in Russia during the seventeenth and eighteenth centuries, entitled *On the History of the Persecution of the Jews* (in Hebrew).

Given this strong Jewish background, Iliia Iakovlevich's career in Russian politics is remarkable. Apparently the first in his family to pursue an advanced secular education, Gurliand, after completing his secondary school studies in Kharkov, enrolled in the Demidov Juridical Lycee in Iaroslavl, one of the pre-eminent centers of legal studies in the Russian Empire. An outstanding student, he graduated in 1891 with a gold medal for his paper on "The Roman Jurist Gaius and His Works."

He continued his studies in preparation for an academic career, and in 1893 passed the examination for the Magister degree in police law. A year later he began to teach commercial and administrative law at the Lycee as a *privatdocent*. He also worked on a dissertation on "The Idea of Patronage as a Concept of Internal Administration." For some reason, he did not defend his dissertation at the Lycee but instead wrote another dissertation on a topic in seventeenth-century legal studies at Kiev University. In 1902 he was promoted to what we would call full professor at the Lycee, specializing in state and administrative law. He continued to publish extensively (including some fiction), and in 1901 he also began to work as a councilor for the Ministry of Education and the Ministry of Internal Affairs in Iaroslavl. It is not clear how he obtained all these positions, but we do know that he was a favorite of the governor of Iaroslavl, B. V. Stürmer, a conservative if not a reactionary, who in 1916 served as prime minister for about five months and then as foreign minister for some four months.[60]

By this time Gurliand occupied such high academic and government posts that he must have been a Christian, but the date of his conversion is unknown. It may be that he joined the Russian Orthodox Church some time before 1894, the year he began to teach at the Lycee. Certainly, the conversion could not have taken place later than 1902, the year he was appointed professor.[61] He would then also have been eligible for the full-time position he assumed in 1904 in the Ministry of Internal Affairs in St. Petersburg, where Stürmer now occupied the post of director of general affairs. In 1907 Gurliand received another promotion, this time to the Council of the Ministry of Internal Affairs, a post of considerable authority and prestige. In addition, Prime Minister Stolypin now looked to him as his close advisor.[62]

Even a cursory examination of Stolypin's papers in the Russian State Historical Archive for the years after 1906 demonstrates the prime minister's dependence on Gurliand. On every important subject—the nationalities question, provincial reform, administrative procedures, the labor movement, electoral reform, and the agrarian question—the prime minister sought Gurliand's advice. Stolypin regularly asked his adviser to draft legislative proposals or bills for submission to the Duma and, most important for the prime minister's goal of generating public support for his program, to write articles for the press, and in particular for *Rossiia*, presenting the government's case on highly sensitive political issues. Frequently, Gurliand drafted speeches that the prime minister delivered to the Duma and to other audiences.

Gurliand was not only an indefatigable official with a fertile imagination—people suspected that some of Stolypin's most notable bon mots were formulated by Gurliand—but also a ruthless polemicist who could produce articles and pamphlets at short notice. He made it a point to follow developments on all domestic matters that interested Stolypin. The Department of Police sent Gurliand reports on the activities of oppositional groups, and governors from various regions of the empire provided him with detailed information on local unrest. Governors also sent him articles on political subjects for publication in *Rossiia*.

Some of Gurliand's more highly charged writings appeared under a pseudonym, N. P. Vasilev. It may be that he had misgivings about the propriety of a high official engaging in vitriolic polemics. It is also possible that he did not want some of the views expressed in these tracts, most notably their virulent anti-Semitism, to be traceable to Stolypin. The prime minister was known to be well disposed to Jews, so much so that ultraconservatives began late in 1906 to attack him for being too friendly to them. By allowing Vasilev-Gurliand to voice anti-Semitic views Stolypin may have been trying to placate the extremists on the right. Right-wing activists who closely followed politics knew full well that Vasilev was Gurliand, one of Stolypin's right-hand men.[63] For Stolypin, Gurliand served many useful purposes, not the least important of which was to secure his right flank.

Vasilev-Gurliand's two most notable brochures, both financed out of Kryzhanovskii's slush fund, were printed in large numbers and distributed to everyone in a responsible position in public affairs. They were directed at the Kadets and Trudoviks, the two largest oppositional groups in the First and Second Dumas. He berated both parties for their antigovernment policies, and to buttress his case against them he charged Jews with exercising enormous influence in the two movements. The venomous tone of the attacks bears all the marks of the most strident expressions of Judeophobia.

Gurliand paid special attention to the Kadet party's left wing, which, he asserted, gave the movement its revolutionary thrust. And it was precisely this wing that the Jews allegedly dominated. "The overwhelming majority of this group is, of course, Jewish. To be exact, as we have said above—the militant sector of the Jewish intelligentsia [constitutes this group]."[64] According to Gurliand, the Jewish intelligentsia was "irreconcilably" hostile to the Russian people, whom it considered to be "dull, stupid, talentless." Moreover the Jewish intelligentsia "hates Russia, the Russian double-headed eagle, the glory and power of Russia, [and] its importance among European states."[65]

Gurliand acknowledged that the Jewish intellectuals' hostility to

Russia could be explained as a response to wounds that had been inflicted upon them at every turn in their lives, but he clearly did not believe that this in any way justified their bitterness. He granted that as students in high school [gymnasium] they were insulted at being called *zhid*; that they resented the quotas that prevented many of them from studying at a university; and that if they did obtain a university education they felt frustrated at not being appointed "assistant barristers." Many young Jews were also deeply hurt when the parents of "Russian ladies" whom they wanted to marry expressed astonishment and refused to give their consent. "The wound never heals," Gurliand concluded without a trace of sympathy. In fact, even Jewish intellectuals who pursued successful careers and married Jewish women remained bitter for the rest of their lives. "The blood continues to trickle from the wound and causes the entire nervous system to tremble morbidly, [and their] only thought is about Russia, the Russian state, about its double-headed eagle."[66] The disaffected Jews rallied to the revolutionary cause not only to achieve the destruction of all that was unbearable for them, but also to rise politically. Gurliand was convinced that ultimately the Jews' attraction to radical activities stemmed from a predisposition firmly ingrained in Jewish culture. By participating in agitation and conspiracies, he asserted, "the Jews find satisfaction of their basic national instincts."[67]

In his second polemic of 1907, Vasilev-Gurliand painted a stereotypical picture of the pushy Jew. After discussing two categories of people, most of them without higher education, who led the Trudoviks, he turned to a group he considered particularly dangerous: "Third—there is the clever Jew, who not long ago modestly rang at the doorway and for a long time wiped his clammy hands on the skirts of his frock coat before deciding to stretch them out to the [Gentile] owner of the house."[68] The Jews, invariably militant, comprised a small contingent within the Trudovik movement, but they exerted a powerful influence because they became teachers in the special school established in St. Petersburg for the uneducated Trudovik deputies. Through their work in the school, Jews had helped to radicalize the Trudovik delegation in the Duma.[69]

Not surprisingly, Gurliand tried to establish good relations with extremists on the right; if successful, he could neutralize a group of activists who were increasingly badgering the prime minister. In 1908, Gurliand befriended V. M. Purishkevich, the flamboyant spokesman of the ultrarightists in the Second Duma, which he did his utmost to discredit.[70] But, interestingly, the Union of the Russian People, the largest right-wing movement, refused to have any truck with a person of Jewish origin no matter how conservative or anti-Semitic he might be, a stance that can legitimately be characterized as racist. A few weeks after the union was founded in November 1905, one of its leading members, I. I. Baranov, proudly informed the tsar that the organization would not accept Jews into its midst even if they had become Christians.[71] Thus, the union's paper, *Russkoe znamia*, was following a consistent line when, on September 30, 1908, it published an article on "The Gentlemen Government Journalists," which included a reference to the "clever Jewish Gurliand who has suddenly risen to the top." In another issue, *Russkoe znamia* accused Gurliand of having received "huge amounts of money" for an article he had allegedly written for *Russkoe Gosudarstvo*,* and of being "under the aegis of Count Witte," a sworn enemy of Stolypin. In a note to Stolypin, Gurliand denied having written any article for *Russkoe Gosudarstvo* and pointed out that he had met Witte only once. As a government official, Gurliand felt that he could not enter into a polemic over "gutter slander," but he was deeply offended and upset. In a rare display of humor, the prime minister sought to soothe his adviser's hurt feelings by telling him that "if you are slandered it means that you are definitely a valuable person."[72] At first glance, Stolypin's comment seems flippant and insensitive. But in fact it indicated that for him a person's religious background was irrelevant and did not disqualify him from holding a high government position.

Less polemical and less offensive were the editorials in *Rossiia* that Gurliand either solicited or, more likely, wrote himself. They almost always supported Stolypin's policies and principles. One of the most debated issues in educated circles in Russia after the convocation of the Duma revolved around the nature of the empire's political system. Had the country been transformed into constitutional order by the Manifesto of October 1905, as most Octobrists and many people to their left claimed? Or was the country still ruled by an "unlimited autocracy," as the tsar, officials at court, and the ultraconservatives insisted? Stolypin subscribed to neither position, which made his stance on this vital question extremely complicated, almost to a point of obscurity.

Rossiia's editorials frequently touched on this issue in an attempt to elucidate Stolypin's views.[73] The prime minister contended, according to the paper, that the ultraconservatives were wrong to insist that despite the October Manifesto the monarchy remained an unlimited autocracy. An important change had taken place, and the Russian polity

---

Russkoe Gosudarstvo had been established by Witte and was the forerunner of *Rossiia*.

could now be described as a constitutional order. But it was a constitutional order of a special kind, sui generis, quite different from the constitutional forms found in the United States and in Central and Western Europe. Stolypin elaborated on this point in an interview late in 1906, in which he asserted that the polity of the United States could be classified as constitutional because the people had agreed to such a system of government; the term might even be applicable to Prussia, where the throne and the people had entered into an agreement on a constitution. "But in our country the Manifesto of October 17 and the Fundamental Laws had been granted by the autocratic Sovereign. The difference, of course, is enormous and has still not received its correct legal construction."[74] In Russia, Stolypin contended, there had developed a merger between autocracy and a popularly elected assembly, a signal achievement. As he put it in a speech to the Duma on November 16, 1907: "[T]he most precious merit of the Russian state system" was the "autocratic authority and the free will of the monarch that have evolved historically." Only this "authority and this will" were capable of saving Russia at times of national convulsions and leading the country along the path of "order and historical justice."[75] And the monarch, in this reading of Russian history, had chosen voluntarily to permit the creation of an elected legislature, whose powers, however, were limited to effecting changes in the details of the legislative and political program determined by the government. Under no circumstances did the legislative body have the right to assume the authority of the executive branch.

On occasion, Stolypin described his political outlook somewhat differently: he said that he was a constitutionalist but not a "parliamentarist," by which he meant that he wished to maintain the system of government established by the Fundamental Laws. The monarch would retain his authority but would govern in accordance with the rule of law.[76]

The legal theory and history underlying this contention are open to challenge. True, the tsar had granted the October Manifesto, but he had not done so voluntarily; he made the concession at a time when he faced a general strike that threatened the country with anarchy. Moreover, in the manifesto the tsar had committed himself not to enact any measure without the approval of an elected legislature, a commitment that undermined the claim of continuing autocratic power. The Soviet historian Diakin contended that in Stolypin's conception of Russia's political system the state remained "an autocracy in essence and in the extent of its authority and was limited [only] in the forms of its manifestations."[77] There is some truth to this contention. By the same token, the tsar's concession in the October Manifesto on the prerogatives of the Duma meant that the sovereign was no longer an autocrat. In short, there was a contradiction between Stolypin's claims and political realities after October 1905.

This became evident almost from the moment he took charge of the government. Numerous conflicts arose between the government and the legislature, even when the majority in the latter were moderates and conservatives. On those occasions, Stolypin's political conception turned out to be quite fuzzy and unhelpful on the division of functions between the monarch and the government, on the one hand, and the legislature, on the other. It was unrealistic for him to assume that a representative assembly elected even on the basis of a limited suffrage would forever kowtow to the tsar. The issues at stake were too weighty and impinged on too many vital interests for them to be resolved in the way Stolypin considered ideal. Time and again, the Duma refused to accept the limited role he assigned to it; the ensuing clashes proved to be his undoing.

In truth, Stolypin was much more effective and convincing in spelling out his program and policies than he was at providing abstract justifications for his conduct of affairs. He was a practical man with practical solutions for Russia's ills, but whenever he ventured into the realm of theory he almost invariably lost his footing. His pragmatic bent of mind and his candor enabled him to charm most of the journalists, scholars, and diplomats whose goodwill he sought to cultivate. In wooing Westerners, Stolypin no doubt sought to shore up support for Russia by foreign financial institutions, but his aim seems to have been much broader than that. He spoke to ambassadors and foreign journalists so frequently and openly that he seems to have been seeking legitimacy among people who represented countries he admired. It vexed him, for example, that the reports on developments in Russia in the British press were consistently "critical and hostile," and he did not hesitate to tell British visitors that journalists did not understand the country's problems or the government's goals.[78] In short, he wanted to persuade Western dignitaries that his aim was to modernize Russia and to transform the country along Western lines, economically and socially, even if not politically.

Stolypin's success in cultivating goodwill among foreigners was remarkable. One of the first to interview him was D. M. Wallace, the British journalist who in 1877 had published a detailed and insightful book on his travels in Russia in which he vividly described the customs of the peasants in various parts of the country. He was fluent in Russian and knew Russia well. Wallace interviewed Stolypin on July 24, 1906, just two weeks after the change in government, and came away with a "favorable impression." Wallace was impressed by the prime minister's appearance and "sympathetic manner" but also by his views and common sense. "He speaks remarkably well," Wallace reported, "especially when he is using, as he did on this occasion, his native language. Unlike many of his countrymen, he never indulges in vague philosophical phrases, but speaks simply, clearly, earnestly, and to the point. His whole manner and bearing suggest a large reserve supply of quiet determination, energy, and perseverance—qualities in which the Russians are too often very deficient. If he succeeds, his success will be due, I believe, rather to those qualities, combined with a large amount of common sense, than to any exceptionally brilliant intelligence."[79] It is a tribute to Wallace's acuity that after one interview he grasped so accurately the personality of Stolypin and understood the sources of his strength as a political leader.

Stolypin wasted no time in letting his administrators know that his leadership would be much more energetic than Goremykin's, that the lax days of recent months had come to an end. On July 11, two days after the change of government, he sent a telegram to all governors-general, governors, and the *namestnik* (viceroy) of the Caucasus informing them that he had been granted authority by the tsar to unify the operations of local authorities; he was therefore directing them to establish order "firmly, quickly, and steadfastly" and "without any hesitation." Disturbances must be "rebuffed unremittingly." The tone was somewhat more severe than the tone of a similar directive he sent to local authorities after taking over the Ministry of Internal Affairs some two and a half months earlier. But he added an admonition that was consistent with his overall conduct of affairs as governor of Saratov. He stressed the importance of resorting to legal methods of struggle against disturbers of the peace. "Revolutionary plans must be handled with all legal means. The measures that are adopted must be characterized by firm, careful planning; therefore indiscriminate repression must not be approved. Illegal and imprudent operations provoke bitterness instead of calm and are [therefore] unacceptable."

Stolypin added that the tsar and the government were committed to a "renewal of the old order": laws that were obsolete and did not serve their purpose would be abolished and changed. In the meantime, "order must be fully preserved. In this you must demonstrate initiative, and the responsibility for this is yours." The prime minister was certain that the firm exercise of authority in accordance with his directives would "undoubtedly" receive the support "of the best sectors of society."[80]

Nevertheless, Stolypin continued to worry about the preparedness of these officials. On September 15, he sent a circular marked "Strictly Confidential" to all governors-general, governors, and city governors outlining what he considered to be the most effective methods of dealing with the opposition to government authority. The methods were based, as he acknowledged, on his experiences in Saratov during the stormy days of October 1905. Stolypin warned senior officials in the provinces that in his view the revolutionaries, though defeated in their attempts to provoke a general uprising in July,* were preparing for a new onslaught, for a "decisive action against the entire [political] system." But force alone would not suffice to crush the insurgents. In Stolypin's view, the best way to defeat the radicals was to cut the ground from under them by depriving them of popular support. The prime minister spelled out in much detail how this could be done, and the circular, running to some twenty printed pages, was a strikingly comprehensive set of recommendations, in effect a handbook on how to outfox and defeat the radical left.

For example, the peasants, on whom the revolutionaries were counting for support, were, according to Stolypin, interested primarily in increasing their landholdings, not in waging a political struggle. "Therefore it is necessary above all for local authorities to take measures to eliminate as quickly as possible those economic factors [of distress] on which the agitation [by radicals thrives]." If local authorities discover that peasants in their regions were waiting for the Peasants' Bank to conclude loans for the purchase of land, every effort should be made to speed up the transactions. That would be one of the "most positive and effective means of calming the village population."[81] At the same time, governors ought to make a point of visiting areas of unrest and speaking in person to peasants with grievances. The governors should emphasize the "inflexible firmness of governmental authority," but they should also protect the peasants against excessive and illegal demands by landlords. Finally, governors should enlist the help of local institutions such as the zemstvos and the Church to persuade peasants to refrain from violence.

The police, too, must be trained to take action to prevent disorder, not merely to put it down. They should maintain a close watch on agitators; outsiders bent on trouble-making should be quickly removed from

*On these attempts, see below pp. 130–37.

the region. And if the police learned of impending unrest in a locality, a senior official should immediately appear on the scene and attempt to restore calm. If that failed, the authorities should quickly send additional forces to the area, "keeping in mind that the appearance in advance of sufficient forces can prevent a misfortune." On the other hand, if violence erupted, local officials must take the "most decisive measures." Recent developments had demonstrated that "permissiveness and indecision" by officials lead to "grave consequences."[82]

Governors should also be vigilant in keeping an eye on associations such as unions and educational institutions, which often focused on antigovernment campaigns. Similarly, the authorities should maintain surveillance over the press, which, in Stolypin's view, frequently abused the law on free speech by printing articles "overtly hostile to the government." Legal action should be taken against journalists and editors who advocated violation of the law.[83]

Stolypin conceded that he was placing "a complicated task" on the representatives of governmental authority in asking them to conduct the struggle against the revolution on so many fronts. But he assured them that they were being asked to perform a great service to the state, which was experiencing an "historical moment, when new political structures were emerging." He made a passionate appeal to the country's officials to set aside petty bureaucratic conflicts so that they could devote all their energies to implementing the directives from the central government, which was determined to enact the reforms promised by the monarch. He informed the local officials in no uncertain terms that "high policy" would be set by the government and not by "subordinate administrative organs." In an effort to inspire the bureaucrats, he urged them to carry out that "high policy" with enthusiasm. "The servants of the state must fight sedition not with faint-heartedness and compromises but with energy, firmness, and real resolution for the throne and well-being of Russia. . . . Panic in society and impudence by revolutionaries are caused precisely by the confusion, flabbiness, and apathy of government authorities, who at the present time must demonstrate all the positive qualities that can help the government lead the country from disturbances to tranquillity. By stopping revolutionary actions at the very beginning, even with the most severe legal measures, local organs instill in the population trust in the strength of the authorities and the stability of the law. There can be no doubt that it is the duty of the head of the province to inspire the second level of officials with these principles; [the governors] must provide all their subordinates and the population with an example of civic valor, raise their spirits and bear the responsibility for the grave consequences of [any] successes by the revolutionary movement."[84]

The circular of September 15, 1906, removed any doubts in the minds of Russian civil servants that the new prime minister would force them to change their customary ways of doing the government's business. Stolypin planned to mobilize the entire bureaucracy in his drive to realize his vision for revitalizing the country. The impetus for re-establishing order and for introducing change would come from the center, from the government under his direction, from the highest organs of the state. In driving his subordinates to expend maximum effort to implement his policies, Stolypin was asking no more of them than he did of himself.

He maintained a demanding schedule of work that amazed bureaucrats unaccustomed to taking their tasks seriously. "My father," the prime minister's daughter recalled, "always worked past midnight, usually until two a.m. Sometimes he did not sleep all day unless one considers the rest which he took each day before dinner. He would lie down on the divan in his study and quickly fall asleep for fifteen minutes, after which he was entirely refreshed and cheerful. By half past nine in the morning, all his life he was always completely dressed, drinking coffee. Some kind of exercise was essential to him, preferably an hour's walk in the fresh air. But every walk or ride which Papa attempted away from the [Winter] Palace [where the Stolypins were then living] was charged with such danger for his life that some time passed before there was any workable plan for such excursions."[85]

Stolypin's disciplined work habits enabled him to master the intricacies of a wide range of issues facing the government. He devoted his mornings to reading newspapers, domestic and foreign, as well as new books on contemporary issues, especially those dealing with questions of public law. He also received reports from senior officials working in one or another department or in the provinces. In the afternoons, he frequently attended sessions of the Duma and State Council, where he listened to the debates and made a point of defending government policies. Some of his interventions in the legislative chambers were extemporaneous, but most were carefully crafted. For days before he delivered a major speech, employees in various departments familiar with the topic would do the preparatory research, examining stacks of documents and checking the facts Stolypin wished to include in his presentation. After the prime minister had read the material he would often ask for more information, forcing bureaucrats to remain at their desks until daybreak. Stolypin was especially eager for information on legislative precedents for his proposals in Western countries, which he liked to cite to buttress his arguments. To a very large extent, his speeches, highly polished and invariably filled with facts and allusions to historical events relevant to his theme, were his own creation.[86]

Stolypin was also meticulous in preparing himself for meetings with the cabinet, advisory committees, or individual ministers and legislators, and insisted that they begin exactly on time. He wished to inculcate in Russian officials the importance of punctuality, a "lesson" that foreigners in particular thought was very much needed. S. I. Timashev, the minister of trade and industry after 1909, recalled that Stolypin always received visitors promptly. If the prime minister himself was late, he would apologize and explain why he had been delayed. The discussions were then businesslike and brief.[87] Visitors and cabinet members soon got into the habit of arriving five minutes before meetings were to begin. "In a corner of the room where we met," according to one participant, "there was an English clock. When this clock had struck the first of its nine strikes, Stolypin entered, and went into the assembly room, and when the last of us had entered, the door was locked from the inside. If anyone had arrived late, he would have to stay outside."[88]

Once the deliberations began, the atmosphere was surprisingly informal. Cabinet meetings were held twice a week, on Tuesdays from 10:00 P.M. until two or three o'clock in the morning, and on Fridays from 3:00 P.M. until 6:00 or 7:00 P.M., and they were like "friendly conversations," even though they were attended not only by ministers but also by members of various departmental councils. Stolypin encouraged everyone to speak freely. Indeed, Rediger complained that the minister of finance, Kokovtsov, frequently delivered inordinately long speeches, which sometimes took up half the time and never lasted less than fifteen minutes. Kokovtsov justified his long disquisitions with the claim that virtually every issue before the cabinet in some way affected the national budget, which he felt obliged to protect. But he tended to ramble: "He began every speech with an apology that he must again ask the Council to pay attention to him for a few minutes; then he followed with an exposition why this question was important, with a history of his familiarity with it, pointing out the reasons why he cannot touch on [all of] them, and, finally, with an account of the subject under discussion." Most of the audience soon tired of the orations, and Rediger, who always submitted a report to the tsar early in the morning on Tuesdays, could barely stay awake. Whenever Kokovtsov took the floor, Rediger could not help recalling that Bismarck insisted that all his ministers confine themselves to speeches lasting no more than ten to fifteen minutes even when they dealt with the most complicated questions.[89] But Stolypin never interrupted the minister of finance, the one man in the cabinet who was treated with a degree of deference by the prime minister, who felt inadequate in dealing with financial questions. He often resented Kokovtsov's insistence on keeping expenditures to a minimum, but he respected the man, who was older than he and had had many more years of government experience. In any case, Stolypin was used to working till all hours in the night and listening to Kokovtsov did not tire him.

For Stolypin, the cabinet meetings were important in thrashing out policy options and, even more, in implementing the procedures of a united government, under which the prime minister played a key role in formulating policies in all spheres of governmental authority. As Timashev recalled in his memoirs, ministers who sought the approval of the cabinet for a specific measure needed to secure the support of Stolypin before the meeting. The prime minister encouraged free-wheeling discussions of proposals, but he made sure that the outcome would be to his liking. Once the cabinet reached a decision he sent the recommendations with a breakdown of the vote to the tsar for final action.

Stolypin's predominance within the government was beyond question. He set the agenda and he took the lead in seeking support for government policies, but he was not skilled at small talk or backslapping, which prevented him from developing a large personal following, a serious defect for a politician dependent on the support of parliamentary representatives. "At a dinner," one official recalled, Stolypin "could be quite apathetic, and his remarks were commonplace."[90] He did make a practice of inviting members of the Third Duma and State Council as well as senior officials to his house for tea, but even at these informal gatherings the focus was on business, on the attempt to find a common language on political issues. In his relations with colleagues he was always affable and listened attentively to their opinions on issues, but once he had made up his mind no arguments could cause him to change course. There was a streak of inflexibility in him, making it almost impossible for him to yield on details to win support for the essentials of his position. In short, he lacked the ability to compromise, a serious shortcoming for a statesman operating in a pluralistic political system. The same rigidity hampered him in his personal relations with colleagues and political leaders in general. He was charming in his contacts with people who agreed with him but could be merciless toward political opponents or ministers who differed with him. Officials who voiced opposition to his policies were encouraged to resign quickly, and if they insisted on remaining in office and engaged in "intrigues" they would be sent a formal notice of dismissal, as happened to the state comptroller, P. Kh. Schwanebach.[91]

Stolypin adopted a very broad view of his role as prime minister. From time to time he went on extended trips—the most notable was to Siberia—to familiarize himself with conditions outside the capital. He also took an interest in the administration of the capital itself. He was especially concerned with improving the water supply in the city and with efforts to contain the cholera epidemic that struck the city in 1908. Finally, he went out of his way to play a role in designing and implementing the empire's foreign policy, a sphere that the tsar considered to be his own preserve. Stolypin insisted that as prime minister of a united government he could not be indifferent to so vital an aspect of the country's affairs. He not only accompanied the tsar at some international meetings but also exercised a strong influence on the overall course of Russia's relations with foreign countries.[92] It would be misleading to suggest that Stolypin exercised the kind of authority wielded by the British prime minister or the German chancellor, but there is no question that Stolypin was unique among the long list of imperial ministers in the scope of his influence on national policy. Some previous ministers may have been as energetic as he but none intervened directly in so many aspects of governmental affairs.

Although his political interests were wide-ranging, Stolypin's main concern was domestic reform and in particular agrarian reform. But for over two months after he took over as prime minister events forced him to focus on the maintenance of public order. The first such event was an eruption of unrest on July 17, 1906, in Sveaborg, an island fortress in Helsingfors (Helsinki) harbor, where discontent was rife among the soldiers and sailors. Despite urgings by the military organizations of the Socialist Revolutionaries and Social Democrats in Helsingfors as well as the Social Democrats in St. Petersburg to postpone any violent action, local militants staged a mutiny to protest the arrest of some two hundred men for "minor misdeeds." The mutineers secured the support of some infantrymen and gained control of several small islands in Helsingfors. At the same time, the Red Guards in Helsingfors, composed of Finnish workers, declared their support for the uprising and called for a general strike in the city. The workers' response, however, was half-hearted, in large part because the Finnish Social Democrats did not wish to get involved in what they regarded as a conflict of concern only to Russians. Fierce fighting broke out in Sveaborg and continued for two days, but as soon as two companies of Finnish infantrymen arrived in Helsingfors the tide began to turn in favor of the government. Violence also erupted in Kronstadt on July 19, but that unrest, too, was quashed quite quickly. One other successful mutiny broke out, on the cruiser *Pamiat Azova*, as the ship was approaching Revel. In the scuffle, mutineers killed several officers and seriously wounded the captain. The violence apparently frightened many of the sailors who had not participated in the seizure of the boat, and when no other ships joined the mutiny they overwhelmed the mutineers and regained control.

In view of the brevity of these mutinies, revolutionary activists were hard put to provide effective support. Nevertheless, Bolshevik leaders in St. Petersburg felt they could not stand aside. On Lenin's recommendation, an appeal was issued, most probably on July 19, in the name of "The Soviet of Workers' Deputies," calling on workers to initiate a general strike. By this time, the Central Committee of the Russian Social Democratic Workers Party (RSDWP) also issued a call for all workers to walk out in protest against the dissolution of the Duma. The workers' response was tepid, in part no doubt because news had reached St. Petersburg and other areas of the empire that the mutinies in Sveaborg and Kronstadt had already been quelled. Discontent was still widespread in Russia, and the revolutionary fervor of radicals remained at a high pitch, but the masses' enthusiasm for strikes and demonstrations clearly had diminished substantially.[93]

Stolypin, however, took no chances. Even before the dissolution of the Duma, on July 7 and 8, the police had arrested a number of leading SDs and SRs in the capital; V. M. Chernov and A. A. Argunov, members of the SR central committee, avoided arrest by jumping out of the window of an apartment as the police were entering. Two weeks later, on or about July 22, the police took into custody twenty-seven members of the St. Petersburg Committee of the RSDWP.[94] At about the same time, Stolypin, always determined to have at his disposal an overwhelming amount of military force to nip any disturbance in the bud, informed the tsar that the garrison in St. Petersburg was too small. He therefore requested that two more divisions be immediately brought to the capital. The prime minister wanted to crush the protest movement quickly, "since the smallest revolt in Petersburg will evoke an echo throughout the entire country and will compromise us in Europe."[95]

The quick collapse of the uprising greatly bolstered the government's self-confidence. Never shy about claiming credit for his achievements, Stolypin attributed the failure of the left primarily to the firm measures taken by the authorities. "This experience," he boasted, "demonstrates anew that in Russia, more even than in other countries, order can be maintained only when the government demonstrates its real power without fear and without being influenced by sentiment." He was convinced that the revolutionaries were now thoroughly demoralized and that the "organs of order" had been revitalized. The masses, on the other hand, had come to realize that a "strong arm" ruled over them, and that would make it possible to restore respect for order and private property and to institute far-reaching reforms.[96]

The government provided abundant evidence of its resolve to use its strong arm to punish the mutineers and the participants in the political strikes. On August 5, a navy field court sentenced 17 members of the *Pamiat Azova's* crew and 1 civilian agitator to death. Twelve sailors were sentenced to hard labor for periods ranging from six to twenty years; another 13 were placed in penal battalions or jail for varying terms; 15 received unspecified disciplinary punishments, and 3 civilians were handed over to the procurator for further judicial proceedings.[97] In Sveaborg, a military court ordered the execution of 17 men and the incarceration of 71, again for varying periods of time.[98] Of the 118 men arrested at the Konstantin Fortress, the one place the insurgents had captured and had controlled briefly, 10 were sentenced to death, 18 were found innocent, and the rest were punished with imprisonment at hard labor or placed in penal battalions.[99]

Workers at the city's printing office in St. Petersburg who had gone out on strike had to sign a statement drawn up by the authorities indicating that they wished to be reinstated and that they promised not to participate in any sort of meeting or join any strike at an "establishment that is important to the public or the state."[100] In the capital and in Moscow, the police deprived many unions of their legal status. In several other cities of the empire, police actions against unions were somewhat less drastic but nonetheless stern.[101]

The failure of the mutinies to spark a national general strike did not signify an end to civil disorder. A new avalanche of terror, emanating both from the right and the left and more brazen as well as widespread than ever before, swept across the country. The first major incident during Stolypin's ministry occurred on July 18, 1906, when M. Ia. Herzenstein, a Kadet deputy who specialized in agrarian matters, was assassinated by a person hired by the reactionary Union of the Russian People (URP). At about the same time terrorists on the left stepped up their campaign of violence. The reliable journal *Pravo* reported on August 13 that no fewer than twenty-eight assassinations had recently occurred in various cities of the empire; in virtually all of them the victim either died or suffered serious injury. A week later the same journal reported twenty-three such incidents.[102] The daily press contained so many accounts of violence that its very absence was considered newsworthy. "Today was an exceptional day [in Warsaw]," *Rech* reported on September 9; "there was no bloodshed and no robbery."[103] Terrorists frequently targeted policemen of various ranks, but they also proved adept at gunning down senior officials. To a large extent, the funds for acquiring weapons came from the so-called partisan actions, or armed robberies, carried out by bands of terrorists. In Latvia alone, there were 643 incidents in the six-month period from the spring until the fall of 1906. Fifty-seven involved arson, 211 were armed attacks on and assassinations of officials, and 372 were attacks on district administrations, post offices, inns, or government liquor stores; the other three were cases of sabotage, all involving the deliberate wrecking of telegraph equipment.[104] This account of violence in the empire in 1906 could be vastly expanded. Virtually no region remained entirely immune, though some areas were harder hit than others. All in all, from October 1905 through September 1906, 3,611 government employees, including village policemen, mid-level officials, as well as generals and governors, were killed.[105]

Although the violence could not overturn the old order, many Russians feared that it would lead to unbearable lawlessness.[106] That possibility was dramatized by the terrorists' most notorious exploit, the bombing of Stolypin's summer home on August 12, 1906. As it turned out, the bombing led to one of the most sustained, brutal, and also most controversial campaigns of government repression and, ironically, strengthened Stolypin's hand as prime minister.

August 12 was a Saturday, which is why Stolypin was at his dacha on Aptekarskii, one of the many islands in the Neva River where prominent citizens of St. Petersburg spent their weekends. As was his custom, Stolypin devoted several hours that day to receiving petitioners with special requests. Many people were therefore in and around the residence early in the afternoon, when three Socialist Revolutionary Maximalists* entered the scene, two in army officers' dress and one in civilian attire, each carrying a briefcase loaded with bombs. The guards became suspicious of one of the three men, and when they tried to inspect his briefcase, all three, shouting revolutionary slogans, threw their bags to the ground, producing an enormous explosion. The would-be assassins died on the spot.

*The SR Maximalists were an ultraradical offshoot of the SR party.

Although they did not succeed in killing Stolypin, who was in a room that somehow remained essentially intact, their bombs did cause a tremendous amount of damage and many casualties. The facade of the house was completely destroyed. Twenty-seven people died instantly—among them General Zamiatin and three other senior officials—and another seventy were injured, most of them seriously. "Fragments of the balcony and the roof were strewn about everywhere. A shattered carriage and the injured horses were covered by the fragments. Everywhere one could hear the groans of the wounded, everywhere one could see shreds of human flesh and blood." Stolypin's assistant and friend, Syromiatnikov, rushed to the prime minister's home and was shocked by the devastation: "Stolypin," he recalled, "flushed with excitement, came into his half-demolished study, with plaster stains on his coat and an ink spot on the back of his neck. The top of his writing-desk had been lifted right off by the explosion, which took place in the hall at a distance of about thirty feet from the study, and the inkstand had hit his neck." Stolypin was understandably distraught over the injuries to one of his daughters and his son. "When I carried out my daughter from under wreckage," he told Syromiatnikov, "her legs hung like stockings. My son has one knee broken and his head is injured. He is all crumpled up."[107] At first, the doctors thought that they would have to amputate both of the young woman's legs. But after a few days they decided to let nature run its course and within a year she was able to walk again. The three-year-old boy recovered faster.[108]

Stolypin, who had suffered a minor cut on his face, remained remarkably calm and took charge of the rescue efforts as soon as he had arranged for the care of his children. He moved his family to the Winter Palace, which was more secure than their quarters on Fontanka, the official residence of the prime minister. The police now took elaborate measures to conceal his moves outside the palace. Whenever he left the palace, Stolypin would be kept in the dark about the exit at which his carriage would be waiting for him. If he planned to take a walk, he would not know where the carriage would stop to allow him to start. After he had completed his stroll, usually for an hour or so in one of the suburbs, the police would take him back to his apartment along a route they had decided upon without informing the prime minister. Stolypin bristled under these restrictions, but there had been so many reports of assassination plots that he reluctantly agreed to the precautions.[109]

Other than that, he continued his normal routine as head of the government. The cabinet met one day after the explosion, and Stolypin acted "as if nothing unusual had happened." His show of fortitude revealed a character trait that he had displayed often in Saratov but not yet in St. Petersburg, and it did much to raise his "moral prestige."[110]

Many hundreds of telegrams and letters—carefully preserved in five bound volumes—were sent to Stolypin and his wife by individuals and various associations and local organs of self-government throughout the country congratulating him on having survived the assassination attempt. Even foreigners—from England, France, and the United States—took the trouble of writing to him to express their relief that he was not seriously hurt. One Englishman, T. O. Underwood, a retired army officer who had served in India, advised Stolypin on how to cope with the terror: "Get a few well known Englishmen at the head of a Department or Departments." Underwood was sure that there were some "good Russians, but the population have been put off so often by promises that they believe nothing and nobody. . . . I hope you will excuse this earnest attempt to do some good. As for you and your terrible trials, I say: Strive on, and Buck up and Serve your Country and trust the Great Ruler of all."[111] The tsar, who rarely displayed warmth to his officials, sent the prime minister a personal message in which he stated that Stolypin's escape was a "divine miracle; one cannot view it any differently." He ended with the following words: "My thoughts are with you. With sincere esteem."[112] Deeply moved, the prime minister responded with an expression of unflinching loyalty: "My life belongs to YOU, YOUR MAJESTY." He prayed to the Almighty, he continued, to grant him his "greatest happiness," which was "to help YOUR MAJESTY lead our unhappy country along the path to legality, calm, and order."[113] According to Kokovtsov, after the assassination attempt Stolypin was no longer criticized for "provincialism"; he "gained in stature and was unanimously acclaimed master of the situation."[114]

Right-wing extremists, who still supported Stolypin, also sent telegrams congratulating him on having escaped injury, but often these messages contained highly inflammatory advice on how to deal with the terror. On September 9, 1906, the members of the Russian Assembly, a monarchist association, sent their warmest regards to Stolypin and his family, but at the same time considered it their "moral duty" to point out that "no kind of indulgence or concessions by the government to the revolutionary parties would stop their bloody activities [aimed at the] destruction of Russia, [that] none of the most liberal bills will satisfy the anarchists, socialists, democrats, and separatists." Order could be preserved only by unrestrained use of force. The ultrarightists went on to claim that "[in] all bloody events of recent years the instigators, organizers, and executors are more often than not Jews." Wherever Jews live, "they are hated by Christians, offend their most sacred feelings, and in every way torment the peaceful population." This message, sent to Stolypin by telegram, ended with a plea to the prime minister to enforce rigid quotas on the number of Jewish children in Russian schools; the government must protect Russian children from being corrupted by the "impertinent and criminal" Jewish youngsters.[115]

Other extremists on the right demanded a drastic reorganization of the political system to facilitate a campaign against terror. "We need a *dictatorship,*" *Moskovskie vedomosti* asserted; "we need a government of struggle. Only by purging the state of the bloody coalition of anarchists and brigands can the authorities turn their attention to peaceful, constructive work. . . . We must not wait. Either ruin or a *dictatorship.*"[116] Stolypin did not share this cataclysmic view of Russia's plight. Nor did the other ministers, none of whom proposed changing the form of government at the first meeting of the cabinet after the assassination attempt. Some ministers actually proposed a conciliatory measure, convoking the Duma earlier than planned. But most members of the cabinet recommended that energetic action be taken against the "anarchist gangsters."[117]

Stolypin intended to root out terrorism, but he did not want the government to act without respect for the law, as he had frequently noted in his directives to governors and other officials urging stern handling of revolutionaries. Even after the attempt on his life, he insisted that the introduction of unduly harsh measures would probably not be effective and would only deepen the hostility of society toward the government. But he came under intense pressure to take more drastic steps than he favored. For one thing, the United Nobility, supported by several important people in the court entourage, stepped up its pressure for the establishment of a dictatorship and, according to A. S. Izgoev, a writer who belonged to the Kadet Party, Stolypin believed that the only way he could prevent a dictatorship was to intensify the campaign against terror.[118] This is not to suggest that the prime minister in any way minimized the danger of terrorism. On the contrary, late in August he told Nicolson, the British ambassador to St. Petersburg, that he expected more terror and had recommended to the tsar that he form "'Ministres de réserve' for the more important Departments, so that should he [Stolypin] or another Minister be assassinated, there would be someone ready to take their place immediately. He did not wish any interim to occur." The only question in Stolypin's mind was *how* best to combat terror.[119]

Two days after the assassination attempt, Tsar Nicholas applied strong pressure on Stolypin to crack down on the revolutionaries. In a letter to the prime minister, Nicholas warned that the rash of murders and robberies was producing "a condition of complete anarchy." He reminded him that in the manifesto he had issued at the time of the dissolution of the Duma he had vowed not to tolerate lawlessness any longer. The time had come to act. Nicholas directed Stolypin to let him know as soon as possible "what measures [the cabinet ministers] consider most appropriate for the implementation of my inexorable will to eradicate sedition and to restore order."[120] Fearful that if he did not produce a new, tough policy the tsar would adopt the drastic measures that the reactionaries were advocating, Stolypin reluctantly decided to bring the matter before the cabinet. The result was the notorious law on field courts-martial.[121]

Apparently, only one member of the cabinet, the minister of justice, Shcheglovitov, shared Stolypin's misgivings. Like the prime minister, Shcheglovitov considered such courts undesirable for legal and political reasons.[122] Everyone else took a position along the lines of Gurko's: "The 1906 revolutionists were fighting the government openly, and, to my way of thinking, the government was not only justified but even duty bound to take every legal step to prevent the breakup of the state and to insure a normal course of administration in the country. False sentiment and mock liberalism toward the enemies of the state affected the entire workings of the state apparatus and consequently violated the interests of millions of people."[123]

Invoking Article 87 of the Fundamental Laws, which accorded the government the power to issue decrees with the ruler's approval when the Duma was in recess, the cabinet adopted the law on field courts-martial on August 17; the tsar approved it two days later. True, the mandate of such decrees automatically expired unless the legislature voted to retain them within two months of its first meeting. But at the time the law on field courts-martial was enacted no decision had been made as to when the Second Duma would meet. Months would surely elapse before the law could be rescinded. In the meantime, many citizens accused of terrorism would have received extremely severe punishments; the death penalty was to be liberally imposed. The law was so sweeping that it quickly became one of the most contentious issues of Stolypin's entire tenure as prime minister, and it is no exaggeration to say that it shaped the prime minister's reputation, at the time and in the history books, almost as much as his agrarian reforms.

The decree applied to all areas under martial law or under Extraordinary Security—in effect, most of the empire. It stated that whenever it was "so obvious" that a civilian had committed a crime that no investigation was necessary, the case was to be handed over to a field court composed of five military officers selected by the governor-general, the chief local administrator, or individuals invested with comparable authority. Within twenty-four hours of his arrest, the accused would appear before the court, which was obliged to conclude the trial within two days. All of the court's work was to be conducted "behind closed doors" according to legal procedures established for the military services. Once sentences had been handed down, they "immediately acquire the force of law" and had to be carried out within one day. Thus, the entire process from start to finish would take no more than four days.[124]

In an attempt to clarify the intent of the law on the field courts, Stolypin on October 10 sent a directive to all senior officials in the empire. He indicated that the law should be applied only to people charged with "murder, robbery, [or] attacks on sentries in military guards, [or] with armed resistance to authorities, assaults on officials of the military and police and on officials in general, [or] with having been involved in the illegal manufacture, acquisition, storage, carrying, or sale of explosives or shells." He stressed that the sentences passed down by the field courts must not be abrogated or submitted to any other court for further review.[125]

The law was, of course, a travesty of due process and even of military justice. As the historian William C. Fuller notes, "If guilt was so obvious, why have trials at all?"[126] Actually, the use of military courts to try civilians was not new. Since mid-1905, in areas under the emergency decrees a growing number of civilians charged with crimes had been handed over to such courts, but the rules of the Code of Criminal Procedure had not been abandoned. Due process, even if on a limited scale, continued to be honored until the law of field courts was promulgated.[127]

Virtually all leaders of society and most of the press vehemently denounced the law. With characteristic understatement, the British ambassador to Petersburg informed his superiors in London that "the reception accorded to [the law] in the press is the reverse of favourable." He could find only three newspapers that supported the government, all the others "stigmatizing" it as "reactionary."[128] Shipov, fervent only in his devotion to political moderation, declared that the law placed "in the hands of the authorities an extraordinary weapon of terror."[129] Even V. P. Pavlov, the chief military procurator, a man denounced in the Duma for his harsh treatment of radicals, expressed reservations about the law.[130] Public opinion abroad, especially in Great Britain, also took a dim view of the Russian government's abandonment of due process. The pro-Russian sentiment that had been on the rise in Britain suffered a temporary setback.[131]

The Octobrist A. I. Guchkov was the only prominent figure in society to come out publicly for the field courts-martial, which, he claimed, were necessary to put down the revolution and preserve the political freedoms secured since 1905. In an interview published in *Novoe vremia*, he went so far as to announce that "I deeply believe in Stolypin. We have not had such able and talented persons in power."[132] Appalled by Guchkov's announcement, Shipov resigned from the Union of October 17. In a widely publicized letter, he declared that he "had nothing in common with A. I. Guchkov" and warned that the measure praised by Guchkov would promote "the process of demoralization and extremism in society."[133] Citizens from all corners of Russia sent telegrams to Shipov congratulating him on his break with the Octobrist party.[134]

The extensive and vivid coverage in the press of the trials was bound to inflame public passions. From the moment the law was enforced on August 31, newspapers devoted many columns to detailed accounts of the trials and punishments, emphasizing the harshness of the procedures, the cruelty of the authorities, and the heroism of the victims.[135] During the first sixteen days of their operation the field courts sentenced 27 people to death, and during the eight months the law was on the books 1,102 people were executed, 329 people were sentenced to hard labor, 443 to prison terms of varying periods, and 7 to exile. Only 71 of the accused were acquitted.[136] By the standards of the post-1918 era, these figures do not seem particularly disturbing, but it must be kept in mind that during the nineteenth century European governments did not mete out large numbers of capital punishments. Even in autocratic Russia, during the eighty years preceding 1906 the average annual number of executions was nine.[137]

The law on the field courts-martial left deep scars in society long after it had lapsed. Critics of Stolypin in the liberal and radical camps referred to them as the most glaring evidence of his cruelty and of his contempt for the rule of law, and rarely missed an opportunity to berate him for his role in establishing them. In the end, the resort to these courts most probably hindered rather than aided the prime minister in his quest for political stability.

Despite his initial lack of enthusiasm for the field courts-martial, Stolypin defended them as necessary in the struggle against disorder once they had been introduced. Whether he did so out of a sense of duty or from conviction is hard to say. A revealing incident related by A. I. Shingarev, a Kadet member of the Duma and the minister of agriculture in the Provisional Government in 1917, provides support for either interpretation. Shingarev recalled that when, in the spring of 1907, he asked Stolypin to intercede in behalf of several men he believed had been unjustly sentenced to death for the murder of a landowner, the prime minister became very agitated. "You always think," Stolypin said, "that you can ask the authorities to act on the basis of starry-eyed idealism. The authorities have a terrible responsibility. I have the facts here, look . . . you demand the abolition of the military field courts, [but] look at this chart. Each day, the more the Duma deliberates [about abolishing capital punishment], the greater the number of victims, dead policemen, constables. Terror continues and grows. I have a responsibility in this. You do not have the right to demand that I abolish capital punishment." Shingarev retorted that no kind of governmental responsibility compelled the authorities to execute innocent people. Disappointed, Shingarev left the prime minister's office, but later he learned that Stolypin ordered a new trial after all. The men were again found guilty and executed.[138]

Stolypin, as has already been noted, was not a bloodthirsty tyrant who believed in indiscriminate killing of the regime's opponents. On the other hand, at times it seemed to him that the authorities had no alternative but to resort to capital punishment to prevent large-scale violence. He voiced this view clearly in December 1906, when the tsar sought his advice on a recommendation by Admiral Dubasov that he pardon the man who had tried to assassinate him (Dubasov). Stolypin was moved by the admiral's "moral sensitivity," but then pointed out that a year earlier, during the uprising in Moscow, Dubasov had not hesitated to suppress the rebels with an "iron fist." The prime minister now considered it his duty "to Your Majesty, to Russia, and to history" to argue against leniency for the would-be assassin: "[It] is grievous and shameful that only the execution of a few will prevent a sea of blood."[139]

When all is said and done, the controversy over the moral justification and effectiveness of the field courts-martial is not easily resolved. Even if they had been effective in restoring order, and that cannot be proven beyond a doubt, there remains the question of whether pacification secured at so heavy a price in human and political terms could help Stolypin to achieve his broader goal, the creation of a polity based on the rule of law.

Stolypin unquestionably faced unrest of staggering proportions, and none of the means previously used to end it had succeeded. However, the evidence on the effectiveness of the field courts is scanty and inconclusive. Stolypin himself provided statistics that only muddied the waters. He claimed that substantially more officials and private citizens were killed and wounded by terrorists in 1907 than in 1906, which, he insisted, argued for the effectiveness of the field courts. But since he did not give a breakdown of the number of assassinations before and after the courts operated—that is, before August 19, 1906, and after the law elapsed on April 20, 1907—it is impossible to gauge their impact. Moreover, he acknowledged that in 1908, well after the law on field courts was no longer in effect, the number of assassinations had declined significantly.[140] On the other hand, the British ambassador in St. Petersburg, who closely followed the incidence of crime, reported in mid-October 1906 that although lawlessness was still rampant, "reports coming from different parts of the country are to the effect that the summary retribution meted out by the courts-martial is gradually producing its deterrent effect." The German consul in Moscow thought that as a result of the field courts, public safety had improved in the city, though he noted that progress was very slow and predicted that it would take a long time to bring the unrest to an end. Toward the end of October 1906, the British ambassador again referred to the effectiveness of the summary trials and informed the Foreign Office that "the country is said by competent observers never to have been so quiet since the beginning of the revolutionary agitation." Yet he also conceded that though the "new measures are directed primarily against the revolutionaries, [they] leave Liberals, who are not revolutionaries, at the tender mercies of the provincial Governors and the secret police." The reaction of society to the government's crackdown was therefore ambivalent. "Public opinion is not, for the moment, revolutionary, as it was a year ago, but it may be doubted whether it is for that reason any more reconciled to a continuance of the present regime."[141]

The last point is critical. Even if the authorities had succeeded in reducing terrorism through the field courts-martial, pacification achieved by such means was bound to widen the chasm between state and society. Admittedly, reliance on due process by the government would have been more expensive, since it would have required a larger police force and an expanded judiciary. But that approach to disorder would have gained the sympathy of large sectors of society. Equally important, it would probably have engendered a greater respect for the law in the people. As the prime minister rightly saw, the traditional weakness of respect for law and the pervasive hostility toward authority were major obstacles that would have to be overcome if he was to succeed in his efforts to create a state based on the rule of law. Disregard by the government of judicial procedures generally accepted as fair and just only made matters worse. It served as a bad example, encouraged contempt for the law, and impeded the emergence of a genuine sense of citizenship.

Other aspects of Stolypin's campaign against the opposition were less harsh but nonetheless severe and arbitrary. Immediately after the dissolution of the Duma, the prime minister initiated a crackdown against the press that continued for months. Determined to prevent the dissemination of the Vyborg Manifesto, which urged passive resistance to the government, he ordered his subordinates to secure signed statements from all owners of printing presses in the country that they would not print the document.[142] Local officials adopted additional measures. Thus, on September 2 the governor of Viatka, S. D. Gorchakov, prohibited "the dissemination in the press of works that by their content might provoke distrust of the government and public authorities or might arouse unrest among the population." According to *Pravo*, Gorchakov's directive made editors in the province very apprehensive, since, in their view, even the dissemination of official announcements and of the governor's own decrees could well arouse such unrest.[143] In another province, Zhitomir, policemen ordered vendors at the railway station not to sell any "progressive newspapers."[144] Throughout the country the police either confiscated specific issues of newspapers and journals judged to be seditious or closed them down altogether.[145]

In addition, the police conducted innumerable searches of offices and private homes and arrested thousands of citizens. The roundups began in July, immediately after the dissolution of the Duma, and their scope increased over the next several months, as the following figures demonstrate. During a five-day period in early September, 420 people were arrested in St. Petersburg; in Warsaw the police seized 1,400 on one day alone (September 1); in early October the Moscow authorities jailed 1,011 political prisoners. Many of the new prisoners were undoubtedly revolutionaries, but a substantial number were activists in the liberal movement or simply "untrustworthy" people.[146] Reports from several provinces indicated that so many teachers had been arrested that some schools had to be closed.[147]

The government's campaign was directed with special rigor against the Kadets. Prior to the issuance of the Vyborg Manifesto, the repression of Kadet organizations had been confined largely to the provinces. Now the government began to repress them in the capital as well by closing down their offices. Late in the summer the Kadets, never registered by the government as a legal party, asked Stolypin for permission to hold a congress. He refused, and ordered governors not to permit a congress to be held in their provinces. He also ordered the police to keep an eye on the Kadets in case they planned to convene a congress abroad. If such a congress met and drafted an appeal to the people, the police were to take "all measures" to prevent its distribution within Russia, and to apply "the most repressive measures" against the Kadet leaders who composed the appeal.[148]

In the fall, N. N. Kutler, a former minister of agriculture and now a Kadet, made a personal plea to Stolypin to permit the party to reopen its central club in St. Petersburg. The prime minister turned him down on the grounds that the actions of the Kadet Duma faction, and in particular its advocacy of passive resistance, had demonstrated the party's "revolutionary character." Stolypin never could be generous or forgiving toward political activists who sought to overturn the country's political system. Kutler contended that the party viewed passive resistance not as a revolutionary but as a legitimate form of struggle by the opposition. Stolypin was not impressed: "This is only playing with words," he said, "and it does not change the essentials of the matter."[149]

Punishing the men who had signed the Vyborg Manifesto became something of an idée fixe for Stolypin, and it was because of his relentless determination to settle scores with those he perceived to be his and the state's political enemies that radicals would refer to the police as "Stolypin's Oprichniki" (the vicious political police under Ivan IV).[150] Generally, Stolypin kept his passions under control, but when he allowed himself to be carried away by anger he tended to lash out at his opponents. Thus, in mid-1906, in a rage over the protests against the dissolution of the First Duma, he directed governors to take the "most decisive measures" against former deputies who circulated the Vyborg Manifesto among peasants or agitated for militant action against the government. He also saw to it that formal charges under Article 129 of the Criminal Code were brought against every deputy (about 230) who had signed the manifesto, even though the Kadet party within a matter of days backed away from the tactic of passive resistance. It was a year and a half before the case came to trial, but in the meantime the accused were disqualified from standing for election to the Second Duma. The former deputies were tried not for drafting the manifesto but for conspiring to distribute it, a more serious charge that carried the penalty of imprisonment and deprivation of political rights. Altogether, 166 were found guilty, sentenced to prison for three months, and prohibited from ever engaging in political activities.[151]

Although Stolypin's repressive measures were not nearly as brutal as

those of his predecessor as minister of internal affairs, they were extensive and harsh. But they did not constitute his only weapon against the
left. He never lost sight of his reformist agenda, which, as will be seen in
the next chapter, he considered as important as the resort to force in
pacifying the country.

4

Fighting the Revolution, August 1906-June 1907

True to his word, Stolypin moved quickly to act on his pledge not to rely solely on repression to restore order. He was convinced that his predecessor, Goremykin, had committed a "grave error" in failing to prepare a program of reform for submission to the First Duma. The consequence of that mistake, he told Bernard Pares, was "that all the new Bills came from the Duma, so that they were very silly. It was just the opposite of what happens in other countries with constitutional governments. All the Bills, all the definite proposals [in Russia] came from the Opposition. This was an impossible position. Here is the first main article of my programme, consecutive work from the Ministry itself, to be submitted to the Duma later." Stolypin believed that he could "persevere" over the radicals in the legislature only if he confronted them with a carefully designed set of proposals.[1]

The ideological underpinnings of Stolypin's strategy are contained in a statement he drafted to clarify his own thinking, a practice he followed whenever he faced difficult decisions. The statement, in Stolypin's handwriting, was discovered by the historian V. S. Diakin, who agreed with the conclusion of archivists that Stolypin probably composed it early in 1907. The dating seems plausible, and it accurately reflects his credo, to which he had subscribed at least since his days in Saratov. Pithy and thoughtful, it is worth quoting in full before examining the specifics: "Reform at a time of revolution is necessary since in large measure revolution is caused by the defects of the internal structure [of the country]. If we concern ourselves exclusively with the struggle against the revolution, then at best we will eliminate the consequences but not the causes: we would heal the ulcer, but the infected blood will generate new ulcers. Moreover, the path to this reform has been triumphantly proclaimed. The State Duma has been created, and it is impossible to turn back. That would be a fatal mistake—[in those countries] where governments vanquished revolutions (Prussia, Austria), they succeeded not by resorting exclusively to physical force but by relying on strength, by taking the lead in instituting reform. For a government to devote all its creative talents to police measures—that is an acknowledgment of impotence by the ruling authorities."[2]

As a guide to action for a conservative who wished to avoid both inflexibility and weakness at a time of revolutionary turbulence, the statement is hard to fault. It emphasized both the restoration of order and the need to come to grips with the social and political causes of the turbulence, a two-pronged approach that had served him well in Saratov. But, as Stolypin would soon discover, it was not easy to find the right balance between repression and reform. In part because of pressure from the tsar and right-wing extremists and in part because of his own conviction that overwhelming force was necessary to cow the opposition, Stolypin at times placed more weight on repression than on reform. But there can be no doubt that ideologically the statement quoted above accurately described the thrust of the program he wished to pursue. This was made abundantly clear in the communiqué on the government's intentions that he issued on August 24, 1906.

Published on the front page of all the major newspapers, the communiqué began with a reference to the revolutionary upheaval of the preceding two years and the intensification of unrest since the spring of 1906. "Hardly a day passes without some new crime [being committed]." After listing the senior officials who had been killed, the communiqué asserted that the revolutionaries planned to create panic throughout the country, bring the government to its knees, and seize executive power. But the authorities would not yield to "wicked designs: it is possible to kill individuals, but it is impossible to kill the idea that animates the government. It is impossible to destroy the will of the government which is directed at restoring the possibility of living and working freely." The government intended to suppress "criminality" without hesitation and would meet "force with force," but would employ only "legal means." Failure to adhere to that principle would destroy the entire state system. Yet the government could not ignore the reality that normal judicial procedures had proven inadequate for the suppression of criminal unrest. Hence it had been necessary to issue "temporary" regulations establishing field courts-martial to deal with the spread of violence. Stolypin emphasized that these courts were designed as a means to "safeguard the freedom to live and toil" and not as a permanent feature of the state order.

In keeping with the position Stolypin had formulated in his unpublished statement, the communiqué vowed to disregard the advice of political groups urging the government to devote all its energies either to the struggle against sedition or to the cause of reform. Its tasks were more complicated. It must "protect order with decisive measures, it must protect the population against revolutionary manifestations, and, at the same time, direct all its energies along the path of construction in order to create a new and stable order based on legality and a reasonable concept of freedom."

To achieve such an order, the government would propose far-reaching reforms, the more urgent ones to be enacted immediately under the powers granted to the government under Article 87; others would be submitted to the next Duma. The list of legislative proposals was long and touched on virtually every national institution and every aspect of national life: freedom of religion; inviolability of the person; civil equality; improvements in peasant land-ownership and in the conditions of workers, including a system of state insurance; reform of local government with the aim of establishing direct links between provincial and district administrations; introduction of zemstvos in the Baltic and in the northern and northwestern regions; introduction of zemstvos and urban self-government in the provinces of the Polish Kingdom; reorganization of local courts; reform of secondary schools and universities; introduction of an income tax; reform of the police; further measures to safeguard public order; convocation of an all-Russian assembly of church officials to propose reform of religious institutions.

The communiqué did not propose any limitations on the tsar's prerogatives, and that was bound to irritate the oppositional movement. Nor did it offer any details about the content of the listed reforms. But it was a remarkably ambitious program of reform. Unprecedented in scope, its implementation would have produced vast changes in the Russian polity and in society. Stolypin called for support from all "sensible sectors of the state which yearn for calm, not for the destruction and disintegration of the State." For its part, the government promised not to restrict citizens in expressing their opinions on the program either in print or at public meetings. It would restrict only the propagation of revolutionary ideas and then only by resort to "all legal measures"; the sole purpose would be to protect the people against violence.

The urgent measures that would be introduced immediately would enhance the freedom of peasants, the Old Believers, and, to the dismay of right-wingers, of Jews. "On the Jewish question there will be an urgent examination [of measures] that only arouse irritation and are clearly obsolete and can therefore be immediately abolished." On the other hand, broader issues affecting "the relations between Jews and the native population [and which] are matters of national conscience" should be left for consideration by the Duma.[3]

Stolypin wasted no time in acting on his reform proposals. Even before the communiqué was issued, the government designated 5.5 million rubles for the establishment of new public schools, the first step in the planned introduction of a system of universal primary education and raising the pay scale for teachers.[4] In mid-October the government issued a ukase lifting various restrictions on Old Believers and other dissenting sects, recognizing them as legitimate religious associations whose rights would be virtually equal to those of the official Orthodox Church. The one remaining distinction would be that only the Orthodox Church would be permitted to proselytize among other faiths.

Stolypin's most ambitious initiative by far, and the one to which he devoted more time and energy than to any other, was the enactment of agrarian reform under Article 87 of the Fundamental Laws. It was also to be his most notable and most controversial achievement. During Stolypin's years as prime minister probably no governmental measure evoked as much anger and as many polemical writings as the agrarian reform, which, after all, would touch the lives, in one way or another, of an overwhelming majority of the population. Designed radically to transform the structure of economic and social relations in the countryside, the reform inevitably aroused the interest not only of the peasants, but also political activists throughout the political spectrum. An analysis and evaluation of the arguments and claims advanced for and against Stolypin's initiative would require a sizable monograph. And if the voluminous work of scholars over the past eight decades on the implementation of the reform—often focused on individual provinces or districts—were included, the monograph would become a very large tome. Of course, no discussion of Stolypin's agrarian reform can avoid these matters; the feasibility of his undertaking bears very directly on any assessment of his achievements as a statesman. But for a biographical study, it may be more instructive to pay special attention to his overall aims and to the means he favored to realize them. Both have often been misrepresented. Contemporaries widely accused the prime minister of caring only about the kulaks, the relatively affluent peasants, and of sanctioning violence to implement the agrarian reform against the wishes of most villagers. These charges, frequently repeated by historians, cannot be substantiated and have led to serious misunderstandings of the entire enterprise.

Although innovative in the deepest sense, the agrarian measures Stolypin enacted cannot be said to have been his brainchild. Ever since

the emancipation of the serfs in 1861, there had been a growing awareness in Russian society that drastic steps were required to cope with the
country's economic backwardness and to stimulate economic growth.[5]
The emancipation had freed the serfs, but it had also strengthened the
commune,* an institution whose importance for the peasants can hardly be exaggerated. In central and northern Russia, where it was primarily
located, the great majority of peasants lived in a village commune,
which was the legal owner of the peasants' land, provided local self-
government for them, and had a large say in regulating the peasants'
economic affairs.† "It is nearly impossible," a recent study of the commune noted, "to find a single significant social act of the peasant (within
the commune, to be sure) or a significant event in his life that was not
influenced by the commune, through either its formal or its informal
structure. . . . [The commune] embraced not just a part of his life activity, not just certain parts of his personality, but his entire being and existence."[6]

About 80 percent of the communes periodically redivided land
among villagers to maintain the equality of allotments assigned to peasant families, whose size would naturally vary over the years. Thus, there
was no tradition of private land-ownership among the bulk of the country's population, and as long as the peasants did not own the land they
worked, they lacked the incentive to modernize their farms and improve
efficiency. Moreover, because of the sharp increase in Russia's population from 1861 to 1905 (by some 40 percent), the average allotment assigned to peasants, in most cases not overgenerous to start with, declined by about 25 percent. The various commissions the government
established in the late nineteenth and early twentieth centuries to study
the deficiencies of agriculture all agreed that indolence, low productivity, alcoholism, and indigence were the main features of the countryside. Many statistics could be cited to demonstrate the wretched conditions in the countryside, but none are more telling than the following
two: the death rate in Russia was almost double that in England; taxes
and the redemption payments imposed on the peasants at the time of
the emancipation were so onerous that by 1875 total peasant arrears
amounted to 29 million rubles. Peasants who failed to make their payments could be subjected to whipping by a birch rod or to confiscation of
their property. Yet in 1895 the total peasant arrears had risen fourfold, to

---

*Mir and obshchina in Russian.
†Not as widespread in northeastern Russia and Siberia, the communes in these
regions were also somewhat different from those in the central parts of the country.
There were very few communes in the Ukraine and in eastern European Russia.

119 million rubles.[7] In an endeavor to rectify these conditions, the commissions set forth a series of proposals that would become the basis of Stolypin's reform program.[8]

Stolypin's signal achievement was to translate the abstract ideas on agrarian reform into reality. He himself had favored those ideas as far back as the late 1880s and 1890s, when he supervised work on his estate in Kovno and became aware of the defects of Russian agriculture. And the set of recommendations he had sent to the tsar from Saratov in 1904 and 1905 adumbrated the reforms of 1906. Now, as prime minister, he was the driving force behind their implementation, taking the initiative and conveying a sense of urgency for speedy action. Whenever officials raised objections, especially to the use of Article 87, Stolypin "was adamant, answering that for him the peasant problem would permit of no compromise."[9] He was absolutely convinced that the commune was the root cause of most of Russia's woes, and he was never at a loss for words in denouncing it. Late in December 1906, for example, he told a foreign journalist: "Our agrarian commune is a rotten anachronism that thrived only thanks to the artificial, unsound sentimentalism of the last half century, in defiance of common sense and the most important needs of the state." He went on to blame the commune for the ignorance, indolence, and alcoholism of the peasants, as well as for their failure to assume the responsibilities of citizenship.[10]

Soon after assuming leadership of the government, Stolypin directed A. V. Krivoshein, the head of the Peasant Bank, and Gurko to prepare recommendations for the issuance of a ukase on agrarian reform. Once that task had been completed, Stolypin undertook to ward off the opposition of influential Slavophiles like F. D. Samarin, who were nostalgically attached to the commune as the bedrock of stability in the countryside. But the Slavophiles were not the only ones who revered the commune, as was noted by Carl Andreas Koefoed, an enterprising Dane who had moved to Russia in 1878 and over the next three decades became an expert on Russian agriculture as well as a leading opponent of the mir. Koefoed discovered that for a large number of peasants he encountered in his extensive travels "it was enough that . . . [the commune] was genuinely Russian, and therefore indisputable—[to them that it was] something holy."[11]

Stolypin's agrarian reform also faced opposition in the Council of Ministers. At a cabinet meeting of October 16, Kokovtsov, B. A. Vasilchikov and N. D. Obolenskii referred to the attitude of the villagers and argued that "it has still not been demonstrated that the peasants themselves had a negative view of the commune."[12] The three ministers actually feared that the reform would provoke unrest in the countryside, and they urged Stolypin not to act on his own but to submit his proposals to the next Duma for its consideration. But Stolypin did not believe that the legislature would approve any land reform that did not provide for the expropriation of privately owned lands. In view of the First Duma's handling of the agrarian issue, there is little doubt that Stolypin was right. Gurko strongly supported Stolypin, arguing that under normal conditions the approach recommended by the three ministers would be appropriate, but given the prevailing turbulence, extraordinary procedures were necessary. "The vital interests of the country," he insisted, "must be placed above this or that provision of the law."[13] Since it was known that the tsar supported Stolypin, the prime minister prevailed in the Council of Ministers. On November 9, Nicholas gave his formal approval to the ukase on agrarian reform, which was promulgated that day.

In sponsoring the agrarian reforms, Stolypin was motivated by much more than a desire to improve the country's economy. For him, they constituted the linchpin of the entire array of reforms that he intended to introduce for the transformation of Russia into a stable and prosperous country. It was his focus on the broad arena of social and political institutions that distinguished Stolypin's conception of agrarian reform from that of previous statesmen and public figures who had advocated dismantling the commune.

In the prime minister's view, the planned changes in the countryside would affect the peasants' attitudes on a whole range of issues, fundamentally altering the *mentalité* of most of the people in Russia. The most critical problem in Russia, according to Stolypin, was that the peasants, who composed the vast majority of the population, were wholly lacking in civic spirit (*grazhdanstvennost*); they did not respect the laws, and they had no developed sense of civic obligation. In short, the peasants were not yet citizens in the full meaning of the word. His goal, Stolypin stressed, was to transform them into citizens by giving them a stake in society, by making them realize that order and discipline were in their own interest. "Private peasant ownership," Stolypin had written in the memorandum he had submitted to the tsar in 1905, "is a guarantee of order, because each small owner represents the nucleus on which rests the stability of the state."[14] Unless the masses in the countryside were converted into citizens respectful of order, a state based on law was inconceivable.[15] Stolypin's model, no doubt, was the West, where, as one historian put it, "property rights have historically provided the basis for other civil and political rights. Ultimately, the person has assumed the inviolability granted to property."[16] In sum, Sto-lypin aimed at nothing less than a transformation of the peasantry's psychology in the deepest sense of the word.

In various speeches justifying the reforms—delivered after they had already been introduced—Stolypin used phrases that gave the impression that the reforms were designed to help only the well-to-do kulaks. Thus, in 1908 he declared that the Ukase of November 9 "placed a wager not on the wretched and drunken, but on the sturdy [*krepkie*] and strong." But in the very same speech, he also made it clear that he was not speaking of a small sector of the peasantry. The "strong people" he had in mind were the "majority in Russia." As he put it in 1910, the government had a responsibility to care for the "relatively weak, the relatively feeble, the relatively incapacitated," but it must focus on un-leashing the energies of the entire nation: "All the powers of both the legislator and the government must be exerted toward raising the pro-ductive forces of the sole source of our well-being—the land. By applying to it personal labor, personal property, by applying to it the powers of all our people without exception, we must raise up our impoverished, weak, exhausted land, since the land is the pledge of our strength in the future; the land *is* Russia."[17]

In an earlier speech, delivered on May 10, 1907, he made a similar point: "The aim of the government is completely definite: the govern-ment wishes to lift up peasant landholding, it wishes to see the peasant rich, satisfied, since where there is sufficiency, there, of course, is en-lightenment, there also is real freedom. But for this we must give a chance to the capable, industrious peasant, that is, the salt of the Rus-sian earth, to free himself from the vise in which he now is caught. . . . Such a peasant proprietor the government is obligated to help with counsel, to help with credit, that is, money. We must forthwith turn to the much neglected job of considering all those small-landed peasants who live by agriculture. We must give all these small-landed peasants a chance to make use, out of the existing land supply, of such a quantity of land as they need, and on favorable terms. . . . At the present time our state is ailing: the most ailing, the weakest part . . . is the peasantry. We must aid it. . . . The idea that all the forces of the state must come to the aid of the weakest part of it may be termed the principle of socialism; but if this is the principle of socialism, it is state socialism, which has been applied more than once in Western Europe and has achieved real and substantial results."[18]

A careful reading of these statements makes it clear that when Stolypin used the word "strong" he was thinking not of peasants who were economically strong (that is, rich), but of peasants who were psychologically strong: rational beings who understood their own interests and were prepared to take initiatives to better their lives. They were, in short, energetic and enterprising, strong in willpower. Every peasant so inclined would be given an opportunity to abandon the old habits of work, which had proved so disastrous, and to adopt modern, rational methods of farming.

Stolypin's stress on individual initiative emerged with particular force in his criticism of the Social Democratic proposals on the agrarian issue, which called for nationalization of the land. If that project were adopted, he warned, "everything would be equalized—and one can make everyone equal only at the lowest level. It is impossible to make the lazy man equal with the industrious, the stupid equal to the man capable of work. . . . The good manager, the inventive owner, by the very nature of things will be deprived of the chance of applying his knowledge to the land."[19] Although conservative proprietors tended to support Stolypin's reforms because they did not involve the compulsory confiscation of land, the prime minister's long-range goal was not to preserve the nobility as a privileged estate. According to Guchkov, Stolypin realized that the emergence of an economically strong peasantry might harm the economic interests of the nobles, but that did not deter him. "Let the nobles," he declared with a trace of impatience, "reorganize their own economic affairs. That is their business." He had a much larger vision of Russia than the protection of the nobility. In fact, he assumed that eventually the nobility would cease to exist as a separate group and that there would be only one agricultural class, a class of independent farmers.[20]

The Ukase of November 9 was actually the capstone of a series of agrarian reforms introduced in 1906. In August the government announced that it would make available for sale to peasants a modest amount of land (1.8 million desiatinas) from the state, the tsar's personal holdings, and the properties of the imperial family. Stolypin had persuaded the tsar and the grand dukes to take this action, though he failed to persuade them to donate the land.[21] At this time, he himself sold his estate in Nizhnii Novgorod to the Peasants' Land Bank in the hope of setting an example for other landowners.[22] Stolypin also took steps to facilitate the purchase of land by the Peasants' Bank and, more important, the sale of land to peasants by reducing the interest on loans charged to villagers.[23] Many landlords, frightened by the unrest and by the possibility that their land would be confiscated, were eager to sell, often at relatively low prices. Capitalists did not rush to buy the land because they too feared confiscation, and peasants did not show nearly as much interest in purchasing it as Stolypin hoped because they expected all the land to be distributed to them free of charge. Still, the Peasants' Bank did substantially increase its landholdings. Between 1896 and late 1905, it acquired 2,785 estates totaling 4.9 million desiatinas; over the next fourteen months, it acquired 7,617 estates with 8.7 million desiatinas of land.[24]

On September 19, the government enacted a law opening up to colonization a substantial amount of land that belonged to His Majesty's Cabinet in the Altai region of West Siberia, where communes were not widely established. The next ukase on the agrarian question, promulgated on October 5, was more far-reaching; it provided for an extension of civil and personal rights to the peasants, narrowing the distinction between them and other classes and thereby conferring many of the attributes of citizenship on them. Peasants were now permitted to work in administrative agencies of the state, to attend educational institutions without prior permission from the commune, and to retain ties with their village communities if they entered the civil service or some other profession. In addition, peasants could now become members of another village community by acquiring land there without forfeiting membership in their own community. They could move freely from one region to another as long as they received the appropriate permits from their new place of residence. The election of peasants to zemstvos no longer had to be approved by the provincial governor. Finally, the peasants were freed from various punishments previously imposed by the communal assembly and the land captains* for the infraction of regulations.[25]

The key article of the Ukase of November 9, the most far-reaching of the agrarian reforms, read as follows: "Every head of a peasant family holding allotment land [nadel] by right of communal tenure is entitled at any time to claim the appropriation as private property of his due share of the said land." If no redistribution had been conducted during the preceding twenty-four years, the peasant would receive all the land he was cultivating at the time he requested separation from the commune. If redistribution had taken place within that period, the peasant

---

*The post of land captain was created in the late 1880s as part of the counter-reforms. Appointed by provincial governors, the land captain assumed a vast amount of arbitrary power in the countryside. He could overrule decisions of all local institutions, appoint personnel to important government positions, and order the imprisonment of a peasant for five days or impose five-ruble fines without resorting to judicial proceedings. For more on the land captains, see below, pp. 224–25.

could still obtain the amount of land he was cultivating, but only until the next scheduled redistribution, at which time changes might be made in the size of individual holdings. The peasant was also guaranteed the use of the same quantity of meadowland to which he had been entitled as a member of the commune. Before the promulgation of the ukase, a peasant could leave the commune as owner of the land he worked only with the approval of the communal assembly, a cumbersome procedure that discouraged separation.

In addition, the Ukase of November 9 made it easier for peasants to bring about consolidated ownership of the strips into which the land was divided and thus to dissolve the commune. The strip system had been introduced centuries earlier to provide peasants with an equal share of different types of land in the village—in some provinces, the number of strips per peasant household ranged from eleven to over a hundred. Because the strips were widely scattered, the peasants were forced to spend a part of their working day walking from one strip to another, a waste of time and energy that reduced productivity. Strip farming also militated against the use of machinery.[26] Prior to the reform of 1906, a unanimous vote of the communal assembly was needed before any consolidation could be enacted; now an affirmative vote by two-thirds of the assembly sufficed.

To help communes in the difficult task of reallocating the land in their villages, the government established land organization commissions. Stolypin wanted the entire process to be voluntary; peasants who wished to stay in the commune might do so. "The Law of November 9," Stolypin assured the State Council early in 1910, "avoiding all violence, all compulsion in its attitude both toward the communes and family property, only . . . cleared the path that until now has prevented the peasants from exercising their free will, counting on [the likelihood] that once they are no longer constrained, their abilities and intelligence and strength will manifest themselves [and that this] will give free rein . . . to the . . . initiative of the Russian national spirit."[27] On the whole, a scholar of the subject noted recently, the government lived up to this commitment and displayed a fair amount of flexibility "in dealing with peasants' demands during the implementation of the . . . reform."[28] But the prime minister kept a close watch on the process, and he did his best to encourage it. In mid-1909, for example, he sent the following message to the governor of Perm: "According to the records I have received, the progress of the land settlement in Perm province is not developing as successfully as it should given the local conditions in the province."[29]

He also pressed for additional legislative measures to facilitate the breakup of the commune. Thus, in 1910 the Duma passed a law (at the government's prompting) that provided for the creation of hereditary landholdings in all communes not subjected to a general redistribution over the preceding twenty-three years. The Law of May 29, 1911, made it easier to consolidate the strips, a majority vote rather than a two-thirds vote being sufficient. This legislation also gave the peasant the right to demand part of the undivided land, such as the meadows.[30]

The opposition rejected Stolypin's agrarian reforms. Many liberals and all the radicals denounced the Ukase of November 9 because it did not provide for the expropriation of land, which, they insisted, was a key demand of the peasants, who would refuse to abandon the commune. For that reason they predicted that the entire enterprise would fail. But some radicals implicitly conceded that the policy Stolypin was pursuing might divert the masses from a revolutionary course. Although Lenin voiced conflicting views on the reform program, on several occasions he sounded a note of warning that the prime minister's initiatives could undermine the strategies of the left. In 1907, he granted that it was creating "a peasant bourgeoisie." In 1908, he declared flatly that Stolypin's program could succeed: "If Stolypin's policy is continued . . . then the agrarian structure of Russia will become completely bourgeois, the stronger peasants will acquire almost all the allotments of land, agriculture will become capitalistic, and any 'solution' of the agrarian problem—radical or otherwise—will become impossible under capitalism."[31] The SRs, strong supporters of the commune as an institution that facilitated socialist agitation in the villages, now began to stress cooperation between peasants rather than the socialization of the land, a tacit acknowledgment that the commune was losing support among peasants.[32] Kadet leaders disagreed among themselves about the desirability of preserving the commune, but all of them opposed the Ukase of November 9 because Stolypin had bypassed the Duma by resorting to Article 87 of the Fundamental Laws.[33] Not until the spring of 1910, almost four years after the enactment of agrarian reform, did the Duma and State Council adopt legislation affirming the ukase. The debates were long and intense and in the State Council the division between supporters and opponents of the bill was so close that Stolypin had to make special efforts to secure the votes of councilors who were sitting on the fence.[34]

Even the reactionary United Nobility, the staunchest opponents of expropriation, at first lobbied against any agrarian reform on the assumption that it would provide for forcible alienation of private lands. But when Stolypin's program failed to contain such a provision, the United Nobility quickly changed its stand.[35] However, his most implacable enemies among the rightists, most notably Witte and Durnovo, never ceased to attack the agrarian reforms. Witte charged the government with imposing the reform against the peasants' will and claimed that it had brought few benefits to the people in the countryside, only confusion and harm. It seemed to him impossible, he said contemptuously, to implement the principle of private property "with one stroke of the pen." It was pointed out to Witte that Stolypin's reforms did not differ in any fundamental way from proposals the former prime minister himself had made a few years earlier, but that did not impress him.[36] Witte could not bear the thought that anyone could succeed where he had failed.

Moderate conservatives (especially the Octobrists) proved to be Stolypin's most fervent supporters on the agrarian question. After the Revolution of 1917 they became effusive in their praise of the prime minister's policy, claiming that "had it not been for the war [of 1914], this law . . . would have saved Russia from revolution." The measure, V. A. Maklakov asserted, "found among the peasants themselves an unexpected, sympathetic response, in spite of its shortcomings."[37]

Stolypin himself was confident that the agrarian reform he had introduced would transform Russia, that it was the "last link in the emancipation of our agrarian class," the logical extension of their emancipation in 1861.[38] But he conceded that it would be a gradual and slow process stretching over two decades.[39] Some of the ardent supporters, frustrated at the slow and inept implementation of the measure, looked for scapegoats, arguing, as one observer put it in 1909, that "the chief objection which can be raised against it is that in execution it may be faulty, and tend too much to go to extremes, and that advantage may be taken of this weakness by the capitalist and the Jew to the detriment of the thriftless Russian peasant."[40] However, experts on the Russian countryside who had all along voiced doubts about the entire project were much less optimistic than the prime minister. For example, Kutler, the former minister of agriculture who supported the Kadet agrarian program,* claimed that it would take at least a hundred years for Stolypin's policy to have a decisive impact on the country.[41]

Although scholars differ in their overall assessments of the agrarian

---

*The Kadet land program called for extensive expropriations of land with compensation and its distribution to "land-starved peasants."

reforms, their studies suggest that Stolypin was in fact too sanguine.[42] To be sure, many peasants showed interest in the reforms, but the obstacles impeding implementation were immense.[43]

Even with the best of intentions, the government was incapable of implementing the reforms with as much dispatch as it hoped. It had at its disposal far too few surveyors (only five thousand), whose services were needed in deciding on the details of the transfer of land from communal to private ownership. Furthermore, a large number of peasants for one reason or another rejected the very idea of seceding from the commune. Sheer inertia, the unwillingness to change a lifetime of habits, played an important role in inhibiting peasants from taking advantage of the new law. And peasants did not necessarily find separation economically advantageous. Often a peasant with a separated farm would not have access to roads, wells, or the drainage system; the division of lands of widely different quality into equitable plots was bound to be controversial and frequently unfeasible; many poor peasants worried that the final division of communal lands would leave them with insufficient grazing land. At the same time, many villagers committed to the principle of egalitarianism feared that the new law would inevitably produce greater inequalities in the villages. Finally, personal and social considerations militated against the success of the reform. Women, especially those whose husbands spent large parts of the year working in distant cities, felt comfortable with the social life in the village and feared the isolation that would invariably accompany secession from the commune. They would have to live on farms far removed from their previous neighbors.[44]

Although the government had promised that the reform would be enacted on a purely voluntary basis, in some localities officials pressured communes to proceed with secession. But there is little hard evidence on the extent of such pressure.[45] On the other hand, the opponents of the agrarian reform were also known to twist arms. At times, enraged peasants even tried to stop a secession by resorting to violence against the separators, forcing the police and army to step in. "Hostile manifestations," according to one contemporary account, "towards separating members of communes often assumed bitter and barbaric forms. Fires, murders, and conflicts involving bloodshed were by no means rare occurrences. There was even a case of almost unbelievable atrocity in the drenching with oil of a departing member by his fellow villagers, who burnt him like a live torch."[46] The conflicts between the supporters and opponents of separation became so intense that in some areas of the empire it seemed as though a "social war" had broken out in the country-side.[47]

An unqualified judgment on the effectiveness of Stolypin's agrarian reform is difficult to make. His most ardent defenders claim that because of the outbreak of World War I and the Revolution of 1917 the reforms could not be fully implemented; and that it is unfair to belabor them for failing to change Russia's political landscape.[48] But an examination of the reform process indicates that it was very slow to begin with and had become markedly slower well before 1914. The number of applications for secession reached its high point early in 1909 and declined sharply thereafter. Some 508,000 households left the commune in 1908, 580,000 in 1909, and 342,000 in 1910. In 1913 the number shrank to 135,000. By 1914, only about 20 percent of the peasants had obtained ownership of their land, while 14 percent of the land had been withdrawn from communal tenure. Strip consolidation developed at an even slower pace. By late 1916, 10.7 percent of the peasant households in European Russia worked land that was enclosed.[49] On the other hand, Stolypin's contention that his agrarian reform was not designed to benefit only or primarily the richer peasants was substantiated. The main beneficiaries were peasants with "average-sized holdings," who proved to be the most eager to take advantage of the new regulations.[50] Nonetheless, the process of privatization and consolidation would have taken many years to reach even a majority of the peasants. Whether in the meantime political stability, one of Stolypin's primary goals, could have been achieved is an open question.

Nonetheless, the promulgation of the Ukase of November 9 was a bold and imaginative stroke on Stolypin's part, almost certainly the most effective response to Russia's agrarian crisis. But because of the inevitably slow pace of so complex a process, a new eruption of political turbulence probably could not have been avoided. On the other hand, had the war not broken out in 1914, the turbulence might not have been as radical as it was in 1917. A substantial number of peasants did acquire their own property, and their attitudes toward economic and political issues were likely to change. Given more time for implementation, the agrarian reform might have contributed to a more moderate resolution of the political crisis than the one of 1917. That would not have been a mean achievement.

At about the same time that Stolypin enacted the agrarian reform he launched another initiative that affected far fewer people and yet seems to have provoked no less interest and concern within the cabinet, at

court, and in conservative circles generally. In fact, this proposal, designed to lift some of the restrictions long imposed on the Jewish population, so deeply troubled the tsar that in the end it ran afoul of his
prejudices and was never enacted. An account of how the reform measure fared reveals much about Stolypin's views on the vexing Jewish
question, his surprising naiveté regarding the tsar's attitude toward the
Jews, and the determination of right-wing extremists to maintain the
Jews in a position of legal inferiority. Perhaps most important, Nicholas's handling of the issue speaks volumes about his exalted conception
of his role as monarch and his readiness to assert his prerogatives on issues dear to his heart.

Although scholars have generally depicted Stolypin as more liberal
toward Jews than most senior officials in Late Imperial Russia, they
have ascribed different motives to his Jewish policy. Some historians
have insisted that his relatively favorable attitude was not a matter of
deep conviction;[51] others have contended that he advocated ameliora-
tion of conditions for Jews primarily for opportunistic reasons, to placate foreign investors repelled by the government's harsh policies and to
wean Jews away from radicalism.[52] Some contemporaries even accused
him of outright hostility toward the Jews, a charge he denied by insisting that he was "by no means an anti-Semite." He adopted a cautious
stance, contending that it would be unwise "to solve the Jewish question by one stroke of the pen as absolute justice would demand." Such
an action would not serve the interests of the Jews, he argued, for it
would only arouse popular hostility toward them and probably would
provoke a new round of pogroms. As evidence of this hostility, Stolypin
disclosed that he and the tsar received between twenty and thirty telegrams a day from all parts of Russia opposing any concessions to the
Jews and "accusing [Stolypin] of having sold himself to the Hebrew
race."[53]

He was hardly guilty of that, but he did feel impelled to abolish some
of the most egregious restrictions imposed on the Jews and sought to do
so by invoking the government's emergency powers under Article 87.
For one thing, the October Manifesto, which granted civil rights to the
people, seemed to him to be applicable to all inhabitants of the empire,
including the Jews. For another, he was eager to lessen the appeal of
radicalism to the Jews; the disproportionate number of Jews active in
the revolutionary movement was a matter of endless concern to conservatives, including the prime minister himself. "Of late," he cautioned
the tsar, "the Jewish question has significantly intensified; the dissatisfaction with the present constraints, compared to those imposed on the

rest of the population of the Empire, as well as the growing irritation with and hatred of the Russian government and Russia itself that has reached extreme proportions, have pushed the Jews into a desperate struggle against the prevailing state system in order to achieve a lightening of the burdens of the legal restrictions on their property and civil rights." To achieve the political stability that the tsar desired, Stolypin continued, the government could not avoid the "urgent question of an immediate improvement in the life of the Jewish population."[54] The prime minister was also determined to blunt the criticisms of foreign bankers, some of whom were troubled by Russian anti-Semitism.[55] At first glance, then, Stolypin seems to have been guided by opportunistic considerations on the Jewish question. However, a careful reading of published sources and relevant archival documents suggests that this interpretation does not adequately account for the prime minister's complicated and at times inconsistent policy toward the Jews. Stolypin was in fact committed to easing the lot of the Jews in the Russian Empire on moral grounds as well as pragmatic.

In October 1906, Stolypin placed a modest proposal on the Jewish issue before the Council of Ministers. It did not call for the abolition of the Pale of Settlement,* the principal demand of Jews and liberals; nor did it propose to change the law prohibiting Jews from buying or leasing land in rural regions of the pale, another major grievance of the Jews. Stolypin's measure would merely permit those Jews who had engaged in trade or worked as artisans outside the pale for ten years to remain outside it. Wives, children, and "other direct descendants" as well as brothers and sisters (who were still minors) of a man who had lived outside the pale for ten years would be permitted to live with him. And in areas within the pale where Jews were allowed to engage in trade and industry, the various restrictions on them would be abolished, placing them "on a nearly equal footing with other Russians." Jews would also be allowed to live in villages and certain towns within the pale from which they had been excluded. Fines imposed on families of Jewish draft-evaders would be eliminated. In addition, the official documents of Jews who had converted to Christianity would no longer have to indicate the original affiliation of the converts. Stolypin's reform would also have made it easier for Jews to secure permission to serve in management positions in partnerships and corporations. Finally, Stolypin indicated that he intended to submit to the next legislature reform proposals on other aspects of the Jewish question. Although the entire package was not

*On the Pale of Settlement, see above, p. 23.

very far-reaching—the prime minister himself referred to it as "modest"—its adoption would have pointed to a shift in government direction.[56]

Before Stolypin submitted the measure to the tsar, he sought the approval of his cabinet. The ministers' deliberations were lengthy, stretching over three meetings, and incredibly confused and contentious, demonstrating once again that any mention of the Jewish question in government circles aroused the deepest passions. V. I. Gurko, the assistant minister of internal affairs, who attended most cabinet meetings at Stolypin's request even though he was not a minister, claimed that V. N. Kokovtsov, the minister of finance, generally inclined to consider "matters from the point of view of their reaction on the stock market," defended the project. Kokovtsov acknowledged that he did not like Jews but saw no alternative to easing their lot. "The Jews are so clever," Kokovtsov asserted, "that no law can be counted upon to restrict them. It is useless to lock a door against them, for they are sure to find a passkey to open it." He also argued that existing laws only angered Jews and served as pretexts for officials inclined to abuse their authority.

Astonished at Kokovtsov's statement, Gurko could not let it "pass unchallenged." It seemed to him farfetched to remove locks from doors just because "someone uses a passkey." He contended that "either the Jews are harmless, in which case the government must abolish all restrictions against them, especially those concerning Jewish settlements; or their presence is a pernicious influence, in which case, since locks are inefficient, we must use bolts or anything that will serve that purpose." Gurko granted that lifting restrictions on the Jews might be the wiser course, for the population would then have to "develop in itself some resistance against them" and "our intelligentsia might cease to be so sympathetically concerned for the fate of the Jews." But the concessions to the Jews that Stolypin had proposed would be useless because they would not satisfy them. In fact, the concessions would "put into their hands a weapon which will facilitate [the Jews'] fight against the government. Everybody knows what part the Jews played during the recent upheaval. Now, as a reward, the government is about to give them privileges!"

According to Gurko, after he had his say, Stolypin was so confused that he postponed further discussion until the cabinet met again. Realizing that the ministers had been annoyed by his intervention, Gurko told Stolypin that he would not attend the next meeting, though he repeated his opposition to the entire project. Stolypin decided on an unusual procedure: he asked the cabinet at its next session to adopt the decision of the majority by acclaim so as to spare the tsar any responsibility for the government's action. Stolypin did not want the tsar to be in the position of having to antagonize either the extremists on the right or the Jews.[57] The cabinet voted for the reforms after Stolypin made a strong case for lifting some restrictions on the Jews, arguing that this was necessary to wean them away from radicalism and to counter anti-Russian propaganda in the United States. All the ministers agreed with Stolypin and even offered to make specific suggestions on which restrictions to abolish.

As soon as the cabinet reached a consensus, Stolypin sent the measure to the tsar in a document that ran to no less than sixty-one printed pages. The document began with a detailed account of the legal status of the Jews ever since 1772, when Catherine II annexed parts of Poland-Lithuania with a sizable Jewish population. With his usual thoroughness, Stolypin sought to familiarize the monarch with the background to the "Jewish question" and to explain why reform was necessary. During the cabinet's deliberations, Stolypin had not referred to the tsar's views on the project, but every minister assumed that Nicholas favored it. It did not occur to anyone that Stolypin would bring up so sensitive a matter without first talking things over with the tsar. In this instance, they overestimated Stolypin's sagacity.

Strangely, the prime minister seems not to have been aware of the depth of Nicholas's hostility toward the Jews. Or perhaps Stolypin assumed that while the tsar profoundly disliked Jews, he would nevertheless rise above his personal feelings and approve the reforms for reasons of state—that is, to remove a source of political instability. In any case, had Stolypin realized that Nicholas's prejudices ran very deep and overrode all other considerations, he would surely not have asserted in the document he sent to the tsar that opposition to the reforms could be expected from various groups and individuals "united by a general feeling of intransigent hostility toward Jewry." But the Council of Ministers, Stolypin continued, was firmly convinced that such opposition should not deter the government or the tsar from carrying out the promise regarding Jews made in the official communiqué of August 24. "However great the difficulties in implementing the program of the aforesaid report, the program must nevertheless be carried out." If the government wavered, it would be accused of not honoring its promises to transform the country and would lose the confidence of "right-thinking groups of society."[58] It was a strong statement that left no doubt about Stolypin's commitment to improving the legal status of the Jewish community.

Weeks passed without any word from the court on the ministers' proposals. "We often asked Stolypin," Kokovtsov recalled, "what its fate had been and why it had not been returned, and his replies were always assured and confident."[59]

When the tsar's response finally arrived on December 10 in a letter to Stolypin, the cabinet was understandably stunned. Nicholas indicated that he had thought about the Jewish question "night and day" long before he had received the Council of Ministers' recommendation and concluded that he could not agree to any relaxation of the restrictions. "An inner voice," the tsar revealed, "keeps insisting more and more that I do not take this decision upon myself. So far, my conscience has not deceived me. Therefore, I intend in this case also to follow its dictates. I know that you too believe that 'the heart of the Tsar is in God's hands.' So be it. For all those whom I have placed in authority I bear an awesome responsibility before God and am ready at any time to account to Him."[60] Even Kokovtsov, a fervent believer in the autocratic principle, found this an extraordinary statement. "None of the documents in my possession shows so clearly the Tsar's mystical attitude toward the nature of his imperial power as this letter to the Chairman of his Ministers' Council."[61]

On the very day Stolypin received Nicholas's letter, he drafted a penitent reply. He had no intention of creating difficulties for the tsar; and he would not try to get him to change his mind. But since word of the cabinet's decision had been leaked to the press, perhaps a flat veto of the project was not the best course. That would place the blame for the failure of the Jewish reform proposal fully on Nicholas's shoulders. Instead, the tsar should send an entirely new message indicating that he was not opposed to the prime minister's proposal in principle, but considered it unwise to introduce changes of such complexity hastily two months before the Duma was scheduled to meet. An announcement along these lines, Stolypin added, would also have the advantage of dispelling any notion that the tsar lacked confidence in his cabinet. If this approach was agreeable to the tsar, the Council of Ministers' journal would be changed to indicate that the cabinet had not insisted on issuing a decree on the Jewish question but had merely sought the monarch's permission either to invoke Article 87 of the Fundamental Laws or to submit the matter to the Duma. On December 11 Nicholas agreed to follow Stolypin's advice.[62]

This strange sequence of events raises a series of questions about Stolypin's attitude toward the Jewish question. Was he well disposed toward Jews or were the claims of some contemporaries accurate, that he was in fact hostile toward them? Did he abandon the reforms so quickly out of loyalty to the tsar, or was the Jewish question simply not a matter of high priority for him? His public statements and his policies on the Jewish question after 1907 are inconsistent and do not constitute, as Hans Rogger has put it, "a clear goal or unifying principle."[63]

One of Stolypin's personal memoranda in his archive on the reform proposal, a two-page handwritten document, is helpful in answering these questions. Written for himself alone to clarify his own thinking, there was no reason for him to dissemble. No one reading the document can fail to be struck by the absence of any of the pejorative references to Jews that were the stock-in-trade of Russian conservatives.[64] On the contrary, in two separate places he indicated understanding for the hurt felt by Jews at their treatment by the Russian authorities. After raising the question of whether policies toward the Jews should be liberalized, Stolypin made the following point: "Naturally—is it not abnormal to arouse and embitter a race of five million people? Clearly, this is wrong and the [Jewish] question must be diagnosed." Elsewhere, in the document he declared that the "government can take into account only moral necessity and moral principles. It cannot tolerate a situation under which a part of its citizens can justly consider itself offended and looks for relief in violence."[65] According to Syromiatnikov, at about the time Stolypin composed the note on the Jews he made the following, rather remarkable statement in a personal conversation: "The Jews throw bombs. And do you know the conditions under which they live in the Western parts [of the empire]? Have you seen the poverty of the Jews? If I lived under such conditions perhaps I too would start to throw bombs."[66] These views of the prime minister, incidentally, are consistent with attitudes he had formed during his long stay in Kovno, the center of a sizable Jewish community. Stolypin's daughter recalled that when she was growing up in Kovno, her father demonstrated in various ways that he was well disposed toward Jews.[67]

But if Stolypin favored a more liberal policy toward the Jews as a matter of principle, he was also a cautious politician sensitive to powerful pressures from different directions. As was his wont, he adopted a thoroughly pragmatic approach in evaluating the specific measures of reform that might be launched. In the very first sentence of his memorandum, he insisted that every initiative on the Jewish question must be undertaken under conditions of "complete calm" and always with an eye on "political and state needs." At the same time, the authorities must shun the practice—prevalent in the First Duma—of evaluating "all the principal questions from a purely theoretical standpoint." Nor would it be wise to tackle all the "evils of contemporary life" at once. In his view, the Jewish question deserved immediate attention, but he warned against yielding to the demands of the most passionate advocates of one policy or another. As he put it, there must be "no concessions to the revolutionaries' impudence and no harm to the native population, the Russian people."

Taking this as a basic principle, Stolypin ruled out the immediate abolition of the Pale of Settlement, which was one of the Jewish community's most pressing demands. It would be "frivolous," he insisted, to undertake such a major change without careful deliberation by the legislature. Nor did he think the time had come to grant Jews the same rights as other subjects to acquire landed property because of the "great financial means at the disposal of the Jews." He feared that Jews would succeed in buying up an inordinate amount of state lands available for purchase. Stolypin then made a general reference to abolishing some of the restraints imposed upon Jews in the Pale of Settlement—clearly the measures that he eventually submitted to his cabinet. But even while confining himself to modest reforms, Stolypin was by no means confident that he would succeed in implementing them. "We do not know whether the government will be able to do anything in this sphere or to what extent it can lighten the law [concerning Jews], but it is evident that the government cannot contemplate any measures beyond these limits." Stolypin feared resistance to his initiative but was vague on the likely sources of opposition. He did not so much as hint at the possibility of being overruled from above, by the tsar. He thought that his reforms might be attacked from two quarters: "People seized by passion [here he no doubt had in mind the extremists on the right] will not attempt to understand the issue and will begin to cry about betrayal"; on the other hand, "the Jews, wishing to prevail politically, will consider themselves offended by 'half measures.'"

In the last paragraph of the memorandum, very roughly drafted, Stolypin suggested that once the restraints on the Jews had been lightened in the cities and small towns of the Pale of Settlement without "immoral" consequences—that is, violence—it might be possible to consider eliminating the pale altogether. Fear of kindling massive attacks on the Jews was a constant theme in Stolypin's stress on gradual steps to ameliorate conditions for them.[68]

The contents of the personal note in Stolypin's archive leave no doubt about the sincerity of the prime minister's commitment to reform on the Jewish question. This conclusion is reinforced by comments Stolypin made in private conversations with the British ambassador to Russia, Sir Arthur Nicolson. On at least six different occasions during a two-year period, from July 1906 until June 1908, Nicolson and Stolypin had long confidential conversations on Russia's domestic situation, and each time the Jewish question came up. Inevitably, Stolypin reiterated his support for reform, going so far as to say that "he would be quite willing to see the Jew enjoying without stint all the rights appertaining to the Russians," though he persisted in his opposition to hasty action.[69]

One suspects that Stolypin did not fight harder for the implementation of his reform proposals on the Jewish issue because he was totally unprepared for the tsar's unequivocal opposition. That he did not initially consider this a possibility is suggested by his unpublished personal memorandum in which he made no mention at all of the monarch's likely attitude toward his initiative. If it had occurred to Stolypin that Nicholas might take so adamant a position, he would not have pressed the issue as hard as he did. An ardent believer in monarchical rule, the prime minister would not have taken a public stance in opposition to the tsar. In view of the tsar's hostility toward the Jews it is actually surprising that Stolypin expressed support for a more liberal policy in his conversations with the British ambassador. It is also surprising that late in 1906 he favored granting Jews the right to take part in elections for municipal councils (dumas), to serve on council boards, and to occupy certain administrative positions. Moreover, he expressed support for more lenient policies on various other issues: in 1907, on the expulsion of Jews from interior provinces; in 1908, on the barring of Jews from the armed services; and, finally, in 1909 on the raising of quotas for them in secondary schools.[70] Stolypin's subservience to the tsar was not unqualified.

Stolypin's defeat on the Jewish question demonstrated the prime minister's political weakness. Even on relatively modest reform proposals he could accomplish little if the tsar opposed him. But that was not his only concern. He needed a legislature that would ratify the measures he had introduced under Article 87 and that would go along with further reforms. The election for the Second Duma was in full swing in the fall of 1906, and the prime minister decided to make every effort to influence the outcome. Unlike Witte, the prime minister at the time of the election to the First Duma, he intended to intervene actively. As he told one of his supporters, government leaders in every country with elected parliaments helped candidates of their choice, and he saw no reason why he should abstain.[71] But he was clearly nervous about his ability to influence the voting. In late October he already feared the worst, and in a confidential conversation with the German ambassador he made it clear that if necessary he would dissolve the Second Duma more quickly than the first, "without giving the deputies an opportunity to create scandals."[72]

Stolypin's most serious problem in the electoral campaign, one that would bedevil him throughout his premiership, was that he did not have his own political party. There is no doubt that he understood the importance of mass parties in providing him with personal and legislative support, but unlike political leaders in other countries with parliamentary systems, he was hamstrung. He was, after all, utterly beholden to the tsar, the source of his political legitimacy. Would Nicholas, who was notoriously suspicious of any group with a defined political program, have tolerated the formation of a mass party led by Stolypin and providing him with an independent base of power? Merely to raise the question is to answer it. Not surprisingly, there is no evidence to indicate that Stolypin ever seriously thought about forming his own party. He knew that any move on his part in that direction would have spelled the end to his career as prime minister.

Without a party completely to his liking, Stolypin did the next best thing in the election: he supported in various ways parties he thought would support his program. His government legalized the reactionary Union of the Russian People and the Octobrists and, after some hesitation, the Group for Peaceful Renewal, a small party somewhat to the right of the Kadets. But the authorities continued to turn down all requests from the Kadets for registration as a political party, which meant that the liberals were not recognized as a legal association, could not maintain offices or clubs, and were prohibited from campaigning. But such were the oddities of political affairs in Russia that the Kadets were permitted to field candidates for the Duma and managed at times to circumvent other restrictions, on campaigning for example, that were imposed on them.

The government actively courted the extremists on the right. In September 1906 Stolypin sent a telegram to B. M. Insevich, chairman of the Monarchist Party and of the Kiev section of the Russian Assembly, to express his appreciation for the support he had offered the government.[73] In January 1907 *Pravo* reported that the Ministry of Internal Affairs had given the reactionary Union of the Russian People (URP) in Warsaw one thousand rubles to publish a new journal and three thousand rubles to cover the expenses of running the organization.[74] In St. Petersburg, several members of the URP held meetings at a number of police stations, where they conducted readings of a "special character" and then passed out appeals printed by the Black Hundreds. In one office the chief of police attended the reading, and when it was over, he ordered his men to lift the "lecturer-reader" on a chair as a mark of esteem.[75] Despite his later misgivings about the extremism of the URP, Stolypin always expressed gratitude to the organization for its help to the government when it was most needed. In March 1909, he wrote to General I. N. Tomachev, the governor of Odessa, about his personal recollections of the "important, one might say historical, role of the Union of Russian People during the troubles of 1905–1906 in the suppression of the revolutionary movement."[76] As a consequence, Stolypin found it difficult to break with the URP and to crack down on it even when it attacked him mercilessly.

Some years later, after the collapse of tsarism, it emerged that Stolypin had given small sums of money directly to A. I. Dubrovin, the head of the URP, even though his newspaper, *Russkoe znamia*, viciously attacked the prime minister. The details are not known because Stolypin, according to Kryzhanovskii, the deputy minister of internal affairs, had destroyed all the relevant documents. When Kryzhanovskii was asked if he was troubled by the expenditure of large sums of money to right-wingers and to selected newspapers without any receipts or accounting, he simply replied, "I represented Stolypin." As if to assuage his conscience, Kryzhanovskii claimed that the large sums of money he gave to the press did not yield anywhere near as many articles favorable to the government as he would have liked. He attributed his failure partly to his own inexperience and to his inability to devote sufficient time to cultivating the press. But he also claimed that the main reason for his poor showing was that he could not find enough experienced journalists to do his bidding, which, in his view, was not surprising, since most newspapers were controlled by the opposition and "people of Jewish descent."[77]

In the electoral campaign of 1906–7 the authorities also manipulated the electoral process and harassed the opposition in numerous ways. Thus the Senate issued a series of so-called clarifications that reduced the number of peasants, workers, and intelligentsia allowed to vote; and officials at all levels of government sought to restrict the activities of parties they considered to be untrustworthy.[78] But in the end, none of the government's efforts to influence the election succeeded. The results can only be described as an ignominious rout for Stolypin and his supporters. The Second Duma turned out to be far more radical than the first. The Octobrists increased their strength from 13 to 44, and the extremists on the right, without any representation in the First Duma, succeeded in electing 10 deputies and could count on the support of some 54 from other factions. But the number of left-wing deputies jumped from 111 to 222, with the Social Democrats, Socialist Revolutionaries, and Popular Socialists winning a total of 118 seats (as against 17 in the First Duma), and the other party of the left (the Trudoviks) 104. The parties of the center suffered a serious decline: the Kadets and their adherents won 99 seats; in the First Duma these groups were supported by 185 deputies. The Muslim group elected 30 and the Cossack group 17. The Polish Kolo ("Circle") raised its number of deputies from 32 to 46. The nonpartisans suffered the steepest decline, from 112 to 50.[79]

Ultraconservatives, the tsar's advisers at court, and the government could hardly have been more stunned. Although it had been clear for some time that the opposition would do very well, apparently no one in authority had expected so resounding a defeat. Rumors now began to circulate in the capital that Stolypin's government would be dismissed, to be replaced by Kokovtsov, who would reassure foreign bankers of Russia's stability. Stolypin had lost the confidence of the court because he had lost his gamble of holding another election without changing the electoral system.[80]

On February 7, 1907, the tsar's entourage* took the highly unusual step of convoking a meeting of the cabinet and senior court officials in Tsarskoe Selo to discuss the crisis. On only one previous occasion had a minister (Stolypin) ever attended a formal meeting of court officials. The agenda consisted of two items: the election and the stance to be taken toward the new Duma. Kokovtsov argued that the government had to

---

*"Entourage" is, admittedly, an imprecise term. On the other hand, it is less pejorative than "camarilla," the word widely used by contemporaries critical of the government. Whichever word is used, the point is that Nicholas did not rely only on the heads of various ministries for information and advice. He repeatedly sought the counsel of what can be called, for lack of a better word, his entourage, which, it should be stressed, was not a fixed group. At any particular time, it might include palace officials, close relatives, prominent citizens, and simply friends whose company the tsar enjoyed. General A. A. Mossolov, who occupied the senior post of director of the chancellery at court, claimed that many people "grossly exaggerated" the entourage's influence on the tsar. It is true that at times Nicholas reached critical decisions on his own, but there is little doubt that the court and outside advisers played a key role in his thinking on many issues of national importance. The most prominent member of the entourage in the years from 1905 to 1911 were Count V. B. Frederiks, the minister of the court; Count P. K. Benkendorf, the palace marshal; the Grand Dukes Nicholas Nokolaevich, Sergei Aleksandrovich, Alexander Mikhailovich, Michael Aleksandrovich, and Paul Aleksandrovich; Prince V. P. Meshcherskii, editor of the ultraconservative *Grazhdanin*; and K. P. Pobedonostsev, former procurator of the Most Holy Synod. For more details on the entourage, see Mossolov, *At the Court*, passim; and Verner, *The Crisis of Russian Autocracy*, pp. 67–69.

spell out its attitude toward the legislature quickly, since foreign stock exchanges were very nervous about political developments in Russia. The Western Europeans, he pointed out, feared an intensification of conflict in the empire and also feared that the people would not remain as calm as they had been during the period of the First Duma and its dissolution. Stolypin was more sanguine. It had come to his attention that the Kadets, "remembering the history of the First Duma," had decided not to pursue a revolutionary tactic; on the contrary, they intended to adhere strictly to the principles of constitutionalism. Stolypin expected the left to adopt revolutionary tactics immediately, but he assured the group that as long as the Kadets did not support the radicals, the extremists would be unable to muster a majority for such an approach. Consequently, he was not convinced that relations between the government and the legislature would immediately turn sour. He suggested that the government wait until the situation had become clearer before reaching any decision on how to deal with the Duma.

Stolypin's comments made a strong impression on several members of the tsar's entourage, which continued to meet after the departure of the ministers. The entourage had indeed been considering a change in government before the Duma met, but now some members of the group began to waver. In the end, the tsar's advisers decided to delay a final decision until Count Frederiks had a chance to consult with various public figures. They met twice more before the Duma was convened, but they were still unable to reach a decision on Stolypin's fate. When news of the various meetings at court appeared in *Russkie vedomosti*, the St. Petersburg Telegraph Agency, a government organ, denied that they had ever taken place. But there is good reason to dismiss the denial. The reporter who broke the story was a very well informed man with close connections to high officials. Moreover, his article was so detailed as to have the ring of truth.[81]

Politically weakened, Stolypin made a daring move to undermine the Kadet party, which was still not officially registered as a legal political party. He invited Miliukov, the party's leader, to his office, and in a state of great agitation proposed a deal. If the Duma would condemn political assassinations, he would legalize the Kadet party, whose votes would be essential for a condemnation of terrorism by the legislature. Although the defeat of terrorism was a paramount concern to Stolypin, he had an ulterior motive in making the overture to Miliukov. The prime minister thought that a repudiation of terror by the Kadet leadership might split the party, encouraging the right wing to align itself with the Octobrists and moderate conservatives. The result would be a pro-

government majority in the Duma. It is not clear that Miliukov immediately grasped all the implications of the prime minister's proposal, but
he was taken aback by its boldness. He told Stolypin that he could not
speak for the entire party, which for reasons of "political tactics" refused to condemn revolutionary terror. In any case, it seemed to Miliukov unrealistic to expect the Kadets to yield on this issue to government officials who themselves regularly murdered political opponents.
Stolypin then appealed to Miliukov not as the leader of a Duma faction
but as a contributor to *Rech*, a paper with close ties to the Kadets.
"Write an article denouncing assassinations; I will be satisfied with
that." Miliukov still demurred, though he was tempted by the thought
that he might be able to end the persecution of his party. Finally, he
agreed to run an article on condition that he would not sign it. Stolypin
accepted the condition, which seemed to him to be meaningless, since
Miliukov's style was easily recognizable. Miliukov then added another
condition. He would have to secure the agreement of other Kadet leaders. Once again, the prime minister yielded. If the article appeared, the
party would be legalized.

Miliukov could not, however, secure agreement from other party
leaders, and the deal fell through. In his memoirs Miliukov claimed that
at the time of the discussion with Stolypin he did not realize that "the
fate of the Duma" depended on his making the necessary gesture, that
is, issuing a statement uttering the "sacred words" denouncing political
terror. Stolypin, Miliukov acknowledged years after the meeting, was
then under great pressure from the right, and he needed "some sort of
paper or some sort of gesture from the leading party in order to strengthen and perhaps even to save his own position. Otherwise he faced having to surrender to the right."[82] Certainly, Miliukov's rejection of
Stolypin's proposal lent weight to the prime minister's—and even more
to the ultraconservatives'—conviction that the liberals still banked on a
popular upheaval to bring them to power. It seemed to them that the
Kadets could not sever their ties, however tenuous, to the revolutionaries. This did not augur well for the future of the Duma, scheduled to begin its meetings on February 20.

The extraordinary meetings at court on the government's future
dramatized, at one and the same time, the strength and political precariousness of Stolypin, seven months after he took office. On the one hand,
he had established himself as a forceful and respected leader with a clear
vision of the country's future direction. He had enacted several notable
reforms, and he had taken firm action to suppress terrorism. No one
doubted that the prime minister himself had been the moving force be-

hind all these measures. He had, moreover, had considerable success in asserting the principle of cabinet unity, a significant change in the administration of public affairs in Russia. The tsar acknowledged Stolypin's pre-eminence in a rescript he sent to the prime minister on January 1, 1907, in which he lavished praise on the Council of Ministers for its achievements "under your leadership" in restoring order. This was not an isolated expression of the tsar's confidence. He also bestowed upon Stolypin the rank of Steward of the Household and the Order of St. Anna I of the First Degree, with the following laudatory words: "In recognition of exemplary, dedicated, and selfless service."[83] A few weeks earlier, Nicholas had written his mother that "I cannot tell you how much I have come to like and respect [Stolypin]."[84]

However, there were also good reasons for the prime minister to be apprehensive. Not only had he failed to secure a favorable outcome in the elections; there were also signs of disharmony within the government. The most serious rift was with the minister of war, Rediger, who had been much impressed with Stolypin when he became prime minister, describing him as "young, energetic, confident in Russia's future, [a man who] undertook reforms decisively." By the late summer of 1906, however, relations between the two men had begun to fray because, in Rediger's words, the prime minister wished "to be the boss over the army." Initially, the specific point at issue was the use of the army to put down unrest. Stolypin endlessly pressed Rediger to deploy troops for police work: to protect railroads, banks, post offices, and liquor stores. As a result, in the Caucasus and Warsaw, many soldiers spent all their time on duty patrolling the streets. In the first ten months of 1906, Rediger complained, civilian authorities called on the military to carry out police functions on no fewer than 2,330 occasions. In 158 instances, soldiers fired their weapons on civilians. These were duties that the men did not relish and for which they had not been trained. They would, Rediger warned, "quickly cease to be soldiers." The minister of war sent one protest after another to the prime minister about the "abuse" of the military, but to no avail. In one letter, Rediger declared that "I have the honor to inform Your Excellency that I deem my primary task to be the preservation of the troops in order that they might above all answer to their chief function," which was external defense.[85] The solution to the problem would have been to increase the police force, but Kokovtsov refused to allot additional funds for that. Hence Stolypin argued that the army must be used to deal with the most urgent problem facing the government, the "establishment of order and security."[86]

Rediger was also deeply angered by the prime minister's practice of bestowing special rewards and promotions to senior officers of the gendarmes and police without consulting the Ministry of War, even though that was a legal requirement. This issue came to a head when in October 1906 Stolypin on his own authority promoted Baron Nolken, a colonel in the gendarmes, to the rank of major general. In response to Rediger's formal protest to the Council of Ministers, Stolypin stated that the tsar had approved the promotion. Rediger raised the matter with the tsar, who told him that he had directed the prime minister to obtain his (Rediger's) agreement. When Rediger confronted Stolypin with this information, the prime minister flew into a rage and threatened to resign. Rediger, according to his own account, remained cool, declaring that it was not up to him to make any judgment on Stolypin's political future. He had to protect the prerogatives of the Ministry of War. At this Stolypin "began to tell me about the burdens and dangers of service in the Ministry of Internal Affairs." Rediger sympathized but refused to budge, and Nolken did not receive the promotion. From that moment, relations between the two ministers remained strained, so much so that Rediger refused to attend sessions of the Council of Ministers.[87]

Stolypin thus was under considerable stress when, in December 1906, he granted an interview to P. A. Tverskoi (pseudonym for Petr Dementev, Americanized as Peter Demens), in which he revealed more about his aspirations and apprehensions and about his strengths and weaknesses as a political leader than in any other conversation. Tverskoi had left Russia for the United States in 1881, made a fortune as a railroad promoter and in several other businesses and also wrote articles on various subjects, many of which appeared in *Vestnik Evropy*. Before he set sail for Russia, Tverskoi had been asked by Melville Stone, the head of the American Associated Press, to share with him his impressions of Russia. Stone was not satisfied with the reports from the Associated Press's representative in St. Petersburg, a certain Mr. Conger, who was a capable man but knew no Russian and did not understand conditions in Russia. Tverskoi had good connections with political and literary circles in St. Petersburg, who helped him to meet influential people in the capital and provided him with interesting information, but he quickly concluded that only Stolypin himself could enlighten him about the state of affairs in Russia. After all, it was a widely held view that in "Stolypin [the country] had at last found that Bismarck who had been sought in vain for a long time, a man of fervor and steel, who stopped at nothing in striving to attain a set goal. . . ." Stolypin agreed to see him on a Saturday afternoon and agreed to talk with him uninterruptedly until all of Tverskoi's questions had been answered. The interview lasted two and a half hours. That same evening Tverskoi wrote down the prime minister's answers, which were remarkably candid, and he was certain that his notes accurately reflected Stolypin's comments. His account of Stolypin's views and his analysis of his personality are more detailed and insightful than those of any other person who knew Stolypin.

Strangely, Tverskoi waited almost six years before publishing an article on the interview. He gave an interesting explanation for the delay. He sensed that despite Stolypin's candor the prime minister was not really his own man and was therefore not the person to enlighten him about the direction in which the country was moving. To be sure, Stolypin had made a very strong impression on Tverskoi. The prime minister was clearly an "energetic, quick-witted man, with all the resources of an executive, a man with an iron will, who, however, adjusts himself and will always adjust himself to someone else." Although he was not reticent, his responses were always ambiguous. Not once did Tverskoi have the sense that the prime minister was giving completely independent and spontaneous answers. "If he was a Bismarck, then he was an entirely one-sided" replica of the German chancellor. "Bismarck combined in his person both a powerful locomotive and the driver of the machine—but Stolypin seemed to me to be only the locomotive."[88]

Stolypin made several statements to suggest this portrait. When Tverskoi asked whether there were issues on which the prime minister felt obliged to act with extreme caution and whether there were limitations on his willingness to act against his own better judgment, Stolypin responded that "I am first of all loyal to the Tsar and am the executor of his plans and commands." Elsewhere during the interview, he repeated this point, insisting that "I and the cabinet are only executors, not lawgivers. We are doomed to wait."[89] Tverskoi pressed him on the point by asking the prime minister about his intention to resign, for Stolypin had indicated that on several occasions he had thought of leaving his post. His answer revealed much about his sense of duty, but it also revealed a sense of pride in his influence. In other words, although he was the tsar's servant and could not resist him on issues on which the ruler was adamant, there were many areas in which he could affect the ruler's decisions. Stolypin had not resigned, he said, because he knew that he would inevitably be replaced by someone like Durnovo or Stishinskii, both of whom opposed him and his policies. "I am firmly convinced that such a change would be harmful for the government and for society. It would put a halt to the tranquillity that has begun to set in, would delay the transition [from martial law] to normalcy, [and] could even provoke God knows what. Our society is still in ferment. Politically, it is still extremely shortsighted and insufficiently educated; otherwise it would be clear [to society] that under existing conditions a more liberal government than mine is unthinkable, whereas the possibility of [moving to] the opposite direction is essentially unlimited."[90] Stolypin's assessment of his precarious political position was correct. He was situated between the reactionaries on the right and the liberals on the left. Whether he would survive politically would depend on the person who continued to be the final arbiter of politics, the tsar.

Stolypin made it clear that in his view this state of affairs was not likely to change in the foreseeable future. True, the October Manifesto had introduced important political changes, but the tsar's authority had not been vitiated.* And that authority, Stolypin said in response to a pointed query by Tverskoi, was the legal basis for placing much of the country under some form of emergency rule. He insisted that there could be no doubt that conditions warranted resort to such an extreme measure. "It is impossible to deny and one cannot overlook the fact that in the recent period the spirit of anarchy had seized not only the people and society but even the personnel of the governmental authorities. It was a kind of measles or scarlet fever. And this personnel was disorganized as never before, as was everyone else. The entire country was derailed." He went on to point out that in many parts of the country there was no authority at all, and for some months dozens of small republics had flourished. The government's impotence, in fact, had "compelled me more than once to think of resigning." Nothing, he declared, would please him more than to be convinced that normal conditions had returned and that he could abandon martial law and "remove from my shoulders, . . . from my conscience[,] a terrible burden."[91]

On the whole, Stolypin was cautiously optimistic, though he foresaw serious difficulties for his government. Russia was experiencing a "transitional period," and basic changes in the "state system" were impossible without "zigzags." The process would be slow and full of pitfalls, but gradually the country would be transformed along the lines he envisioned. The next major test would be whether the government and the Second Duma would be able to cooperate. He had his doubts but insisted that, if the legislators showed interest in serious work, his government would cooperate to the best of its abilities. "If not, we will dissolve [the Duma]." After the experience with the First Duma, such a

---

*For a discussion of Stolypin's views on the nature of the Russian autocracy after the October Manifesto, see above, pp. 126–28.

course of action did not seem to him to be "so terrible." After all, in the transition to a representative system the Prussian authorities had frequently dissolved parliament, and he suggested that he was prepared to do the same. And he promised not to change the electoral procedures under any circumstances. "Absolutely. There will not be the slightest change in this respect. This would be a revolution from above. We intend to achieve order with . . . [procedures] we now have. The present system [of voting] is absolutely firm insofar as this depends on the government."[92]

Initially, when the Second Duma met on February 20, 1907, it appeared as though relations between the legislature and the government might be harmonious. On the very day of the first meeting, Stolypin expressed satisfaction to the tsar about the chamber's conduct of affairs. To be sure, the left did not join the rightists in cheering when the deputy P. N. Krupenskii shouted "Long Live the Sovereign Emperor! Hurrah!" but neither did the left stage a counterdemonstration. The Kadet president of the Duma, F. A. Golovin, had given a brief address that Stolypin considered "decent."[93] His expression of willingness to work with the monarch was especially welcome, and his cordial reception by the tsar at a private audience encouraged the Kadets. Two weeks later, after Stolypin gave an address to the Duma (on March 6), the prime minister was still hopeful about working with the legislature, despite some sharp attacks on him. "The mood of the Duma," he told Nicholas, "is very different from that of last year, and during the entire time of the meeting there was no shouting and no whistling." The prime minister thought that a majority consisting of Kadets, Octobrists, rightists, and the Polish Kolo might be formed. Such a moderate right-center coalition might well prove capable of cooperating with the government.[94] Most of the deputies initially shared Stolypin's optimism about the legislature's ability to work constructively.

Stolypin still feared, however, that the left-wing deputies, a sizable contingent in the Second Duma, would again become disruptive and would go to great lengths to arouse the public to take up arms against the government. On February 24, 1907, he sent another circular to senior officials throughout the empire, this time urging them to maintain vigilance over mass meetings where deputies were scheduled to speak. Meetings of revolutionary organizations should be prohibited "without delay or hesitation."[95] Yet there can be no doubt that the prime minister sincerely hoped to avoid a break with the Duma. His motives were broadly ideological as well as personal. On the one hand, he wished to

institutionalize the structure of government established by the Fundamental Laws. On the other hand, he believed that his own political fate
was closely linked to the fate of the Second Duma. If he were forced to
dissolve the legislature, he told a French correspondent, he would not be
able to remain at his post. Stolypin revealed that P. N. Durnovo and
Goremykin were engaged in fierce intrigues against him and were only
waiting for him to falter. By the same token, if the cabinet resigned,
things would go badly for the Duma, "since it has many enemies and
few defenders in the highest circles." For his part, Stolypin did not intend to dissolve it so long as it remained "innocent"—that is, as long as
it did not become unruly.[96]

The goodwill between the Duma and the government did not last
very long. For one thing, Golovin's relations with Stolypin quickly
soured. Golovin conceded that he was partly responsible for a series of
misunderstandings between them, but he placed most of the blame on
Stolypin, who, he claimed, tended to regard the legislature as little more
than a department subordinate to the government and its president as
merely a department head bound to take orders from the bureaucrats. In
addition, Golovin never trusted Stolypin, which surely contributed to
the bad blood between them. Some of their disagreements appear to
have been trivial, but they reflected real conflicts over the respective
prerogatives of the prime minister and the president and, by extension,
over the independence of the legislature.

By law, the prime minister, not the president, controlled the guards
at the entrance of the Tauride Palace, where the Duma met. The officers
in charge of the guards, an *Okhrana* colonel, Baron N. D. Osten-Sacken,
and his assistant, a captain of the gendarmes, Ponomarev, kept careful
watch over the gate and would allow no one to enter who did not have a
pass approved by Stolypin's office. Golovin managed to bring some of
his friends into the building only by personally accompanying them. But
the wife of the Duma secretary, Mme. Chelnokova, was stopped at the
gate when she wanted to visit her husband. The ostensible reason for the
tight security was to protect ministers against assassination, but in fact
Stolypin applied the rules against outsiders very broadly to prevent experts from participating in committees that sought their advice. On
March 26 the Famine Relief Committee was forced by an official of the
Ministry of Internal Affairs to ask several experts, who had somehow
entered the building, to leave before testifying. Golovin protested to
Stolypin, who upheld his ministry's authority over outsiders. But he
then allowed G. E. Lvov, a well-known figure in society, to testify before
the committee. In this instance, Stolypin was willing to relax the rules

because Lvov was a member of an official committee on the famine. In a subsequent exchange of letters, Stolypin and Golovin quibbled over the interpretation of the rules on outsiders; Stolypin seems to have had the stronger case in claiming the right to decide on the invitation of outsiders, but in insisting on this right he inevitably gave the impression of favoring traditional bureaucratic procedures. He announced that he would allow experts to testify at committee hearings only when the president and the prime minister agreed that the testimony was necessary. It was not a satisfactory agreement.[97]

The two men also quarreled over the jurisdiction of the police within the Tauride Palace. A particular source of irritation for the deputies were the frequent attempts by *Okhrana* agents to prevent journalists from speaking to them. Golovin protested to Baron Osten-Sacken, who claimed that he was simply carrying out orders. Golovin then complained to Stolypin, who in March announced that he had ordered police agents to stop their "activities" within the building.[98]

At bottom, the problem was that, despite Stolypin's wish to work with the Duma, he deeply distrusted the deputies, many of whom, not only the avowed radicals, he considered sympathetic to the revolutionary cause. Police spies kept a close watch on the legislators, and late in March, Stolypin sent a circular to all governors ordering them to put an immediate stop to peasant meetings that some deputies were organizing and to punish the deputies for engaging in illegal actions. To hamper contact between the capital and local activists, the government also directed the main telegraph office in St. Petersburg to screen all telegrams sent out by left-wing deputies. In some localities the police ordered telegraph offices not to accept any telegrams emanating from the State Duma.[99]

Another source of Stolypin's irritation with the Duma was his growing suspicion that the deputies had little interest in constructive work. On March 14, only eight days after he had expressed satisfaction with the chamber's conduct of business, the prime minister wrote to the tsar that "in the State Duma a spate of inflammatory words continues [to be uttered], and nothing is heard about work [on legislative proposals]."[100] Nicholas, too, expressed impatience with the Duma; as early as March 3 he told the German ambassador that the new Duma would soon dig its own grave. Golovin made a special effort to assure the monarch that the Duma could work effectively, but he did not succeed. Not long after the meeting with Golovin, Nicholas told Stolypin that the intemperate speeches of the deputies "constitute a serious danger to tranquillity in the villages." And more revealingly, he wrote to his mother that he was getting telegrams from everywhere asking him to order a dissolution. "But it is too early for that. One must let them [the deputies] do something manifestly stupid or mean, then—slap! And they are gone."[101] Both the tsar and Stolypin had become unnerved by the tenor of the Duma debates, which, if anything, were even more intemperate than those of the first legislature.

The Kadets, again the dominant force in the Duma, had not changed their program on any major issue, but they had modified their tactics to reflect their basic concern, "to preserve the Duma." They went to great lengths to avoid supporting measures the authorities might consider provocative. Instead of concentrating on projects of fundamental consequence to the political and social order, they planned to focus on more incremental changes. To maintain their moderate stance, they would seek to form two different majorities. They would vote with the rightists on procedural and tactical questions but on programmatic issues they would side with the left. But such a neat division soon turned out to be unfeasible. As soon as two key issues, terror and agrarian reform, came up for consideration it became obvious that their approach would not work. Whatever stand they took on either one of these issues would inevitably infuriate either the right or the left. The Kadets therefore opted for a policy of delay; and for several weeks they succeeded in preventing a vote on any major issue, tactical or substantive, so as not to antagonize the government. But the strategy enraged the leftists, who accused the liberals of abandoning their principles. At the same time, right-wing deputies reviled the Kadets, in particular the Kadet president, for not muzzling the radicals, who persisted in using the Duma as a tribune from which to agitate for revolution. In truth, the extremists on the right and the left were much more interested in theatrics than in legislation. The left-wing firebrands expected their denunciations of the government to incite the masses to undertake a new assault on the old order. The firebrands on the right expected those antics to expose the impotence of the Duma and the treachery of many of the deputies. Once that became clear, the rightists presumed, the tsar would be faced with the necessity of doing what they wanted—dissolve the despised legislature. Count V. I. Bobrinskii, the right-wing Octobrist, was not wrong when in a moment of great agitation he said to Bernard Pares, the English historian of Russia, in the corridor of the Tauride Palace: "It's bedlam! It's madness!"[102]

Hardly any session of the Duma was wholly free of rancor, but the deputies managed to avoid a major confrontation until the fifth session, on March 6, when Stolypin gave his first address. It was a measured but

also a lofty speech in which he presented the overall goal of the government and outlined the projects it planned to introduce for the Duma's
consideration. The principle that guided the cabinet, he asserted, was
"to create the material norms in which will be embodied the new legal
relations that flow from all the reforms of the recent period. Reorganized
according to the will of the Monarch, our country will be transformed
into a state based on law. . . . [The government will present an entire series of bills] to create the firm foundations for a new political system in
Russia."[103]

The program he now spelled out was consistent with the one he had
published in the newspapers on August 25, but he provided the Duma
deputies with far more details. Stolypin had directed officials in six departments (Internal Affairs, Justice, Finance, Trade and Industry, Transportation, and Education) to develop reform proposals for submission to
the Duma. On January 12, 1907, the cabinet discussed and approved
forty-two measures for the tsar's consideration. Then, two weeks later,
the cabinet devoted two meetings (on January 26 and 30) to three proposals of the Ministry of Education for the creation of a system of universal primary education, a subject of special interest to Stolypin ever
since his days as governor of Grodno. "Every child of both sexes," the
ministry's statement began, "must have the opportunity, on reaching
school age, to take a full course of study in an appropriately organized
elementary school." The forty-five proposals of the six ministries,
touching on virtually every aspect of the country's domestic affairs,
were approved by the tsar and became the basis of Stolypin's first address to the Second Duma.[104]

Stolypin began his speech with a brief reference to the agrarian
measures he had already enacted under Article 87 and which would now
come up for consideration by the Duma and the State Council. Beyond
that, the first item on the government's schedule was to "develop legislative projects . . . [to establish] the legal foundations that were promulgated by the Manifesto of October 17 [and] for which no laws have [as
yet] been enacted." Specifically, that would entail laws to guarantee
freedom of speech, assembly, press, association, inviolability of the individual, freedom of worship, and privacy of personal correspondence.
Stolypin promised to introduce bills to place "local affairs on new principles"—namely, that local organs of self-government would be based
on the principle of the legal equality of all citizens. The estate principle,
according to which the votes of certain privileged classes counted for
more than the votes of the rest of the population, would be abolished.
The administrations of local authority, including the police, would be

thoroughly overhauled. He also promised to introduce self-government (zemstvos) in the Baltic and western regions and in the Polish Kingdom; on that issue he gave a hint of future problems, for he indicated that the "special interests" of "the purely Russian population [living there] from olden times" would receive favorable consideration. This suggested that he meant somehow to deal with conditions that placed ethnic Russians in a politically subservient position. The prime minister also vowed to reform the court system and to submit a bill on "the civil and criminal responsibility of civil servants" charged with misconduct.

In his list of reform proposals Stolypin did not neglect social measures. He promised to take up the issue of the peasants' need for more land and the unsatisfactory conditions in the industrial workplace. The main benefit for industrial workers would be a system of insurance to cover medical expenses, help for those injured at work and for invalids, and pensions for retirees. He reiterated his support for a system of compulsory primary education for every citizen and promised to submit legislative proposals for the creation of an extensive network of schools. Finally, Stolypin promised to develop legislative projects to protect the interests of Russian commerce and industry in the Far East as well as to expand the country's transportation system. He acknowledged, toward the end of his speech, that his wide-ranging program would require huge financial outlays and asked the Duma and the State Council to offer him advice on his program. He then extended his hand to the deputies in a conciliatory gesture: "The government is ready," he said, "to apply the greatest efforts in this direction [of reform]: its work, its goodwill, the experience it has accumulated, will be placed at the disposal of the State Duma, which will receive the cooperation of a government conscious of its duty to preserve the historical traditions of Russia and to restore order and calm, that is, of a firm and purely Russian government, such as the government of His Majesty should be and will be (*stormy applause from the right*)."[105]

If a liberal had delivered the prime minister's speech, a large number of deputies would have applauded most of it. After all, Stolypin was calling for a radical reordering of Russian society. His comments on the agrarian question did not please the liberals or the left, but other than that he proposed many of the reforms demanded by the opposition. But Stolypin was a conservative. He spoke in the name of the tsar, and he was using the mailed fist in seeking to crush the revolution. So it was not surprising that the prime minister's address pleased few in the chamber. Still, the intensity of the attacks on it were astonishing. The first to rise was I. G. Tsereteli, a twenty-five-year-old Georgian who had already demonstrated so remarkable a gift in practical politics that he had been elected chairman of the sixty-five Social Democrats in the Duma.

An eloquent and fiery speaker, Tsereteli let loose with a barrage of attacks on Stolypin and the government so savage that it provoked catcalls by the rightists. Many people may have been surprised, Tsereteli said, at the "deathly silence" with which the deputies had listened to the first address by the "government that had dissolved the Duma, the government of field courts-martial." But that silence reflected the "full force of our protest, the full depth of our indignation." He went on to denounce the government for having placed the entire country under martial law, for having imprisoned its best sons, and for having squandered funds meant to aid starving people. It was an autocratic government "indissolubly linked" to a small group of "landlords who advocate serfdom and live at the expense of millions of hapless peasants." At this point, the right began to shout "Away with him, lies," while the left applauded. After a brief interruption, Tsereteli continued in the same vein, accusing the government of having provoked pogroms and of having refused to subordinate itself to the legislature. "Only with the direct support of the people will it be possible to stop the wild outburst of violence that has devastated the country." Several deputies vehemently protested this obvious call for mass action, and Golovin asked Tsereteli "not to issue appeals for an armed uprising." Tsereteli denied making such an appeal; he was merely pointing out the obvious, that the "government invites an armed uprising."[106] Several other left-wing deputies joined in the attack on the government, and at one point a few of them demonstratively left the chamber.

Prince P. D. Dolgorukov, a Kadet, tried to bring the vituperation to an end, but few responded to his appeal. The nasty exchanges continued, with V. M. Purishkevich, one of the more colorful and impulsive leaders of the right wing in the Duma, unleashing a stinging attack on the opposition. But it was Stolypin himself who delivered the most eloquent and dramatic response to the left. Enraged by the tenor of the debate, he asked for the floor toward the end of the session. He repeated the government's commitment to act only within the limits of the law and warned that even if the Duma failed to support the government, it would not shirk its responsibility. It would not give up its role as protector of the state and the unity of the Russian people. He did not intend to restrain deputies who wished to work for the well-being of Russia from pursuing their deliberations, even if they differed with his proposals. And he would welcome the unmasking of any violation of the law, any abuse. Whoever was guilty would be brought to justice. But having said that, he also vowed that the government would react differently to those who attacked it intemperately and encouraged open defiance of the authorities. "Such attacks are aimed at paralyzing the government, they all amount to two words addressed to the authorities: 'Hands up.' To these two words, gentlemen, the government must respond, in complete calm and secure in the knowledge that it is in the right, with only two words: 'Not afraid.'"[107] When Stolypin returned to his seat, all the other ministers gave him an ovation such as no other minister had ever received in the Duma. Maklakov, then a Kadet deputy, recalled that "many of us were only prevented by party discipline from applauding. [His speech] made an enormous impression throughout the country. . . . March 6 was the climax of Stolypin's popularity."[108]

The accolades from all over the empire were so numerous and heartwarming that the prime minister's office placed them in a huge, leatherbound volume that was entitled, in golden script, "6 March 1907." Most of the telegrams, letters, and postcards came from solidly conservative organizations or individuals such as church officials and army officers. But at least thirteen letters of congratulation were sent by local branches of the Octobrist movement. Also, a fair number seem to have been written by ordinary people moved by his show of defiance, courage, and patriotism. One wrote: "Today, dear Petr Arkadevich, you have once again presented a bright and lofty moment to all Russians who live in their country." Another citizen wrote in French: "Felycitons [sic!] chaleureusement admirable discours [d'un] vrai homme d'etat" (We warmly congratulate the admirable speech of a true statesman).[109] Stolypin's conduct shortly after the attempt to assassinate him in August 1906 had raised his moral stature at court and in political circles generally; his speech on March 6, 1907, turned him into a hero among all those who yearned for calm and stability. According to V. V. Shulgin, a highly intelligent right-wing deputy, the prime minister's words resonated throughout Russia. "Having lost the ground from under our feet, we [again] had faith in the people in authority, [and believed] that Russia had again found a strong government. The army, the bureaucracy, the police, and every citizen who did not want a revolution became more cheerful and self-confident. This was accomplished by two words: Not afraid."[110]

Golovin, no admirer of Stolypin, later conceded that the government and the right generally had emerged from the skirmish of March 6 with a "moral victory." Although the prime minister was widely distrusted, he had indicated a willingness to work with the Duma. The deputies on the left, however, refused to put him to the test. And the silence of the center during the debate was interpreted as a reluctance to cooperate with the government even when the two did not disagree. It would have been much wiser, according to Golovin, for the Duma to have been more forthcoming, at least until the government's intentions had become clearer.[111] It is hard to quarrel with Golovin's judgment.

Indeed, it soon became apparent that the extremists on the right and the left were more interested in debating the virtues of mass action of one kind or another than in passing legislation on concrete issues. The subject under discussion varied, but at bottom the controversies centered on the legitimacy of seeking change by revolutionary means. Both the rightists and the leftists had been traumatized by the turbulence of the preceding two years, and none of them could come to grips with the need to focus on any issue less cosmic than revolution itself. With tedious regularity, debates degenerated into brawls.[112]

By late March 1907, rumors began to circulate in the capital that the court was seriously considering dissolving the Duma. According to other rumors, intrigues against Stolypin at court were proceeding at a feverish pace. Ultraconservatives, troubled by the prime minister's advocacy of reform and willingness to work with the Duma, denounced him as "untrustworthy" and "two-faced"; in favoring equal rights for Jews he "is playing a dangerous game." Some even referred to him as the "Kadet minister." There was talk of his being replaced soon by either Krivoshein or Durnovo. Some ultraconservatives advocated the establishment of a dictatorship under Admiral F. V. Dubasov, the suppressor of the Moscow uprising in December 1905.[113]

Stolypin's speech in the Duma on March 13 on the field courts-martial further undermined the rightists' confidence in the prime minister. Stürmer contended that Stolypin had given a bad speech that convinced listeners that the "government was weaker than the opposition."[114] It is true that Stolypin had made some conciliatory statements to the opposition. In keeping with his appeal to Miliukov for a denunciation of terror, he urged the deputies on the left to utter "a conciliatory word [indicating] that you will stop the bloody madness [that is, the terror]." If that were done, the government would undertake to "limit the harsh law to only the most exceptional cases of the most insolent crimes." Moreover, if the Duma encouraged Russia to pursue the path of "calm work" the government would not ask the deputies to vote on an extension of the law on field courts-martial but would allow it to lapse. Stolypin was in effect offering the Duma the same deal he had offered Miliukov. But Stolypin also made it clear that so long as the terror continued the government would not abandon the law. "When the state finds itself in danger, it must, it is obliged to, resort to the most severe, the most exceptional laws to protect itself against disintegration. This was, this is, this will always be immutable." He justified this principle by telling the deputies that when "a house is on fire, . . . you break into a stranger's house, you break the doors, you break the windows. When a person is ill, you treat his body with poison; when an assassin attacks you, you kill him. Every state recognizes [the legitimacy] of such conduct."[115] This defense of the field courts-martial did not satisfy the ultraconservatives. But in fact there was not much the government could do. It was clear that the Duma would never vote to confirm the ukase establishing the courts. Stolypin had no choice but to allow the ukase to lapse as of April 20, the last day on which it remained constitutionally on the books.

Stolypin's insistence on maintaining the courts till the last moment was not one of the prime minister's wiser decisions. He had known all along that the Duma would never consent to extending the life of the courts, and he also knew that the system of summary justice deeply offended not only left-wing but also centrist deputies. He could have earned much goodwill both among the Kadets and among the moderates had he abolished the courts in February, when the Duma was convened, or soon thereafter. He believed he needed the special courts to fight terrorism, but in addition he attached great symbolic and political importance to the question. If he could persuade the Duma to issue an outright condemnation of terror, the revolutionary left would be discredited and that, in turn, would help restore tranquillity to the country. Stolypin thus retained the field courts-martial as a bargaining chip in his desperate hope of inducing the Duma to repudiate terror. The ploy did not work.

On the contrary, relations between the government and the Duma continued to deteriorate at an alarming pace. On April 16, a storm erupted in the Duma over remarks by A. G. Zurabov, a thirty-four-year-old Social Democrat from Armenia denigrating the Russian army. According to Stolypin's daughter, that evening her father appeared at the dinner table "with an exceedingly disturbed face. . . . The leftists had permitted speeches by so many revolutionaries that he had begun to wonder whether it would ever be possible to work with the people who occupied such an irreconcilable position with regard to existing authority."[116] The uproar began when Zurabov, during a discussion of a bill to fund the recruitment of 463,050 men for the army and navy for 1907, called for a people's army to replace the regular army and then cast aspersions on the military forces, claiming that they "will never be fit for external defense." He also predicted that the army would be used to crush the opposition and the Duma.[117] Outraged by these comments, the rightists unloosed a barrage of howls so loud and persistent that Golovin could barely restore order. When Golovin, hoping to mollify the right, suggested that Zurabov had been misunderstood, the Social Democrat repeated, more forcefully than before, that "the army of autocratic Russia always was and will be defeated." The right became even more indignant and shouted: "Away with him! Get out!" Several right-wingers ran up to the rostrum shaking their fists at Zurabov, who turned pale. It looked as though the Social Democrat would be physically assaulted then and there. Golovin rang the bell in an effort to restore calm, but to no effect. All the ministers and other officials demonstratively stalked out of the hall. Golovin recessed the meeting.[118]

After failing to pacify the officials in the ministerial pavilion, Golovin returned to his office, where he received a telephone call from an angry Stolypin. The prime minister asked for details about the incident and told Golovin that the tsar was astonished that neither the Duma nor its president had protested Zurabov's attack on the army. Stolypin also indicated that the emperor was considering disbanding the legislature. Golovin tried to assuage Stolypin's anger: Zurabov, he said, was himself an army officer, and he had spoken only for himself and not for the Duma. Moreover, because of the tumult created by the right-wingers, he (Golovin) had not been able to respond properly to Zurabov on the floor of the chamber. Stolypin was not mollified by these arguments.[119] In a desperate effort to appease the government, Golovin secured enough support in the Duma to authorize him to prevent Zurabov from resuming his speech on the army. It was an unusual punishment for a deputy, a clear reprimand, but it did not satisfy the right-wing deputies.

Several leading Kadets warned Golovin that the authorities also did not consider the Zurabov incident closed. Determined to avoid dissolution of the Duma, Golovin immediately telephoned Stolypin, who invited him to his office at the Winter Palace. It was then 1:00 or 2:00 A.M. The prime minister was still in a rage over the entire affair. "I could not but tell Golovin," Stolypin informed the tsar, "that in every foreign parliament a person such as Zurabov would be torn to shreds or, at least, would be given a lashing."[120] Nevertheless, Stolypin let Golovin know that he did not want to dissolve the Duma, but warned that the tsar might well decide to do so. Nicholas's decision would hinge on Rediger's report, due early that morning. Golovin asked the prime minister to urge Rediger to advise the tsar against dissolution and to set up a meeting between the president and minister of war before the latter's meeting with the tsar. As soon as Golovin reached his hotel, Stolypin called him. He had arranged an appointment with Rediger at eight o'clock, one hour before the minister was to leave for his audience with the tsar. Stolypin stressed that Golovin's conversation with Rediger would be critical. When Golovin met Rediger, he implored the minister of war to submit an "objective" report to the tsar and assured him that Zurabov misspoke and had not intended to insult the army. Rediger was satisfied and promised to advise Nicholas not to dissolve the legislature. The tsar followed the minister's advice.[121]

On the surface, the political crisis caused by Zurabov's speech seemed to have ended on a harmonious note. Stolypin was still eager to work with the Duma and had therefore intervened to calm ruffled feathers. In testimony to the Commission of Inquiry in 1917, Golovin contended that although the Zurabov affair gave Stolypin a perfect pretext for dissolving the Duma, he did all he could to avoid doing so. Stolypin, in Golovin's view, still wanted to retain the Duma and hoped it would pass bills, "of course, along the lines that would please him."[122] However, it soon became evident that the prime minister's attitude toward the legislature had changed. He now seemed to be much less interested in its affairs, rarely attended its sessions, and did not initiate any discussions with the president, Golovin.[123]

Two letters that Stolypin sent to the tsar in April indicate that the prime minister had in fact become disillusioned with the Duma, and that it was simply a matter of time before he turned against it completely. On April 9, he wrote Nicholas that the legislature "is rotting at the core, and many leftists, realizing this, would like a dissolution now so that they can create a legend that the Duma would have achieved miracles but that the government killed it and everything was thrown into confusion."[124] A week later, at the time of the Zurabov affair, Stolypin decided that if the Duma rejected the military bill it would have to be sent packing. And at a meeting of the cabinet on April 17, virtually all the ministers argued that the legislature should not be allowed to remain in session. Stolypin agreed with the majority, but he wanted to wait until a new electoral law was completed.[125]

It was not until late May, when it became evident that the Duma would not support his agrarian program, that the prime minister fully committed himself to drastic action against the legislature. When the agrarian issue first came up for discussion, Stolypin hoped that he could influence the course of the debate. But once it became apparent that all of the measures introduced by the various parties rejected the reforms Stolypin had introduced under Article 87, the prime minister became enraged. In a private meeting with the Kadet deputy P. B. Struve, Stolypin indicated that while he was prepared to make concessions on political and legal questions, he would not agree to abandon his agrarian program. Stolypin's chief concern was that the Duma committee on agriculture, which was proceeding in secret, would come up with a new proposal that he would find totally unacceptable. And that might force him to dissolve the Duma over the agrarian question, which he did not want to do because it might provoke unrest in the countryside. If the Duma was intent on passing a bill he could not accept, he wanted to know about it well in advance so that he could find another pretext for dissolving the legislature.[126] All hope of a compromise ended on May 9 with the adoption by the Duma committee of a measure favoring the expropriation of large amounts of privately owned lands. The Kadets, fearful of losing the support of the increasingly militant peasant deputies, supported the measure.[127]

The next day, May 10, Stolypin appeared in the Duma for a last-ditch effort to persuade the deputies to support his agrarian program. He began his speech with a conciliatory gesture. He granted that everyone who had spoken on the agrarian issue was sincerely concerned to find appropriate solutions. Consequently, he would pay no attention to the insults and charges leveled at the government. He would concentrate on an impartial and calm exposition of the government's views. He warned that the proposal of the left, nationalization, could not possibly solve the problem of the peasants' land hunger because there simply was not enough land available in European Russia. He cited an elaborate array of statistics to support his claim. He also warned that nationalization would undermine all existing legal relations, since it would abrogate the right of private property; it would produce a "social revolution" on a scale unprecedented in human history. The planned redistribution of the land might temporarily place everyone on an equal footing, but the outcome would be to depress the economic and cultural level of the country as a whole. Moreover, the equality would not last, since not all human beings were equal in their willingness to work or in their abilities. Eventually, the more gifted and industrious would re-establish private ownership of land. In the meantime, Russia would have endured a period of economic devastation. (From the vantage point of 2000, Stolypin's prognosis seems a remarkable prediction of the fate of Soviet policies of nationalization.)

Even though the Kadets opposed nationalization, their proposal for compulsory expropriation, according to Stolypin, also abrogated the principle of private property. Even under their plan no one's land would be safe any longer. Moreover, if the peasants expected to secure land where they lived, very few of them would move to other areas of the empire, such as Siberia. (Colonization of the Far East was part of Stolypin's reform program.) Furthermore, all 130,000 landowners would be deprived of their property in the end, which would mean "the destruction . . . of [local] centers of culture." Thus, the Kadet program would produce the same results as that of the socialist left, the ruin of the country.

Stolypin insisted that the only sensible alternative was the plan already in place. His government intended to create a prosperous, satisfied peasantry, a goal that could be reached only if the people in the countryside were freed from the restraints now imposed on them. "It is necessary to give them the possibility of increasing the fruits of their labor and to present them with an inalienable right to property." And that, the prime minister stressed, would be possible only if the commune ceased to exist. To encourage the peasant to leave the commune, the government planned to provide advice and financial credit. Stolypin granted that in addition to these measures, it might be necessary to confiscate some privately owned lands, but such confiscations would be exceptions, "not the general rule." The government would resort to such extreme measures only when they would be economically beneficial to society. He gave examples: the construction of a water trough or a well to facilitate pasturing, or the construction of a road passing through strips of land. In endorsing confiscations under exceptional circumstances, Stolypin made a very modest concession to the Kadets, but the overall thrust of his remarks was that the reforms introduced under Article 87 must remain intact. He ended with a powerful rhetorical flourish that was quoted almost as often as his "not afraid" declaration on March 6. "The opponents of the state system," he said, "would like to choose the path of radicalism, a path alien to Russia's historical past, alien to its cultural traditions. They need great upheavals, we need a great Russia!"[128] To underline the importance he attached to his message, Stolypin sent a copy of his speech to all governors, with a request that they distribute it to local officials, who were to post it on public walls in all towns and cities and to have it read at peasant meetings.[129]

The Second Duma never voted on the agrarian issue. Fearful of provoking Stolypin into dissolving the chamber, the Kadets decided simply to leave the issue in the hands of the committee charged with drafting a bill. The committee stalled. But that did not satisfy Stolypin, who continued to suspect that without warning the Duma would adopt a bill he could not live with.

By this time, the prime minister pursued a two-pronged approach to warn the Duma. On the one hand, in his speech to the Duma on the agrarian question he made a conciliatory gesture. He sought to woo the Kadets by offering to expropriate some privately held lands on a very limited basis. Preservation of the Duma was still his preferred policy. On the other hand, he sought to placate the tsar and the court entourage, who, he knew, were increasingly critical of his stance toward the legislature. Sometime in early May or late April he asked Kryzhanovskii, the deputy minister of internal affairs, to draft a new electoral law that would produce a majority of deputies from the "more cultivated strata of the population."[130]

Perhaps more important, sometime in April, Stolypin charged A. V. Gerasimov, the head of the St. Petersburg *Okhrana*, with locating documents that would implicate Social Democratic deputies in a conspiracy against the state. Even then, Stolypin still hoped to avoid dissolution. Not until late in May, when it was clear that the legislature would not vote for his agrarian program, did he abandon all hope of productive cooperation with the Duma.[131]

The stage was set with a routine police action, a raid of the apartment of a Menshevik deputy, I. P. Ozol. The police claimed to have found documents incriminating Ozol and fifty-four other deputies in a conspiracy to overthrow the government. When thirty-one deputies introduced an interpellation addressed to the ministries of Internal Affairs and Justice, accusing both departments of a "series of illegal actions" in connection with the entry into Ozol's apartment, Stolypin decided to respond personally and quickly. As far as he knew, he told the legislators, the police in the capital had received information that there would be a meeting in Ozol's apartment of the "central revolutionary committee," which was in touch with the local military-revolutionary committee. "Under the circumstances, the police could not have acted otherwise than to invade this apartment . . . and to conduct a search of this apartment. Don't forget that the city of Petersburg is under Extraordinary Security, and that in this city extraordinary events are taking place. Thus, the police had the right to do what occurred in the apartment." Stolypin conceded that a group of deputies were in the apartment, but he claimed that incriminating documents were found on some of them. He suggested that since no one was physically harmed, the police could not be accused of having acted inappropriately. Moreover, a day later, on May 6, further police searches of Ozol's apartment had turned up evidence linking the deputy to the military-revolutionary committee, "whose aim is to provoke an uprising within the army." Stolypin added that "besides protecting the deputies' immunity, we, the bearers of authority, have another responsibility, to protect the public safety."[132]

The liberal press and many deputies were shocked by the police raid and the searches of Ozol's apartment. In violating the immunity of a parliamentary representative, the government had disregarded one of the most important rights guaranteed in constitutional states. But once Stolypin had decided that the Duma had to be dissolved, he refused to be deterred by such considerations. Exactly when he reached that decision is not clear, but by May 30 his plans had been carefully formulated. That day he informed the tsar on his course of action and indicated that both the manifesto announcing the dissolution and the ukase on new electoral procedures would be sent to him for his signature on June 1.[133]

Early on June 1, Stolypin sent a brief note to Golovin requesting the floor at the next sitting of the Duma. The prime minister also invoked Article 44 of the chamber's regulations, which permitted him to request that the session be closed to the public. Golovin immediately took the appropriate measures to comply with Stolypin's wishes.[134] As soon as the session began, early in the afternoon of June 1, Stolypin stepped up to the tribune to address a tense chamber. Every deputy knew that the prime minister would level serious charges against the Social Democratic delegation. In a short speech, Stolypin announced that the procurator of the St. Petersburg Provincial Supreme Court, P. D. Kamyshanskii, had decided to indict some of the deputies, who, according to documents found in Ozol's apartment, belonged to a criminal organization. Further details, Stolypin continued, would be provided by the prosecutor and the minister of justice. Stolypin warned that if the Duma failed to cooperate with the authorities in this matter, his administration would be unable to maintain order in the empire.[135]

The procurator then asked the Duma to lift the immunity of fifty-five Social Democratic deputies who, the police claimed, were members of an organization dedicated to the overthrow of the government and its replacement with a democratic republic. Kamyshanskii indicated that the police would launch a full investigation of the deputies, sixteen of whom would be taken into custody immediately for questioning.

The Duma, at a loss on how to respond to the government's demands, appointed a committee of twenty-two deputies to be chaired by a highly respected Kadet, the historian A. A. Kizevetter. The committee was to report on its examination of the case against the Social Democrats by 7:00 P.M. the next day (June 2). If it worked through the night, it

would have about nineteen hours to complete its task, an impossible assignment given the vast amount of material to be analyzed. The committee worked diligently on the mountain of material that had been presented by the prosecutor, and the more evidence it examined "the
clearer it became that the SD fraction had not organized any kind of
military conspiracy."[136] At 7:00 P.M. on June 2 the committee informed
the Duma that it had not yet completed its work and that it would need
two more days to study the material. Golovin telephoned the prime
minister to let him know about the delay and to ask whether the Duma
would be disbanded if the committee did not conclude its work that
evening. Stolypin's "answer was entirely reassuring."[137]

The authorities, however, had already taken measures that told a different story. As early as June 1 the police searched the apartments of
several SD and SR deputies and began a massive roundup of citizens.
The arrests were especially widespread at various railway stations. Also
on that day, a large number of policemen had been stationed near the
Tauride Palace. Whenever a crowd of citizens appeared on a street of the
capital, mounted patrols as well as numerous agents from the secret police were sent to the area. Toward evening, additional policemen were
deployed in various parts of St. Petersburg.[138]

In a desperate attempt to stay Stolypin's hand, four Kadet deputies
who had secretly met with him from time to time (V. A. Maklakov, P. B.
Struve, M. V. Chelnokov, and S. N. Bulgakov) took it on themselves to
visit the prime minister again. They had decided that Stolypin must be
warned that it would be "sheer madness" to dissolve the Duma now.
They arrived at the Elagin Palace at 11:30 P.M. on June 2; Stolypin received them immediately, even though he was then in the midst of a
meeting of the Council of Ministers. The conversation began on a sour
note. When the Kadets claimed that the charges against the Social
Democrats were unfounded, Stolypin shot back: "I will not discuss this
with you: if the judicial authorities say that there is proof, this must be
accepted as the starting point for action, for us and for you. . . . While we
talk here, Social Democrats are roaming from one factory to another inciting the workers." After several such exchanges, the four Kadets all
wondered whether they should not simply get up and leave.

In a final effort to prevent a collapse of the talks, Struve asked
Stolypin why he had changed his attitude toward the Duma so drastically. Why was he making such impossible demands just when the legislature was working more effectively than ever before? Stolypin indicated that now it was his turn to be puzzled. He had not noticed any improvement in the way the Duma was conducting its business. Sadly, he

noted that he could not possibly agree with the Duma on the agrarian question. The Kadets were taken aback; Chelnokov reminded Stolypin that he had recently expressed satisfaction with the way the Duma was proceeding on this issue. Chelnokov pointed out that the legislature was considering the agrarian bill clause by clause, a procedure that would permit the kind of amendments Stolypin favored. Unimpressed, Stolypin reminded his interlocutors that Kadet orators had insisted that the party would never abandon its agrarian program. Bulgakov, who was a member of the Agrarian Committee, informed Stolypin that the committee did not intend to adopt the plan on the compulsory expropriation of private lands. Now Stolypin perked up and began to show great interest in his visitors' remarks. It seemed as though an important misunderstanding had been cleared up, and that agreement might be reached with the prime minister after all.

Stolypin's tone became more conciliatory, but still he would not yield on the demand for the expulsion of the Social Democrats. If the Kadets had abandoned their agrarian program, he asked, why would they not yield to his government's demands? "Liberate the Duma of [the Social Democrats], and you will see how well we will be able to work together." The Kadets would command the support of a majority in the legislature and would be able to implement their program. "You will see," Stolypin continued, "how everything will then go well. Why don't you want this?" In addition, Stolypin claimed that expelling the SDs was essential to the attainment of a legal order in Russia, a goal that the liberals shared with him. The Kadets were once again taken aback, not having expected this turn in the conversation. Maklakov replied for the four men: "You present your demand in such a sharp and exaggerated form that the Duma cannot accede to it. After this, we would be ashamed to look each other in the face." Stolypin asked point blank: "Does this mean that the Duma will refuse [our request]?" "Certainly," Maklakov said. "I myself am a rightist Kadet and will vote *against* you." Stolypin looked straight at the other three Kadets, all of whom indicated agreement with Maklakov. "Well," he announced, "then there is nothing to be done. . . . [O]nly remember what I say to you: now it is you who are dissolving the Duma."

One of the Kadets asked the prime minister whether he expected any unrest in response to the dissolution. "No. Perhaps purely local [incidents]; but this is not important." Stolypin could confidently make that prediction. Since mid-May he had received two detailed and cautiously optimistic assessments from the Department of Police on how the people throughout the country were responding to the deliberations of the

Duma. Although there were pockets of strong hostility toward the government, overall the country was calm, and the authors of the reports did not anticipate any major explosions in the near future. The assessments were based on reports submitted by provincial and city governors, who carefully monitored the political mood of the people under their jurisdiction.[139]

The prime minister concluded the meeting with a surprisingly cordial statement: "I hope to meet all of you in the Third Duma. My only pleasant memory of the Second Duma is my acquaintance with you. I hope that when you get to know me better, you will not regard me as such a villain as people generally consider me." Maklakov could not contain his anger: "I will not be in the Third Duma. You have destroyed all our work, and our voters will turn to the left. Now they will *not* elect *us*." Stolypin grinned enigmatically. Maklakov posed one final question: "Or will you change the electoral law, effecting a coup d'état? That would not be better." Stolypin did not answer. The Kadets left, having accomplished nothing.[140]

The last-ditch appeal by the four Kadets was bound to fail. Although Stolypin had resisted the intense pressure for dissolution for three months, he had now concluded that he could never cooperate with the Duma as it was then constituted. The differences over the agrarian issue were no doubt very important in leading him to that conclusion, but the final conversation with the four Kadet deputies suggests that political considerations were also critical. Even Bulgakov's revelation that the Kadets had decided to abandon the plank on compulsory expropriation did not prompt Stolypin to change his mind. Stolypin may simply not have trusted the Kadets on this issue, but it is also possible that he had become convinced at this point that nothing short of a fundamental political change would do. After all, his conflicts with the legislature ever since March 6 had not centered on the agrarian question alone. He had believed all along that most deputies did not appreciate the necessity of restoring law and order, which to him was a sine qua non for the restructuring of Russian society. Stolypin did not accept the ultraconservative view of the Duma as an institution whose very existence was incompatible with the preservation of the monarchical order. Deep down, however, he too distrusted the Duma because it had never abandoned the demands for radical change in the political system. The Kadets had modified their tactics since the First Duma, but the prime minister simply did not have any confidence that they would hue to a clear-cut course.

In mid-May, according to Sir Arthur Nicolson, Stolypin "regretted that he found it impossible to come to any understanding with the [K]adets, but their tactics were so vacillating and so uncertain that no confidence could be placed in them. In the Duma they alternately fluctuated between the Left and the Moderates, and it was difficult to predict from day to day what policy they would adopt. They never seemed to have the courage to take a decided line and follow it consistently, and [Stolypin] was quite unable to follow their devious course."[141] The prime minister suspected, with good reason, that the Kadets envisioned a far greater role for the Duma than it had been accorded by the Fundamental Laws. He, on the other hand, was a firm believer in the primacy of the monarchy. In the last analysis, then, the political question of who was to rule was no less important to Stolypin than the agrarian question.

In any case, by the time the four Kadets visited him, Stolypin had already let the tsar know that he now favored dissolution. The pressures from the court were too strong for him to change his decision even if he had been so inclined. On May 30 he had informed the tsar that on June 1 he would ask the Duma to expel fifty-five SD deputies and to agree to the arrest of the sixteen deputies who were "most guilty" of conspiring against the state. The Council of Ministers, he continued, considered it unwise to demand the arrest of all fifty-five deputies, for that would smack of political revenge. But if any of the fifty-five went into hiding the police would pursue them and take them into custody. Three days later, on June 2, he indicated that while there were some differences among the ministers on details, all of them agreed that it was necessary to dissolve the Duma. "I firmly believe," Stolypin wrote at the end of the second letter, "that the Lord will lead Russia to its predestined path, and that Your Majesty will have the good fortune of seeing [the country] pacified and extolled."[142]

Tsar Nicholas himself, by this time determined to disband the legislature, advised Stolypin in no uncertain terms that he would brook no delay. At 11:30 P.M. on June 2, he wrote to the prime minister that he had signed the new electoral law, and that "I waited all day long with impatience for notification from you that the dissolution of the accursed Duma had been completed. But at the same time I feel in my heart that things are not moving along smoothly and are being dragged out. This is intolerable.—The Duma must be dissolved tomorrow, on Sunday morning. It is necessary to display decisiveness and firmness to Russia. The dispersal of the Duma is now the right [thing to do] and vitally necessary. There must be no delay, not one minute of hesitation! God favors the bold."[143] Once again Nicholas demonstrated that on issues about which he felt strongly he had a mind of his own and could be decisive.

At 6:00 A.M. on Sunday, June 3 (the First Duma had also been dissolved on a Sunday) several *Okhrana* agents entered the Tauride Palace
as others posted the manifesto disbanding the legislature at the doors.
The city remained quiet throughout the day. Although the army was in
a state of alert, not a single unit was summoned from the barracks. Policemen arrested over two hundred people, including the sixteen Social
Democratic deputies at the center of the controversy. Other SD deputies
received notices to appear in court the next day. The police continued to
arrest people suspected of being revolutionaries, and by June 6 the total
number in custody in St. Petersburg had reached six hundred. The police
conducted similar roundups in many other cities of the empire.[144]

In launching the crackdown, the police followed instructions Stolypin had sent to senior provincial officials in several circulars. The
prime minister informed officials that the emperor was ordering them to
"take all measures, even the most extreme, to maintain calm and order
after the dissolution of the State Duma." No agitation directed at
"distorting" the manifesto on the dissolution should be allowed. In this
connection, officials must pay special attention to the press, which
might attempt to mislead the people on the tsar's intentions. Stolypin
reminded them that in areas under emergency regulations, a large part of
the empire, they had the authority to close down presses that published
materials "clearly hostile to the government" and that posed a danger to
public order.[145]

In the manifesto dissolving the Duma (drafted under Stolypin's direction), Tsar Nicholas went into considerable detail to explain his action: "To Our regret, a significant portion of the members of the Second
Duma did not justify Our expectations. Many of those sent by the people to work [for them] did not go with a pure heart, with a desire to
strengthen Russia and to improve its system, but [went rather] with an
explicit intention to increase unrest and to promote the disintegration
of the state." He charged the deputies with having failed to consider
many of the projects introduced by the government (all told, there were
about 150 such projects) and with having refused to condemn terror.
Moreover, they had resorted to interpellations for the sole purpose of
arousing hostility to the government among large sectors of the population. Finally, the tsar pointed to an "action unprecedented in the annals
of history": the participation of a group of elected officials in a plot
against the state and tsarist authority. For these reasons, Nicholas
claimed, he had no choice but to disband the Duma. He announced that
a new Duma would meet on November 1, but he also indicated that he
would take appropriate measures to ensure that the new legislature

would be devoted to the strengthening of the Russian state. "[T]he State Duma," the manifesto declared, "must be Russian in spirit."

To achieve that, a new electoral law for the selection of deputies had been sent to the Senate for promulgation. The manifesto spoke in only general terms of the principles underlying the new law. The tsar simply vowed to remain faithful to the Manifesto of October 17 and the Fundamental Laws by ensuring representation to all segments of the population. But he made one important exception. In those regions of the empire where the population had not attained the proper level of civic consciousness (*grazhdanstvennost*), elections would be temporarily suspended.[146] To secure the widest dissemination of the tsar's decision, the Most Holy Synod sent a telegram to all dioceses directing them to see to it that priests read the manifesto and the new electoral law at the conclusion of church services.[147]

The task of designing the electoral law had been entrusted to Kryzhanovskii, the deputy minister for internal affairs and a man highly accomplished in the art of drafting governmental statements and projects. But this time even Kryzhanovskii was baffled. Stolypin had given him only vague instructions. He was to devise a scheme that would ensure the election of a Duma composed of "the more cultivated strata of the population," by which the prime minister meant, of course, a Duma in which a majority of the deputies would be conservative and sympathetic to his program. But Stolypin also directed Kryzhanovskii to remain faithful to the general scheme of the previous elections so that the new regulations would not appear to be a total rejection of the concessions the autocracy had made in October 1905. Stolypin indicated that it was his wish and the wish of the tsar that no category of the population represented in the first two dumas be completely deprived of representation in the Third Duma. Although Kryzhanovskii thought that he was being asked to square the circle, as a loyal servant to the tsar he accepted the assignment.[148]

After submitting various options to the government, Stolypin expressed preference for the one that Kryzhanovskii considered the "most brazen." He would introduce numerous changes in the existing electoral law by radically altering the number of seats in the Duma assigned to particular geographical regions, social groups, and ethnic minorities. "Trustworthy" citizens would simply be given the lion's share. Even then, the Senate issued several interpretations of the law to further limit the franchise of various categories of voters. It was all thoroughly arbitrary and transparent, and it made for extraordinary complexity, but it worked in producing a Duma the authorities considered acceptable.

The essential features of the law can be briefly summarized. The size
of the Duma was reduced from 542 to 442, almost entirely at the expense of the outlying regions of the empire. The Steppe and Turkestan
regions, the vast Turgai, Ural, and Iakutsk oblasts, the nomadic peoples
of Astrakhan and Stavropol, and the Siberian Cossacks lost their representation completely. The Duma delegations of the Poles, Armenians,
and Tatars were sharply reduced. Thus, the Poles, with a population of
about 11 million, would elect fourteen deputies, two of whom had to be
Russian. In the Second Duma, it will be recalled, the Polish delegation
numbered forty-six. The roughly 6 million people of Transcaucasia
could elect seven deputies, one of whom had to be Russian. (The requirement that some of the deputies from non-Russian regions must be
Russian was designed to satisfy the demands of the local Russian communities and ensure that the new Duma had a truly Russian cast.) By
contrast, the province of Kursk, with a population of 2.5 million, the
vast majority of them ethnically Russian, was assigned eleven deputies;
the 3 million citizens (also overwhelmingly Russian) of Tambov would
elect twelve. In addition, the law favored the affluent over the masses.
The peasants would choose only half as many electors (those who made
the final selection of deputies) as they had in 1906, and the landowners a
third more.

In the fifty-one provinces of European Russia, landowners would select roughly 49.6 percent of the electors, the urban population 26.2 percent, the peasants 21.7 percent, and industrial workers 2.3 percent. In
slightly over half these provinces, landowners by themselves selected a
majority of the electors, and in the remaining provinces they could obtain a majority by forming alliances with one or another urban group. To
reduce the election of liberals in cities, eighteen of the twenty-five urban centers were deprived of the right to choose their own deputies. The
eighteen cities were merged with the provincial constituencies. In the
seven cities that still elected their own deputies (St. Petersburg, Moscow, Kiev, Odessa, Riga, Warsaw, and Lodz), the enfranchised population was divided into two categories: men of substantial wealth and everyone else. Each category elected the same number of deputies. Women,
men under the age of twenty-five, students, soldiers, sailors in active
service, and people who had been dismissed from the civil service or
convicted of a criminal offense were entirely excluded. Although the
voting was fairly straightforward and direct in the large cities, elsewhere
"the system of indirect voting is developed to such an extent as to make
elections resemble walking through a labyrinth." The elections were to
proceed in three different stages, and the electors who survived the

process would meet in the capital of the province to choose the deputies. As one contemporary observed, "The system is so calculated that in the end, the big landowners are almost certain to secure a majority, and the peasants returned are usually those who seem to the landowners fairly safe."[149]

The dissolution of the Duma and the new electoral law made it possible, as will be seen in the next chapter, for Stolypin to obtain what he had longed for, a legislature with a majority of moderates and conservatives. Although some unrest and lawlessness continued to plague the country for two months or so, the people generally reacted apathetically to Stolypin's drastic actions. After two years of revolutionary turbulence and political activism, the national mood had changed quite dramatically. Observers noticed a significant decline of interest in domestic politics. Newspapers no longer dwelt on internal affairs and devoted an increasing number of articles to foreign affairs. A year earlier the press had almost completely ignored that subject. "The Russian people, generally speaking," the British ambassador to St. Petersburg concluded early in August 1907, "is at present tired of the ceaseless internal troubles of the past two, or nearly three years."[150] In less than a year as prime minister, Stolypin appeared to have achieved one of his two goals, the defeat of the revolution and with that the restoration of order. Now he turned his attention to his second goal, the reform of Russia's economic and political institutions, which proved to be far more elusive than the first, in large part because many of the people, some of them very influential, who had wished him well in his battle against the left showed nothing but contempt for his efforts at reform.

There was another reason, however, for Stolypin's difficulties in enacting reform. His arbitrary actions on June 3 repelled many moderates and liberals to such an extent that they refused to have any dealings with Stolypin's government, which was derisively dubbed the "3 June System." These opponents of the old order, as well as the left in general, insisted that Stolypin's dissolution of the Duma and the promulgation of the new electoral law amounted to nothing less than a coup d'état, a deliberate violation of the constitution created by the Manifesto of October 17, by far the most significant achievement of the revolution. Was that a correct assessment of Stolypin's actions of June 3?

Some defenders of the old order claimed that the events of June 3 could not be considered a coup since the authorities had simply dissolved the Duma, not eliminated it. The tsar, according to this interpretation, merely changed the Fundamental Laws, which was his prerogative.[151] It is not a convincing argument. To be sure, the tsar acted legally in dissolving the Duma, but the critical question is whether he also acted legally in changing the electoral law. Even conservatives such as the German ambassador to St. Petersburg, who applauded Stolypin's move, acknowledged that "in reality, the decree on the electoral law is in a formal sense a coup d'état, a breach of the constitution."[152] Kryzhanovskii himself conceded that it was "indisputable" that "formally" the promulgation of the new electoral law violated the Fundamental Laws. He offered two justifications, one legalistic and the other pragmatic. In his testimony in 1917 to the committee investigating the causes of the empire's collapse, he pointed out that Stolypin did not believe the tsar had violated the law because he had never taken an oath to uphold the Manifesto of October 1905. Consequently, Nicholas still retained autocratic powers and could deal with the Duma and the electoral system as he wished.[153] Kryzhanovskii also mentioned this line of reasoning in his memoirs, asserting in addition that the manifesto dissolving the Duma was not issued under Article 87 of the Fundamental Laws but enacted by the tsar himself; and an act promulgated by the sovereign did not need the approval of the Duma.

Kryzhanovskii's pragmatic argument seems more plausible. He insisted that in view of the circumstances at the time, the government could not have followed a different course. Had new elections been held under the old procedures, a Duma capable of constructive legislative work could not possibly have been elected. It would then have been necessary either to abolish the representative system altogether and establish a dictatorship, or to change the electoral system at a later date. According to Kryzhanovskii, an "influential group" at court argued vigorously in favor of suspending elections for the next Duma for five to ten years. Stolypin, however, wished to preserve the Duma as an institution and at the same time create conditions for the selection of a legislature that would be capable of "re-educating society."[154] Kokovtsov agreed with this interpretation: "In making this change [in the electoral system] without the consent of the Duma [Stolypin] violated the Tsar's earlier decree, but he did so solely in the name of preserving the principle of public representation."[155] Gurko in his memoirs made the same point in defending Stolypin's conduct. The prime minister "really intended not to violate the constitution but to strengthen and preserve it."[156]

Interesting as these arguments are, the simple fact is that the government had indeed staged a coup d'état. A reading of the Fundamental Laws of 1906, enacted by Tsar Nicholas himself, makes that clear. Article 87 stated specifically that this emergency article could not be used to "introduce changes either in the Fundamental State Laws or in the Organic Laws of the State Council or of the State Duma or in the provisions on elections to the Council or to the Duma."[157] Moreover, two senior officials actually acknowledged that Stolypin deliberately violated the constitution with the intention of changing the political structure. In his memoirs, A. A. Mossolov, the director of the Chancellery in 1907, bluntly stated that because the prime minister knew that he could not secure passage of the electoral law in the Duma, he effected a "*coup d'état* from above."[158] And on the same page on which he invoked the pragmatic argument in favor of dissolution, Kokovtsov noted that Stolypin was fully aware of what he was doing and "had a great struggle with his own conscience before he had undertaken the task of revising the electoral law."[159] Kokovtsov's recollection is consistent with our knowledge of the prime minister's attitude toward the electoral procedures. As will be recalled, only seven months before the second dissolution Stolypin had vowed in his conversation with the journalist Tverskoi that he would not arbitrarily change the electoral law. To do so, the prime minister had noted, would be to stage a "revolution from above," another term for a coup d'état. In the end, he overcame his scruples and knowingly violated the constitution, not by breaching minor technicalities but by radically transforming the empire's political system.

Even now the clock had not been fully turned back to 1904. True, the tsar still claimed to rule as an autocrat, but so long as the Duma continued to function the claim was not convincing. Neither he nor the bureaucracy could operate as arbitrarily as they had before the Revolution of 1905. On many vital questions the tsar and his officials needed the support of the legislature. Although the electoral law of June 3, 1907, deprived the masses of much of their representation, the Duma did not become a mere rubber stamp for the government, as Stolypin would soon learn to his dismay. The prime minister had done much in one year to quell the revolution and to weaken the opposition, but in his quest for reform he still had to contend with a parliament that was not as pliant as he would have liked.

5

Fighting for Reform

Eleven days after dissolving the Duma, Stolypin was sufficiently confident that the repercussions would be minimal to take an eight-day cruise on the yacht *Neva* that the tsar had placed at his disposal. For the first time in months the prime minister freed himself from work to relax with his family, and it was an exhilarating experience for him and his wife. "They had become young and gay, had revived so much that they were entirely altered," their daughter recalled. "Smiling, calm, they would not be parted and spoke as if they were experiencing a second honeymoon. . . . It was obvious that [in St. Petersburg] they had felt deprived of the opportunity to converse, to move freely, to live their own lives."[1]

Stolypin remained in good cheer for some time after returning to work. The British ambassador, Sir Arthur Nicolson, who held two lengthy conversations with him in August and October, found him to be "in excellent health and spirits; he was living in a Palace granted to him by the Emperor on one of the islands, and surrounded by high palisades, triple rows of barbed wire entanglements, and a large force of mounted and foot gendarmes holding watch round the grounds, while water patrols keep guard on the river." Never before had the prime minister exuded as much confidence about future political developments. Economic conditions generally were improving, and peasants "were purchasing land whenever they had an opportunity." Workers, Stolypin was convinced, were turning away from politics and concentrating on the formation of trade unions, which he believed to be a healthy trend so long as the unions abstained from politics. Stolypin was no doubt referring to the early signs of a movement among Mensheviks, the more moderate wing within Russian Marxism, to emphasize legal rather than underground activity, a movement that Lenin would later denounce as liquidationism (that is, a desire to liquidate the Social Democratic Party in Russia).[2]

Stolypin thought that the "landed interests" and members of zemstvos, two groups likely to be sympathetic to the moderate opposition but not to the radicals, would be strongly represented in the Third Duma. He expected the Kadets not to do well in the upcoming elections since they "had lost much ground in the country." Consequently, it seemed probable that a "solid Centre party would be formed" in the Duma, making it possible for him to cooperate with the new legislature in enacting his program.

Stolypin, however, was apprehensive about the extremists on the right and left, who together might secure enough seats to be capable of disrupting the proceedings of the legislature. Significantly, he feared the extremists on the right more than those on the left. Now that the revolution was in retreat, he expected the right to become emboldened and to offer the most formidable opposition to his program of reform. On no fewer than three different occasions in the interviews he spoke of this danger, declaring that "reaction must not be allowed to gain the upper hand." "The spirit of reaction," he insisted, must be "subdued." His warnings about the rightists proved to be remarkably prescient; and how to deal with the new danger turned out to be one of the most challenging tests of his political skills. Stolypin was confident that the government could "without difficulty" deal with the revolutionary parties, since the army was entirely trustworthy. But he remained curiously silent about how he would handle the radicals on the right, no doubt because he had to be cautious in taking on opponents with strong ties to the court.

He himself intended, as his interlocutor put it, "to continue on the path of a liberal policy, while repressing sternly all disorders and revolutionary propaganda." But he insisted that Russia could not be governed in the way that Western European countries were governed because "political life and parliamentary ideals were enigmas to the enormous majority of the nation, ignorant and unlettered as they were." If he proceeded "gradually," he would eventually be able to establish a "thoroughly Liberal regime." His most important task was to "convince the country that the Government was strong and able to stand by itself."[3]

The prime minister's immediate concern was the electoral campaign for the Third Duma. In the two previous elections the government had miscalculated badly and had unexpectedly been forced to confront hostile legislatures. This time it was determined to take the necessary measures to prevent such an outcome. In addition to enacting the new, restrictive electoral law, it encouraged local electoral committees to apply a variety of dubious measures to reduce the number of eligible voters even further. A few statistics will suffice to indicate the success of the government's electoral policies. Only about 19 percent of eligible voters in sixty-seven cities of European Russia (roughly 10 percent of all the cities) participated in the elections for the Third Duma, compared to about 55 percent in 1906. The total number of voters in these cities dropped from 307,930 to 195,000. In some cities, the decline was at least 50 percent, and in a few the decline was even greater, ranging from 65 to 84 percent. Even in some rural areas with sizable numbers of large landowners, the registration lists declined by 30 to 40 percent, the result of the exclusion by officials of voters considered politically unreliable.[4]

When the final returns came in, Stolypin's expectations appeared to be justified. The composition of the Third Duma was as follows: Rightists, 51 deputies; Moderate rightists, 96; Octobrists, 154; Progressives, 28; Kadets, 54; Trudoviks, 14; Social Democrats, 18; Polish Kolo, 11; Polish-Lithuanian-Belorussian Group, 7; Muslim Group, 8.[5]

Since the Octobrists had by now swung decisively to the right, the government could reasonably count on the support of about 300 deputies out of a total of 441. However, 32 of the deputies in this coalition had clearly identified themselves as candidates of the Union of the Russian People, which meant that slightly over 10 percent of the legislators in the conservative camp were not simply progovernment but extremists who wished to undo the political concessions of 1905 and 1906. On some issues, however, several Progressives also supported the government, giving it an even more decisive majority. Put differently, if all the national groups are counted as part of the opposition, which was true only to a degree, the combined strength of the parties that favored a radical reordering of the country's political system amounted to no more than a third of the Duma. One need only compare these figures with those for the First and Second Dumas to note how drastically the empire's structure of politics had been transformed.* The opposition, the dominant force in the first two legislatures, had been reduced to virtual impotence.

The social group that now emerged as the dominant political force was the land-owning nobility, which was represented by 173 deputies, almost 40 percent of the Duma's membership. These gentry deputies were elected by some thirty thousand families, who represented about 0.1 percent of all the families in the empire. Although not all the gentry deputies voted consistently with the right, most did; a mere handful of men thus exerted a powerful influence on the affairs of state in a country whose population numbered about 130 million. The rightists could also count on the support of 53 deputies who were Orthodox clergymen—a much larger contingent than in the two preceding legislatures—and of

*On the First and Second Dumas, see above, pp. 86–87, 174–75.

the one deputy who was a Roman Catholic priest. Twelve more who could be relied on to side with the authorities were the government officials. Significantly, only 38 legislators came from the professions, and only 7 were businessmen. Of the remaining deputies whose social origins are known, 68 were peasants, 27 workers, and 17 Cossacks.[6]

The reassertion of the conservative gentry's predominance in the country's political life had been presaged at a zemstvo congress in Moscow, which met on June 10, 1907, only one week after the dissolution of the Duma. Of the 158 representatives from thirty-two provinces at the congress, 33 belonged to rightist movements, 33 were members of the moderate rightist or nationalistic organizations, and 44 were Octobrists. The Kadets and their allies, who predominated in previous zemstvo congresses, were represented by fewer than 20 delegates, most of whom had not been prominent in the liberal movement. Except for M. A. Stakhovich, none of the leaders of Russian liberalism were in attendance.[7] Not surprisingly, the congress expressed support for Stolypin, whom it greeted as "a loyal servant of our Sovereign, who did not lose faith in this difficult time in the vital forces of the Russian land." In making this point, the delegates were voicing their approval not only of the political changes introduced by the prime minister but also of his successful resistance to those at court and in the State Council who advocated abolition of the Duma. For the landed gentry, the new political settlement appeared to be ideal, since it ensured them a place of pre-eminent influence. At the same time, the congress avoided any reference to the tsar as autocrat, preferring instead the appellations "all-merciful Sovereign" or merely "Sovereign." Thus the delegates left unresolved the question of the relative powers of the monarch and the representative institution.[8]

The drift to the right also manifested itself on the local level in the zemstvo elections held in various localities in the four weeks following the dissolution of the Duma. In the provinces of Poltava and Samara, only rightists won seats; in Tambov, 20 Octobrists, 6 members of the Union of the Russian People, and only 1 Kadet were elected.[9] These results marked a continuation of trends that had emerged in late 1906 and early 1907. A comparison of the political allegiances of chairmen of zemstvo assemblies in 1905 and 1907 graphically demonstrates the changes that had occurred. In 1905 the Kadets occupied fifteen chairmanships, the Progressives six, the Octobrists thirteen, and the rightists none. Two years later the figures were: Kadets, one; Progressives, three; Octobrists, nineteen; rightists, eleven.[10] Thus at all levels of the political arena the opposition suffered devastating defeats.

Stolypin and Kryzhanovskii had reason to be pleased with their

handiwork. They had finally secured the election of a Duma not dominated by the opposition; the election itself had been conducted without
any serious incidents; the country appeared to be content with the new
political arrangements. But, as one astute foreign observer noted, it
could not be assumed that the population had completely abandoned
liberal ideals or even revolutionary aspirations. Rather, many people
who favored a fundamental reordering of political institutions were relieved that a representative body, however vitiated, continued to play a
role in shaping the country's affairs.[11]

The national mood can best be described as one of reluctant resignation. On November 1, when the deputies gathered for the opening ceremonies of the Duma, "[t]here was no excitement or enthusiasm noticeable in the streets as on the two previous occasions, nor were there any
crowds [to welcome the deputies]. A general holiday was not given in
honour of the occasion. . . . A great number of policemen could be seen,
and they had been given orders to disperse crowds of more than about
fifty persons, and the people were warned that no demonstration of any
kind would be tolerated."[12] Beneath the surface, discontent and the "old
hatred" for the government were palpable, and this "chronic malady"
seemed likely to plague Russia for a long time.[13]

Count Friedrich von Pourtalès, who arrived in St. Petersburg early in
1908 as the new German ambassador, was in fact amazed at how little
the country had changed since his last stay there eighteen years earlier.
Despite the country's defeat in war and the "prodigious convulsions" of
the revolution one could not detect the "beginning of a new era. . . . Everywhere one still encounters the old Russia with an all-powerful bureaucracy that is hostile to the modern state system of Western Europe."
Most astonishing, according to Pourtalès, those in authority persisted in
minimizing the seriousness of the events of 1905–7, which, the ambassador was told time and again, were not nearly as far-reaching as the upheaval of 1789 in France. During the French Revolution the entire political system had collapsed, whereas Russia had experienced only local
unrest instigated by "Jewish agitators." Some Russian dignitaries,
among them General Kuropatkin, who was the minister of war in 1904
and should have known better, even claimed that Russia could have defeated Japan had it not been for the interference by diplomats. Pourtalès
granted that Stolypin was committed to pursuing moderate policies of
reform, but he feared that the prime minister faced so much pressure
from ultraconservatives that he might be forced to move sharply to the
right.[14]

In truth, when the Duma was about to begin its deliberations

Stolypin seemed to be walking a political tightrope. He hoped to establish cordial relations with the Duma, but the tsar complicated his task because he could not overcome his deep distrust of the legislature even though it was no longer dominated by members of the opposition. Contrary to Stolypin's wishes, Nicholas flatly refused to meet the deputies, as he had when the First Duma was convened, on the grounds that they had not demonstrated to his satisfaction that they were prepared to work constructively with the government. "We must avoid," Nicholas informed Stolypin, "any premature public appearances or precedents on my part." To emphasize his resolve, Nicholas pointed out that his views were "unconditionally shared" by the empress.[15]

Nicholas's stand undercut Stolypin's political strategy, but, ever the loyal servant of the tsar, he immediately assured the monarch that he would take appropriate steps to have the deputies' request for a meeting with the tsar formulated in the most general terms "so that the failure to receive the Duma will not have the character of a refusal on the part of Your Majesty to meet [the deputies]. Of course, not a single person knows that I have reported to Your Majesty on this matter." At the same time, the prime minister politely indicated that he regarded the tsar's refusal a blunder. He considered it his duty, he told Nicholas, "not to hide from Your Majesty the fact that a majority of the members of the State Duma have a very strong and sincere desire to see their Tsar. These are all people animated by the most loyal feelings toward Your Majesty. Regardless of their future work in the Duma, they are worthy by themselves of gracious attention from Your Majesty." Stolypin ended with a plea that the tsar not abandon his original intention of granting an audience to individual groups of deputies.[16]

Nicholas's refusal to meet the Duma was not simply an expression of petulance. He was making a pointed statement about the nature of Russia's political system, which had once again become a subject of fierce debate. During the first meetings of the Duma, right-wing deputies insisted that the Address to the Throne must contain the word "autocracy"; their aim, of course, was to send a message to the nation that the October Manifesto had not altered the structure of government. On the other hand, the Kadets wished to include the word "constitution" in the address precisely because they wanted to emphasize that the political order had been transformed and that there would be no abandonment of the principles enunciated by the tsar in the October Manifesto. The Octobrists, who held the balance of power on the issue, rejected both words, opting instead for a reference to the "renovated" state established by the October Manifesto. The Kadets and the moderate rightists accepted the compromise, as did most of the opposition press. *Tovarishch*, a left-wing paper, declared triumphantly: "The debate shows that autocracy has been buried once and for all; the danger from the Right scarcely exists." And the Kadet paper *Rech* claimed that the Octobrists had shown beyond a doubt that they did not subscribe to the views of the extreme right. Miliukov, the leader of the Kadets, hailed the Octobrists for having demonstrated their support for constitutionalism; he now believed that his party would be able to cooperate with the moderate liberals. Most significantly, *Rossiia*, the paper controlled by Stolypin, voiced satisfaction with the compromise worked out by the Octobrists and declared that "[t]he time has arrived when the Duma will know how and when to sink party differences for the good of the country."[17] It seemed as though Stolypin had succeeded in forging a right-of-center coalition in the Duma, precisely what he had hoped for.

But the tsar and his entourage at court were not at all pleased. They viewed the compromise, correctly, as a victory for the constitutionalists, and that they could not abide. A. P. Izvolskii, the foreign minister and one of the more liberal members of the cabinet, confided to the German ambassador that he did not feel free even to raise the subject of the nature of the Russian polity among his circle of acquaintances, and indicated that, in his view, it would have been the better part of wisdom for the Duma to have avoided the issue altogether. The tsar, Izvolskii revealed, was "deeply distressed" over the debates in the Duma; he, Izvolskii, and Stolypin were extremely apprehensive about the mood at the tsarist court. The issue, Izvolskii warned, "touches on matters on which the Tsar, consistent with his mode of thought, tolerates very little criticism or suggestions for change."[18]

There is no evidence that Stolypin and Nicholas ever aired their differences over the Duma. It seems likely that both restrained themselves to avoid a clash. But the prime minister did not conceal his view that while he believed in the pre-eminence of the tsar, he also believed that the October Manifesto had introduced a constitutional order, which he differentiated from a parliamentary order, in which the legislature is the pre-eminent authority.* At the time the Third Duma debated the issue, Stolypin tried valiantly to remain in the good graces of both the tsar and the deputies who abhorred the word "autocracy." He did his best to explain to A. I. Guchkov, the chairman of the committee that drafted the Address to the Throne, why the tsar's rage over the omission was under-

---

*See above, pp. 126–28, for a more detailed discussion of Stolypin's view on this issue.

standable. "If you forgot to address me as 'Your Excellency,' I should not mind, but if you struck the word, perhaps I should."[19] For Nicholas, a fundamental principle was at stake, and he never forgave Guchkov. From that time, relations between the court and the Octobrist leader remained frosty. But the more pragmatic Stolypin continued to work for the tsar and with Guchkov.

In the meantime, the Duma had started its deliberations, and there could be no doubt that this legislature differed markedly from the first two. "The members [of the Duma]," an astute foreign observer noted, "were no longer the dubious figures of peasant agitators or people whose faces revealed that they could neither read nor write; also missing were the many Jewish professors and lawyers as well as the costumes of deputies from Poland, southwestern Russia, and the Caucasus. They have to a large extent been replaced by members of the right, whose appearance gives an entirely new character to the image of the [group]. Many deputies wore the ribbon of the Stanislav Order, an even larger number wore uniforms that indicated that they were former military men or representatives of the civil service. If one adds the fifty clergymen, then there remain relatively few deputies who remind one of the previous deputies. In short, it seems that the old Russia, which has been so little noticed and which has been much underestimated abroad, is at the battleground of internal politics—that Russia in which the Court, the Church, and the barracks, supported by a self-conscious civil service, play a decisive role. These deputies could, after the long domination of the democratic opposition, sing the national anthem with satisfaction and enthusiasm . . . and shout 'Hurrah' after every verse."[20]

In one of its first actions the Duma elected N. A. Khomiakov as its president, a clear sign of the Octobrists' influence in the chamber. A former marshal of the nobility in Smolensk and senior official in the Department of Agriculture, the fifty-seven-year-old Khomiakov was a highly respected leader of the Octobrist Party widely admired as a judicious and principled man. His success in receiving the support of most rightists, providing him with a majority of 371 out of some 440, seemed to augur well for the Duma's ability to avoid polemics and to concentrate on legislative work. In his first speech as president, he let it be known that he would be his own man and would not kowtow to the rightists or the liberals. On the one hand, he indicated his support for the principle of the unity of the Russian Empire, a comment directed at the Polish deputies who had abstained from voting on the Address to the Throne because it did not state that the Duma would honor the "legislative strivings of the nationalities." On the other, he made clear his view that the Duma was an authentic legislative body, not simply an institution that offered advice to the monarch. But he was adroit in formulating his positions, which were carefully crafted to give minimum offense to Nicholas and the Poles. "I have confidence in the future of an undivided and unified Russia. I believe in the will of the Duma, [and believe that] through its work, [it will] bring about the long awaited peace in the country and, in accordance with the wishes of the Tsar, do good work as a legislative body."[21] Khomiakov's public optimism should not be interpreted as naiveté. He realized, for example, that the tsar was slippery. Privately, he told F. A. Golovin, the president of the Second Duma, that Nicholas "does not lie, but he also does not tell the truth."[22]

Stolypin worked reasonably well with Khomiakov, but his closest ally among the Octobrists was A. I. Guchkov, a founder of the movement in 1906 and now the leader of its faction in the Duma. A fervent patriot and a believer in monarchy as a symbol of national unity and a center of political authority, Guchkov shared many of the prime minister's political predilections. When the field courts-martial were instituted in August 1906, Guchkov was one of the very few public men to support Stolypin.* Yet he also believed deeply in the principles of the October Manifesto and did not hesitate to make that clear to the tsar and the ultraconservatives. The Third Duma, in his view, must dedicate itself to a wide range of reforms, especially in the area of national defense but also in other spheres that particularly interested Stolypin, the one man, Guchkov insisted, who could revitalize Russia. Guchkov was willing to accept incremental reforms and gradual increases in the influence of the Duma, positions that Stolypin found acceptable. Although the two men were never personally close and although they differed on some issues, they maintained a good working relationship during the early years of the Third Duma.[23] So long as that held, the enactment of reform seemed feasible.

Stolypin outlined his legislative plans on November 16, 1907, in his first address to the Third Duma. Although he had recently described the government's program in his speech to the Second Duma and did not contemplate any major changes, he declared it necessary to present his program once again. In saying this, Stolypin was less than candid. He himself pointed out at the beginning of his talk that "conditions have not remained unchanged," a clear reference to the fact that the new Duma was more conservative, leaving him free to deliver a speech dif-

*See p. 144.

ferent in tone and substance from the one he had made only eight months earlier. His nods to liberalism in the speech of March 1907 were replaced by a much harsher and more nationalistic thrust.

To be sure, Stolypin reiterated his call for reform of local and provincial self-government and of the educational system and the courts, as well as the reorganization of the police, and the introduction of a system of workers' insurance. He also expressed the hope that exceptional measures would soon be abandoned and that steps would be taken to promote respect for a legal order. And he urged the Duma to pass legislation confirming the agrarian reforms he had introduced under Article 87. Missing from the second speech was any reference to the October Manifesto, whose implementation, he had vowed earlier, would transform the country into a state based on law. Nor did he promise to submit bills guaranteeing civil liberties and religious toleration.

Moreover, no one could fail to notice his renewed emphasis, right at the beginning of his speech, on the government's intention to use force to put down unrest by the "foes of society," the extremists on the left. "It has now become clear to everybody that the disruptive movement started by the Extreme Left parties has degenerated into open brigandage, and has brought to the fore all the elements inimical to society and the law, thus ruining honest workers and demoralizing the younger generation." This statement was greeted by "vehement applause on Right and Centre benches."

After Roman Dmowski, the leader of the Polish Kolo, had criticized the prime minister for mistreating the "subject races" and in particular the Poles, and the Kadet V. A. Maklakov had attacked him for failing to promise guarantees for the liberties of the people, Stolypin stepped up to the podium a second time and, "stammering with excitement," he assumed a far more militant and conservative tone. Now he dwelt on the virtues of the "historical autocratic power" of the sovereign, which not only was the "repository of the Russian ideal of the State" and embodied "its might and unity" but in times of "upheaval and danger to the State" was also the only force capable of saving Russia and leading the country "to a path of order and historical veracity." The "autocracy of the Moscow Tsars" had, no doubt, undergone changes over the past three centuries, yet "[t]he Russian Empire owes its origin and development to its Russian roots, and with its growth grew and also developed the autocratic power of the Tsars. To this Russian stem no foreign and alien flower may be grafted. (Cheers, Center and Right.) Let our Russian flower bloom on it." He then returned to a point he had briefly touched on in his previous address, the temporary suspension of the irremovability of judges, which he claimed was necessary to enhance the government's capacity to deal with disorder. And his response to Dmowski was hardly designed to placate the Poles. He urged the Poles to "take our point of view, and acknowledge that the greatest blessing consists in being a citizen of Russia; hold up that emblem as high as it was held by citizens of Rome and you will then style yourselves citizens of the superior kind, and will receive all manner of rights." Put differently, the national minorities could enjoy the privileges of citizenship, but only if they renounced demands for special political status within the Russian Empire.

Toward the end of his speech Stolypin, as was his custom, turned to rhetorical flourishes to energize his supporters. "The Government must seek to avoid superfluous words; but there are words which have caused the hearts of Russians to beat for centuries past, and such words and sentiments must be kneaded into the mind, and must be reflected in the acts of the Government. These words are: undeviating loyalty to Russian historical traditions. These words form a counterpoise to Socialism, and magnify the country in opposition to those who desire its disruption, and finally they express loyalty to the death to [our] Tsar, who personifies Russia. This, gentlemen, is all I desire to state. I have stated what I think, and have spoken to the best of my ability. (Loud applause.)"[24]

It cannot be said that the views Stolypin expressed in this speech differed substantially from what he had said on previous occasions. There could never be any doubt about his devotion to the monarchy or his patriotism. But he had never been as unqualified and bombastic in expressing these sentiments. He did not really wish to revoke the October Manifesto, and he claimed to be a constitutionalist. Was he, then, carried away by the fact that many deputies of the Third Duma were conservative and nationalistic? Or was he trying to placate the tsar and his advisers at the court, who were deeply suspicious of the legislature regardless of its political makeup?

Whatever his intentions, the liberals would not allow his remarks to go unanswered. The next day, on November 17, they unleashed an attack on the prime minister that provoked what one observer called a "tumult such as had not been known in the two previous Dumas." Miliukov censured the prime minister for not bothering to mention the October Manifesto, and F. I. Rodichev accused the Russian authorities of having sought to threaten the Poles by warning them that Germany would invade the Polish Kingdom if order were not re-established. This comment was greeted with cries of "lies" and "enough" so loud that the president could not hear Rodichev's speech. But that was followed by an even noisier ruckus set off by a remark by Rodichev that he could not complete: "At the time when the Russian authorities were struggling with the excesses of the revolution they saw only one means, one safeguard for our victory: the rope which [the ultrarightist] Purishkevich has called the Muraviev collar,* and which the descendants of Purishkevich will perhaps call the Stolypin necktie." As he said this, Rodichev used his arms to indicate how the rope was fastened around the neck of victims of the field courts-martial. Stolypin, angry and pale, stalked out of the chamber together with the other ministers, and within short order the prime minister challenged Rodichev to a duel. Within the chamber, there was an uproar. "It seemed," the reporter for the *Novoe vremia* noted, "that an electrical current was passing through the benches. Deputies ran from their seats, shouted, banged on their desks; the cries and expressions of indignation blended into an incredible noise; it was almost impossible to hear anyone or the President's bell." The deputies appeared to be on the verge of attacking each other physically, and the president, incapable of maintaining order, adjourned the session for one hour. Rodichev apologized to Stolypin, explaining that he had not intended a personal slur. The prime minister was mollified and accepted the apology, but the Duma voted overwhelmingly to suspend Rodichev for the next fifteen meetings of the legislature.[25]

So long as Stolypin was under attack for his suppression of the left, conservatives of all shades of opinion rallied to his support. But the prime minister took seriously his promises of reform, which meant that he would encounter fierce resistance from some of his allies. In a sense, he had little choice. Once he had enacted the agrarian reforms in 1906, which encouraged peasants to leave the commune and become private landowners, the existing institutions of peasant self-government, based on the principle that the peasants constituted a separate estate (*soslovie*) with rights different from those of other estates, could no longer be justified. He made this point to the Council of Ministers on December 11, 1906, when he provided the rationale for the reform of local institutions: "[T]he grouping of Russia's population by estates represents something concrete only to the extent that this division corresponds to real differences among distinct class elements; when it exceeds these limits, it is a purely fictitious construct."[26] Eight days later, he stated categorically,

---

*A reference to the repressive measures of Count Muraviev when he was governor-general of Vilna in 1863.

also at a meeting of the cabinet, that the "estate organs of the peasants (on the *volost* and village levels), and also the special institutions that now manage peasant affairs (the land captains, district congresses, and provincial offices) are to be abolished."[27] Privately, the prime minister told A. A. Naryshkin, a leader of the United Nobility, in no uncertain terms that the estate principle was outdated and should be abolished.[28]

In addition, Stolypin was determined to embark on a far-reaching restructuring of local government because he was convinced that the prevailing system was inefficient, "thoroughly decrepit." Many marshals of the nobility, key figures in the structure, paid little attention to administrative affairs, leaving the work to deputies. Not infrequently, marshals spent long periods away from their districts; over one-fourth of them resided there only rarely. As a consequence, there was no coherence to the administration of local affairs; civil servants from the various ministries such as Finance, Justice, Postal Service, and Forestry operated on their own and at times at cross-purposes. Moreover, Stolypin had noticed as governor of Saratov that the police could not cope with civil unrest. All this seemed so evident to him that he refused to believe that anyone could in good conscience contend that reform of local institutions of government was unnecessary. He took as his models Prussia and France, where the *Landrat* or *Prefet* coordinated policies for localities.[29]

The reference to Prussia was especially noteworthy because it signaled the Russian nobles that the changes Stolypin proposed would not necessarily mean an end to their political pre-eminence in the state or an end to monarchical rule. Indeed, on June 3, 1907, *Rossiia* carried an article specifically urging Russian nobles to study how conservatives in Prussia had managed to defend the monarchical principle by constitutional means.[30] This was Stolypin's way of reassuring the nobility that he planned to create institutions that would enlist support from the new property owners (peasants leaving the commune), who would have a stake in the prevailing monarchical order.

In making his case for administrative reform, Stolypin also indicated that he was troubled by the politicization of the civil service, and not only in a leftward direction. No doubt, a sizable number of officials in the ministries of Justice and Finance openly supported liberal causes. But a number of governors and police officers had in various ways helped right-wing organizations that promoted violence against the left and against Jews. Stolypin, as had Witte, denounced such conduct and insisted that officials desist from it. Despite his general defense in the

Second Duma of the police, Stolypin dismissed the governor of Suwalki when it became evident that he was partially responsible for the pogrom in Bialystok in June 1906.[31]

Several ministers had previously recognized the deficiencies of local self-government. In 1902, Plehve and in 1904–5 Witte had established several commissions to formulate reform proposals, but they did little beyond enunciating general principles. Stolypin, however, considered the matter a cornerstone of his entire program and devoted himself much more systematically than his predecessors to producing concrete measures for change. Shortly after his appointment as minister of internal affairs he directed trusted members of his department, most notably the talented Kryzhanovskii and Gurliand, to devise specific proposals.

Apparently fearful that conservatives in the Third Duma would undermine his initiative, he decided to mobilize support by convoking the Council on the Local Economy, an institution conceived by Plehve to advise the Ministry of Internal Affairs on local issues. It never met during Plehve's tenure, but Stolypin wished to accord the assembly an important role in the legislative process. As he told the tsar in 1910, the council, widely regarded in society and in the press as a kind of "Pre-Duma," was designed to provide civil servants, ministers, marshals of the nobility, urban leaders, and zemstvo activists an opportunity to work together in a friendly spirit and to examine as well as improve projects before their consideration by the Duma.[32] It is surprising that he clung to this view as late as 1910, since by that time it was evident that the Council on the Local Economy would not assume the role he envisioned.[33]

The first meeting of the council in March 1908, held in St. Petersburg to maximize the prime minister's influence over the proceedings, was attended by twenty-three government officials (seventeen from the Ministry of Internal Affairs) and representatives chosen by all thirty-four zemstvo assemblies and by twelve city dumas. Stolypin himself addressed the first session and immediately sought to confront the skepticism of the audience, which included a sizable number of conservative nobles. "I know that many believe that as long as the countryside is not completely calm it is necessary to retain the old system. But the government believes otherwise and considers it its duty to undertake an improvement in the system of local administration." He invited the members of the council to "invigorate" the proposals his ministry had formulated and hoped that during the deliberations "misunderstandings" would be removed.[34] Moreover, he went out of his way to reassure the assembly that the government would insist on maintaining the "influence and importance [in the zemstvos] of the most cultivated, most educated element," the group with the most experience in zemstvo work—that is, "the class of local landowners."[35]

The prime minister's appeals and reassurances proved to be wasted effort. It quickly became evident that Stolypin had misjudged the mood of the council and the nobility in general: his proposals encountered the most intense resistance.

From the moment Stolypin broached the idea of local reform, however, he believed that he should not lightly abandon his efforts. He knew firsthand that the deficiencies of government in the provinces to which he had referred told only part of the story. In fact, the entire system was archaic and cumbersome and shot through with incompetence, arbitrariness, and corruption. The heart of the problem can be traced to the attempt of various governments since the emancipation of the serfs in 1861 to accomplish what was impossible: to reconcile the principle of autocracy with that of local initiative. Fearful that the institutions of self-rule established in the 1860s would seek to play a role in national affairs, the authorities in St. Petersburg maintained traditional organs of local power alongside the new ones and even created an additional governmental body to hold the old ones in check. The result was a jumble of local organs of government with overlapping authority that were frequently at odds with each other.

But there was another reason for the deficiencies in the administration of European Russia.* Neither the central government nor the local organs ever provided adequate resources for the staffing of bureaucratic agencies; the pay of civil servants at the lower rungs of the civil service was abysmal, making it extremely difficult to recruit well-educated, dedicated, and honest people. Only too often, the temptation to take bribes was hard to resist. The endless tales of corruption that fill the pages of Russian literature of the nineteenth and early twentieth centuries do not distort reality.

The governor stood at the apex of the bureaucratic hierarchy in the provinces. Invariably a man from the nobility, the governor was appointed by the tsar and was answerable to him, although he directed the bulk of his reports to the Ministry of Internal Affairs, which, of course, was accountable to the monarch. Although the ministry sought to fill

---

*The situation in the rest of the empire was no better, but Stolypin's reform proposal was to be introduced only in European Russia and in large parts of the Ukraine, thus excluding the six provinces in Lithuania and White Russia and the three provinces in southwestern Ukraine, in which zemstvos had not been established.

the governorships with men who were educated and had extensive administrative experience, favoritism still played a part in the selection process.

Even the most conscientious and diligent governor faced a daunting assignment, however, for his responsibilities and powers were very extensive. His main task was to maintain law and order, and in times of acute unrest he would be authorized by St. Petersburg to enforce special emergency measures that vastly enhanced his powers.* But at all times he was responsible for such matters as famine relief and public health (especially during plagues, a fairly frequent occurrence). The governor also could veto the appointments by zemstvos of their sizable staffs, a power he would invoke to keep politically unreliable individuals off the public payroll. He also could impose limits on the zemstvo budgets, and he regularly made tours of inspection of the province to familiarize himself with local conditions and to gauge the effectiveness of the administration. In short, the governor's decisions affected virtually every sphere of public life. Yet governors faced numerous limitations on their authority. Power in the provinces was fragmented, as Richard G. Robbins has pointed out, and consequently governors were often frustrated in seeking to implement their policies in their jurisdictions.[36]

For one thing, governors had to contend with the provincial marshals of the nobility, who occupied the second most prestigious post in the provinces. Elected by assemblies of the gentry for three-year terms and confirmed in their posts by St. Petersburg, the marshals as a group represented the very top stratum of the nobility and were viewed as spokesmen of the gentry estate.[37] The marshals had certain specific administrative tasks such as chairing the provincial zemstvo assembly and serving on all major standing committees, but their influence reached beyond these functions. More often than not, a provincial marshal was well connected in high circles in St. Petersburg, and in conflicts with governors it was not at all predictable who would prevail. In addition, in each district (uezd) the local nobility elected a district marshal of the nobility, who chaired district zemstvo assemblies as well as various committees that dealt with peasant affairs.

District and provincial zemstvos had been established in 1864 and had been assigned extensive powers in such areas as the improvement of agricultural production, health services, the building and maintenance of roads and bridges, public education, and charity. The members of the zemstvo assemblies were elected but on the basis of an unequal suffrage;

---

*For details on the emergency powers, see below, p. 263.

42 percent of the seats in the district zemstvo assemblies were held by nobles, and in the provincial assemblies nobles held 74 percent. Nevertheless, the zemstvos' achievements in their areas of competence were considerable. But they were frustrated by their limited powers and by the central government's increasing interference in their work. Not surprisingly, many zemstvo activists as well as a very large number of full-time employees (teachers, agronomists, engineers, statisticians, and doctors) became increasingly vocal in advocating far-reaching political reform. In the years immediately preceding the Revolution of 1905, governors frequently found themselves in conflict with them (as noted in the chapter on Stolypin's three years as governor of Saratov).

To complicate matters further, the peasants had their own institutions to handle some of their affairs. These institutions operated at the level of the *volost* (canton), which consisted of anywhere from three hundred to two thousand male peasants, who elected assemblies, which, in turn, chose officials to maintain order and to control the issuance of passports. The volost also had its own courts that could mete out punishments for minor offenses and could settle disputes between peasants involving a sum no larger than one hundred rubles. The *volost* institutions were based purely on the estate principle—that is, participation in their affairs was limited to peasants.

In 1889, during the era of counterreform, the government created a new post, that of land captain, and invested it with so much authority over peasant affairs that the system of peasant self-rule, allegedly characterized by "chaos and wild abuse," was greatly diluted. The procedures for the selection of the land captain indicate the importance the government attached to the post. The district marshals of the nobility were to prepare lists of suitable candidates from which the governor made his selection, but the final choice remained with the Ministry of Internal Affairs. If the ministry did not like the governor's nominee, it could make its own appointment. A land captain was to be a nobleman from the area in which he would serve, and he was to have completed some higher education or to have sufficient experience in administration.

The land captain exercised vast powers over peasant affairs. He could nullify decisions of peasant assemblies and of communes, he could add items to their agendas, and he could remove peasant officials from their posts if he considered them to be "unreliable." The land captain could also void decisions of the *volost* courts and could on his own decide certain civil and criminal cases. As a group, the land captains pretty much enjoyed a free hand in their work. The districts marshals, who were to

keep an eye on their actions, often looked the other way. And the conferences of land captains that were supposed to supervise the captains
could hardly be expected to be objective. A land captain could be dismissed only by the Ministry of Internal Affairs. All in all, the government could be satisfied in having found a way of prolonging the peasants' condition of tutelage. It had created an administrative structure
that blocked the peasants from gaining experience in self-government
and in fulfilling the rights and obligations of citizenship.[38]

Clearly, the nobility played so commanding a role in governing the
provinces that no effort at fundamental administrative reform could
succeed without diminishing the prerogatives of that class. Yet there is
no evidence that Stolypin anticipated unyielding opposition from the
gentry to his program, the outlines of which he first made known in a
presentation to the cabinet late in 1906. He seemed to have been confident that the debates and negotiations, which dragged on for over two
years and were almost always rather complex and often acrimonious,
would persuade the nobility that his approach best served the interests
of the state and deserved support. In this tortuous process, the government felt obliged to retreat on one issue after another, but even then it
could not secure the necessary support. Still, the principles underlying
Stolypin's efforts deserve attention because they cast light on his conception of how Russia should be governed.

The prime minister sought to achieve several goals. He wanted to ra-
tionalize and streamline local government, make it more efficient, define its functions clearly and more broadly, and involve a larger number
of people than heretofore in its operations. At the same time, the central
government would increase its overall role in the administration of the
provinces. Of course, Stolypin did not intend to abandon the goal of reconciling autocracy and local initiative. He believed that he could devise
a more effective machinery to achieve that goal. At first glance, the various parts of the reform plan seem to be at odds with each other, but it is,
in fact, quite coherent.

One of its key features was the creation of a new post, the district
commandant, to be filled by the Ministry of Internal Affairs. The district
commandants would replace the district marshals of the nobility and
would assume some of the functions of the land captain, a position that
would be eliminated. Although the new officials' duties would be primarily administrative, they could rule on the legality of measures
adopted by a new cantonal assembly, the zemstvo. In addition, the
authority of governors, also appointees of the Ministry of Internal Affairs, was to be broadened. In the event of threats to public order, they

would have greater latitude in imposing emergency measures. Governors as well as district commandants would also be granted full control over the actions of officials from the various ministries working within their provinces, and both would be accorded the right to attend meetings of zemstvo assemblies and of city dumas, and, if they requested it, would be the first to speak.

At the same time, Stolypin's reform proposal, in keeping with his vow to undermine the estate principle, called for the dismantling of the elaborate cantonal (*volost*) structure, which managed only the affairs of peasants. The new primary units of government in the cantons would be zemstvos elected by men from all social groups. The powers of the reformed zemstvos were to be expanded into such areas as elementary education, famine relief, public health, communication systems, and economic affairs generally. But in the event of civil disorder, the authorities in St. Petersburg would have the right to intervene in the zemstvo's conduct of affairs. This was designed to prevent the oppositional activities of the zemstvos, which were widespread before 1905.

To break down the estate system of voting further, Stolypin recommended a substantial broadening of the suffrage in elections to zemstvos throughout the country. Ever since the establishment of zemstvos in 1864, elaborate regulations were enforced to ensure the gentry a dominant position, as has already been noted. All told, only 129,000 people out of a population of some 130 million could participate in the elections for zemstvo deputies. Stolypin proposed that the number be increased sixfold, to 765,000 taxpayers. This marked a significant democratization of the electoral system, but property qualifications remained very important in determining eligible voters. And, as previously noted, Stolypin also favored extending to Jews the right to participate in elections to urban dumas, though they were not permitted to elect more than one-fifth of the deputies of any one council.[39]

To reassure the nobles further that the reform of local self-government would not render them impotent as a political force, Stolypin proposed granting certain special privileges to rich nobles. Landowners whose wealth amounted to more than 150,000 rubles would be granted membership in district zemstvos without having to stand for election, though the total number of such deputies was not to constitute a majority in any assembly. The prime minister also stipulated that both the land-owning class and the peasantry would be guaranteed a certain minimum number of seats. His overall goal was to ensure a membership of the zemstvos with a sufficient level of education to handle complex issues of government. Rich landowners, he argued, composed a significant percentage of the educated class and therefore deserved special consideration in determining the composition of the zemstvos. Stolypin's proposals on local government would have produced a distinct weakening of the estate principle, but they would not have eliminated it completely.[40]

Nonetheless, most nobles, apprehensive over the loss of power, rejected Stolypin's proposals for reform of local government. In the face of mounting criticism, Stolypin made additional concessions to assuage their fears. Late in 1908, for example, he promised them that marshals of the nobility would be the "first candidates" for the new posts, though he did not promise that they would definitely be appointed.[41] It was to no avail. In the nobles' view, even if Stolypin's proposals for local reform did not immediately end their influence they were a first step in that direction. The recent vote in the Third Duma, apparently abetted by the prime minister, not to include the word "autocracy" in the Address to the Throne only added to the nobility's anxiety. Stolypin, it appeared to them, had crushed the revolution, but he had not done so to save the old order. He too wanted to change that order, and that seemed to be as great a threat as the proposals of the left.

Rightists had begun to be suspicious of Stolypin very early during his tenure as prime minister, even before the proposals on local government had surfaced. Late in 1906, the Second Congress of the United Nobility expressed strong reservations about the drift of the prime minister's reform program, warning in what were still restrained words, that "our interests as an estate might diverge from those of the government." By early 1907, when the specifics of the local reform proposal had become widely known, Count S. D. Sheremetev, a wealthy and influential landowner, wrote to F. D. Samarin, also a rich landowner, that the prime minister's plan was nothing less than "an attempt to speed up the transition to a new form of government" and smacked of "governmental cynicism."[42] At about the same time, Stolypin received a memorandum drafted in the name of a group of rightists in the State Council by Count K. I. Pahlen, a former minister of justice, denouncing the plan in the most strident terms. The rightists rejected the basic elements of the projected reform: the removal of marshals of the nobility from the leading role in the affairs of the districts, the formation of nonestate zemstvos in the cantons, and the extension of the suffrage in elections of zemstvos generally. In the rightists' view, the government's proposal would provoke "a fundamental disruption of the entire administrative mechanism in the heat of a revolution that is also a war, but one with an internal enemy that is much more dangerous than any foreign foe."[43]

The militancy and strident language reflected the despair of a large part of the nobility, a social group that had been declining steadily as an economic and political force ever since the emancipation of the serfs in 1861 and that by the early twentieth century feared that it was facing a loss of the last vestiges of its influence. Constituting no more than 1.5 percent of the population, the *dvorianstvo*, according to the census of 1897, was a highly diversified group of rich and poor, owners of large estates or of modest summer homes in the countryside. About a fifth were professionals, and a fair number were civil servants or military officers. Close to 50 percent of the nobles were ethnically non-Russian. Although nobles were the main prop of the autocracy, they were not politically homogeneous. A sizable portion supported reactionary movements, others favored the conservative cause, and quite a few had turned to liberalism in the early twentieth century.[44]

Until the emancipation, the nobility had performed important functions in the body politic, though it did not enjoy the kind of independence from the state that its counterpart in France (or other Western European countries) had achieved by the late eighteenth century. The Russian nobility was subservient to the monarch, who, in turn, maintained the political order that enabled the gentry to serve as a leading force in society. The nobles exercised vast authority over the roughly 45 percent of the peasants who were serfs, manned the judicial posts in their districts, supervised the collection of the soul tax, and oversaw the recruitment of men for military service. A few nobles, moreover, owned large estates that yielded a surplus for the export market. No matter how other classes viewed these arrangements, they could not deny that the *dvorianstvo* discharged obligations useful to the state. After the reforms of the 1860s, however, the nobility began to lose much of its raison d'être and standing in society, though that was not the government's intention.

In fact, Alexander II's government, which had implemented the emancipation decree, went to great lengths to prevent the decline of the nobility. It designed the decree in such a way as to provide the nobles with a maximum amount of land. It also granted them tax privileges and ensured them a dominant role in the local organs of government, the zemstvos. Tsar Alexander III (r. 1881–94) continued to be solicitous about the *dvorianstvo*, which he regarded as the pre-eminent class in society and in the state.[45] In 1885 the government created the Gentry Land Bank, which offered loans at low interest rates to noble landowners. But neither that measure nor several others undertaken by the government in the late 1880s and the 1890s halted the decline of the *dvori-anstvo*.

The most striking manifestation of the nobility's decline was its loss of land. Unable or unwilling to administer their estates on a capitalist basis, many nobles sold their land to townsmen or peasants. In the period from the Great Reforms until 1905, the nobility surrendered about one-third of its total landholdings. To appreciate the magnitude of the transformation of land ownership, it should be kept in mind that in the 1860s the privileged classes owned one-half of the privately held arable land.

Economic trends played an important role in the nobility's decline. The severe agrarian crisis in the last decades of the nineteenth century, a worldwide phenomenon that caused a sharp drop in the prices of major crops, hindered the development of large-scale farming in Russia.[46] Moreover, most nobles never mastered the rudiments of scientific farming and made only the feeblest efforts to obtain up-to-date machinery.[47]

In the last analysis, the nobles' inability to turn their estates into profitable ventures was rooted in their psychological disposition. Under serfdom, noble landlords had never been known for hard work, managerial skills, or frugality. Accustomed to receiving state handouts and dues as well as services from their serfs, they failed to develop the drive and initiative necessary for success in a market economy. The emancipation of the serfs made matters worse for the nobility. They became even more paralyzed, for now they had to fend for themselves under circumstances thoroughly alien to their experience.

Early in the reign of Tsar Nicholas II, senior officials became alarmed at the nobility's declining role in public institutions. So many nobles had fled the countryside that the supply of personnel qualified to hold positions of authority was seriously depleted. At times, not enough nobles could be found to fill all the seats to which they were entitled in the zemstvo assemblies. It has been estimated that in fifty provinces out of seventy-eight the *dvorianstvo* was no longer capable of exerting a measurable influence on local affairs. The government was at a loss on how to reverse the trend.[48]

The agrarian unrest in the fall and winter of 1905, the most extensive and destructive disturbance in Russia since the eighteenth century, stunned and alarmed the nobles, prompting many of them to turn sharply to the right.[49] One consequence of that turn, the reassertion of the conservative gentry's predominance in the zemstvos, has already been noted. Another consequence was their increasing militancy, which took two forms, an organized campaign to promote their cause at court and a campaign to vilify Stolypin, seen as a threat to their survival as an influential force in society.

Early in April 1908 a delegation from the United Nobility led by A. A. Bobrinskii gave the tsar a letter summarizing the resolutions of the Fourth Congress attacking the proposal on local government. In response, Nicholas, clearly undermining his prime minister, promised not to permit a diminution of the authority of the district marshals of the nobility. Two months later Gurko, forced to resign in disgrace late in 1906, passed on to the tsar a report of the Fourth Congress that accused the government of undermining state institutions that "defend tsarist autocracy and Russia's historical structure" and of failing to reform the schools, press, and jury system, allegedly the breeding ground for rebellion.[50] On January 31, 1908, a meeting of the nobility of Moscow province adopted a resolution, by a vote of 198 to 122, that in effect called for a disavowal of the Manifesto of October 1905. The Duma, the resolution stated, should be deprived of legislative authority, and the autocracy, "responsible only to God," should be restored. The nobility of Kursk province passed a similar resolution and sent it to the tsar.[51]

At private gatherings of dignitaries in St. Petersburg and Moscow and elsewhere, the campaign against Stolypin became highly personal and even vicious. L. A. Tikhomirov, a man who in the 1880s had moved from the extreme left to the extreme right, reported late in 1907 that whenever he met with friends the main topic of conversation was Stolypin's perfidy. No one trusted him, and the general view was that he "makes promises very easily and then begins to have second thoughts."[52] Every few weeks rumors circulated that the prime minister had resigned, was about to resign, or would soon be asked by the tsar to leave office. Late in February 1908, the rightist and former minister Shirinskii told Tikhomirov that Stolypin had been deeply offended by the tsar's favorable reaction to an address at an imperial audience by a deputation from Tula that in effect expressed lack of confidence in the government. Stolypin, Shirinskii reported, tendered his resignation to Nicholas. The tsar refused to accept it, but Shirinskii gleefully insisted that Nicholas did not appreciate such behavior by his ministers and that soon Stolypin would be forced to leave office.[53] Invariably, the presumed successor to Stolypin would be someone congenial to the extremists of the right. The names most frequently mentioned were Goremykin and P. N. Durnovo.[54] The list of dignitaries who in late 1907 and early 1908 attended the salons in St. Petersburg where the prime minister was regularly savaged is long and impressive: it included powerful nobles, prominent civil servants, former ministers, and one future prime minister (B. V. Stürmer).[55]

Perhaps the most persistent, and certainly the most vicious, foe of Stolypin was Prince M. M. Andronikov, whom Bernard Pares called "one of the most sinister personalities in the public life of Russia." If true, and apparently it was, Andronikov must have been a very talented man, because in early twentieth-century Russia the competition for notoriety and nastiness was very keen indeed. Even so gifted an intriguer and slanderer as Witte was appalled by the man's behavior. Witte conceded that Andronikov was not a stupid man; he knew several languages and yet he could "hardly be considered an educated man. After leaving school he entered on his chosen career—swindler and police agent." He had attended the aristocratic Corps of Pages and that, together with his title of prince, gave him entree to high society in St. Petersburg. A man of some charm, he managed to insinuate himself into the good graces of men in positions of power and prestige: he would send these men gifts of icons and, perhaps more important, information—gossip is a better word—hoping to obtain other gossip in return. Despite his "most unsavory moral reputation," he exerted considerable influence at court, where he was regularly received by the tsar, the minister of the court, and the commandant of the palace. Not a rich man, he relied for his income on speculation, loans, and handouts from the police, apparently in return for information on men in positions of authority.[56] Another source of income was his work for the so-called reptile press, a reference to newspapers that bribed journalists to write articles with a particular slant.

Andronikov was convinced that Stolypin's policies would not succeed in pacifying Russia, and in mid-1907 he tried to warn the prime minister that he would court disaster if he did not change course. Stolypin received him at his office, listened to his advice, and decided to ignore him. Andronikov, not accustomed to such treatment, became the prime minister's irreconcilable enemy, determined to topple him from power. He launched a campaign of vituperation, telling anyone who would listen that Stolypin was politically bankrupt, that whatever he did was bad, rotten, and bound to lead to new catastrophes. In his private conversations and his newspaper articles he also raised the question of whether the prime minister was preparing himself to replace the tsar, who, in Andronikov's imagination, was thinking of renouncing the throne. And Stolypin, in this version of his ambitions, was bent on forming his own dynasty. In 1910, Andronikov, who liked to boast that he was an "A.D.C. [aide de camp] of the Almighty," noted maliciously that Stolypin had already moved in that direction by giving important posts to relatives: S. D. Sazonov, his brother-in-law, was the minister of foreign affairs after September 1910; and L. A. Kasso, also related to Stolypin by marriage, was the minister of education. It is a sign of the poisoned political atmosphere in Late Imperial Russia that a man such as Andronikov was taken at all seriously in political circles.[57]

Stolypin was not impervious to criticism, and on occasion he complained about newspaper attacks on him. Generally, however, he maintained his composure and would not allow himself to be diverted from his policies. "In talking to Mr. Stolypin," the German ambassador, Pourtalès, noted early in 1908, "one gets the feeling that one is dealing with a man with a straightforward and loyal character, a man who systematically follows the path he considers the right one."[58] In noting Stolypin's tenacity, Pourtalès put his finger on a key aspect of the prime minister's character. Despite the fierce opposition of the nobles to his project on local government, Stolypin throughout 1908 and in 1909 continued to seek support for it in the Duma. He made concessions to the nobles, but he refused to abandon the essentials of his program. Early in 1909 he personally urged rightists and moderates in the Duma, among them G. G. Zamyslovskii and P. N. Balashov, to support his proposals. He made a similar appeal to the president of the Duma, Khomiakov. But the forces arraigned against him were too powerful. As Kryzhanovskii ruefully put it in his memoirs, Stolypin's "attempt to affect the special position of the nobility in local administration, which, to be sure, he decided not to press to the ultimate, stirred up strata that had great influence over the throne: . . . [The tsar's] retinue openly condemned . . . [the reform proposals]."[59]

Even though Stolypin did eventually obtain the support of the majority of the Council on the Local Economy for his project, it was a pyrrhic victory. Three-fourths of the votes for his project came from government officials; two-thirds of the representatives from the zemstvo provinces voted against it. In the face of the irreconcilable opposition of the nobles and without active support from the tsar, Stolypin had no choice but to give up and shelve the project.[60] The reforms never came up for a vote in the Duma. It was Stolypin's first major, and arguably his most devastating, defeat. If he could not reduce the influence and power of the nobles he would not be able to reorganize and modernize the country's political system, one of the two linchpins—the other was the agrarian reform—of his entire reform program.

Stolypin's initiatives in educational and labor reform, two areas of long-standing interest to him, also ran into fierce resistance, but the government did achieve some of its goals in both areas. The prime minister understood that the nation's economy could not be modernized and the people's standard of living could not be raised substantially unless the level of education throughout the empire was greatly improved. Statistics on literacy confirm his contention that Russia was unprepared to undertake the technological advances that had transformed Central and Western Europe. In 1897, only 21 percent of the empire's population could read and write. In 1904, only about 3.5 million children attended elementary schools administered by the Ministry of Education. In addition, close to 2 million children were educated in schools run by the Church. In other words, a mere 27 percent of all the children of school age were exposed to what in most cases amounted to a rudimentary education. To grasp the significance of these figures, it is worth noting that in Japan, which also had recently undergone a process of modernization, some 93 percent of all boys and girls of school age were attending school in 1903.[61]

Reform of elementary education was high on Stolypin's agenda from the moment he became prime minister. When his newly formed cabinet considered its overall program, early in August 1906, it explored the question in some detail and then returned to it on January 26 and 30, 1907, five weeks before Stolypin's speech to the Second Duma outlining his goals. The proposals formulated at the first meeting, which the tsar approved on September 30, 1906, became the centerpiece of Stolypin's educational policy for the next five years. They were notably ambitious and had they been fully implemented they would have produced major social and economic changes.

Within ten years a system of universal primary education was to be introduced throughout the empire. All children of both sexes, beginning at the age of eight, were to be offered four years of education. The responsibility for establishing new schools and for administering them would rest with the zemstvos and urban city councils, but the central government would continue to finance much of the cost (about 85 percent of the funds would come from St. Petersburg) and would retain ultimate supervision over the schools. No teacher in an elementary school was to be assigned classes larger than fifty, and for each such group of students there would be one teacher for secular subjects and one for religious instruction. No school would serve an area larger than two miles in radius. Salaries for teachers, which were pitiable (360 rubles a year at zemstvo schools and 60 rubles a year at Church schools), could be raised, but only if the local authorities assumed the extra cost.[62]

The educational reforms quickly encountered vigorous opposition.

The Orthodox Church raised two objections even though the government made clear that the Church would also be permitted to open new schools. The first objection was financial. Stolypin's legislative proposal did not provide for any funds from the Ministry of Education for the establishment and maintenance of Church schools; the Holy Synod, a government institution that funded existing religious schools, would have to finance new ones from its budget. In addition, the Holy Synod feared that the secular schools would not impart the proper religious training to youngsters. Activists in the zemstvos raised a different objection. They pointed out that the government's plan for compulsory elementary education would place a severe financial burden on local authorities. The government therefore made a concession: it stipulated that the zemstvos' financial means could be taken into account in undertaking the construction of new schools. This meant that in some regions of the empire not enough schools might be built to accommodate all the children of school age. The government's proposal ran into opposition for yet another reason. The original bill allowed instruction in areas where minorities predominated to be in languages other than Russian, but the State Council insisted that in all subjects except religion the language must be Russian. No agreement could be reached on this contentious issue, and the first bill (introduced in 1907 in the Second Duma) providing, in a systematic way, for universal compulsory elementary education floundered. In June 1912 it was finally rejected by the State Council.[63]

The government, however, was not deterred by its failure to secure legislative approval for its program. The Ministry of Education offered sizable sums of money to district zemstvos and city councils willing to build new schools; in the course of two years it transferred about 4.5 million rubles to local authorities committed to educational expansion. Then, in May 1908, the Third Duma adopted a government bill that contained several features of the bill that had been submitted a year earlier to the Second Duma. The result was a steady growth in elementary education. By 1913, the annual expenditure on elementary education amounted to 62.9 million rubles. Three years later, in 1916, of 441 district zemstvos in the empire, only three had failed to enter an agreement with the government in St. Petersburg for financial subsidies to build schools; 494 out of 789 towns with institutions of local self-government had done the same. By 1915, 33 towns including all the major cities had built enough schools to provide every eight-year-old with an elementary education. In the course of ten years, from 1905 to 1915, the number of schools in the empire rose from 92,295 to 123,754, and in the four years from 1911 to 1915 the number of pupils rose from 6,180,510 to 7,788,453. In 1915, slightly over 50 percent of all children between the ages of eight and eleven were attending school.

This increase in students required, in turn, an increase in the number of seminaries and institutes to train teachers. The government launched a program to establish both types of training centers. By 1916, 189 seminaries and 48 institutes were in place. At the time of the Revolution of 1917, primary education was still not universal, but when it is kept in mind that in 1897 only 21 percent of the population was minimally literate, it is clear that Stolypin's initiative had made a strong impact on education in Russia. A historian of Russian education has, in fact, referred to the "phenomenal expansion of educational opportunity" in the decade from 1905 to 1914.[64]

In the field of labor reform, Stolypin's government also had to overcome strong resistance. The prime minister had long favored such reform. As provincial marshal of the nobility in Kovno in 1902 Stolypin had advocated the establishment of insurance schemes for industrial and agricultural workers. His model was Bismarck's reform, which he praised for having directed the labor movement into a "calmer course." The underlying assumption was that the so-called labor question posed a serious social and political problem for the country, a notion by no means universally acknowledged in government circles. In fact, until 1905 the Ministry of Internal Affairs, the very department that Stolypin headed after April 1906, was in the forefront of those who claimed that there was no labor problem at all, that relations between employers and their workers were patriarchal in character, comparable to the relations between landlords and peasants. Consequently, the advocates of this position argued that the Russian worker, who was in any event less well educated than his counterpart in Western Europe and still tied to the land, would not succumb to the enticements of outside agitators, the alleged fomenters of labor unrest. Many officials knew that these assertions were baseless, but frank acknowledgment by imperial authorities that the patriarchal relationship was inapplicable to the urban setting would have constituted a confession that the social order of tsarism was based at least in part on myth.[65]

Bloody Sunday shattered the last remnants of the illusions about the docility of the industrial workers. Within months, a commission under the direction of Kokovtsov, the minister of finance, made some surprisingly progressive recommendations: the legalization of certain workers' associations, the creation of special funds for medical assistance for workers, shortening of the workday, and the establishment of a state in-

surance system for workers. Only Germany had a more generous program of labor legislation for the industrial sector.[66] But the opposition of
industrialists to these reforms proved to be insurmountable, and they
were not enacted in 1905.

Stolypin's government sought to revive several key measures proposed by the Kokovtsov Commission. Acknowledging that labor unrest
threatened to undermine public order, the cabinet in 1907 stated, in language similar to that used by Stolypin in 1902, that "the guiding principle of [the government's] policy is to bring about the maintenance of order in the factories and calm among the workers."[67] The prime minister
directed Gurliand, his advisor and senior official in the Ministry of Internal Affairs, to develop a program of labor legislation for workers, and
that was then refined and revised by the Ministry of Trade and Industry,
which in June 1908 introduced four bills in the State Duma. The centerpiece of the legislation was the creation of insurance schemes against
illness and accidents for industrial workers in factories and mines as
well as for employees in shipping and other transportation enterprises.

As had happened in 1905, the industrialists, although claiming to be
in favor of legislation to improve conditions for workers in principle,
raised one objection after another to the government's bills, claiming
that the insurance scheme would be too expensive and that it would
give too much power to the workers, who were to elect representatives
to a committee administering the insurance funds. Some officials also
began to have doubts about the latter provision, and in the prolonged deliberations, stretching over some four years, the original plan was inevitably watered down. Nonetheless, the final bill, approved by the tsar on
June 23, 1912, marked a significant breakthrough for industrial workers
in Russia. Stolypin was no longer alive, but there is little doubt that he
deserves much of the credit for it.

The main features of the final bill can be easily summarized. Workers in large factories and mines and those employed by railroad companies and shipping firms in European Russia and the Caucasus would be
insured against illness and accident. This would amount to some three
million workers, roughly 20 percent of the country's workforce, according to the Soviet scholar V. Ia. Laverychev.[68] Both workers and employers were to finance the insurance funds, the former contributing between 1 and 3 percent of their earnings and the latter about two-thirds of
that amount. Workers idled by an accident or illness would receive two-
thirds of their average daily wage. An elaborate administrative structure
including both workers and employers was charged with the supervision of the program. In a study of the workers' legislation of 1912, Ruth

A. Roosa concluded that "in its provisions for medical care [the program] went well beyond that offered by any other country."[69]

A reform program as ambitious and wide-ranging as Stolypin's was bound to provoke opposition from conservatives who feared change as a matter of principle and from groups who believed that their interests were at risk. But they were not the only ones to obstruct the implementation of his policies. Some recalcitrant subordinates undermined the second aspect of his overall program, the pacification of the country. His acerbic exchange of letters with one such subordinate, Count I. I. Vorontsov-Dashkov, is particularly noteworthy because it highlights, among other things, the complex character of the Russian bureaucracy and the limitations on the authority of even so forceful a prime minister as Stolypin.

No one familiar with the biography of the seventy-year-old Vorontsov-Dashkov would have thought him capable of challenging the tsar's authority and of deviating in any way from conservative principles. In 1881, Vorontsov-Dashkov had belonged to the ultraconservative *Sviashchennaia druzhina* (Holy Host), which dedicated itself to hunting down and eliminating revolutionaries. For sixteen years, from 1881 to 1897, he served as minister of state domains without showing any signs of discontent with the established order. But when he was appointed viceroy* of the Caucasus in 1905 he became, in the words of one historian, "an exceptionally liberal administrator," adopting tolerant policies toward the Armenians, as well as favoring "liberal economic reforms" and the establishment of zemstvos in the Caucasus.[70]

It is difficult to account for Vorontsov-Dashkov's change of heart. It may be that the deep social unrest and ethnic conflicts in the Caucasus persuaded him that the traditional policies of the government could no longer be effective. In any case, he chose to follow his own instincts and adopted a rather casual attitude toward the growing unrest.

In February 1907, Stolypin expressed alarm over the failure of the authorities in the Caucasus to restore order, and in a sharply worded telegram to Vorontsov-Dashkov gave the viceroy specific advice on how to deal with civil disorder. The prime minister's immediate concern was the spread of strikes in the oil industry in Baku. It had come to his attention that local businessmen did not think that they could resist the demands of disaffected workers, who were being supported by local au-

---

*The authority of a viceroy (*namestnik*) was comparable to that of a governor-general.

thorities. Stolypin feared that the consequence of capitulation to the workers would be an "incalculable calamity" that he and the Council of Ministers believed could be prevented only if the viceroy acted immediately and forcefully. The viceroy was to assemble a large armed force to protect local industry and suppress disturbances. The local administration was also to make clear its opposition to the "reckless demands" of the workers. Stolypin indicated that the tsar fully approved of the government's stand and was confident that "you will not refuse to take extreme measures to prevent the approaching disaster." Six weeks later, the prime minister sent another telegram to Vorontsov-Dashkov informing him once again about his and the tsar's alarm over developments in Baku and other Caspian ports. To maintain order and to prevent interruption of shipping, the viceroy must resort to the "most energetic measures," including the immediate expulsion of several hundred workers who had gone out on strike. New crews should be formed and these should be guarded by soldiers. Also, the garrison of Baku should be immediately reinforced. Such steps, the prime minister contended, "would have a morally calming effect" in the region. He asked Vorontsov-Dashkov to send him a telegram outlining the measures he was taking so that he could write an appropriate report for the tsar.[71]

Whatever measures the viceroy took seemed inadequate to Stolypin, who a year after the initial prodding sent Vorontsov-Dashkov a letter (dated April 11, 1908) that ran to fifteen printed pages. It amounted to nothing less than a blanket indictment of the local administration's failure to maintain order in the Caucasus. The prime minister surveyed conditions in one region after another, claiming that the authorities had generally abdicated their responsibilities and that in some areas authority had completely collapsed. The bill of particulars was staggering: in 1907 alone there had been 3,060 incidents of terror in the Caucasus; 1,239 people had been killed and 1,253 injured. Various groups had openly waged campaigns to promote nationalist causes. In the town of Telaev, revolutionary proclamations and newspapers advocating an armed uprising had been distributed and posted on buildings "before the eyes of the police." Armed individuals roamed the streets unmolested. The Ministry of Internal Affairs had also discovered that in one region twenty-three out of thirty-three policemen were openly sympathetic to radicalism. In 1907, the city of Novorossiisk had been nominally under martial law, and yet conditions there were totally anarchic: assassinations, robberies, and pillaging appeared to be normal occurrences. Well-to-do citizens and various institutions were being compelled to pay "taxes" to criminals. Stolypin listed several towns and regions where left-wing parties had taken control of judicial and administrative functions. He was especially disturbed by the activities of the Dashnaktsutiun, the Armenian Revolutionary Federation, a "criminal organization" committed to revolution and to Armenian nationalism. Stolypin placed the blame for this state of affairs directly on the shoulders of the local authorities, which had failed to discharge their obligations. Their failure to undertake the "simultaneous, decisive, planned rebuffs to all ... actions of criminal organizations and individuals" had caused the breakdown of law in the Caucasus. The prime minister ended his angry missive with the hope that Vorontsov-Dashkov would now take steps to safeguard "vital state and local interests."[72]

It took Vorontsov-Dashkov over three months to respond, and when he did (on July 23, 1908) he was as feisty and unyielding as the prime minister. The viceroy contended that the Ministry of Internal Affairs was both ill-informed and one-sided in its conclusions about the Caucasus. For one thing, other regions of the empire, most notably the Baltic provinces, had witnessed as much unrest and criminality as the Caucasus. Moreover, the people in the area over which he exercised authority were culturally less developed than the citizens of many other parts of the empire, and that explained the unruliness of the population under his charge. The natives in southern Russia were more impressionable; they reacted quickly and strongly to changes they did not understand. In saying this, the viceroy was of course conceding that Stolypin was not completely off the mark in his charges. But Vorontsov-Dashkov also insisted that the poor means of communication and transportation in the Caucasus made it difficult for him to maintain order. Having said that, the viceroy accused Stolypin of exaggerating the incidence of terror and crime in the area under his authority. And he dismissed as insulting the charge that local authorities had entered into cooperative arrangements with the Armenian revolutionary movement. "To this charge I am obliged to reply that representatives of the party 'Dashnaktsutiun' have not anywhere or at any time taken over the functions of the police." Nor was it true that the Armenians had established an "organized military force." Indeed, he claimed that his administration had cracked down on the Armenian activists, arresting and exiling many of them. He bristled at the very notion that officials under his authority had been less than efficient: they did not deserve to be "reproached for inaction."

To be sure, the police could be more effective, but the viceroy placed much of the blame for its failings on the central government in St. Petersburg. The police force was too small, was poorly paid, armed with obsolete weapons, and was asked to do work not normally required of policemen, such as escorting mailmen and guarding prisons. The latter tasks were a drain on resources that left the police with too few men to perform their normal duties. Moreover, the police were hampered by another problem: the central government had not assigned sufficient funds for the building of prisons. Jails built for 280 inmates now were forced to accommodate over 700. In sum, Vorontsov-Dashkov not only rejected many of the charges Stolypin had hurled at him; he charged the government in St. Petersburg with a failure to take adequate measures to maintain order in the outlying regions of the empire.[73] What he did not reveal to the prime minister was his inclination to be much more tolerant toward political activists than officials in St. Petersburg. Stolypin, of course, suspected that, and yet he did not dismiss Vorontsov-Dashkov; there is no evidence that he even tried. Perhaps the viceroy had some powerful protectors at court, or perhaps the administration in the capital was simply too lax or incapable of finding a more acceptable person to take over the unenviable task of administering the Caucasus, certainly one of the most explosive regions of the empire. In any case, despite his harsh exchange of letters with the prime minister, Vorontsov-Dashkov remained at his post until 1915.

The institutions of higher education, another hotbed of unrest during the revolutionary period from 1905 to 1907, also resisted Stolypin's program of pacification. In an attempt to restore order during the heady days of August 1905, the government had issued a decree (known as the Regulations of August 27) restoring to the universities and advanced institutes the autonomy of which they had been deprived in 1884. Councils of faculty members could once again elect the rector, and the faculty could elect the deans. The councils also assumed authority over educational matters and student affairs. For example, they could permit students to hold meetings on school grounds and, in the event of disorders, could close down the institutions. Courts of professors were established to rule on student infractions of disciplinary codes. Although the new dispensation seemed to be a sensible and workable arrangement, it soon led to endless conflict between students and university administrators, and between universities and governmental authorities. Students, interpreting the right to hold meetings very broadly, organized blatantly political gatherings, at which the tsarist regime came under severe criticism. At times speakers advocated the overthrow of the autocracy, and money was collected for organizations planning armed uprisings. Deans and rectors would plead for restraint, and were sometimes heeded but often ignored. Time and again, officials ordered the police or the army onto the university grounds to stop the political agitation, and when that happened the schools often closed down altogether, either by order of the administrations or as a result of student strikes. From late 1905 until the summer of 1906 the institutions of higher education held no classes at all.[74]

For Stolypin, these institutions posed a particularly acute challenge to his dual program of reform and repression. On the one hand, he was by no means hostile to higher education. On the contrary, as a university graduate himself he appreciated the importance of advanced education for Russia. The kind of modernization he envisioned required large cadres of trained citizens. Only a reformed educational system, he told the minister of education, A. N. Schwartz, on September 6, 1908, could save "our youth, and, consequently, Russia."[75] When conservatives wanted to reduce expenditures for education, the prime minister argued vigorously against them, and generally he prevailed. For example, in April 1907 he voted with the majority in the Council of Ministers in favor of funding the opening of a new university (it was founded in Saratov in 1909). The number of students at Russian universities continued to rise after he took over as prime minister, and by 1908 there were 35,329 in attendance, an increase of about 80 percent since 1904.[76]

On the other hand, Stolypin was uncompromising in his opposition to what he considered to be the politicization and therefore corruption of educational institutions. He frequently wrote letters to the minister of education and to his most trusted advisers, especially Gurliand, outlining his views on how the schools should cope with student activism. He also wrote a lengthy memorandum for his own eyes only on the subject, a clear sign that this was a matter of the utmost importance to him. Stolypin's campaign against the politicization of the universities was, of course, an integral part of his campaign against radicalism. He was convinced that the experiences of young Russians at the troubled institutions of higher learning often led them to embrace the revolutionary cause. Although he believed that the government could play a significant role in stemming the tide of radicalism at universities, he thought that the primary obligation lay with the professors. They must see to it that there was no interruption in the work of the universities, that learning proceeded in a calm atmosphere. "The professors," he declared, "must exclude from the educational establishments the instigators of unrest and should not shift [responsibility] to the government to take urgent measures. This only provokes new unrest."[77] If Stolypin had remained faithful to this doctrine of benign neglect, his government's university policy might have been much more effective.

When Stolypin became prime minister in July 1906, the minister of education, P. M. von Kaufmann, was a moderate conservative with little experience in higher education and few fixed views on how universities should be administered. His main concern was the reopening of the schools in September with as little trouble as possible. To that end, in July of 1906 he recommended a series of liberal measures, such as the admission of women, the abolition of the Jewish quota, granting the faculty the right to introduce an elective curriculum, and the abolition of the inspectorate (which kept an eye on student conduct). Only the last item was approved by the cabinet, leaving the other matters to the Duma. Von Kaufmann also adopted a relatively tolerant policy toward student meetings: they would be permitted so long as they did not openly aid revolutionary organizations and did not include nonstudents.[78] For about a year, von Kaufmann's pragmatic approach seemed to work reasonably well. There was some unrest, occasionally one or another school was closed for a short period, but on the whole the institutions of higher education remained much more peaceful than they had been during the heyday of the revolution.

Nevertheless, Stolypin was not satisfied. Although most students devoted themselves to their studies, he insisted, early in October 1906, that "the revolutionary minority is still in charge. . . . Students at Saint Petersburg University are so used to being free to hold meetings and discussions in the university that the latter has become a 'Republic in the Capital of the Autocracy.'" He made it clear that he favored the use of troops to break up student meetings that included outsiders—that is, nonstudents.[79] A month later, early in November, Stolypin told his minister of education that he agreed "in a most decisive way" with the city governor of Moscow, A. A. Reinbot, who had refused to make any concessions to students at Moscow University who were demanding, among other things, freedom of association and freedom of speech.[80] Von Kaufmann, however, continued to favor a much more relaxed approach to student activism, for which he came under increasing criticism from the prime minister. As Stolypin put it to the tsar on December 22, 1907, the Ministry of Education must be led by a "firm" hand. It seemed to him a mistake to drag out the conflict between the authorities and the students. If it became evident that the Ministry of Education was impotent, "a shadow of uncertainty and deceptiveness would be cast over the entire political course of the government."[81] In viewing the government's relations with the universities in such cosmic terms, Stolypin virtually foreclosed the possibility of compromise.

Tensions at the universities began to mount in response to the government's new guidelines on student organizations, which were issued on June 11, 1907, four days after the dissolution of the Second Duma. Henceforth students were prohibited from forming organizations on a universitywide basis, and only student meetings with a clear "academic character" would be allowed. If the meetings took up nonacademic issues, the police would immediately disperse them. Many students opposed the guidelines, but they did not mount a major campaign against it.

The turning point in student activism came early in 1908, when Stolypin dismissed von Kaufmann and replaced him with a primitive hardliner, A. N. Schwartz. A former professor of classics with some administrative experience as curator of the educational districts in Riga and Warsaw, Schwartz initially rejected Stolypin's offer of the post because he himself believed that he was so right wing, even reactionary, that he would arouse intense opposition. In dismissing Schwartz's concern, Stolypin stated a conception of effective leadership, which gives a rare insight into how he viewed his own role as head of the government: "For success one needs to have not only confidence but faith. At the present time a program and the will to implement it are not enough. You must have a cold, iron will and passionate faith in success." Stolypin disregarded Schwartz's demurrals and on January 1, 1908, appointed him minister of education.[82]

True to his word, Schwartz wasted no time in adopting very harsh and, in a literal sense, reactionary policies. In a memorandum drafted in the spring of 1908, he favored a return to the program of Russification. He would try to revoke concessions granted to non-Russian peoples; he would impose strict quotas on Jews at all levels of education; and he would abandon the relatively lax regulations enacted since August 1905. He also let it be known that he considered the students and many of the professors hostile to the prevailing order and a threat to the security of the state. In keeping with these views, he demanded that the faculty councils at the universities of St. Petersburg, Moscow, and Kharkov outlaw all student organizations.[83] Early in October 1908 the Ministry of Education made public a Draft Statute of new regulations that embraced the principles of the memorandum. In many respects, the statute rescinded the concession made in August 1905 and thus amounted to a virtual return to the harsh conditions that had been imposed in 1884.[84] Inevitably, the new approach to university governance aroused deep resentment among students, who at a meeting of various organizations early in September appealed for a nationwide academic strike. Within a couple of weeks, student meetings at the universities of Moscow,

Kharkov, Kazan, Kiev, and Odessa voted to support the strike. But public support for the students was tepid, and early in October the strike was called off.

In the meantime, Schwartz had overreached himself. He had announced his opposition to the practice of some professors to permit women to attend their classes as "auditors" on the grounds that many of them were intellectually unprepared for advanced studies. He would allow women enrolled in university courses to remain in class for the semester, after which they would be excluded. But that was too much even for Tsar Nicholas, who informed the prime minister that the policy on women auditors was not to be changed. Stolypin drafted a statement reflecting the tsar's wishes, which enraged Schwartz and prompted him to tender his resignation.[85] The prime minister appealed to Schwartz to remain in office. There are times, Stolypin told the minister of education, when one must yield to popular moods on specific issues. Such concessions to opportunism were trivial and meaningless. What mattered was that he and Schwartz agreed on fundamentals and that they would continue to pursue policies best for higher education. "I see the disintegration of the schools," Stolypin told Schwartz. "I know the Russian revolutionary, a good-natured ignoramus, who thinks the highest perfection can be attained not by sticking to the long and beaten track of education and determination, but by one leap . . . with bombs in his hand directed at the authorities!" Schwartz agreed to stay at his post but only if he were permitted to inform *Rossiia* that he had offered to resign and had changed his mind only because the prime minister had asked him to.[86]

Early in 1908, in a personal memorandum not intended for distribution on unrest in the institutions of higher learning, Stolypin formulated his overall strategy. His aim, he said, was not government control over the universities; his goal was to prevent activists from coercing students to engage in political agitation. He also noted that the cabinet believed that the controversies between students and the authorities turned on the students' misinterpretation of the autonomy decree of August 27, 1905. They claimed that they had been accorded the right to engage at will in political agitation on university grounds, but the councils of the schools as well as the government defined autonomy as the right of professors to regulate academic life. In addition, the government in 1905 had committed itself to the abolition of the inspectorate, which had, in fact, been done.

Over the preceding two years, however, new and contentious issues had emerged. Universities had been overwhelmed by an influx of students unprepared for advanced studies. Unauthorized organizations had been created to influence the decisions of the councils of professors. Under the circumstances, Stolypin insisted, the government could not shirk its obligation to restore what he considered to be normal conditions. The government had no intention of abolishing all institutions of student self-government. It would not, for example, interfere with student elections of "elders," who served as intermediaries between professors and students. But the government would refuse to permit the various student organizations to unite into one universitywide organization, which, it was feared, would invariably turn to politics. This, in Stolypin's view, was the crux of the issue between the authorities and the students that led to the call for a strike early in 1908. He was committed to keeping the schools open and to protecting the professors and students who wished to devote themselves to academic affairs. The prime minister vowed not to resort to any forceful measures so long as the strikes remained peaceful. However, if the students on strike sought to prevent others from attending class, then the police should be summoned to the university to arrest the strikers.[87]

The tone of Stolypin's private memorandum was relatively moderate. Though firm in expressing opposition to the kind of autonomy demanded by activists and many professors, it was not strident and it did not denounce or denigrate anyone. But in a letter to Gurliand on September 7, 1908, urging him to write an article (almost certainly for *Rossiia*) on developments at the universities, the prime minister adopted a rather different tone. Stolypin wanted his assistant to emphasize that in 1905 the high schools and universities had become an "arena for political struggle" and that every honorable head of the Department of Education must, "regardless of his political credo," devote himself to "cleansing the schools of political scum [*nechisti*]" and to establishing law and order. No doubt, Stolypin warned, such an educational leader would be furiously attacked by citizens from many walks of life, an inevitable "result of the social flabbiness, compassion, [and] sentimentality [that many people adopt] with regard to young people, who are no longer accustomed to being disciplined and to taking school [work] seriously." With considerable anger, Stolypin declared that the government could not adapt itself to an ephemeral mood of society and could not forget that students marched on school grounds with Brownings in their hands and that professors tried to ingratiate themselves with the revolutionaries and "danced to the tune of rebellious S[ocialist] R[evolutionary] students." The government must also make clear that it would not allow professors to gain political influence by "hypnotizing" students into

supporting them in their struggle against the authorities. "All the whin-
ing about the government's arbitrariness, about imaginary infringement
upon academic autonomy and so on will not compel the government to
deviate from establishing order [and] legality; it will not compel [the
government] to give the masses of Russian youngsters over to the intrigues of left-wing professors as material for manipulation." Such
dreams, the prime minister declared, "must be abandoned, and politics
must be abandoned, [and there must be] a return to study."[88]

The harshness of the prime minister's letter to Gurliand was uncharacteristic of Stolypin, a man not given to displays of rage; even during his most trying days as governor or head of government he expressed
his views in more temperate language. But student unrest appears to
have unnerved him. He thought that intellectuals and educated people
in general were ultimately responsible for the revolutionary turbulence
in Russia. Without their "dreams" and agitation, he believed, the country would be in a better position to enact a program of sensible reforms
such as he favored. Fear that student unrest would undermine his efforts
to stabilize Russia seems to have become an obsession for Stolypin.

For the next two years, from 1908 to 1910, Schwartz's tenure as minister of education was uneventful. Student strikes occurred from time to
time, but they remained minor. But the government had not given up its
determination to rein in the universities, and early in 1910 the cabinet
decided to send Schwartz's reactionary Draft Statute of 1908 to the
Duma for consideration as a prelude to implementing its provisions.
The president of the legislature, N. A. Khomiakov, rejected the plan outright, contending that it would cripple the universities. Rightists such
as Purishkevich, on the other hand, thought that Schwartz was altogether too lenient in his treatment of student activists. Facing opposition from moderates and rightists, the government withdrew the statute
shortly after Schwartz's departure from the Ministry of Education in
September 1910.

By this time, dissatisfaction with Schwartz as leader of the Department of Education had become widespread. A. A. Bobrinskii, a
prominent conservative supporter of Stolypin, contended that while
Schwartz's views were perfectly sound, he was, like professors generally, incapable of administering the Department of Education.[89] At the
same time, Schwartz's relations with the prime minister had turned
sour. In his autobiography, Schwartz suggested that the initial tension
between them arose over the question of the Jewish presence in Russian
schools. By 1909, in the schools in Beliaev, Poland, 36 percent of the

students were Jews rather than the officially acceptable 10 percent. Similar trends were noticeable, he claimed, in other parts of the empire. The tsar asked Stolypin to explain this unexpected and unwelcome development. At the prime minister's request, Schwartz formed a committee of individuals from various departments (Education and Justice) to examine the matter, and in June of 1909 it submitted a report recommending that steps be taken to reduce the number of Jews in educational institutions. But when the subject came up for discussion Stolypin, according to Schwartz, behaved "strangely" and seemed uncharacteristically ignorant of the relevant facts. Schwartz hinted at the possibility that Stolypin was trying to distance himself from the report in order to play up to the "pseudo-liberal camp." It may well be that given his generally benign attitude on the Jewish question Stolypin was uncomfortable with any proposals to limit the number of Jews in educational institutions. Whatever the reason, Schwartz was very distressed and astonished at the "ease with which . . . [the prime minister] betrayed his colleagues by exposing them to the hatred of the Jews." Schwartz now had doubts about the political and personal reliability of Stolypin.

He also began to resent the prime minister's interference in the affairs of the Ministry of Education and concluded that Stolypin was really a dilettante in the field of education. At times, he came up with "very fantastic plans." For example, he pushed an idea advanced by a certain Professor Boklevskii that the government assign tens of thousands of rubles for the purchase of equipment for some sort of "flying game" to deflect students from politics. Schwartz wrote a long memorandum dismissing the project as foolish, but he persuaded none of the ministers. According to the minister of education, another pet project of Stolypin's was a proposal advanced by V. M. Purishkevich: the formation of special academic associations with a military character to meet off campus. These "clubs" were to serve as a counterpoise to leftist organizations within the universities. Schwartz argued against the project because he was convinced that conservative students were interested in studying academic subjects, not in learning how to fight. He also feared that the plan, if implemented, would prompt left-wing students to form similar "clubs." Schwartz was overruled in the cabinet, and when he learned, allegedly from newspaper accounts, that the plan would be implemented, he decided in the fall of 1910 that the time had come for him to leave office.[90]

The new minister of education, L. A. Kasso, was also very conservative and also a former professor (of law), but he was more pragmatic than

his predecessor. He announced his willingness to live with the rules enacted on August 27, 1905, which granted the universities a relatively
liberal degree of autonomy. If he thought that his moderate stance
would usher in a prolonged period of calm at the universities, he was
soon to be deeply disappointed.

A new wave of student unrest erupted after the death of Lev Tolstoy
on November 7, 1910. Students were angered by the decision of the Holy
Synod to prohibit any religious ceremony in his memory because he had
been excommunicated as a heretic in 1901 for his anarchist views and
his rejection of the dogmas of the Church and insistence that love, self-
denial, and the return of good for evil were the essentials of Christianity.
Within days, thousands of students in St. Petersburg, Moscow, Kiev,
Kharkov, Warsaw, and Odessa held memorial services, at which
speeches were made in support of one of Tolstoy's favorite causes, the
abolition of capital punishment. Fearful that revolutionaries would attempt to join forces with the students, several thousand of whom had
gathered outside the Kazan Cathedral, the authorities in St. Petersburg
deployed a large contingent of policemen and soldiers, which unceremoniously dispersed the crowd and arrested some of the demonstrators.
The police also used rough tactics in handling a similar crowd in Moscow, arresting about 150 students. But neither the radical parties nor the
workers joined the meetings, and by November 15 the unrest had subsided.[91]

Had Stolypin and the ultraconservatives not panicked and overre-
acted to the demonstrations, the ruckus would most probably have
ended then and there. But on December 11, 1910, a right-wing zealot, M.
O. Menshikov, sounded an alarm in a column in *Novoe vremia*. He
warned that "the second round of the revolution had already begun" and
urged the prime minister to expel students who participated in demonstrations. Only too ready to attribute revolutionary aims to the students, Stolypin was probably also alarmed by a report from the *Okhrana*
that students were taking the lead in promoting revolutionary movements. On January 11, 1911, he issued a directive "temporarily" ban-
ning meetings on the grounds of universities and ordering the police to
break up meetings even if there had been no requests for such action
from faculty councils. In a confidential memorandum to governors-
general and police chiefs, the prime minister declared that the universities had ceased to be corporate bodies and had become political enti-
ties.[92] Stolypin felt confident that he would succeed in defeating the
student activists in short order.[93]

The government's repressive measures were extensive. The ban on meetings amounted to a recision of autonomy and was seen as a threat even to various apolitical student organizations such as credit societies and the social associations of students from the same geographical regions (*zemliachestva*). In St. Petersburg a large number of students were arbitrarily expelled from the university, several were exiled to remote areas of the empire, and some leading professors were dismissed for protesting the entrance of the police onto university grounds. In Moscow, the appearance of armed police in university buildings led to "clashes, arrests, punishments." Enraged by these measures, the students called for a general strike, which began on January 26 and lasted for much of the spring semester. The German consul in Moscow warned his superiors in Berlin that there would soon be "enormous pressure" by Russian students to secure admission to German universities. The consul was concerned about the potential impact of the influx of Russians on the schools in his country. "It would be a good thing if our universities right at the beginning undertake a strict sifting of those [Russians] who show up."[94]

The conflict between the university and the government became especially acute in Moscow, where the rector, A. A. Manuilov, resigned in protest over police intervention. He declared that the police action, undertaken without request from his office, created a system of "dual power" in the university, making his role superfluous. Two of his senior assistants, M. A. Menzbir and P. A. Minakov, also resigned. On second thought, Manuilov and his colleagues withdrew their resignations, but that did not impress the government, which accepted the resignations of the three administrators and, in addition, stripped them of their professorial appointments. Now some 130 professors and instructors resigned out of solidarity with the three men. The government retaliated by expelling Manuilov and Professor V. I. Vernadskii from the State Council, to which they had been elected by the university. Moscow University was teetering on the edge of chaos.[95]

Inevitably, the government's conduct inflamed public opinion, and the criticism was not limited to the left wing of the political spectrum. "Sixty-five of the leading merchants and manufacturers of Moscow have even gone so far as to issue a declaration protesting the course adopted by the Government, whom they hold responsible for what has occurred. While condemning the strike and the methods of . . . obstruction employed by the students, they consider the Government's repressive measures wholly unjustifiable, and declare that they cannot look on in silence while the universities are being ruined."[96]

The author of this report, George Buchanan, the British ambassador to St. Petersburg, could not understand why the prime minister was resorting to such heavy-handed methods. "The disturbances at the universities are a small matter in themselves," but excessive force against them was likely to make matters worse. Buchanan concluded with a prophetic warning: "Should the good harvests with which Russia has been favoured for the past two years be followed by a succession of bad ones, or should there be a serious outbreak of plague or cholera, the Government might find themselves confronted with a recrudescence of the revolutionary movement which is likely to gather increasing force the longer that they refuse to adopt a more progressive policy."[97]

Stolypin's harsh tactics toward the student movement are something of a puzzle. He surely had an inordinate fear of student radicals, who, he believed, were being manipulated by "committees established in Paris and other foreign towns." He was convinced that the universities were "almost the only field open to . . . [the radicals'] machinations, now that the peasants were contented and that the army would no longer lend an ear to their propaganda."[98] For Stolypin, then, much was at stake in the campaign against student unrest. Yet he had always warned against the use of excessive force because that invariably incensed the opposition and increased antigovernment demonstrations. No doubt the intense pressure from the right to take a tough stand influenced him. But in this instance he seems not to have acted with the sense of proportion shown in other confrontations. In 1910 and 1911 the prime minister was involved in his most serious political crisis (to be discussed in Chapter 8), and there is evidence to suggest that he was deeply agitated and that his political instincts were not as sound as they had been in the past.

Whatever the reason for his response to the student strikes, his policies toward the universities did not have the desired effect. The government expelled 1,871 students and suspended 4,406. The authorities encouraged the formation of right-wing student organizations, which were given financial support and were granted audiences by the tsar and the prime minister. The government also promised employment to students who remained aloof from the strike movement. But these initiatives did not produce the results that Stolypin hoped for. Only in Kiev did right-wing students succeed in establishing organizations of any influence. More important, the strike continued until April, and the government's harsh policies drew serious criticism from many Octobrists, whose support in the Duma was essential for Stolypin. The Octobrists charged the prime minister with overreacting to the student demonstrations after Tolstoy's death.[99] By every measure, Stolypin's educational policies must be considered a failure.

Stolypin's somewhat erratic and harsh attitude toward institutions of higher education stands in striking contrast to his views on foreign policy, which were remarkably consistent and invariably moderate. Strictly speaking, he was not authorized to play any role in shaping Russia's relations with foreign countries. According to the Fundamental Laws of 1906, the minister of foreign affairs was to report not to the cabinet but only to the tsar. But Stolypin took a broad view of the concept of united government and insisted that he be informed of all major decisions of his ministers and that he contribute to the formulation of foreign policy. In this, the prime minister was not motivated by a lust for power. He thought of himself as the pre-eminent leader of the government, and he realized that there was a close link between foreign and domestic policies. He understood that foreign policy decisions had profoundly affected internal developments in 1904, when Russia embarked on the ill-fated adventure in the Far East and lost the war against Japan. He was determined to avoid new foreign entanglements that could undermine his domestic program.[100]

That Stolypin was no dilettante in the field of international affairs is evident from his discussions with foreign ambassadors. He closely studied foreign leaders and had a good grasp of their intentions as well as the strengths and weaknesses of their countries. In the fall of 1909, for example, he expressed concern over the naval rivalry between Germany and Great Britain, "which was by no means a guarantee for peace, but rather an incentive to war." Because of internal discontent in Germany, there was the danger, he warned, that the German government might feel it would have to justify the large expenditures on the navy by some action that would enhance the country's power and prestige. He was also worried about Turkey's intentions; nor did he have any confidence in Aehrenthal, the foreign minister of Austria-Hungary, whom he considered to be "not a statesman in whom any trust could placed." He feared that Austria-Hungary might undertake "fresh surprises" that would destabilize Europe. And he thought that the "close union" between Germany and Austria-Hungary "was in a sense disquieting." Even though Germany might wish "to remain quiescent, Austria might drag her into some adventures," an acute premonition of what happened after the assassination of Archduke Ferdinand in Sarajevo on June 28, 1914. Stolypin had no confidence in King Ferdinand of Bulgaria, a man he considered to be "exceedingly clever and exceedingly untrustworthy." He was also well informed about conditions in Greece and Persia; in the latter country "there did not appear to be a single individual . . . capable of mastering the situation." Finally, the prime minister voiced opposition to the right-wing extremists in his own country, who distrusted "perfidious Albion" and wanted Russia to form a close alliance with Germany. Stolypin, on the contrary, favored close relations with England.[101]

The thread that runs through these comments by Stolypin is his desire for international stability and peace. Whenever he participated in discussions of Russia's foreign policy he insisted that the country must avoid any action that could lead to military conflict, a real danger in view of the tensions between the Great Powers. Germany's program of naval armament, started in the late 1890s in its effort to become a world power, was seen as a serious threat by Great Britain, which after 1902 drew closer to France. France, on the other hand, still nursed grievances against Germany over the loss of Alsace-Lorraine in 1871. It therefore established close ties with Russia, in large measure by extending generous loans to the tsarist government. Austria-Hungary, fearful of losing control over the Slavic minorities within its borders, retained a close alliance with Germany, by the early twentieth century the most powerful country on the continent. By themselves, the alliances and understandings between the Great Powers and the formation of two blocs did not mean that military hostilities were inevitable, but they did promote nationalist fervor in all the major countries of Europe and engendered a sense of anxiety about the stability of the international order.

Stolypin knew that Russia was too weak to exert significant influence on the system of alliances. He also realized that foreign diplomats had no illusions about his country's strength, though he probably did not know the depth of contempt in which Russia was held by foreigners. A confidential memorandum distributed within the German Foreign Office in April 1908 was utterly dismissive of Russia. The tsar's army, the memorandum stated, was in worse shape than it had been in 1905 and could not wage war effectively. No one should be misled by the recent maneuvers of the Russian army. "The Slav is an actor" and puts on a good show. In fact, the military was incompetent from top to bottom, and any foreign army, even that of Turkey, would trounce the Russians. "Russia has at present no justifiable claim to be treated as a great power."[102] Although Stolypin would have been shocked by the bluntness of this memorandum, his approach to foreign policy was consistent with its conclusions.

This became clear at a meeting, on August 11, 1907, of senior officials under the chairmanship of the prime minister to consider the details of a possible agreement with Great Britain with regard to Afghanistan, where Russia and England had been vying for influence. Izvolskii, the foreign minister, who generally shared Stolypin's views on foreign policy, had negotiated a settlement with the British according to which Afghanistan was to be a British sphere of influence and Persia was to be divided into three zones, one of which would be dominated by the Russians. In seeking support for the agreement, Izvolskii spoke candidly about the fact that "the War of 1904–5 and the internal disorders have placed Russia in a difficult position." Only an agreement with Britain would enable Russia to extricate itself from its awkward situation in the Far East, where Britain was allied with Japan. If the country continued to be mired in the Far East, Russia would decline into a "second rate power" totally incapable of influencing events in Europe. This would be "the greatest calamity for Russia."[103]

Stolypin, the second speaker at the conference, was even more candid about Russia's plight. Describing the agreement with Britain as a truly great achievement for the state, the prime minister conceded that "[o]ur internal situation does not permit us to conduct an aggressive foreign policy. The absence of anxiety about international relations is for us very important, since it gives us a chance to devote all our energies in [an atmosphere of] complete calm to settling the internal affairs of the country." Under the circumstances, the agreement with Britain must be recognized as the most promising for our interests.[104] All the dignitaries agreed with Stolypin, and thus a consensus emerged on foreign policy that remained in effect for some seven years. The watchword of Russian diplomacy would be restraint: Russia would do its utmost to avoid foreign entanglements that might increase the risk of war.

This is not to say that there was no challenge to the consensus. By 1908, Russia witnessed a new upswing of nationalism, the nature of which was, like everything else in Russian politics, complex. Part of the complexity resulted from the fact that there were two distinct, though related, aspects to Russian nationalism. On the one hand, it connoted a concern with the defense, stability, and power of the state. The proponents of this form of nationalism sought to create institutions that would enable the state effectively to administer and defend a specified territory; often they also took a special interest in enhancing the power and prestige of the state in the international arena. In substance and tone, their ideas were not markedly different from those of nationalists in Germany, France, and Great Britain.

In Russia, however, nationalism also touched on another, highly sensitive, matter, the integration of the numerous (well over one hundred) minorities, who composed no less than 55 percent of the empire's population and most of whom had retained their own language, religion, and customs and could justifiably claim to be the heirs of a long and proud history. And then there was the vexing Jewish question. The five million Jews did not constitute a majority in any juridically separate region of the empire and therefore made no claims to political autonomy. But many Jews did speak a language other than Russian and insisted on retaining their religious traditions, which posed a challenge to Russian nationalists committed to the integration of the minorities.

In a real sense, the Great Russians, who, it must be kept in mind, were a minority of the empire's total population, had been remarkably successful in dominating the state politically and culturally. Until very recently, in fact until the early 1990s, it was not uncommon for educated people around the world to refer to the citizens of the Russian Empire and the Soviet Union simply as Russians, which, strictly speaking, was an accurate term for only one of the ethnic groups in that large country. Moreover, most of the works of history on that country were written from the standpoint of the Great Russians, and they contained relatively little information about the minorities. Only during the past few years has it become clear to the general public that the vast region known as Russia was populated by a large variety of peoples with distinct cultures.

The Great Russians' assertion of dominance was a natural consequence of their success in creating the empire. This cannot be attributed to conscious decisions of any one ruler or any one group of expansionists determined to conquer lands adjacent to Russia. It may be an overstatement to suggest that the clever comment by the historian J. R. Seeley that Great Britain acquired its empire "in a fit of absence of mind" could also be applied to Russia, but it would not be completely off the mark. The expansion of the Muscovite state, which began in the sixteenth century and lasted for over three centuries, did not proceed according to a master plan.

Initially, the Muscovites extended their military and political power into so-called open lands—that is, regions that were sparsely populated, to a considerable extent by nomadic cattle raisers. Generally, rule by the Russians did not involve a sudden and fundamental reordering of the social and economic life of the conquered peoples. Nor did the conquerors embark on a conscious policy of eradicating, physically or culturally, the nationalities. Russian rule meant essentially, as Marc Raeff has noted, "the extension of sovereignty which the ruler exercised through his household or court (*dvor*). He depended on a small number of military servitors to keep control over the territory." Over the course of some three centuries, the expansion proceeded in three phases: acquisition, incorporation, and assimilation or integration.[105]

Although this pattern was essentially maintained in Russia's expansion into the vast regions of Siberia, the country's expansion into the Ukraine was motivated by a desire for additional agricultural land and a concern with enhancing the military security of the empire. But Russia's extension of its power over the Baltic provinces, Finland, and Poland proceeded differently. It was a consequence of military conquests and was in each instance ratified by international treaties. Moreover, in these three regions Russia initially committed itself to maintaining the autonomy of the local ruling groups. Significantly, much of the expansion (especially during the early period of the process) was so gradual and so frequently accompanied by peasant settlement of the conquered lands that relatively few people in what had been Muscovite Russia realized that their country was being transformed into a multinational empire.

However, by the time Stolypin came into office several minorities, having retained much of their cultural heritage, had developed national self-consciousness. Among the Poles, Finns, Ukrainians, Georgians, and Armenians, to mention only a few, movements clamoring for extensive autonomy and in some cases even for independence became active and were viewed with alarm in St. Petersburg. And a growing number of younger Jews expressed open resentment of the restrictions imposed on them by joining one or another oppositional movement. For those in power, the danger appeared to be twofold: internal disintegration of the empire and/or weakening of the country at strategically important borders such as Poland and Finland, which would be the flash points in the event of a European war.

The proposals considered by the authorities in St. Petersburg on how to deal with the two dangers are too numerous to be taken up here, but they can be lumped into two broad categories: repression, which implied the outlawing of political associations sympathetic to national aspirations and aggressive promotion of the Russian language and culture as well as Russian Orthodoxy; the second, liberal approach implied concessions that would permit the national minorities a maximum amount of cultural and political autonomy consistent with the maintenance of a unitary, federal state.

Thus, in formulating their policies Russian nationalists had to take into account a wide range of domestic and foreign political issues, which accounts for the difficulty in defining Russian nationalism. There is considerable merit to Geoffrey Hosking's suggestion that broadly speaking it took two forms by the early twentieth century. The first, which he calls dynastic, stressed cultural integration in one form or another of the national minorities within the empire to create a unified state based on the culture of the Great Russians together with a cautious policy vis-à-vis foreign powers. The second, which Hosking calls constitutional, emphasized liberal policies toward the nationalities and an expansionist foreign policy.[106] Although the distinction between the two strands of nationalism was not always clear-cut, the difference between them was nevertheless real and helps clarify the divergent thrusts in the country's foreign policy and in its policy toward the national groups within the empire.

The striking feature of Stolypin's nationalism was its eclecticism. It consisted of ardent patriotism, extreme caution in foreign policy, and, with some notable exceptions to be discussed in Chapter 7, a fairly moderate stance toward the minorities. His paramount concern was to turn the Russian Empire into a nation state whose stability and power would be ensured, in large measure because it would command the loyalty of its diverse population. If not exactly unique, Stolypin's nationalism was favored by only a small minority within the establishment.

Early in 1908, an eloquent appeal for the ideas of constitutional nationalism emanated from the liberal camp. P. B. Struve, a right-wing Kadet, published two articles in a journal widely read by the intelligentsia, *Russkaia mysl*, in which he argued for the adoption by the government of a new course on the international scene. The first article was provocatively entitled "Great Russia," a reference to Stolypin's famous statement in the Second Duma that "[t]hey need great upheavals, we need a great Russia." From the context of Stolypin's speech it is clear that by a "great" Russia he meant a politically stable and prosperous Russia. Stolypin wanted to bind the nation together so that it would be great economically and culturally. There is no mention in the speech of foreign expansion. But Struve defined the word "great" differently, arguing that every state was an organism that "wishes to possess external power." Specifically, Struve held that Russia should extend its influence "in the entire basin of the Black Sea, that is, in all the European and Asiatic countries 'that face' the Black Sea." In that region Russia should strive for "economic supremacy," and once it had achieved that, the country would also acquire political and cultural "predominance in all of the so-called Near East." Although Struve favored the use of peaceful methods in extending Russia's power, he insisted that an assertive foreign policy would require a strong army and navy. Russia would need a military force capable of landing at any point along the Black Sea and at the same time would have to be strong enough to protect the country fully from hostile forces in the region.

Unlike Stolypin, who always placed primary emphasis on domestic considerations in formulating his stand on foreign policy issues, Struve argued for the primacy of foreign policy. "The touchstone and the yardstick of all so-called domestic politics of the government as well as [political] parties ought to lie in the answer to the question: in what measure does this policy further the so-called external power of the state?" Thus, Struve argued for a liberal policy toward the Jews, including the elimination of the Pale of Settlement, in part because the Jews would constitute a "very valuable element" as "pioneers and middle men" in the country's economic expansion in the Black Sea region. At the same time, Russia should pursue an "intelligent" policy toward the Poles: Russification should be abandoned, the Poles should be granted full autonomy, but the Polish Kingdom must remain part of the empire to enable Russia to maintain "natural links" with Slavs in the Austro-Hungarian Empire.[107]

Many Kadets repudiated their colleague Struve for his advocacy of assertive nationalism, imperialism, and for what they regarded as his glorification of war. Strangely enough, Izvolskii, the foreign minister who only six months earlier had pursued a cautious foreign policy, changed course dramatically early in 1908 and began to act like the representative of a Great Power determined to embark on an assertive foreign policy. His motives are still not altogether clear. Most likely, as William Fuller has suggested, he considered it necessary for Russia to prove to the world that it was still a major power capable of flexing its muscles. But there can be no doubt that Izvolskii was abandoning Stolypin's commitment to restraint in foreign affairs.[108]

The change in Izvolskii's policy became manifest when he entered into negotiations with Count Aehrenthal, the Austro-Hungarian foreign minister, over an agreement to permit Austria-Hungary to annex Bosnia-Herzegovina in return for which the Straits of the Bosphorus and Dardanelles would be opened to Russian warships. Tsar Nicholas, no more astute in foreign policy than in any other matters, approved the scheme, which was bound to arouse the most vigorous opposition from the Serbs, the Turks, and Great Britain. No doubt because he feared opposition to his scheme, Izvolskii neglected to inform Stolypin or any other member of the cabinet of his negotiations with Aehrenthal. The tsar also remained silent on his own role in the negotiations.

In September 1908 the foreign minister went to Buchlau, in Styria, and struck a final deal with Aehrenthal, though no date was set for its implementation. Izvolskii proceeded to various Western capitals to prepare the leaders for the announcement of the agreement. But when he reached Paris early in October he received a surprise: a telegram from Aehrenthal that he was going ahead with the annexation of Bosnia-Herzegovina without waiting for the outcome of Izvolskii's discussions with Western ministers.

When Stolypin learned of the Buchlau agreement, he was enraged, not only because he opposed the specifics of the deal but also because the principle of united government had been violated. The prime minister told N. V. Charykov, the acting foreign minister (Izvolskii was still abroad), that under no circumstances would he approve of the agreement and if it were not changed he would resign. Stolypin insisted that "any kind of risk of foreign complications for Russia" was "inappropriate." Nor did he wish to give his consent to the "annexation of a Slavonic land by a Germanic State, whatever political advantages this might bring to Russia." The minister of finance, Kokovtsov, fully supported Stolypin. Charykov urged Stolypin not to resign and promised that as acting foreign minister, he would not support Izvolskii on the Buchlau agreement.

Stolypin, accompanied by Admiral A. A. Birilev, minister of the navy, and Charykov, then presented a report to the tsar on the tangled affair. "The Emperor listened in silence to Stolypin's arguments against Russia giving her approval to the annexation of Bosnia and Herzegovina." As promised, Charykov agreed with Stolypin. The tsar's demeanor was "frigid reserve"—he had, after all, approved the deal; Charykov was certain that if the prime minister had submitted his resignation at the meeting the tsar would not have tried to dissuade him.[109] In the end, Russia swallowed its pride and did not raise any objections to Austria-Hungary's annexation of Bosnia-Herzegovina, but no attempt was made to enforce the provisions relating to the straits. It was not the outcome Stolypin had hoped for, but at least he had reasserted the principle of united government and he had preserved the essentials of his foreign policy. As he told the British ambassador, "Baron d'Aehrenthal had scored a temporary victory, but this was preferable to a general European war."[110]

Even then, Stolypin did not consider the incident closed. At a meeting of the cabinet on October 25, attended by Izvolskii, the prime minister indicated that he still could not understand why he and the other ministers had been kept in the dark about the negotiations with Aehrenthal. He reminded his colleagues that when, in mid-September, he learned of the meeting with the Austro-Hungarian foreign minister he had indicated in no uncertain terms that "such important events must not be allowed to take place behind the government's back." Forcing Turkey to make extensive concessions could, he warned again, lead to war. And he was certain that public opinion in Russia did not favor a belligerent foreign policy any more than he did.

The entire affair placed Stolypin in a difficult political position. He was furious at Izvolskii but did not want him to resign because his departure from the cabinet could be interpreted as a sign that Russia intended to jettison the agreement he had engineered and might consider going to war to force Austria-Hungary to withdraw from Bosnia-Herzegovina. The prime minister was also nervous about the reaction of the Duma to the foreign policy fiasco. His support there came from rightists and Octobrists, many of whom favored an aggressive foreign policy. In this instance, the Kadets would support the prime minister, but for two reasons he was reluctant to appeal to them. He had broken off relations with them after the dissolution of the Second Duma, and, in any case, he believed that "it is impossible to pursue two policies: one for internal affairs and a second for foreign affairs." Izvolskii, realizing that he had undercut Stolypin and complicated the government's conduct of foreign policy, apologized for his indiscretion. This did not undo the damage, but it was an acknowledgment of the cabinet's primacy even in the formulation of foreign policy.[111]

Stolypin remained faithful till the end of his days to his conviction that Russia must pursue a pacific foreign policy. On July 28, 1911, some five weeks before his death, he wrote a long letter (in French) to Izvolskii, now ambassador to Paris, outlining his general views on Russia's role in international affairs. It was a friendly missive and did not address any specific issue. Clearly, the difference of 1908 between the two men had been pushed aside, if not forgotten. The prime minister praised Izvolskii for the agreement he had reached with Great Britain in 1907, which, he was sure, would preserve peace for the foreseeable future. The determination to avoid armed conflict was, in fact, the central theme of the entire letter. "We need peace," Stolypin wrote; "war in the course of the next few years, especially if [it broke out] for reasons that the people do not understand, would be fatal for Russia and the dynasty. On the other hand, every year of peace strengthens Russia, not only militarily and in its naval power but also financially and economically. Moreover, and this is essential, Russia is maturing from year to year; we see there the emergence of a [public] consciousness and of public opinion. . . . However bad . . . [our parliamentary institutions] may be, over the past five years Russia has been radically transformed under their influence, and when the time comes it will conscientiously face up to the enemy. Russia cannot sustain, and cannot emerge victorious from, a war unless it is a popular war." Stolypin was moved to express these views to Izvolskii because he was troubled by the failure of Russia's press, which he derided as a "distorted mirror," to help shape a sound public opinion on foreign affairs.[112]

The scholarly literature on Stolypin tends to focus on his domestic policies and on the extent to which they succeeded in undermining the ability of the left to mount a new offensive against the old order. Those who argue that his policies initiated the transformation of Russia into a modern and stable state contend that with his death in 1911 and the outbreak of war in 1914 the process of economic and social renewal ended prematurely. But this school of thought does not place sufficient emphasis on Stolypin's insistence that Russia must avoid war if it was to succeed in modernizing itself, a policy that was followed for two and a half years after his premiership ended. It was only in 1914 that Tsar Nicholas, reasserting his pre-eminence in international affairs, abandoned Stolypin's principle, with disastrous consequences, though it is worth noting that he was not eager for war. In fact, he acceded to the pressures of leading generals to issue the fatal order for full mobilization (on July 29, 1914) that made war inevitable only after considerable hesitation and vacillation. Nicholas hoped that his long-standing personal relationship with Kaiser William II would somehow enable him, at the last moment, to prevent a conflagration.[113]

Now it may well be, as David McDonald has argued, that it is "difficult to conceive of any Russian government that could have held back from action in support of Serbia in July 1914."[114] But the absence of so forceful a figure as Stolypin during the fateful month of July certainly weakened the opposition to war, reducing the chances of a serious debate within the political class. Ironically, Stolypin's old enemy, the archconservative P. N. Durnovo, was a member of the State Council and made precisely the point that Stolypin had made for years, that for Russia a military conflict would spell disaster, "a social revolution in its most extreme manifestation."[115] But Durnovo, who favored close ties with Germany to avert war, failed to muster much support. Whether Stolypin could have gained more of a hearing for Durnovo's prediction of doom is, of course, conjectural. But even for a highly disciplined historian such speculation is sometimes warranted. In this instance, it helps us to achieve a better understanding of the diverse strands in Stolypin's political outlook and of the significance of his assassination in 1911.

Top: P. A. Stolypin at age
seven (on right) with his
younger brother, A. A.
Stolypin. Source: G. I.
Lystsov, *Petr Stolypin*.
Moscow, 1997 (a collection
of memoirs about Stolypin).

Right: Stolypin in Vilna
gymnasium (high school) in
1876. Source: Lystsov.

Left: Stolypin as university student, 1884. Source: Khotulev.

Bottom: Stolypin as university student, 1881. Source: Viacheslav Khotulev, *Petr Stolypin*. Moscow, 1998.

Top: Stolypin as governor of Saratov. On a journey to town of Kamyshin, August 31, 1903. Source: Khotulev.

Left: Stolypin as prime minister. Source: Harold Williams, *Russia of the Russian*. New York, 1918.

Left: Stolypin and his wife, Olga Borisovna, in 1906. Source: Khotulev.

Bottom: Stolypin and his family on the terrace of the Elagin Palace, 1907. Source: Khotulev.

Top: Stolypin in his office in the Winter Palace, 1907. Source: Khotulev.

Left: Stolypin on the day of his assassination, September 1, 1911. Source: Lystsov.

Top: Stolypin, wounded (on September 1, 1911), being carried to car to take him to a hospital. Source: Khotulev.

Right: Dmitrii Bogrov, Stolypin's assassin. Source: Reproduced for me by the New York Public Library from *Dmitrii Bogrov i ubiistvo Stolypina*. Berlin, 1931.

Monument to Stolypin, placed outside Kiev City Council
building on September 1, 1912. Source: Lystsov.

Nicholas in 1890, became Tsar Nicholas II in 1894. Source:
New York Public Library.

Top: Mariia Feodorovna, dowager empress. Persuaded Tsar Nicholas to retain Stolypin in office in spring 1911. Source: New York Public Library.

Left: Tsar Nicholas II. Source: Russian Pictorial Collection/ Hoover Institution Archives.

Top Left: A. I. Guchkov, leader of the Union of October 17 (or Octobrists).
Source: Slavonic Library of Helsinki University (postcard).

Top Right: Count V. N. Kokovtsov, minister of finance in Stolypin's
cabinet. Source: *Gosudarstvennyi Sovet*, Petrograd, 1915, p. 52.

Bottom Left: A. P. Izvolskii, minister of foreign affairs in Stolypin's
cabinet. Source: *Niva*, no. 34 (1906), p. 537.

Bottom Right: S. Iu. Witte, minister of finance from 1892 to 1903 and
prime minister from October 1905 to April 1906. Then, as a member of
the State Council, he fiercely criticized Stolypin. Source: *Sovremennaia
Rossiia v portretakh i biografiiakh vydaiushchikhsia deiatelei.*
St. Petersburg, 1904, p. 1.

Left: P. N. Durnovo, minister of internal affairs, 1905–6; thereafter member of the State Council and strong opponent of Stolypin. Source: *Sovremennaia*.

Bottom: "Great Historical Day—April 27, 1906." Arrival of diplomatic corps at the Winter Palace on day that First State Duma opened. Source: *Niva*, no. 18 (1906), p. 286.

Top: Military patrols outside St. Petersburg post office to guard against terrorism. Source: *Niva*, no. 50 (1906), p. 800.

Bottom: Group of men sentenced to death in Baltic provinces in 1906 for alleged terrorist activities. Source: S. I. Mitskevich, ed., *Albom pervoi russkoi revoliutsii 1905–1907 g.g.* Moscow, 1926.

Уголокъ въ Таврическомъ саду.

Деталн круглой оазы въ Государственной Думѣ.

Видъ на Таврическій дворецъ съ юго-востока.

Left: State Duma. Source: *Niva*, no. 8 (1907), p. 122.

Bottom: The Duma building. Source: Harold Williams, *Russia of the Russians.*

Видъ на Таврическій дворецъ со стороны сада.

Государственная Дума. По фот. Н. Ольшанскаго, лит. «Нивы».

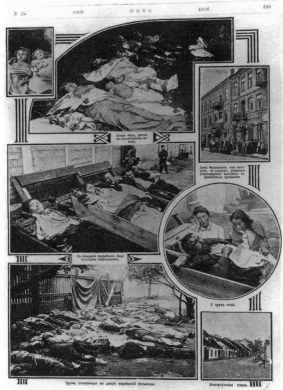

Left: Anti-Jewish pogrom in Bialystok, June 1906. Source: *Niva*, no. 25 (1906).

Bottom: A Jewish delegation presents sacred Torah to Stolypin in Kiev on August 30, 1911. Source: Lystsov.

6

Embattled

Early in 1908, only eighteen months after assuming the post of prime minister, Stolypin faced an uncertain future. It seemed as though the furious attacks from powerful groups on the right would undermine his authority; rumors of his impending resignation circulated widely and more frequently than ever before. Stolypin dimissively denied that there was any substance to the rumors, but one of his colleagues in the cabinet suggested that the prime minister tended to treat the campaign against him "a little too lightly" because he did not understand the intensity and maliciousness of the intrigues against him.[1]

Some of the charges were in fact so absurd that Stolypin can hardly be faulted for shrugging them off. For example, one anonymous leaflet, entitled "On the Eve of a State Coup," accused Stolypin and Guchkov, two ardent royalists, of having hatched plans to overthrow the monarchy.[2] But not all the charges against the prime minister were that bizarre, and Stolypin's public stance of indifference to the campaign of vituperation belied his real feelings. He was angry and in the early months of 1908 began to fight back. He issued a circular prohibiting government officials, specifically mentioning military orchestras, from participating in the activities or festivities of ultrarightist organizations. He made a point of naming the largest such organizations, the Union of the Russian People, as one of the movements to be shunned.[3] To Stolypin's acquaintances it was apparent that the political struggles had taken their toll. Bernard Pares, who saw him in May 1908 after a lapse of two years, found the prime minister "somewhat aged; his features were somewhat sharper set. There was no difference of manner except for a slight reserve."[4]

The most ominous development was the steady erosion of Stolypin's political support. Although he could still count on most of the Octobrists and moderate rightists, many conservatives, appalled by his persistent advocacy of reform, turned against him. Moreover, his relations with the tsar, critical for his effective exercise of authority, were not without ambiguity. In his communications with the prime minister,

Nicholas maintained a correct and businesslike tone, but he rarely displayed warmth. True, the tsar prized Stolypin as a loyal servant who had beaten back the revolution, and he continued to heap honors on him. On January 1, 1908, he bestowed upon him the title of secretary of state, a rank that accorded him the privilege, held by only about twenty men in the entire empire, of passing on to officials unwritten orders from the sovereign. But the tsar's advisors raised strong objections to the appointment, contending that "M. Stolypin is still too liberal in his views and policy."[5] Although Nicholas remained adamant on the appointment, he let it be known in various ways that he did not share his prime minister's enthusiasm for reform and that Stolypin could not take his support for granted. He graciously received delegations of right-wing extremists who reviled Stolypin, he distanced himself from the Duma, with which Stolypin wished to cooperate, and he continued to assert his prerogatives as an autocrat.

The tsar's most conspicuous demonstration of support for the extremists of the right was his frequent grant of pardons to ultraconservatives convicted of serious crimes. Throughout 1908, *Pravo*, the legal journal, carried almost weekly announcements of such leniency. For example, in February the Union of the Russian People succeeded in obtaining a pardon for nineteen people in Chernigov province who had been deprived of their rights by local courts as a punishment for having engaged in criminal unrest. At about the same time, the tsar pardoned eleven peasants who had participated in pogroms against Jews in Kishinev. In May, eighteen people sent to jail in the village of Smel, near Kiev, for a similar offense were pardoned. In April, the tsar granted amnesty to V. I. Gurko, the former assistant minister of internal affairs who only six months earlier had received the very light punishment for corruption of disqualification from occupying any public office for three years. Within three months, Gurko, a conservative firebrand, was received by the tsar at Tsarskoe Selo. Stolypin was then away from the capital on a five-week yachting trip and was therefore unable to prevent Gurko's rehabilitation. According to newspaper reports, the prime minister's opponents were planning to bring Gurko back into the government, a move, they hoped, that would so embarrass Stolypin that he would feel compelled to resign. On hearing of the plan, many Octobrists were thoroughly alarmed, fearing a "conspiracy by reactionaries."[6]

Even the prime minister's policies to restore order after the turbulence of 1905–6 now came under attack, not only from the left, which considered them too harsh, but, surprisingly, also from the right, which dismissed them as ineffective. Stolypin himself was certain that tranquillity was returning to the country, and that, he claimed, had encouraged people to shun revolutionary agitation and to devote themselves instead to commerce and industry, which once again flourished. In mid-August 1908, he contemplated modifying the emergency regulations imposed in the Baltic provinces, Odessa, Kharkov, and elsewhere, though he did not think that would be possible in Poland or the Caucasus.[7] Over the next few weeks, martial law in the Baltic provinces was replaced by "Reinforced Security," and in Dvinsk, Vitebsk province, "Extraordinary Security" was replaced by "Reinforced Security."[8]

Such modifications cannot be dismissed as minor matters. The Edict of August 14, 1881, had granted vast arbitrary powers to local officials (governors-general, governors, and city governors) in the implementation of emergency measures during periods of unrest. Under "Reinforced Security," which could be imposed by the minister of internal affairs or a governor-general acting with the minister's approval, officials could keep subjects in prison for up to three months, impose fines, prohibit public gatherings, exile alleged transgressors of the law, transfer blocks of judicial cases from criminal to military courts, and dismiss local government and zemstvo employees. Under "Extraordinary Security," which could be imposed only with the approval of the tsar, a region was placed under the authority of a commander in chief who could dismiss local elected zemstvo deputies and could even dissolve zemstvos completely. The commander in chief could also suspend journals, close universities, and other centers of advanced study for up to one month. By the spring of 1906, about 69 percent of the provinces and regions of the Russian Empire were either completely or partially subject to one of the emergency codes.[9] Even though Stolypin modified the emergency regime in only a few areas, his action did indicate the government's interest in abandoning some of the harshest features of the regime introduced during the revolutionary period.

In some measure at least, the tranquillity trumpeted by Stolypin had been achieved by enlarging the prison population. Studies conducted by the Ministry of Justice reported that within a span of about three months, from the end of 1907 until February 1908, the number of persons incarcerated had jumped from 156,716 to over 165,000. Of these, about 13,000 were political prisoners, including a fair number of peasants who had been involved in agrarian unrest. The statistics on the prison population do not include the persons arbitrarily exiled to Siberia and other outlying regions. According to the Department of Police, more people were sent into exile by administrative order or by judicial actions in 1907 than in 1906 or 1905. The increase was 31 percent under the former procedure and 60 percent under the latter. All told, throughout 1907 some 74,622 people had been exiled, of whom 88.2 percent were punished for what was perceived to be political misconduct. And these statistics did not include the people who were still being investigated.[10] The statistics on capital punishment tell a similar story: in 1906, there were 144 executions; in 1907, 1,138; in 1908, 825. Only in 1909 did the number of executions begin to diminish significantly.[11]

The enlargement of the prison population aggravated a social problem that had been troublesome for some years, the overcrowding of jails. The government had built very few new prisons; in some regions, it rented private premises for use as jails as a stopgap measure. In Kiev, for example, the prisons were designed to accommodate 690 but had a population of 2,207; in Odessa, there were 1,610 prisoners in facilities built for 804; in Ekaterinoslav, there were almost three times as many prisoners as could be accommodated. It was not unusual for the men and women to sleep on floors, in corridors, or to be forced to sleep in a sitting position.[12]

Civil disorder of various forms, a serious problem for the authorities during the revolution, had subsided but remained widespread. "Cases of murder, robbery, and other acts of lawlessness," one observer noted, "continue to be very general throughout the country, more especially in the south." The police reported that throughout 1907 they had confiscated 147,000 revolvers. In March 1908, there was evidence of "an increased daring on the part of the criminal classes in . . . [St. Petersburg]. Cases are reported of bands of armed robbers entering private houses and 'holding up' the inmates while they rifle the premises. A few days ago a goods train was boarded only four miles out of St. Petersburgh [sic!] by an armed gang; they were, however, driven off and one of their number wounded."[13] Political terrorism had declined by 1908, but here too the government still faced a serious problem. In 1906, terrorists killed 1,126 persons and wounded 1,506; in 1907, they killed 3,001 and wounded 3,046; in 1908, the numbers had declined to 1,820 and 2,083, respectively. In 1909, there was a marked decline in terrorist acts; in the first four and a half months, 203 were killed and 210 wounded.[14]

Of course, Stolypin had never claimed that he could crush the revolutionary movement and restore order instantly. On taking office as prime minister he had told the tsar that it would take five years to "stamp out the embers of the revolution," and so he could take comfort from the fact that by 1908 he had gone some distance in realizing his goal. Nor was he able in a matter of a few months or even a year to inspire the population with a sense of civic consciousness and with a respect for law. Traditional distrust of authority was too deeply rooted, as was noted in an amusing but nevertheless telling report of the British Embassy in March 1908: "Another great source of pecuniary loss to the State railways in Russia is to be found in the general conduct of the travelling public. Passenger railways rates are notoriously low in this country, but not sufficiently so to satisfy universal requirements. Many people travel first class with third-class tickets. Others, even when travelling considerable distances, do not take a ticket, but content themselves with giving a gratuity to the guard, who in return for this attention consents to shut his eyes to the irregularity of their proceedings. What, they argue, is the good of buying a ticket when the money will never get further on its way to the State Exchequer than the pocket of some one or other of the railway officials. A third and more numerous category of travellers refrain from either purchasing tickets or tipping the officials, but trust to good fortune to be able to conceal themselves at the moment that the ticket collector makes his rounds. In these circumstances it is a matter of small wonder that the State railways in Russia are not paying concerns, and that the Government has been obliged to introduce a general increase in the passenger and goods tariff."[15] The corruption described by the British ambassador was not limited to the railways, which is one reason for Stolypin's slow progress in establishing a legal order in the empire.

Inevitably, as Stolypin pursued his ambitious goals of pacification and reform the list of his enemies grew at a rapid pace. Some despised his policies, others despised him because of his success in wielding power. The most notable among the former was Lev Tolstoy, who, as already noted, had befriended Stolypin's father during the Crimean War. Since that time, Tolstoy had become a critic of institutionalized religion and rejected the state as well as private property. But he remained a devoted adherent of Christianity, whose doctrines he reinterpreted by contending that Christ was not the son of God but a moral teacher. As noted in the preceding chapter, the Holy Synod of the Russian Orthodox Church excommunicated him in 1901.

On political issues, and in particular on the revolutionary upheaval of 1905, Tolstoy was ambivalent. He refused to identify himself as an anarchist because he thought that all anarchists wished to change society by violent means. Yet as a proponent of the doctrine of nonviolence, he rejected the institution of government, which was based on the use of violence. Evil, he believed, should be resisted not by force but by persuasion. He had also become a great admirer of the "unspoiled" peasantry and advocated a return to pastoral simplicity, a stance that shaped his position on agrarian reform.[16]

While he hated the violent methods of struggle adopted by the revolutionaries he was most passionate in his denunciation of government violence. In September 1906, he publicly excoriated Stolypin as the head of a government that perpetrated "senseless, stupid," and "unnecessarily harmful horrors," a reference to the executions of the field courts-martial. In July 1907, Tolstoy sent a personal letter to the prime minister, referring to him as "the son of my friend." He made a stirring appeal for a change in direction: "Two courses are open to you. Either you will continue in the way you have begun, condoning and even directing the policy of exile, hard labor, and capital punishment, and, without accomplishing your aims, leave a hated name behind you and, which is more serious, lose your soul; or taking the lead among all the countries of Europe, you will strive to abolish the oldest and greatest injustice of all, which is common to all peoples: the individual ownership of land." It was a stinging rebuke that Stolypin pondered for a while, and when he sent a reply, drafted by his brother, Aleksandr Arkadevich, he ignored Tolstoy's criticisms of the government's repressive policies. The prime minister simply defended his agrarian program, stressing his view that the right to private ownership in land must be recognized as flowing directly from the "innate instincts" of human beings. Undeterred, Tolstoy in January 1908 again wrote to Stolypin asking why he was continuing two mistaken policies: the destruction of the commune to create a class of small landowners and the resort to force to put an end to violence, both of which only made matters worse in Russia. A year later Tolstoy sent two more letters, one to Stolypin's brother (A. A.) and one to a certain Popov, attacking the death penalty as "shameful, repulsive." There is no evidence of any further replies by the prime minister to Tolstoy's criticisms.[17] But in the summer of 1910, when Tolstoy was on his death-bed, Stolypin indicated that he would have been pleased if the Church lifted the excommunication. Apparently, the government and the Holy Synod discussed the matter, but the synod remained intransigent. Tolstoy died a heretic, and priests were prohibited from participating in a mass for him.[18]

Politically more threatening to Stolypin were the venomous attacks by Count S. Iu. Witte, formerly the prime minister and minister of finance and now an influential member of the State Council, which had to approve bills passed by the Duma before their submission to the tsar for final action. In many ways a brilliant man, Witte was also vain, emotionally unstable, and vindictive. He was also an inveterate intriguer who enjoyed nothing more than to plot the downfall of his enemies, real or presumed. He devoted much of his time after retirement to savaging Stolypin, and his membership in the State Council provided him with a golden opportunity to undermine the prime minister. Whenever he perceived a slight by the prime minister, however trivial or unfounded, he launched a campaign of vilification. More to the point, he became a mainstay of the right-wing clique in the State Council determined to bring down Stolypin.

In his memoirs, Witte claimed that when he learned of Stolypin's appointment as prime minister, he was pleased because the former governor of Saratov was reputed to be a man of "strong character and iron will." But Witte immediately added that Stolypin was also known to be a man "not possessed of great ability," which raises the question why Witte approved the appointment. In fact, Witte went on to say that Stolypin's only virtues were his "audacity and courage," that he lacked the "mind, the education, and the experience" to amount to anything more than a "bayonet Junker." Even then, he might have served well in his office "had he remained a bachelor." But he had married a woman "who could do anything she pleased with him," and his deference to her and to her family (the prominent Neidgardts) "gradually corrupted him." By the end of his life he had lost interest in his work, and his only concern was to amass "honors and material advantage, in ways that would have been unthinkable under his predecessors."[19] For the rest, the memoirs are filled with attacks on the prime minister for virtually every policy he adopted and every decision he made. Witte accused Stolypin of being stupid, cynical, duplicitous, brutal, and venal. He attacked his policies as at once right wing and too moderate, sometimes in the very same paragraph. Thus, he thought that Stolypin was too restrained in his foreign policy because he did not plan to incorporate the northern provinces of Persia, "just as we incorporated the provinces of the southern Caucasus. But this requires that the inhabitants of the Caucasus, who shed so much blood in our behalf, be treated as sons of the Russian Empire, and not as aliens, as that so-and-so Stolypin tried to do." The latter comment referred to what Witte considered to be Stolypin's mistreatment of national minorities within the empire.[20]

For some four years, Witte nursed his grievances against Stolypin without openly challenging him, though he did play a role in most of the intrigues against Stolypin. Early in May 1910, he adopted a new tactic. He sent Stolypin a letter that runs to seven long, printed pages outlining the evidence for a charge he had nurtured for three years: that the prime minister had been privy to all the assassination attempts made on Witte and had taken no measures to prevent them. Witte claimed that during the night of April 29–30, 1907, policemen had discovered two "infernal machines" in the chimney of his house that were designed to produce an explosion so powerful as to kill everyone inside. A few days later Witte had received two anonymous letters warning him that further attempts on his life would be made. He handed one letter over to the director of the police and another one to an *Okhrana* agent on duty at his house. Subsequently, in May 1907, I. P. Shipov, a member of the State Council, warned him that a bomb would soon be thrown at the car taking him to a meeting of the council. He evaded the attack by walking to the meeting. The next day there was a report in a newspaper that an explosion had killed a person on a street in St. Petersburg. An investigation disclosed that the explosives had been planted by a policeman and that the aim had indeed been to kill Witte. Witte claimed that three years later, in 1910, evidence came to light that Aleksandr Kazantsev, known as a right-wing hit man, had carried out the wishes of men "in state service," who, in turn, were in direct contact with the *Okhrana*. In short, Witte alleged that the secret police were behind the attempts to assassinate him. His suspicions were confirmed when he learned that the Russian government considered it "undesirable" to conduct a thorough investigation of the attacks on him.

Witte assured Stolypin that if he were a private person he would appeal to the public for support by publishing the information on the assassination attempts. But because of his present position as a member of the State Council and his past service as prime minister, "such a course of action" was completely out of the question, an assertion he did not support with any argument. He was confident that since he had given Stolypin all the pertinent facts the prime minister would show his letter to the cabinet and would take measures "to stop the terrorist and provocative conduct of secret organizations, [and of] employees of both the government and political parties" and thus spare other government officials from the "disagreeable position in which I was placed."

Stolypin waited seven months before answering Witte's letter. The delay was insulting to Witte, but Stolypin can be forgiven. It may well be that initially the prime minister was at a loss as how to respond to the far-reaching charges, which had already received a great deal of attention from him and the police. Stolypin pointedly declared that "your letter did not provide me with anything new." The prime minister had often insisted that the government had not been indifferent to threats to Witte and that the authorities had thoroughly investigated every incident. At no time had the police been "timid" in following up leads. "I absolutely reject this reproach and the arguments you provide to corroborate it." Stolypin then took up each one of Witte's charges and offered evidence to refute them. Stolypin did not go so far as to accuse Witte of paranoia, but any objective reader would conclude that for himself.

It took Witte only two weeks to respond. After a cutting remark about Stolypin's long delay in writing to him, Witte repeated all the charges and then suggested that the State Council be requested to appoint a respected dignitary to investigate the matter and reach an objective conclusion about his charges. He named several men as suitable candidates for the task, among them Durnovo, one of Stolypin's fiercest enemies.[21]

In the meantime, there had been a nasty confrontation between Witte and Stolypin in the corridors of the State Council. If Witte's account can be credited, the altercation began when Stolypin derided Count K. I. Pahlen, who had allegedly been convinced by the evidence of police negligence, as a man who "has taken leave of his senses." Stolypin further enraged Witte by asking him whether he considered him, the prime minister, an idiot or an accomplice in the assassination attempts. "Spare me from replying to so delicate a question," Witte shot back.[22] Stolypin wrote once more to Witte, informing him that the Council of Ministers had considered the charges of police negligence, found them to be without merit, and had therefore decided not to take any further action in the matter.[23] Relations between the two men were now so strained that they rarely spoke to each other. A few months later, during the prime minister's gravest political crisis, Witte took his revenge. He played a major role in the intrigue that undermined Stolypin's authority. Unable to regain the position to which he believed he was entitled, the prime ministership, he could comfort himself with having achieved the next best thing, the humiliation of his nemesis. It was hardly an edifying achievement for a man who had made signal contributions to his country, first in promoting economic development and then in bringing to an end the war with Japan and the chaos of the general strike in October 1905.

Although no evidence has ever emerged to corroborate Witte's charge that the police had conspired to have him killed, it is conceivable that the former prime minister, by nature an inordinately suspicious man with a festering grudge against Stolypin, sincerely believed that his accusations were true. About fifteen months before he confronted Stolypin, some revelations about the police had come to light that suggested that the security forces were capable of the most cynical and ruthless conduct.

In May 1908, A. A. Lopukhin, formerly the director of the Department of Police in the Ministry of Internal Affairs and governor of Estland, made a startling revelation to V. L. Burtsev, a radical historian who devoted himself to unmasking spies in left-wing movements. Lopukhin disclosed that for some years Evno Azef, the head of the Combat Organization of the Socialist Revolutionary (SR) Party, a movement that was sympathetic to terrorism and contended that Russia could bypass capitalism and move directly to agrarian socialism, had been an employee of the police ever since 1893. He had thus been a double agent who had supplied the authorities with a large amount of very valuable information about the revolutionary movement. But that was only part of Azef's role. After about ten years as a police spy, Azef, a rather unsavory character who would betray any cause or person for money, decided on a new role, that of agent provocateur. When several attempts on the life of the despised minister of internal affairs, V. K. Plehve, failed, several SRs in the Combat Organization, which directed the party's terrorist activities, began to suspect Azef of having betrayed them to the police. To protect himself, Azef then decided to demonstrate that he was indeed a bona fide terrorist; he helped arrange the successful assassination of Plehve on July 15, 1904. It has also been suggested that Azef, a Jew, was motivated in part by his anger at Plehve for his anti-Jewish actions, in particular his alleged sponsorship of the pogrom in Kishinev in 1903.[24]

Lopukhin's motives in exposing all this are still somewhat murky. His detractors, of whom there were many, contended that he was an extraordinarily ambitious man who falsely claimed to be committed to liberalism. Appointed director of the police (one of the most important departments in the empire) in 1902 at the rather young age of thirty-eight, Lopukhin, eager to please his superiors, resorted to harsh police measures to contain the opposition. He became embittered when he was removed from his post early 1905 for negligence in failing to prevent the assassination of Grand Duke Sergei Aleksandrovich, an uncle of the tsar. Even though he received another post, the governorship of Estland, he was determined to seek revenge by embarrassing the government at every turn. Allegedly, Lopukhin administered Estland willfully and managed to arouse "great discontent among the population," which became openly hostile to him. After he was recalled from Estland in 1907 he lived lavishly and squandered his wealth. According to his detractors, Lopukhin exposed Azef in revenge for the agent's role in organizing the murders of Plehve and Sergei Aleksandrovich. The two assassinations undermined confidence in the police and therefore in Lopukhin, forcing him to retire from a very prestigious post.[25]

Lopukhin's defenders, and more recently the historian Charles A. Ruud, have portrayed him as a true liberal who "stood firm for the rule of law." In this version, Lopukhin sought the post as director of police because he was interested in reforming the department. His liberalism prompted him early in 1906 to inform prime minister Witte that in October and November 1905 a secret press in police headquarters in the capital had printed thousands of proclamations urging the massacre of Jews and of advocates of reform who wished to limit the powers of the tsar. An investigation confirmed the accuracy of Lopukhin's allegation and Witte ordered the destruction of the press and the remaining proclamations. His revelations to Burtsev thus appears to have been consistent with his liberalism, his desire to undermine authoritarianism in Russia and to promote the principles of legality.[26]

Whatever Lopukhin's motives, his revelations stunned the SRs, who conducted an investigation that corroborated the charges against Azef. Late in 1908 and early in 1909 the SR party officially announced that Azef was not only a police spy but that he had also played a key role in several terrorist acts. It emerged that Lopukhin had named Stolypin and A. V. Gerasimov, head of the St. Petersburg *Okhrana*, as Azef's most important patrons within the government. Lopukhin had actually been a friend of Stolypin's and thus could speak with authority about the prime minister's deep interest in police activities. He revealed that Colonel A. V. Gerasimov, an unrepentant hardliner on domestic unrest, gave daily reports to Stolypin and that both Gerasimov and Stolypin had full confidence in Azef. In fact, the prime minister was eager to meet Azef to find out more about the mood and plans of the terrorists. No such meeting took place, but there is no doubt that Stolypin was fully aware of Azef's work for the police.[27]

The news about Azef's role as an agent provocateur created a sensation in Russia and was widely reported, even in the international press. And it caused such an uproar in the Duma that the deputies voted to conduct two interpellations of the government's role in the Azef affair. Stolypin decided that the charges against him and his administration were serious enough to warrant his personal response.

Early in the evening of February 11, 1909, he appeared in the crowded chamber accompanied by no fewer than eight ministers. Count V. A. Bobrinskii, a right-wing Octobrist who acted as the reporter on the measure to interpellate the government, began the debate with a plea to all the speakers to focus on the facts of the case so as to enable the legislature and the country to reach a fair judgment on Azef's actions. But it immediately became clear that both sides in the debate were more interested in scoring points than in establishing the facts. None of the deputies wished to speak until the prime minister had delivered his speech, and Stolypin did not wish to speak until the socialists, who had claimed to have in their possession two letters from Azef himself proving his involvement in terrorist acts, submitted their evidence. After an awkward delay, the Social Democrat I. P. Pokrovskii broke the deadlock and delivered a brief speech on Azef's career and his role in promoting terrorism. Then A. A. Bulat, a Trudovik, addressed the chamber, concentrating on quotations from Azef's letters, which he had sent to the tribunal of the SR Party investigating his conduct and which appeared to substantiate the charge that Azef had been an agent provocateur.[28]

At that point Stolypin stepped up to the podium to deliver a long and detailed defense of the government. He offered to share with the Duma all the information at his disposal in an entirely "impartial" way, confident that his report would clear the government of all charges of having acted illegally or improperly. Previous speakers, Stolypin pointed out, had branded Azef a provocateur, but that was precisely how revolutionaries mislabel anyone who provides the authorities with information about their movement. And the revolutionaries were now intent upon placing the blame on the government for ghastly terrorist acts that had taken the lives of innocent citizens and children. That explained their focus on Azef; if he could be held responsible for the many murders of officials, the government would be branded as ruthless murderers. "Is it not advantageous for the revolution to disseminate monstrous rumors about the government's crimes, to shift on to the government all the odium of the affair, charging its agents with criminal machinations which have demoralized the members of the revolutionary parties and the revolution itself?"

But in charging Azef with criminal conduct, Stolypin insisted, the left offered an incorrect definition of an agent provocateur. A provocateur was a person who undertook to commit a criminal act and persuaded another person to participate in that act. However, a police agent such as Azef, who joined a revolutionary movement for the purpose of providing the police with information about the movement, could not be regarded as a provocateur. According to Stolypin, Azef had never over his long career as a police agent, which began in 1892, done anything other than pass information to the authorities, much of it helpful in nipping in the bud terrorist acts that could have caused great harm to the government. But several assassination attempts by groups not associated with the Socialist Revolutionary Party had not been stopped because the police had not penetrated them. Stolypin assured the deputies that if he had received information implicating any police spy in terrorism, he would immediately have ordered his arrest, "whoever it may have been." Under no circumstances would his government resort to provocation "as a method, as a system," a point he subsequently reiterated: "I loudly declare that the government does not and never will tolerate criminal provocation."

Having said that, the prime minister conceded that "ugly occurrences are always possible!" suggesting that some police spies may indeed have initiated terrorist actions, despite the government's disapproval. The evidence is, in fact, overwhelming that Azef was an agent provocateur, not simply a police spy. But did Stolypin know that when he delivered his speech denying Azef's role in terrorist actions? Did he have information, other than Lopukhin's charges, that Azef had planned assassinations? The available sources do not permit a definitive conclusion, but it seems highly likely that the prime minister had been privy to Azef's involvement in Plehve's assassination, not to mention other attacks on high officials. Lopukhin, whom he now denigrated as unreliable, was well informed about the work of the secret police and was in frequent contact with the prime minister. Eight years after the Azef affair became a cause célèbre, Lopukhin testified before the Commission of Inquiry on the Collapse of the Old Regime that as early as 1906 he had personally informed Stolypin about Azef's "role as an agent provocateur" and that the prime minister had expressed no indignation. General A. V. Gerasimov testified before the same commission that Stolypin was "always in the know" about Azef's activities.[29]

Unfortunately, Azef himself never made a public statement about his work in the Socialist Revolutionary Combat Organization and could not be questioned by the police because he managed to escape to Germany shortly after Lopukhin unmasked him. He succeeded for some ten years in evading the SRs, who, he assumed correctly, were looking for him and planned to kill him. In Germany, Azef lived under an assumed name and made his living playing the stock market. His motives in acting as a double agent remain unclear to this day. It seems that he never fully identified with the police or with the revolutionaries. Apparently, what he most wanted was to acquire as much money as possible to support his penchant for high living. As a police informant, he regularly pressured officials for an increase in pay, and by 1906 he received six hundred rubles a month, a very substantial sum in those days. At the same time, as head of the Combat Organization he had at his disposal a large amount of SR money, to which he helped himself quite liberally. For Azef, police work proved to be highly lucrative, enabling him to travel extensively and to support a mistress in grand style.

No matter how much Stolypin knew about Azef's various activities, the prime minister was deeply concerned about the charges leveled at his government, which badly tarnished the security forces and weakened them in their endeavors to stamp out the revolutionary opposition. That explains his painstaking attempt to rebut the charges of the SRs, which seemed persuasive to many people, including the British ambassador to St. Petersburg. The prime minister's apprehensions about the charges may also explain the ending of his speech, which was obviously designed to deflect criticism of his government and to put the revolutionaries on the defensive.

In his last two paragraphs Stolypin spoke about Russia's need to recover from its recent turbulence; while the monarch had taken the initiative to begin the recovery, Duma deputies must assume much of the burden in the future. "We, the government, can only put up the scaffolding, which facilitates your work in [creating] the building. Our opponents point to the scaffolding as an ugly building raised by us, and furiously rush to destroy its foundations. And this scaffolding will inevitably collapse and perhaps crush us under the debris, but this will [only] happen when out of the wreckage there is already noticeable at least the main outline of a renovated building, [whose inhabitants will be] free in the best sense of the word, free from poverty, from ignorance, from injustice, and devoted, as one person, to the Sovereign of Russia. (*Stormy applause from the right and center.*) And, gentlemen, this time will come, it will come despite all the revelations, since on our side is not only force but the truth."[30] It was a standard ending for Stolypin— emotional, uplifting, eloquent, and vaguely optimistic—but it did not succeed in diverting attention from the issue at hand, the government's sponsorship of an agent provocateur who played a major role in the assassinations of a minister of internal affairs and other dignitaries. In the newspapers, many commentators praised the lucidity and candor of the prime minister's remarks, but their assessments of the contents varied according to their political allegiances.

Stolypin bore a deep grudge against Lopukhin and resolved to punish him by bringing him to trial on the charge that he had betrayed the government. Realizing that the trial would be sensational, the prime minister sought the tsar's assent to the proceedings. Nicholas, who disliked Lopukhin for his disclosure in 1906 of the secret press in police headquarters that printed proclamations calling for pogroms, gave his approval. It was a speedy trial (in April 1909), at which Lopukhin was prevented from making a statement exposing the role of the police and Stolypin in the Azef affair. Astonishingly, the court found Lopukhin guilty of belonging to the Socialist Revolutionary Party because he had spoken to some of the SRs about Azef and sentenced him to penal servitude for five years. A higher court then reduced the sentence to five years of exile in Siberia. In 1912, the government granted him an amnesty and restored his civil rights.[31]

However embarrassing and painful, the Azef affair, the conflict with Witte, and the intrigues of right-wingers did not seriously undermine Stolypin's authority as prime minister. But they diverted him from his major concerns and added to a growing perception that he was embattled, forced to fend off enemies ready to pounce on him as soon as he faltered. They thus created an atmosphere that made Stolypin rather edgy, and on two occasions, the first in May 1908 and the second in May 1909, the prime minister spoke openly of resigning. That both incidents were unexpected and seemed initially to be fairly trivial only points up Stolypin's growing sense of isolation.

The first occurred on May 7, 1908, when Kokovtsov, the minister of finance, made the following thoughtless and provocative remark during a routine speech in the Duma on the financing of railway construction: "Thank God we have not got a parliament yet." Kokovtsov had, of course, formulated his comment very carelessly; Russia did have a parliament. What he meant was that parliamentarism had not been established—that is to say, parliament did not exercise decisive control over governmental policies. But in the heat of the moment that distinction between "parliament" and "parliamentarism" was overlooked. A huge cry of protest from the liberal and left-wing deputies greeted the minister's remark. Kokovtsov, who had never concealed his disdain for the Duma, ignored the noise and continued his speech without bothering to explain. Immediately after he left the podium, Miliukov, the leader of the Kadets, sharply criticized Kokovtsov, and a day later an Octobrist denounced the minister. Other deputies then tried to speak on the subject, but Khomiakov, the president, cut off further discussion.

However, he made a point of deploring Kokovtsov's remark as "unfortunate," a rather mild rebuke. Kokovtsov was deeply offended and submitted his resignation to Stolypin. After consulting with Kokovtsov and Khomiakov, the prime minister sent a letter to the president of the Duma threatening to resign as prime minister unless the criticism of the minister of finance was withdrawn. A relatively minor altercation had mushroomed into a ministerial crisis. The Octobrist deputies and the deputies to their right thought that the tsar might use the conflict as a pretext to dissolve the Third Duma. The opposition, on the other hand, was gearing up for a fight to the finish. The Kadets proposed that Khomiakov resign as president and that the Duma then re-elect him unanimously, a move that would have sharpened the conflict with the government. But Khomiakov was not in a mood to jeopardize the Duma over what he considered to be a trivial issue. He publicly declared in the Duma that in characterizing Kokovtsov's remark as "unfortunate" he had acted "incorrectly." Kokovtsov withdrew his resignation, and Khomiakov was rewarded with an invitation to Tsarskoe Selo, where he was graciously received by the tsar.

Although it ended happily, the incident demonstrated, once again, the contempt with which conservatives regarded the Duma. Stolypin, as we know, did not share that sentiment, but he nevertheless felt called upon to defend Kokovtsov. It was widely rumored that he had done so "under pressure from the highest quarter." But he may have come to Kokovtsov's defense on his own because the minister of finance belonged to the more conservative wing of the cabinet, which had strong links to the entourage at court, where the prime minister was regarded as too liberal. At the same time, Khomiakov's quick retraction indicated that the moderates in the Duma did not want Stolypin to resign, because they realized that their political fate depended on his remaining in office. "While Stolypin is in office," one observer noted, "the Duma feels comparatively safe, and the Duma consequently clings to Stolypin with pathetic energy." On the other hand, the deputies distrusted Kokovtsov, who was often mentioned as a possible prime minister. He was "the most hated Minister" in the Duma, a fact, it was widely assumed, that "did not disturb him greatly."[32]

The second, far more serious and more complex, political crisis again involved the vexing question of the prerogatives of the Duma and the monarchy. Its origins can be traced to the government's request, early in 1908, for thirty million rubles a year for a four-year period to rebuild the Russian Navy, badly mauled during the war with Japan in 1904–5. The plan was to construct four battleships of the Dreadnought class to be maintained in the Baltic Sea. In his appearance before the Duma Committee for Imperial Defense on March 3, 1908, Stolypin made a valiant effort to secure support for the bill, which had come under strong criticism. Half the committee opposed the measure on the grounds that Russia was not a naval power and that for the protection of its coastlines ships were unnecessary; the other half of the committee believed in a strong navy but opposed the expenditures because the Naval Ministry was poorly administered and the program of naval construction was poorly conceived. Stolypin rejected the arguments on both power political grounds and on constitutional grounds. If Russia failed to build a strong navy it would be forced to "retire to the interior of the country," an option the prime minister considered highly undesirable. Rejection of the funds would be "directly prejudicial to the international position of Russia, removing . . . the very corner-stone of the plan of Imperial defense now being developed by the government." It would also force many shipbuilders to go out of business, causing a loss of a large number of blue-collar jobs. And he could not agree with the second group of opponents to the credits, those who wished to delay construction of the navy until reform of the Naval Ministry had been completed because this suggested that the legislature could dictate to the tsar on these matters. He buttressed his argument by reminding the deputies that the structure and administration of the army and navy were constitutionally the prerogatives of the monarch. And he pointed out that the tsar treasured those prerogatives so dearly that he would not even disclose to the Duma the details of the administration's naval plans or the nature of reforms the Naval Ministry was contemplating. The constitutional issue was to loom ever larger as the debate over the naval question unfolded over the next fifteen months.[33]

As expected, the Duma Defense Committee turned down, by a vote of nineteen to fourteen, the government's request for the thirty million rubles. In accordance with the Fundamental Laws, the government could implement the budget of the previous year, which sufficed to begin naval construction. Though disappointed, Stolypin let it be known that the defeat on the credits would not lead to an all-out conflict between the government and the Duma. However, the tsar seems to have been far more distressed than Stolypin. On March 11, 1908, he wrote to the prime minister: "The naval question troubles me very much; we will discuss it when you give your report."[34] Stolypin's options were not promising, for the opposition to the credits was by no means confined to liberals and left-wingers. A large number of Octobrists and a good many rightists were disinclined to support the government despite their yearnings for a powerful Russia.

When the bill came up for consideration in the Duma itself on May 24, 1908, Stolypin once again spoke for the credits of thirty million rubles. Now, much more than in his first speech on the subject two months earlier, he stressed nationalistic themes in urging the deputies to support the government's proposal. He granted that many legislators who opposed the measure were not motivated by antistate sentiments; their concern was to prod the Ministry of the Navy to improve efficiency and to eliminate abuses. But that could not be achieved by the Duma, which, as he had already noted, did not have the authority over the administrative details of a department directly under the monarch's control. If the deputies continued to vote against the credits, they would undermine the government's goal of establishing Russia as a naval power capable of defending its coastlines. For every country "a fleet is a matter of national pride; it is the external proof of the fact that a nation has power, has the possibility of maintaining control over the sea. For this, a few fortresses are insufficient; it is not possible with a few armed fortresses to defend the shorelines. For the defense of the shores we need mobile fortresses that can sail freely, we need a fleet of battleships." In short, to be defenseless at sea was as dangerous as being defenseless on land.[35]

Stolypin's resort to a patriotic appeal made little impression, even on deputies who could normally be expected to follow his lead. About three weeks after he had given his speech, Guchkov, leader of the Octobrists, leveled an attack on the Department of the Navy so fierce that it had the effect of a bombshell. Bernard Pares, who was in the chamber at the time, described it as the "most effective speech ever made in the Duma"; he also noted that "no speech ever did so much to raise the consequence of the Duma."[36] Guchkov, it must be recalled, was a moderate liberal who in 1906 had become an enthusiastic ally of Stolypin. He was also a deeply patriotic man who had fought bravely in the Russo-Japanese War. A strong advocate of monarchy though not of autocracy, uncompromising in his opposition to any plan that even remotely suggested a federal system of government, Guchkov's criticism of the Naval Ministry was motivated not by any hostility to the authorities but by a conviction that they were mismanaging the affairs of state and weakening the country. Three days before his most sensational speech, Guchkov had dwelt on the country's humiliating defeats at Port Arthur and the Straits of Tsushima, blaming these catastrophes on the senior officials in the navy. Specifically, he charged the ministry with mindlessly concentrating on the construction of ships without at the same time training personnel properly or developing an efficient administrative structure. In view of the government's negligence, the legislature was duty bound to inform the tsar that the state's armed forces were in disarray. "And if we did not fulfill this . . . duty, then I would say that the Manifesto of October 17 was written in vain; we have been assembled in this hall in vain. Our first duty is to tell the truth to the Emperor, and we should remember that the old order collapsed [in 1905] exactly because of lies."[37]

These harsh words were mild compared to the attack Guchkov delivered on the tsarist administration on May 27. After repeating the charge that the central government had recklessly gone to war in 1904 and then had failed to prosecute it effectively, he criticized the military leadership for not undertaking necessary reforms in the aftermath of the defeats. He referred to the Council of State Defense, still presided over by an appointee of the tsar, as a moribund institution and urged that it be placed under the chairmanship of the prime minister. Most dramatically, he called for the retirement of several grand dukes, who headed military inspectorates, which were important positions in the structure of the army and navy. He went so far as to name a number of the grand dukes who should be dismissed and made pointed remarks about the incompetence of the president of the Defense Council, Grand Duke Nikolai Nikolaevich, a reactionary who, however, had played a crucial role in persuading the tsar to issue the October Manifesto in 1905. The speech created a great stir in the Duma and in the press, all the more so because it was widely known that the minister of war, General Rediger, and the president of the Duma, Khomiakov, were not at all displeased with Guchkov's remarks. Rediger chafed under Grand Duke Nikolai Nikolaevich's arrogant handling of the affairs of the Defense Council and also resented the tsar's meddling in the administration of the military departments. When Nicholas ordered Rediger to reply to Guchkov's attack on the grand dukes, the minister of war took the courageous and unprecedented step of declining on the grounds that his comments would be less than forceful since he believed Guchkov's comments to be on target.[38]

Guchkov had not informed Stolypin that he intended to make a public issue of the inefficiency of the military services because he did not wish to "compromise" the prime minister. At the time, Stolypin was in Revel (Tallinn) at a meeting of the tsar and King Edward VII, and as soon as he returned to St. Petersburg he confronted Guchkov: "What have you done! The Emperor is outraged by your speech. He said to me that if you have some objection to the participation of the grand dukes in the administration, you might have expressed it to him personally and ought not to have exposed it on a public tribune or, furthermore, listed them by name." From that time, relations between Guchkov and the court, already strained, became decidedly hostile. But, significantly, Stolypin told Guchkov that he was "essentially in complete agreement" with him, and that the tsar had actually been inclined to remove the grand dukes from their posts in the military establishment. Stolypin feared that now Nicholas would not go ahead with the dismissals because he would not want to be seen as caving in to Guchkov.[39]

In truth, Stolypin took two conflicting positions on the Naval Ministry, one in support of the tsar and one in favor of increasing the Duma's involvement in determining military policy, not an uncommon course on his part when the sensitive issue of the tsar's prerogatives was under consideration. Stolypin did believe that the military forces needed to be reformed if Russia was to have an efficient navy and army, but he also feared that if he took an unambiguous stand in favor of the Duma, his tenure as prime minister would end. And there was no doubt in his mind that Guchkov had made a mistake in taking so forceful a stand. The Octobrist had needlessly poisoned the political atmosphere and had needlessly played into the hands of the extremists on the right. Indeed, Purishkevich, the right-wing firebrand, lost no time in rebuking Guchkov on the floor of the Duma on the grounds that it was "inadmissible" even to discuss matters "constituting the prerogatives of the autocratic leader of the Russian army." Purishkevich held that Guchkov had established a "precedent that is leading the State Duma along an extremely undesirable and dangerous path."[40]

Stolypin felt called upon to reply to Guchkov, though he did it without indicating that he was responding directly. On June 13, 1908, he appeared before the State Council to appeal for support for the credits to build the four battleships. He began with a justification for a large navy, which touched on his general views on Russia's foreign policy. As noted in Chapter 5, Stolypin strongly opposed an aggressive foreign policy, but this did not mean that he wanted Russia to sink into the position of an uninfluential power. "Great world powers," he told the state councilors, "have world interests. Great world powers must take part in the international system [of alliances], they cannot renounce the right to have a voice in the settlement of world events. A fleet is the lever that makes it possible to exercise this right, this necessary appurtenance of every great power with a sea coast."[41]

Stolypin urged the State Council not to attach any conditions to the bill providing funds for the navy, such as the reorganization of the navy's administrative structure. The government in Russia, unlike governments in Western Europe, is responsible to the monarch, not to the legislature. If the State Council succeeded in interfering with the executive operations of the government, "complete irresponsibility would ensue" with no clear lines of authority. Under those circumstances, Russia could lapse into a "pernicious" political system with "a change of government ... every two or three months because of an unfavorable vote in the legislative chambers." Stolypin then deplored the Duma's failure to pass the credits for ship construction; it had acted as it did, he pointed out, not because it opposed the enlargement of the navy but because it lacked confidence in the competence of the Naval Ministry. And in the process the Duma had claimed prerogatives not granted by the Fundamental Laws. Stolypin argued that passage of the credits by the State Council would restore the balance of constitutional authority. "We are sentinels," he said at the conclusion of his speech, "charged with defending a line of demarcation, and if our own people or outsiders attempt to violate it, we will not be cowards and look the other away. And we ask you, if you believe that a fleet is necessary, if you believe that Russia is not so impoverished that it must renounce the sea, then gentlemen of the State Council, do not shirk the responsibility from which neither the law nor the Sovereign has freed us."[42] The State Council was impressed: it voted 113 to 35 in favor of the credits, but the Duma did not approve the measure until 1911.

It seemed as though the controversy of the navy's administrative structure had been settled. But it flared up again in a different context. It turned out that the leadership of the Naval Ministry had been considering some administrative reforms on its own for some two years. The measure that the ministry finally introduced in the Duma on May 24, 1908, was moderate: it called for the establishment of a naval general staff at a total cost of seventy-four thousand rubles, not a very large sum, and it included lists of the positions, specifying the salary of each, that would make up the new office. The sponsors argued that the war with Japan had demonstrated the need for an institution that would concern itself with the overall planning of strategy and with the mobilization of the navy. The Council of Ministers had adopted the measure without any discussion. According to Kokovtsov, the measure did not at first particularly engage the interest of the prime minister, though he did favor it. The Duma itself considered the bill so routine that it voted for it on May 24 without any debate.[43]

In the State Council, however, the bill met a different fate. In the council's finance committee the reactionary intriguer Schwanebach claimed that the bill was constitutionally defective because the Duma had not only voted the credits but had also taken it upon itself to establish the new lists; that was a violation of the Fundamental Laws, which left such matters in the hands of the tsar. Although it was clearly a rather trivial matter, the rightists seized upon it to undermine Stolypin.

There was no better way to do that than to accuse him of trespassing on the monarch's authority. Nicholas was paranoid when it came to his prerogatives, as the rightists well knew. Once Schwanebach had made the first charge, other state councilors swung into action. Durnovo, long Stolypin's foe, spoke against the measure, and soon the cry was heard that a "very serious question of principle" was at stake. In the end, the council rejected the bill, which marked the first occasion on which the upper chamber rejected an initiative of Stolypin's. The vote was not only a personal blow to Stolypin. It also struck at the prime minister's strategy of cooperating with the Octobrists, who had supported the bill in the Duma. If the rightists succeeded in destroying his alliance with the Octobrists, his entire program would be jeopardized. Stolypin had no choice but to meet the rightists' challenge head-on.

Late in 1908 the government reintroduced the bill, and in mid-December the Duma passed it without amendment. All attempts to persuade the Duma deputies to reach a compromise with the State Council failed; the deputies would not agree to vote solely on the credits and leave out the item on the creation of the lists. The finance committee of the State Council decided to go along with the Duma's bill with the proviso that the lower chamber should be informed that in the future no violations of the Fundamental Laws would be tolerated by the upper chamber. Apparently Stolypin let it be known that he agreed with the State Council that the measure violated the law, but nevertheless he favored its adoption in the present form because he considered the immediate establishment of the naval staff absolutely essential. Thus, the prime minister defended both the inviolability of the Fundamental Laws and the deviation from those laws on this occasion. So long as he sought to retain the confidence of the tsar and of the Duma he could not do otherwise.[44]

In private conversations at the time, Stolypin insisted that Articles 14 and 96 of the Fundamental Laws were ambiguous in delineating the respective prerogatives of the crown and the legislature with regard to military matters. A careful reading of the relevant pages supports that judgment. Stolypin confessed that because of "political considerations" he had decided to favor the Duma's interpretation; he wanted to fend off the "reproach that the crown was attempting to enlarge [its] prerogatives too far." He also defended his stand in favor of the Duma by pointing out that according to the Fundamental Laws the crown was authorized to consult with the legislature in matters that were not constitutionally within its competence. For example, the Duma had no say in foreign policy, but the tsar had often authorized the minister of foreign affairs to inform it on his dealings with foreign countries and to seek its counsel. Hence, it was appropriate for the monarch to have turned for advice to the Duma on the naval staff bill. Stolypin thus suggested that the Duma's action on the list of positions was not out of line.[45]

After the affirmative vote in the finance committee, the measure was referred to the State Council, where in March and April of 1909 the debate reached unprecedented levels of intensity. The rightists, led by Durnovo, Witte, and V. F. Trepov, all men who despised Stolypin, took the high road and argued that the government was proposing a measure that would change the political structure of the country and would permanently destroy the effectiveness of the country's military establishment. Durnovo put the military and constitutional argument most succinctly and dramatically. He warned that if adopted the bill would create a dangerous precedent, and, in time, the State Council and the Duma would assume complete control over the military services. Not only would that violate the Fundamental Laws; it would also shatter the "foundations on which rests the power of the Russian state," the authority of the tsar, which was the key factor in creating Russia "and [which still] embodies the strength and might of Russia."[46]

The government took the challenge seriously and discussed the matter in two cabinet meetings, at which the ministers preferred a compromise solution; but if this proved to be unfeasible, they agreed to support the measure as passed by the Duma.[47]

Stolypin intended to appear in person before the State Council to argue for the measure, but he took sick and, at the insistence of his doctors, left the capital to spend about a month in the Crimea. The nature of his illness is not clear. According to one report, Stolypin was suffering from a mild form of lobar pneumonia. But Nicholas's comments to his mother on March 4, 1909, suggest that the ailment was more serious. "Stolypin's illness has now abated, but for one day it alarmed everyone. It seems that his heart is not in order, [and] that, of course, is dangerous when there is an inflammation. He became ill on the very night that he returned from [the palace] after having delivered a report to me."[48] In any case, his condition was serious enough for him to ask Kokovtsov, the minister of finance, to take his place at the State Council, though he indicated that he would understand if Kokovtsov did not wish to assume the burden. But if Kokovtsov refused, Stolypin would leave his bed to make a last effort to persuade the state councilors to follow his lead on the naval general staff measure. Kokovtsov agreed to speak on Stolypin's behalf and took the prime minister's rough notes to guide him in his presentation. His only condition was that no one "must hold it against me if I failed and the general session adopted a decision other than that of the State Duma."[49]

Kokovtsov's arguments, which barely deviated from Stolypin's, were straightforward and telling. He pointed out that at previous sessions the State Council had already approved measures very similar to the one now before it. He warned that further delay would surely harm the efforts to improve naval efficiency and strongly rejected the charge that the authority of the tsar would be diminished by the bill as passed by the Duma.[50] He acknowledged that an article of the Fundamental Laws had "not been observed" but rejected the argument that this constituted a dangerous precedent. After all, the "ministry responsible for the error promised not to repeat it in the future."[51]

In the end, on March 19, 1909, the State Council voted for the measure, but the result was no triumph for Stolypin. Seventy-five councilors voted against, and of the eighty-seven who voted in favor, seven were members of the cabinet. The conservative newspaper *Novoe vremia* expressed shock that "a Russian Ministry, responsible solely to the Emperor" had allied itself with the "liberal center," the Kadets, and the Poles, in limiting the "prerogatives of the monarch." If the ministers had voted against the bill, as the editors of the paper thought they should have, the rightists would have won and the prerogatives of the tsar would have been maintained.[52] The final disposition of the bill was now up to the tsar himself. The rightists immediately launched a vigorous campaign, employing all their persuasive powers, influence, and skills at intrigue, to persuade Nicholas to reject it. For about three weeks, St. Petersburg was extraordinarily tense. The political class realized that the country faced a turning point: the tsar's rejection of the bill could lead to Stolypin's fall from office and the re-establishment of the kind of autocratic regime that had held sway before 1905.

Stolypin wasted no time in seeking to mobilize support for his position. Soon after returning from the Crimea, he called an urgent meeting of the cabinet, which lasted until 2:30 A.M.; the ministers decided that if the tsar rejected the bill, they would all resign.[53] Convinced that his prestige and influence hung in the balance, Stolypin made every effort to persuade the tsar not to use his veto power. In a special letter to him, the prime minister rejected outright the charge that the bill in any way diminished the legal rights of the sovereign. The government, Stolypin insisted, had acted in accordance with legislative norms. He warned that rejection of the bill would create "excessive and insurmountable difficulties for him." He also sought to exploit Nicholas's deep dislike of Witte by predicting that the former prime minister, "together with other intriguers," would accuse the "seditious government" of under-mining the tsar's authority.[54] As it turned out, that is exactly what Witte's allies did at the March 13 meeting of the State Council. Durnovo and Trepov attacked the government's "wide interpretations" of the Fundamental Laws and its broadening of the competence and authority of the legislative institutions.[55]

At a private meeting with the monarch a few days before Nicholas handed down his decision, Stolypin seemed to sense that he faced de-feat. Deeply distressed, he is reported to have made the following re-mark: "Your Majesty apparently wants to lean for support on right-wing extremists [while] maintaining a moderate cabinet." To which Nicholas responded: "No, I know the right-wing extremists very well. However, Markov II* passed on to me the greetings of [his] faction."[56] Both re-marks are revealing: Stolypin's was a shrewd assessment that succinctly explained his own precarious position. He was committed to reform, but the man to whom he was accountable favored the program of the reac-tionaries. Nicholas's comment suggested that notwithstanding his doubts about the character of the extremists he was well disposed to-ward them because they supported him.

Our best source for Stolypin's thinking during the crisis is contained in the reports of foreign ambassadors, to whom the prime minister talked freely, no doubt because he felt confident of their support. He let it be known that the extremists on the right were using the bill on the naval general staff to undermine his position by telling the tsar that the government had participated in an effort to encroach upon his preroga-tives. The right-wingers, he told the British ambassador, met regularly in the home of Count P. G. Sheremetev, a wealthy man who had enjoyed entree to the court ever since the reign of Tsar Alexander III. Sheremetev was a hard-line reactionary unwilling to make any concessions to the changes introduced since the Revolution of 1905. He was so enraged at the tsar for having granted the October Manifesto in 1905 that he "re-moved His Majesty's portrait from his *salon*." Witte regularly attended the meetings at Sheremetev's house, convinced that even though he was deeply distrusted and disliked at court the financial situation in Russia would deteriorate, and then his services as a minister would again be needed.[57] Stolypin was persuaded that his enemies wanted him to acqui-esce in the rejection of the bill, if the tsar so decided, and stay in office

---

*N. E. Markov, known for some reason as Markov II, was one of the more viru-lent rightists. In 1917 he predicted (approvingly) the extermination of all Jews in a new wave of pogroms. In the 1920s he lived in Germany and supported the Nazis. Laqueur, *Black Hundred*, p. 24.

because that would be the ultimate humiliation and "they would like to see him discredited in the country."

The intrigues against him, as Stolypin characterized them, were "low and base." He had just returned from his convalescence, and he had been approached by several people, who he knew had been "most active against him," to assure him of their loyalty. They claimed not to have lifted "a finger against him" and declared that they would be deeply distressed if he resigned. Even Witte, "the head and front of the whole campaign," had assured him that he had done nothing to harm the prime minister and "earnestly trusted that M. Stolypin did not believe a word of the rumours which had been circulated as to his having participated in any intrigues against him." Stolypin related all this in a calm demeanor; it was as though this was standard behavior of his enemies in high circles, which in fact it was. He was obviously repelled by the machinations of the intriguers, a kind of political in-fighting for which he never developed a taste. His disdain for intrigues was an admirable trait but a serious failing in a political leader in St. Petersburg, and it would cost him dearly.

For several days, Stolypin remained in the dark about the tsar's position. Nicholas had received him "most graciously," but he could not divine Nicholas's intentions. On the other hand, Stolypin left no doubt about the depth of his own views: "I have the feelings of a loyal subject towards his Sovereign, but I feel more than that. His Majesty and I have worked together for three troublous [sic!] years, and we have had to face many difficulties together. I have the highest opinion of His Majesty's straightforwardness and sincerity of purpose, and I feel bound to him by very close ties. But on this question, I must stand firm." He pointed out that the cabinet had pressured hard for the bill and could not retreat, even though he acknowledged that "the bill in itself is a trifling one." But he believed that nothing less than the future direction of his government was at stake. Events would prove his judgment to have been sound.[58]

For days on end, politicians, patrons of the capital's salons, and the newspapers seem to have devoted themselves entirely to the political intrigues in the highest circles of government and the fate of the prime minister. On March 25, Guchkov, well informed about the thinking of the court, noted privately that "the resignation of Stolypin and part of the cabinet is possible." The newspapers once again named likely successors to Stolypin: I. G. Shcheglovitov, the minister of justice, A. V. Krivoshein, the minister of agriculture, or V. N. Kokovtsov. Even *Rossiia*, a paper financed by the government and run by Stolypin loyalists, at first (on March 27) issued an ambiguous denial of the rumors about the prime minister's departure from office. Only a week later, on April 4, did the paper state categorically that there was no basis to the rumors.[59]

In the meantime, there had been various indications that the influence of the rightists at court was rising. On March 10, 1909, the tsar dismissed Rediger as minister of war because he had failed to offer a strong defense of the military in the Duma at the time of Guchkov's criticisms. But many observers believed that the real reason for the dismissal was that Rediger had refused to respond to Guchkov's criticisms of the grand dukes. The tsar replaced Rediger, a highly competent and independent officer, with V. A. Sukhomlinov, a frivolous man whom Stolypin could not abide and whom he regarded as "unsuitable, unreliable, and incapable of inspiring respect."[60] But Nicholas felt comfortable with Sukhomlinov, politically a man after his own heart. At the time he was considering the bill on the naval general staff, he confided to Sukhomlinov that "I created the Duma not to have it give me orders but to give me advice," precisely the position of the rightists who were heavily lobbying for a veto of the bill. On several other senior appointments Stolypin's wishes were also disregarded by the court in favor of men recommended by the ultraconservative United Nobility.[61]

Finally, on April 25, after five weeks of rising tension in the capital, the tsar let Stolypin know that he would not approve the bill on the naval general staff. Nicholas said that he had "constantly" thought about the question and had decided that he could not accept the measure, but he gave no reason for his action. However, he could not ignore the fact that his own chief minister, that is, Stolypin, had not only made clear his full support for the bill but had also indicated that rejection of it would make his position untenable. Nicholas therefore stated categorically that "[t]here can be no question of confidence or no confidence. Such is my will." Then Nicholas made a point that went to the heart of the controversy over the action taken by both houses of the legislature: "Remember that we live in Russia, and not abroad or in Finland . . . , and therefore *I do not permit anyone to think about resigning*. Of course there will be talk about this in Petersburg and Moscow, but the hysterical cries will soon die down." Nicholas then directed Stolypin to draw up new rules clarifying the authority of the Duma and State Council in legislating on military and naval bills. He ended the note with a firm refusal to accept anyone's resignation: "I warn you that I categorically reject in advance your or anyone else's request to be relieved of his office. Respectfully your Nicholas."[62]

To emphasize his concern about the protection of his prerogatives, three days after he had rejected the bill Nicholas sent an imperial rescript to Stolypin officially requesting him to formulate "rules showing what legislative acts or affairs concerning the Military and Naval Departments of the Government shall be subject to my direct decision in the manner laid down by Article 96 of the said laws, and what acts in this respect shall be submitted to me for confirmation by the ordinary legislative procedure. Such rules, after discussion of the same in the Council of Ministers and after they have received my approval, shall be made known and strictly carried out." Nicholas ended the rescript with a reiteration of his confidence in Stolypin: "The entire activity of the Council of Ministers under your presidency, which merits my complete approbation, being directed towards strengthening the fundamental principles of State organization which I have firmly established, gives me the assurance that you will successfully execute this my present commission in accordance with my instructions."[63]

Stolypin faced a dilemma. He had been unambiguous about his intention to resign if the naval general staff bill were rejected, and he knew that if he remained in office his position would be substantially weakened. He could hardly deny the claim of the rightists "that the victory was already theirs." The monarch's failure to take his advice could not be viewed as anything other than a humiliating blow. And there would be harmful political consequences. The Octobrists would surely distance themselves from him, removing the linchpin of his entire Duma policy (a right center coalition). On the other hand, as a loyal monarchist the prime minister found it impossible to disobey his ruler, to engage in an act that would be widely perceived as derogation of duty.

A very practical, political consideration also played a role in Stolypin's thinking. If he resigned, the tsar would appoint an outright reactionary in his place. Stolypin was not alone in fearing such an outcome. A senior official in the British embassy was so disturbed by that possibility that he sent to London an urgent, handwritten note pointing out that "I can see nothing but drawbacks in the substitution of a reactionary Prime Minister for M. Stolypin. Even if it results in failure (which it doubtless would) it would throw Russia back and undo much good which M. Stolypin had done." Interestingly, the anonymous author of this note also feared that Russian foreign policy would change drastically if Stolypin left office. A new, reactionary government might well throw Russia "into the arms of Germany." Great Britain could strengthen Stolypin's hand by inducing the Russian government "to maintain complete solidarity with us, notably in Persian affairs, which we are trying to do."[64] Still, no one could be sure whether Stolypin would succeed in re-establishing his authority after his humiliation. The only indisputable conclusion one could reach about the ministerial crisis, as the British ambassador pointed out, "was that Russia has a considerable distance to travel before she becomes a constitutional State in the Western acceptation of [the] term."[65]

Stolypin put up a good front after the crisis had abated. He told the French and Japanese ambassadors that he was satisfied with the outcome. After all, the bill itself was of "comparatively minor importance." Moreover, Stolypin took comfort from the fact that the tsar had expressed full confidence in the cabinet—a reference to the rescript of April 28—and he had made clear that he did not blame the government for the passage of the bill on the naval general staff in the Duma and State Council. The tsar also had indicated that he was satisfied with the government's determination to uphold the Fundamental Laws. Finally, Stolypin took satisfaction from the tsar's decision to permit him and not the president of the State Council to submit to the tsar the names of individuals to be appointed to the upper chamber. This was important since the president of the council, Akimov, was a right-winger and would have nominated like-minded men to bolster his faction.[66]

Privately, however, Stolypin's assessment was different. "My authority has been undermined," he is quoted as having said to a foreign acquaintance in St. Petersburg, "I will be kept for some time so that they can make use of my abilities, and then I will be thrown overboard."[67] Stolypin was a realist, and he understood that the rightists had good reason for their exultation.[68] He was also sure that they would soon resume their campaign of vilification. True, Stolypin had managed to inflict some defeats on his enemies, such as the prevention of a large demonstration by reactionaries at the time of the festivities marking the two hundredth anniversary of the Russian victory at Poltava in 1709. But at the same time, as the German ambassador to St. Petersburg noted ruefully, six weeks after the crisis had abated, rumors continued to circulate that the prime minister would resign after all, probably in the fall of 1909. Stolypin's position still appeared to be precarious.[69]

The political consequences of the tsar's veto of the naval general staff bill became evident very quickly. Many Octobrists, still committed to reform generally and to the principles of the October Manifesto in particular, were profoundly disappointed and frustrated that their efforts to reinvigorate the command structure of the navy had come to naught. This failure raised doubts about the ability of the Duma to work effectively and produce the changes they considered necessary for the modernization of the country. These Octobrists distanced themselves from the prime minister, and although they did not formally join the opposition they no longer could be considered his reliable ally.[70] The right-center coalition in the Duma, on which Stolypin had based his hopes for majorities in favor of his reforms, was thus undermined. Without a political party of his own, he now looked for support to the moderate rightists, who late in October 1909 formed the Russian National fraction (soon to be known as the National Party) under the leadership of P. N. Balashev, a large landowner in Podole with strong views and a strong personality. His great wealth enabled him to pay out of his own pocket for much of the party's activities and thus to play an important role in shaping its policies.

Stolypin's reliance on the Nationalists was bound to produce a shift in his priorities if not in his long-range policies, for the new party favored a program that in some respects differed markedly from his. It was not reactionary pure and simple; it favored such reforms as universal education, old-age pensions, reorganization and improvement of the courts of law and legal procedures, the extension of local self-government to all nationalities, and the maintenance of representative institutions, which were to keep an eye on the legality of the government's conduct of affairs, and they wished to maintain the monarchy as a "supreme authority." The Nationalists also were committed to establishing the predominance of "true Russians" in all parts of the empire. Indeed, they were uncompromising in their support of the "unity and indivisibility" of the Russian Empire, which meant opposition to the strivings for autonomy by many of the minorities. The Nationalists were especially harsh on the Jewish question, holding that the Jews could not have rights granted to other minorities.

When Balashev was asked by the British ambassador why his party was so "hard" on the Jews, he replied that "it was necessary to take a decided attitude on that question" but conceded that it might have to be modified. The Jewish problem, he noted, was "an almost insoluble problem" for Russia, but he did not exclude the possibility of supporting proposals "for ameliorating the lot of the Jews, were such ever put forward."[71]

The key element in the Nationalists' program was Russian nationalism. It was not the liberal nationalism referred to in the previous chapter. It focused not on the expansion of the state but on the integration of the minorities into the empire. The precise form that the promotion of Russian nationalism would take would become clear only as specific issues arose. But the idea of Russian nationalism was sufficiently broad and appealing to attract conservative Octobrists and some other, smaller groups in the Duma. Depending on the issue the Nationalists could count on 100 to 150 votes in the Duma. That was not enough to provide Stolypin with a clear majority, but it did give him a solid basis of support. The new alignment helps explain the prime minister's shift in emphasis in his policies on the national question. Stolypin accepted the inevitable: if he were to remain in office he would have to adjust to the hard reality that the ultimate authority in Russia, the tsar, did not favor the reform policies he had sought to pursue during his first three years as prime minister. As Orlando Figes put it, "[As] far as the Tsar was concerned, Stolypin's political programme threatened to shift the balance of power from the court to the state institutions."[72] Unless he wished to oppose the tsar, which was temperamentally and ideologically inconceivable for Stolypin, he would have to change course, even though he knew that without reform and modernization neither the dynasty nor Russia's imperial interests could in the long run be protected.

This is not to say that Stolypin caved in completely to the right. Partly out of revenge but also to weaken the extremists, he launched a campaign against the Union of the Russian People. As already noted, he prohibited the right-wing extremists from taking part in the celebrations of the victory at Poltava in 1709; he also agreed to the request of a Finnish court to arrest the organizer of the murder of the Kadet deputy, M. Ia. Herzenstein (Gertsenshtein), and he attempted to place people willing to cooperate with the government in leading positions of the union.[73] Given the tsar's sympathies for the union and for the right-wing extremists generally, these moves by Stolypin were risky. He seems to have decided to send a signal to his enemies on the right: he may have lost a battle but he would not capitulate and concede total defeat. He would continue to pursue his overall goals even if he had to make some tactical adjustments.

In the year of his first serious crises, from the spring of 1908 to the spring of 1909, whenever he felt thoroughly embattled, Stolypin sought relaxation by traveling abroad incognito on the royal yacht *Almaz*, which the tsar placed at his disposal. On these trips, he engaged in playfulness that he never displayed as a public figure. In the summer of 1908, for example, he decided to surprise his daughter, Maria, who was then living in Berlin with her husband, a junior diplomat at the Russian Embassy. Russian officials had managed with remarkable efficiency to keep all the arrangements secret, and no one in Germany knew that the prime minister was on German soil. He traveled to other cities, and in Hamburg he

toured the city, frequented stores, attended the theater and "was in a fes-
tive mood all the time. . . . Papa enjoyed his incognito to the utmost."
Eventually, however, the German authorities learned about the famous
person in their country, and Kaiser William II sent a message to the Russian Embassy inviting Stolypin to his palace. But Stolypin refused, unwilling to give the impression that he was taking the initiative in matters of foreign policy, constitutionally still the tsar's domain. Stolypin
feared that a meeting with William "might lead to more harm than
benefit."[74]

In the fall of 1908, Stolypin and his family went on another trip on
the *Almaz;* after meeting Maria in Stettin he traveled to Libava, Latvia,
where the prime minister again enjoyed moving about incognito. The
local police knew that Stolypin was on the *Almaz,* which had docked in
the harbor, and made extensive preparations to accompany the prime
minister when he came ashore. They had expected him to travel in the
city in a car or in the port commander's carriage. But instead Stolypin
sneaked out of the boat and rode on the city's trams. The family spent
hours touring the city, sightseeing, shopping, and when tired, stopped
for tea at a sidewalk cafe. After dark, the Stolypins returned to the yacht,
again by tram, and as they approached the boat they overheard the
comments of one of the policemen on guard: "Well, thank God, he
passed the day in safety. Stolypin did not come ashore in spite of all our
preparations. Now we can rest." Papa, with amusement in his eyes, signaled us to be silent. He then gave an order "for a message of thanks to
be sent to the police chief for such exemplary order in the city, which he
had examined in detail."[75]

7

Religion, Nationalism, Migration

In an interview in October 1909, with a journalist from the regional newspaper *Volga*, Stolypin sought to dispel the widely held perception that his political cooperation with the Nationalist fraction signified a repudiation of his reformist agenda. But he also took pains to phrase his views carefully so as not to give offense to his conservative allies. It was a classic example of the prime minister's strategy of ambiguity, to which he resorted with growing frequency after the crisis of the spring of 1909: please the right without offending the center.

Stolypin chose a provincial newspaper as his forum because he believed that the press in the major cities, St. Petersburg and Moscow, devoted too much space to "high politics," party squabbles, and political intrigues. Journalists tended to focus on "fruitless" disputes over the nature of the Russian polity and thus failed to understand the essential feature of the country's system of rule. Ever since the issuance of the Manifesto of October 17, Russia had been developing a "purely Russian state structure" in keeping with its "historical traditions and the national spirit," a reference to his view that while the tsar was pre-eminent, the Duma, too, had a definite role to play in national affairs.

In the interview Stolypin also claimed that in harping on the "pessimism and general depression" that had allegedly gripped the nation, the press in the two capitals misread the mood of the people. For his part, he had observed quite the contrary, a distinct improvement in the nation's state of mind, a change particularly noticeable in the provinces. It seemed to him that much of the nation was beginning to be drawn into "cheerful labor," and that large numbers of Russians were optimistic about the country's future. He attributed the "cheerful optimism" to the agrarian reforms, which had enabled many people in the countryside to become landowners and to acquire the rights of citizenship. No longer limited to a lifetime of labor as peasants, who at most could hope to reach the status of a "muzhik-kulak," the masses in the countryside now faced "other, brighter horizons." As private landowners, they could take the initiative in planning their future. Referring to his many years in the western regions of the empire, Stolypin noted that at that time he had discovered the advantages of the "peasant khutor economy." He was struck by the way the "free tillers of the soil" were "cheerful and self-confident."

Although pleased with the agrarian reform's accomplishments, the prime minister insisted that further reforms were needed. He spoke specifically of the government bill, then languishing in the Duma, to put an end to the election of zemstvos on the basis of the estate principle. In yet another attempt to calm the fears of the rightists, he assured them that landowners, "this important cultural force in the great work of the state apparatus," would retain their influence in Russia. Stolypin ended the interview with an expression of optimism frequently quoted in the literature on Late Imperial Russia: "Give the state twenty years of internal and external peace, and you will not recognize present-day Russia."[1] It was a bold prophecy predicated on the assumption that he would succeed in reviving his reform program, which had been blocked in 1908 and 1909.

Nonetheless, after the defeat of the naval general staff bill, Stolypin did move "perceptibly to the right."[2] He slowed down his efforts at reform and he paid increasing attention to the national question. But his comments in *Volga* suggest that his retreat was tactical, not motivated by second thoughts about the validity of his principles. He had not abandoned his goal of transforming Russia into a state in which all citizens would enjoy the rights of citizenship and in which legal class distinctions would be reduced.

Soviet historians, following the lead of Avrekh, have subjected Stolypin to intense criticism for his change of direction, accusing him of "maneuvering" simply to stay in power. But what was his alternative? He could have resigned, but his departure from office, as he and his supporters reiterated time and again, would have opened the door to the appointment of an outright reactionary, who would have sought to turn back the clock to the political order of 1904. It is also likely that a reactionary prime minister would have pursued a nationalist program far harsher than the one he adopted. Stolypin's options in the spring of 1909 were not alluring.

Although conscious of the precariousness of his political standing, Stolypin gave the impression in mid-1909 of "great calm" in carrying out his functions as prime minister. He even felt personally secure enough to leave the apartment in the Winter Palace that he had occupied since the assassination attempt in August 1906 and to move into the official residence in the city. To a foreign observer in St. Petersburg, it seemed that the prime minister was right to feel politically secure: every "moderate and sensible" person in the capital believed that Nicholas would not allow himself to be persuaded to be "separated from this excellent [and] loyal servant."[3]

Stolypin's tilt to the right first manifested itself when he modified his stand on religious reform. For some time, moderate liberals such as the Octobrists and the Kadets had pressed for changes in the legal position of citizens who did not profess Orthodox Christianity, a demand that aroused passionate resistance not only from leaders of the Church but also from political conservatives. According to the Fundamental Laws, the Orthodox Church was "pre-eminent and predominant" and thus enjoyed the rights of an established church of the Russian Empire. The tsar was the head of the Church, and its administrative leader, the procurator of the Most Holy Synod, a layman, was a member of the cabinet. Clearly subordinate to the state, the Church hierarchy tended to buttress the autocracy. Not infrequently priests used their pulpits to indoctrinate the flock in loyalty to the secular authorities. Only the Orthodox Church was authorized to proselytize and engage in missionary work. Conversion from Orthodoxy to a non-Christian faith was considered an offense punishable by the state.

Although the Russian Orthodox constituted a majority of the population in the empire (about 70 percent), a substantial minority of the people belonged to various sects or religions. The largest sect, the Old Believers, who had split off from the Church in the seventeenth century over questions of ritual and prayers, probably numbered at least eleven million people. Until the mid-nineteenth century the Old Believers were subjected to outright persecution—the government would often close their churches, discipline their priests, and seize their property—but even in the twentieth century they chafed under numerous restrictions. Other religious groups, such as Jews, Muslims, and Protestants, were also a sizable presence in the empire—about five million Jews and fourteen million Muslims—and also endured a wide range of disabilities. Ever fearful of a dilution of Russian Orthodoxy, the government imposed strict regulations on such matters as intermarriage, conversions, and the movement of Jews from the Pale of Settlement to the interior of Russia. Sometimes the government's concern touched on matters that seemed to border on the bizarre. In the summer of 1911, for example, the Ministry of Internal Affairs asked the Senate to rule on the following questions: if a Jew converted to Russian Orthodoxy, would he be permitted to adopt a new patronymic? And if he could do so, would his children be allowed to use the new patronymic or must they retain the old one? Utterly baffled, the Senate responded that there was no legislation covering either contingency.[4]

During the Revolution of 1905, the government took several steps to ease the restrictions on non-Orthodox Christian religions. In April 1905, it issued the Edict of Toleration, which applied to all Christian groups and especially mentioned the Old Believers as a sect that should not be subject to restrictions. Over the course of several weeks, some sixteen hundred people who had been punished for religious dissent were either granted pardons or allowed to return from exile. But, determined to preserve the pre-eminence of Orthodoxy, the government appointed a "special commission" to seek ways of reconciling the principle of religious freedom with the maintenance of special privileges for the Orthodox Church. In the meantime, the October Manifesto went beyond "toleration of religions" by proclaiming "freedom of conscience."

Under Stolypin, the Ministry of Internal Affairs sought to deal with the religious issue in a more comprehensive and systematic way. Stolypin himself took a personal interest in the issue, overcoming resistance from officials within his department who saw no need to address the widespread discontent with the government's policy on religion that had surfaced during the period of revolutionary turbulence. For Stolypin, religious reform was part of the process of modernization; but he also conceived of it as a means of disarming the radicals, who exploited the deep hostility toward the government's restrictions on non-Orthodox citizens. Under Stolypin's direction, the cabinet discussed a wide range of religious subjects, including the introduction of civil procedures for registering births, deaths, and marriages and the elimination of religious instruction in schools. It even considered the possibility of recognizing atheism as an acceptable belief.[5]

Stolypin's support for such far-reaching changes did not betoken indifference to the place of religion in society. He was a pious man and believed that Russia should remain a Christian country in which the government would continue to play a significant role in religious affairs. It also seemed natural to him that the government should give preference to Orthodoxy, the faith of the majority of the population. But he did not favor severe restrictions on other religions and wanted the state to be as unintrusive as possible in matters of personal belief. He wished to extend to religious organizations the same rights accorded to any other association, though he was not prepared to go so far as to extend these rights to religious institutions of the Jews, who were widely viewed with suspicion. Still, Stolypin's approach, as one historian has noted, amounted to "a radically different view of relations between temporal and spiritual authorities from anything which the Russian state had previously envisaged."[6] Between September 1906 and February 1907, some fourteen bills on religious matters were taken up by the Council of Ministers for subsequent submission to the Duma. Among other things, the measures granted the Old Believers and other sects that had split off from Orthodoxy the right to form parishes. They also facilitated conversions, permitted approved religions to proselytize, and allowed people of different Christian faiths to intermarry and to determine their children's faith without state interference.

Even before the lengthy process of parliamentary debate began, the government enacted some significant reform under Article 87, most notably the legalization of the Old Believers' parishes, and toward the end of 1906 the tsar took the unprecedented step of receiving a delegation of Old Believers at his palace, which had the effect of extending official recognition to the sect. Although grateful for these conciliatory moves by the imperial authorities, the Old Believers indicated that they would not feel secure until their newly won rights had received the imprimatur of the legislature. Stolypin was sympathetic, but it was not until March 1909 that the Duma Commission on Religious Affairs approved several bills that for the most part reflected the prime minister's views, though on some relatively minor issues they were more liberal than Stolypin's proposals. One bill permitted the Old Believers to establish their own communities and to preach and proselytize freely. Another allowed Russians to convert from one Christian religion to another. The proposals marked the first attempt to secure legislative approval for the promise of religious freedom contained in the October Manifesto of 1905, and they enjoyed strong support in the Duma.

The Duma's delay in considering religious reform can be attributed to the fierce campaign by leaders of the Orthodox Church against Stolypin's proposals, which appeared to them to place all non-Orthodox Christian religions on the same footing as Orthodoxy. Whenever word circulated in the press that the government was considering liberalizing any aspect of the rules on religion, Church dignitaries would swing into action. For example, early in 1908 the Ministry of Internal Affairs let it be known that it favored abolishing the obligation of a married couple from different Christian religions to sign a statement that the children would be raised in the Orthodox faith. The government justified the change as consistent with the Imperial Edict of Toleration issued in 1905. Enraged, the Holy Synod denounced the proposal as a desecration of the "very sacrament of marriage," since both partners had agreed to an Orthodox marriage ceremony. The fact that only one of the couple belonged to the Orthodox faith was irrelevant.[7]

On May 5, 1909, when the bills finally reached the Duma, opposition to religious reform came from an unexpected source. That day, the assistant to the procurator of the Most Holy Synod and thus a member of the government, A. P. Rogovich, denounced the measures before the Duma for going far beyond the government's intentions and urged that they not even be debated. Interestingly, the Kadet paper *Rech* was so surprised and taken aback by Rogovich's attack on the bills that it concluded that his speech must be part of a "cleverly conducted" intrigue against Stolypin, who, after all, had favored it.[8] But on May 12, S. E. Kryzhanovsky, the assistant minister of internal affairs, participated in the Duma debate on the bills on religious freedom and made it clear that Rogovich was not involved in an intrigue in this matter: the government had changed its position. After praising the overwhelming majority of Old Believers for always having been "true sons of Russia," Kryzhanovsky asked the legislators to strike the provisions granting ministers of non-Orthodox sects the right to be entitled "priest" and the right to proselytize. The exercise of these rights by the non-Orthodox, he now asserted, would undermine the Orthodox's claim to be the "true Church." To buttress the government's new position, the assistant minister declared that "nowhere in the world" did "absolute freedom of religion" prevail. Even in Switzerland, he contended, Jesuits were prohibited from propagating their views, and "even in America the propagation of Mormonism is prohibited."[9] The Duma understandably refused to accept what amounted to emasculation of their bills.

The Kadets and the left generally supported the original bills. But the leader of the Octobrists, Guchkov, scion of a prominent Old Believer family, favored them with his customary fervor. When some members of the Octobrist delegation in the Duma opposed the measures, he resigned in anger as their leader, although he quickly withdrew his resignation at the urging of colleagues. But despite his energetic support the bills continued to encounter fierce and in the end insurmountable opposition.[10]

The Church and the rightists, convinced that the bills contained "within [their] . . . . scope ominous dangers to the safety of the true Church," became increasingly militant. They expressed shock at the very idea that a secular body such as the Duma would dare to arrogate to itself the right to tamper with purely ecclesiastical matters. Worse still, the prime minister himself, charged with preserving the sacred institutions and traditions of Russia, was promoting such encroachments.[11] Tikhomirov, one of the more colorful polemicists of the ultraright, could not contain his rage. He called the prime minister a "swine" who had behaved dishonorably and with "colossal stupidity" on the religious issue. Tikhomirov claimed to be deeply saddened by the government's initiative because "morally" Stolypin "has been severely damaged in my eyes."[12]

However the opposition to liberalizing the laws on religious issues was not confined to extremists. P. P. Izvolskii, the procurator of the Most Holy Synod, and thus a member of the cabinet and, in addition, a man reputed to be a political moderate, expressed strong reservations about religious reform. He did not wish to grant other religions, even Christian ones, the right to proselytize, and he opposed the abolition of penalties for converting from Orthodoxy. These measures, Izvolskii argued, would undermine the predominance of Orthodoxy over other faiths, and that he considered totally unacceptable. In February 1909, Stolypin forced Izvolskii to resign. But three months later, in May 1909, the tsar ignored Stolypin's recommendation for a successor and selected as procurator S. M. Lukianov, who had a reputation for "firmness," a clear message to the prime minister that the court was not pleased with the thrust of his policies.[13] Lukianov was not suited for the post. According to Witte, he was a physician who "should have stuck to his calling."[14]

That Stolypin was once again walking a political tightrope became apparent on May 22, 1909, when he addressed the Duma on the various bills it was considering on religious freedom. Deliberately avoiding the specifics of the reform proposals, he concentrated on a general discussion of religious freedom, a tack that enabled him to ignore the most contentious questions. His approach indicated that he and the government had retreated and that they no longer favored the lifting of the restrictions on non-Orthodox religions that had been originally proposed. But he wanted to "dispel certain misunderstandings that have arisen about my opinions." It soon became evident that Stolypin was trying, at one and the same time, to admit abandonment of his reform proposals and still claim that he was committed to religious reform.

He reminded the Duma that the tsar himself had started the process of introducing religious freedom in Russia with the issuance of three decrees (December 12, 1904, April 17, 1905, and October 17, 1905), but he conceded that there remained a "broad area of the current law" that needed to be changed to implement the sovereign's principles fully. For complete freedom to prevail, people must be permitted to convert from

one Christian faith to another without prior approval from the civil
authorities, to conduct services according to their rituals, and to build
houses of worship. There were thus certain legal issues that needed to be
resolved, such as the rights of citizens to form religious associations, the
relationship between the state and the different faiths, and the scope of
freedom of conscience. These rights had to be reconciled with the "privileges that are to be preserved in the Fundamental Laws for the Orthodox Church." Stolypin insisted that in dealing with questions of conscience the government and the state "must act with great care and caution." In themselves, these points were not new for the prime minister;
what was new was that he placed so much emphasis on them and that
he failed to spell out clearly the changes he wanted the Duma to enact.[15]
In truth, he was vague because he was once again trying to find a middle
ground between the reactionaries and the moderates.

The difficulty he faced was similar to the one he faced in clarifying
his views on the new political dispensation in Russia. Just as he wanted
to fuse tsarism with an elected legislature, so he wanted to reconcile the
predominance of Orthodoxy with freedom of conscience. On the one
hand, he would not press for a complete renunciation by the state of the
right to regulate religious affairs, since that would lead to a "rupture of
that ancient link which has existed between the state and the Church, a
link from which the state extracted spiritual force and the church extracted strength, a link that gave life to our state and yielded invaluable
rewards. This rupture would mean the approach of a new era of mutual
distrust, [and] suspicion between Church authorities and the legislative
authorities, and the natural character of a union between [secular]
authority and Church would be lost. In the eyes of the Church, the state
would lose the significance of being an Orthodox State, and the Church,
in its turn, would be placed in a difficult position; it would have to secure for itself political and civil rights with all the dangerous consequences flowing from such a situation."[16]

On the other hand, Stolypin acknowledged that the relationship between the state and the Church had to be changed because citizens of
different Christian faiths as well as non-Christians now played a role in
the country's political life. But the only significant change he proposed
was to end state interference in questions of canon law or dogma. In
those spheres, the Church must be independent. Yet he also insisted on
maintaining the pre-eminence of the Orthodox Church. As he put it, he
wanted to harmonize the principle of religious freedom and the interests
of the state with the "interests of the predominant [and] pre-eminent
Church, and with this goal in mind [the government] should enter into

prior contacts with it on these questions."[17] In short, the prime minister had learned a painful lesson, that he would not be able to introduce far-reaching changes on religious issues unless he secured the approval of the Church hierarchy. But these general statements did little to clarify his position on the specific issues under debate.

When Stolypin touched on those issues, he also displayed a penchant for taking positions that were, at one and the same time, progressive and traditional. He held, for example, that if a parishioner wished to convert from Orthodoxy to another Christian faith, he should be required immediately to inform his priest, who would admonish the parishioner but would refrain from any coercion or insult. Coercion, Stolypin argued, would violate the principle of freedom of conscience. The prime minister also believed that citizens who wished to convert from Christianity to a non-Christian religion should no longer be punished, but he strongly opposed the Duma commission's proposal that this right should be openly proclaimed by law, since even Western European countries did not go that far. To do so in Russia would be to proclaim that other religions stood on a par with Russian Orthodoxy, a judgment that neither the government nor the Russian people would be willing to accept. He ended his speech with an appeal for a pragmatic approach to freedom of conscience, suggesting that otherwise the tsar might not accept the Duma's measures: "Gentlemen, our task is not to adjust Orthodoxy to some abstract theory of the freedom of conscience but to light the torch of religious freedom of conscience within the limits of our Russian Orthodox State. Gentlemen, do not burden our legislative project with extraneous appendages that are not understood by the people. Remember that the religious law will operate in a Russian state and that it will be ratified [and implemented] by the Russian Tsar, who for more than a hundred million people was, is, and will be an Orthodox Tsar. [*Applause from the right and center.*]"[18]

This speech thus sought to appease every major interest group. In referring to the primacy of Orthodoxy he sought to satisfy the Holy Synod. In reaffirming his support of the October Manifesto he was reassuring the centrists, and in particular the Octobrists, that he still stood for genuine liberalization of the laws on religious freedom. His stress on the "Russian spirit" was designed to please the Nationalists. And his invocation of the tsar as the ultimate authority on religious matters was a sop to the rightists. But according to liberal newspaper *Rech*, he failed in the end to satisfy fully any of the political groups to whom he pitched his speech.[19]

The Duma wasted little time in demonstrating its dissatisfaction with the prime minister's new course by refusing to amend the bills that had been approved by its commission. Stolypin, in turn, under growing pressure from the right and apparently from individuals at court as well, then backed away from one reform after another. He informed the cabinet that the Orthodox Church should continue to enjoy a monopoly in proselytizing, and that the bill on mixed marriages, which he now said violated canon law, should be withdrawn from the Duma. In October 1909, the bills on mixed marriages and on freedom of worship were removed from legislative consideration and never resubmitted. Even the bills that applied only to the Old Believers, extending their rights minimally, were not enacted because of opposition in the upper chamber, the State Council. And early in 1910 the government actually issued regulations that imposed certain new restrictions on the organizational activities of non-Orthodox religions aimed at making it more difficult for them to attract new members.[20] Stolypin's three-year effort to move the country toward religious freedom ended in ignominious defeat. Religious reform aroused too many passions for him to prevail. Not only did he face the resistance of extremists on the right and his personal enemies; but he had to deal with officials in his Ministry of Internal Affairs, who feared that any weakening of the Orthodox Church would undermine the social fabric.

Defeated in his attempts at reform, Stolypin, in the view of many historians, cynically turned to fervent nationalism in a desperate attempt to shore up his political position. Formulated in such stark terms, this interpretation is hard to sustain. For one thing, he never deviated from a pacific view of foreign policy. Stolypin had always been profoundly patriotic, and almost from the moment he assumed the leadership of the government he expressed concern about the decline of Russian influence in some of the outlying regions of the empire. But unlike the rightists and unlike the tsar, he avoided insensitive remarks about the minorities, and he did not advocate the destruction of their cultural institutions. He sought to protect Russian cultural interests throughout the empire and to preserve its political unity.

His policies toward Finland are a case in point. In the period of Stolypin's tenure as prime minister, no national issue was more complicated. According to the legal scholar N. M. Korkunov, there were three views on the status of Finland: the first, generally favored by the Finns, held that Finland was a sovereign state that had entered into a "personal [*realnoi*] union with Russia"—that is, the country recognized the emperor of Russia as its grand duke but retained its own institutions and laws; the second held that Finland had been incorporated into the empire but had remained a province with an extensive degree of autonomy; the third maintained that Finland had no valid claim to sovereignty since it had been annexed to Russia by force. Korkunov, who subscribed to the third position, argued that it all came down to a question of whether Finland had joined the Russian Empire as a result of a personal agreement between the Russian ruler and Finnish authorities or had been forcefully incorporated into the empire. The answer, according to Korkunov, must be sought in the history of the relationship between Finland and Russia.[21]

Finland had joined the empire in 1808, and for most of the nineteenth century the issue of sovereignty did not arise, since the Finns were allowed a substantial degree of autonomy. The Grand Duchy of Finland, as the region was officially known, retained its own legislature, which enacted the laws for the principality, its own political and legal administrations, its own currency and police force, and even a small army of its own. Moreover, the Finns imposed a special civic and legal status on ethnically Russian citizens living in Finland, which rankled the prime minister no end. These citizens of the empire could not vote for deputies to the Seim (Finnish diet or parliament), could not be elected to the legislature, could not occupy any other elective office, and if they were businessmen they had to operate under special restrictions. In addition, only citizens who had attended Finnish schools or could pass a special examination administered by the Alexander University in Helsinki could be employed as civil servants in Finland. The Finns justified their treatment of the Russians in their midst as self-defense, to protect the weak against the strong. With a population of less than three million, they feared that they would be overwhelmed by the majority in the empire of 130 million.[22] True, the Senate, which acted as the executive authority in Finland, was known as the "Imperial Senate" and reported directly to the tsar, who held the title of grand duke of Finland, but that had little bearing on the governance of the region, since the Russian authorities made no effort to restrict the Finns' autonomy.

From a strictly legal standpoint, Korkunov had a strong case in arguing that Finland's claim to sovereignty was groundless. In 1808, Russia had defeated Sweden, seized Finland, and in March 1809, Tsar Alexander I promised the Finnish Diet at Poorvoo that he would permit the Finns to exercise all the liberties, quite extensive for the time, that they had enjoyed under the Swedish crown. The promise was not exactly a voluntary act by the tsar, since Alexander wished to pacify the Finns, who had not been overjoyed at being annexed by Russia and had, in fact, offered armed resistance to the Russian conquerors. Yet it is also true that Finland's adhesion to the Russian Empire was not the result of a treaty or any other agreement between two sovereign states. Indeed, as Korkunov pointed out, Finland had not been a sovereign state when it was part of Sweden and therefore could not have entered into an agreement as a state with Russia.[23] Whatever the legal niceties, for over eighty years the untidy arrangement under which the Finns conducted their affairs within the Russian Empire worked rather well. Formally, the Finns were subjects of the empire and subordinate to St. Petersburg in foreign policy, but beyond that they exercised virtual sovereignty in their land. On the other hand, the Russians could legitimately assert that Finland was part of the empire even though their control was severely circumscribed.

In the late 1890s this amicable relationship began to crumble, and the Russian authorities came to view Finnish autonomy as a threat to the security of the empire. The main reason for the change was that revolutionary agitation, a growing problem within the empire, was not proscribed in Finland. Not only did Russian revolutionaries operate freely on Finnish soil and move easily from the Karelian Isthmus to Russia proper, they could also count on the sympathy of the police and on help from local activists. Moreover, Russian political and military leaders feared that foreign powers hostile to Russia might use Finland as a jumping-off point for attacks on St. Petersburg, only twenty miles from the Finnish border. And by the early twentieth century some quasi-military organizations favoring Finnish separatism were beginning to appear in Helsinki and elsewhere. Russian conservatives also feared that the Finnish political system, based on universal suffrage after 1906, would serve as a model for other minorities within the empire. And Russian industrialists increasingly feared competition from the Finns, who in the 1880s and 1890s had made considerable progress in developing modern industry, most notably in timber and textiles.[24]

Troubled by all these developments, the authorities in St. Petersburg began to look for ways to restrict Finnish autonomy, inevitably provoking sharp polemics couched in abstruse language about the rights of the Finns and the rights of the Russian government. In seeking to penetrate the tangled history of these conflicts one is reminded of the pithy comment uttered in a mood of despair by the British prime minister, W. E. Gladstone, about the Irish question: "that it passed the wit of man to devise a satisfactory distinction between matters of local and matters of Imperial concern."[25] Both the Russians and the Finns came up with ingenious arguments to buttress their claims, but it is hard to avoid the conclusion that many of these were little more than self-serving justifications by two camps locked in a power struggle.

The appointment of General N. I. Bobrikov as governor-general of Finland in 1898 can be taken as a turning point in the relations between Russian and Finland. A heavy-handed chauvinist, Bobrikov quickly enacted policies designed to integrate Finland more closely into the Russian Empire. Within weeks of his appearance in Helsingfors (Helsinki), he issued a decree requiring Finns to serve five years in the military services, a more onerous obligation than that imposed on Russians. The Finnish draftees, moreover, could be placed in Russian units, and Russian officers could henceforth be assigned to command Finnish units. Until this time, Finns had to serve for only ninety days, spread over three years, and they were assigned to Finnish units. Bobrikov and his superiors in St. Petersburg claimed that the military measures were justified because the Finns were protected by the Russian Empire and should therefore contribute to the realm's defense. It was not an argument that carried much weight among the Finns, many of whom insisted that their country enjoyed the status of a separate state and should therefore attend only to its own defense.[26]

Bobrikov delivered the most serious blow to Finnish autonomy when he issued the Manifesto of 1899, which transformed the Finnish Seim from an institution with the authority to legislate into a merely advisory body. For decades, the Seim had enjoyed wide latitude in adopting legislative proposals, which the tsar could either ratify or veto. Henceforth, the only power reserved by the Diet was to comment on legislative proposals that the tsar and the State Council could ignore if they so wished. Bobrikov also directed the Finnish civil service to conduct its official business in Russian. Opposition to these measures developed quickly throughout Finland, taking the form of passive resistance. "Pastors refused to proclaim the law [of 1899] in their churches, judges refused to carry it out, conscripts refused to obey the call to service." Bobrikov responded to the resistance by adopting ever harsher measures: in 1903 he suspended the constitution altogether, enlisted Russian bureaucrats to carry out his orders, and then ruled the region as a virtual dictator. In June 1904, Bobrikov was assassinated by Eugen Schaumann, the son of a former senator.[27]

Any hopes of Russian officials that they would be able to exploit tensions between the Swedish elite (about 8 percent of the population) and the Finns (over 90 percent of the population) proved to be illusory. The Swedes made up the bulk of the landlords and upper business class and had for decades exercised a disproportionate degree of political power,

but unlike the German minority in Latvia and Estonia, they were prepared to yield some of their privileges. Moreover, the Swedes supported
the Finns in their endeavor to maintain the autonomy of Finland.

Many Finns took an active part in the Revolution of 1905, and in October of that year Finland, like many cities of the empire, was paralyzed
by a general strike. On November 4, the tsar, informed by his officials
that the Russian administration in Finland faced a complete loss of
authority, beat a hasty retreat. He issued a manifesto suspending the ill-
conceived law of 1899 and other decrees enacted by Bobrikov and restored full civil freedoms to the Finns. The manifesto also directed the
Finnish Senate to formulate a new electoral law and to propose legislation on the powers and function of a newly elected Seim. The Finns had
won a major victory, but the unrest continued. By now, some Finns were
demanding full independence from Russia, a new factor in the bitter
conflict between Finland and the tsarist government. Throughout 1906,
there were reports of weapons being smuggled into the country; in addition, some activists called for a general strike, and a serious mutiny
broke out in Viapori.[28]

It was not until late 1907 that Stolypin launched a major initiative
on the Finnish question, and when he did, he revealed his acute sensitivity to Russian national interests in Finland. In a missive of October 16,
1907, to General C. F. A. Langhoff, the minister secretary of state for
Finnish affairs, he expressed his concern about the use of Swedish in
administrative documents, even though a Russian translation was always provided for Russian officials. The date is significant, because it
demonstrates that Stolypin's interest in the so-called national question
was not simply a consequence of the political crisis of the spring of
1909, the standard explanation for his turn to nationalism. Although
Stolypin conceded that the use of Swedish in documents relating specifically to internal Finnish affairs conformed to the Imperial Decree of
April 20, 1906, he claimed that it ran counter to Article 3 of the Fundamental Laws and to other imperial legislation. He also complained that
he found the use of Swedish "extremely inconvenient" and could not
approve of a practice that assigned "priority to the Swedish language
over the common language of the state." He asked Langhoff to explain
why Russian could not be the first language in all documents that touch
on imperial affairs, as specifically required by the Law of August 1, 1891.
Clearly unwilling to provoke the Finns on what he considered to be a
minor issue, Langhoff replied with a long account of the usage of both
Swedish and Finnish in official documents and pointed out that in the
past the tsar had seemed unperturbed by the practice. Stolypin was not

mollified; he continued to pressure Langhoff to issue a directive to the Finns to use Russian in documents that had any bearing on imperial affairs.[29]

At about the time of this acerbic correspondence, in the autumn of 1907, Stolypin formed a Special Conference on the Affairs of the Grand Duchy of Finland, composed of several government ministers, the governor-general of Finland, and legal experts, to discuss issues relating to Finland before they came up for consideration by the cabinet. Stolypin himself chaired the committee, but he knew relatively little about conditions in Finland and tended to rely on the advice of several hardliners whom he named to the conference. One member, for example, V. F. Deitrikh, had been Bobrikov's deputy in Finland, and wags in St. Petersburg claimed that the only difference between the two was that Bobrikov was killed by irate Finns and Deitrikh was merely injured.[30] In March 1909 Stolypin obtained the tsar's approval for the formation of yet another Special Commitee on Matters Dealing with the Grand Duchy of Finland. Composed of five Finns and five Russians, the committee was to come up with a permanent solution to the "Finnish problem." The state controller, P. A. Kharitonov, a confidant of Stolypin's, was appointed chairman, and could be expected to do Stolypin's bidding.

The committees met with some regularity, but it soon became evident Stolypin intended to exert personal control over Finnish affairs. Having decided that only an unyielding stand by the government would protect Russian interests, he became constantly involved in the government's dealings with Helsingfors. On December 22, 1907, he informed the tsar that at a meeting with N. N. Gerard, governor-general of Finland, and Langhoff, he had considered it "not superfluous to declare aloud that Your Majesty has firmly decided that in the event of a violation of the law by Finns and failure by them to heed the law, [we will] apply force 'manu militari.' Apparently, [the people] in Helsingfors have begun to understand that these are not empty threats, and it seems to me that events will take a satisfactory turn."[31] These words were music to Nicholas's ears. A man filled with bigotry toward all the minorities in the empire, he especially disliked the Finns. In a surprisingly candid conversation with the German ambassador in mid-January 1907, the tsar had declared the Finns to be at a very low cultural level, "especially with regard to morality, and nothing good is to be expected from them."[32] The tsar's role in promoting a hard line vis-à-vis Finland had been a crucial factor in the government's assertion of greater control over that country ever since the late 1890s.[33]

Stolypin closely monitored developments in Finland and frequently corresponded with the governor-general, involving himself endlessly in administrative procedures and political developments, many of which were hardly so momentous that they would normally require the attention of the prime minister of a large empire. To be sure, some of the issues discussed by the governor-general and Stolypin touched on important matters, such as the introduction in Finland of compulsory elementary education. But Stolypin also was asked to approve the building of a new highway, the construction of a new telephone line and a new building for the Seim, the extension of the Saimaa canal, and various measures the Finns proposed to take to protect their forests. It was not uncommon for Stolypin's office to draft a response within four days after receipt of a memorandum or letter from the governor-general. The Finnish question was a matter of the highest priority for the prime minister.

An examination of the frequently testy correspondence between Stolypin and the governor-general of Finland makes it abundantly clear that whatever issue was discussed, minor or major, the prime minister was always guided by one underlying concern: that Finland not be permitted to assert its sovereignty or to expand its jurisdiction in any way. A rather trivial incident early in 1908 vividly demonstrates this. The governor-general of Finland, Gerard, had sent a request to the Ministry of Internal Affairs to pass on to the captain of a Dutch ship, the *Gelderland*, four gold watches, purchased by the Finnish Senate, to be presented to his crew for having saved the men of a Finnish ship, the *Fortuna*, that had run aground. The watches carried the following inscription (in English): "To N. N. from the Finnish Government for saving the crew of the wrecked Finnish ship 'Fortuna.'" Stolypin informed Gerard that Izvolskii, the foreign minister, was unwilling to deliver the watches since Finland, an "indivisible part" of the Russian state, had no right to give gifts in the name of the Finnish government. Moreover, Finnish ships traveled under the Russian flag, and the Russian government, not the Finnish authorities, represented their interests. Stolypin made clear that he "fully share[s] the views" of the foreign minister. "Underlying the inscription by the Finnish Senate," Stolypin declared, "is the mistaken notion of Finland as an independent state with its own government and [that it was] only associated with the [Russian] Empire." The Finnish administration, the prime minister insisted, was not a government "recognized in public law and is not invested with any authority in international relations." Stolypin directed the governor-general to have the inscription on the watches altered. Stolypin considered the incident so important that he discussed it at a cabinet meeting and secured the tsar's approval for his directive to the governor-general.[34] It is not known whether the four brave sailors ever received their reward.

In the meantime, within Finland the national mood turned increasingly hostile toward the Russians. In the elections for parliament (Seim) in March 1907, the socialists captured eighty-three out of two hundred seats, and with the support of deputies committed to Finnish nationalism they dominated the chamber's proceedings. Stolypin now feared that the parliament in Helsinki might launch a grab for power. On several occasions, he reminded the governor-general, whom he considered to be too lenient, that it was his duty to prevent the Finnish legislature from usurping the prerogatives of the tsar. He was especially disturbed by Gerard's agreement to a reduction of funds for his office that had been voted by the Seim. The prime minister directed Gerard to reconsider and to let him know what actions he would take to reverse the Seim's decision.[35] Early in March 1908, Tsar Nicholas, who also followed developments in Finland closely, informed Stolypin that he thought the time had come to dissolve the Seim.[36]

Two weeks later, on March 22, the governor-general sent the Seim packing. Stolypin justified the action with the claim that the legislature had acted inappropriately toward the imperial government. For example, on January 30, 1908, the speaker, P. E. Svinhufvud, had launched an "inadmissible condemnation" of the deputy governor-general, F. A. Zein. In addition, the speaker had made it a practice of referring to the emperor as grand duke—his formal title as nominal head of Finland—a deliberate display of disrespect for the monarch. More serious, the parliament had adopted, by a vote of seventy-one to forty-seven, a motion of no-confidence in the Senate for its compliance to a request by the Russian government to hand over to administrative courts Russian citizens accused of "political crimes." The government warned that if a newly elected Seim did not abandon "extremism," further "decisive measures," including a second dissolution, would be enacted.[37]

The prime minister now made his first public statement in defense of his Finnish policy. Responding to three interpellations in the Duma (by Octobrists, Nationalists, and rightists) that had apparently been formulated with his knowledge if not approval, Stolypin began his long speech (on May 5, 1908) by rejecting the claims that Finland was either an entirely independent state or even a region such as the Caucasus, which enjoyed a unique degree of autonomy. Finland, Stolypin stressed, was a constituent part of the Russian Empire, and the empire was administered by a unified government responsible to the tsar for "everything that occurred in the state." To buttress this claim, Stolypin rehearsed the history of Russia's incorporation of Finland early in the nineteenth century, to which reference has already been made. But with his usual fondness for excursions into scholarly justifications for his policies, he went even further back into Russia's past and cited an obscure Treaty of Orekhovsk of 1323 that, he asserted, had placed part of eastern Finland under Russian control.[38]

But Stolypin's determination to maintain a tight rein over Finland was rooted not only in history but also in current politics. The network of revolutionaries that operated freely on Finnish soil worried him. He reminded the Duma that radicals planning to overthrow the Russian government had held many conferences in Finland, that weapons had been freely imported for transshipment to Russia, and that many of the assassinations of Russian officials had been planned on Finnish soil (including the attempt to kill him in August 1906). Unable to operate in Finland without the permission of local officials, the Russian police found it virtually impossible to protect imperial interests. Under the circumstances, the government had no choice but to resort to "emergency measures. This was, unquestionably, its duty since, to repeat, some 26 versts [about 18 miles] from the Sovereign's residence preparations were being made every minute for villainous assassinations." Stolypin warned that if the dangerous revolutionary organizations in Finland were not liquidated the entire Vyborg province would be placed under martial law.[39]

Stolypin contended that the government did not wish to impose a regime that harsh on the Finns. Nor did it wish to abrogate the rights of autonomy that the Finns had enjoyed for close to a century. On the contrary, the authorities in St. Petersburg would consult the Finns on matters of concern to Finland, but "the supreme power, [must] of course, [remain] in the hands of Russia." If Finnish claims that no imperial law could be valid unless ratified by the Seim were accepted, there would be endless conflict between St. Petersburg and Helsingfors. In a private conversation, Stolypin held that the Finns should understand that, as Tsar Alexander II had told the Finnish Senate in 1863, they "belonged to a large family at the head of which stands the Russian Emperor."[40]

Stolypin listed the following as distinct imperial prerogatives: defense of the entire empire, including supervision of fortresses and protection of the coastlines, supervision of postal services, administration of the telegraph system, customs, and some branches of the railways. In addition, the rights of Russian natives living in Finland, a particularly thorny issue, must be regulated by imperial authorities.

To prevent further "intolerable" conflict, Stolypin called on the Duma to review the relationship between Finland and Russia and to adopt legislation establishing it on a sound basis. The deputies from the right and center greeted Stolypin's speech with prolonged applause and shouts of "bravo."[41] The prime minister could count on solid support within the Duma for his Finnish policies.

Before the Duma took formal action on the Finnish question, however, the government acted on its own. On May 20, 1908, it required the Council of Ministers to review all legislative measures touching on imperial interests that the Finnish authorities planned to enact. Hitherto, bills adopted by the Finnish authorities were submitted to the secretary of state for Finnish affairs and then to the tsar himself for final approval. Now the various ministries in St. Petersburg would have a voice in deciding which bills passed by the Seim and agreed to by the Senate were acceptable. Apparently, Stolypin took the initiative in issuing the regulation without bothering to consult the Duma, or anyone else for that matter, because he feared that if he sought legislative approval he might not get exactly what he wanted. He also did not wish to go through the entire legislative process before implementing his new Finnish policy.[42]

In his speech to the Duma, Stolypin had said that it was his intention to reduce conflict between St. Petersburg and Helsingfors to a minimum. In fact, his actions produced precisely the opposite effect: conflicts multiplied and became increasingly bitter as the government involved itself more and more in the details of Finnish affairs. Some are worth noting because they reveal the complexity of the "Finnish problem." The Finns were convinced that Stolypin was determined not simply to defend imperial interests but also to interfere in purely Finnish affairs. The prime minister, on the other hand, suspected every move of the Finnish authorities as somehow designed to harm or ignore Russian interests and was extraordinarily touchy on what seem to have been fairly trivial matters. But, then, where national pride was involved no slight appeared to be too trivial to cause deep distress to a man as patriotic as Stolypin.

Even mere rumors about Finnish assertions of their national identity provoked the prime minister to action. In November 1908, he heard that several Finnish newspapers had raised, not for the first time, the question of designing a special flag for the Grand Duchy of Finland that would be flown on public buildings. Stolypin informed the newly appointed governor-general, V. A. Bekman, that this would violate the Imperial Decree of December 21, 1896, and asked for confirmation that the law was being enforced. The governor-general assured the prime minister that the authorities were upholding the law and that the newspapers were ill informed. Nowhere in Finland had a new flag been in evidence.[43]

Late in June 1908, Stolypin sent a confidential missive to Bekman protesting several actions being considered by the Senate. On the assumption that Bekman would be more forceful than his predecessor (Gerard) in restraining the Finns, the prime minister, speaking in the name of the entire cabinet, questioned him about the Senate's decision to establish two new schools at Alexander University, one to concentrate on the improvement of butter production and the other on the raising of cattle, without describing them as "Imperial" institutions. "Such a systematic absence of the title 'Imperial,'" Stolypin asserted, "can, in the view of the Council [of Ministers], have a tendentious character and must not be permitted in governmental documents published by Finland." Stolypin also complained about the Senate's plan to levy taxes on playing cards. A law to that effect would infringe on the "prerogatives of the monarch." The cabinet expressed a general wish that Bekman would "carefully protect the sphere of administrative legislation that falls within the prerogatives of the Sovereign's authority" and not allow the Senate to enlarge its authority. Stolypin indicated to Bekman that the cabinet was determined to "revive and strengthen the authority of the governor-general" and asked him to let the Finns know that in the event of a jurisdictional conflict between him and the Senate the matter at issue would be passed on to the tsar for final resolution.[44]

When Stolypin asked Bekman to take legal action against two newspapers (*Tyomies* and *Raivaaja*) for having published some "harsh and undesirable" articles about the Russian authorities, the governor-general, inclined to avoid provocative actions over minor issues, declined on the ground that neither the law on the press nor the Criminal Code had been violated. The prime minister refused to accept the explanation. He referred to an article in the Finnish Criminal Code enacted in 1865 that made it absolutely clear that not only "abusive language about the Emperor but also any disrespect with regard to the Imperial personage is punishable." He then asked Bekman what steps he planned to take to curb two other newspapers that had published articles with "extremely disgraceful contents and that were filled with impertinent outbursts against Russia and the Russian government."[45] The prime minister maintained the pressure on Bekman over the "extremely unruly and intolerant" tone assumed by Finnish newspapers. Early in February

1909, Stolypin complained that he learned of "impertinent outbursts" against the imperial authorities almost every day, and not infrequently the papers even insulted the tsar and derided "everything Russian." These developments "lead me to believe that it is urgently necessary as soon as possible to regulate the law on the press . . . and thus place limits on the further corruption of a local, close knit group of journalists." He wanted Bekman to enact "temporary administrative" measures to curb the press, and he directed him to urge the Senate to formulate legislation to restrict the press.[46]

Once again, Bekman was reluctant to carry out Stolypin's directives. The governor-general noted that the Manifesto of October 22, 1905, had put an end to prior censorship, and therefore any enactment of a law that restricted the Finnish newspapers would conflict with the expressed will of the tsar. Moreover, legislative procedures in Finland did not allow for the kind of "temporary" emergency measures permitted under the Fundamental Laws, a reference to Article 87. And if such an emergency measure were enacted in Finland, no one would enforce it, according to the governor-general. Only a vote for the reimposition of censorship by the Seim would be effective. But Bekman was certain that the Seim would never take such action.[47] At every turn Stolypin seemed to be stymied.

That, however, did not deter him. By now he seems to have been obsessed with the Finnish question, and he simply continued his barrage of directives on matters small and large. In August 1909, he was enraged over the Senate's decision to release Matti Reinik from prison; the man had been charged with an attempt to assassinate the governor of Vyborg, Miasoedov. Stolypin had learned about the release from a newspaper, and he wanted to know if the Senate had even bothered to inform the governor-general's office about the release. The deputy governor-general, F. A. Zein, made the appropriate inquiry and informed the prime minister that Reinik had in fact been released some two weeks before the matter was reported in the press. Zein also noted that the Senate had acted within its rights; the Legal Department of the Senate, according to various statutes, had the authority to discharge a prisoner before he completed his sentence. But Zein added that it might be necessary to review the statutes, given the "extraordinary aspect of this political crime." Infuriated, Stolypin now turned to Bekman, the governor-general, and asked him to suggest measures to be taken to prevent the recurrence of such actions, which "discredit" the authority of the highest representative of the Russian state in Finland, the president of the Senate, meaning Bekman himself. Embarrassed at not having known about the release, Bekman explained that the Senate had not placed the status of Reinik on the agenda because it was not considered particularly important. Since the Senate's vote on Reinik, he had asked the chairman of the Legal Department for the names of other individuals incarcerated for political crimes. For the rest, Bekman declared that although he considered the release of Reinik "biased and unjust" there was nothing he could do to reverse the decision, since the Senate had acted legally.[48]

The Russian authorities were not only offended by challenges to their political authority in Finland; they were also troubled by efforts of local Finns to humiliate them and to reduce their cultural influence in the region. Late in 1909, for example, S. M. Lukianov, the procurator of the Most Holy Synod, complained to the prime minister that from time to time Finns approached Russian monasteries in Sortanlakhti and Serdobol at night and hurled "insults" at the monks. Lukianov did not describe the insults, but he indicated that he had heard from the fathers superior of the monasteries that the Finns, who could not be identified because they did their work after dark, would generally appear during Christmas time and during the Easter season. Stolypin immediately directed the governor-general to put a stop to the hooliganism, which he considered to be of "very serious significance." It was, he said, "completely unacceptable that in the Russian State, places sacred to the Orthodox faith found themselves under constant threat of insults from the local population." His majesty, he continued, insisted that "extraordinary measures" be taken to prevent the insults. Zein appealed to the commander of the 22nd Army Corps in Helsinki, Olkhovskii, to protect the monasteries. Olkhovskii sent small detachments of soldiers to the two monasteries from time to time, but he complained that he did not have enough troops at his disposal to maintain a permanent military presence in the area. Zein then asked the prime minister for additional troops, not only to protect the monasteries but also to counter "Pan-Finnish propaganda among the Orthodox [Christians] in Karelia." The minister of war, Sukhomlin ordered more soldiers to the two towns, but it proved to be impossible to stop the incidents completely.[49]

By this time the cabinet had formally adopted certain principles on the governance of Finland that would serve as the basis of legislation to be taken up by the Duma. The Grand Duchy of Finland was declared an "indivisible part of the Russian State," although the Finnish people would continue to be "free in internal affairs, exercising rights guaranteed by their constitution." But the cabinet insisted that the Russian monarch would remain the final authority in Finland; he would rule the country with the assistance of the Finnish authorities. The secretary of state, the tsar's representative, must receive all reports on actions taken by the Finnish authorities. The Seim would have no right to pass judgment on the legality of actions of Russian officials. In brief, the government rejected the Finnish claim that Finland was a separate state and contended, instead, that it was a province of the empire with autonomous rights in a wide range of internal affairs. On October 14, the tsar approved the cabinet's decision.[50]

Realizing that the government's actions would be considered provocative by the Finns, Stolypin in October and November of 1909 held two special meetings of the cabinet to make plans in the event of an outbreak of unrest. Stolypin told the ministers that although order had so far not been violated on a large scale in Finland, "the internal situation in the *krai* is very alarming." Almost all the "social forces" in Finland, the political parties, the newspapers, the public institutions, and even the civil service, were "deeply imbued" with the "false" idea that Finland was a separate state and were prepared to support any movement hostile to the Russian state. A few oppositional groups, Stolypin continued, had succeeded in obtaining "extensive stores" of weapons and bombs, and some of the police reserves had been turned into "cadres" for a future mutiny to be launched by major elements of the Finnish army. Plans had also been laid for a general strike, at which point Finnish rebels would attempt to disarm the Russian garrison and seize control over the post offices and railways. Finally, Stolypin claimed to have information that some units of the Russian army were sympathetic to the Finnish cause and might lend support to the Finns. In the prime minister's view, Russian forces in Finland were inadequately prepared for a large-scale rebellion.

At Stolypin's suggestion, the cabinet agreed to send additional military units to Finland, to bolster Russia's naval presence there, and to reinforce units stationed at strategic points such as railways, bridges, and in towns with large concentrations of workers. Within Russia, the military command was to purge Russian units of "unreliable" soldiers and develop plans for the speedy dispatch of troops in the event of major unrest. The navy would immediately halt all contacts at sea between Finns and foreign ships. If government officials went on strike, the authorities must resort to force and, if necessary, to repressive measures, "including the most extreme." Speedy action and "steady firmness" on the part of the Russian authorities were critical. The cabinet agreed to authorize the minister of internal affairs (that is, Stolypin) to use his judgment on whether to ask the tsar to impose martial law. Nicholas, who actually wished to send more troops to Finland than did the prime minister, approved the cabinet's decision, and on December 4, 1909, Stolypin so informed Zein, who had recently been appointed governor-general.[51] Early in 1910, Stolypin had made further plans to deal with unrest in Finland. He wrote to Zein that once martial law was imposed, the tsar would appoint a special commander-in-chief over the Baltic fleet and would place all customs guards under the authority of the commander of military guards, the senior officer in the Petersburg military district.[52] Stolypin expected the worst in Finland and was determined at all costs to retain control over the country.

On March 14, 1910, the government submitted a bill to the Duma delineating, once and for all, the sphere of authority of the Finns in administering their affairs and the areas (nineteen in all) that were considered to be of imperial significance and therefore under the jurisdiction of the tsar and of imperial institutions such as the Duma. Not only did the bill grant St. Petersburg control over such matters as customs, education, communications, and civil liberties; it also specifically allowed the Russian government to revise the list of items to be considered of imperial significance, giving the tsarist authorities the option of further limiting Finnish autonomy. Kokovtsov warned that the measure would be deeply resented by the Finns as an encroachment of their most fundamental rights, and the foreign minister, Izvolskii, feared it would provoke unrest in Finland and complicate Russia's relations with foreign countries. But Stolypin was unmoved.[53]

On May 21, 1910, the prime minister delivered a passionate defense of the government's bill in the Duma. He granted that the relationship between Russia and Finland was extraordinarily complicated and that the contradictory claims of the Finns and the Russians, mired in numerous documents and official pronouncements, could not easily be sorted out. But given the recent tensions in the relationship and the violations of various agreements by the Finns, the Russian government had no choice but to attempt once and for all to clarify the status of Finland within the empire. One particularly vexing violation, he noted, was the failure of the Finns to live up to an agreement that had been reached in 1905 on the military service of Finns in the imperial army. The government had abolished the requirement for universal service for Finns on the understanding that the Seim would vote ten million marks a year to compensate the imperial authorities for its losses of manpower. But the payments had not been made, raising a fundamental question about the relationship between Finland and the empire.

According to Stolypin, two diametrically opposed points of view emerged, that of the Russian state and that of the Finns. The government in St. Petersburg, representing the interests of the state as a whole, maintained that the arrangement on military obligations and the payments to be made to Russia had an unhealthy effect on general imperial interests because the Russian population had to bear an unfair share of the burden. The Finns, on the other hand, claimed that their constitution granted the Seim the authority to decide on the military obligations of their citizens. The conflict between the two points of view could not be resolved without action by the Duma, which is why the bill on Finland had been submitted to the legislature.

Stolypin reiterated that the Finns were entitled to a wide range of autonomy in administering their own affairs, but at the same time he insisted that the authorities in St. Petersburg must assert another principle: "that those subjects that affect the entire empire, or those Finnish laws that affect the interests of Russia, are outside the limits of competence of the Finnish Seim. Any other interpretation would lead us to an historical cul-de-sac." That the Finns were citizens of the empire was beyond dispute, as was proved by the presence of Finnish deputies in the Duma enjoying rights equal to those of every other deputy.

The prime minister concluded with an appeal filled with emotion and nationalistic rhetoric: "It will be pointed out to us that with this . . . [legislation on Finland] the bureaucracy is striving to destroy the high local culture and public education. I will answer you with the words of the reporter [on the bill], who said that aside from the Finnish sense of justice there also exists the Russian sense of justice; it will be pointed out to you that the government does not take into account the interests of all the people; to that I answer that the Sovereign entrusts the matter to you and not to the bureaucracy and that without you not a single Imperial law will be enacted; finally, triumphantly reference will probably be made to European public opinion expressed by signatures at thousands of meetings [organized by] Finns living abroad; to this I reply, and all of Russia replies, that many people apparently still do not understand that under the new system of Russia we do not dismember [our country], we do not break apart, but we become stronger and get to know each other.

Gentlemen, eliminate a dangerous specter, which is worse than enmity or hatred—it is contempt for our country. One senses contempt in the threat of passive resistance by certain Finns, one senses contempt on the part of unsolicited advisers, one senses contempt, unfortunately, in some sectors of our society that do not believe either in justice or in the vigor of the Russian people. Gentlemen, shake off this evil dream and, embodying Russia, challenged by the Tsar to perform a serious deed, the equal of which you have never performed, prove that in Russia there is nothing higher than the law that leans on the power of the people."[54]

Stolypin's passionate speech elicited the desired response. Most deputies hailed it as a masterpiece, and several rightists and Octobrists spoke enthusiastically in favor of turning Finland into an integral part of the empire. On June 10, 1910, the Duma passed the bill by a vote of 164 to 23 after a debate that lasted only a couple of hours. As one contemporary noted, the legislature "disposed [with extraordinary speed] of one of the most complex problems that can form the subject of legislation, and adopted proposals perhaps more far-reaching than any with which it has yet been called upon to deal."[55] Even the Kadets, who were committed to a liberal policy toward the minorities, were split on the bill, but in the end they did not vote for it. The rightists could not contain their joy at the outcome; when the vote was announced, Purishkevich shouted triumphantly and provocatively, "Finis Finlandiae." The bill sailed through the State Council without any difficulty, and on June 17 the tsar approved it, making it the law of the land.[56]

That, however, did not end the tensions and conflicts between the imperial government and Finnish authorities. One of the more contentious conflicts had to do with a charge Stolypin had made in his speech of May 21, that in Finnish schools youngsters were imbued with hostility toward Russia and the Russian language.[57] Early in November 1910, Governor-General Zein informed the prime minister that Russian history and the geography of Russia received short shrift in Finnish schools, and when they were part of the curriculum they were taught in a "strongly distorted form," which he considered "not normal and entirely incongruous with the interests of the Russian state." Zein proposed to take measures immediately to improve the level of instruction in these subjects, which "of course must be conducted in a Russian spirit." The goal must be not only the "formal" teaching of the history of Russia and of instruction on current conditions there, but also the "awakening of a feeling of respect, loyalty, and devotion" to Russia. He expected a "long and hard road" in the endeavor to overcome the "scornful" attitude of the Finns toward the empire and to counteract the support for "separatism" among the local population. The most pressing task was to produce textbooks that devoted appropriate attention to Russia and Russian culture. He urged the prime minister to secure the participation of the Ministry of Education in the project, and hoped to introduce new courses in the elementary schools in the academic year 1911–12 and in secondary schools a year later. Zein intended to bring the matter before the Finnish Senate and indicated that he expected the Finns to provide the funds for the textbooks.[58]

Stolypin approved of Zein's plan, which he immediately passed on to a special imperial committee.[59] Early in May 1911, L. A. Kasso, the minister of education, inspected eighteen Russian schools in seven regions of Finland and was shocked to note that even in these institutions students lacked a solid grounding in Russian language and culture. More troubling still, even the children of Russian families did not receive solid training in Russian. In Karelia, where a sizable number of Russian Orthodox lived, the local authorities had opened a series of Finnish schools to counteract the influence of the Russian schools. In these new schools, "Russian culture is . . . gradually disappearing," and "loyalty to Orthodoxy is weakening, while sympathy for Russia is disappearing, especially in the younger generation." Kasso argued that the state should support the Russian schools in Finland, "which alone can paralyze the separatist aspirations of the Finns." More specifically, Kasso proposed that funds be made available by the treasury to establish more Russian schools in Karelia and in the province of Vyborg, the Finnish areas adjacent to Russia. He also called for the founding of a seminary to produce teachers who would be fluent in Russian as well as Finnish, "well trained in pedagogy, and imbued with the Russian state idea."[60]

Stolypin liked Kasso's report, as did the tsar, who on July 15 formally expressed his approval. The prime minister suggested an empty building (a former military school) in Fredrikshamm for the seminary, but Kasso rejected the offer; he wanted the seminary to be in Serdobol, a town with a large Orthodox population. In the meantime, Stolypin sent Zein a copy of Kasso's report with a directive to act speedily in implementing its proposals.[61]

Although relations between Finland and Russia continued to be strained and the Seim frequently refused to consider bills that had been passed by the Duma, Stolypin probably achieved a measure of success in increasing Russia's control. Even on so trivial a matter as the establishment of a new salary scale for doctors at Finnish hospitals, the governor-general in 1911 made sure to secure the approval of the government.[62]

When Stolypin became prime minister, he faced an anomalous situation. Finland was essentially a state within a state. And so long as Finland enjoyed that status and continued to serve as a haven for revolutionaries and terrorists, Stolypin's goal of subduing the revolutionary opposition, still a paramount concern for him, remained elusive. It was Stolypin's commitment to the two closely related goals of strengthening the Russian state and eliminating the revolutionary threat that explain both the passion with which he pursued his policies in Finland as well as his success in implementing them.

Stolypin's other nationalist initiative, the incorporation of Kholm, part of the former Kingdom of Poland, into the Russian Empire, also shows that his emphasis on national issues after 1909 was not a cynical ploy to curry favor with the rightists. He made his most passionate speech in favor of incorporation at a meeting of the Council of Ministers early in 1907, more than two years before his first major political setback. He feared, as he did in Finland, the diminution of Russian influence in the region. Local Poles, he pointed out, were gaining adherents for Catholicism and thus succeeded in weakening the influence of the ethnic Russians. In addition, he feared that if his plan to introduce zemstvos in the Polish areas of the empire materialized, the organs of local self-government would be dominated by Poles, who already occupied a pre-eminent position in the economy. He considered the matter so urgent that he proposed annexing Kholm under Article 87 of the Fundamental Laws, which allowed the government to act by decree. The cabinet restrained him and persuaded him to adopt the more prudent course of submitting the proposal to the Duma.[63] Over the next few years, the "Kholm question" became one of the more complicated political issues and provoked an astonishing degree of nationalist fervor.

The region under dispute, which in 1912 came to be known as the Kholm province, consisted of eleven districts in the eastern provinces of Siedlce and Lublin, both of which were predominantly Polish and Catholic and had been part of the Congress Kingdom of Poland established in 1815. Adjacent to the provinces of Grodno and Zhitomir, their population included 310,000 Catholics, 305,000 Orthodox, 114,000 Jews, and 28,000 people professing various other faiths. But these figures tell only part of the story, since about two-thirds of the Orthodox were former Uniates,* who a generation earlier had been more or less coerced into converting to Orthodoxy. The converts were not firm adherents of Orthodoxy, a fact of considerable importance in the evolution of the conflict over Kholm. To add to the complexity, not all the Ukrainians in Kholm, whom the government considered to be ethnically Russian, were Orthodox or Uniate, and some Poles were not Catholic.[64]

The idea of transforming the eleven districts into a new province had

---

*The Uniates recognized the authority of the pope but differed from Catholicism in their rites and discipline. The lower clergy of the Uniate Church, for example, were permitted to marry.

surfaced after the Polish rebellion in 1863, and from 1896 until 1905 the idea was broached on eight different occasions at the highest levels in St. Petersburg. The advocates of the proposal believed that only such a bold measure would permanently guarantee the predominance of the Orthodox in the region. But in the end the government held back, fearful that it would be difficult to administer the new province and that it would be unwise for "military-strategic" reasons to separate the area from Congress Poland and antagonize a large portion of the local population.[65]

Totally unexpected developments in the eleven districts in 1905 prompted the Russian government to abandon its restraint. In April of that year, Tsar Nicholas issued a decree granting religious toleration that specifically permitted citizens to convert from one Christian creed to another without penalty. In what was to become the Kholm province, many thousands, amounting perhaps to 168,000 people, most of them former Uniates, left Orthodoxy for Catholicism. It was a great shock to the Russian authorities and to the Orthodox Bishop Evlogii, who on May 2, 1905, sent an alarming telegram to K. P. Pobedonostsev, the procurator of the Most Holy Synod: "The Orthodox Russian cause is perishing."[66]

Bishop Evlogii, a determined and energetic man dedicated both to Orthodoxy and militant nationalism, immediately launched a campaign for the separation of Kholm from Congress Poland and its annexation by Russia. He was also a highly intelligent man, adept at organizing mass meetings and at framing his views, however provocative, in spiritual language, in words of love. He secured the help of such dignitaries as Count V. A. Bobrinskii, an influential conservative, and P. N. Durnovo, minister of internal affairs from late 1905 until April 1906 and then a prominent member of the State Council. Over the course of several years, the bishop visited one parish after another to drum up support for his project. In June 1910, a group of Duma Nationalists arrived in Kholm to attend a well-organized mass meeting at which peasants pleaded for legislation that would separate Kholm from Poland and incorporate it into the empire.[67] Within some five years, the bishop had succeeded in turning the Kholm project into a nationalist cause with substantial popular support.

In the meantime, Stolypin had taken up the cause again and urged the Duma to consider legislation for the formation of a new province in Kholm. According to the newspaper *Slovo*, in June 1909 the prime minister submitted a seventy-six-page report with an "explanatory note" to the Duma setting forth the case for incorporation. Beyond the newspaper article, there is very little information on the prime minister's views, but this report leaves little doubt that Stolypin was deeply fearful of the non-Russian population in the borderlands.

At the time, Stolypin was at work on a proposal to introduce zemstvos and organs of municipal self-government in the western provinces (to be discussed in the next chapter), and he was much troubled by the possibility that the new institutions would be dominated by non-Russians, in particular by Poles whose loyalty to imperial interests he questioned. Kholm, a region he claimed had been "Russian since earliest times," made him especially apprehensive. He accused the Catholic clergy, in his view a tool of Polish nationalists, of having engaged in a relentless campaign of propaganda to convert the local population to Catholicism. Many defections from Orthodoxy had already occurred, and Stolypin warned that if the region were not integrated into the empire, the Poles would succeed "in taking into their hands the entire local economy as well as education, compelling [the Russian population] little by little to convert to Catholicism." In this report to the Duma, Stolypin came closer than in any other statement to suggesting that there was a region of the empire in which non-Russians posed a serious threat to Russian residents who, he believed, had a legitimate claim to supremacy. But even here his primary concern was to ensure the predominance of Russian state interests, not to crush an indigenous culture. He warned that by itself the separation of Kholm from the Polish Kingdom would not safeguard Russian interests in the region. A "fundamental reorganization" of law and administration would be necessary, but that would take many years and perhaps even decades. He envisioned a gradual integration of Kholm into the Russian Empire.[68]

A Duma committee began to consider the Kholm question in May 1909, but it did not submit its report until May 7, 1911, and the entire Duma did not begin its deliberations until late in November 1911, by which time Stolypin was no longer alive. No bill, according to one historian, evoked as much pandemonium in the Third Duma as the debate over the future of Kholm, and that is remarkable for a chamber known for its unruliness. No fewer than 107 deputies spoke on the measure, but when the debate ended late in April 1912, the vote was one-sided, 156 in favor and 108 against. The State Council followed suit early in May, and on June 23 the tsar signed the bill, turning Kholm into an integral part of the Russian Empire.[69]

Despite Stolypin's focus after mid-1909 on the national question, he maintained a strong interest in agrarian reform, which, after all, had been his first and most important achievement. On several occasions he coaxed the Duma into expanding the measures he had introduced in 1906. And late in August 1910 he undertook a three-week tour (accompanied by the minister of agriculture, A. V. Krivoshein) of the vast stretches of Siberia to obtain firsthand knowledge of the possibilities of further economic development in that region. It was a tour devoted solely to "business [and] hard work," Stolypin wrote his wife from one of the stops, but he did not complain. "I have at least seen and learned things that one cannot learn from documents."[70]

When Stolypin introduced the agrarian reforms in 1906, one of his aims was to encourage peasant migration to the Far East, where uninhabited land was still available, much of it belonging to the state. (Other major landowners were Cossack army units and his majesty's cabinet.) The government, in a position to offer newcomers land on relatively generous terms, developed an elaborate plan for the encouragement of settlement in Siberia. Districts in European Russia were granted a certain number of allotments in the Far East; local zemstvos or land tenure commissions appointed envoys or scouts representing groups of peasants who showed interest in migrating. After inspecting the available land, the scouts, if they were satisfied, would make a formal claim to portions of the land and report to their neighbors at home. Peasants still interested in colonization would then join groups for a long journey on new railway trains popularly known as "Stolypin trains." Accurate statistics are hard to come by, but there is little doubt that for a few years after the Revolution of 1905 migration was substantial. In 1907, close to 570,000 peasants moved to Asiatic Russia, and during the two succeeding years the number rose to over 700,000 per annum. By 1914, the population of that vast region had reached 21.1 million, as compared to about 10 million in 1897. But in 1910 the movement to the east had begun to decline. Part of the problem was that the best land had already been appropriated; and in 1910 there was a crop failure in Siberia that prompted an alarming number of colonists of that year, about 20 percent, to return to European Russia.[71] That the decline in migration was uppermost in the minds of the two ministers is clear from the first sentence of their report: "The most important concern of the state in Siberia is [the promotion] of migration."[72]

Stolypin and Krivoshein covered a vast amount of ground in the short span of three weeks: six districts in four provinces and extensive areas in Siberia and the Steppe. They traveled by railway and on waterways and even rode horseback for some 550 miles to reach remote settlements. Everywhere they made a point of talking to a wide range of people from officials to ordinary farmers. They spoke to old settlers, Cossacks, newly arrived settlers, and to Kirghiz as well as other people from various indigenous groups. The 170-page report they published in 1911 on their impressions was full of graphic details about life in Siberia and, on the whole, its tone was optimistic. It did not hide their strong support of colonization and took great pains to describe the benefits to the colonizers and to Russia. Yet it also acknowledged that migration was often hard and dangerous. Only substantial aid and advice from the government could ensure its success.

Privately, Stolypin adopted the same cautious tone. In a letter to the tsar some days after he had returned from Siberia, he wrote that "my general impression is more than comforting." Russia had at last overcome the ill effects of the recent political convulsions and was now "undoubtedly experiencing a strong economic and moral upsurge." Siberia was growing "fabulously." In the Kulunda steppe, located in southwestern Siberia between the rivers Irtysh and Ob, which two years earlier had been unfit for colonization, there had emerged not only settlements but what he called "almost cities." He was also impressed by the mix of people who had gone to Siberia: rich and poor, strong and weak, registered and unauthorized migrants. And many of these colonists had a "correct, pure, Russian outlook." In his meetings with them, the people had proudly declared their belief in God and had asked for the construction of churches and schools. In each village he and Krivoshein had encountered people who expressed their love for the tsar and the hope that he would enjoy a long life.[73] Stolypin wrote in a similar vein to his wife from Perm, where the local zemstvo put on a special exhibit of handmade products manufactured locally. "In general, I observed a very serious and considerate attitude of public groups toward our travels!" And deputies from zemstvos and towns in the neighboring localities made the trip to Perm to inform the prime minister of their needs and sorrows. A local priest greeted the prime minister with special warmth and gave his blessings to the entire group from St. Petersburg. In several other towns, newspapers generally described the official delegation in positive terms as a "solemn procession."[74]

Stolypin also detected potential problems or "complications" that "we are preparing for ourselves" that in time could undermine the benefits. He was referring to the government's policy of granting land to the peasants worth up to one hundred rubles a desiatina and at the same time "artificially" establishing communes in a region accustomed to private property. He had encountered migrants "perishing without earnings" and yet "we have not thought . . . of establishing private landed property," the only form of ownership that can be profitable. The consequence of the growth of communes, Stolypin warned, would be the emergence of "an enormous, rudely democratic country [in the Far East], which will soon throttle European Russia."[75] Stolypin did not elaborate on this apprehension, but he presumably feared that the egalitarian society emerging in Siberia would counteract the individualistic yet authoritarian system he was trying to promote.[76]

On the other hand, in the Volga valley, which Stolypin and Krivoshein also visited, the effect of land settlement on the psychology of the people seemed entirely wholesome. To the prime minister's delight, he had noticed that some of the peasants were "apostles of land settlement and agricultural improvements." He had even met "peasant revolutionary" members of the First Duma who "are [now] passionate homesteaders and supporters of order." He praised the tsar for having understood that this would happen. "And how right you are, Your Majesty, how correctly you fathomed what is happening in the soul of the people, when you write that the basic questions for the government are land settlement and migration. It is necessary to apply enormous energy to these two questions and not permit them to languish."[77]

For the most part, the published report by Stolypin and Krivoshein on their tour concentrated on practical matters: the area's richness in natural resources, the size of the new settlements, the quality of the transportation system and the schools, the price of grain and other products, living conditions, economic prospects, and the possibilities for expanding agriculture into such fields as cattle-raising and the production of butter and other dairy commodities. They did not believe that Siberia would in the foreseeable future enjoy significant industrial development: capital was in short supply, there was no large and trained workforce, and the local markets for industrial goods were too small. Still, Stolypin and his colleague were much impressed by the "rapid and solid growth of Siberia" and strongly favored increased government encouragement of migration to the Far East. In keeping with their longstanding advocacy of private land ownership, they recommended that this principle be applied in Siberia: "The right of land ownership must serve as the main guarantee for raising the productivity of the peasant households and the renewal of migration. But Siberia needs not only small-scale peasant land ownership. It is also necessary to guarantee a supply of migrants with larger private landholdings."[78]

Stolypin believed that the movement eastward was, economically, more important for Siberia than for European Russia. The migration could have a truly significant impact on the western parts of the empire only if several million people a year emigrated, and that had not happened and was not likely to happen in the near future. He was not even convinced that migration on so vast a scale was advisable economically or politically. He apparently feared that a large decline in the human resources of European Russia would weaken the western borders of the Russian state. If that happened, the country would face in the west a problem it had faced in the east and that, in fact, had been one reason for Stolypin's interest in the colonization of Siberia. In his view, the Far East needed a larger population for the protection of the country's borders. He quoted the aphorism of a Chinese dignitary to buttress his argument: "Just as a tree without bark dries up, so a state without firm borders ceases to be a [sovereign] power."[79]

The report on Siberia by Stolypin and Krivoshein did not materially affect the government's policies on the Far East. By the time it was published in 1911, Stolypin, the principal advocate of migration, was no longer alive and conditions for colonization had become less attractive. The poor harvest of 1911 prompted a very large number of the migrants who had left their homes that year to return to European Russia. It has been estimated that in 1911 some 60 percent of the new migrants pulled up stakes, and that from 1912 to 1916 about 30 percent did so each year.[80] Not until 1954 was a new effort undertaken, now by the Soviet government, to encourage migration to the so-called "virgin and idle lands," mainly in northern Kazakhstan and western Siberia, and to spur agricultural production. The campaign launched by the Communists seems to have been modestly successful, though it encountered problems similar to those encountered by Stolypin.[81]

8

The Last Defeat

Despite the painful setbacks he had endured, Stolypin remained a man of remarkable optimism and self-confidence. In mid-1910, on the eve of his severest political crisis, he impressed foreign dignitaries with his resolve to implement his program. Now that he had recuperated from his winter illness, which had forced him to spend several weeks in the Crimea, he let it be known that he would resume active leadership of the administration. To be sure, in his absence from the capital right-wing extremists, unimpressed by his focus on nationalistic themes over the past year, had stepped up their intrigues against him and had increased their influence at court. Still, he vowed to remain faithful to the program he had pursued over the preceding four years.[1]

When Stolypin heard that many people feared that he might "go backward altogether," he responded with considerable emotion: "We are not fools; it would be utter madness. We know how to learn our lessons. Perhaps the extreme Right want something of the kind: you remember ([he said] with a smile), those who wished for a 'Restoration' in France. But you can freely contradict it. The rumours are without any foundation. The Duma, it is true, has more work than it can do. But it depends on what you call backwards and what forwards. For instance, the Socialists would say that the Land Settlement (private farms instead of communal property) is a step backwards; the Liberals were against the village commune, and now that I go against it, they attack me. If the commune was a step forward, then we are going backward; but I myself think that individual property is a step forward. So, too, with the reduction of exceptional administration [a reference to emergency measures]. I think that we are going forward fast enough."[2]

In an interview he gave in mid-January 1911 to A. Ksiunin, a journalist for *Novoe vremia*, Stolypin also voiced optimism about his reform measures. The Third Duma, in the prime minister's view, had been much more effective in passing legislation than his enemies—whom he criticized as prejudiced—were prepared to acknowledge. He conceded that he had suffered some defeats in the legislature, but that was to be

expected. Overall, the situation was not all that bad. Although at present "the [political] machine was screeching . . . the country lives." He
recalled a statement he had made after the dissolution of the Duma in
June 1907: "The First Duma was red, the Second was many-colored, and
the Third will be gray." The Third Duma was indeed "drab," but it had
adopted some very important bills on the national question, such as the
law on Finnish self-government, and on the agrarian question (approval
of his reforms of 1906), which, he proudly claimed, were changing the
lives of millions of peasants. More could have been achieved if there had
been a "strong center" in the legislature, and he was hopeful that the
Fourth Duma, to be elected in 1912, would have such "a firm center
with a nationalistic hue." He called on all moderate parties to unite for
the upcoming electoral struggle. Ksiunin suggested that because Stolypin was such a dynamic leader and splendid orator his optimism
might not be misplaced.[3]

Not everyone shared Ksiunin's optimism. According to one keen
foreign observer, society seemed to be gripped by a certain fatalism
growing out of a sense that "everything is going to pieces." The younger
generation, moreover, widely subscribed to the motto "Live and enjoy
yourself" and paid little attention to politics. "We are sleeping," complained one citizen who deplored the new mood of resignation. And
within the political class, which still took an interest in public affairs,
there were increasing doubts about Stolypin's ability to survive much
longer as prime minister, let alone his ability to make good on his promise to restructure Russia and consolidate the tranquillity he had established after the turbulence of 1905.

The foreign observer suggested that there were two principal reasons
for the malaise in 1910. As it became clear that the revolutionary tide
had been turned back, more people than ever before subscribed to the
view, already widely held in conservative circles in 1907 and 1908, that
the upheaval had not been the result of deep discontents in Russia. On
the contrary, "the entire misfortune of the revolution," it was claimed,
had been "caused by foreign, mainly Jewish, influences. As a consequence, it was widely preached that the subjugation of Judaism and of
the 'modern idea' is the panacea for restoring the spiritual health of Russia." This "reactionary nationalistic tendency" was gaining momen-
tum, and the tsar himself "did not distance himself from it." The country, so it seemed to many, no longer needed a leader such as Stolypin,
who believed in modernization.[4]

At the same time, many moderates, in particular the Octobrists,
were disappointed with the prime minister for not defending the pre-

rogatives of the Duma more aggressively during the debate over the naval general staff bill. He seemed to care more about holding onto office than defending the principles of constitutionalism he claimed to favor. The moderates also took Stolypin's gradual but perceptible moves to the right, especially on the national question, as cynical maneuvers to help him keep power.

Pourtalès, the German ambassador to St. Petersburg who reported on these attitudes toward the prime minister, believed that the Octobrists were mistaken in depicting Stolypin as a man without the gifts of statesmanship, as a leader incapable of asserting his independence and pursuing his vision for Russia. True, Stolypin was above all an honest and loyal servant of the monarch, merely a "'chinovnik' [bureaucrat], but [he was one] in the best sense of the word."[5] At critical moments he had demonstrated personal courage and a willingness to sacrifice himself for causes he believed in. That is why he doggedly held onto his office.

Late in 1910, Stolypin indicated in various ways that he still contemplated a wide range of domestic reforms. In November, he informed the tsar about three specific proposals that had been discussed by the Council on the Local Economy before their consideration by the cabinet: the reorganization of financial institutions that provided credit for cities and zemstvos, measures to help citizens in economic distress due to crop failures, and the construction of new roads in various regions of the country. He favored all three projects and hoped to involve citizens at the local level in their implementation so that they would not be the "creation of bureaucrats alone."[6]

At about the same time, I. Ia. Gurliand, Stolypin's close advisor at the Ministry of Internal Affairs, sought the prime minister's reaction to an article he was writing for *Rossiia* praising the Duma for tackling some difficult issues and predicting further productive work by the legislature. "We have a right to expect a great deal from the fourth session [of the Third Duma]," Gurliand wrote. He expected the Duma "to take serious steps to promote the broadest development of the moral and material forces of the Russian people," by which he meant reforms to extend elementary education and to restructure the organs of local self-government throughout the empire.[7] Stolypin supported all these measures, but at the time he was preoccupied with one particularly difficult project, a sweeping change in local self-government in several western provinces. It was a project dear to his heart, one that would change the political landscape in a large and important region of the empire. He anticipated some opposition, but he never suspected that it would produce a firestorm more threatening to his position as leader of the government than any of the many intrigues against him over the preceding four years.

To understand the incredibly complicated and contentious debate over the government's proposal, one must be familiar with the history and demography of the nine provinces in the southwest, Belorussia, and the northwest that would be affected by the changes (Vitebsk, Volhynia, Kiev, Minsk, Mogilev, Podolia, Grodno, Vilno, and Kovno). In all these provinces the Great Russian population was a distinct minority, ranging from 3.28 percent in Poldolia to 13.29 percent in Vitebsk, whereas Ukrainians and Belorussians constituted a substantial majority. In Stolypin's view and in the view of nationalists generally, the Ukrainians and Belorussians, most of whom were of the Orthodox faith, belonged to the Russian ethnic stock and therefore could be relied upon as loyal citizens of the empire. Each one of the nine provinces had sizable Jewish communities, ranging from 11.69 to 17.20 percent, and their loyalty to the empire, in the eyes of many officials and Duma deputies, was suspect. Finally, each province had a minority (ranging from 1.03 to 10.08 percent) of Poles, who exerted a powerful political and social influence in the region because many of them were large landowners.[8] In 1864, when zemstvos were introduced in European Russia, the government decided not to establish them in any of the nine provinces. The Polish rebellion of 1863 had only just been suppressed, and since the law creating the zemstvos ensured a predominant place to the gentry by virtue of an unequal and indirect suffrage, it was feared that the Poles would be dominant in a large region of the empire. It was a region, moreover, that in part was adjacent to the former Kingdom of Poland, where nationalist sentiment continued to run high.

Yet almost from the moment Stolypin assumed leadership of the government, he contemplated extending local self-government to the western provinces. No doubt, his many years of residence in that part of the empire disposed him to take a special interest in the region. But it is noteworthy that late in 1906, when he first brought up the issue, he tended to view the Polish gentry with less suspicion than most officials. He told the cabinet that the Poles were no longer hostile to the Russian state and seemed willing to devote their energies to improving conditions in the area. Moreover, he noted that in some parts of the western provinces Russians owned more land than the Poles, which lessened the danger of Polish domination. He was so eager to introduce the zemstvos in the western provinces that he proposed doing so immediately under the emergency regulation of Article 87 of the Fundamental Laws. There was no reason, he contended, to deprive the area of an institution that had proven to be beneficial in other parts of the empire. He also thought that the introduction of zemstvos would demonstrate the government's commitment to the principles of the October Manifesto. Although Stolypin's proposal in 1906 made some provisions for separate voting of the national groups, that was not an issue to which he attached great importance. Nothing came of Stolypin's proposal because the government decided on a general reform of the zemstvos throughout the empire and did not wish to embark on piecemeal changes before the final plan was completed.[9]

However, the political crisis over the zemstvos in the western provinces erupted before a master plan was formulated, by Stolypin or anyone else. As is so often true of dramatic historical events, the origins of the crisis were quite mundane, and no one involved in the first deliberations expected the outcome to be the deadliest of all clashes between the rightists and the prime minister. Early in May 1909, D. I. Pikhno, a fervent nationalist and editor of the reactionary newspaper *Kievlianin*, introduced a proposal in the State Council in the name of thirty-three councilors to change the procedures in the nine western provinces for the election of members of the upper chamber, the State Council. In most of European Russia, the zemstvos chose the councilors, but since there were no zemstvos in the western provinces, congresses of landlords with sizable landholdings made the selection. As already noted, Polish landlords predominated in the region and, consequently, the councilors from all nine provinces were Poles. Politically, the Polish members of the State Council were quite moderate, but that was irrelevant to Pikhno. He feared that eventually the Poles might become hostile to the empire and, in any case, as a chauvinist he simply wanted more Russians in the upper chamber.

Pikhno's project was simplicity itself: the nine provinces were to be divided into three groups, each representing three provinces; two congresses, one of Russian landlords and one of Polish landlords, would meet in Vilno, Mogilev, and Kiev to select twenty electors, who, in turn, would meet separately to choose the members of the State Council from their midst. But each electoral region would be required to select two Russians and one Pole, giving the Russians a total of six members and the Poles three. For a conservative such as Pikhno, the scheme had two advantages. It gave the Russians two thirds of the councilors from the nine provinces, and it kept the selection of the councilors in the hands of well-to-do landlords.[10] It was thus consistent both with the emerging nationalist ideology and with the principle underlying the original establishment of the zemstvos, that the landed gentry should be the paramount social and political force in the countryside.

Stolypin wasted no time expressing the government's agreement with the nationalistic thrust of the proposal by Pikhno and his thirty-two colleagues. On May 8, he informed the State Council that the government considered the prevailing law on the election of members to the State Council from the nine western provinces "imperfect" and in need of change. Three weeks later, in the Duma, he referred to the law as "abnormal and unjust." All in all, the Poles constituted 4 percent of the total population in the western region, and yet they elected all nine state councilors. It could be argued, Stolypin conceded, that such a state of affairs was desirable: state councilors, unlike Duma deputies, were supposed to be selected from the "most cultured, most prosperous, [and] most stable" elements of society, and in the nine provinces the Poles were the upper crust of society. However, Stolypin rejected this line of reasoning by pointing to the rest of European Russia, where state councilors also came from the upper strata of society but were elected through a system in which citizens from various social groups participated. He was referring to the election of state councilors by the provincial zemstvo assembly, an "institution representing the economic interests of the entire province."

The key problem in the nine provinces, as Stolypin saw it, was the absence of such an institution, the zemstvo. The time had come, he argued, to establish it in the west, and that called for a far more extensive political change than envisioned by Pikhno and his thirty-two colleagues. The introduction of zemstvos would not only provide the western areas with the kind of self-government prevalent in the rest of European Russia, but would also create an institution for the selection of the councilors. At the same time, Stolypin made a crucial promise. He assured Pikhno that in devising a bill on the zemstvos he would be guided by the nationalist idea. The electors who would select the members of the zemstvos would be divided along national lines so that the interests of the Russian population would be "fully protected." The new procedures would, as Stolypin put it, restore "justice for the 15 million Russians in the Western region."

However, the entire matter was too complicated to be settled during the current session of the Duma, which would have to vote on the measure. The prime minister therefore suggested that the project of the thirty-three councilors be shelved temporarily and that for one year the old procedures for the election of state councilors remain in effect. He intended to appoint a special commission to examine the issue and produce a bill as soon as possible.[11]

Stolypin tried to reassure the Poles that in taking the initiative on the zemstvos he was guided solely by state interests and not by any desire to degrade the Poles: "The government is not guided by hatred," he told the Duma on May 30, 1909, "nor by a wish gratuitously to insult the Poles—that would be not only ungenerous but unstatesmanlike. The government is guided by a notion that should always guide every government, the notion that we must listen to the just demands of the native Russian population in the outlying districts and if these demands are well grounded we must support them with all the force of governmental authority."[12] The rightists and centrists in the Duma greeted these words with applause, but the Poles were understandably nervous about the prime minister's intentions.

Stolypin was right in warning that the establishment of zemstvos in the nine provinces would be complicated, but there is no evidence that he had any inkling that he was stirring up a hornet's nest. Not only would he have to take into account the conflicting interests of various national groups in the nine provinces. He would also have to be sensitive to the divergent economic interests of several social groups; the estate principle still governed the election of zemstvo deputies, and any deviation from that principle was bound to arouse the deepest fears among many nobles in the empire, not simply among the upper crust in the western regions. If property qualifications for the election of zemstvos in the western provinces were eliminated or even changed, the Russians might indeed emerge as the dominant force in local government, but many of the new voters would inevitably be untutored citizens, and Stolypin did not consider them capable of administering provincial affairs. More than that, his enemies in the State Council and at court would be appalled by such a democratic innovation, which would set a precedent for the entire country. They were watching his every move, ready to pounce on him as soon as he took any step that they viewed as subversive of the prevailing order.

Once he had committed himself to the Western Zemstvo project, Stolypin made it his legislative priority and spared no effort to prepare a bill for the Duma that would enlist wide support. According to the minister of finance, Kokovtsov, "he had given the matter his personal attention from the start, defending the project most energetically, and often stating that after the peasant agrarian reform and the revision of the gubernatorial administration he attributed great importance to this matter, for—this was his favorite expression—'I have nursed the problem in my heart since my early youth and during the period of my first contact with local life in the northwestern region to which I gave my best years.' Therefore he listened most attentively to every observation made both in the Duma and in the Council; he attended every session until the Duma expressed its approval of the project's basic principles."[13] Stolypin also sought to mobilize support outside the Duma by giving speeches in which he emphasized that large "state interests" were at stake in the endeavor to extend the zemstvos to the west. In a speech on October 6, 1909, at a meeting of the Council on the Local Economy he stressed the government's fear that the Russian inhabitants of the nine provinces would be economically overwhelmed by the richer Poles and culturally "absorbed" by them. He contended that it would be "imprudent" not to support the "state idea" with "the very force of law" in a province such as Vilno, where the "state idea was inadequately rooted."[14] Stolypin was sending an emotionally charged message: the very basis of the Russian state would be endangered unless the zemstvos in the west were elected on the basis of the national principle.

When the cabinet conducted its analysis of the plan to establish zemstvos in the nine provinces with clear-cut Russian predominance, the ministers quickly realized that however desirable, it could not be easily implemented. The proposed division of all voters into national curiae (to be discussed below) presented no insuperable problems in most of the nine provinces. But the Russian landowners in Kovno and Vilno owned so little land that it did not seem feasible to assign them a significant role in the elections to the zemstvos. It must be kept in mind that Stolypin did not wish to give a predominant political voice to the landless peasants, who he believed were not sufficiently educated for such a role. And Grodno presented yet another problem. It was administratively part of the governor-generalship of the three provinces (Kovno, Vilno, and Grodno). Therefore, the cabinet decided in December 1909 to drop these three provinces from the project altogether and to propose the introduction of zemstvos only in the remaining six provinces in the southwestern region of the empire. The official reasoning on the matter, as reported in the press, was remarkably candid: "Considering it impossible to guarantee in Kovno and Vilno provinces a majority for the Russian population and recalling at the same time the wish of the Council on the Local Economy [which had discussed the project], expressed repeatedly, that it is better not to have any zemstvo rather than a Polish one, the Ministry of Internal Affairs reached the conclusion to introduce zemstvos only in Kiev, Volhynia, Podolia, Mogilev, and Vitebsk . . . [and

Minsk]."[15] The three provinces in the northeast would retain the old administrative structure.

A few months later Stolypin publicly defended the exclusion of the three provinces from the new arrangement. He repeated the argument that the zemstvos must not fall into Polish hands, but he also sought once again to reassure the Duma deputies that the government did not wish to offend the Poles. "Do not think, Gentlemen, that the government has any kind of prejudice, that there is any kind of hostility toward the Polish population [a remark that evoked shouts from the left: "and how"]. On the part of the government that would be stupid, and on my part this would be even ridiculous because precisely in those provinces about which I am now speaking I learned to appreciate and respect the high culture of the Polish people and I can say with pride that I still have many friends there." At this there was an outburst of derisive noise on the left side of the chamber.[16]

In truth, there is virtually no evidence that in pressing for zemstvos in the southwestern provinces Stolypin was motivated by prejudice. His concerns were to uphold what he liked to call the "Russian idea" and the power of the state. Hence, he wanted Russians to be politically predominant throughout the empire, and particularly in those areas where they constituted a majority of the population. What he seems not to have understood was that in seeking to manipulate the electoral system in the southwestern provinces to ensure the Russian population political predominance he was in effect snubbing the Polish minority. Nowhere else in the empire were electoral procedures based so blatantly on the national principle. For all his acuity, he did not realize that what he considered to be sound political policy would be deeply offensive to sizable minorities in the empire.

The legislative proposal he submitted to the Duma in January of 1910 was a masterpiece of complexity. Its single most important provision was the replacement of elections on the basis of the estate principle with elections on the basis of the national principle. Property qualifications for the suffrage would remain, but they would be drastically reduced. In every one of the six provinces, two curiae, one Russian (in which all non-Poles entitled to vote would participate) and one Polish, would select the electors who would make the final selection of zemstvo deputies. This procedure would be applicable for the election of district and provincial zemstvos. But the precise number of zemstvo deputies to be selected by each national group would be determined in accordance with yet another set of rules. The authorities would establish the percentage of a national group in the total population of a given province and the percentage of the value of the group's landholdings and immovable property; these two figures were added and then divided by two. The result was the number of deputies the national group could elect. An example of how this would work may be helpful. If in a province the Poles constituted 2 percent of the population and the immovable wealth of the Poles in a particular district amounted to 38 percent of the total wealth in the province, the two figures would be added, giving the sum of 40, which would be divided by two. In that province, the Poles would be guaranteed twenty seats in the zemstvo assembly.

However, the government realized that a rigid application of these rules would enable the peasants to elect a majority of the deputies in all the district and provincial assemblies, since the newly established, lower property qualifications gave many of them the vote. This the authorities considered unacceptable. Therefore, another rule was established: the number of peasant deputies in any district must not exceed one-third of the total number in the zemstvo assembly. Elected by district zemstvo assemblies, the provincial zemstvo assemblies thus would not be inundated by peasants. In addition, the Orthodox clergy was granted the right to be represented by three priests in the district assembly and four in the provincial assembly, a significant increase. According to the regulations of 1890, the clergy was entitled to only one deputy in the district and provincial assemblies. To ensure Russian control of the administration of the zemstvos, the government's bill stipulated that the chairman and not fewer than half the members of the zemstvo boards must be Russian. Finally, the bill included a special statute excluding Jews, no less than 10 percent of the population in each one of the six provinces, from zemstvo elections. The statute was gratuitous, since the Regulations of 1890 had already disenfranchised the Jews. But the government wanted to "avoid any misunderstanding."[17]

During the lengthy debates of the bill in the Duma Committee on Local Self-Government and in the Duma itself, many amendments were added, most of them unacceptable to the government, which only further complicated the measure.[18] In the end, the bill was cluttered with provisions that appeared to be at cross purpose with each other. But that hardly mattered because the committee, in a strange denouement, turned down its own creation. As a result, the government's bill was the one that was formally under consideration by the chamber. But it contained many controversial features. Only the rightists and the Nationalists found it acceptable more or less as drafted. A sizable number of Octobrists had reservations. They were prepared to support the idea of national curiae as a temporary evil, but they were uncomfortable with what appeared to them to be signs of the government's distrust of local government and excessive suspicion of the minorities. "I am ready," said the Octobrist Iu. N. Glebov, "to support what is dictated by national pride, but not what is dictated by hatred for everything non-Russian."[19] The Kadets found the bill totally unacceptable. Their spokesman, A. I. Shingarev, repudiated the creation of national curiae, which would only intensify national animosities, and he attacked the provisions that limited the number of peasants who could serve in the zemstvos and that continued the disenfranchisement of the Jews. The Kadets viewed the bill as a clear deviation from the principles enunciated in the October Manifesto.[20]

Stolypin took it upon himself to defend the government's project in two addresses to the Duma in the spring of 1910. With characteristic candor, he left no doubt about his intentions in sponsoring the extension of zemstvos to the western provinces: it was necessary, he declared on May 7, 1910, to "subordinate the zemstvo idea to the state idea," a view that was consistent with his entire political philosophy. As he read Russian history, the government had imposed its will on the nation in stages. Initially, it had pursued its goal of realizing the state idea by armed force; then it did so by administrative measures, which achieved predominance for the "Russian state elements" in the various regions of the empire. Thus the government had reached out from the center of the empire and had provided the impulse for the building of the state and for the penetration of the "Russian state cells" in the localities. Now every effort must be made to penetrate the western region, where the "state cells" were weaker and "more disconnected" than the "robust citadels of Polish culture, which for centuries have implanted themselves in Western Russia." Stolypin warned against allowing events in the area to run their natural course without decisive intervention by the government. "Is it really possible at the present time in the political arena in the Western region to permit a free contest, a free competition between two political and economic factors, the Russian and the Polish? Is it an appropriate role for the Russian government to be an outside observer, an outside spectator (applause from the right and center and a shout of Bravo), standing on this historical hippodrome, or in the capacity of an impartial judge at the [final] post, simply registering the victory of one or another nationality?" A power such as Russia, he asserted elsewhere in the speech, "cannot and does not have the right to refuse to carry out its historical tasks without being punished for it. But, Gentlemen, we have forgotten our historical tasks." Always a patriot, Stolypin had now adopted the language of the chauvinist. Rightist and centrist deputies appreciated his words. They applauded heartily and shouted, "Bravo, splendid!"[21]

Stolypin placed all the blame for the tensions in the southwestern provinces on the Polish landlords and intelligentsia. Even though the Poles made up only 4 percent of the population they had gained control of vast stretches of land far out of proportion to their numbers. And they had not made these acquisitions legally or in the natural course of economic development. They had established their economic supremacy "by virtue of a historical squall that swept over this area and overthrew everything Russian."[22]

Even now the Poles sought to extend their control over the area. Stolypin recalled that as recently as 1906 the Poles had rebuffed efforts to conciliate them. That year, a society of Russian landlords had been formed in the southwest for the specific purpose of establishing amicable relations with the Poles. The society sent a delegation to St. Petersburg to ask the government to abolish all restrictions imposed on the Poles. But the "alliance" between the two national groups collapsed within months when Polish conferences in Kiev and Zhitomir proclaimed "that Polish culture was superior to Russian culture and that the Poles in the southwestern region occupied a special place." Stolypin urged the Duma deputies to read the *Dnevnik Kievskii* for the month of October 1906; it contained a letter from a Polish landlord claiming that the Poles were so strong that they needed neither an alliance with the Russians nor their help. All these "historical facts" made it necessary for the Duma to approve the establishment of national curiae in the southwestern provinces. It was the only possible way to protect Russian interests, the only way to guarantee that "the Western region is and will be a Russian region, for ever and ever."[23]

The debate in the Duma, at times rather spirited, continued for some three weeks, until May 29, 1910, but in the end the measure passed with a comfortable if not overwhelming margin, 169 to 139. The rightists' and the Nationalists' support for the measure was, of course, assured. How the Octobrists would vote was uncertain for some time, in large measure because the faction was leaderless at the time. Ultimately most Octobrists voted for the bill, having concluded that it was the best compromise they could obtain. As one of their leaders, V. K. Anrep, put it, the bill "has one merit: it brings new life into the region."[24] Still, it was supported by substantially less than half the 440 deputies. The bill was then forwarded to the State Council, where Stolypin expected easy passage. It was to be his greatest and most costly miscalculation.

For several months a committee of the State Council debated the bill, and the government had every reason to remain confident. The committee not only failed to voice any serious criticisms but actually voted to eliminate many of the amendments adopted by the Duma and opposed by the government. But when the debate began in the State Council itself in January 1911, the bill suddenly came under sharp attack. On the first reading it still received the votes of almost all the rightists and passed with a solid margin. By this time, however, there was a clear danger signal: the rightists lined up so solidly behind the bill only because they had received word that "the highest sphere" wanted them to vote for it. That rightists did not defy the tsar's wishes is a point to be kept in mind as this story unfolds.

It turned out that the rightists objected to central features of the bill and voted for it only reluctantly. They were very uneasy about the abandonment of the estate principle in the elections, the lowering of the property requirement, and the creation of national curiae. One consequence of the new procedures would be to assign the peasants in the western district zemstvos a larger share of the representation than peasants in the rest of the empire. Would the next step not be to change the electoral system throughout the empire, greatly weakening the gentry? Even centrists in the State Duma were alarmed by this possibility and tended to support the conservatives on the issue. As Witte, a leader of the bill's opponents, noted: "Moderate nobles opposed the bill because of its divisive character, which would pit Russian nobles against Polish nobles, when in fact the two groups shared common interests."[25]

In addition, the rightists objected to the national curiae out of fear that their establishment would encourage and in a sense legitimize antistate sentiments and would thus undermine the unity of the empire. It would, Witte warned, send a dangerous message to the country: that the imperial authorities did not trust the non-Russian inhabitants of the empire, that they believed that the interests of ethnic minorities differed fundamentally from those of the Russian people. The curiae, in short, rather than strengthen the Russian state would weaken it. A similar point was made by a Polish member of the State Council, Meysztowicz: "It would seem that after the sad experience of the recent past it would follow that people should be divided not according to nationalities but into the adherents of social order and the social system. However, the bill divides Russian and Polish conservatives into national chambers and so strengthens disunion."[26]

Stolypin was aware of these objections. He attended all the discussions of the bill in the State Council commission before the measure reached the full council, but he did not consider "the opposition from the Right members . . . particularly important." In fact, he was so confident that "he did not consider it necessary to have all ministers who were members of the State Council attend the session so as to increase his support, though there were a few such members. . . . Stolypin's optimism in this matter was further strengthened by the attitude of the Chairman of the State Council, M. G. Akimov, who belonged to the Right group and was well informed as to its opinions."[27]

Still, on three different occasions Stolypin replied forcefully to criticisms of various councilors. He categorically denied that the government had "accidentally" devised the plan to restructure the zemstvos in the west in response to Pikhno's proposal to change the procedures for the election of state councilors. He pointed out that he had favored the restructuring of local government in 1906 and claimed that he had not submitted a bill to the Duma earlier only because he considered the chances of passage very slim. He seized the opportunity to proceed as soon as it became clear to him that a bill "in keeping with state interests" could be adopted.[28] For the rest, he repeated his arguments about the need to curb the Poles, in language even more strident than the language he had used in the Duma. "The Poles," he declared on February 1, 1911, "are the former rulers of the land; they have lost their authority there but preserve their wealth, preserve their culture and preserve their [historical] recollections, which accustomed them to rule, accustomed them to dominate." To permit a small minority of the population to occupy such a position of superiority was intolerable, all the more so since the Poles were determined to defend "their national interests" at all costs and view every question in the region from the vantage point of those interests.[29]

A month after uttering these remarks, Stolypin returned to the State Council and once again stressed the importance he attached to the creation of national curiae, a proposal that by now seemed to have become an obsession with him. The western region, he pointed out, was "a rich land, a land that needs zemstvo self-government, [it is] a Russian land that, however, has an influential upper stratum of the population that is Polish. If the electoral assemblies are not divided along national lines the upper stratum of the population will, of course, acquire predominant [and] supreme influence." Stolypin charged that those who disagreed with him on this question clearly subscribed to a view of the state different from his. They understood the state as the aggregate of different individuals, tribes, nationalities, all united by one common law and one common administration. Such a state, which he called an amalgam, guarded and protected the existing "correlation of forces." But he had in mind a different conception, which is worth quoting in full because it demonstrates his somewhat mystical views of the state: "[It] is possible to think of the state as a force, as an association that embodies national [and] historical principles. Such a state, acting in accordance with national traditions, has the will, strength, and authority to apply coercion, such a state subordinates the rights of individuals [and] of separate groups to the rights of the collectivity. I consider Russia to be such a collectivity. I consider the successive bearers of such a state system to be the Russian lawgivers. The decision is yours, Gentlemen."[30] In uttering these words, Stolypin came as close as he ever did to articulating support for what has come to be known as integral nationalism, a much more intolerant form of nationalism than he generally espoused. Not surprisingly, the Poles—and other minorities—found the prime minister's words chilling. However much he disavowed any prejudice toward the minorities of the empire, his words now gave a different impression.

On the other hand, Stolypin remained confident about the chances of the Western Zemstvo bill because he knew that his words would resonate in the upper chamber. The State Council was, after all, essentially a conservative body. The rightists and moderate conservatives together controlled about 55 percent of the votes, and the nationalist appeal could be counted upon to persuade some moderates to support the prime minister's initiative. But in fact the political lineup was much more complicated than Stolypin realized. He could count on the firm support of only a small group, led by his brother-in-law, A. B. Neidgardt. None of the others on the right or center felt any obligation of personal loyalty. His failure to build a political party under his own leadership and his failure to cultivate close friendships among the political elite proved to be costly. There were very few councilors to whom he could appeal on personal grounds to vote for his proposal.

The prime minister furthermore had fierce enemies in the State Council who wanted nothing more than to bring him down. Durnovo had disliked Stolypin from the moment he met him and bore a grudge against him ever since he was replaced by Stolypin as minister of internal affairs in 1906. Others on the extreme right, most prominently V. F. Trepov, regarded Stolypin as a liberal in sheep's clothing who was conspiring to overthrow the autocracy and the old order in general. Trepov told Count V. B. Frederiks (minister of the court) in all seriousness that "part of the Duma project was a revolutionary move pure and simple, eliminating all from zemstvo work who were cultured and educated in the region, and that it was being advanced to please the petty Russian intelligentsia, who were eager to take everything into their own hands and to get a bite of the 'zemstvo pie.'"[31] During the debates in the State Council, Trepov gave yet another reason for voting against the bill. He would do so, he said, "for no other reason than that Stolypin's 'game was up.'"[32]

And then there was Witte, the central figure in the intrigues about to unfold. Witte, as we have noted, could not abide Stolypin, whom he envied for his skills as a statesman and whom he suspected of endless plots to humiliate him and even to have him killed. At this time, late in 1910, Witte had yet another reason for despising the prime minister. In Odessa, Witte's home city, a street had been named for him when he was prime minister. Witte reveled in the honor and derived enormous pleasure from taking walks on a street that bore his name. But now the city council planned to rename the street. Witte made a personal appeal to Stolypin to order the city council to abandon its plan, but the prime minister indicated that he had no authority to intervene in such a local issue; the city council could do as it wished. (According to one account, Stolypin actually raised the issue with the tsar, who refused to intervene in behalf of a man he despised.) But Witte persisted in pressuring Stolypin, who remained adamant that he could do nothing. At this, "Witte almost sank to his knees, repeating this request over and over." As he left the prime minister's room, Witte "turned around, staring malevolently at . . . [Stolypin and] said that he would never forgive him."[33]

Witte had been a very successful minister of finance and an able prime minister. Once he retired from those posts he applied his considerable intelligence and talents to intrigue. He was masterful in organizing the opposition to the Western Zemstvo bill. Even at the last minute before the balloting on the zemstvo bill, no one outside the intrigue, least of all Stolypin, expected anything but a clear-cut victory for the government. But on March 4, 1911, the bill was voted down, ninety-two to sixty-eight, with twenty-eight rightists—who had initially expressed support for the bill—siding with the opposition. Stolypin, in the chamber at the time, was stunned. According to eyewitnesses, his facial expression changed and remained frozen for some time. Then he "left the room, and everybody saw clearly that something momentous had happened."[34]

A. I. Guchkov, who a year earlier had been elected president of the Duma, let it be known that he intended to reintroduce the bill on the western zemstvos in the lower chamber and that it would come to a vote within the thirty days prescribed by the regulations on the handling of defeated legislative proposals. Within fifteen minutes after Guchkov's announcement, more than two hundred signatures had been collected to support such a move. There seemed little doubt that the bill would again be adopted and that the government's initiative was not dead. There would then be time to mount a more vigorous campaign in the State Council to secure the necessary votes.[35]

The prime minister, however, showed no interest in pursuing normal parliamentary procedures to overturn the State Council's decision. He was in a rage and wanted not only a reversal of the decision but also revenge on the people who had humiliated him. Hours after the vote he told Krivoshein that under no circumstances could he accept "this revolting decision." At a cabinet meeting two days later, he indicated that he "had definite information that the events in the State Council were but the result of an intrigue against him." He had learned that P. N. Durnovo had submitted a memorandum to the tsar claiming that the creation of special bodies of peasant electors would antagonize the Polish landowners, "who heretofore had maintained a loyal attitude toward Russia." Durnovo also warned that the bill would promote anti-Russian hostility among persons "openly harboring Austrian sympathies." As a result, the "more cultured class of landowners" might refuse to have anything to do with the zemstvos, leaving the work of local government in the "hands of people incapable of handling it."[36]

What Stolypin apparently did not yet know was the tsar's complicity in the intrigue. Whether Nicholas had been deliberately devious in order to undermine Stolypin's authority or had acted without understanding the consequences of his behavior is still not clear. It is clear, however, that the rightists were given contradictory information on the tsar's wishes. On the one hand, Akimov, the president of the State Council, informed the rightists that "the highest sphere" still favored the passage of the Western Zemstvo bill. This would have sufficed to persuade enough rightists to vote for it and to ensure its adoption. But shortly before March 4, the tsar told Trepov that the rightists should feel free to vote as they wished, a message Trepov was only too eager to pass on to his colleagues. The message made the difference in the balloting.[37] In an entry in his diary on March 5, 1911, Count A. A. Bobrinskii suggested that the tsar was going through a difficult period, and that this might account for his failure to give clear-cut instructions to his followers in the State Council. Nicholas was said to be "nervous, did not know what to decide, . . . is upset. They say that he is worried about family troubles, the health of the Empress and so on."[38]

Be that as it may, Stolypin concluded that he could not possibly remain in office, and on March 5 he submitted his resignation during an audience with Nicholas. Detailed and moving accounts of the meeting are contained in a set of notes jotted down by Stolypin and in a report by the German ambassador, who almost certainly obtained his information from the prime minister himself. Although Stolypin appears to have been too agitated to formulate his recollections and thoughts in a fully coherent way, the thrust of his comments is clear enough. He wanted to resign but the tsar would not permit it because, he said, he knew of no one who could replace Stolypin. Having declared his willingness to leave office, Stolypin felt free to speak candidly about the men who had undermined his authority: "I told . . . [the tsar] that the rightists are not rightists but shady, smooth-tongued, and mendacious reactionaries, mendacious because they resort to shady methods of [political] *struggle*."[39] In an obvious effort to justify his having told Trepov that the rightists were free to vote their consciences, the tsar indicated that Trepov had claimed that nobles from three provinces had been unduly pressured by the government to lobby for the passage of the Western Zemstvo bill. Enraged at this revelation, the tsar had fulminated: "So I have once again been betrayed."[40] The prime minister dismissed Trepov's charge as totally groundless and again denounced his enemies for intriguing against him. The rightists, he told Nicholas, did not consider it "necessary to legislate"; they believe "it is necessary only to administer." Stolypin added the following, revealing remark: "But apparently this pleases the monarch and he himself believes it," another indication of a serious political difference between the prime minister and the ruler.[41]

Stolypin again brought up the subject of his resignation. He told the tsar that he felt he had no choice, since "I no longer have [your] support." And as a minister beholden to the tsar, he could not look for support in society or seek the backing of a political party. Here, Stolypin was referring to a fundamental weakness in his position as prime minister: his authority depended entirely on the goodwill of the tsar. Without it, he could achieve nothing. Nicholas must have understood Stolypin's point, but he did not repudiate, or even criticize, Trepov. He wanted the support of people like Trepov, and he wanted Stolypin as prime minister. When Stolypin reiterated his determination to leave office, Nicholas "*only cried and embraced me. I genuinely feel sorry for him! He believes in mysticism, he listens to prophesies*, believes in relying on the rightists."[42]

In part, Nicholas's unwillingness to let Stolypin go was related to the monarch's belief that a change of government after a legislative defeat of a government bill would be seen as a victory for parliamentarism. But as he had told Stolypin during a previous crisis, Russia was not Western Europe. A Russian government defeated in the legislature was not obliged to step down; only the tsar could force ministers to leave office. Nicholas made the same point now. He was afraid, he told Stolypin, of creating a "precedent. What would become of a government responsible to me if ministers came and went, today because of a conflict with the State Council, tomorrow because of a conflict with the Duma?"[43] Still, Stolypin seemed to believe that in the end the tsar would allow him to retire. He had concluded that there were two possible resolutions of the crisis: a reactionary government would be appointed or a bureaucratic government would be installed under Kokovtsov to carry on the policies of the previous five years. He was confident that the second path would be chosen, and as if to reassure Nicholas about the country's future, he told him that over the *past five years I have come to know the revolution very well, and I know that it is now smashed and because of my efforts it might be possible to hold on for another five years. But what will then happen depends on those five years.* It seemed to Stolypin that the tsar feared being overshadowed by his prime minister, which might explain Nicholas's inconsistency on the zemstvo bill. "Above all," Stolypin noted, "I feel sorry for the Sovereign."[44]

There is one other report on the confrontation between the tsar and Stolypin, also based on information provided by the prime minister, that gives a slightly different version. The tsar, it seems, suggested that the Western Zemstvo bill be reintroduced in the Duma and promised to use his influence in the State Council to secure passage of the measure. But Stolypin rejected the offer on the grounds that the State Council would never accept the establishment of national curiae and, in any case, would never reverse itself because "it would never admit its mistake." Nevertheless, the tsar left open the door to a solution of the crisis other than Stolypin's resignation. In refusing to let him go, the tsar told the prime minister: "Think of some other way out and let me hear it."[45]

Inevitably, news of Stolypin's resignation was quickly leaked to political dignitaries and became the major topic of conversation among them and in the press. The right-wing publicist Tikhomirov heard of it on March 7, and a day later he received one telegram after another claiming that Nicholas had in fact accepted the resignation. He also heard rumors that Kokovtsov would replace Stolypin and remain in office till the end of the Duma's session. Then Durnovo would be appointed prime minister on the understanding that he would stage a coup d'état and "reshape" the Fundamental Laws of 1906 with regard to the Duma and the State Council. Tikhomirov published an editorial in *Moskovskie vedomosti* expressing sympathy for the prime minister and criticizing the state councilors who had hatched the plot to overthrow him and thus had damaged national interests. The rightists, and especially Witte, were furious at having been exposed, all the more so because the source was a conservative newspaper.[46]

Without much hard information on the political crisis, newspapers could do little more than speculate about Stolypin's fate. The liberal *Rech* published a long article on March 9 analyzing the prime minister's record over the past five years and concluded that Stolypin's political career was finished. *Rech* did not approve of his program, but it grudgingly expressed admiration for the man. Although his policies were often harsh, he never avoided responsibility for the government's actions. In one of his first speeches in the Duma, he had announced that he had "received full authority and [that in his hands] lay the entire burden of responsibility" for the conduct of state affairs. But eventually he abused his authority, moved too far to the right, and lost the support of the right center. Yet he had failed to win over the right-wing extremists, and that was the principal reason for his present predicament.[47]

Another article in *Rech* reported that Stolypin was making a desperate effort to hold on to power. He had allegedly authorized his assistant in the Ministry of Internal Affairs, Kryzhanovskii, to sound out the Kadet leader S. A. Muromtsev about forming a Kadet ministry in which Stolypin would remain the minister of internal affairs. *Rossiia*, the paper sponsored by the government, categorically denied this rather fanciful story.[48]

Birzhevye vedomosti, a moderately conservative paper, published what seemed to have been the best informed and certainly the most judicious articles on the crisis. On March 11, it declared that no one in St. Petersburg, not even Stolypin himself, knew whether the government would fall. "The news emanating from the most competent sources literally changes every hour. In the morning people whose knowledge is unimpeachable confirm as correct the news that the crisis has been overcome and that P. A. [Stolypin] will return to power; in the evening, one of the most prominent members of the cabinet asserts with equal certainty that P. A.'s departure is irrevocable."[49]

In fact, the crisis had not yet been resolved. Late one evening (probably on March 10), Stolypin met with his cabinet and insisted that he would not yield on the Western Zemstvo bill. He claimed not to be motivated by a desire for revenge against the opponents of the bill, not even against his long-standing enemies Durnovo and Trepov. He remained unyielding, the prime minister told the ministers, for only one reason:

he was absolutely convinced that the bill was necessary to advance the interests of the state. Those interests were being harmed by a "small group of people pursuing their own personal interests," which included, above all, ousting him from office. Stolypin further contended that if he did not prevail on the zemstvo bill, he would not be able to get any bills passed in the State Council and would thus not be able to conduct the government's affairs effectively.

At this juncture the prime minister, who had been summoned back to the palace, revealed a daring and, as it turned out, dangerous plan to get the bill enacted after all. He would inform the tsar that he would agree to stay in office only on condition that the two legislative chambers be prorogued for three days, during which time the Western Zemstvo bill would be enacted as law under Article 87 of the Fundamental Laws, which granted the authorities the right to issue decrees as emergency measures when the Duma was in recess. The declaration made a strong impression on the cabinet. "Every member fully shared the point of view of the head of government."[50]

In his memoirs, Kokovtsov claimed that after the cabinet meeting he warned Stolypin that his plan to prorogue the legislatures was a "political mistake" and also predicted that another, previously undisclosed, part of his plan—to demand that the tsar discipline Trepov and Durnovo—would backfire. Kokovtsov was convinced that if Nicholas yielded, he would never forgive Stolypin for having pressured him to punish two loyal state councilors.[51] Stolypin was not deterred.

The sequence of events that ended the crisis must surely be one of the most bizarre in the history of the tsarist autocracy. On March 9, four days after he had personally informed Nicholas of his resignation, Stolypin was summoned by the dowager empress to Gatchina. "As he entered the door of Empress Maria Fedorovna's study," Stolypin's daughter reported, "he met the sovereign. The Emperor's face was red from weeping and, without exchanging greetings with my father, he walked swiftly past, wiping tears with his handkerchief." But the empress greeted the prime minister "with exceptional warmth." She immediately raised questions about Stolypin's intention to resign and then indicated that she had just discussed the matter with Nicholas. "I have informed my son of my deep conviction that you alone possess the strength and ability to save Russia and bring her back to the true way." She also revealed that Nicholas's wife, Empress Alexandra Fedorovna, had exerted the wrong kind of influence over the ruler, but in the end she—the empress dowager—had convinced him not to let Stolypin go. The empress dowager then "implored" Stolypin to withdraw his resignation. "Her words breathed deep love for Russia," Stolypin's daughter wrote, "and such firm assurance that my father had a mission to save Russia that he came away from her agitated, disturbed, and beginning to hesitate in his decision."[52]

The dowager empress's intervention in Stolypin's behalf quickly became the talk of the political class and a source of embarrassment to the tsar. The German and British ambassadors learned about it as early as March 13, four days after the emotional meeting between Stolypin and the tsar's mother. The German ambassador was also informed that it was the rightists' rigidity that at the last moment prevented the replacement of Stolypin by Kokovtsov. Kokovtsov was said to have insisted that he, like Stolypin, be appointed minister of internal affairs as well as prime minister. But the "reactionary elements" insisted that someone from their ranks must be given the second most important post in the government. If this account is credible, and it very well may be, the extremists on the right had outfoxed themselves.[53]

Several hours after Stolypin returned from his meeting with the dowager empress, at 2:00 A.M., a messenger arrived from the tsar with an "amazing letter" of sixteen pages confessing "all matters in which he had not been sufficiently candid with Papa." Nicholas vowed in the future to "work hand in hand" with the prime minister and "to conceal nothing from him of government affairs." No copy of this letter has survived, but a copy of the handwritten note Nicholas sent to Stolypin on March 9 was found in the archives. It is so emotional and so full of admiration for the prime minister that it is worth quoting in its entirety:

> Petr Arkadevich,
>
> For the past four days since our conversation I have thought about my answer from every angle.
>
> I do not wish to permit your departure. Your devotion to me and to Russia, your five-year experience in the post you have occupied and mainly your steadfast conduct of the principles of Russian policies in the outlying regions of the state impel me with all the means at my disposal to retain you. I say this to you with full sincerity and conviction, and not impulsively.
>
> Now let us examine what is being said and thought about you. What unanimous regret, even dejection, is being provoked by the mere rumor of your departure. In the light of all this can you really continue to be stubborn? Of course not. I know in advance that you will agree to remain. I demand this, every true Russian wants this. I request that you, Petr Arkadevich, come to me tomorrow morning, on Thursday, at 11 o'clock in the morning. Remember—my confidence in you remains as complete as it was in 1906. Very sincerely yours, Nikolai.[54]

Stolypin appeared promptly—it must have been on March 10—and agreed to stay at his post, but only if the tsar agreed to prorogue the Duma and the State Council for three days and to banish from St. Petersburg Durnovo and Trepov for "an unspecified leave of absence abroad."[55] Nicholas, who had been informed of Stolypin's conditions, agreed to them. According to one report, the Tsar had implored him to remain in office "with tears in his eyes."[56] Nicholas's acquiescence makes him look extraordinarily weak, but in truth he was subject to very powerful pressures. Not only his mother but also several grand dukes had urged the tsar to keep Stolypin at his post. The grand dukes Alexander Mikhailovich and Nikolai Mikhailovich had argued that without Stolypin Russia would face disintegration.[57]

Stolypin had been warned by men well disposed toward him that he was making a mistake in invoking Article 87 to enact the Western Zemstvo bill. A. I. Guchkov, one of his staunchest defenders ever since 1906, sent him a personal letter predicting that the drastic actions the prime minister was contemplating would produce "utter chaos" in the country. "You know what an ardent and convinced supporter of yours I have been . . . how hateful to me are your enemies, how in particular I supported the Western Zemstvo bill. Nevertheless, I must say to you: the step you are taking is a fateful one, not only for you personally, . . . but for Russia, for the new reformed Russia which is so dear to you, and for which you have done so much."[58] Three other prominent Octobrists made a similar appeal to Stolypin. The prime minister conceded that his plan was a "strain on law," but he nevertheless insisted that it could not be regarded as undermining the Duma since the legislature had already passed the bill. His only concern, he indicated, was to weaken the rightists in the State Council so as to bolster his chances of securing approval of necessary reforms in the future.[59]

Unmoved by appeals to desist, the prime minister on March 12 prorogued the two legislatures, forced the two state councilors, Durnovo and Trepov, to leave St. Petersburg—officially, they were placed on leave of absence until January 1, 1912—and then enacted the zemstvo project by decree. It was a victory that proved to be Stolypin's greatest political blunder as well as one of his most serious violations of the constitution. He had on occasion overstepped the bounds of legality—in revising the electoral law in 1907 and in drafting the decree on the field courts-martial—but never quite so blatantly and provocatively. Article 87 of the Fundamental Laws was designed to enable the government to cope with emergencies at times when the legislatures were not in session. True, in invoking the article to introduce agrarian reform in 1906 the prime minister had interpreted the word "emergency" rather loosely, but the Duma was in recess at the time. Now, in 1911, the Duma was in session and Stolypin could have reintroduced the bill. Even the German ambassador to St. Petersburg, Pourtalès, who held Stolypin in high esteem, concluded that the prime minister's conduct was clearly an "arbitrary interpretation of . . . an article of the Fundamental Laws that is difficult to reconcile with constitutional principles."[60] And in insisting on punishing Durnovo and Trepov, the prime minister appeared to many political leaders and observers to be acting out of pure spite. He had placed the tsar, his source of authority, in the position of having to punish men who were among the most fervent advocates of the autocratic principle.

The reaction to Stolypin's dramatic moves was swift and almost entirely hostile. Appalled by what they considered to be "a huge, unprecedented triumph for Stolypin," the rightists denounced Stolypin's vengefulness, which reminded them, "*mutandum mutandis*, of the era of Biron," when Russia was administered with extraordinary ruthlessness and greed by a foreigner, Biron, who had become a favorite of Empress Anna in the 1730s. On March 14, Count Bobrinskii noted in his diary that "[t]he indignation of Petersburg is boundless. People of every political tendency agree that Stolypin has reached Herculean limits of impudence." Rumors circulated that he had been given the right to exile up to twenty-five members of the State Council, a charge that has never been substantiated. Many people in the ultraconservative camp now feared what they believed to be the prime minister's cardinal vice, his "murderous ambition."[61] At a dinner party of rightists on March 21 the host and the guests were extremely nervous and uncomfortable. "Everyone feels that the *danse macabre* has still not ended and . . . every member of the [State] Council expects Stolypin's [policy of] ostracism will affect him. They look upon themselves as the 'Girondins of the modern era,'" which implied that they regarded Stolypin as another Robespierre.[62]

When Guchkov learned that his advice had been disregarded, his distress turned to anger and despair. He told A. A. Polivanov, the assistant minister of war, that within the short span of a few days the prime minister had managed to offend, irretrievably, every political party and to lose the confidence of all of them. The State Council would never forgive him for having banished two "loyal servants." And the Kadets, Guchkov predicted, would be the ultimate beneficiaries of the political turmoil; they would make significant gains in the upcoming elections for the Duma. Stolypin's political authority would be so severely undermined that he would not survive in office for very long.[63]

Guchkov himself contributed to weakening Stolypin by resigning as president of the Duma. During a personal encounter he told the prime minister that "I cannot work with you any more." The government's "clearly unconstitutional actions" simply left him no choice but to register his disapproval in the strongest possible way. Stolypin "was very much surprised." He simply could not understand, as Guchkov put it, that he had "dealt a blow to our not yet firmly consolidated constitution" and that he had "committed political suicide." Stolypin offered only one defense, which he repeated whenever Duma deputies criticized him during the crisis: "But I have issued the law in the form approved by the Duma." He refused to grasp that the issue was not the substance of the law but the arbitrary way in which it was being enacted.[64]

Guchkov's prediction that public opinion would turn against Stolypin proved to be accurate. Left-wing Octobrists and the Kadets were so outraged that they indicated "they would prefer to see an out-and-out reactionary at the head of the Government rather than a man who had proved false to all his early promises, while he still paraded under the mask of a constitutionalist."[65] And the tsar appeared to be nursing a deep grudge against the prime minister. Every few days, rumors circulated in the capital that Nicholas, still angry at Stolypin, was considering his dismissal.[66]

Two months after the ministerial crisis had abated, the outrage remained at a high pitch. At a social gathering at Tsarskoe Selo in mid-May, Pourtalès, the German ambassador, talked to many prominent people at court and to Duma deputies as well as state councilors, and all of them, friends as well as enemies of Stolypin's, agreed that during the conflict over the Western Zemstvo bill the prime minister, acting from "passion and malice," had committed a serious political blunder. It was an act of "incomprehensible short-sightedness" on Stolypin's part to have antagonized the State Council, an "influential and powerful body in the Russian state." Powerful men in the court entourage would now try to convince the tsar that Stolypin was attempting to assume "omnipotent dictatorial power." But Pourtalès was not persuaded that Nicholas would go so far as to dismiss Stolypin, at least not immediately. At the court function "relations between the monarch and his Prime Minister appeared to be natural and cordial." Several dignitaries assured Pourtalès that the tsar was still grateful to Stolypin for having crushed the revolution "and so far will not agree to his downfall."[67] As was so often the case, Nicholas found it excruciatingly difficult to come to a firm decision on the personnel in his administration. He deeply distrusted strong leaders and yet he sensed that he needed such leaders for the efficient conduct of affairs.

Foreign diplomats and journalists in St. Petersburg sent innumerable reports to Western Europe on the political crisis, describing the intrigues in graphic detail. A. P. Izvolskii, the Russian ambassador to Paris, feared that the accounts reflected so badly on his country that the French authorities might have second thoughts about Russia's stability and its reliability as an ally. On March 14 he sent a telegram to A. A. Neratov, a senior official at the Ministry of Foreign Affairs, asking for more information and clarification of the course of recent events. At the very least, he wanted to clear up the contradictory interpretations of the political situation that had appeared in the French press. Evidently, the ambassador did not know that the Russian press was also putting out conflicting stories. Izvolskii asked whether it would be advisable for him to give an interview to representatives of the local press so as to provide guidance to journalists.

Stolypin was sufficiently concerned to take it upon himself to dictate an immediate response to Izvolskii. He repeated his version of events: right-wing extremists had created an "unnatural alignment of [political] parties" and had thus succeeded in defeating the Western Zemstvo bill. He acknowledged that there had been much distress over his handling of the crisis and conceded that some turbulence in the two legislative chambers could now be expected. But he was confident that calm would soon return, a judgment he based on the belief, soon to be disproved, that the Octobrists had decided against joining the opposition. "It is desirable," Stolypin advised, "for you to direct the press along the proper lines," although he did not think it was necessary for Izvolskii to make personal appeals to journalists. The tone of Stolypin's message suggests that he was not overly perturbed over the repercussions to the crisis.[68]

His sang-froid is surprising, but so is his entire behavior during the crisis, which baffled commentators at the time and has led historians to speculate about Stolypin's equilibrium in the spring of 1911. One respected scholar concluded that Stolypin's decision to prorogue the Duma and the State Council and to punish two of the principal intrigants against him "was not a rational act of statesmanship, but the step of a man driven to nervous exhaustion by the continual struggle against intrigue and now determined to root it out at one blow."[69] Another has argued that the prime minister's behavior "raises questions about his mental state not only at the time of the crisis but in general."[70] Even Solzhenitsyn, who idolizes Stolypin, thought that his conduct in March 1911 was "too hot-headed and too stubborn."[71] There is no doubt that his behavior after the State Council voted against the Western Zemstvo bill was ill-considered and at odds with his usual demeanor. He was a man of strong convictions, and he frequently defended his views vigorously and passionately. But he was not known to be normally ill-tempered or vengeful. Nor was he in the habit of acting impetuously. Whenever he faced a major decision he would carefully consider his options and analyze the various aspects of the problem. On such occasions, he would go to the trouble of jotting down his thoughts on paper to elucidate the grounds for his decision. Stolypin was not a man who rushed to judgment.

To be sure, early in 1911 the pressures on him were formidable, and contemporaries sensed that he was not himself, not as self-assured as he had been.[72] He was clearly under a severe strain. Yet it would be a mistake to ascribe his harsh behavior simply or even primarily to a loss of equilibrium, as mere irrationality. In his mind, serious issues were at stake. If the reactionaries succeeded in blocking his proposals, there would be no chance of realizing his vision of a rejuvenated Russia. He had already suffered several legislative defeats, and if he endured one more—on a matter on which he had staked his personal reputation—his political future would surely be bleak. True, he might have resubmitted the bill to the Duma, but however committed he was to establishing a working partnership between the government and the legislature, he did not want the latter to be an equal partner in that relationship. He still believed in monarchical rule and therefore did not want to be in a position of having to rely too heavily on the legislative branches of the government to secure adoption of his program. At the same time, if he were to function effectively in a monarchical order he needed the full support of the tsar. If the reactionaries succeeded in undermining Nicholas's confidence in him, he would be a spent bullet. The conditions he imposed on the tsar for remaining in office can thus be seen as serving three different goals: to assert his supremacy over the reactionaries, to reaffirm his primacy over the legislature, and to re-establish his authority as the person enjoying the ruler's confidence. His conduct was brazen and provocative. It could also be argued that he was taking a huge risk, a gamble that might backfire. But was his plan irrational, was he acting as a man emotionally out of control?

Very quickly it became clear that the prime minister's actions would not succeed in bending the two legislatures to his will. On March 15, the

Duma adopted, with a lopsided vote of 174 to 88, no fewer than four interpellations questioning the legality of the government's prorogation of the legislature. In the State Council the president, Akimov, tried to prevent a vote, but he failed. On the very same day that the Duma voted the council also voted in favor of an interpellation, again with a decisive vote, 98 to 52. Stolypin thus faced what can only be described as a rebellion in both chambers of the legislature. The deputies and the state councilors wanted the government to respond to some difficult questions. How could it justify invoking Article 87 when no emergency existed? Did the government not take it upon itself to enact a bill that the upper house had rejected, thus undermining the authority of the country's legislative institutions and violating the principle enunciated by the tsar in the October Manifesto that no law would be enacted without approval by the people's representatives?

Stolypin decided to respond to the State Council's interpellation—an unprecedented action by the upper chamber—quickly and resolutely. He was no doubt encouraged by an unusually warm, handwritten note of support from the tsar: "I wish you, Petr Arkadevich, peace of mind and complete success at the State Council. Nikolai."[73] The note, written on the tsar's initiative one day before Stolypin's appearance at the State Council, raises some difficult and interesting questions about the widely held view that Nicholas was so furious at the prime minister for having compelled him to yield to his conditions to prevent his resignation that he would never be reconciled to him. And, inevitably, it raises questions about the view, just as widely held, that Stolypin's days as prime minister were numbered.[74] It may well be, as the historian Manfred Hagen has suggested, that the relationship between Stolypin and Nicholas was not as contentious as has generally been assumed.

Hagen presents some interesting evidence to support his interpretation. In his personal correspondence at the time of the political crisis, the tsar, not known for discretion in his letters to members of his family, never even mentioned Stolypin. It is also known that several people close to the tsar told Stolypin that they continued to support him. Grand Duke Nikolai Mikhailovich assured the prime minister on March 14 of his "deepest respect," "great sympathy and warmest feeling for him." The grand duke also alluded in a derogatory way to the "tactics of those people." Finally, some important political dignitaries, among them the president of the Nationalist fraction, P. N. Balashov, voiced support for the prime minister. Even among the Octobrists there were some who remained loyal to Stolypin. M. V. Rodzianko, a leader of the party and later president of the Fourth Duma, warmly congratulated the prime minister for having overcome the political crisis of March 1911 and expressed the hope that he would have the necessary "courage" and "endurance" to carry on.[75] All this evidence in support of Hagen's thesis fits in with a comment of Pourtalès, the German ambassador, made on May 15, 1911: "A highly placed person in the Tsar's entourage told me recently that one must concede that in the conflict [in March] Mr. Stolypin made mistakes, but his [previous] services and the difficulty in replacing him are so great that one cannot now think of a successor."[76]

Aside from the right-wing extremists, the most influential enemy of Stolypin was undoubtedly the empress, who, it can be safely assumed, resented the prime minister not only because she resented anyone who threatened to overshadow her husband but also because Stolypin had let it be known that he was appalled at the growing influence of Rasputin. A Siberian peasant turned mystic and mountebank, Rasputin greatly impressed the empress and to a somewhat lesser extent the tsar with his presumed ability to hypnotize and save the life of the tsarevich, who suffered from a potentially fatal disease, hemophilia. But Rasputin was also a notorious lecher who had beguiled numerous women at the court. Even Witte and his wife were believed to be taking Rasputin seriously, though some people speculated that Witte displayed fondness for the holy monk only to ingratiate himself with the tsarina in the hope that he would be rewarded with a high government position. On the other hand, many conservatives were outraged that "[t]his good for nothing is at all times admitted to the Palace."[77] Stolypin considered it his duty to warn Nicholas that Rasputin's role at court was widely viewed as a disaster, as a scandal that cast a shadow over the throne. He delivered a report to the tsar on Rasputin's disgraceful misconduct, but Nicholas was not prepared to ignore his wife's wishes by banishing the monk from the court.[78] Early in 1911, the prime minister took the bold step of ordering Rasputin to leave St. Petersburg. Rasputin obeyed, but the empress remained in touch with him; later that year he was allowed to return to the capital.[79]

In view of the empress's hostility toward Stolypin, it is surprising that the tsar, who loved his wife deeply and often followed her advice, plucked up the courage to resist the pressure to dismiss his prime minister. In fact, he even bestowed a new honor on Stolypin. Early in April 1911, Nicholas issued an imperial rescript expressing his appreciation for Stolypin's services to the state and made him a "Knight of the Saint, Grand Duke Aleksandr Nevskii."[80]

Nonetheless, to many of his colleagues Stolypin appeared to be "greatly changed." The widespread and intense hostility toward him seemed to have sapped his self-assurance.[81] Yet on occasion he still gave the impression of being fully in charge and of taking a strong interest in national affairs. This is borne out by a report by P. P. Stremoukhov, governor of Suwalki province. Sometime in the spring of 1911, he went to St. Petersburg to be briefed about his new assignment as governor of Saratov, then a center of right-wing agitation. Since "everyone in the city said that Stolypin was leaving office," Stremoukhov thought it would be pointless to discuss Saratov with him. Still, Stremoukhov kept his appointment with the prime minister, and, to his surprise, Stolypin was "entirely composed" and acted as though he expected to remain in office for a long time. Stolypin spoke authoritatively about Saratov and informed the new governor that he had just ordered the banishment from the province of the chief troublemaker, the monk Iliodor. When Stremoukhov asked if the tsar agreed with the decision, Stolypin answered categorically that the tsar wanted to put an end to Iliodor's "scandalous behavior."[82]

The truth is that the relationship between Nicholas and Stolypin was ambivalent on both sides, and it is best not to be dogmatic about how that relationship, severely tested in the spring of 1911, was destined to end. The tsar needed a forceful prime minister and yet felt uncomfortable with Stolypin, a man with strong opinions that occasionally clashed with his desire to maintain the old order, the order that had prevailed before 1905. Stolypin, on the other hand, revered the monarchy and wished to retain an authoritarian system of rule but at the same time believed that Russia must be modernized socially, economically, and politically. The tsar, it was clear, did not fully appreciate, and probably did not fully understand, Stolypin's vision for the empire and therefore remained reluctant to give his prime minister unqualified support. It was, in short, an uneasy relationship based on the conviction of each that he needed the other.

The mutual ambivalence manifested itself strikingly in an exchange of letters late in April and early in May of 1911. Only Stolypin's letter has survived, but it is evident that he was responding to a note from Nicholas indicating a wish to pardon Durnovo and permit him to return to the capital after only three of the twelve months in the original order of banishment. The tsar's leniency has been interpreted not only as a sign of his fondness for the rightists but also of the weakness of Stolypin's position.[83] But that is not the most plausible interpretation of the exchange of letters. Stolypin's very firm and lengthy response to the tsar, in which he argued against a pardon for Durnovo, suggests that the prime minister felt secure enough to oppose the monarch on a matter about which Nicholas had strong opinions. Indeed, Nicholas heeded Stolypin's advice and did not permit Durnovo to return to the capital until the fall of 1911, when Stolypin was no longer on the scene. Although in the relationship between the two men the tsar enjoyed the upper hand, Stolypin was not without influence.

In his letter, Stolypin acknowledged that he had wrestled for some time with his conscience in deciding how to respond to the tsar's wish to pardon Durnovo. Much as he tried, he could not forget "Durnovo's indefatigable activities" in the State Council in seeking to obstruct the government's work. And from various press accounts it was clear that even after his banishment he continued to attack the government. In any case, pardoning Durnovo at this time would serve no practical purpose. He was scheduled to leave the country for two to three weeks, and when he returned the council would no longer be in session. A pardon would therefore be interpreted as a change of policy by the government; it would appear to the Duma and the State Council that the government was wavering in its determination to enact the Western Zemstvo measure on the basis of Article 87. Stolypin concluded that it was his "firm belief that the wisest course would be to postpone the question of a pardon until a more suitable time—when . . . [Durnovo] would be able to resume his work in the legislature." In a postscript, Stolypin sought to appear reasonable without, however, retreating an inch. "Forgive me, Your Majesty, for the boldness [with which I voice] my candid views, which are expressed by me out of a sense of duty and out of regard for my oath of office; believe me, the last thing I would want to do is to affect your freedom to decide."[84] The tone of this letter was not that of a man in despair over his lost authority, of a man who felt crushed by setbacks.

On the contrary, it was the tone of a man convinced that he had not made a mistake in bypassing the legislatures. That is also the approach he adopted in his speeches in both chambers in the month preceding the letter to the tsar. His appearance in the State Council on April 1 was eagerly awaited; "the entire city is once again agitated. What will he say?"[85] It would not be easy for him to face so hostile an audience. In the debates on the interpellation before the prime minister's appearance, which no minister attended, the denunciations of the government had been fierce. Prince Trubetskoi made a point of emphasizing that even though the upper chamber had the right to challenge an action by the government it has almost never done so. But now the State Council had no choice but to discharge "a great and sacred responsibility to both the throne and the homeland." The prime minister's conduct had been unprecedented and amounted to nothing less than a breach of the Fundamental Laws of the empire. The government, Trubetskoi concluded, had an obligation to explain its conduct to legislators, many of whom were normally well disposed to it.[86] In his reply, Stolypin immediately took responsibility for the government's action, asserting that he had been guided only by his understanding of "state necessity" and not by any desire to disregard or show disrespect for the rights and opinions of "that lofty institution in which I have the honor to present my explanation."

As Stolypin perceived the drift of the debate, his critics had raised three closely related questions. Was the resort to Article 87 legal? Did an emergency exist that justified the application of Article 87? Did Stolypin establish a precedent for disregarding and insulting the two legislatures? Stolypin granted that suspension of the legislative chambers should be undertaken only under extraordinary circumstances, but he insisted that it was the duty of the government to defend the prerogatives of the crown and that there could be no doubt that the tsar had the constitutional right to suspend the chambers at any time he considered such action warranted. In support of his position he referred to several Russian scholars and to "a whole galaxy of German and Austrian scholars." He also contended that Article 86 of the Fundamental Laws, which stipulated that bills became law only after passage by both chambers and acceptance by the monarch, was not intended to "paralyze" the applicability of Article 87. If that were the case, the authority of the sovereign would be weakened to an unacceptable and unprecedented degree. In no state with a constitutional provision for the application of emergency measures was the legal authority of the government limited in this manner.

Stolypin also insisted that Western scholars generally agreed that only the government had the right to decide on the specific conditions justifying the application of emergency measures. The claim by state councilors that this right belonged to the legislatures "contradicts the spirit of our Fundamental Laws as well as the established practice of Western European states." He rejected as absurd the notion that he had established a dangerous precedent. After all, Article 87 did not empower the government to rule permanently without participation of the two legislative chambers. Any decree enacted under Article 87 must be presented for a vote to the Duma and the State Council within two months after the two assemblies reconvened. If the assemblies voted down the decree it would become null and void. But the principal guarantee against abuse of Article 87 lies in the "control" exercised by the "highest authority." "In a state administered in accordance with monarchical principles, there cannot be a more powerful, a more important guarantee." After all, that authority, the tsar, was also entrusted with an even more awesome responsibility, the prevention of an unjustified declaration of war by the legislative branch.

To be sure, invocation of Article 87 may not be an ideal instrument of government, but sometimes it was necessary to resort to it; he compared it to a tracheotomy, a procedure doctors used "when an ill person is suffocating and it is necessary to insert a pipe in the throat to facilitate breathing." Similarly, drastic measures were occasionally inevitable in the political realm "when friction absorbs all . . . [the] work" of a new representative body. As the political culture of a country matured, such measures would become superfluous, and, he assured his listeners, they would disappear in Russia. He also assured the state councilors that he intended to resort to them only rarely and with "extreme caution and circumspection." It pained him, he declared at the end of his speech, that the State Council felt abused and insulted by the government's action on the Western Zemstvo bill. It was not his intention to denigrate the legislatures. His only concern was to prevent serious harm to national interests, which would have been the consequence of the failure to enact the Western Zemstvo bill.[87]

Stolypin's speech to the State Council was a spirited and uncompromising defense of his recent conduct, interesting not only for its justification of his every action but also for its capacious definition of monarchical rule in Russia. But if he thought that his arguments would secure him wide support in the State Council, he was to be deeply disappointed. By a vote of ninety-nine to fifty-three the chamber upheld the interpellation and thus declared that the prime minister had failed to refute the charges against his government. It could not have been much consolation to him that there was not an official vote of censure because his opponents failed to muster a two-thirds majority.

About four weeks after the debacle in the State Council, Stolypin sought to persuade the Duma to abandon its interpellations, again without success. For the most part, his arguments were identical to those he had presented in the upper chamber. But a careful reading of his comments reveals somewhat different emphases in the two speeches. In the more conservative upper chamber, he stressed the role of the tsar in the administration of the state. In the Duma, he dwelt on the dangers that the State Council's rejection of a measure passed by the lower house posed to its authority. In the future, all major reforms would be at risk because the upper chamber would now feel freer to veto measures passed by the Duma. He also contended, in an obvious attempt to remind the deputies of their newly won power, that never before had "a question of such deep national significance . . . been introduced for action by [elected] representatives." The deputies should not lose sight of the historical significance of this fact: "[O]nly in the reign of Nicholas II has faith in the people resulted in a summons of the people to decide national affairs" on a matter crucial for the creation of a new Russia. "We are protecting the future of our country and are boldly hammering the nails—together with you—of the structure of Russia, which we are not ashamed to say will be Russian; and this responsibility is the greatest pleasure of my life." Many deputies greeted these words with shouts of "Bravo."[88] But the appeals to the Duma's nationalism and to the principle of popular participation in government were dismissed even more dramatically than the appeal to the principle of autocracy in the upper house. The deputies voted, 203 to 82, in favor of a Kadet motion rejecting as unsatisfactory Stolypin's explanation of his resort to Article 87. This was a two-thirds majority, and according to the Fundamental Laws, whenever two-thirds of the Duma rejected a minister's explanation in response to an interpellation the case could be referred to the tsar for adjudication. But the deputies, no doubt expecting defeat, failed to submit the matter to the sovereign.

In the short run, the government faced a more serious threat than the adverse votes in the two chambers. By law, Stolypin had to submit the Western Zemstvo measure to the Duma for its consideration within sixty days after it reconvened. Anticipating certain defeat, he decided to adjourn the legislature on May 13, some six weeks before its planned adjournment and one day before the deadline for the resubmission of the bill. When the two legislatures reconvened late in 1911 they voted in favor of the Western Zemstvo bill, but this happened months after many of its provisions had already been implemented. Much of the rancor had dissipated, since Stolypin was no longer alive. Moreover, the results of the elections in the southwestern provinces seemed to justify Stolypin's prediction that the bill would serve Russia well.

For over two months, from early March through mid-May, Stolypin had survived, against all odds and almost all predictions, one crisis after another and had prevailed in the struggle with the Duma and State Council. Still, most knowledgeable contemporaries believed that he had paid a very high price for his survival and that his tenure as prime minister remained precarious. The tsar was said to be smarting from the humiliation of having been compelled to accept Stolypin's conditions to prevent his resignation. A majority of the Octobrists had announced their withdrawal of support from the prime minister, a decision that ended the alliance between the moderate liberals and the government.

The extremists on the right remained as hostile as ever to Stolypin, whom they now seemed to despise and fear almost as much as the Kadets or people to the left of them. The newspapers carried a stream of reports, some true and some false, about elaborate intrigues against the prime minister. Only the Nationalists remained loyal to Stolypin, but that was not enough to secure adoption of legislation he wished to enact. The British embassy's judgment in mid-June 1911 about Stolypin's tenuous hold on power seems to have reflected the consensus of the political class in St. Petersburg: "[It] would need but some comparatively trifling incident to lead His Majesty finally to decide upon accepting his resignation."[89]

The crisis had taken its toll on Stolypin, who was physically exhausted and appeared to be thoroughly dejected. Bernard Pares, who saw him in July, reported that Stolypin was "sunken and listless" and "talked a great deal of resigning."[90] Kokovtsov recalled that although Stolypin never told him whether the crises had affected his relations with the tsar, the prime minister "was greatly changed—everyone agreed on this. Something inside him seemed to have snapped; his former assurance had left him as he had perceived the hostility with which he was surrounded."[91]

Yet, some astute observers refused to rule out a change of attitude toward the prime minister by the political class and even anticipated his survival in office. In the very report in which Bernard Pares spoke of Stolypin's political vulnerability, the scholar also pointed out that people did not exclude the possibility that "passions will subside before the autumn." Although Duma deputies still resented the government's "rough-handed methods," they might still accept their "own bill" on the western zemstvos. For all the talk that Stolypin was worse than a reactionary, they feared that if a reactionary actually replaced Stolypin conditions would be worse. "This is not a country where the condemnation of certain actions in the Minister can secure an opposite policy." If the reactionaries succeeded in ousting Stolypin, the consequence would be "the loss of a great deal of the progress which has been made so painfully." Moreover, no one to the left of the Nationalists could think of a successor to Stolypin who would be better. "Men have been used up terribly fast in Russia . . . [and there] are too few of them to start with."[92] Pares, to be sure, was generally sympathetic to Stolypin, but his analysis was not implausible.

Certainly, the early results from the elections to the district zemstvos in the western provinces tended to strengthen Stolypin's hand. These elections, it should be recalled, were held in accordance with the provisions of the imperial edict issued under the emergency regulations of Article 87, the application of which had caused the political crisis in March. The rightists' prediction that the elections would provoke intense hatred between the Poles and Russians proved to be unfounded, as did their warning that zemstvo assemblies would be composed of "ultra-democratic" deputies devoid of the education and culture necessary for public service. The Poles, in fact, succeeded in winning anywhere from 8.5 to 17 percent of the seats, considerably more than their proportion of the population. Many leading Polish landowners were elected, as were many wealthy Russian proprietors. And a sizable number of the peasant deputies represented agricultural associations, which were either conservative or Nationalist in their politics. Even though questions had been raised about the fairness of the elections and the size of the turnout, very few contested the outcome, which was clearly a victory for the government and a good omen for the government in the upcoming elections to the Fourth Duma.[93] It was also seen by some as a vindication of Stolypin's decision to establish the zemstvos in the west, and that could hardly have gone unnoticed at court. Certainly, the Nationalists did not stint in their praise of Stolypin. "Hail this great man," a columnist in their paper, *Podolianin*, wrote on July 16, "who, with his strong hand, guided the Russian ship of state along the path of national renewal. West Russia will not forget P. A. Stolypin."[94] When Stolypin left the capital in the summer of 1911 for his summer retreat at Kolnoberzhe, he left behind a hostile Duma and State Council and a monarch still suspicious of him, but his political standing appears to have improved more than anyone would have believed possible only two months earlier.

9

Assassination

The eight-week ordeal, beginning on March 4 with the State Council's rejection of the Western Zemstvo bill and ending with the votes on the interpellation of the government late in April, had left Stolypin politically wounded but unshaken in his conviction that he had pursued the right policies. "I do not doubt in the least," he told A. V. Zenkovsky sometime in May, "that ultimately both legislative institutions will fully applaud my position about elective zemstvos in the Western provinces."[1] In the meantime, he worked on an ambitious master plan of national reconstruction, as if to demonstrate to foe and friend alike that the recent attacks on him and the defeats in the legislative chambers had not paralyzed him. The resulting report called for a thorough reorganization of the country's administrative structure and for a series of reforms, some new and some revivals of reforms that had previously been quashed or defeated in the legislatures. The report itself has not survived, but a detailed statement of his plans, dictated to Zenkovsky over four days in May, appeared in the West in 1956. According to Stolypin's daughter and Zenkovsky's associate, A. F. Meyendorf (formerly assistant president of the Duma and a cousin of Stolypin's), the statement was among Stolypin's papers in Kolnoberzhe and mysteriously disappeared shortly after his death, apparently during a government commission's screening of the materials in the prime minister's study. But Zenkovsky, who emigrated from Russia in 1920, had retained a copy of the statement, which for some reason he chose not to make public until the 1950s.[2]

Stolypin had no illusions about the tsar's attitude toward him. He knew that he did not share his commitment to reform and that he felt that the prime minister had exerted undue pressure on him to banish two loyal rightists from St. Petersburg. Nevertheless, Stolypin believed that Nicholas would be moved by his love for Russia to approve the proposals in his report. On the other hand, Stolypin was not at all sure that the Duma and State Council would vote for them. If his initiatives were in fact turned down in the legislative chambers, he was inclined to dissolve the Third Duma and launch a campaign for a more amenable Fourth Duma. In the interval between the dissolution and the elections, he would again seek to invoke Article 87 to implement his reforms.[3] Stolypin's recent clashes with the legislatures and his defeats had not mellowed him.

His plan for the reorganization was bold and far-reaching, the most detailed articulation of his vision for Russia. But before taking up its contents, it should be noted that the authenticity of the document has been questioned. The Soviet historian A. Ia. Avrekh claimed to have found some serious mistakes in Zenkovsky's work, which included not only Stolypin's statement on the reorganization of Russia but also several chapters on the prime minister's dealings with the Duma and the State Council and a brief account by Zenkovsky's son on how the manuscript came to be published. In addition there is a description by Alexander Zenkovsky of his personal contacts with Stolypin and an explanation of why the prime minister chose him as the person to take down his views on future reforms. Zenkovsky claimed to have been both a professor and head of the financial and budget division of the Kiev zemstvo from 1903 to 1919; it was in the latter capacity that he traveled on business to St. Petersburg on several occasions and met the prime minister. Stolypin chose him as the interlocutor in 1911 because he did not trust the bureaucrats in the Ministry of Internal Affairs to carry out his wishes to expand the authority of the zemstvos. Zenkovsky, on the other hand, had extensive experience in local self-government and, in Stolypin's view, was therefore much more likely than the bureaucrats to be sympathetic to his plan to delegate more powers to the zemstvos.

Avrekh challenged the veracity of Zenkovsky's account. In the first place, he asserted that Zenkovsky could not have been an employee of the Kiev zemstvo before 1911 because it was only in that year that such an institution was established in the city. Avrekh also noted that Zenkovsky claimed to have been a professor but never told the reader when and at which institution he held that title or what subject he taught. In general, Zenkovsky supplied very little autobiographical information; he referred only to acquaintances in Russia who were no longer alive, and thus his account could not be verified. And why, Avrekh asked, did he wait some thirty-odd years before making his document public? According to a handbook on Kiev (*Ves Kiev*) for 1912, Alexander Vasilevich Zenkovsky was a bookkeeper at the Kiev Provincial Office (or Board) on the Economy. In the handbooks for previous years, the name Zenkovsky does not appear at all. "Thus . . . Zenkovsky was not and could not have been acquainted with Stolypin."

Some of Avrekh's doubts can be readily overcome. It is true that before 1911 there was no elected zemstvo in Kiev, but in 1903 the government established provincial and district committees and boards, whose members were appointed by the Ministry of Internal Affairs, with jurisdictions very similar to those of zemstvos. In fact, they were popularly known as "margarine" zemstvos, which no doubt explains Zenkovsky's reference to the agency for which he worked as a zemstvo—strictly speaking not correct but hardly a gross distortion. In any case, he worked there until 1919, and in 1911 it had become a zemstvo in the strict sense. As for the professorial title, it is known that Zenkovsky was a professor at the Juridical Faculty of the Russian University in Prague in the 1920s and 1930s.

There is reason, furthermore, to question Avrekh's motives in challenging the authenticity of Zenkovsky's book. Avrekh bore such deep animus toward Stolypin, evident in all his scholarly writings, that he seems to have been predisposed to distrust and distort Zenkovsky's book, which depicts the prime minister favorably. For example, Avrekh claims that Zenkovsky portrays the prime minister as a "one hundred percent liberal."[4] But that is simply incorrect. In the statement reproduced by Zenkovsky, Stolypin makes it clear that his concern was to neutralize "Russia's internal enemies who wish to overthrow the monarchy and the existing social order." Nor did Stolypin so much as hint at the possibility of reducing the tsar's authority; he referred to him as the "Sovereign [who] was completely responsible before God and his people to select as Chairman of the Council of Ministers the most capable of national leaders."[5] It is true that many of the changes that Stolypin proposed in his statement were designed to liberalize social and economic conditions in Russia, but that did not make him a full-fledged liberal as the term was understood at the time. He did not favor the replacement of monarchical rule with a parliamentary system of government, as Avrekh surely knew.

There is another reason for giving Zenkovsky the benefit of the doubt about the authenticity of his book. Not a single idea in the statement that he attributed to the prime minister is inconsistent with the reforms Stolypin had championed ever since the 1890s. The plan for the reorganization of Russia that he put forth in 1911 was much more elaborate and specific than any he had previously proposed, but it did not mark a significant shift in outlook. It could actually be viewed as a summary statement of his vision as a public servant and statesman.

The contents of the plan can be easily summed up. Stolypin recommended the establishment of seven new ministries, each one of which would be charged with formulating legislative proposals to improve conditions in its jurisdiction. A Ministry of Labor was needed, Stolypin argued, to study working-class conditions in Western European states and America and to report to the Council of Ministers on the feasibility of emulating the policies of those countries, in all of which progress had been made in improving the lot of the masses. "After the workers' cultural and economic needs are met, they will not be that revolutionary proletariat which they were in 1905 but will enjoy equal rights with the conscientious citizenry and petty bourgeoisie. As participants in the national structure they will not yield to propaganda from Russia's internal enemies. In fact, they will doubtless become defenders of the newly reorganized regime of Russia."[6]

A new Ministry of Local Self-Government would supervise the work of local political institutions, whose authority was to be expanded. Property qualifications for participation in zemstvo activities would be "reduced to one-tenth" of the prevailing level and, "with the exception of lunatics and criminals," every citizen "regardless of nationality or creed" would be granted the suffrage in local elections. A new Ministry of Nationalities would seek to improve conditions for all the nationalities; the goals would be to end conflict between them and to turn them into "loyal subjects of Russia." A Ministry of Social Security would be charged with developing a system of "guarantees" for every citizen "in case of disability, illness, unemployment, and so forth." A Ministry of Creeds would undertake to reorganize the institutions of the Orthodox Church, restore the patriarchate in Russia, and establish new ecclesiastical academies. To promote economic development, Stolypin proposed the establishment of a Ministry for Investigation, Utilization, and Exploitation of the Natural Resources of Russia. Finally, he urged the creation of a Ministry of Public Health Care to provide additional funds to the zemstvos, which supervised medical facilities throughout the country. The ultimate aim should be to develop a program that would "render free medical assistance to the people."[7]

Stolypin also urged the radical reorganization of every other ministry to turn them into more efficient institutions. To achieve his overall program, he believed it would be necessary to institute a progressive income tax from which the poor would be entirely exempt, raise salaries of policemen and of certain higher-ranking civil servants (to reduce corruption), establish a system of "free minimal education" for all children, enlarge the network of railways, and take "unusually stern measures" to stamp out both pogroms and internal disorders. In discussing the need to cope with the "feeble development of industry," Stolypin bemoaned the fact that the Jews of Russia, a large group, had not been allowed to participate fully in the country's economy. "One cannot deny that Jews are talented financiers and merchants" and that they had made significant contributions to various sectors of the economy in other European states. It seemed to him "desirable to remove all restrictions on Jews in Russia," a proposal that clearly included the abolition of the Pale of Settlement. Although Stolypin stressed that primary responsibility for the operation of governmental agencies rested with the tsar, he reiterated the importance of the principle of united government. "All ministers presented by the Chairman of the Council of Ministers to the Sovereign must be responsible to the Chairman. And reports by specific ministers to the Sovereign must always have prior approval of the Chairman."[8]

In the last part of his statement, Stolypin focused on foreign policy. He had insisted all along that Russia was too weak to pursue an assertive foreign policy and that the government must devote its energies to domestic rejuvenation. Now, in 1911, he urged the creation of an international parliament composed of representatives of all states, to resolve misunderstandings between nations by peaceful means. It may well be that he made this proposal to please Tsar Nicholas, one of whose pet projects ever since 1898 had been the convocation of international conferences "for the maintenance of universal peace and a possible reduction of the excessive armaments." In 1899 and again in 1907 such conferences were held at The Hague, both on the initiative of the Russian government. They did not achieve their primary goal, but they did outlaw some especially inhumane weapons and created the Permanent Court of Arbitration.[9] Now Stolypin proposed an international parliament to focus not only on political conflicts but also on economic questions; it would create an international bank to provide credits and advice to countries "to avert those periodic economic crises in both industry and agriculture which inevitably occur first in one state and then in another."

Interestingly, Stolypin singled out the United States as a country with which he wished to develop closer relations. Like Russia, the United States was so rich in natural resources that it had no interest in enlarging "its territory nor [in] seiz[ing] any colonies or [in] exploit[ing] people." He also admired the United States for its great economic achievements and for the "exceptional energy" of its people. He considered it likely that the United States would gradually overtake England as the most powerful country in the world. Unfortunately, the "propaganda from Russia's internal foes" had predisposed Americans to dislike Russia. He wished to correct the false impressions of Americans and for that purpose planned, "with the Sovereign's approval," to visit Washington in the near future. He also intended to invite prominent Americans to Russia so that they "might see for themselves that freedom exists in Russia and not oppression of nationalities as charged by Russia's foes." American visitors would quickly realize that the average "Russian is as friendly and goodhearted as the Russians have always been."[10]

No definitive conclusion about Stolypin's motives in preparing the grandiose plan is possible. Did he believe that he would remain at the helm of the government for some time to come and therefore wished to map out his future policies, building on the creation of zemstvos in the western provinces? Did he intend to impress the tsar with his energy and imagination, making it more difficult for Nicholas to dismiss him? Or was he resigned to leave office and wanted to establish a legacy to his liking?

Stolypin's personal and public conduct in the weeks following the drafting of the report provide clues to his state of mind but nothing more conclusive. When, early in June, Stolypin went to his beloved Kolnoberzhe for the summer, even his own family was not privy to his innermost thoughts and feelings. He had asked Kokovtsov to handle many of the administrative duties during his absence from the capital, but he continued to be actively involved in affairs of state and remained in constant touch with St. Petersburg. But he did appear to be a man under a terrible strain. His daughter "had never seen him so exhausted," and he himself confessed that he "felt on the verge of exhaustion." Before leaving St. Petersburg, he had visited his doctor for a checkup and discovered that he suffered from angina pectoris. The doctor recommended a complete and long rest. The prime minister told his son that he planned to follow the doctor's advice at Kolnoberzhe "without harm to business, and then go south in the fall." Ominously, he added: "I do not know if I will live that long." A post mortem revealed that both his liver and heart were severely diseased, and his doctors believed that he probably did not have long to live.[11]

Late in August, Stolypin was scheduled to travel to Kiev for a series of major ceremonies and celebrations attended by the tsar and numerous dignitaries: the unveiling of a statue for Tsar Alexander II, the consecration of the Pedagogical Museum, the one hundredth anniversary of Kiev High School (gymnasium), the laying of the foundation for the planned agrarian and industrial exposition in 1913. In addition, the visiting officials planned to attend some large military maneuvers in several towns near Kiev.

For several months, local authorities made elaborate preparations to ensure smooth traffic and security during the tsar's stay. A large number of police officers from St. Petersburg, Moscow, Riga, Kharkov, Warsaw, and even from Siberia and the Caucasus, as well as some three hundred detectives and numerous *Okhrana* officials, were to be assembled in Kiev. General P. G. Kurlov, the assistant minister of internal affairs and chief of the Corps of Gendarmes; M. N. Verigin, the deputy director of police; General A. I. Spiridovich, chief of the security police protecting the emperor; and some of their senior assistants, came to the city to exercise overall supervision over security arrangements. As the senior police official, Kurlov had ultimate responsibility for security during the tsar's presence in Kiev. The detectives conducted thorough searches of some three hundred buildings "from the roof to the cellars" and made many arrests of suspects, all of which naturally aroused the interest of local citizens and especially of hotel owners. The preparations were so extensive that many inhabitants of Kiev knew long before the tsar's arrival not only that their city would be visited by Nicholas but also the precise route of the royal entourage from St. Petersburg through the Ukraine.

The festivities began in Kiev on August 29. Large crowds lined the streets and gave Nicholas an enthusiastic welcome.[12]

Citizens had been warned not to throw flowers at the tsarist carriage, and on August 20 they were informed that tickets to various celebrations would be distributed by employees in Kurlov's office. Kurlov had instructed his subordinates to screen applicants carefully and not to issue passes to anyone who aroused their suspicions. Security seemed to be airtight.

Stolypin had arrived in Kiev during the night, at about 12:45 A.M. on August 27 and had stayed at the home of the governor-general. Early in the morning he attended prayers and then began to receive delegations from the local nobility, zemstvos, and the city council and spent some time working on matters that had been referred to him by his office in St. Petersburg. Kokovtsov arrived on the morning of August 29 and immediately paid Stolypin a visit. "I found him in a gloomy mood. During later conversations I learned that he was being almost ignored at court; no court carriage had been assigned to him, nor had room been found for him on the Imperial boat for the trip to Chernigov. He was very gracious to me, however, going out of his way to thank me for the work I had done as Minister of Finance."[13] This characterization of Stolypin as a man in an unhappy frame of mind can be found in several memoirs written years after his death. Guchkov even went so far as to claim that the last time he saw Stolypin, the prime minister was "very depressed . . .

He had said : 'I am sure I shall be assassinated by a member of the secret police.' It was noted in Kiev that Stolypin was . . . left out of the special measures taken for the protection of the sovereign. Inviting Kokovtsov to share his carriage, he himself commented on this, and spoke again of assassination." Guchkov also sensed that Stolypin no longer felt capable of dealing with the "irresponsible court influences." He was bitter over the support that he believed the tsar was giving the "fanatic Iliodor," a monk who engaged in "Black Hundred propaganda" in Saratov and who was undermining the authority of the government. No longer confident that he could withstand the pressures from his enemies, Stolypin, it seemed to Guchkov, "was coming to a decision to give up his post."[14]

Kryzhanovskii, the prime minister's loyal assistant, also recalled that in the summer of 1911, Stolypin feared that he might not survive the trip to Kiev. But for some reason Kryzhanovskii chose not to include this rather interesting information in his published recollections, which appeared in Germany in 1938. A brief account of his last meeting with the prime minister can be found in the unpublished portions of his memoirs. In contrast to Guchkov, Kryzhanovskii claimed that Stolypin feared not assassination but a natural death. "I am afraid," Stolypin is quoted as having said, "that I will not come back [from Kiev]." He revealed that his heart was in very poor condition, that he had had two fainting fits, and that he had a premonition that he did not have long to live. Determined to avoid alarming his wife, he asked Kryzhanovskii to remain silent about his illness. Stolypin then gave Kryzhanovskii four large, sealed packages that contained his "secret archive," with the request that he burn them in the event of his death. Stolypin did not want his successor to "rummage" through them. But at the end of the meeting the prime minister also stipulated that if Kryzhanovskii could safeguard the packages he should retain them and pass them on to Stolypin's son when he reached his twenty-first birthday. All that Kryzhanovskii knew about the packages' contents was that they included Stolypin's reports to the tsar and materials touching on the political crisis of March 1911 and the financial scandal involving V. I. Gurko. Kryzhanovskii noted that he burned the packages during the night of March 2, 1911. He obviously meant early in March 1917, in the early stages of the revolution that overthrew tsarism.[15]

These recollections of Stolypin's pessimism and gloom during his stay in Kiev late in August 1911 have often been cited by publicists and historians to buttress the notion that Stolypin's tenure as prime minister was coming to a close and that he himself realized it. However, there is evidence to suggest that the recollections may have been retrospective reflections on what Stolypin's mood should have been, given his fate on September 1, rather than on his actual mood.

Certainly, the one extant, personal letter by Stolypin written at the time, in the evening of August 28, probably the last letter or document he wrote, does not convey the image of a man in total despair and ready to give up the ghost. If anything, it gives the impression that Stolypin was enjoying his busy schedule and taking delight on learning of various developments in the western provinces that confirmed his optimistic assessments of the region's political future.

The letter was sent to his wife, whom he addressed with his usual warmth: "My dear angel, I thought of you throughout my journey." He noted that in Vilna his train was coupled with one carrying L. O. Kasso, the minister of education, and V. K. Sabler, procurator of the Most Holy Synod. Even though he arrived late at night, he was met at the station by senior officials, a group of nobles, and members of zemstvos from three provinces. He also noted, without complaint, that "he was in harness" all day long, first at church services, then at the Museum of Tsarevich Alexei, and, finally, at the "highlight," a meeting with some two hundred zemstvo deputies from the six western provinces where zemstvos had only recently been established at his insistence under Article 87. The group, which included magnates, middle-level nobles, and peasants, had come to Kiev to greet the tsar. "I gave a short speech. Representatives from all 6 provinces responded. My general impression was that [the group] was full of elation bordering on enthusiasm." There could be no doubt, he wrote his wife, that the zemstvo men who responded to his speech—in his view, "true Russians"—were enthusiastic about their work. "This was denied by the left and the extremists on the right. I was guided by my faith, and now even the blind have begun to see clearly."[16] The friendly meeting with the zemstvo officials was yet another indication to Stolypin that his policy on the expansion of the zemstvos was the right one; he clearly felt vindicated.

On September 1, Stolypin attended a performance of Rimsky-Korsakov's *The Tale of Tsar Sultan* at the Municipal Kiev Theater, the major entertainment scheduled for the dignitaries visiting the city. Every notable in Kiev at the time seems to have been present: the tsar and the young grand duchesses, three ministers aside from Stolypin, members of the court, senior government officials, and many local dignitaries. Stolypin occupied a seat in the first row of the pit, not far from the governor-general's box in which the tsar and his daughters were seated. During the second intermission, Stolypin stood up, faced the audience, most of whom were in the foyer, and talked casually to people who approached him. Baron Frederiks, the minister of the court, and Sukhomlinov, the minister of war, were standing nearby, also chatting amiably. Suddenly, a young man dressed in evening clothes walked toward the prime minister from the rear of the theater without ever being stopped or questioned by any of the policemen and detectives in the building. However, according to one report, "Stolypin seems to have noticed him, and to have looked interrogatively at him, as if to ask him what he wanted. Before . . . he could say anything the young man drew a revolver and fired two shots point blank at his Excellency. One ball struck M. Stolypin's right hand, and the other entered his body just beneath the right breast, striking the cross of one of the orders which he was wearing." Without losing consciousness, Stolypin sunk into his seat, tried to open his jacket, and looking up at the imperial box made what witnesses interpreted as a sign of the Cross.[17] It was a fitting act of a seriously wounded man who was both deeply religious and utterly devoted to the monarchy.

On hearing the shots, the audience panicked and pandemonium broke loose; in the confusion the assassin almost managed to escape, but one of the police officials recognized him and took him into custody. The audience rushed at the assassin, who would have been lynched had policemen not come to his rescue. The tsar, who was in a drawing room with his daughters at the time of the shooting, made an uncharacteristically imaginative gesture: he returned to his box, stepped up to the front row, and pointedly faced the audience. "He was enthusiastically acclaimed"; at the request of the audience the orchestra played the national anthem, which was sung by the entire opera company kneeling on the stage.[18]

In the meantime, Stolypin had been rushed to the Makovskii Hospital, where he languished for four days. At first, the medical reports were encouraging: on September 2, the doctors indicated that the prime minister's general condition was "entirely satisfactory." He had not lost much blood, the pulse stood at seventy, and the bullet that had penetrated his body seemed not to have caused serious injury. His liver had been damaged, but the doctors did not consider it necessary to perform an operation to remove the bullet.[19] For two days Stolypin seemed to be on the road to recovery: he engaged in lively conversation with Kokovtsov and continued to show interest in administrative affairs. On September 3, his wife arrived and found him in a cheerful mood. On that day the tsar also came to the hospital and briefly spoke to Stolypin, though Nicholas later claimed that Olga Borisovna would not let him see the patient for fear of agitating him unduly. By nightfall that day he suddenly took a turn for the worse and began to lapse into periods of unconsciousness. The next morning the doctors concluded that his condition was hopeless. Doctors tried to talk to him, but he was incoherent much of the time. Only one word that he repeated several times could be clearly deciphered; it was "Finland." In a letter of September 9, 1911, to the tsar, Olga Borisovna (Stolypin's wife), thanked the monarch for his kindness toward her and ended with an account of the prime minister's last words, uttered twenty minutes before his death: "The main thing is that the word *Finland* has been heard."[20] If he was still in command of his mental powers when he uttered that single word, it would be a further confirmation of how much importance he attached to Russian hegemony over Finland.

Toward the evening of the fifth he spoke one more sentence, "Turn on the light!" and then died. The next day Nicholas returned from Chernigov to Kiev and immediately went to the hospital. "He sank to his knees before the body of the faithful servant and offered prayers for a long while. Those present heard him repeat over and over the words, 'Forgive me.' Afterward, the requiem was said in his presence."[21] The tsar's words are not easy to interpret. Were they the general comments of a pious Christian asking for forgiveness for any wrongs he may have done against him throughout their five-year period of collaboration? Or was Nicholas apologizing for having been cool toward the prime minister during the preceding five months, since the ministerial crisis in March?

Two letters Nicholas wrote to his mother only days after Stolypin's death do not provide conclusive answers to these questions, but they do demonstrate once again the extraordinary callousness of the tsar. In the first, Nicholas recounted in some detail his activities in Tsarskoe Selo during the last days before his departure for Kiev: he attended various meetings, official receptions, two weddings, and several military maneuvers—all these events went off splendidly. Then he mentioned the meetings and receptions he attended in Kiev, including a talk with the son of the Bulgarian tsar, before touching on the most dramatic event, the "dirty assassination of Stolypin." When he heard what turned out to be the shots he thought at first that some binoculars had fallen down somewhere in the theater. He immediately returned to his box and saw Stolypin, who "slowly turned toward me and crossed himself with his left arm." Nicholas heard the cries of members of the audience who wanted to do away with the assassin. Astonishingly, he expressed regret that the lynching did not succeed. "In my view, unfortunately the police removed him to a separate location for the first interrogation. Still, he was severely crumpled and two of his teeth were knocked out."

As for the slain prime minister, the tsar referred to him simply as "poor Stolypin" and noted his acute suffering during the night after the shooting, when he had to be given injections of morphine. He briefly mentioned the funeral, describing the demeanor of Stolypin's wife: "The poor widow stood like a statue and could not weep." Then, in the very same paragraph Nicholas told his mother about the "splendid" parade of the army that he had observed in a town some thirty miles from Kiev. He left Kiev by boat for Sevastopol on September 7: "It was a great pleasure to board the yacht again!" Nicholas expressed no sadness at all about losing so loyal a servant as Stolypin and said nothing about his contributions to Russia. But Nicholas was not totally incapable of expressing emotions: he voiced great pleasure over the fine condition of the Black Sea fleet that he had inspected in Sevastopol: "The ships and the cheerful fellows who command them were a truly brilliant sight, and it was a delight to note the difference between them and what we had recently. Thank God!"[22]

In the second letter to his mother, written on September 11, Nicholas said nothing at all about the assassination and again failed to express any appreciation of Stolypin's services to him personally and to Russia. Uppermost in his mind was his difficulty in finding a suitable person to head the Ministry of Internal Affairs. He had decided to appoint Kokovtsov as prime minister, but for the second position, also occupied by Stolypin, he considered it necessary to find someone well acquainted with the Department of Police, "which is now in a terrible condition." Kokovtsov recommended A. A. Makarov, a hardliner who as assistant minister in the department under Stolypin had been in charge of the police.[23] Nicholas accepted Kokovtsov's recommendation, but Makarov was an ineffectual administrator and headed the department for only about fifteen months.

If the tsar was indifferent to Stolypin's fate, the empress could not conceal her relief over the change in leadership. Early in October, she berated Kokovtsov for constantly comparing himself to the late prime minister. "You seem to do too much honor to his memory," she said, "and ascribe too much importance to his activities and his personality. Believe me, one must not feel so sorry for those who are no more. I am sure that everybody does only one's duty and fulfills one's destiny, and when one dies that means that his role is ended and that he was bound to go, since his destiny has been fulfilled. Life continually assumes new

forms, and you must not try to follow blindly the work of your predecessor. Remain yourself; do not look for support in political parties; they
are of so little consequence in Russia. Find your support in the confidence of the Tsar—the Lord will help you. I am sure that Stolypin died to
make room for you, and this is all for the good of Russia."[24] It would be
hard to find a comment that more vividly reflects both the insensitivity
and mysticism prevalent at the highest echelons in the tsarist court. Or
one that provides more insight into the monarchy's loss of authority
during the last years of the empire.

The tsar and Kokovtsov were right to believe that they must shore
up the country's confidence in the police forces. The assassination
"evoked feelings of horror and indignation," and many citizens feared a
general outbreak of unrest. According to one observer, Kiev had been
transformed within one day from a city radiating with bright lights to
one plunged into darkness, "fully in harmony with the mood of dejec-
tion that has gripped the inhabitants." The main street, Kreshchatik,
was completely deserted; only one person could be seen strolling along
the boulevard.[25]

The assassin had been identified as a Jew, leading to much speculation that there would be an eruption of pogroms. The declaration on
September 5 by three rabbis condemning the assassination and disassociating the Jewish community from the crime did little to deflect attention from the Jews. Immediately after the requiem for Stolypin in the
Vladimir Cathedral on September 6, some twenty men began throwing
stones at Jewish students and attacked Jewish salesmen on Aleksandr
street with knives. Elsewhere in the city, members of the Union of the
Russian People delivered a series of inflammatory speeches to sizable
and attentive crowds. The police dispersed them, but they marched to
another location to resume their agitation. Merchants in Lodz, fearing
further violence and the destruction of Jewish businesses, halted the
shipment of goods to Jewish merchants in Kiev.[26] Large numbers of Jews
in the city, seized by "indescribable anxiety," began to flee to other parts
of the country; the railway station was so crowded with Jewish families
carrying what belongings they could pile onto trains that it was impossible for people planning to travel to reach the platform. By September 7,
some twelve thousand Jews were reported to have left the city.[27]

Kokovtsov, it should be noted, did his utmost to calm the Jews of
Kiev. When a delegation visited him on September 2, he announced that
"[e]very attempt to stage a pogrom will be rooted out with the most decisive measures." He ordered the dispatch of three Cossack regiments to
Kiev, all to be stationed in districts populated largely by Jews. According

to some reports, the news of Stolypin's death was kept secret for several hours to give the authorities time to bring in the troops to "prevent a massacre of Jews on a large scale."[28] Not everyone was pleased with Kokovtsov's stance. One local official berated him: "Well, Your Excellency, by calling in the troops you have missed a fine chance to answer ... [the assassin's] shot with a nice Jewish pogrom." In an effort to forestall encouragement by local officials of anti-Jewish disorders—there were reports of anti-Jewish agitation in Odessa, Saratov, and Nizhnii-Novgorod—Kokovtsov sent a telegram, approved by the tsar, to provincial and city governors demanding that they do all in their power to prevent pogroms. The firm measures worked. By September 11 many of the Jews who had left Kiev began to return to their homes.[29]

The alleged Jewishness of Stolypin's assassin, however, again became a public issue some six weeks after the murder. At the time, the Duma was considering three interpellations that raised questions about the apparent negligence of senior officials in protecting the prime minister. In its very first sentence, the Octobrists' interpellation referred to "the Jew Bogrov," wording that the Kadets criticized as offensive and inflammatory. The Nationalists' interpellation was even more inflammatory; it also emphasized Bogrov's Jewish background and then added that "not a few Jews" were "irreconcilable enemies of Russia and its political system."[30] Right-wing extremists, on the other hand, opposed the interpellations on the grounds that they implied a lack of confidence in the official investigation of the assassination that had been launched at the initiative of the tsar himself. In any case, the rightists were convinced that the Jews had engineered Stolypin's murder. One of their leaders, the Duma deputy Markov II, declared on the floor of the chamber: "There is an upsurge of the revolution. World Jewry had found new forces, has found new money; it buys these assassins, it buys these villains, [and] sends them off to fight the Russian people."[31] Hearing these charges, the British embassy in St. Petersburg feared that a "new anti-Semitic campaign" was being contemplated in right-wing circles.[32]

One way or another, many contemporaries, scholars, and writers referred to Dmitri G. Bogrov as a Jew. Even the British ambassador to St. Petersburg described him as a "christianized Jew," the Russian press spoke of him as a "converted Jew" (a term used subsequently by some historians), and Kryzhanovskii, the assistant minister of internal affairs, declared in his memoirs that Stolypin was killed by a "traitor—a Jew." More recently, Solzhenyitsyn made much of Bogrov's Jewish roots and asserted flatly that the assassin was motivated to kill Stolypin to avenge the wrongs inflicted upon the Jews. "It was only four years ago now,"

Solzhenitsyn wrote, "and still he [Bogrov] had not exacted revenge for the Kiev pogrom of November 1905, from which he had allowed himself to be carried to safety."[33]

In fact, Bogrov can be considered a Jew only if Jewishness is defined in strictly racial terms. As the deputy L. N. Nisselovich, a Kadet and one of two Jewish representatives in the Third Duma, pointed out during the debate on the interpellations, the assassin had "never had anything in common with the Jewish people," which is not surprising since his grandfather and father had converted to Christianity. Nisselovich stressed that it was simply wrong and mischievous to suggest that Bogrov was in any way a representative of the Jewish community, which "took no part whatsoever in this affair."[34] Even when he was about to be executed, Bogrov reacted dismissively to an official's offer to let him speak to a rabbi before meeting his Maker. To seek spiritual comfort from a rabbi, or apparently from anyone else, was clearly not of interest to him.[35]

Bogrov's religious background is certainly not the most important, or the most controversial, aspect of the assassination. The entire episode, like almost every assassination of a political leader, quickly gave rise to numerous conspiracy theories that still preoccupy journalists, novelists, and historians, and that still evoke a wide range of conflicting conclusions. All the Russian newspapers and many diplomatic reports at the time focused on one question: given the extensive security measures of the authorities, how could the assassin have managed to kill the prime minister so easily? Inevitably, journalists and editorialists pointed a finger at the police, who were accused of apathy, thoughtlessness, and negligence, at the very least. The questions and the charges multiplied quickly when it turned out that the assassin had been an *Okhrana* agent for some time, a piece of information that had reached the press within two days of the assassination.[36] As more details emerged about Bogrov's background and his state of mind in 1911, his motives for killing Stolypin as well as the ease with which he eluded the police became ever more mysterious. But in the end, an examination of his biography may provide better answers to these mysteries than even the most ingenious of conspiracy theories.

Dmitrii Bogrov was born in 1887 into a well-to-do family in Kiev. His father was a prominent lawyer whose estate was said to have been worth about half a million rubles, a very substantial sum at the time. For many years he was a member of the Kievan Gentry Club, which was restricted to the city's elite. It is inconceivable that he would have been admitted into this prestigious club had he not been converted to Christianity. Dmitrii received a very good education: he attended gymnasium, studied foreign languages, and on several occasions visited Western Europe. In 1905 he enrolled in the Law Faculty at Kiev University, but long before completing his studies he went to Munich, where he stayed over a year. At this point his biography turns murky: it is not known why he went to Munich. Apparently, he had decided to continue his education on his own, concentrating on subjects that interested him. Late in 1906 he returned to Russia and within a year the police searched his living quarters on suspicion that he belonged to a revolutionary movement. There is some evidence that as early as 1905 Bogrov had joined the Socialist Revolutionary Party, quickly lost interest in that movement, and joined an anarchist group.

For the next few years, Bogrov led a remarkably unsettled existence. According to his brother, in mid-1907 he became an agent of the *Okhrana*, though he may in fact have started working for the secret police six months earlier, in late 1906. In any case, it is known that he reported directly to Colonel N. N. Kuliabko, the chief of the *Okhrana* in Kiev. Bogrov told Kuliabko that he badly needed money, having "lost" fifteen hundred francs abroad—he seems to have been an inveterate gambler. He had to repay the debt, and his father, whom he described as very stingy, would not help him. Kuliabko agreed to give him an advance of one hundred rubles and to pay him one hundred rubles a month, in return for which Bogrov would supply the police with information about anarchists and the Maximalists.

There is no evidence that Bogrov actually had a change of heart and now supported the tsarist regime, as was the case of some other revolutionaries who became police informers. But during his interrogation in 1911, he claimed that he had become disenchanted with the radicals, who, he had concluded, were for the most part thieves and mercenaries. He remained active in the movement, he said, only to expose them to the *Okhrana*. He did admit that the money from the *Okhrana* was important to him, though he did not indicate why he needed it.[37] Some scholars have speculated that he worked for the *Okhrana* to realize his "revolutionary" goals and that he planned all along to kill Stolypin or even the tsar. In truth, we do not know what he was planning to do, and it is conceivable that he himself did not know.

We do know that the information he passed on to the police proved to be accurate, and thanks to his tips several expropriations, attacks by revolutionaries on banks and other institutions to steal money, were prevented and a number of revolutionaries were arrested. Bogrov spent some time in the years from 1907 to 1910 abroad, where he continued to supply information to the *Okhrana* on revolutionary student groups. Inexplicably, in September 1908 he was arrested by the police but released after three weeks. It may be that the police, too, were confused about Bogrov's loyalties and intentions. Shortly after his scrape with the authorities, he returned to his studies at Kiev University, and in February 1910 he was awarded a degree in law. He moved to St. Petersburg, where he worked for Iu. Kalmanovich, a prominent lawyer who seems to have been active in left-wing movements. The head of the *Okhrana* office in the capital, M. F. Von Kotten, made contact with Bogrov, who, however, did not at this time pass along any valuable information on revolutionaries. Nevertheless, Bogrov received 150 rubles a month from Kotten, and after he went to France in November 1910 he sent one letter to the *Okhrana* with some moderately valuable information about the SRs. He also asked for more money.[38]

It may be that Bogrov had now decided once and for all to throw in his lot with the radical left. While still in St. Petersburg he visited E. E. Lazarev, a prominent Socialist Revolutionary, and asked the SRs to approve his plan to assassinate Stolypin. Without providing any details about his motives, Bogrov simply indicated that he was moved by personal and ideological considerations, which is so vague as to allow for a wide range of interpretations. One historian has suggested that his "basic motive must have been the desire to expiate his sin [informing on revolutionaries] before the revolutionary cause, to gain redemption through assassination—and this was a desire which he could not openly and fully admit to a revolutionary."[39]

At first, the SRs were not inclined to oblige. Lazarev discussed Bogrov's proposal with his colleagues, who were divided over the advisability of his scheme to kill the prime minister. Some SRs noted that "there are bad rumors about" Bogrov and therefore did not want to have anything to do with him. The strain of playing so many different roles overwhelmed Bogrov; he suffered a nervous breakdown, and at the urging of a doctor and his parents he went to southeastern France to recuperate. He returned to Kiev in February 1911, apparently fully recovered, and began working for a law firm.

In June, his past activities for the *Okhrana* came back to haunt him. He learned that revolutionaries in Paris suspected him of having betrayed them; six weeks later, on August 16, a former comrade named Stepa visited him in Kiev and told him that an anarchist tribunal had condemned him to death for his betrayal. When Bogrov insisted on his innocence, Stepa let him know that he could rehabilitate himself only by committing some act of terrorism during the upcoming celebrations early in September when a large number of dignitaries would be in Kiev. Stepa suggested Kuliabko, the senior *Okhrana* official, as a suitable target for assassination, but when Bogrov learned of all the other officials who would be at the festivities he apparently assumed that the radicals really wanted him to aim at someone more important. For Bogrov, the most inviting target was the prime minister.[40] He laid his plans very carefully and implemented them with brilliance and remarkable aplomb. Bogrov was clearly a very troubled man, but his inner stresses had not affected his intellectual sharpness. But, impressive though he was in misleading the police and covering his tracks, it must be noted that he was greatly assisted by officials who displayed astonishing gullibility and incompetence.

On August 26, Bogrov resumed contact with the *Okhrana* in Kiev after having been out of touch for some nine months. He told two senior officials, Kuliabko and Spiridovich, that Lazarev and other SRs were planning to assassinate Stolypin and the minister of education, L. A. Kasso. He dismissed Spiridovich's suggestion that the SRs might also try to kill the tsar; the SRs, according to Bogrov, feared that such an action would provoke anti-Jewish pogroms. Bogrov named a certain "Nikolai Iakovlevich" as the person most likely to carry out the assassination. For some reason, Bogrov would not divulge "N. Ia's" last name, but he gave a detailed description of the man: tall, handsome, about thirty years old, who sported a pointed beard, wore an English coat, a bowler hat, and dark gloves. The information was passed on to Verigin and to Kurlov, the highest security officials in Kiev, and they directed a large force of agents to scour the streets and the railway station. They made numerous arrests and searches, but no one fitting the description given them by Bogrov was found. Since Bogrov, known under the code name of "Alenksi," would be the central figure in thwarting the plot, he was promised by Kuliabko access to all places where celebrations would take place. He was counted upon to spot the conspirators and to inform the police of their whereabouts. Convinced that Bogrov was a "very valuable agent," Kuliabko, Spiridovich, and Verigin planned to have Bogrov lead the SR plotters to his apartment, where the police would arrest them. The *Okhrana* put a watch on Bogrov's apartment, and several agents were assigned to follow his every move.[41]

On August 31, Bogrov called a police supervisor named Bubnov and asked for a ticket for the ceremonial event at the Merchants Garden, where Stolypin was scheduled to make an appearance. When Bubnov failed to produce the ticket, Bogrov called Kuliabko, telling the *Okhrana* chief that Nikolai Iakovlevich had arrived in Kiev together with a certain Nina Aleksandrovna and had asked him to participate in the assassination. Bogrov had refused, but told Kuliabko that it was essential for him to be at the Merchants Garden to spot the accomplices of Nikolai Iakovlevich. He warned Kuliabko that if he could not go to the garden his plan to foil the assassination would "flop." Bogrov now received the ticket, gained entrance to the garden, but he saw only the tsar, not Stolypin. He moved about freely, and since he did not find his quarry he decided to go to the theater the next evening.

On September 1, Kuliabko informed F. F. Trepov, the governor-general of Kiev, of the plot to kill Stolypin. Esaulov, an adjutant at the governor-general's office, was delegated to warn Stolypin and to advise him not to leave the house that day. Kasso received the same warning. Stolypin dismissed the danger, claiming, "All this is not serious." The prime minister's dismissal of the warning raises another question about the reliability of Guchkov's claim that shortly before his departure for Kiev Stolypin believed he would be assassinated.

Be that as it may, Bogrov pressed on with his plan. To obtain a ticket to the opera from Kuliabko he concocted an elaborate story. He told the *Okhrana* official that Nikolai Iakovlevich had indeed arrived in Kiev on a train from Kremenchug accompanied by Nina Aleksandrovna; the two terrorists had a suitcase containing two Browning revolvers and planned to arrive at his—Bogrov's—apartment the next day, September 1, between 12 noon and 1:00 P.M. Bogrov also told Kuliabko that Nikolai Iakovlevich had been at the Merchants Garden but because of darkness and the large number of people had not been able to get close to Stolypin. Nikolai vowed to try again, and that was why Bogrov needed a ticket to the opera. Kuliabko was impressed with Bogrov's information and promised to supply him with a ticket. Kuliabko told his police agents that Bogrov would light a cigarette when he was close to the would-be assassins at the Municipal Theater, which would be the signal for the police to make their arrests.

Kuliabko's gullibility is astonishing. He even believed Bogrov's claim, made to him personally by Bogrov during the fatal day, September 1, that Nikolai Iakovlevich and Nina Aleksandrovna had visited him in his apartment and had shown him the two Brownings as well as a bomb. This meant that the two conspirators had managed to evade the police who were keeping a close watch on Bogrov's apartment, but Kuliabko did not seem to find that strange. Early in the evening, after receiving another call from Bogrov, he sent Bogrov the ticket. Police agents followed his every step and were to be on the alert in case he met someone in the streets of the city who appeared to be a terrorist.

Bogrov went to the opera and during the first intermission met Kuliabko, who was becoming increasingly nervous. Bogrov assured Kuliabko that Nikolai Iakovlevich was still in his apartment. During the second intermission, Bogrov located Stolypin's seat, but before he could implement his plan he ran into Kuliabko again; highly irritable and worried, the *Okhrana* chief asked Bogrov to go home and keep an eye on his guest. Bogrov excused himself, indicated he would leave, but instead walked to the stalls, approached the prime minister, took out his loaded Browning, fired the two shots, accomplishing the deed he had planned so carefully.[42]

During his first interrogation, on September 2, Bogrov cleared up some of the mysteries surrounding the assassination. He revealed that he had invented the story about "Nikolai Iakovlevich" and "Nina Aleksandrovna" to mislead the police. When he was asked why he became a revolutionary again after having worked for the *Okhrana*, he at first refused to answer but then made the following comment: "It may be that for you there is no logic [in all this], but I had my own logic." He went on to explain that he had decided to kill Stolypin "since I regarded him the main architect of reaction and decided that his activities were very harmful to the people." During that first interrogation and in two subsequent ones he emphasized that he had acted completely on his own without any help from anyone else. "I confirm that I carried out the assassination of State Secretary Stolypin alone, without any accomplices and without any kind of directive from any party."[43]

The authorities acted with utmost speed in disposing of the case. On September 9, Bogrov was tried in secret by a military district court in Kiev. The entire proceedings lasted three hours; twelve witnesses testified, all of them against Bogrov. He himself did not speak and mounted no defense at all. The court deliberated for twenty minutes, found Bogrov guilty, and sentenced him to death by hanging. During his last interrogation on September 10, Bogrov for the most part repeated the story he had given in his deposition of September 2, but in addition he made some strange claims. He asserted that he had never received any money from the *Okhrana*, which was vehemently disputed by several officials. He also claimed that he had carried out the assassination "without any criminal intent and [that it was] even a surprise to me." Finally, he said that he had shot Stolypin because he was the most prominent person in the country, the focus of everyone's attention.[44] Bogrov was hanged early in the morning of September 11. Moments before the execution, Bogrov again behaved peculiarly. He was asked if he would like to speak to a rabbi. "I want to, but without the police present." When he was told that was impossible, he replied, "If that is the case, then let's proceed."[45]

Although the court did not suggest that Bogrov had accomplices in the assassination, it did raise serious questions about the competence of the police and in particular of Kuliabko. The judges found it incomprehensible that the chief of the Kiev *Okhrana* had been informed by Bogrov that an assassination was being planned and yet did not undertake an independent investigation of the conspiracy. They also criticized Kuliabko for giving Bogrov tickets to the Merchants Garden and to the Municipal Theater without keeping him under closer surveillance and without searching him when he entered the two public spaces. The judges directed that the appropriate authorities be informed of the lapses by the police.[46]

In pointing out Kuliabko's incompetence, the judges certainly made a correct assessment of police failings. Kuliabko himself realized that he had mishandled the security arrangements. Minutes after the assassination he ran into Kurlov in the lobby of the theater and, leaning against a wall with one hand on his head and another on his holster, muttered, "I am guilty, there is nothing left for me to do but to shoot myself." But he thought better of it and did not pull the trigger. In fact, after he had regained his composure he defended himself with the argument that he had every reason to trust Bogrov, who in the past had been very helpful to the *Okhrana* and had never come under suspicion.[47]

Still, the notion that one man acting completely on his own and without help from anyone could, in the face of the vast precautions by the authorities, have killed the second most important man in the empire seemed implausible and provoked much skepticism. The government therefore appointed an official investigation, led first by Senator M. I. Trusevich and then by Senator N. E. Shulgin, and it concluded, in a report issued in 1912, that police incompetence had been even more widespread than originally suspected. It appeared that General P. G. Kurlov, the assistant minister of internal affairs, had for some time been dissatisfied with Kuliabko's work in the Kiev *Okhrana*. The Kiev office did a poor job in tracking revolutionaries and often failed to respond in any meaningful way to requests for information from the Department of Police or higher officials in the Ministry of Internal Affairs. Yet no measures had been taken to improve the performance of the staff in Kiev. The committee also concluded that Kuliabko, Verigin, Spiridovich, and Kurlov had bungled the security arrangements at the time of the celebrations in Kiev. It specifically noted that Kurlov had been negligent in failing to send police officers to Bogrov's apartment after he had been told that revolutionaries committed to terrorism were there. Also, Kurlov should have ordered Kuliabko not to give Bogrov a ticket to the opera.[48]

Even before the investigating committee's report was issued, more serious charges against senior officials began to circulate in the press and in the halls of the Duma. Guchkov, a leader of the Octobrists, charged on the floor of the legislative chamber that four senior officials of the *Okhrana* were guilty of "direct sufferance [of the murder]." Twenty-five years after the assassination, Guchkov still believed that the murder "was at least tolerated by those in high positions." The officials had planned to remove Stolypin from St. Petersburg by creating "a high post of viceroy in Siberia" for him, but when for some reason that scheme failed they decided not to prevent the plot to kill the prime minister.[49]

The Soviet historian Avrekh was only too eager to seize on such comments and the admittedly suspicious conduct of officials in Kiev to declare, "There are serious grounds for believing that the assassination of Stolypin . . . was the work of the *Okhrana*."[50] Other scholars, in Russia and in the West, have taken up this theme, contending that right-wing extremists, some of them in the imperial palace, so despised Stolypin that they decided that he must be removed from office. When all their intrigues appeared to have failed, they connived with senior officials in the secret police to have the prime minister killed.[51] Kurlov became the prime suspect in the conspiracy against Stolypin. The most telling evidence for the conspiracy theory has been presented by Avrekh, who pointed out that Kurlov and Stolypin had for some years been involved in fierce bureaucratic conflicts. An indefatigable intriguer against the prime minister at court, Kurlov had gone so far as to intercept Stolypin's mail to find material with which to blacken his reputation. On occasion, Kurlov even countermanded Stolypin's orders. Avrekh also claimed that Kurlov was a thoroughly disreputable man who squandered government funds, frequented elegant restaurants beyond his means, and was always in debt; in short, he lived very much as did his future friend, Rasputin. Kurlov, in Avrekh's view, had reason to fear that Stolypin would dismiss him.[52]

Avrekh offered additional arguments to bolster his interpretation. For example, Bogrov was tried and executed much more quickly than the assassins of Grand Duke Sergei Aleksandrovich and Plehve. The only plausible reason for the great haste was to prevent Bogrov from telling the truth about the assassination. Moreover, such fast executions could only be carried out if powerful persons at court—he specifically named General V. A. Dediulin, the commandant of the court, who also did not get along with Stolypin—favored it and lobbied for it. As additional evidence, Avrekh also pointed out that Kokovtsov suggested that Kurlov was involved in the assassination. Finally, Avrekh raised the question why the tsar did not permit a trial of Kurlov and other senior officials charged with incompetence. Nicholas, it seemed to Avrekh, wanted to cover up the entire affair.[53]

There are compelling answers to all these charges, and they all undermine the conspiracy theory. Immediately after the assassination, the police conducted extensive searches of Bogrov's papers and took into custody everyone named in them. Altogether, about one hundred searches of possible accomplices were made, and over five hundred people were arrested and questioned—not only revolutionaries but also "prominent" citizens (lawyers and doctors). Not a shred of evidence was found to shed light on the assassination.[54] Avrekh's contention notwithstanding, speedy trials and executions were not that unusual in Russia after 1906, so the treatment of Bogrov can hardly be considered unique. And Kokovtsov's statement, cited by Avrekh, does not accuse Kurlov of having led a conspiracy. Kokovtsov simply pointed out that Trusevich's committee found that "General Kurlov and his staff had been crassly negligent."[55] Even the granting of Bogrov's ticket to the opera had a precedent: according to Kurlov, in 1906 a double agent had been allowed into the Municipal Theater to foil the assassination of a governor-general.[56]

There remains one other question: why was there no trial of the four senior officials found to have been negligent? Such a trial could proceed only with the approval of the tsar, and his unwillingness to sanction it may have been motivated by several considerations. In view of his recent difficulties with the prime minister, Nicholas may have been conflicted over the assassination. Stolypin was a powerful personality; he was recognized as an accomplished leader; and many influential people supported him. It would not have been easy to dismiss him even if the tsar were convinced he should no longer lead the government. Much as Nicholas deplored terrorism, he may have believed that this particular assassination spared him from making a painful decision. It is also known that Nicholas was very fond of Spiridovich, one of the four officials charged with negligence, and would not have wanted to hurt him. "I see him at every turn," the tsar said. "[He] follows me about like a shadow* and I simply cannot see this man so crushed by grief; surely he

---

*Spiridovich was the commandant of the guard at the imperial residence in Tsarskoe Selo.

did not want to do any harm and is guilty of nothing except his failure to take every measure of precaution."[57] But probably the most important reason for the tsar's opposition to a trial was his reluctance to expose the incompetence of the police; a public airing of its mistakes would have undermined confidence in his regime. From Nicholas's vantage point, it was much better simply to conduct a shakeup of the Kiev Police Department, which did take place. Kuliabko's punishment was the mildest: he was temporarily suspended from his post in Kiev. The authorities granted Verigin's and Kurlov's requests that they be relieved of their posts in the Ministry of Internal Affairs.[58]

Finally, the conspiracy thesis is suspect for yet another reason. The very historians who advance it most forcefully also insist that by the summer of 1911, Stolypin was politically finished, that his days in office were numbered, and that every knowledgeable observer of Russian politics at the time knew that. But if the *Okhrana* and right-wing extremists were certain that Stolypin's political demise was at hand, why would they take the risk of conspiring to have him killed?[59] There are gaps in our knowledge about Bogrov's action and serious questions remain about the conduct of the authorities both before and after the assassination, but the charge of a conspiracy by police officials and members of the tsarist entourage to eliminate Stolypin is not convincing. One should not rule out incompetence by tsarist officials as a major factor in allowing Bogrov to achieve his goal. Those officials were not noted for diligence and professionalism.

In the end, after all the conspiracy theories have been found wanting, one is led to conclude that Stolypin's life was cut short by a troubled man whose motives may never be clarified to everyone's satisfaction. He may have wanted to make amends for having betrayed the revolutionary cause, or he may simply have sought to carve out a place in history for himself. By 1910, Bogrov was desperate. In a letter written late in 1910 or early 1911, Bogrov said: "I have no interest in life. Nothing, aside from an endless series of cutlets, which lie ahead for me to eat. And that, if I can afford it. I am depressed, bored, and most of all lonely."[60] A man in such distress is capable of murder without being part of a conspiracy.

However uncertain the motives or the machinations behind the assassination, its impact on Russia is clear: it marked the end of an era, an era of extraordinary governmental activism. Political leaders and commentators from a wide range of political parties and movements recognized this even though they differed sharply in their assessments of Stolypin's policies. "Stolypin was both a knight and a hero," declared one prominent Left Octobrist, identified as "P," who had been interviewed by Bernard Pares late in 1911 for a survey of the reactions of political leaders to the assassination. "The loss of such a man, especially in Russia, which is so poor in public men, is a very great one. And then the part played in this tragedy by the Government itself, as represented by its servants, fills every true Russian with shame and alarm."[61] "P" himself thought well of Stolypin's successor, Kokovtsov, portraying him as intelligent, well informed, sensible, and patriotic, but at the same time he pointed out that the "position of the Prime Minister is anything but easy, and whether he can master it no one knows." Indeed, many Russian dignitaries doubted whether Kokovtsov possessed the "strong personality" needed to govern effectively; he did not command great influence at court and was generally regarded as a colorless man, without the broad vision and drive of his predecessor.

Another Left Octobrist, "N," did not expect Kokovtsov to be able to curb the two groups that the moderates most feared, the extremists on the right and the Kadets. Nor was he "strong enough at court to govern," especially since he had no party that backed him. He did not rule out the possibility of a coup d'état by Durnovo and Witte. Yet another Left Octobrist, "O," contended that no matter how much Kokovtsov committed himself to Stolypin's overall program, he would follow a different course, for he "has no interest at all in programs and conflicts and will try to avoid them as much as he can."[62]

A prominent Right Kadet, "V," echoed the sentiments of most Kadets in expressing relief that the "exclusive domination of Stolypin" had come to an end. His rule had "meant the irresponsibility and absolutely uncontrolled domination of the officials, [and] senseless persecution of all nationalities of the Empire." He thought it likely that now there would be a "cautious liquidation of all the predilections of the late Premier, and an attempt to conduct Russia along a path of legality and moderation without the disturbance of exciting impulses."[63]

The right-wing extremists were equally relieved to be rid of Stolypin as prime minister, and they also thought that Russia would now take a new path—but, of course, their reasoning was quite different from that of the Kadets. The rightists' great fear had been that Stolypin would succeed in undermining the old order. Durnovo, speaking in strictest confidence, said to Pares that "I am certainly sorry for Stolypin's death, but at least now there is an end to all reforms." True to his penchant for intrigue, Durnovo poured scorn on the man who had been one of his chief coconspirators against Stolypin: "I am afraid that I already see signs of a return of the old bribery system of Witte."[64]

Among the political elite, only the Nationalists, the one group in the Duma that by 1911 could be considered Stolypin's loyal followers, felt deeply aggrieved over the assassination. The Nationalists did not believe that Kokovtsov, despite his long association with Stolypin, was really committed to his program, and they feared that he would seek to undo all that had been achieved over the preceding few years. They exaggerated, but there was some basis for their apprehensions. Kokovtsov had voiced misgivings about Stolypin's Finnish policy and about the Western Zemstvo bill. He had also expressed interest in lessening the restrictions on the Jews—in this he did not differ from Stolypin, but it nevertheless made the Nationalists nervous. Shortly after the assassination, the Nationalists and others hostile to the new prime minister began a whispering campaign that accused Kokovtsov of favoring moves to conciliate "the revolutionary elements in the country," a charge that was, of course, absurd. Still, Kokovtsov considered it advisable to publish a statement of his policies in the semiofficial newspaper, *Rossiia*, declaring that he planned no fundamental changes in the government's program. He stressed that he would resist any attempts by "aliens" to undermine Russian national unity, a pointed reference to the Nationalists' preoccupation with the alleged disloyalty of the minorities in the empire. The Nationalists were relieved, but they never felt comfortable with Kokovtsov.[65]

The belief that Stolypin's death signified a sharp break in Russian politics was not limited to mainstream parties and politicians. Within weeks of the assassination, Lenin contended that it marked an end to the "first period in the history of the Russian counter-revolution." He referred to "the Stolypin period" as a "definite entity" during which the liberal bourgeoisie, collaborating with the landed nobility and Tsar Nicholas, had turned "its back on democracy." Stolypin's goal had been to "pour new wine into old bottles, to reshape the old autocracy into a bourgeois monarchy." But the prime minister's policy had failed, and "a new grave-digger of tsarist autocracy"—he meant the masses of the Russian people—"is knocking at the door." In the end, according to Lenin, Stolypin had taught the Russian people a useful lesson: they must either place themselves under the direction of the proletariat in a new onslaught against the autocracy or "sink deeper into slavery."[66] Lenin's analysis was crude and polemical, but, as he did so often, he displayed great political acuity by putting his finger on Stolypin's greatest failure, his inability to revitalize the monarchical system of rule. Lenin also sensed, correctly, that with Stolypin's departure from the political scene, no one in high authority would even attempt to undertake social and political modernization of the monarchical order. The Bolshevik leader was right in concluding that the "Stolypin period" had come to an end.

Throughout Russia, people from every walk of life, sensing the gravity of the moment, reacted with shock and apprehension to the news of Stolypin's murder. The stock exchange panicked and stocks tumbled precipitately. The national mood is captured nicely in a newspaper description of how the citizens of Ekaterinoslav, an industrial city in the Ukraine, coped with the announcement of the assassination: "[P]eople were confused, mournful, listened to the funeral dirge; in all social and governmental institutions people listened to requiems. Every issue of the newspapers was filled with details about the crime and about the last minutes of the loyal protégé of the Tsarist Throne and the mother country."[67] Thousands of letters and telegrams of sympathy from all over the country poured into the Stolypin estate at Kolnoberzhe.

The funeral, attended by leaders of most of the political parties and by huge crowds from all sectors of the population, was held in Kiev—Stolypin had expressed the wish to be buried wherever he died. The casket with his remains was placed in the wall of the Pechersk Monastery, "alongside the tombs of Iskra and Kochub[ey], having given, like they, his life for Tsar and Fatherland."[68] Within a year, memorials were built to the late prime minister in Kiev, Grodno, and Samara. The statue in Kiev prominently displayed some of Stolypin's most memorable words: "Not afraid," "You want great upheavals, we want a great Russia," and "I firmly believe that, having lighted the flame of a Russian national idea in the west of Russia, it will not be extinguished until it illuminates the whole of Russia."[69] These utterances do not adequately reflect all of Stolypin's policies over his many years of public service, but they do sum up the policies that embroiled him in his fiercest conflicts and brought him his greatest triumphs as well as his most painful failures.

Conclusion: Stolypin's Legacy

Stolypin as prime minister pursued five major goals, all of them consistent with views he had held ever since he entered public life in the 1880s: the defeat of the revolutionaries and liberals who had challenged the autocratic system of rule in 1905 and the reestablishment of civic order; the maintenance of monarchical rule although an elected representative body would participate in the formulation of government policies; the transformation of the Russian Empire into what he considered to be a modern state, one in which the peasants would be encouraged to abandon the commune, the traditional estate system would be abolished, the rights of citizenship would be extended to peasants and various other social or ethnic groups, and the government would sponsor a wide range of social legislation; the strengthening of the empire in the western regions by enhancing the political role of ethnic Russians and by curbing the autonomy of Finland; and, finally, the pursuit of a nonaggressive foreign policy, a prerequisite for the achievement of domestic tranquillity and stability. It was an enormously ambitious undertaking touching on every sphere of national life—political, economic, social, educational, and religious. Considering the chaotic and underdeveloped state of Russia in 1906, Stolypin could well be charged with hubris in assuming that he could effect changes of such vast magnitude within a reasonable period of time. Even his acknowledgment that his measures would take hold only if the country enjoyed twenty years of peace does not make his ambition any less prodigious.

As it turned out, many of Stolypin's reform proposals were never enacted, and those that were produced social and political changes at a much slower pace than the government had hoped for. Stolypin's five-year tenure as prime minister has therefore been widely characterized by historians as a failure, a failure virtually inevitable given the intransigence of the tsar and his supporters and the intense pressure from below for more fundamental, revolutionary change. According to these historians, the social and political order was so polarized and rigid that its reform was out of the question. At first glance, so bleak an interpretation of the Stolypin era seems persuasive, but close scrutiny of developments in Russia from 1906 to 1911 raises serious questions about it.

For all his many failures, Stolypin's achievements were not derisory, and they were largely due to his personal initiatives. By dint of his determination and a willingness to resort to harsh measures, Stolypin succeeded in imposing his will in several critical areas. He took the lead in defeating the revolution and in restoring a measure of calm throughout the empire. The introduction of agrarian reforms, the most notable initiative by a Russian government in some fifty years, is inconceivable without his drive and persistence. That is also true of the imposition of Russian hegemony over Finland, the extension of zemstvos in the western provinces, and the promotion of public education and workers' insurance. In addition, Stolypin succeeded in implementing the principle of united government, an important step in rationalizing the administrative procedures at the highest levels of authority. Under his successor, Kokovtsov, that principle was undermined, not because Kokovtsov was opposed to it but because he was too weak to enforce it. The truth is that however much Kokovtsov wished to follow Stolypin's policies (some he did not wish to follow), he had neither the force of personality nor the political skills to do so effectively. The widely held views that the social and political divisions in Russia were so intense that the identity of the person who led the government was irrelevant and that the kind of upheaval that occurred in 1917 was unavoidable are hard to sustain.

On the contrary, the weakness of Russia's political leadership from 1911 to 1914 points in an opposite direction and suggests that Stolypin's assassination may in fact have been a misfortune for the country. Conventional wisdom holds that under no circumstances could he have remained in office if he had not been killed. The tsar no longer had confidence in him, the court entourage despised him, the reactionaries wished to be rid of him, many Duma deputies distrusted him, and, in any case, he himself no longer had the energy or the will to serve as prime minister. It is as though he was politically dead before he was physically dead. Yet his conduct during his last months suggests that he himself did not rule out the possibility of holding on to power. He prepared a long list of reforms, and during his first days in Kiev in September 1911 he acted like a man determined to carry on, as is clear from his last letter to his wife. His health had no doubt declined, and if he had grown much weaker physically he would have been obliged to leave office. But it is not certain that Nicholas would have taken the initiative in ousting him. By all accounts, the tsar had wanted to let Stolypin go during the ministerial crisis of 1911 and yet was prevailed upon to retain him. Then, after the ministerial crisis had abated, Nicholas wished him well in his feud with the State Council, which raises the question of how firm the tsar was in his decision to dismiss him. Nicholas was not as weak a person as has often been claimed, but he also was not a man of iron will. His mother and some of the grand dukes, all of whom greatly valued Stolypin, could influence the tsar, as in March 1911 when they persuaded Nicholas to retain Stolypin. And Nicholas and many of his closest advisers knew of no one who could fill Stolypin's shoes. Overall, the prime minister had served his master well, and Nicholas was fully aware of that.

Still, even if the tsar had decided not to dismiss him, it is far from certain that Stolypin after 1911 would have succeeded in securing passage of the reforms he considered essential for Russia's stability and prosperity. Even though the Third Duma was far more conservative than the First or Second, Stolypin never dominated it. Without a party of his own, he had to rely on coalitions—usually of the moderate conservatives and Octobrists. And after the ministerial crisis of March 1911 the Octobrists became increasingly hostile to him. They doubted his commitment even to the limited parliamentary regime promised in October 1905, and they no longer believed that it was in their interest to cooperate with him.

The one party Stolypin could now rely on was the Nationalists, who in the elections to the Fourth Duma in 1912 won only 91 out of 432 seats. Many of the 31 Centrists might have cooperated with the Nationalists, making this right-center coalition the largest in the chamber. But it would not have been large enough to dominate the proceedings. The 63 rightists were not inclined to support the kind of reforms Stolypin favored. And the remaining 247 deputies (Octobrists, Progressisty, Kadets, Trudoviks, Social Democrats, and several national groups as well as Nonparty men) would have opposed most if not all of his initiatives.[1] Stolypin was a much more talented leader than his successors, but the odds against him in the Fourth Duma would have been staggering.

There remains one critical question about Stolypin's influence on the direction of government policy. Had he been in office in 1914, could he have prevailed upon the tsar to pursue a nonbelligerent course during the tense days of July, when Austria, backed by Germany, was bent on military action against Serbia? The question may seem purely speculative. After all, nationalist passions ran high in all the continental countries, and the mutual fears of all the states were deep, based on years of suspicion and conflict. But as Dominic Lieven has shown, there was nothing inevitable about the outcome of the diplomatic maneuvers after the assassination of the Austrian Archduke Francis Ferdinand in Sarajevo on June 28. For much of July the Council of Ministers was extremely important in devising Russia's response to Austria's bellicose moves against Serbia. Only during the last days of July did the diplomats and generals take charge of that response.[2] To be sure, the final decision was always in the hands of the tsar, but he took seriously the cabinet's recommendations. The procedures for the cabinet's role in foreign affairs that Stolypin had insisted upon at the time of the Buchlau crisis in 1908 remained intact. The decisive voice in the cabinet's deliberations in July 1914 was that of Krivoshein, the minister of agriculture, generally considered the most powerful figure in the Russian government. A highly intelligent and cautious person, Krivoshein was by no means a warmonger. But he had decided that Russia must adopt a "firm stand" against Germany; his statement to that effect to the Council of Ministers, the minister of finance (Peter Bark) recalled, "was the most instrumental in influencing our decision."[3]

Krivoshein, it is worth recalling, was very close to Stolypin, and it is not farfetched to assume that he would have deferred to Stolypin on so critical a matter as the response to Austria's ultimatum to Serbia. It seems very likely, given his previous insistence that Russia must avoid war, that even in 1914 Stolypin would have tried to keep Russia at peace. He was not alone among conservatives in fearing the consequences of war. The arch-conservative P. N. Durnovo, his bitter enemy, sent a memorandum to Tsar Nicholas in February 1914 warning that a European war would be prolonged and would surely provoke a social revolution with shattering consequences for the old order. Durnovo's influence on the government during the crisis in July was slight, since the State Council, in which he served, had no role in determining foreign policy.[4] Still, he might well have sided with Stolypin in pressing for avoidance of war, and they, supported by other rightists fearful of war, might have had an impact at the court. This is all speculation, to be sure, but it is worth pondering in any endeavor to assess Stolypin's place in Russian history.

In the end, the historian seeking to understand Stolypin and to assess his historical significance must focus on his achievements and failures in the five years he actually headed the government. Even such a dispassionate approach does not necessarily yield answers that will satisfy every student of Russian history. It would be a simple matter to describe his legacy if he had been simply a reactionary, a tyrant, a great visionary, a reformer, a patriot, or an opportunist determined, above all, to hold on to power. Too often in the literature, Stolypin is portrayed in such absolute terms, and the result is a gross distortion of the man and his work. It is true that at various stages in his career he publicly stressed different issues; and in 1909 he appeared to be embarking on an entirely new course by embracing Russian nationalism, albeit a nationalism that bore his own stamp. No doubt these shifts are partly responsible for the divergent interpretations of his role in Russian history. In fact, however, there was an underlying unity to his career, but, like all eminent statesmen with a large vision, he was a complicated man prepared to pursue his goals by different means. Political stability, economic prosperity, and national solidarity were his guiding principles as a public official. Convinced that neither a return to the political order that had existed prior to 1905 nor a revolutionary upheaval could achieve these goals, Stolypin argued for major reforms that, he believed, would transform Russia into a modern and orderly state. The point is that Stolypin was not a reactionary. He was a conservative in the classic sense: he revered Russia's historical traditions and established institutions, and he placed a high value on social stability, but at the same time he understood that without major changes the country's entire social and political structure would be at risk.

In truth, long before he became a national leader and long before the revolutionary turbulence of 1905, Stolypin had favored a series of major reforms. As an official in the provinces, he had advocated the abolition of the peasant commune, the creation of a network of elementary schools, and the establishment of a system of social security and workers' health insurance. His persistent advocacy of these reforms when he became a national leader prompted some contemporaries and historians to place him in the tradition of Russia's great reformers, such as Peter the Great, Michael Speransky, and Alexander II. But in fact, his model was the German chancellor, Otto von Bismarck. In his speeches in favor of one reform or another Stolypin frequently referred to the experiences of Western European countries, but the country he most admired was Germany, not only because of its apparent efficiency but also because it was undergoing a fundamental political transition, from absolutism into a monarchical order tempered by parliamentarism. In 1906, as already noted, Stolypin was widely regarded as Russia's Bismarck. Stolypin, too, was said to be "a man of blood and iron," determined at all costs to impose his will on the country and, like Bismarck, he was guided by two principal concerns, to strengthen the state and to preserve as much as possible of the existing political order. Just as Bismarck had to contend with political enemies on both flanks, Stolypin had to fend off the fierce opposition not only of the left but also of many on the extreme right, who were convinced that his changes would not preserve the essentials of the old order but would undermine it completely. And, again like Bismarck, he was prepared to use a variety of means—progressive as well as repressive—to achieve his goals.

The analogy between Stolypin and Bismarck is far from perfect. Bismarck was not nearly as subservient to the head of state. The principle of monarchical rule still had many adherents in Germany, but it was a far cry from the doctrine of autocracy that was deeply embedded in the political culture of Russia in the nineteenth and early twentieth centuries. The kaiser was not perceived as a ruler with unlimited power, as the fountainhead of law; in fact, Germany was a *Rechtsstaat*, a state based on law, which Russia clearly was not. Emperor William I played a much less prominent role in setting policy than did Tsar Nicholas II, who never abandoned his exalted conception of his authority as head of state. Much more than William I, Nicholas retained control over major governmental decisions as well as over the appointment of senior officials. On several occasions, as has been noted in this study, Nicholas overruled his own prime minister on critical issues.

This important difference between Stolypin and Bismarck notwithstanding, the legacy of the two men for their respective countries was in one central respect similar. They both guided their countries at a time of profound political and social change but failed to prepare the nation to cope with those changes and to adjust to new institutional arrangements. In a celebrated essay published in May 1918, entitled "Bismarck's Heritage," Max Weber made this point forcefully about Germany. Bismarck, according to Weber, "left behind a nation *totally without political education*" because he misused "monarchical sentiment" to impose his will on the nation and refused to countenance any political leader who demonstrated independence, anyone who had a will of his own. He mercilessly discredited such people as "hostile to the military" or as "enemies of the Empire."[5] For Bismarck it was not enough to achieve his goals; he was determined to destroy his political opponents.[6] In short, he tolerated a parliament but did all he could to prevent the emergence of a mature citizenry capable of sustaining a parliamentary system of government.

With important qualifications, Weber's criticism of Bismarck can also be leveled at Stolypin. Stolypin, too, favored the maintenance of a parliament and he also did little to enable political leaders to obtain appropriate experience in the art of responsible government. He did not vilify his opponents nearly as fiercely as Bismarck did, but, consciously or unconsciously, he exhibited some of the personality traits of the German chancellor: arrogance and rigidity in dealing with political opponents. His insistence on excessively severe treatment of student activists did more to inflame the opposition than to restore calm to the universities, which, as he acknowledged, were indispensable in training the manpower needed in a modern state. In June of 1907 he dissolved a Duma that would not do his bidding and then changed the electoral system drastically to produce what he hoped would be a pliant legislature. When the upper chamber refused to endorse his plan for the establishment of zemstvos in the western provinces, he sent the Duma and the State Council packing for three days and enacted his zemstvo measure under the emergency regulations of the Fundamental Laws. There was thus a disjunction between his conduct on the one hand and his avowal of support for a popularly elected legislature and his expressed desire to imbue the people of Russia with a sense of citizenship on the other.

In the Russia of the first decade of the twentieth century, when the country was still emerging from the revolutionary turbulence of 1905–7 and when a pluralistic system of government was only just beginning to emerge, there was perhaps a need for a leader who governed with a firm hand. But that by itself was not enough. There was a need also for a leader with flexibility, who could persuade associates and even opponents to accept policies they did not find congenial, and who knew how to compromise. Stolypin lacked those attributes, and that helps explain his failure to reach a modus vivendi with the two legislative chambers.

The disjunction between Stolypin's goals and his methods of government also manifested itself in his attempt to promote the rule of law. He realized, correctly, that without a legal order Russia could not develop into a stable and prosperous country. He undertook various measures to promote respect for the law, but when it suited his purposes he violated it. The most prominent example, of course, was the field courts-martial in 1906, a travesty of the principle of legality. He was loath to adopt this drastic measure and agreed to it only after considerable pressure from the tsar, but once the courts had been established he defended them as a necessary tool for the restoration of order. It was not a stance that could promote respect for law in a population unaccustomed to its workings.

The most serious obstacle Stolypin had to overcome in his quest to modernize Russia, however, was the tsar's resistance to change. Nicholas had never reconciled himself to the concession that had been wrested from him in October 1905. Nicholas never accepted the Duma as a genuine partner in governing the country. He still looked upon himself as an autocrat and relied for support on the most reactionary groups in society, such as the United Nobility and the Union of the Russian People. Although not unintelligent, he was short-sighted and full of prejudices toward ethnic non-Russians, prejudices that he made little effort to conceal. In an empire in which about 55 percent of the population was ethnically not Russian, that was a recipe for disaster. Stolypin adopted policies that were injurious to the interests of some of the minorities, in particular the Finns and the Poles, but he did not harbor any deep-seated prejudices against them. He was not known as a person who disparaged their culture or considered them inferior as human beings. His primary concern was to strengthen the Russian state, and he believed that his policies were necessary to bolster the state. In fact, on the Jewish question Stolypin favored policies that were distinctly progressive; he wished to introduce measures that would have marked a first step in extending to Jews the rights of citizenship. But the tsar, claiming to be guided by the hand of God, overruled him on this issue, and frequently indicated unwillingness to consider non-Russians as equals to Russians.

The tsar's opposition was not the only obstacle that Stolypin had to overcome in pursuing his program. Paradoxically, many nobles and ultraconservatives from other classes never understood that Stolypin's reform proposals were more feasible and more likely to lead Russia out of the abyss than any other. The rightists insisted on retaining the autocracy and their own privileges, a stance that was utterly unrealistic in twentieth-century Russia. Stolypin had sensed the futility of this position, but he could not persuade the one group that had most to gain from his program—survival as an influential force in the empire—that he was leading Russia along the right path.

Thus, although Stolypin saw the revolutionaries and the liberals as his primary political opponents, his differences with the tsar and the extremists on the right were also very deep, in fact unbridgeable. So long as he focused almost exclusively on suppressing the revolution, for about nine months in 1906 and 1907, he was fairly secure as prime minister. Once he sought to change the political institutions of the country, his position became tenuous. Under the circumstances, it is remarkable that he survived in office for five years and that he achieved as much as he did.

In the end, Stolypin's legacy was ambivalent. On many issues—the agrarian question, the rights of private property, local self-government, religious reform, education, social legislation—he proposed changes essential for Russia if the country were to achieve the status of an efficient, stable, and vibrant nation. Today, almost ninety years after his departure from office, the issues he addressed remain unresolved, which is why Stolypin's policies have attracted so much attention in the former Soviet Union. That his unrealized goals should have become live issues decades after his tenure in office is itself striking testimony to his understanding of Russian realities, to the cogency of his assessment of Russia's failings and his pleas for reform. Ironically, the academics and politicians who are now resurrecting Stolypin's reform proposals seem to be oblivious to the prime minister's flaws, his willfulness and authoritarianism, which partially explain his failure to implement much of his program.

The last authoritarian reformer in Imperial Russia, Stolypin made heroic and worthy efforts in behalf of his country. He grappled with the country's most vexing problems, but it would be short-sighted not to perceive that he left an ambivalent legacy. He did much to highlight the deficiencies in Russia's social and political order that hampered the empire from developing into a modern state, and he proposed some compelling correctives. But he seems never to have understood that the means used to implement reform can be as decisive in shaping a country's institutions as the reforms themselves, however worthy they may be.

Reference Matter

Notes

The following abbreviations are used in the Notes. Complete authors'
names, titles, and publication dates are given in the Bibliography, pages
437–57.

BAKH   Bakhmetev Archive, Columbia University, New York City.

BDFA   British Documents on Foreign Affairs. Public Record Office,
            London.

British   *British Documents on Foreign Affairs: Reports and Papers*
Documents   *from the Foreign Office Confidential Print.* Ed. Dominic
            Lieven. Vols. 4–6, n. p., 1983.

Dokumenty   *Revoliutsiia 1905–7 gg. v Rossii: dokumenty i materialy.*
i materialy Eds. A. Pankratova et al. 8 vols. in 17 parts. Moscow,
            1955–65.

GARF   Gosudarstvennyi Arkhiv Rossiiskoi Federatsii, formerly
            Tsentralnyi Gosudarstvennyi Arkhiv Oktiabrskoi Revoliu-
            tsii (TsGAOR), Moscow.

HHSA   Haus-Hof-und-Staatsarchiv. Russland, Berichte. Vienna.

Otchety,   Gosudarstvennaia Duma. *Stenograficheskie otchety.* 22
Duma   vols. St. Petersburg, 1906–12.

Otchety,   Gosudarstvennyi Sovet. *Stenograficheskie otchety.* 5 vols.
Sovet   St. Petersburg, 1906–11.

PAAA   Politisches Archiv des Auswärtigen Amts. Abteilung A,
            Russland. Bonn.

RGIA   Rossiiskii Gosudarstvennyi Istoricheskii Arkhiv, formerly
            Tsentralnyi Gosudarstvennyi Istoricheskii Arkhiv (TsGIA),
            St. Petersburg.

VA KKK   Valtionarkisto, Kenraalikuvernöörinkanslia (State Archives,
            Governor-General's Chancellery Archive), 1906–11. Hel-
            sinki.

VSV   Valtionarkisto, Valtiosihteerinvirasto (State Archives, Office
            of the Minister State Secretary), 1906–11. Helsinki.

Introduction

1. For the most extensive depiction of Stolypin as a villain, see Witte's *Vospominaniia*, passim. An uncritical, contrary view can be found in Syromiatnikov, "Reminiscences of Stolypin."

2. See, for example, Lenin, "Stolypin i Revoliutsiia," *Sochineniia*, vol. 17, pp. 217–25. In his writings from 1906 to 1911, Lenin frequently castigated Stolypin.

3. These themes are repeated in virtually all of Avrekh's writings listed in the bibliography.

4. See, for example, Conroy, *Peter Arkad'evich Stolypin*; Figes, *A People's Tragedy*, pp. 221–32; Hosking, *The Russian Constitutional Experiment*; Hosking, *Russia*, pp. 431–47; Pipes, *The Russian Revolution*, pp. 166–91; Wcislo, *Reforming Rural Russia*, passim; Levin, "P. A. Stolypin."

5. Vinogradoff, "A Patriot and His Enemies"; Strakhovsky, "Stolypin and the Second Duma," p. 12.

6. Solzhenitsyn, *August 1914*, pp. 530, 577.

7. Goriachkin, *Pervyi russkii fashist*.

8. For an interesting analysis of Putin's speech, see Paul Goble, RFE/RL, web page, July 10, 2000; for an English translation of the speech, see Russia TV, Moscow, July 8, 2000.

9. Glagolev, "Formirovanie," pp. 67–68.

10. For a brief discussion of the adulation of Stolypin in the late 1980s, see Diakin, "Byl li shans," p. 113.

11. *P. A. Stolypin i Istoricheskii Opyt Reform v Rossii.* I have not had access to the papers delivered at this conference.

12. Ludwik Bazylow, *Ostatnie lata Rosji carskiej; Rzada Stolypina.* Warsaw, 1972.

13. See, for example, the review by Edward Chmielewski in the *Slavic Review* 3 (Sept. 1973), pp. 609–10.

14. *Dokumenty i materialy.*

15. For more on the archive, see Sominich, "Lichnyi fond."

16. The archives of the French Foreign Ministry did not contain any dispatches relevant to my topic; I was told that a fire during World War II destroyed many of the reports from Russia.

17. McDonald, *United Government*, p. 151.

Chapter 1: The Early Years

1. Izgoev, *Ocherk zhizni*, pp. 5–7; Zyrianov, *Politicheskii portret*, pp. 5–6.

2. For more details on Stolypin's family, see Von Bok, *Reminiscences*, pp. 22–27; Conroy, *Peter Arkad'evich Stolypin*, pp. 1–2; Sominich, "Lichnyi fond," p. 90.

3. Zyrianov, *Politicheskii portret*, p. 64.

4. Von Bock, *Reminiscences*, p. 37; Zyrianov, *Politicheskii portret*, pp. 8–9.

5. Izgoev, *Ocherk zhizni*, p. 12.

6. Von Bock, *Reminiscences*, p. 43.

7. Ibid., p. 3.

8. Ibid.

9. RGIA, f. 1662, op. 1, d. 228, l. 1.

10. RGIA, f. 1662, op. 1, d. 228, l. 5.

11. Stolypin to Olga Borisovna, May 15, 1904, RGIA, f. 1662, op. 1, d. 230, l. 22.

12. RGIA, f. 1662, op. 1, d. 230, l. 16.

13. Ibid., l. 138 ob.

14. Ibid., d. 229, l. 1.

15. Ibid., d. 228, l. 17.

16. Ibid., d. 229, l. 5.

17. Ibid., d. 230, l. 105 ob.

18. Von Bock, *Reminiscences*, p. 13.

19. Ibid., p. 78.

20. Ibid., pp. 11, 148–49.

21. P. A. Stolypin, *Ukazatel knig, zhurnalnykh i gazetnykh statei po selskomu khoziastvu za 1886 g.* (Moscow, 1887) For more details on this volume, see Glagolev, "Formirovanie," p. 69.

22. Von Bock, *Reminiscences*, p. 21.

23. Ibid., p. 22; Zyrianov, *Politicheskii portret*, p. 13.

24. RGIA, f. 1662, op. 1, d. 229, l. 1.

25. Ibid., d. 16.

26. Ibid., items 29 and 31.

27. Von Bock, *Reminiscences*, p. 14.

28. For more details, see the account in Becker, *Nobility and Privilege*, pp. 20–22, 144, and passim.

29. Von Bock, *Reminiscences*, p. 12.

30. Ibid.; Glagolev, "Formirovanie," p. 70.

31. Von Bock, *Reminiscences*, p. 32.

32. Ibid., pp. 84–85.

33. On the financial difficulties of Kovno farmers, see Zyrianov, *Politicheskii portret*, p. 12.

34. For additional statistics on the population and the distribution of land ownership in the western provinces, see Weeks, *Nation and State*, pp. 86–87.

35. Rogger, *Jewish Policies*, pp. 199–206. For more information on the restrictions imposed on Jews, see Stanislawski, *Tsar Nicholas I*, pp. 36–42, On prevailing attitudes toward Jews, see Klier, *Imperial Russia's Jewish Question*.

36. Von Bock, *Reminiscences*, pp. 50, 54. Originally, "maiufess" (generally spelled "mayufes") referred to a song that Jews sang during the midday meal on the Sabbath. In the course of the eighteenth and nineteenth centuries the song somehow became transformed in what is today Poland and acquired a derogatory connotation. In its new form, it had a strong rhythm, was performed before non-Jewish audiences, and was accompanied by "coarse, comic movements of the performer, part of an improvised mock-ritual." According to a Yiddish dictionary published in 1911, "Polish noblemen seeking

entertainment would compel Jews who came to them with requests or on business matters to sing this song." Mayufes also came to be a "popular pejorative term for a person who fawns and grovels before someone more powerful." In his authoritative article on the subject, Chone Shmeruk pointed out that Polish squires would enjoy watching Jews making themselves look ridiculous in performing the dance; any Jew who refused to do so "could expect to feel the consequences across his back." Shmeruk cites no example of a nobleman participating in the humiliating dance. It seems highly unlikely that Stolypin would have been unaware of its negative connotations; his participation in the dance suggests indifference on his part to the generally held view of mayufes. See Shmeruk, "*Mayufes.*"

37. "Doklad P. A. Stolypina ob eksporte v Gemaniiu zhivogo skota i miasa v sviazi c polozheniem veterinarnago dela v gubernii," RGIA, f. 1662, op. 1, d. 59, ll. 1–17. For a somewhat revised version of this report that Stolypin sent to the Ministry of Agriculture, see "Predstavlenie Kovenskago Obshchestva Selskago Khoziaistv Ministerstvu Zemledeliia i Gosudarstvennykh Imushchestv po voprosu o novom torgovom dogorove s Germanieiu," ibid., d. 60.

38. RGIA, f. 1662, op. 1, d. 66.

39. On Nabokov's changes in the selection of juries, see Baberowski, *Autonomie und Justiz*, pp. 213–15.

40. On Stolypin and the western zemstvos, see Zyrianov, *Politicheskii portret*, pp. 16–18.

41. Obolenskii, *Moi vospominaniia*, pp. 78–80.

42. Izgoev, *Ocherk zhizni*, p. 15.

43. Von Bock, *Reminiscences*, pp. 83–84.

44. *Entsiklopedicheskii slovar*, vol. 9, pp. 748–51.

45. *Trudy mestnykh komitetov*, p. 76.

46. Ibid., pp. 1–9, 76.

47. Izgoev, *Ocherk zhizni*, p. 19.

48. *Trudy mestnykh komitetov*, pp. 22, 28–29.

49. Ibid., pp. 31–32.

50. Ibid., p. 32.

51. Von Bock, *Reminiscences*, p. 88.

52. Avrekh, *P. A. Stolypin i sudby*, p. 17.

Chapter 2: Governor of Saratov

1. Von Bock, *Reminiscences*, p. 98 (with some emendations).

2. Conroy, *Peter Arkad'evich Stolypin*, p. 11; Willetts, "The Agrarian Problem," p. 117; Raleigh, *Revolution on the Volga*, pp. 17–20.

3. Von Bock, *Reminiscences*, p. 98.

4. For more on conditions in Saratov, see Raleigh, *Revolution on the Volga*, pp. 17–74.

5. RGIA, f. 1662, op. 1, d. 229, l. 2; Bock, *Reminiscences*, p. 99.

6. For a full account of these conflicts between Stolypin and the Balashov zemstvo, see Fallows, "Forging the Zemstvo Movement," pp. 262–71.

7. GARF, f. 102, op. DOO 1903, d. 559, l. 4.

8. On Chenykaev's earliest involvement in politics, see Melancon, "Athens or Babylon?" pp. 76, 79–80.

9. Fallows, "Forging the Zemstvo Movement," pp. 762–64.

10. GARF, f. 102, op. DOO 1903, d. 559, l. 1 ob.

11. Ibid.

12. Ibid., ll. 5, 5 ob.

13. Ibid., ll. 6 ob. and 7.

14. Ibid., l. 18.

15. Seregny, "Politics and the Rural Intelligentsia in Russia," pp. 178–79. I have used Seregny's translation of Anikin's recollection of his meeting with Stolypin, which he related at a session of the First Duma.

16. RGIA, f. 1662, op. 1, d. 230, l. 4.

17. Ibid., l. 13.

18. Ibid., ll. 5, 8–10.

19. Von Bock, *Reminiscences*, p. 101.

20. On the war and its impact on Russian politics, see Ascher, *The Revolution of 1905*, vol. 1, pp. 44–73.

21. RGIA, f. 1662, op. 1, d. 231, l. 9.

22. Von Bock, *Reminiscences*, p. 119.

23. Ibid., pp. 101–2.

24. RGIA, f. 1662, op. 1, d. 230, pp. 32, 33–34, 37.

25. Ibid., l. 81 ob.

26. Ibid., l. 78 ob.

27. Izgoev, *Ocherk zhizni*, p. 23.

28. RGIA, f. 1662, op. 1, d. 230, ll. 79–80.

29. Ibid., ll. 100, 104.

30. Ibid., ll. 106–9.

31. Ibid., ll. 114–15.

32. *Novoe vremia*, July 16, 1904, p. 1.

33. Ascher, trans. and ed., "The Coming Storm," pp. 154–55.

34. RGIA, f. 1662, op. 1, d. 230, ll. 134–35. See also Von Bock, *Reminiscences*, p. 112. As she put it, Plehve's assassination "produced an exceptionally heavy impression on Papa."

35. RGIA, f. 1662, op. 1, d. 230, pp. 112 i ob., 134–35, 137–38.

36. Ibid., l. 141.

37. Ibid., p. 149 ob.

38. Ibid., l. 162.

39. Ibid., ll. 166–67.

40. Santoni, "P. N. Durnovo," pp. 32–40.

41. RGIA, f. 1662, op. 1, d. 230, ll. 166, 168–69.

42. Ibid., ll. 174–80.

43. Fallows, "Governor Stolypin," pp. 163–64; Sanders, "Lessons from the Periphery," pp. 233–34. For an account of the entire campaign, see Emmons, "Russia's Banquet Campaign."

44. Quoted in Askew, "An American View," pp. 41–42.

45. On the strike movement in Saratov, see Derenkovskii, "1905 god v Saratove," pp. 76–79; *Dokumenty i materialy*, vol. 1, pp. 378–79, 383–87, 399.

46. *Dokumenty i materialy*, vol. 1, pp. 377–78.

47. Ibid., pp. 385–87.

48. On the zemstvo congress, see Pipes, *Struve: Liberal on the Left*, pp. 366–70.

49. Derenkovskii, "1905 god v Saratove," p. 79.

50. *Dokumenty i materialy*, vol. 1, pp. 388–91.

51. Robbins, *The Tsar's Viceroys*, pp. 183–86; Weissman, *Reform in Tsarist Russia*, p. 11. For a thorough discussion of the "security police system" in Late Imperial Russia, see Daly, *Autocracy under Siege*, passim, but esp. pp. 49–123.

52. *Dokumenty i materialy*, vol. 1, pp. 388–91.

53. Ibid.

54. "K istorii agrarnoi reformy Stolypina," pp. 86–87.

55. Wcislo, *Reforming Rural Russia*, pp. 201–2.

56. Ibid.

57. "K istorii agrarnoi reformy Stolypina," pp. 83–84.

58. Ibid., pp. 84–86.

59. On this point, see Glagolev, "Formirovanie," p. 76.

60. "K istorii agrarnoi reformy Stolypin," p. 85.

61. Ibid., p. 87.

62. Ibid.

63. Ibid., p. 81.

64. RGIA, f. 1662, op. 1, d. 231, ll. 1–2.

65. Syromiatnikov, "Reminiscences of Stolypin," p. 77.

66. Shulgin, "Glavy iz knigi 'Gody,'" pp. 76–77.

67. Von Bock, *Reminiscences*, p. 119.

68. Ibid., p. 128.

69. Pares, *A Wandering Student*, p. 156.

70. RGIA, f. 1662, op. 1, d. 231, l. 2.

71. Argunov, "Iz vospominanii," pp. 144–47.

72. *Dokumenty i materialy*, vol. 1, p. 748.

73. Ibid., vol. 2, part 1, pp. 834–35.

74. Wcislo, *Reforming Rural Russia*, p. 200.

75. RGIA, f. 1662, op. 1, d. 231, pp. 20–21.

76. The quotation and the information on this event are from Seregny, *Russian Teachers and Peasant Revolution*, p. 137.

77. On the background to the conflict between the doctors and the authorities in Balashov, see Fallows, "Forging the Zemstvo Movement," pp. 813–14.

78. RGIA, f. 1662, op. 1, d. 231, l. 17.

79. Ibid., l. 15.

80. Ibid. 231, l. 22.

81. Ibid., l. 31.

82. GARF, f. 102, op. DOO 1905, d. 999, ch. 45, ll. 17 and 17 ob.

83. RGIA, f. 1662, op. 1, d. 231, ll. 29–30.

84. Ibid., ll. 33–34.

85. GARF, f. 102, op. DOO 1905, d. 999, ch. 45, ll. 18 and 18 ob.; RGIA, f. 1662, op. 1, d. 231, l. 30.

86. "Don't alarm yourself, for the moment everything is tranquil. You know that I do not deceive you. No letters from you today . . ." RGIA, f. 1662, op. 1, d. 231, l. 26.

87. GARF, f. 102, op. DOO 1905, d. 1325, l. 27 ob.

88. Argunov, "Iz vospominanii," pp. 148–51; GARF, f. 102, op. DOO 1905, d. 1325, ll. 28 ob., 66–67, 118; Fallows, "Forging the Zemstvo Movement," pp. 816–18.

89. GARF, f. 102, op. DOO 1905, d. 1325, ll. 120–20 ob.

90. *Pravo*, no. 38, Aug. 2, 1905, cols. 2458–59.

91. *Dokumenty i materialy*, vol. 2, part 1, pp. 835–36.

92. Fallows, "Forging the Zemstvo Movement," p. 819.

93. Ibid., p. 818.

94. Ibid., pp. 819–20.

95. Ascher, *The Revolution of 1905*, vol. 1, pp. 213–15.

96. *Vestnik Evropy* 40 (Nov. 1905), pp. 445–46.

97. Gershtein, "Oktiabrskaia politicheskaia," p. 339.

98. GARF, f. 102, op. DOO 1905, d. 135, ch. 20, ll. 70 ob.–73, 75, 75 ob. 78; *Dokumenty i materialy*, vol. 3, part 1, pp. 526–29, 615–18, 629–30; Fallows, "Governor Stolypin," pp. 177–79.

99. RGIA, f. 1662, op. 1, d. 231, l. 44.

100. Gershtein, "Oktiabrskaia politicheskaia," p. 329.

101. RGIA, f. 1662, op. 1, d. 231, l. 43.

102. Ibid., ll. 45–46.

103. Ibid., l. 45. Emphasis added.

104. *Dokumenty i materialy*, vol. 3, part 1, pp. 429, 432; *Syn otechestva*, Oct. 14, 1905, p. 1; *Russkie vedomosti*, Oct. 15, 15, 1905, p. 2; Von Laue, "Count Witte and the 1905 Revolution," p. 31.

105. Ascher, *The Revolution of 1905*, vol. 1, p. 255.

106. GARF, f. 102, op. DOO 1905, d. 1350, ch. 20, l. 80; Raleigh, *Revolution on the Volga*, p. 57.

107. *Russkie vedomosti*, Oct. 22, 1905, p. 1.

108. GARF, f. 102, op. DOO 1905, d. 1350, ch. 20, l. 99 ob.

109. Raleigh, *Revolution on the Volga*, p. 57.

110. *Rus*, Oct. 30, 1905, p. 2.

111. Teitel, *Iz moei zhizni*, p. 183. I owe this reference to Brian Horowitz, who sent me a copy of his article "A Portrait of a Russian-Jewish Shtadlan: Jacob Teitel's Social Solution," which will appear in *Shofar* in the spring of 2000. See also Horowitz's article for a discussion of Stolypin's intervention in behalf of Jewish girls who had come to Saratov without a residence permit and whom the local police sought to expel. Stolypin stopped the expulsions.

112. *Dokumenty i materialy*, vol. 3, part 2, pp. 429–31.

113. See Stolypin's report to the Ministry of Internal Affairs on April 26, 1905, in Karpov, *Krestianskoe dvizhenie*, pp. 143–46.

114. Gokhlerner, "Krestianskoe dvizhenie Saratovskoi gubernii," pp. 198–202; Gokhlerner, "Iz istorii krestianskogo dvizheniia," pp. 228–36.

115. A translation of the telegram can be found in Wcislo, *Reforming Rural Russia*, p. 200. See also Manning, *The Crisis of the Old Order*, pp. 266–67.

116. *Dokumenty i materialy*, vol. 5, part 2, pp. 76–77.

117. Gokhlerner, "Iz istorii krestianskogo dvizheniia," pp. 228–36; Gokhlerner, "Krestianskoe dvizhenie Saratovskoi gubernii," pp. 198–202; *Dokumenty i materialy*, vol. 2, part 2, p. 428.

118. RGIA, f. 1662, op. 1, d. 231, ll. 68–69.

119. Ibid., l. 98.

120. Ascher, *The Revolution of 1905*, vol. 1, pp. 250, 373.

121. RGIA, f. 1662, op. 1, d. 231, ll. 70–71, 102.

122. Ibid., ll. 80–81.

123. Von Bock, *Reminiscences*, pp. 120–21.

124. Derenkovskii, "1905 god v Saratove," pp. 98–101.

125. On the Moscow uprising, see Engelstein, *Moscow, 1905*, pp. 202–25.

126. Fallows, "Governor Stolypin," pp. 181–82; Derenkovskii, "1905 god v Saratove," pp. 101–2; *Dokumenty i materialy*, vol. 4, part 2, pp. 733, 1133.

127. GARF, f. 102, op. DOO 1905, d. 1350, ch. 20, l. 67 ob.

128. Fallows, "Governor Stolypin," p. 184.

129. *Russkie vedomosti*, Nov. 7, 1905, and Jan. 19, 1906, cited in Wcislo, *Reforming Rural Russia*, p. 202.

130. Karpov, *Agrarnaia politika Stolypina*, pp. 172–74.

131. Karpov, *Krestianskoe dvizhenie*, pp. 94–97.

132. For more details on the election, see Ascher, *The Revolution of 1905*, vol. 2, pp. 45–53.

133. *Dokumenty i materialy*, vol. 5, part 1, p. 710.

134. Bogdanovich, *Dnevnik*, p. 377.

135. Gerassimoff, *Der Kampf*, p. 110.

136. Witte, *Vospominaniia*, vol. 3, p. 348.

137. RGIA, f. 1662, op. 1, d. 231, ll. 82–83.

138. *Svod zakonov Rossiiskoi Imperii*, eds. A. F. Volkov and Iu. Filipov (St. Petersburg, 1904), vol. 1, p. 2. For a discussion of the ideology of autocracy and its competing interpretations, see Verner, *The Crisis of Russian Autocracy*, pp. 63–71.

139. *Russkie vedomosti*, Sept. 21, 1905, p. 3.

140. For more details on the Fundamental Laws, see Ascher, *The Revolution of 1905*, vol. 2, pp. 63–71.

141. Byrnes, *Pobedonostsev*, p. 24; Adams, "Pobedonostsev and the Rule of Firmness," pp. 132–39.

142. Bing, ed., *The Secret Letters of the Last Tsar*, p. 160.

143. Witte, *Vospominaniia*, vol. 1, p. 269.

144. RGIA, f. 1662, op. 1, d. 231, l. 83.

145. Ibid., ll. 85, 103–4 ob.

146. For an English version of the speech, see Maklakov, *First State Duma*, pp. 44–45.

147. "Dnevnik A. A. Polovtseva," no. 3, p. 118.

148. Avrekh, *P. A. Stolypin i sudby*, p. 17.

149. Zyrianov, *Politicheskii portret*, p. 55.

150. See the treatment of this subject in Robbins, *The Tsar's Viceroys*, pp. 78–81.

Chapter 3: Fighting the Revolution, April–August 1906

1. Tverskoi, "K istoricheskim materialam," p. 186.

2. Gurko, *Features and Figures*, pp. 463–64.

3. Ibid., p. 464.

4. Kryzhanovskii, *Vospominaniia*, p. 90; Izvolskii, *Recollections*, p. 173.

5. Gurko, *Features and Figures*, p. 468.

6. Syromiatnikov, "Zheleznyi ministr," p. 2.

7. For details on the circular, see Wcislo, *Reforming Rural Russia*, p. 204.

8. *Dokumenty i materialy*, vol. 5, part 2, book 1, p. 74.

9. Ibid., pp. 119–20.

10. Ibid., p. 121.

11. Ibid., p. 75.

12. For an English version of the Fundamental Laws, see Szeftel, *Russian Constitution*, pp. 84–109.

13. *Otchety, Duma, 1906*, vol. 1, cols. 74–76; 154–55; 228, 230, 237, 243; Chermenskii, *Burzhuaziia*, pp. 204–95; Rediger, "Iz zapisok," pp. 111–12; Pares, *My Russian Memoirs*, pp. 107–8; Baring, *A Year in Russia*, p. 108; Vinaver, *Konflikty v Pervoi Dume*, pp. 61–66; Startsev, *Russkaia burzhuaziia*, pp. 56–61.

14. Kokovtsov, *Out of My Past*, pp. 141–42.

15. *Otchety, Duma, 1906*, vol. 1, pp. 566–69; Vinaver, *Konflikty v Pervoi Dume*, pp. 84–85.

16. *Russkie vedomosti*, June 6, 1906, p. 2.

17. *Otchety, Duma, 1906*, vol. 2, cols. 1129–32.

18. Ibid., cols. 1128–29; German Embassy in St. Petersburg to Berlin, June 25, 1906, PAAA.

19. *Otchety, Duma, 1906*, vol. 2, col. 1141.

20. Ibid., cols. 1241–44, 1251–52.

21. For this interpretation, see Manning, *Crisis of the Old Order*, p. 205.

22. *Otchety, Duma, 1906*, col. 1956.

23. *British Documents*, vol. 4, pp. 114–16.

24. Tuck, "Paul Miliukov," pp. 119–20; Miliukov, *Vospominaniia*, pp. 377–79; Chermenskii, *Burzhuaziia*, p. 287; Kokovtsov, *Out of My Past*, pp. 147–49; Riha, *A Russian European*, p. 124; Izvolskii, *Recollections*, pp. 216–17, 219.

25. Izvolskii, *Recollections*, pp. 189–93; Miliukov, *Vospominaniia*, p. 380.

26. *Russkie vedomosti*, July 1, 1906, p. 2.

27. Miliukov, *Vospominaniia*, pp. 380, p. 386; Ascher, *The Revolution of 1905*, vol. 2, pp. 187–89.

28. Shipov, *Vospominaniia*, pp. 445–46.

29. Ibid., pp. 446–48.

30. Ibid., p. 457.

31. Gurko, *Features and Figures*, p. 486; Startsev, *Russkaia burzhuaziia*, p. 105; Zimmerman, "Between Revolution and Reaction," p. 254; Gerassimoff, *Der Kampf*, p. 110; Pares, *My Russian Memoirs*, p. 123.

32. Manning, *Crisis of the Old Order*, p. 261.

33. *British Documents*, vol. 4, p. 166.

34. Gurko, *Figures and Features*, p. 488; Kokovtsov, *Out of My Past*, p. 153; Izvolskii, *Recollections*, p. 203.

35. Kokovtsov, *Out of My Past*, p. 155.

36. "Dnevnik A. A. Polovtseva," no. 3, p. 117.

37. Kokovtsov, *Out of My Past*, p. 152.

38. Ibid., pp. 153–54.

39. Ibid., p. 155; Startsev, *Russkaia burzhuaziia*, pp. 104–5; Kryzhanovskii, *Vospominaniia*, pp. 91–92.

40. *Russkie vedomosti*, July 7, 1906, p. 1; July 8, p. 4; July 9, pp. 2, 4; *Moskovskie vedomosti*, July 11, 1906, p. 2; Bushnell, *Mutiny and Repression*, p. 207.

41. For more details on the Vyborg meeting and its aftermath, see Ascher, *The Revolution of 1905*, vol. 2, pp. 202–9.

42. Shipov, *Vospominaniia*, pp. 464–66.

43. Ibid., pp. 466–72.

44. Ibid., p. 473.

45. Startsev, *Russkaia burzhuaziia*, pp. 116–18.

46. Guchkov, "Iz vospominanii A. I. Guchkova," p. 2.

47. "Perepiska N. A. Romanova," pp. 102–3.

48. *British Documents*, vol. 4, p. 167.

49. Guchkov, "Iz vospominanii A. I. Guchkova," p. 2.

50. German Embassy in St. Petersburg to Berlin, Aug. 10, 1906, PAAA.

51. Kokovtsov, *Out of My Past*, p. 151.

52. *Russkie vedomosti*, July 21, 1906, p. 2.

53. Ibid., July 23, 1906, p. 1.

54. British Embassy in St. Petersburg to London, Jan. 2, 1907, FO 181/899, BDFA.

55. Ibid.

56. Syromiatnikov, "Reminiscences of Stolypin," p. 76.

57. Kryzhanovskii, *Vospominaniia*, pp. 102–3; Shchegolev, *Padenie*, vol. 5, pp. 406–7; Diakin, *Samoderzhavie*, pp. 31–32, 81.

58. "Iz zapiski N. V. Gurliand ot 1953 goda" (by Natalia V. Usacheva), BAKH.

59. RGIA, f. 1629, op. 1, d. 1, l. 1.

60. On Gurliand's biography, see A. V. Likhomanov, "I. Ia. Gurliand i Evreiskii Vopros," pp. 142–53.

61. Russian law permitted converts to change their first names but not their surnames. In the view of the authorities, there was an eternal blemish on the Jews. This law would explain Gurliand's retention of his name. On the law, see Stanislawski, *Tsar Nicholas I*, p. 148.

62. After Stolypin's assassination in 1911, Gurliand ceased to play a major role in government. But in January 1916, when Stürmer was appointed prime minister, he became more influential than ever. For details, see Ascher, "Prime Minister P. A. Stolypin and His 'Jewish' Adviser," pp. 516–17.

63. A. V. Bogdanovich, *Tri poslednikh samoderzhtsa*, p. 409.

64. Gurliand (Vasilev), *Pravda o Kadetakh* (St. Petersburg, 1907), p. 12.

65. Ibid., p. 13.

66. Ibid., p. 14.

67. Ibid., p. 17.

68. Gurliand (Vasilev), *Chto Takoe Trukoviki?*, p. 7.

69. Ibid., p. 49.

70. On Purishkevich, see Laqueur, *Black Hundred*, pp. 23–24; and Ascher, *The Revolution of 1905*, vol. 2, pp. 306–7, 309–12.

71. *Moskovskie vedomosti*, Jan. 15, 1906, p. 2.

72. Likhomanov, "I. Ia. Gurliand i evreiskii vopros," p. 150.

73. For an analysis of the articles in *Rossiia*, see Diakin, *Samoderzhavie*, pp. 30–38.

74. Tverskoi, "K istoricheskim materialam," p. 188. The interview with Tverskoi will be discussed in the next chapter.

75. Diakin, *Samoderzhavie*, p. 33. Stolypin's speech can be found in *Otchety, Duma, 1907–08*, session 1, part 1, cols. 348–54.

76. Pares, *My Russian Memoirs*, p. 126.

77. Diakin, *Samoderzhavie*, p. 37.

78. See, for example, British Embassy in St. Petersburg to London, Aug. 6, 1906, *British Documents*, vol. 4, p. 166.

79. Ibid., p. 167.

80. *Dokumenty i materialy*, vol. 5, part 2, book 1, pp. 76–77.

81. "Tsirkuliar predsedateliia soveta ministrov ot 15 sentiabria," pp. 162–63.

82. Ibid., pp. 164–68.

83. Ibid., pp. 173–79.

84. Ibid., p. 182.

85. Von Bock, *Reminiscences*, p. 178.

86. Paleolog, *Okolo vlasti*, p. 8; Stolypin, *Polnoe sobranie rechei*, p. 25.

87. Timashev, "Kabinet Stolypina," p. 108.

88. Koefoed, *My Share in the Stolypin Agrarian Reforms*, p. 106.

89. Rediger, "Iz zapisok A. F. Redigera," no. 45, pp. 131–32.

90. Koefoed, *My Share in the Stolypin Agrarian Reforms*, p. 105.

91. Timashev, "Kabinet Stolypina," pp. 107–8, 118.

92. Stolypin, *Polnoe Sobranie rechei*, p. 26.

93. Ascher, *The Revolution of 1905*, vol. 2, pp. 230–35.

94. Derenkovskii, "Vseobshchaia stachka," p. 130.

95. *Dokumenty i materialy*, vol. 6, part 2, book 1, p. 272.

96. German Embassy in St. Petersburg to Berlin, Aug. 5, 1906. PAAA.

97. *Pravo*, Aug. 13, 1906, vol. 2610.

98. Ibid., Sept. 24, 1906, cols. 2972–73.

99. Ibid., Aug. 20, 1906, cols. 2664–65.

100. *Russkie vedomosti*, July 30, 1906, p. 4.

101. Bonnell, *Roots of Rebellion*, p. 312; *Obshchestvennoe dvizhenie*, vol. 2, part 1, pp. 294–96.

102. For an account of Herzenstein's murder and the repercussions, see

Rawson, *Russian Rightists*, pp. 132–34, 136; *Pravo*, Aug. 13, 1906, cols. 2602–6; Aug. 20, cols. 2660–62.

103. *Rech*, Sept. 9, 1906, p. 3.

104. Simonova, "Krestianskoe dvizhenie 1905–1907 gg.," p. 224.

105. Geifman, *Thou Shalt Kill*, p. 21.

106. Izgoev, "P. A. Stolypin," pp. 131–32.

107. Syromiatnikiov, "Reminiscences of Stolypin," p. 80.

108. *Russkie vedomosti*, Aug. 13, 1906, pp. 2, 3; *Pravo*, Aug. 20, 1906, cols. 2659–60; Von Bock, *Reminiscences*, pp. 150–57; Gerassimoff, *Der Kampf*, pp. 134–35.

109. Von Bock, *Reminiscences*, pp. 178–79.

110. Kokovtsov, *Out of My Past*, pp. 164–65.

111. RGIA, f. 1662, op. 1, d. 73, ll. 56–57.

112. Ibid., d. 74, l. 1.

113. GARF, f. 601, op. 1., d. 1352, l. 2.

114. Kokovtsov, *Out of My Past*, pp. 164–65.

115. RGIA, f. 1662, op. 1, d. 72, l. 83.

116. *Moskovskie vedomosti*, Aug. 17, 1906, pp. 1–2.

117. *Tovarishch*, Aug. 16, 1906, p. 3; German Embassy in St. Petersburg to Berlin, Aug. 27, 1906, PAAA.

118. Izgoev, "P. A. Stolypin," p. 131.

119. British Embassy in St. Petersburg to London, Sept. 7, 1906, *British Documents*, vol. 4, pp. 209–11.

120. "Perepiska N. A. Romanova," pp. 103–4.

121. Conroy, *Peter Arkad'evich Stolypin*, pp. 94–95; Manning, *Crisis of the Old Order*, pp. 268, 281–82; Levin, "P. A. Stolypin," p. 449; Fuller, *Civil-Military Conflict*, p. 174; Bogdanovich, *Tri poslednikh samoderzhtsa*, p. 388.

122. *Rech*, Sept. 7, 1906, p. 3; Gurko, *Features and Figures*, p. 449.

123. Gurko, *Features and Figures*, p. 449. Kokovtsov claimed that every minister, including the most liberal, agreed on the need to institute field courts-martial. *Out of My Past*, pp. 174–76.

124. The law was widely publicized. See, for example, *Moskovskie vedomosti*, Aug. 29, 1906, p. 1. For a thoughtful discussion of the law, see Fuller, *Civil-Military Conflict*, pp. 174–76.

125. *Moskovskie vedomosti*, Oct. 12, 1906, p. 1.

126. Fuller, *Civil-Military Conflict*, p. 174.

127. Ibid., pp. 169–73.

128. British Embassy in St. Petersburg to London, Sept. 12, 1906, FO 181/865, BDFA.

129. Shipov, *Vospominaniia*, p. 492.

130. Fuller, *Civil-Military Conflict*, p. 174.

131. Harrison, "British Press," p. 92.

132. Chermenskii, *Burzhuaziia*, pp. 332–33.

133. *Tovarishch*, Sept. 5, 1906, p. 4; Sept. 13, p. 3.

134. Ibid., Sept. 16, 1906, p. 3.

135. For details, see Ascher, *The Revolution of 1905*, vol. 2, p. 247.

136. Ibid., pp. 247–48; Diakin, *Samoderzhavie*, p. 27. Precise figures are

hard to come by. For a recent estimate, see Baberowski, *Autonomie und Justiz*, p. 763.

137. Ostrovskii, *P. A. Stolypin*, p. 61.

138. Shchegolev, ed., *Padenie*, vol. 7, p. 4.

139. "Perepiska N. A. Romanova," p. 105.

140. Strakhovsky, "Statesmanship of Peter Stolypin," p. 357.

141. British Embassy in St. Petersburg to London, Oct. 26, Nov. 7, 1906, FO 181/863, BDFA; German Consul in Moscow to Berlin, Oct. 8, 1906, PAAA.

142. *Russkie vedomosti*, July 20, 1906, p. 2; Sidelnikov, *Obrazovanie i deiatelnost*, p. 370.

143. *Pravo*, Sept. 17, 1906, col. 2899.

144. Ibid., Aug. 13, 1906, col. 2597.

145. *Russkie vedomosti*, July 11, 1906, p. 2, July 12, pp. 2, 3, Oct. 17, p. 4; *Moskovskie vedomosti*, July 16, 1906, p. 2; *Rech*, Aug. 30, 1906, p. 2, Oct. 3, p. 3; *Pravo*, Aug. 13, 1906, cols. 2599–2600, Sept. 10, col. 2827, Sept. 17, col. 2903.

146. *Pravo*, Aug. 27, 1906, col. 2736.

147. Ibid.

148. *Russkie vedomosti*, Aug. 31, 1906, p. 3; *Pravo*, Sept. 10, 1906, col. 2823.

149. *Russkie vedomosti*, Nov. 7, 1906, p. 3.

150. *Dokumenty i materialy*, vol. 7, part 2, book 2, p. 117.

151. *Russkie vedomosti*, Aug. 1, 1906, p. 2; *Pravo*, Sept. 24, 1906, col. 2958; Zimmerman, "Between Revolution and Reaction," pp. 293–94.

Chapter 4: Fighting the Revolution, August 1906–June 1907

1. Pares, "Conversations," pp. 104–5; *British Documents*, vol. 4, p. 169.

2. RGIA, f. 1284, op. 185, 1907, d. 5-a, ch. 3, l. 150, quoted in Diakin, "Stolypin i dvorianstvo," pp. 233–34.

3. *Novoe vremia*, Aug. 25 (Sept. 7), 1906, p. 1.

4. On the cabinet's decision on primary education, see *Osobyi zhurnal soveta ministrov 8 Avgusta 1906 goda*, pp. 1–34.

5. This is one of the central themes of Macey's *Government and Peasant in Russia*.

6. Mironov, "The Russian Peasant Commune," pp. 449–50.

7. Rogger, *Russia*, p. 88; Dubrovskii, *Krestianskoe dvizhenie*, pp. 22–23.

8. Ibid.: Macey, *Government and Peasant in Russia*, pp. 43–44.

9. Kokovtsov, *Out of My Past*, p. 160.

10. Tverskoi, "K istoricheskim materialam," p. 191.

11. Koefoed, *My Share in the Stolypin Agrarian Reforms*, p. 18.

12. RGIA, f. 1276, op. 20, d. 4, l. 53–54, quoted in Zyrianov, "Problema vybora tselei," p. 101.

13. Gurko, *Features and Figures*, p. 501.

14. "K istorii agrarnoi reformy Stolypina," p. 84. For a discussion of this memorandum, see above, ch. 2.

15. Tverskoi, "K istoricheskim materialam," p. 191.

16. Wortman, "Property Rights," p. 29.

17. *Otchety, Duma, 1908*, session 2, part 1, col. 2284; trans. in Treadgold, "Was Stolypin in Favor of the Kulaks?" pp. 5–6. See also *Otchety, Sovet, 1909–10*, col. 1601.

18. *Otchety, Duma, 1907*, vol. 2, col. 438; trans. in Treadgold, "Was Stolypin in Favor of the Kulaks?" p. 3.

19. Ibid. For more details on his speech of May 10, see below, pp. 194–95.

20. On these points see ibid., p. 7; and Macey, *Government and Peasant in Russia*, pp. 239–40. The quotation from Stolypin is in Macey, p. 222. See also Pavlovsky, *Agricultural Russia*, pp. 116–17.

21. Manning, *Crisis of the Old Order*, pp. 286–87, 488.

22. Von Bock, *Reminiscences*, p. 176.

23. For details, see Macey, *Government and Peasant in Russia*, p. 226.

24. Preyer, *Die russische Agrarreform*, pp. 159–60; Macey, *Government and Peasant in Russia*, pp. 226, 233–34; Robinson, *Rural Russia*, pp. 209–11.

25. Preyer, *Die russische Agrarreform*, pp. 159–60; Macey, *Government and Peasant in Russia*, pp. 226, 233–34; Robinson, *Rural Russia*, pp. 209–11. For a succinct treatment of Stolypin's agrarian reform, see also Atkinson, *The End of the Russian Land Commune*, pp. 56–79.

26. Pavlovsky, *Agricultural Russia*, p. 82; Pallot, "The Development of Peasant Land Holding," p. 88; on the hardships that strip farming imposed on peasants, see also Robinson, *Rural Russia*, pp. 216–18.

27. *Otchety, Sovet, 1909–10*, col. 1601.

28. Pallot, "*Khutora* and *Otruba* in Stolypin's Program," p. 243.

29. Quoted in ibid., pp. 253–54.

30. Robinson, *Rural Russia*, pp. 212–22; Mosse, "Stolypin's Villages," pp. 261–62; Macey, *Government and Peasant in Russia*, pp. 235–36.

31. Lenin, *Sochineniia*, vol. 15, p. 30.

32. Perrie, *The Agrarian Policy*, p. 184.

33. Zimmerman, "Between Revolution and Reaction," p. 316; Rosenberg, *Liberals in the Russian Revolution*, p. 19.

34. Tokmakoff, *Stolypin and the Third Duma*, pp. 27–59; Waldron, *Between Two Revolutions*, pp. 95–96.

35. Manning, *Crisis of the Old Order*, p. 288; compare with Macey, *Government and Peasant in Russia*, p. 235.

36. Tokmakoff, *Stolypin and the Third Duma*, pp. 50–57.

37. Maklakov, *The First State Duma*, p. 141.

38. *Otchety, Sovet, 1909–10*, col. 1145.

39. He made this forecast in an interview in 1909, which will be discussed in Chapter 7.

40. British Embassy in St. Petersburg to London, Feb. 25, 1909, BDFA.

41. Mosse, "Stolypin's Villages," p. 274.

42. See, for example, Pipes, *The Russian Revolution*, pp. 175–77.

43. For a balanced assessment of peasant attitudes toward Stolypin's reforms, see Macey, "The Peasant Commune and the Stolypin Reforms." Macey argues that "it would be a mistake" to contend that the peasants as a

group opposed "the individualistic goals of the Stolypin Reforms or supported the collectivistic principles of the commune." See p. 230.

44. Mosse, "Stolypin's Villages," pp. 268–71; Owen, *The Russian Peasant Movement*, pp. 51–53; Koefoed, *My Share in the Stolypin Agrarian Reforms*, p. 84; Pavlovsky, *Agricultural Russia*, pp. 123–24.

45. Owen, *Russian Peasant Movement*, p. 82.

46. Alekseev, "Ocherki novoi agronomicheskoi politiki," *Sovremennyi mir*, Sept. 1909, pp. 236–39, quoted in Owen, *Russian Peasant Movement*, p. 83.

47. Gerasimenko, "Obostrenie borby v derevne," p. 21.

48. Tokmakoff, "Stolypin's Agrarian Reform," p. 124.

49. Mosse, "Stolypin's Villages," p. 263; Owen, *Russian Peasant Movement*, p. 63; Atkinson, "The Statistics on the Russian Land Commune"; Pavlovsky, *Agricultural Russia*, p. 135.

50. Pavlovsky, *Agricultural Russia*, pp. 140–41.

51. Rogger, *Jewish Policies*, pp. 90–97.

52. Likhomanov, "I. Ia. Gurliand i evreiskii vopros," pp. 142–53; Conroy, *Peter Arkad'evich Stolypin*, pp. 48–50, 153; Feldman, "On Stolypin's Attempt," pp. 101–30 (in Hebrew), sections of which Gershon Hundert translated for me.

53. *Russkie vedomosti*, Aug. 9, 1906, p. 2; Rogger, *Jewish Policies*, pp. 95–96; British Embassy in St. Petersburg to London, Oct. 22, 1906, *British Documents*, vol. 4, pp. 244–45.

54. *Osobyi zhurnal soveta ministrov, 27 i 31 Oktiabria i 1 Dekabria 1906 goda*, p. 18.

55. "Perepiska N. A. Romanova," p. 106; Rogger, *Jewish Policies*, pp. 94–95.

56. For a full list of the proposed reforms, see *Osobyi zhurnal soveta ministrov, 27 i 31 Oktiabria it 1 Dekabria 1906 goda*, pp. 56–60.

57. Gurko, *Features and Figures*, pp. 504–6.

58. *Osobyi zhurnal soveta ministrov 27 i 31 Oktiabria i 1 Dekabria 1906 goda*, p. 54.

59. Kokovtsov, *Out of My Past*, pp. 167–68.

60. "Perepiska N. A. Romanova," p. 105.

61. Kokovtsov, *Out of My Past*, p. 168.

62. "Perepiska N. A. Romanova," pp. 106–7.

63. Rogger, *Jewish Policies*, p. 95.

64. RGIA, f. 1662, op. 1, d. 308, ll. 1–2.

65. Ibid., l. 2 ob.

66. Syromiatnikov, "Zheleznyi ministr," p. 2.

67. Von Bock, *Reminiscences*, pp. 50, 54.

68. RGIA, f. 1662, op. 1, d. 308, ll. 2, 2 ob.

69. See the dispatches from Sir Arthur Nicolson to Sir Edward Grey dated July 2, 1906, Oct. 22, 1906, Nov. 30, 1906, March 29, 1907, Sept. 7, 1907, in *British Documents*, vol. 4, pp. 115, 210, 244–45, 266, 348; the words in quotation marks are from "Memorandum drafted by Sir Arthur Nicolson in St. Petersburg," June 9, 1908, FO 181/912, p. 2, BDFA.

70. Conroy, *Peter Arkad'evich Stolypin*, p. 50; Conroy, "Stolypin's Attitude toward Local Self-Government," p. 452; Rogger, *Jewish Policies*, p. 96.

71. Kurlov, *Gibel imperatorskoi Rossii*, p. 75.

72. German Embassy in St. Petersburg to Berlin, Nov. 9, 1906, PAAA.

73. *Pravo*, Sept. 19, 1906, col. 2823.

74. Ibid., Jan. 21, 1907, col. 241.

75. Ibid., Oct. 29, 1906, col. 3339.

76. Chernovskii, ed., *Soiuz Russkogo Naroda*, p. 242.

77. Kryzhanovskii, *Vospominaniia*, pp. 100–104; Shchegolev, ed. *Padenie*, vol. 5, pp. 405–9.

78. Miliukov, *Vospominaniia*, p. 421; Kizevetter, *Na rubezhe*, p. 445.

79. Levin, *The Second Duma*, p. 67.

80. *Russkie vedomosti*, Feb. 6, 1907, p. 3.

81. Ibid., Feb. 8, 1907, pp. 2, 3; Feb. 10, p. 2; Feb. 13, p. 3.

82. Miliukov, *Vospominaniia*, pp. 430–32; Riha, *A Russian European*, p. 141; Pipes, *Liberal on the Right*, pp. 55–56; Stockdale, *Paul Miliukov*, p. 167.

83. Verpakhovskaia, ed., *Gosudarstvennaia deiatelnost predsedatelia*, vol. 1, pp. 21–23; Semenov-Tian-Shanski, "Svetloi pamiati," p. 86.

84. "Perepiska Nikolaia II i Marii Fedorovny," p. 204.

85. Quoted in Fuller, *Civil-Military Conflict*, p. 155.

86. Rediger, "Iz zapisok A. F. Redigera," p. 127.

87. Ibid., pp. 128–29. For more details on the strained relations between Stolypin and Rediger, see Fuller, *Civil-Military Conflict*, pp. 155–58, 161–64.

88. Tverskoi, "K istoricheskim materialam."

89. Ibid., pp. 194, 188.

90. Ibid., p. 195.

91. Ibid., pp. 188–89.

92. Ibid., p. 194.

93. "Perepiska N. A. Romanova," p. 108.

94. Ibid., p. 108; Manning, *Crisis of the Old Order*, pp. 295–96.

95. *Dokumenty i materialy*, vol. 6, book 1, pp. 70–72.

96. *Russkie vedomosti*, March 22, 1907, p. 4.

97. Golovin, "Zapiski F. A. Golovina," pp. 132–35: *Russkie vedomosti*, March 30, 1907, p. 4; March 31, p. 2; April 1, p. 4; April 4, p. 2; Levin, *Second Duma*, pp. 134–37.

98. Golovin, "Zapiski F. A. Golovina," pp. 135–36.

99. Pares, *My Russian Memoirs*, p. 133; *Pravo*, April 8, 1907, col. 1090.

100. "Perepiska N. A. Romanova," p. 109.

101. Bing, ed. *The Secret Letters*, p. 229.

102. Pares, *My Russian Memoirs*, p. 142.

103. *Otchety, Duma, 1907*, vol. 1, col. 107.

104. For a full account of the reform proposals considered by the cabinet, see *Osobyi zhurnal soveta ministrov*, Jan. 12, 1907, pp. 1–9; and Jan. 26 and 30, 1907, pp. 1–5.

105. *Otchety, Duma, 1907*, vol. 1, cols. 106–20.

106. Ibid., cols. 120–29.

107. Ibid., pp. 167–69.

108. Maklakov, *Vtoraia Gosudarstvennaia Duma*, p. 96.

109. RGIA, f. 1662, op. 1, d. 80 (an entire volume of congratulations).

110. Shulgin, "Glavy iz knigi 'Gody,'" p. 78.

111. Golovin, "Vospominaniia F. A. Golovina," p. 154.

112. For details on the debates, see *Otchety, Duma, 1907*, vol. 1, cols. 445–50, 565, 954–55, 981–84, 1275–77.

113. Manning, *Crisis of the Old Order*, pp. 300, 302–3; Bogdanovich, *Tri poslednikh samoderzhtsa*, pp. 414–16; *Russkie vedomosti*, March 29, 1907, p. 2; March 30, p. 1; April 10, pp. 4, 5.

114. Bogdanovich, *Tri poslednikh samoderzhtsa*, p. 414.

115. *Otchety, Duma, 1907*, vol. 1, col. 514.

116. Von Bock, *Reminiscences*, pp. 190–91.

117. Levin, *The Second Duma*, p. 295.

118. Golovin, "Zapiski F. A. Golovina," pp. 140–41.

119. Ibid., pp. 141–42.

120. "Perepiska N. A. Romanova," p. 112.

121. Golovin, "Zapiski F. A. Golovina," pp. 145–46; "Perepiska N. A. Romanova," p. 112.

122. Shchegolev, *Padenie*, vol. 5, p. 375.

123. Golovin, "Zapiski F. A. Golovina," p. 147; Levin, *The Second Duma*, p. 303.

124. "Perepiska N. A. Romanova," p. 110.

125. Ibid., p. 111; Kokovtsov, *Out of My Past*, pp. 180–81.

126. Maklakov, *Vtoraia Gosudarstvennaia Duma*, pp. 232–33.

127. Manning, *Crisis of the Old Order*, p. 317.

128. *Otchety, Duma, 1907*, vol. 2, cols. 433–45.

129. *Russkie vedomosti*, May 16, 1907, p. 2.

130. Shchegolev, ed., *Padenie*, vol. 5, p. 418.

131. Zimmerman, "Between Revolution and Reaction," pp. 378–84; Kryzhanovskii, *Vospominaniia*, pp. 107–8; Chermenskii, *Burzhuaziia*, p. 403.

132. *Otchety, Duma, 1907*, vol. 2, cols. 107–8.

133. "Perepiska N. A. Romanova," p. 113.

134. Golovin, "Razgon II," pp. 60–61.

135. Ibid., p. 61; Levin, *The Second Duma*, p. 323.

136. Kizevetter, *Na rubezhe*, pp. 464–65; Golovin, "Razgon II," p. 62.

137. Pares, *My Russian Memoirs*, p. 145.

138. *Russkie vedomosti*, June 2, 1907, pp. 2, 3; *Tovarishch*, June 5, 1907, p. 3.

139. *Dokumenty i materialy*, vol. 7, book 1, pp. 33–46.

140. Maklakov, *Vtoraia Gosudarstvennaia Duma*, pp. 245–47; Shchegolev, ed. *Padenie*, vol. 5, p. 312.

141. *British Documents*, vol. 4, pp. 377–78.

142. "Perepiska N. A. Romanova," pp. 113–14.

143. Hagen, "Nikolaj II an Stolypin," p. 68.

144. *Russkie vedomosti*, June 5, 1907, p. 2; June 6, p. 2; June 7, p. 2; *Tovarishch*, June 7, 1907, p. 3; *Pravo*, June 10, 1907, cols. 1718–19.

145. *Dokumenty i materialy*, vol. 6, book 1, pp. 86–87.

146. *Pravo,* June 10, 1907, cols. 1635–38.

147. *Tovarishch,* June 5, 1907, p. 3.

148. Kryzhanovskii, *Vospominaniia,* pp. 107–8.

149. H. Williams, *Russia of the Russians,* pp. 78–80. The most comprehensive description of the new electoral law can be found in Harper, *New Electoral Law;* for other analyses on which I have relied, see Haimson, ed., *Politics of Rural Russia,* pp. 16–23; Levin, "Russian Voter"; Doctorow, "The Introduction of Parliamentary Institutions," pp. 598–603; and Pares, *My Russian Memoirs,* p. 147.

150. British Embassy in St. Petersburg to London, Aug. 15, 1907, FO 181/906, BDFA.

151. Testimony of M. I. Trusevich, the director of police from 1906 to 1909, at the Commission of Inquiry in 1917, in Shchegolev, ed., *Padenie,* vol. 3, pp. 109–10.

152. German Embassy in St. Petersburg to Berlin, June 19, 1907, PAAA.

153. Shchegolev, ed., *Padenie,* vol. 5, p. 418.

154. Kryzhanovskii, *Vospominaniia,* pp. 114–15; Shchegolev, ed., *Padenie,* vol. 5, p. 418.

155. Kokovtsev, *Out of My Past,* p. 178.

156. Gurko, *Features and Figures,* p. 510.

157. Szeftel, *The Russian Constitution,* p. 99.

158. Mossolov, *At the Court,* p. 141.

159. Kokovtsov, *Out of My Past,* p. 178.

Chapter 5: Fighting for Reform

1. Von Bock, *Reminiscences,* p. 207

2. Ascher, *Pavel Axelrod,* pp. 277–82.

3. *British Documents,* vol. 5, pp. 31–32, 36–37.

4. Levin, "The Russian Voter," p. 666.

5. Manning, *Crisis of the Old Order,* p. 327; Walsh, "Political Parties," p. 148; C. J. Smith, "Third State Duma," p. 202; for slightly different figures, see Hosking, *Russian Constitutional Experiment,* p. 46, Diakin, *Samoderzhavie,* p. 91; and Edelman, *Gentry Politics,* p. 35. These figures are necessarily imprecise because loyalties were not very firm. It was not uncommon for individual deputies to switch from one party to another.

6. C. J. Smith, "Third State Duma," pp. 202–3; Hosking, *Russian Constitutional Experiment,* pp. 47–48.

7. Manning, *Crisis of the Old Order,* pp. 326–27.

8. The information and the quotation in this paragraph are from ibid., p. 328.

9. Manning, "The Zemstvo and Politics," p. 143; Veselovskii, *Istoriia zemstva,* vol. 4, pp. 49–52, 58.

10. Hosking, *Russian Constitutional Experiment,* pp. 29–30.

11. German Embassy in St. Petersburg to Berlin, Nov. 2, 1907, PAAA.

12. British Embassy in St. Petersburg to London, Nov. 20, 1907, BDFA, vol. 5, p. 45.

13. German Embassy in St. Petersburg to Berlin, Sept. 28, 1907, PAAA.

14. German Embassy in St. Petersburg to Berlin, Jan. 24, 1908, PAAA.

15. "Perepiska N. A. Romanova," p. 115.

16. "Iz perepiski P. A. Stolypina," p. 80.

17. British Embassy in St. Petersburg to London, Dec. 4, 1907, BDFA.

18. German Embassy in St. Petersburg to Berlin, Nov. 30, 1907, PAAA.

19. Pares, "Alexander Guchkov," p. 124.

20. German Embassy in St. Petersburg to Berlin, Nov. 14, 1907, PAAA.

21. Ibid.; *Otchety, Duma 1907–8*, vol. 1, cols. 7–8; Chmielewski, *The Polish Question*, p. 45.

22. Golovin, "Zapiski," p. 125.

23. Hosking, "Stolypin and the Octobrists," pp. 144–45; Chmielewski, "Stolypin and the Ministerial Crisis," pp. 5–6.

24. *Otchety, Duma, 1907–8*, session 1, part 1, cols. 307–12, 343–48. Trans. which I have used is in *British Documents*, vol. 5, pp. 48–54.

25. *Otchety, Duma, 1907–8*, session 1, part 1, col. 396. On Rodichev's speech, see also Pares, *My Russian Memoirs*, p. 175; and Riha, *A Russian European*, p. 160. The article in *Novoe vremia* is reprinted in Stolypin, *Polnoe sobranie rechei*, pp. 109–12.

26. Diakin, "Stolypin i dvorianstvo," p. 241, quoted in Becker, *Nobility and Privilege*, p. 167.

27. *Osobyi zhurnal soveta ministrov, 19 i 22 Dekabria 1906 g. i 6 Ianvaria 1907 g.*, p. 1. The basic principles of the reform proposal on local self-government are spelled out in this thirty-two-page report presented to the cabinet by Stolypin. After the cabinet's approval, the report was sent to the tsar on February 11, 1907.

28. Quoted in Hosking, *The Russian Constitutional Experiment*, p. 157.

29. Verpakhovskaia, ed., *Gosudarstvennaia deiatelnost predsedatelia*, vol. 1, p. 6; Kryzhanovskii, *Vospominaniia*, pp. 98–99. See also Diakin, "Stolypin i dvorianstvo," p. 263.

30. Ananych, *Krisis samoderzhaviia*, p. 338.

31. Weissman, *Reform in Tsarist Russia*, p. 129.

32. Stolypin to tsar, Nov. 20, 1910, "Iz perepiski P. A. Stolypina," p. 84.

33. Wcislo, *Reforming Rural Russia*, p. 256.

34. Quoted in Ananych, *Krizis samoderzhaviia*, pp. 459–60; for more on the organization of the council and its deliberations, see Wcislo, *Reforming Rural Russia*, pp. 257 ff.

35. Diakin, "Stolypin i dvorianstvo," p. 258.

36. For a comprehensive study of provincial governors, see Robbins, *The Tsar's Viceroys*.

37. Hamburg, "Russian Marshals of the Nobility," p. 591.

38. Robbins, *The Tsar's Viceroys*, pp. 189–93; Seton-Watson, *The Russian Empire*, pp. 467–69.

39. Conroy, *Peter Arkad'evich Stolypin*, p. 50.

40. For more details on Stolypin's proposals for reform of local government, see, in addition to the report mentioned in note 27, the following: Conroy, *Peter Arkad'evich Stolypin*, pp. 51–69; Conroy, "Stolypin's Atti-

tude Toward Local Self-Government"; Wcislo, *Reforming Rural Russia*, pp. 210–27; Hosking, *The Russian Constitutional Experiment*, pp. 151–70; Weissman, *Reform in Tsarist Russia*, pp. 153–62. The government also sought to replace the canton courts with justices of the peace, who were to be elected by the reformed zemstvos. Thus, the estate system would no longer prevail in the election of local judges. Again, the proposal came under attack and was not acted upon until 1912, after Stolypin's assassination. But the government's proposal had by then been emasculated, and the old system remained with minor changes. See Hosking, *The Russian Constitutional Experiment*, pp. 170–77.

41. *Rossiia*, Nov. 22, 1908, no. 246, quoted in Diakin, "Stolypin i dvorianstvo," p. 263.

42. Diakin, "Stolypin i dvorianstvo," pp. 245–46.

43. Quoted in Wcislo, *Reforming Rural Russia*, p. 231.

44. Rogger, *Russia*, p. 89.

45. Ibid., pp. 90–91.

46. Hamburg, "The Russian Nobility."

47. Queen, "The McCormick Harvesting Machine Company in Russia," pp. 172–73.

48. Rogger, *Russia*, pp. 88–94. For a more detailed treatment of the history of the gentry from 1861 to 1905, see Manning, *The Crisis of the Gentry*, pp. 3–64. I should note that the thesis of the declining nobility has been challenged by Seymour Becker in his interesting book *Nobility and Privilege*. Becker argues, forcefully and plausibly, that noble landowners succeeded in adapting to "significant economic and social change" and, while they became transformed "into something other than their former selves," they did not decline as a social class. For a study of Stolypin, however, the crucial point is that a large number of nobles who were politically active after 1905 behaved as though they were making a last stand to protect their status and privileges.

49. Manning, *Crisis of the Old Order*, pp. 177–202.

50. Diakin, "Stolypin i dvorianstvo," p. 261.

51. Ibid., p. 253.

52. Tikhomirov, *Iz dnevnika*, no. 72, p. 130.

53. Ibid., p. 140.

54. Ibid., p. 133.

55. Diakin, *Samoderzhavie*, p. 98.

56. Pares, *Fall of the Russian Monarchy*, p. 283; Witte, *The Memoirs of Count Witte*, p. 487.

57. For more details on Andronikov, see Solovev, "Politicheskaia smert," pp. 137–53; Pares, *Fall of the Russian Monarchy*, p. 283.

58. German Embassy in St. Petersburg to Berlin, Feb. 24, 1908, PAAA.

59. Kryzhanovskii, *Vospominaniia*, p. 213.

60. Ibid., p. 140. See the analysis in Wcislo, *Reforming Rural Russia*, pp. 274–79.

61. Seton-Watson, *The Decline of Imperial Russia*, pp. 477–78.

62. *Osobyi zhurnal soveta ministrov*, Aug. 8, 1906, pp. 1–34; and Jan. 26 and 30, 1907, pp. 1–25.

63. Waldron, *Between Two Revolutions*, pp. 89–90, 102–3; Alston, *Education and the State*, p. 201; Hosking, *The Russian Constitutional Experiment*, p. 178.

64. These figures are from Anweiler, "Russian Schools," pp. 294, 305–6. See also Hans, *History of Russian Educational Policy*, pp. 211–17; Alston, *Education and the State*, p. 200.

65. Rimlinger, "Autocracy and the Factory Order," p. 91.

66. Snow, "The Kokovtsov Commission."

67. Quoted in Waldron, *Between Two Revolutions*, p. 88.

68. Laverychev, *Tsarizm i rabochii vopros*, p. 241.

69. Roosa, "Workers' Insurance Legislation," p. 452. In addition to Roosa's work, see also Waldron, *Between Two Revolutions*, pp. 88–89, 101–2; Hosking, *The Russian Constitutional Experiment*, pp. 179–80; Avrekh, "Treiteiiunskaia monarkhiia i rabochii vopros"; Laverychev, *Tsarizm i rabochii vopros*, pp. 219–46; Bonnell, *Roots of Rebellion*, p. 381.

70. Suny, *The Baku Commune*, p. 46.

71. *Dokumenty i materialy*, vol. 6, book 1, pp. 114, 120.

72. "Borba s revoliutsionnym dvizheniem na Kavkaze," pp. 187–202.

73. Ibid., part 1, pp. 202–12; part 2, pp. 128–40.

74. Kassow, *Students, Professors, and the State*, pp. 237 ff.; Ascher, *The Revolution of 1905*, vol. 1, pp. 194–206.

75. Shvarts, *Moia perepiska so Stolypinym*, p. 82.

76. Kassow, *Students, Professors, and the State*, pp. 299, 342.

77. RGIA, f. 1276, op. 3, d. 192, l. 19, quoted in Koroleva, "Sovet ministrov Rossii v 1907–1914 gg.," p. 130.

78. Kassow, *Students, Professors, and the State*, pp. 300–301.

79. Quoted in ibid., p. 317.

80. *Dokumenty i materialy*, vol. 6, part 3, pp. 129–30.

81. "Iz Perepiski P. A. Stolypina," p. 81.

82. Shvarts, *Moia perepiska so Stolypinym*, pp. 5–15, 78.

83. For a full discussion of Schwartz's views, see Kassow, *Students, Professors, and the State*, pp. 325–31.

84. Ibid., p. 340.

85. Shvarts, *Moia perepiska so Stolypinym*, pp. 21–31.

86. Ibid., pp. 32, 82–83.

87. RGIA, f. 1662, op. 1, d. 106, ll. 1–6.

88. Ibid., d. 86, ll. 1–2.

89. Kassow, *Students, Professors, and the State*, p. 347.

90. Shvarts, *Moia perepiska so Stolypinym*, pp. 33–45.

91. Kassow, *Students, Professors, and the State*, pp. 348–51; German Consulate in Moscow to Berlin, Nov. 24 and 28, 1910, PAAA; British Embassy in St. Petersburg to London, Nov. 30, 1910, *British Documents*, vol. 6, pp. 70–71.

92. Kassow, *Students, Professors, and the State*, pp. 351–52; Diakin, *Samoderzhavie*, p. 182.

93. British Embassy in St. Petersburg to London, March 6, 1911, *British Documents*, vol. 6, pp. 79–80.

94. German Consulate in Moscow to Berlin, Feb. 22, 1911, PAAA.

95. Diakin, *Samoderzhavie*, p. 183.

96. British Embassy in St. Petersburg to London, March 6, 1911, *British Documents*, vol. 6, p. 80.

97. Ibid.; see also German Consulate in Moscow to Berlin, Feb. 22, 1911, PAAA; Kassow, *Students, Professors, and the State*, pp. 353, 56–57, and passim.

98. British Embassy in St. Petersburg to London, March 6, 1911, *British Documents*, vol. 6, pp. 79–80.

99. Kassow, *Students, Professors, and the State*, pp. 362–63.

100. See McDonald, *United Government and Foreign Policy*, which contains the best discussion of Stolypin's views on foreign policy.

101. British Embassy in St. Petersburg to London, Sept. 12, 1909, *British Documents*, vol. 5, pp. 304–5.

102. Memorandum dated April 4, 1908, PAAA.

103. "K istorii anglo-russkogo soglasheniia," p. 36.

104. Ibid., p. 38.

105. Raeff, "Patterns of Russian Imperial Policy," p. 127. I have relied heavily on this article in the preceding and succeeding three paragraphs. See also Kappeler, *Russland als Vielvölkerreich*, pp. 29–276. Also of interest is Hosking's latest book, *Russia*, in which he argues that Russia's focus on building an empire impeded the creation of a true nation-state. For an account of Russia's methods of rule in the territories of the minorities, see Starr, "Tsarist Government."

106. Hosking, *The Russian Constitutional Experiment*, pp. 215–42.

107. Struve, "Velikaia Rossiia" and "Otryvki o gosudarstve." For an analysis of Struve nationalism, see Pipes, vol. 2, pp. 89–94. The sentence quoted in this paragraph is from Pipes's translation.

108. Fuller, *Strategy and Power*, p. 423.

109. Tcharykow, "Reminiscences of Nicholas II," pp. 448–49; Bestuzhev, "Borba v praviashchikh krugakh," p. 133. Stolypin's daughter also recalled the prime minister's firm statement in opposition to Izvolskii's negotiations: "While I am in authority, I will do everything within the strength of mankind not to allow Russia to go to war because we have not yet accomplished our entire program of internal recovery." Von Bock, *Reminiscences*, p. 241.

110. Sir A. Nicolson to Sir Edward Grey, May 7, 1909, *British Documents*, vol. 5, p. 282.

111. Bestuzhev, "Borba v praviashchikh krugakh," pp. 137–38.

112. Izvolskii, *Au Service de la Russie*, pp. 304–5.

113. Fuller, *Strategy and Power*, pp. 447–48.

114. McDonald, *United Government*, p. 218.

115. Ibid., pp. 199–201.

Chapter 6: Embattled

1. British Embassy in St. Petersburg to London, March 3, 1908, *British Documents*, vol. 5, p. 118.

2. Diakin, *Samoderzhavie*, p. 129.

3. *Pravo*, Feb. 10, 1908, col. 348.

4. Pares, "Conversations," p. 106.

5. British Embassy in St. Petersburg to London, Jan. 15, 1908, BDFA.

6. *Pravo*, Feb. 17, 1908, col. 398; March 16, 1908, col. 650; Apr. 6, 1908, col. 835; May 11, 1908, col. 1212; Diakin, "Stolypin i dvorianstvo," p. 262.

7. *Pravo*, Sept. 2, 1908, col. 1598; British Embassy in St. Petersburg to London, Aug. 27, 1908, *British Documents*, vol. 5, p. 147.

8. *Pravo*, Sept. 7, 1908, col. 1942; Oct. 19, 1908, col. 2801.

9. Harper, "Exceptional Measures in Russia," pp. 92–105; Pipes, *Russia under the Old Regime*, pp. 305–7; Daly, *Autocracy under Siege*, pp. 33–40; *Pravo*, Mar. 6, 1906, cols. 909–16.

10. *Pravo*, Aug. 10, 1908, col. 1761.

11. British Embassy in St. Petersburg to London, June 15, 1909, *British Documents*, vol. 5, p. 295.

12. *Pravo*, May 4, 1908, col. 1161; British Embassy in St. Petersburg to London, March 25, 1908, BDFA.

13. British Embassy in St. Petersburg to London, March 25, 1908, BDFA.

14. British Embassy in St. Petersburg to London, June 15, 1909, *British Documents*, vol. 5, p. 295.

15. British Embassy in St. Petersburg to London, March 25, 1908, BDFA.

16. Marshall, *Demanding the Impossible*, pp. 366–76; Avrich, *Russian Anarchists*, p. 36. For an English version of an important essay by Tolstoy on his political views, see Raeff, ed. *Anthology*, pp. 322–57.

17. Troyat, *Tolstoy*, p. 737; Lure, *Posle*, pp. 47–48.

18. German Embassy in St. Petersburg to Berlin, June 15, 1910, PAAA.

19. *The Memoirs of Count Witte*, p. 656.

20. Ibid., p. 700.

21. "Perepiska Grafa S. Iu. Vitte," pp. 134–51.

22. *The Memoirs of Count Witte*, p. 641.

23. "Perepiska Grafa S. Iu. Vitte," pp. 151–52.

24. Nikolajewsky, *Azeff the Spy*, p. 167.

25. British Embassy in St. Petersburg to London, Feb. 9, 1909, BDFA. Nikolajewsky, *Azeff the Spy*, pp. 1–6, 12–16, and passim.

26. Ruud, "A. A. Lopukhin"; see also Ascher, *The Revolution of 1905*, vol. 1, p. 259.

27. Geifman, *Thou Shalt Kill*, p. 234; Hildermeier, *Die Sozialrevolutionäre Partei*, p. 386. Nikolajewsky, *Azeff the Spy*, p. 179.

28. *Otchety, Duma, 1909*, session 2, part 2, cols. 1365–90.

29. For Gerasimov's statement, see Shchegolev, *Padenie*, vol. 3, p. 13. See also Nikolajewsky, *Azeff the Spy*, pp. 281–84.

30. For Stolypin's speech, see *Otchety, Duma, 1909*, session 2, part 2,

cols. 1418–38; for an eyewitness account of the debate on Azef, see British Embassy in St. Petersburg to London, Feb. 25, 1909, BDFA.

31. Nikolajewsky, *Azeff the Spy*, pp. 280–84; Ruud, "A. A. Lopukhin," p. 162.

32. *Otchety, Duma, 1907–8*, session 1, part 1, col. 1995; Kokovtsov, *Out of My Past*, pp. 205–6; British Embassy in St. Petersburg to London, May 18, 1908, *British Documents*, vol. 5, pp. 129–30.

33. Stolypin, *Polnoe sobranie rechei*, pp. 112–16. For a full account of the Naval crisis, see Hosking, *The Russian Constitutional Experiment*, pp. 74–105.

34. "Perepiska N. A. Romanova," p. 118.

35. *Otchety, Duma, 1908*, session 1, part 3, cols. 1397–1408.

36. Pares, "Alexander Guchkov," pp. 125–26.

37. *Otchety, Duma, 1907–8*, session 1, part 3, cols. 1393–96, quotation as translated in Chmielewski, "Stolypin and the Ministerial Crisis," p. 10.

38. Ibid.; British Embassy in St. Petersburg to London, Aug. 13, 1908, BDFA; Fuller, *Civil-Military Conflict*, p. 235.

39. Guchkov, "Iz vospominanii A. I. Guchkova," quoted in Chmielewski, "Stolypin and the Ministerial Crisis," p. 14.

40. *Otchety, Duma, 1907–8*, session 1, part 3, col. 1632, quoted in Chmielewski, "Stolypin and the Ministerial Crisis," pp. 12–13; see also the analysis in Hosking, *The Russian Constitutional Experiment*, p. 79. Despite the tsar's anger at Guchkov and the furor surrounding Guchkov's speech, the attack on the grand dukes did play a part in prompting some major changes: Grand Duke Nikolai Nikolaevich resigned, other grand dukes were given honorary positions, and the Council of Defense was abolished. See ibid., p. 80.

41. See *Otchety, Sovet, 1907–8*, cols. 1701–9 for Stolypin's speech. The quotation is from col. 1702.

42. Ibid., col. 1709.

43. Chmielewski, "Stolypin and the Ministerial Crisis," p. 16; Kokovtsov, *Out of My Past*, p. 218.

44. Chmielewski, "Stolypin and the Ministerial Crisis," pp. 17–19; see also Kokovtsov, *Out of My Past*, pp. 220–21, on the constitutional issue.

45. German Embassy in St. Petersburg to Berlin, May 22, 1909, PAAA. For more on the contents of Articles 96 and 14, see Hosking, *The Russian Constitutional Experiment*, pp. 74 ff. Hosking's conclusion confirms Stolypin's claims.

46. *Otchety, Sovet, 1908–9*, col. 1350.

47. Chmielewski, "Stolypin and the Ministerial Crisis," p. 19.

48. "Iz perepiski Nikolaia i Marii Romanovykh," p. 187.

49. Kokovtsov, *Out of My Past*, p. 221.

50. *Otchety, Sovet, 1908–9*, cols. 1415–17.

51. Kokovtsov, *Out of My Past*, p. 222.

52. *Novoe vremia*, March 24, 1909, p. 1, quoted in Chmielewski, "Stolypin and the Ministerial Crisis," p. 22.

53. Polivanov, *Iz dnevnikov*, p. 69.

54. Diakin, *Samoderzhavie*, pp. 135–36; Waldron, *Between Two Revolutions*, p. 124.

55. *Otchety, Sovet, 1908–9*, cols. 1349–50.

56. Polivanov, *Iz dnevnikov*, p. 70. Kokovtsov had a different recollection of the outcome of the meeting between Stolypin and the tsar. In Kokovtsov's version, the prime minister was confident that Nicholas would think about the matter for a few days and would then approve the bill, for the monarch's last words had been: "One cannot accuse this Duma of a desire to seize power, and there is no need to fight with it." Kokovtsov, *Out of My Past*, p. 222. But Stolypin's comments to the British ambassador suggest that Kokovtsov's memory may have been faulty in this matter.

57. British Embassy in St. Petersburg to London, May 23, 1909, *British Documents*, vol. 5, p. 286.

58. British Embassy in St. Petersburg to London, May 7, 1909, *British Documents*, vol. 5, pp. 280–82.

59. Diakin, *Samoderzhavie*, pp. 134–35, 137.

60. Kokovtsov, *Out of My Past*, pp. 254. For an incisive assessment of Sukhomlinov, see Fuller, *Civil-Military Conflict*, pp. 237–44.

61. Diakin, *Samoderzhavie*, p. 132.

62. "Perepiska N. A. Romanova," p. 120. I have used, with some emendations, the translation in Hosking, *The Russian Constitutional Experiment*, p. 96.

63. An English translation of the rescript can be found in *British Documents*, vol. 5, p. 284.

64. British Embassy in St. Petersburg to London, May 23, 1909, BDFA.

65. British Embassy in St. Petersburg to London, May 12, 1909, *British Documents*, vol. 5, p. 283.

66. British Embassy in St. Petersburg to London, May 16, 1909, *British Documents*, vol. 5, p. 284

67. Izgoev, *Ocherk zhizni*, p. 86.

68. Polivanov, *Iz dnevnikov*, p. 70.

69. German Embassy in St. Petersburg to Berlin, June 26, 1909, PAAA.

70. Hosking, *The Russian Constitutional Experiment*, pp. 96–97.

71. British Embassy in St. Petersburg to London, Feb. 5, 1910, *British Documents*, vol. 6, p. 2; for a history of the Nationalists, see Edelman, *Gentry Politics*.

72. Figes, *A People's Tragedy*, p. 226.

73. Diakin, "Stolypin i dvorianstvo," p. 269.

74. Von Bock, *Reminiscences*, pp. 231–32.

75. Ibid., pp. 232–33.

Chapter 7: Religion, Nationalism, Migration

1. See Verpakhovskaia, *Gosudarstvennaia deiatelnost*, vol. 1, pp. 3–8, for the entire interview.

2. Chmielewski, "Stolypin and the Russian Ministerial Crisis," p. 37; Diakin, "Stolypin i dvorianstvo," pp. 269–70; Waldron, *Between Two Revo-*

lutions, p. 157; Avrekh made this point repeatedly. In one of his last works, published in 1991, Avrekh said that after the failure of his reform program in 1909, Stolypin "capitulated" to "Durnovo and co." and adopted a policy of "militant nationalism." See his *P. A. Stolypin i sudby reform*, p. 134.

3. German Embassy in St. Petersburg to Berlin, June 26, 1909, PAAA.

4. *Pravo*, no. 25, June 26, 1911, col. 1424.

5. The best study of Stolypin and the religious question is Waldron, "Religious Reform after 1905"; see also Martov et al., eds. *Obshchestvennoe dvizhenie*, vol. 4, part 1, pp. 301–3.

6. Waldron, "Religious Reform after 1905," pp. 119–20. A community of Catholics in St. Petersburg, founded by one of Stolypin's cousins, was tolerated by the authorities because the prime minister protected it. But he did not take any official steps to recognize the community's right to exist. Urged by his cousin to do so, Stolypin responded simply that the Catholics should observe their rituals and that he would "turn a blind eye." See Shkarovskii, "Russkie Katoliki," pp. 439–40.

7. *Pravo*, March 30, 1908, col. 769. See also Waldron, "Religious Reform after 1905," pp. 119–21.

8. Chmielewski, "Stolypin and the Russian Ministerial Crisis," pp. 28–29.

9. *Otchety, Duma, 1909*, session 2, cols. 1023–29; Waldron, "Religious Reform after 1905," p. 135.

10. Hosking, *The Russian Constitutional Experiment*, pp. 99–102.

11. British Embassy in St. Petersburg to London, May 23, 1909, *British Documents*, vol. 5, p. 285.

12. Tikhomirov, "Iz dnevnika L. Tikhomirova," no. 74, p. 165.

13. Koroleva, "Sovet ministrov Rossii v 1907–1914 gg.," p. 119; Chmielewski, "Stolypin and the Russian Ministerial Crisis," p. 29.

14. *The Memoirs of Count Witte*, p. 681.

15. *Otchety, Duma, 1909*, session 2, part 4, cols. 1753–54.

16. Ibid., cols. 1756–57.

17. Ibid., col. 1757.

18. Ibid., col. 1764.

19. Chmielewski, "Stolypin and the Russian Ministerial Crisis," p. 32.

20. Waldron, "Religious Reform after 1905," pp. 136–38.

21. Korkunov, *Russkoe gosudarstvennoe pravo*, pp. 141–52.

22. Stolypin to Zein, Oct. 20, 1910, VA KKK Fb 555, II-2.

23. Korkunov, *Russkoe gosudarstvennoe pravo*, pp. 141–52.

24. Kujala, "The Policy of the Russian Government toward Finland"; Avrekh, *Stolypin i tretia duma*, pp. 44–45; Seton-Watson, *The Russian Empire*, p. 498.

25. British Embassy in St. Petersburg to London, June 11, 1910, *British Documents*, vol. 6, p. 43.

26. Seton-Watson, *The Russian Empire*, p. 498.

27. Hodgson, "Finland's Position in the Russian Empire," pp. 158–59; Kujala, "The Policy of the Russian Government toward Finland," pp. 144 ff.; Seton-Watson, *The Russian Empire*, p. 499.

28. Hodgson, "Finland's Position in the Russian Empire," p. 162.

29. Stolypin to Langof, Oct. 16, 1907, VA KKK, SVKF 275; Langof to Stolypin, Oct. 28, 1907, VA KKK, SVKF 214; Stolypin to Langof, Nov. 12, 1907, VA KKK, SVKF 214.

30. Avrekh, *Stolypin i Sudby*, p. 137.

31. "Iz perepiski P. A. Stolypina," p. 81.

32. German Embassy in St. Petersburg to Berlin, Jan. 28, 1907, PAAA.

33. Kujala, "The Policy of the Russian Government toward Finland," pp. 144–45.

34. The document, untitled, can be found in VA KKK Hd 40.

35. Stolypin to Gerard, Jan. 6, 1908, VA KKK Fb 412, 8–2U, no. 5738; Stolypin to Gerard, Jan. 9, 1908, VA KKK Hg 40.

36. "Perepiska N. A. Romanova," p. 118

37. VA KKK Fb 412, 8–4; British Embassy in St. Petersburg to London, Aug. 13, 1908, *British Documents*, vol. 5, p. 141.

38. *Otchety, Duma, 1908*, session 1, part 2, cols. 2931–32.

39. Ibid., col. 2926.

40. British Embassy in St. Petersburg to London, Aug. 13, 1908, *British Documents*, vol. 5, p. 118.

41. For a full version of Stolypin's speech, see *Otchety, Duma, 1908*, session 1, part 2, cols. 2919–41.

42. British Embassy in St. Petersburg to London, Aug. 13, 1908, *British Documents*, vol. 5, p. 141.

43. Stolypin to Bekman, Nov. 12, 1908; Bekman to Stolypin, Nov. 21, 1908, VA KKK Hd 40.

44. Stolypin to Bekman, June 16, 1908, marked "confidential," VA KKK Fb 418, 47, no. 3083.

45. Stolypin to Bekman, Sept. 18, 1908, VA KKK Hd 40.

46. Stolypin to Bekman, Feb. 1, 1909, VA KKK Fb 465.

47. Bekman to Stolypin, Feb. 11, 1909, VAKK Fb 465.

48. Stolypin to Zein, Aug. 16, 1909; Zein to Stolypin, Aug. 21, 1909; Stolypin to Bekman, Aug. 28, 1909; Bekman to Stolypin, Sept. 10, 1909, VA KKK Fb 454, XXXV.

49. Lukianov to Stolypin, Nov. 24, 1909, VA KKK Fb 454, XLIII, no. 201; Stolypin to Zein, Dec. 2, 1909, ibid., no. 5113; Olkhovskii to Zein, Dec. 12, 1909, ibid., no. 718; Zein to Stolypin, Dec. 16, 1909, ibid., no. 869; Sukhomlin to Stolypin, Dec. 17, 1909, ibid., no. 81774; Stolypin to Zein, Dec. 23, 1909, ibid., no. 5453.

50. *Osobyi zhurnal soveta ministrov*, Sept. 15, 1909, VA KKK, SVKF, 223, no. 4280.

51. Stolypin to Zein, Dec. 4, 1909, VA KKK Fb 531, LVIII-3. On the tsar's militance, see Kujala, "Rossiia i Finlandiia," p. 68.

52. Stolypin to Zein, Feb. 25, 1910, VA KKK Hd 40.

53. Waldron, "Stolypin and Finland," pp. 49, 51; Avrekh, *Stolypin i tretia duma*, p. 65; Kujala, "The Policy of the Russian Government toward Finland," p. 158.

54. *Otchety, Duma, 1910*, cols. 2025–42.

55. British Embassy in St. Petersburg to London, June 11, 1910, *British Documents*, vol. 6, p. 43.

56. Avrekh, *Stolypin i tretia duma*, pp. 64–78; Waldron, "Stolypin and Finland," p. 49.

57. *Otchety, Duma, 1910*, col. 2041.

58. Zein to Stolypin, Nov. 4, 1910, VA KKK Hd 40, no. 1403.

59. Stolypin to Zein, Nov. 17, 1910, VA KKK Hd 40, no. 5391.

60. Kasso to Stolypin, July 12, 1911, VA KKK Fb 625 II.5/5.

61. Kasso to Zein, July 22, 1911, VA KKK Fb 625, II.5/5, no. 23163; Stolypin to Zein, July 30, 1911, VA KKK Fb 625; Stolypin to Kasso, July 30, 1911, VA KKK Fb 625, no. 3737.

62. VA KKK, Fb 620, 2-A-7.

63. Conroy, *Peter Arkad'evich Stolypin*, p. 117; See also Weeks, *Nation and State*, p. 189; Steinberg, "The Kholm Question," pp. 44–45.

64. Weeks, *Nation and State*, pp. 184–88. See also, Chmielewski, *The Polish Question*, pp. 111–37.

65. Avrekh, *Stolypin i tretia duma*, pp. 122–23.

66. Weeks, *Nation and State*, pp. 180–81. The figure of 168,000 is given in Avrekh, *Stolypin i tretia duma*, p. 119. Steinberg, "The Kholm Question," p. iii, gives the figure of 200,000 converts, which seems too high.

67. Avrekh, *Stolypin i tretia duma*, pp. 109–10. Steinberg, "The Kholm Question," p. 39.

68. "P. A. Stolypin o vydelenii Kholmshchiny," *Slovo*, May 22–June 4, 1909, p. 3.

69. Avrekh, *P. A. Stolypin i sudby reform*, p. 168; Weeks, *Nation and State*, p. 191.

70. Stolypin to Olga, Sept. 9, 1910, RGIA, f. 1662, op. 1, d. 231, l. 92.

71. Zyrianov, *Politicheskii portret*, pp. 79–80, 93; Robinson, *Rural Russia*, pp. 250–51; Pavlovsky, *Agricultural Russia*, pp. 177–78; Treadgold, *The Great Siberian Migration*, p. 34.

72. Stolypin and Krivoshein, *Poezdka v Sibir*, p. 1.

73. Stolypin to Nicholas, Sept. 26, 1910, "Iz perepiski P. A. Stolypina," p. 82.

74. Stolypin to Olga, Sept. 9, 1910, RGIA, f. 1662, op. 1, d. 231, ll. 92–93

75. "Iz perepiska P. A. Stolypina," p. 83.

76. On this point, see Treadgold, *The Great Siberian Migration*, pp. 182–83.

77. "Iz perepiska P. A. Stolypina," p. 83.

78. Stolypin and Krivoshein, *Poezdka v Sibir*, pp. 114, 117. For an English summary of the book, see Treadgold, *The Great Siberian Migration*, pp. 160–83.

79. Stolypin and Krivoshein, *Poezdka v Sibir*, p. 18.

80. Zyrianov, *Politicheskii portret*, p. 93.

81. Keep, *Last of the Empires*, pp. 112–13.

Chapter 8: The Last Defeat

1. German Embassy in St. Petersburg to Berlin, June 15, 1910, PAAA.

2. Pares, "Conversations with Mr. Stolypin," p. 109.

3. Verpakhovskaia, *Gosudarstvennaia deiatelnost predsedatelia*, vol. 2, pp. 1–3. The article was originally published as "O vnutrennoi politiki" in *Novoe vremia*, Jan. 13, 1911, without indicating the name of the interviewee, but in the issue of September 10, 1911, p. 4, Stolypin is listed as the source of the interview. See Wcislo, *Reforming Rural Russia*, p. 282.

4. German Embassy in St. Petersburg to Berlin, June 15, 1910, PAAA; Bogdanovich, *Tri poslednikh samoderzhtsa*, p. 477.

5. German Embassy in St. Petersburg to Berlin, June 15, 1910, PAAA.

6. Stolypin to Tsar Nicholas, Nov. 10, 1910, "Iz perepiski P. A. Stolypina," pp. 83–84.

7. Gurliand to Stolypin, Oct. 14, 1910, RGIA, f. 1629, op. 1, d. 55, l. 1.

8. These figures, taken from Conroy, *Peter Arkad'evich Stolypin*, p. 138, are based on the census of 1897.

9. Hosking, *The Russian Constitutional Experiment*, pp. 117–18. See pp. 106–49 for an analytical account of the Western Zemstvo controversy.

10. Avrekh, "Vopros o zapadnom zemstve," p. 66.

11. *Otchety, Sovet, 1908–9*, cols. 1941–42. For Stolypin's speech in the Duma on this topic on May 30, 1909, see *Otchety, Duma, 1909*, session 2, part 4, cols. 2750–57 and 2761–62.

12. *Otchety, Duma, 1909*, session 2, part 4, col. 2756.

13. Kokovtsov, *Out of My Past*, p. 261.

14. Verpakhovskaia, *Gosudarstvennaia deiatelnost predsedatelia*, vol. 1, pp. 15–21.

15. *Pravo*, Dec. 25, 1909, col. 2946.

16. *Otchety, Duma, 1910*, session 3, part 4, col. 779.

17. Avrekh, "Vopros o zapadnom zemstve," pp. 69–70; for an English translation of the bill as enacted in March 1911, see Zenkovsky, *Stolypin*, pp. 129–39.

18. On the amendments, see Hosking, *The Russian Constitutional Experiment*, pp. 123–25. Most of the amendments were later excluded by the State Council.

19. Quoted in ibid., p. 127.

20. Ibid., p. 128.

21. *Otchety, Duma, 1910*, session 2, part 4, cols. 775, 784.

22. Ibid., col. 1391.

23. Ibid., cols. 784, 785, 791.

24. Quoted in Hosking, *The Russian Constitutional Experiment*, p. 131.

25. *The Memoirs of Count Witte*, p. 732.

26. Quoted in Chmielewski, "Stolypin's Last Crisis," p. 108.

27. Kokovtsov, *Out of My Past*, p. 262.

28. *Otchety, Sovet, 1910–11*, cols. 866–67.

29. Ibid., col. 871.

30. Ibid., col. 1241.

31. Kokovtsov, *Out of My Past*, p. 263.

32. *Otchety, Sovet, 1910–11*, col. 927, quoted in Tokmakoff, "Stolypin and the Third Duma," p. 151.

33. Von Bock, *Reminiscences*, p. 259; for a somewhat different version of the incident, see Zyrianov, *Politicheskii portret*, p. 103.

34. Zyrianov, *Politicheskii portret*, p. 104; Kokovtsov, *Out of My Past*, p. 262.

35. Tokmakoff, "Stolypin and the Third Duma," p. 165.

36. Kokovtsov, *Out of My Past*, p. 263.

37. Avrekh, "Vopros o Zapadnom zemstve," pp. 104–5.

38. "Dnevnik A. A. Bobrinskogo," p. 144.

39. RGIA, f. 1662, op. 1, d. 325, l. 1.

40. German Embassy in St. Petersburg to Berlin, March 25, 1911, PAAA.

41. RGIA, f. 1662, op. 1, d. 325, l. 1.

42. Ibid. Emphasis in original.

43. Kokovtsov, *Out of My Past*, p. 264.

44. RGIA, f. 1662, op. 1, d. 325, ll. 1–2. Emphasis in original.

45. Kokovtsov, *Out of My Past*, p. 264.

46. Tikhomirov, "Iz dnevnika L. Tikhomirova," no. 74, pp. 186–87.

47. *Rech*, March 9, 1911, p. 1.

48. *Rossiia*, March 10, 1911, p. 1.

49. *Birzhevye vodomosti*, March 11, 1911, p. 1.

50. Verpakhovskaia, *Gosudarstvennaia deiatelnost predsedatelia*, vol. 2, pp. 80–82.

51. Kokovtsov, *Out of My Past*, p. 265.

52. Von Bock, *Reminiscences*, p. 263.

53. German Embassy in St. Petersburg to Berlin, March 25, 1911, PAAA; see also British Embassy in St. Petersburg to London, March 23, 1911, *British Documents*, vol. 6, p. 93.

54. GARF, f. 601, op. 1, d. 1125, ll. 53–54, in Hagen, "Nikolaj II. an Stolypin," p. 69. There is a translation of the letter in Hosking, *The Russian Constitutional Experiment*, pp. 137–38.

55. Von Bock, *Reminiscences*, pp. 263–64.

56. "Dnevnik A. A. Bobrinskogo," p. 146.

57. Zyrianov, "Politicheskii portret," p. 104.

58. Quoted in Hosking, *The Russian Constitutional Experiment*, p. 139.

59. *Golos Moskvy*, March 15, 1911, cited in Hosking, *The Russian Constitutional Experiment*, p. 139.

60. German Embassy in St. Petersburg to Berlin, April 1, 1911, PAAA.

61. "Dnevnik A. A. Bobrinskogo," pp. 146–47.

62. Ibid., p. 148.

63. Polivanov, *Iz dnevnikov*, p. 104.

64. Pares, "Alexander Guchkov," p. 129; Guchkov, "Iz Vospominaniia A. I. Guchkova," reprinted in Gurko, *Features and Figures*, p. 723; Polivanov, *Iz dnevnikov*, p. 104.

65. British Embassy in St. Petersburg to London, April 6, 1911, BDFA.

66. "Dnevnik A. A. Bobrinskogo," p. 149.

67. German Embassy in St. Petersburg to Berlin, April 1 and May 24, 1911, PAAA.

68. Drabkina, "Iz Zapisnoi," pp. 210–11.

69. Hosking, *The Russian Constitutional Experiment*, p. 159.

70. Edelman, *Gentry Politics*, p. 121.

71. Solzhenitsyn, *August 1914*, p. 591.

72. Kokovtsov, *Out of My Past*, p. 268.

73. Reprinted in Hagen, "Nikolaj II. an Stolypin," p. 69.

74. See, for example, Ananych et al., *Krizis*, p. 495; Weissman, *Reform in Tsarist Russia*, p. 200; Hosking, *The Russian Constitutional Experiment*, p. 147.

75. Hagen "Nikolaj II. an Stolypin," p. 67.

76. German Embassy in St. Petersburg to Berlin, May 15, 1911, PAAA.

77. Bogdanovich, *Tri poslednikh samoderzhtsa*, pp. 475–76.

78. Von Bock, *Reminiscences*, p. 269.

79. Pares, *The Fall of the Russian Monarchy*, pp. 142–43.

80. Verpakhovskaia, *Gosudarstvennaia deiatelnost predsedatelia*, vol. 2, pp. 193–94.

81. Kokovtsov, *Out of My Past*, p. 268.

82. Stremoukhov, "Moia borba," pp. 14–16.

83. Hosking, *The Russian Constitutional Experiment*, p. 147.

84. "Iz perepiski Stolypina," pp. 85–86.

85. "Dnevnik A. A. Bobrinskogo," p. 149.

86. *Otchety, Sovet, 1910–11*, cols. 1405–6.

87. Ibid., cols. 1781–95.

88. *Otchety, Duma, 1911*, cols. 2850–63. Translations of two quotations are from Chmielewski, "Last Crisis," pp. 124–25.

89. British Embassy in St. Petersburg to London, June 14, 1911, *British Documents*, vol. 6, p. 158.

90. *British Documents*, vol. 6, p. 164.

91. Kokovtsov, *Out of My Past*, p. 268.

92. *British Documents*, vol. 6, p. 165.

93. Edelman, *Gentry Politics*, pp. 136–39; British Embassy in St. Petersburg to London, Sept. 1, 1911, *British Documents*, vol. 6, pp. 172–73.

94. Quoted in Edelman, *Gentry Politics*, p. 139.

Chapter 9: Assassination

1. Zenkovsky, *Stolypin*, p. 29.

2. Ibid., p. ix; Von Bock, *Reminiscences*, p. 282. Von Bock refers in general terms to a governmental commission that "carried off" a batch of Stolypin's papers from Kolnoberzhe that dealt with official matters. Among them were some incomplete works by her father "about the future political arrangements of Russia, handwritten in the last day of Papa's life." Von Bock did not know that A. V. Zenkovsky had a copy of these notes. Ibid., p. 283.

3. Zenkovsky, *Stolypin*, p. 28. In 1956 Zenkovsky's son, Serge, wrote that his father had decided to keep the notes secret because Stolypin's policies

"had been sharply attacked both by the left and the extreme right." This would explain his failure to publish the notes in the years from 1911 to 1917, but it does not explain his failure to do so for three and a half decades after he emigrated. See ibid., p. 141.

4. Avrekh, *P. A. Stolypin i sudby*, pp. 242–53, for all his queries about the authenticity of Zenkovsky's book.

5. Zenkovsky, *Stolypin*, pp. 47–48.

6. Ibid., p. 31.

7. Ibid., pp. 31–36.

8. For further details on these proposals, see ibid., pp. 38–49.

9. On Nicholas's role in convoking the Hague conference in 1899, see Morrill, "Nicholas II and the Call for the First Hague Conference."

10. Zenkovsky, *Stolypin*, pp. 50–57.

11. Von Bock, *Reminiscences*, pp. 267–68; Kokovtsov, *Out of My Past*, pp. 268–69; Tokmakoff, *P. A. Stolypin and the Third Duma*, pp. 207–8.

12. German Consulate in Kiev to Berlin, Aug. 3, 1911, PAAA. Gan, "Ubiistvo Stolypina," pp. 961, 962, 974.

13. Kokovtsov, *Out of My Past*, p. 271.

14. Pares, "Alexander Guchkov," p. 129. Guchkov, "Iz vospominanii A. I. Guchkova"; reprinted in trans. in Gurko, *Features and Figures*, p. 724.

15. Kryzhanovskii Archive, Box 2, File 5, Bakh.

16. RGIA, f. 1662, op. 1, d. 231, ll. 96–97.

17. British Embassy in St. Petersburg to London, Sept. 29, 1911, *British Documents*, vol. 6, p. 175; Kokovtsov, *Out of My Past*, p. 272; Von Bock, *Reminiscences*, p. 277.

18. British Embassy in St. Petersburg, Sept. 20, 1911, *British Documents*, vol. 6, pp. 176–77.

19. *St. Petersburg Zeitung*, Sept. 3, 1911, p. 1.

20. GARF, f. 60, op. 1, d. 1352, l. 15; "Nikolai Romanov ob ubiistve Stolypina," p. 210.

21. Von Bock, *Reminiscences*, p. 280.

22. "Nikolai Romanov ob ubiistve Stolypina," pp. 209–11.

23. Ibid., p. 211; Kokovtsov, *Out of My Past*, p. 277.

24. Kokovtsov, *Out of My Past*, p. 283.

25. *Russkoe slovo*, Sept. 3, 1911, p. 1.

26. Ibid., Sept. 8, 1911, p. 1; *Rech*, Sept. 3, 1911, p. 1.

27. *Russkoe slovo*, Sept. 8, 1911, p. 1. For more details on the fear that gripped the Jewish community of Kiev, see Liubchenko.

28. British Embassy in St. Petersburg, Sept. 20, 1911, *British Documents*, vol. 6, p. 176.

29. *Rannee Utro*, Sept. 4, 1911, p. 1; *Russkoe slovo*, Sept. 8, 1911, p. 1; *Utro Rossii*, Sept. 8, 1911, p. 1; *Birzhevye vedomosti*, Sept. 8, 1911, p. 1; *Novoe vremia*, Sept. 7, 1911, p. 1; Kokovtsov, *Out of My Past*, pp. 272–74.

30. *Otchety, Duma, 1911*, session 5, meeting 1, cols. 26–27. See also British Embassy in St. Petersburg, Nov. 2, 1911, *British Documents*, vol. 6, p. 180.

31. *Otchety, Duma, 1911*, session 5, meeting 1, col. 41.

32. British Embassy in St. Petersburg, Nov. 2, 1911, *British Documents*, vol. 6, p. 180.

33. British Embassy in St. Petersburg to London, Sept. 20, 1911, ibid., vol. 6, p. 176; *St. Petersburg Zeitung*, Sept. 3, 1911; Kryzhanovskii, *Vospominaniia*, p. 212; Solzhenitsyn, *August, 1914*, p. 493.

34. *Otchety, Duma, 1911*, session 5, meeting 1, cols. 55–57.

35. Serebrennikov, *Ubiistvo Stolypina*, pp. 23–24. On the question of Bogrov's Jewishness as well as on the assassination, see also Pipes, *The Russian Revolution*, pp. 187–90.

36. See, for example, *Utro Rossii*, Sept. 3, 1911, p. 1.

37. Gan, "Ubiistvo Stolypina," p. 988; Bazylev, "Zagadka 1 sentiabria 1911 g.," p. 120.

38. For the biographical information on Bogrov, see Bazylev, "Zagadka 1 sentiabria 1911 g.," p. 119; Gan, "Ubiistvo Stolypina," pp. 964–65; Tokmakoff, "Stolypin's Assassin," p. 314.

39. Tokmakoff, "Stolypin's Assassin," p. 316.

40. Ibid., pp. 317–18.

41. Gan, "Ubiistvo Stolypina," pp. 966–67, 970–72; Bazylev, "Zagadka 1 sentiabria 1911 g.," p. 121.

42. Gan, "Ubiistvo Stolypina," pp. 978–83.

43. Ibid., pp. 989–93.

44. Ibid., p. 995. Bazylev, "Zagadka 1 sentiabria 1911 g.," p. 123; Tokmakoff, "Stolypin's Assassin," pp. 320–21.

45. Serebrennikov and Sidorovnin, *Stolypin*, pp. 23–24.

46. Gan, "Ubiistvo Stolypina," p. 997.

47. Ibid., pp. 208, 214.

48. Ibid., pp. 194–201.

49. Stepanov, *Zagadki ubiistva Stolypina*, p. 159; Guchkov, "Iz vospominanii A. I. Guchkova," p. 1; *Otchety, Duma, 1911*, pp. 32–33.

50. Avrekh, "Stolypin, liberaly, revoliutsiia," p. 56.

51. Avrekh, *Stolypin i tretia duma*, pp. 367–406; Hosking, *The Russian Constitutional Experiment*, p. 148; Ananych et al., *Krizis samoderzhaviia*, p. 495.

52. Avrekh, *Stolypin i tretia duma*, pp. 396–97; see also Zuckerman, *The Tsarist Secret Police*, p. 193.

53. Avrekh, *Stolypin i tretia duma*, pp. 404–5.

54. Gan, "Ubiistvo Stolypina," pp. 985–86.

55. Kokovtsov, *Out of My Past*, p. 274.

56. Pipes, *The Russian Revolution*, p. 190.

57. Kokovtsov, *Out of My Past*, p. 341.

58. Bazylev, "Zagadka 1 sentiabria 1911 g.," p. 127; Gan, "Ubiistvo Stolypina," pp. 194–95; British Embassy in St. Petersburg to London, November 2, 1911, *British Documents*, vol. 6, p. 180.

59. Pipes argues this point in *The Russian Revolution*, p. 190.

60. Mushin, *Dmitrii Bogrov i ubiistvo Stolypina*, pp. 122–23, cited in Avrekh, *Stolypin i tretia duma*, p. 376.

61. Memorandum for the British government prepared by Bernard Pares, December 23, 1911, *British Documents*, vol. 6, p. 185.

62. Ibid., pp. 186–87.

63. Ibid., p. 188.

64. Ibid., p. 186.

65. British Embassy in St. Petersburg to London, Oct. 4, 1911, *British Documents*, vol. 6, pp. 179–80. See also Edelman, *Gentry Politics*, p. 141, for a discussion of this point.

66. Lenin, *Collected Works*, vol. 17, pp. 247–56.

67. *Zemshchina*, Sept. 3, 1911, p. 1; *Novoe vremia*, Sept. 8, 1911, p. 1.

68. Von Bock, *Reminiscences*, p. 276. German Consulate in Kiev to Berlin, Sept. 20, 1911, PAAA. Iskra was a colonel and Kochubey a high Cossack official who in 1708 warned Peter the Great of a plot by Hetman Mazepa, the king of Poland, and the king of Sweden to unseat the tsar of Russia. Peter did not believe the two men, handing them over to Mazepa, who executed them. A year later, it turned out that the report of a plot was accurate; Peter waged war against Sweden and Mazepa, defeating them in the famous battle of Poltava. The victory elevated Russia into a significant power in Europe.

69. Von Bock, *Reminiscences*, p. 283.

Conclusion: Stolypin's Legacy

1. On the election of the Fourth Duma, see Edelman, *Gentry Politics*, p. 169.

2. Lieven, *Russia and the Origins of the First World War*, p. 60.

3. Ibid., pp. 142–43.

4. On Durnovo's memorandum see ibid., pp. 77–83.

5. Weber, *Gesammelte Politische Schriften*, p. 307; I have used the translation in Pflanze, *Bismarck and the Development of Germany*, vol. 3, p. 441. Emphasis in original.

6. For Weber's article in its entirety, see his *Gesammelte Politische Schriften*, pp. 298–308.

Bibliography

Newspapers and Journals

Birzhevye vedomosti. St. Petersburg. Moderately conservative newspaper.
Moskovskie vedomosti. Moscow. Conservative newspaper.
Nasha zhizn. St. Petersburg. Left-liberal daily; sympathetic to the Socialist
　Revolutionaries.
Niva. St. Petersburg. Moderate conservative magazine.
Novoe vremia. St. Petersburg. Pro-government newspaper.
Pravitelstvennyi vestnik. St. Petersburg. Official government paper.
Pravo. St. Petersburg. Weekly juridical journal. Liberal, close to Kadets.
Rannee utro. Moscow. Liberal newspaper.
Rech. St. Petersburg. Daily of Kadet orientation, though not officially a party
　publication.
Rossiia. St. Petersburg. Newspaper financed by government.
Rus. St. Petersburg. Liberal daily newspaper.
Russkie vedomosti. Moscow. Liberal newspaper; after 1905, close to the
　moderate Kadets.
Russkoe slovo. Moscow. Moderately liberal newspaper.
Russkoe znamia. St. Petersburg. Official organ of the right-wing Union of
　the Russian People.
Syn otechestva. St. Petersburg. Initially a liberal paper; came under the in-
　fluence of the Socialist Revolutionaries.
Tovarishch. St. Petersburg. Left-wing paper.
Utro Rossii. St. Petersburg. Liberal newspaper.
Vestnik Evropy. Moscow. Moderate-liberal historical and political journal.
Vestnik partii narodnoi svobody. St. Petersburg. Kadet paper.
Zemshchina. St. Petersburg. Right-wing newspaper.

Memoirs and Published Documents

Argunov, A. A. "Iz vospominanii o pervoi russkoi revoliutsii," *Katorga i
　ssylka,* no. 1 (1931), pp. 142–61.
Ascher, Abraham, tr. and ed. "The Coming Storm: The Austro-Hungarian
　Embassy on Russia's Internal Crisis, 1902–1906," *Survey: A Journal of
　Soviet and East European Studies,* no. 53 (1964), pp. 148–64.
Askew, William C. "An American View of Bloody Sunday," *Russian Re-
　view,* no. 2 (1952), pp. 35–43.

Balashev, P. N. "Pismo Balasheva k Stolypinu," *Krasnyi arkhiv*, no. 9 (1925), pp. 291–94.

Baring, Maurice. *A Year in Russia*. London, 1917 (original ed., 1907).

Bing, Edward J., ed. *The Secret Letters of the Last Tsar*. New York, 1938.

Bogdanovich, A. V. *Tri poslednikh samoderzhtsa: Dnevnik A. V. Bogdanovicha*. Moscow-Leningrad, 1924.

Bok, M. P. *Vospominaniia o moem otse P. A. Stolypine*. New York, 1953.

———. [Von Bock, Maria Petrovna]. *Reminiscences of My Father, Peter A. Stolypin*. Tr. and ed. Margaret Patoski. Metuchen, N.J., 1970.

———. "Stolypin in Saratov," *Russian Review*, no. 3 (1953), pp. 187–93.

"Borba s revoliutsionnym dvizheniem na Kavkaze v epokhu stolypinshchiny (iz perepiski P. A. Stolypina s grafom I. I. Vorontsovym-Dashkovym)," *Krasnyi arkhiv*, no. 34 (1929), pp. 184–221; no. 35 (1929), pp. 128–50.

Chernovskii, A., ed. *Soiuz Russkogo Naroda: Po materialam chrezvychainoi sledstvennoi komissii vremennogo pravitelstva 1917 g*. Moscow-Leningrad, 1929.

Dillon, Edward J. *The Eclipse of Russia*. New York, 1918.

"Dnevnik A. A. Bobrinskogo," *Krasnyi arkhiv*, no. 26 (1928), pp. 127–50.

"Dnevnik A. A. Polovtseva," *Krasnyi arkhiv*, no. 3 (1923), pp. 75–172; no. 4 (1923), pp. 63–128.

Dnevnik Imperatora Nikolaia II. Berlin, 1923.

Drabkina, F. "Iz zapisnoi knizhki arkhivista. P. A. Stolypin i frantsuzskaia pressa v 1911 g.," *Krasnyi arkhiv*, no. 32 (1929), pp. 209–11.

Drezen, A. K. ed. *Tsarizm v borbe s revoliutsiei 1905–1907 gg.: Sbornik dokumentov*. Moscow, 1936.

Freeze, Gregory L., ed. *From Supplication to Revolution: A Documentary Social History of Imperial Russia*. New York, 1988.

Gerassimoff, Alexander. *Der Kampf gegen die erste Russische Revolution. Erinnerungen*. Tr. Ernst Thälmann. Frauenfeld und Leipzig, 1934.

[Golovin, F. A.]."Iz zapisok F. A. Golovina," *Krasnyi arkhiv*, no. 58 (1933), pp. 140–49.

———. "Razgon II Gosudarstvennaia Dumy," *Krasnyi arkhiv*, no. 43 (1930), pp. 55–91.

———. "Vospominaniia F. A. Golovina o II Gosudarstvennoi Dume," *Istoricheskii arkhiv*, no. 4 (1959), pp. 136–65; no. 5, pp. 128–54; no. 6, pp. 56–81.

———. "Zapiski F. A. Golovina," *Krasnyi arkhiv*, no. 19 (1926), pp. 110–49.

Gosudarstvennyi Sovet. Petrograd, 1915.

Guchkov, A. I. "Iz vospominanii A. I. Guchkova," *Poslednie novosti*, Aug. 9, 1936, pp. 1 ff.

Gurko, V. I. *Features and Figures of the Past; Government and Opinion in the Reign of Nicholas II*. Tr. Laura Matveev. Stanford, Calif., 1939.

Hagen, Manfred, tr. and ed. "Nikolaj II. an Stolypin: Unveröffentlichte Handschreiben des letzten Zaren an den Ministerpräsidenten (1906–1911) in sowjetischen Archiven," *Jahrbücher für Geschichte Osteuropas*, no. 1 (1978), pp. 60–69.

"Iz perepiski Nikolaia i Marii Romanovykh v 1907–1910 g.," *Krasnyi arkhiv*, no. 50–51 (1932), pp. 161–93.

"Iz perepiski P. A. Stolypina s Nikolaem Romanovym," *Krasnyi arkhiv*, no. 30 (1928), pp. 80–88.

[Izvolskii, A. A.]. *Au Service de la Russie: Correspondence Diplomatique, 1906–1911.* Ed. Hélène Izwolsky. 2 vols. Paris, 1919.

———. *Recollections of a Foreign Minister (Memoirs of Alexander Izwolsky).* Tr. Charles Louis Seeger. Garden City, N.Y., 1921.

Karpov, N. I. *Krestianskoe dvizhenie v revoliutsii 1905 goda v dokumentakh.* Leningrad, 1926.

"K istorii agrarnoi reformy Stolypina," *Krasnyi arkhiv*, no. 17 (1926), pp. 81–87.

"K istorii anglo-russkogo soglasheniia 1907 g.," *Krasnyi arkhiv*, no. 69–70 (1935), pp. 3–39.

"K istorii aresta i suda nad S.D. fraktsiei 2-oi Gosudarstvennoi dumy," *Krasnyi arkhiv*, no. 16 (1926), pp. 76–116.

Kizevetter, A. A. *Na rubezhe dvukh stoletii (Vospominaniia 1881–1914).* Prague, 1929.

Koefoed, C. A. *My Share in the Stolypin Agrarian Reforms.* Ed. Bent Jensen. Tr. Alison Borch-Johansen. Odense, Denmark, 1985.

Kokovtsov, V. N. *Out of My Past: The Memoirs of Count Kokovtsov.* Stanford, Calif., 1935.

Kryzhanovskii, S. E. *Vospominaniia.* Berlin, 1938.

Kurlov, P. G. *Gibel imperatorskoi Rossii.* Berlin, 1923.

Liadov, M. N. *Iz zhizni partii nakanune i v gody pervoi revoliutsii (Vospominaniia).* Moscow, 1926.

Liubchenko, V., ed. "'Pogrom visit v vozdukhe': Obshchestvennye nastroeniia v kieve posle pokusheniia na P. A. Stolypina (po materialam perliustratsii)," *Vestnik Evreiskogo Unieversiteta: Istoriia, Kultura, Tsivilizatsiia*, no. 1 (19), (1999), pp. 272–86.

Logachev, V. V. *Sbornik rechei Petra Arkadevicha Stolypina proiznesennykh v zasedaniiakh Gosudarstvennogo soveta i Gosudarstvennoi dumy (1906–1911).* St. Petersburg, 1911.

Maklakov, V. A. *The First State Duma: Contemporary Reminiscences.* Tr. Mary Belkin. Bloomington, Ind., 1964.

———. *Vtoraia Gosudarstvennaia duma (vospominaniia sovremennika).* Paris, 1947.

Miliukov, P. N. *Vospominaniia (1859–1917).* Vol. 1. New York, 1955.

Mitskevich, S. I., ed. *Albom pervoi russkoi revoliutsii 1905–1907 gg.* Moscow, 1926.

Mossolov, A. A. *At the Court of the Last Tsar.* Tr. E. W. Dickes. London, 1935.

Naumov, A. N. *Iz utselevshikh vospominanii, 1868–1917.* 2 vols. New York, 1955.

Nevinson, Henry W. *The Dawn in Russia: Or Scenes in the Russian Revolution.* New York, 1906.

"Nikolai Romanov o revoliutsionnym dvizheniiv armii v 1905–1906 gg.," *Krasnyi arkhiv*, no. 41–42 (1930), pp. 215–30.

"Nikolai Romanov ob ubiistve Stolypina," *Krasnyi arkhiv*, no. 35 (1929), pp. 209–11.

Obolenskii, A. D. *Moi vospominaniia i razmyshleniia.* Stockholm, 1961.

Okreits, S. "Audentsiia u P. A. Stolypina i katastrofa 12-ogo avgusta," *Istoricheskii vestnik,* vol. 131 (1913), pp. 864–79.

Osobyi zhurnal soveta ministrov. Gosudarstvennaia tipografiia, 1906–1911. Microfilm at the library of the University of Illinois, Urbana.

Paleolog, S. N. *Okolo vlasti. Ocherki perezhitogo.* Belgrade, n.d.

Pares, Bernard. "Alexander Guchkov," *Slavic and East European Review,* vol. 15 (1936–37), pp. 121–34.

——. "Conversations with Mr. Stolypin," *Russian Review,* vol. 2 (1913), pp. 101–10.

——. *My Russian Memoirs.* London, 1931.

——. *A Wandering Student.* Syracuse, N.Y., 1948.

Parry Albert. *Full Steam Ahead! The Story of Peter Demens, Founder of St. Petersburg, Florida.* St. Petersburg, Fla., 1987.

"P. A. Stolypin i smertnaia kazn v 1908 g.," *Krasnyi arkhiv,* no. 19 (1926), pp. 215–21.

"P. A. Stolypin i Sveaborgskoe vosstanie," *Krasnyi arkhiv,* no. 49 (1931), pp. 144–48.

"P. A. Stolypin o vydelenii Kholmshchiny," *Slovo,* no. 803 (May 22–June 4, 1909), p. 3.

"Perepiska Grafa S. Iu. Vitte i P. A. Stolypina," *Russkaia mysl,* no. 36 (1915), pp. 134–52.

"Perepiska N. A. Romanova i P. A. Stolypina," *Krasnyi arkhiv,* no. 5 (1924), pp. 102–28.

"Perepiska Nikolaia II i Marii Fedorovny (1905–1906 gg.)," *Krasnyi arkhiv,* no. 3 (1927), pp. 153–209.

"Perepiska Tolstogo s A. A. Stolypinym," in N. Guseva, ed., *Literaturnoe nasledstvo.* Moscow, 1939, pp. 324–29.

Perepiska Vilgelma II i Nikolaia II. Petrograd, 1923.

Petrunkevich, I. I. "Iz zapisok obshchestvennogo deiatela," *Arkhiv russkoi revoliutsii.* Berlin, 1934.

"Pismo predsedateliia sovetov ministrov i ministra vnutr. del P. A. Stolypina na imia namestnika na Kavkaze gr. I. I. Vorontsova-Dashkova ot 11 aprelia 1908 g.," *Krasnyi arkhiv,* no. 34 (1929), pp. 187–202.

Polivanov, A. A. *Iz dnevnikov i vospominanii po dolzhnosti voennogo ministra i ego pomoshchnika (1907–16).* Moscow, 1924.

Polnoe sobranie zakonov Rossiiskoi Imperii, Seriia 3-ia. St. Petersburg, 1885–1916. Vols. 25, 26, 27.

[Rediger, A. F.]. "Iz zapisok A. F. Redigera," *Krasnyi arkhiv,* no. 45 (1933), pp. 92–133.

——. "Zapiski A. F. Redigera o 1905 g.," *Krasnyi arkhiv,* no. 2 (1931), pp. 86–111.

Semenov-Tian-Shanskii, N. "Svetloi pamiati P. A. Stolypina," *Vozrozhdenie,* vol. 118 (1961), pp. 79–100.

Serebrennikov, A., ed. *Ubiistvo Stolypina: Svidetelstva i dokumenty.* Riga, 1990.

Shchegolev, P. E., ed. *Padenie tsarskogo rezhima: Stenograficheskie otchety doprosov i pokazanii, dannykh v 1917 g. v chrezvychainoi sledstvennoi komissii vremennogo pravitelstva.* 7 vols. Leningrad and Moscow, 1924–27.

Shidlovskii, S. I. *Vospominaniia.* 2 vols. Berlin, 1923.

Shipov, D. N. *Vospominaniia i dumy o perezhitom.* Moscow, 1918.

Shulgin, V. V. *Dni.* Leningrad, 1927.

———. "Glavy iz knigi 'Gody,'" *Istoriia SSSR,* no. 6 (1966), pp. 65–91.

Shvarts [Schwartz], A. N. *Moia perepiska so Stolypinym: Moi vospominaniia o Gosudare.* Moscow, 1994.

Skripitsyn, V. A. *Bogatyr mysli, slova i dela.* St. Petersburg, 1911.

Sovremennaia Rossiia v portretakh i biografiiakh vydaiushchikhsia deiatelei. St. Petersburg, 1904.

Spiridovich, A. I. *Les dernières années de la cour de Tsarskoe-Selo.* Tr. M. Jeanson. 2 vols. Paris, 1928.

Stolypin, P. A. *Polnoe sobranie rechei v Gosudarstvennoi dume i Gosudarstvennom sovete, 1906–1911.* Moscow, 1991.

———. "Soobshchenie Saratovskago gubernatora," *Pravo,* no. 30 (Aug. 2, 1905), cols. 2458–59.

Stolypin, P. A., and A. V. Krivoshein. *Poezdka v Sibir i Povolzhe.* St. Petersburg, 1911.

Stremoukhov, P. P. "Moia borba s episkopom Germogenom i Iliodorom," *Arkhiv russkoi revoliutsii.* Berlin, 1925.

Strumillo, B. "Materialy o Dm. Bogrove," *Krasnaia letopis,* no. 9 (1923), pp. 177–89; no. 1/10 (1924), pp. 226–40.

Syromiatnikov, S. N. "Reminiscences of Stolypin," *Russian Review,* no. 2 (1912), pp. 71–88.

———. "Zheleznyi ministr," *Rossiia,* no. 1786 (Sept. 11/24, 1911), p. 2.

Tcharykow, N. "Reminiscences of Nicholas II," *Contemporary Review,* no. 134 (1928), pp. 445–53.

Teitel, Ia. L. *Iz moei zhizni: Za sorok let.* Paris, 1925.

Tikhomirov, L. "Iz dnevnika L. Tikhomirova," *Krasnyi arkhiv,* no. 72 (1935), pp. 120–59; no. 73 (1935), pp. 170–90; no. 74 (1936), pp. 162–91.

Timashev, S. I. "Kabinet Stolypina: Iz 'zapisok' ministra torgovli i promyshlennosti," *Russkoe proshloe,* no. 6 (1996), pp. 95–130.

Trudy mestnykh komitetov o nuzhdakh selskokhoziaistvennoi promyshlennosti. Vol. 11, Grodenskaia guberniia. St. Petersburg, 1903.

"Tsirkuliar predsedateliia soveta ministrov P. A. Stolypina ot 15 sentiabria 1906 g. general gubernatoram, gubernatoram i gradonachalnikam," *Krasnyi arkhiv,* no. 32 (1929), pp. 158–82.

Tverskoi, P. A. "K istoricheskim materialam o pokoinom P. A. Stolypine," *Vestnik Evropy,* no. 4 (1912), pp. 183–201.

Vinaver, M. *Istoriia vyborgskogo vozzvaniia (Vospominaniia).* Petrograd, 1917.

———. *Konflikty v pervoi dume.* St. Petersburg, 1907.

Witte [Vitte], S. Iu. *The Memoirs of Count Witte.* Tr. and ed. Sidney Harcave. Armonk, N.Y., 1990.

———. *Vospominaniia.* 2d ed. 3 vols. Leningrad, 1924.

Zenkovsky, A. V. *Stolypin: Russia's Last Great Reformer*. Tr. Margaret Patoski. Princeton, N.J., 1986. (This includes a translation of Zenkovsky's
Pravda o Stolypine. New York, 1956.)

Other Sources

Adams, Arthur C. "Pobedonostsev and the Rule of Firmness," *Slavonic and
East European Review*, vol. 12 (1953), pp. 132–39.
Agrarnoe dvizhenie v Rossii v 1905–1906 gg. Pub. Imperatorskoe Volnoe
Ekonomicheskoe Obshchestvo. 2 vols. St. Petersburg, 1908.
Alston, Patrick L. *Education and the State in Tsarist Russia*. Stanford, Calif.
1969.
Ananych, B. V. et al. *Krizis samoderzhaviia v Rossii 1895–1917 gg*. Lenin-
grad, 1984.
Anfimov, A. M. *Stolypin i rossiiskaia derevnia*. Moscow, 1992.
———. "Ten Stolypina nad Rossiei," *Istoriia SSSR*, no. 4 (1991), pp. 112–21.
Anweiler, Oskar. *Die Rätebewegung in Russland, 1905–1921*. Leiden, 1958.
———. "Die russische Revolution von 1905," *Jahrbücher für Geschichte
Osteuropas*, n.s. no. 1 (1955), pp. 161–93.
———. *Geschichte der Schule and Pädagogik in Russland vom Ende des
Zarenreiches bis zum Beginn der Stalin-Ära*. Berlin, 1964.
———. "Russian Schools," in Erwin Oberländer et al., eds., *Russia Enters
the Twentieth Century, 1894–1917*. New York, 1971, pp. 287–313.
Ascher, Abraham. *Pavel Axelrod and the Development of Menshevism*.
Cambridge, Mass., 1972.
———. "Prime Minister P. A. Stolypin and His 'Jewish' Adviser," *Journal of
Contemporary History*, no. 3 (1995), pp. 513–32.
———. *The Revolution of 1905*. Vol. 1: *Russia in Disarray*. Stanford, Calif.,
1988.
———. *The Revolution of 1905*. Vol. 2: *Authority Restored*. Stanford, Calif.,
1992.
———. "Soviet Historians and the Revolution of 1905," in Coquin and Ger-
vais-Francelle, eds., *1905*, pp. 476–96.
Atkinson, Dorothy. *The End of the Russian Land Commune, 1905–1930*.
Stanford, Calif., 1983.
———. "The Statistics on the Russian Land Commune, 1905–1917," *Slavic
Review*, no. 4 (1973), pp. 773–87.
Avrekh, A. Ia. "Lenskii rasstrel i krizis treteiiunskoi systemy," *Voprosy is-
torii*, no. 4 (1962), pp. 58–79.
———. "O nekotorykh voprosakh revoliutsionnoi situatsii," *Voprosy is-
torii KPSS*, no. 5 (1966), pp. 30–44.
———. *P. A. Stolypin i sudby reform v Rossii*. Moscow, 1991.
———. "P. A. Stolypin i sudby reform v Rossii," *Kommunist*, no. 1 (1991),
pp. 40–53.
———. "Stolypin, liberaly, revoliutsiia," in Figurovskaia and Stepanskii,
eds., *Gosudarstvennaia deiatelnost P. A. Stolypina*, pp. 34–66.
———. *Stolypin i tretia duma*. Moscow, 1968.

———. "Stolypinskii bonapartizm i voprosy voennoi politiki v 3-ei dume," *Voprosii istorii*, no. 11 (1956), pp. 17–33.

———. "Treiteiiunskaia monarkhiia i rabochii vopros," *Istoriia SSSR*, no. 1 (1966), pp. 42–69.

———. "III duma i nachalo krizisa treteiiunskoi sistemy (1908–1909 gg.)," *Instoricheskie zapiski*, no. 53 (1955), pp. 50–109.

———. *Tsarizm i treteiiunskaia sistema*. Moscow, 1966.

———. "Vopros o zapadnom zemstve i bankrotstvo Stolypina," *Istoricheskie zapiski*, no. 70 (1961), pp. 61–112.

Avrich, Paul. *The Russian Anarchists*. Princeton, N.J., 1967.

Baberowski, Jorg. *Autonomie und Justiz: Zum Verhältnis von Rechtsstaatlichkeit und Rückständigkeit im ausgehenden Zarenreich, 1864–1914*. Frankfurt am Main, 1996.

Babikov, I. I. "Krestianskoe dvizhenie v Saratovskoi gubernii nakanune pervoi russkoi revoliutsii," *Uchenye zapiski Saratovskogo gosudarstvennogo universiteta*, no. 55 (1956), pp. 172–218.

Balabanov, M. *Ot 1905 k 1917: Massovoe rabochee dvizhenie*. Moscow, 1927.

Balmuth, Daniel. *Censorship in Russia, 1865–1905*. Washington, D.C., 1979.

Bartlett, Roger, ed. *Land Commune and Peasant Community in Russia: Communal Forms in Imperial and Early Soviet Society*. New York, 1990.

Bazylev, L. "Zagadka 1 sentiabria 1911 g.," *Voprosy istorii*, no. 7 (1975), pp. 115–29.

Bazylow, Ludwik. *Ostatnie lata Rosji Carskiej: Rzady Stolypina*. Warsaw, 1971.

Becker, Seymour. *Nobility and Privilege in Late Imperial Russia*. DeKalb, Ill., 1985.

Berlin, P. A. *Russkaia burzhuaziia v staroe i novoe vremiia*. Moscow, 1922.

Bestuzhev, I. V. "Borba v praviashchikh krugakh vokrug anneksii Bosnii i Gertsegoviny," *Istoricheskii arkhiv*, 5 (1962), pp. 113–47.

Bogrov, V. *Dmitrii Bogrov i ubiistvo Stolypina. Razoblacheniia "deistvitelnykh i mnimykh tain."* Berlin, 1931.

Bonnell, Victoria E. *Roots of Rebellion: Workers' Politics and Organizations in St. Petersburg and Moscow, 1900–1914*. Berkeley, Calif., 1983.

Borodin, A. P. "Usilenie pozitsii obedinennogo dvorianstvo v gosudarstvennom sovete v 1907–1914 godakh," *Voprosy istorii*, no. 2 (1977), pp. 56–66.

Bovykin, V. I. et al., eds. *Rabochii klass v pervoi rossiiskoi revolitsii 1905–1907 gg*. Moscow, 1981.

Brainerd, Michael Charles. "The Octobrists and the Gentry, 1905–1907: Leaders and Followers?" in Haimson, ed., *The Politics of Rural Russia*, pp. 67–93.

———. "The Union of October 17 and Russian Society, 1905–1907." Ph.D. diss., Columbia University, 1976.

Brock, John Joseph, Jr. "The Theory and Practice of the Union of the Russian People, 1905–1907: A Case Study of 'Black Hundred' Politics. Ph.D. diss., University of Michigan, 1972.

Bukhovets, O. G. "K metodike izucheniia 'prigovornogo' dvizheniia i ego roli v borbe krestianstva v 1905–1907 godakh (po materialam Samarskoi gubernii," *Istoriia SSSR*, no. 3 (1979), pp. 96–112.

Bushnell, John S. "Mutineers and Revolutionaries: Military Revolution in Russia, 1905–1907." Ph.D. diss., Indiana University, 1977.

———. *Mutiny and Repression: Russian Soldiers in the Revolution of 1905–1906.* Bloomington, Ind., 1985.

Byrnes, Robert F. *Pobedonostsev: His Life and Thought.* Bloomington, 1968.

Chermenskii, E. D. *Burzhuaziia i tsarizm v pervoi russkoi revoliutsii.* 2d ed. Moscow, 1970

Chmielewski, Edward. *The Polish Question in the Russian State Duma.* Knoxville, Tenn., 1972.

———. "The Separation of Chelm from Poland," *Polish Review*, no. 1 (1970), pp. 67–86.

———. "Stolypin and the Russian Ministerial Crisis of 1909," *California Slavic Studies*, vol. 4 (1967), pp. 1–38.

———. "Stolypin's Last Crisis," *California Slavic Studies*, vol. 3 (1964), pp. 95–126.

Christian, R. F. "Alexis Aladin: Trudovik Leader in the First Russian Duma: Materials for a Biography (1873–1920)," *Oxford Slavonic Papers*, vol. 21 (1989), pp. 131–52.

Chuprov, A. A. "The Break-up of the Village Commune in Russia," *Economic Journal*, vol. 22 (1912), pp. 173–97.

Conroy, Mary S., ed. *Emerging Democracy in Late Imperial Russia.* Niwot, Colo., 1998.

———. *Peter Arkad'evich Stolypin: Practical Politics in Late Tsarist Russia.* Boulder, Colo., 1976.

———. "Stolypin's Attitude toward Local Self-Government," *Slavonic and East European Review*, vol. 39 (1961), pp. 497–511.

Coquin, Francois-Xavier. *La Révolution russe Manquée.* Brussels, 1985.

———. *La Sibérie: Peuplement et Immigration Paysanne au XIXe Siècle.* Paris, 1969.

Coquin, Francois-Xavier, and Céline Gervais-Francelle, eds. *1905: La Première Révolution russe.* Paris, 1986.

Curtiss, John S. *Church and State in Russia: The Last Years of the Empire, 1900–1917.* New York, 1948.

Daly, Jonathan W. *Autocracy under Siege: Security Police and Opposition in Russia, 1866–1905.* DeKalb, Ill., 1998.

Derenkovskii, G. M. "Vseobshchaia stachka i sovety rabochikh deputatov v iiule 1906 g.," *Istoricheskie zapiski*, no. 77 (1965), pp. 108–53.

Derenkovskii, G. M., et al. "1905 god v Saratove," *Istoricheskie zapiski*, no. 54 (1955), pp. 74–104.

Diakin, V. S. *Burzhuaziia, dvorianstvo i tsarizm v 1911–1914 gg.: Razlozhenie treteiiunskoi sistemy.* Leningrad, 1968.

———. "Byl li shans u Stolypina?" *Zvezda*, no. 12 (1990), pp. 113–24.

———. *Samoderzhavie, burzhuaziia i dvorianstvo v 1907–1911 gg.* Leningrad, 1978.

———. "Stolypin i dvorianstvo: (proval mestnoi reformy)," in N. E. Nosov, ed., *Problemy krestianskogo zemlevladeniia i vnutrennei politiki Rossii, dooktiabrskoi period.* Leningrad, 1972, pp. 231–74.

———. "Zemstvo v treteiiunskoi monarkhii (struktura, izbiratelei i glasnykh)," *Istoricheskie zapiski,* no. 115 (1987), pp. 88–125.

Diakov, I. "Zabytyi ispolin: O Stolypin i ego reforme," *Nash sovremennik,* no. 3 (1990), pp. 131–42.

Doctorow, Gilbert S. "The Introduction of Parliamentary Institutions in Russia during the Revolution of 1905–1907." Ph.D. diss., Columbia University, 1975.

Drezen, A. K. *Armiia i flot v revoliutsii 1905 gg.* Moscow, 1931.

Dubrovskii, S. M. *Krestianskoe dvizhenie v revoliutsii 1905–1907 gg.* Moscow, 1956.

———. *Stolypinskaia zemelnaia reforma.* Moscow, 1963.

Edelman, Robert. *Gentry Politics on the Eve of the Russian Revolution: The Nationalist Party, 1907–1917.* New Brunswick, N.J., 1980.

———. *Proletarian Peasants: The Revolution of 1905 in Russia's Southwest.* Ithaca, N.Y., 1987.

Eklof, Ben. *Russian Peasant Schools: Officialdom, Village Culture, and Popular Pedagogy, 1861–1914.* Berkeley, Calif., 1986.

Emmons, Terence. *The Formation of Political Parties and the First National Elections in Russia.* Cambridge, Mass., 1983.

———. "Russia's Banquet Campaign," *California Slavic Studies,* no. 10 (1977), pp. 45–86.

Emmons, Terence, and Wayne S. Vucinich, eds. *The Zemstvo in Russia: An Experiment in Local Self-Government.* Cambridge, Eng., 1982.

Engelstein, Laura. *Moscow, 1905: Working-Class Organizations and Political Conflict.* Stanford, Calif., 1982.

Entsiklopedicheskii slovar.

Fallows, Thomas S. "Forging the Zemstvo Movement: Liberalism and Radicalism on the Volga, 1890–1915." Ph.D. diss., Harvard University, 1981.

———. "Governor Stolypin and the Revolution of 1905 in Saratov," in Wade and Seregny, eds., *Politics and Society in Provincial Russia,* pp. 160–91.

Feldman, Eliyahu. "On Stolypin's Attempt to Extend the Rights of Russian Jewry in 1906," *Shvut: Jewish Problems in the USSR and Eastern Europe,* no. 12 (1987), pp. 101–30 (in Hebrew).

Ferenczi, Caspar. *Aussenpolitik und Öffentlichkeit in Russland, 1906–1912.* Husum: Matthiesen, 1982.

Ferro, Marc. *Nicholas II: The Last of the Tsars.* Tr. Brian Pearce. New York, 1993.

Figes, Orlando. *A People's Tragedy: A History of the Russian Revolution.* New York, 1996.

Figurovskaia, N. K., and A. D. Stepanskii, eds., *Gosudarstvennaia deiatelnost P. A. Stolypina: Sbornik statei.* Moscow, 1994.

Fischer, George. *Russian Liberalism: From Gentry to Intelligentsia.* Cambridge, Mass., 1958.

Frankel, Jonathan. *Prophesy and Politics: Socialism, Nationalism, and the Russian Jews, 1862–1917.* Cambridge, Eng., 1981.

Freeze, Gregory L. "Handmaiden of the State? The Church in Imperial Russia Reconsidered," *Journal of Ecclesiastical History,* no. 1 (1985), pp. 82–102.

———. "A National Liberation Movement and the Shift in Russian Liberalism, 1901–1903," *Slavic Review,* no. 1 (1969), pp. 81–91.

———. "The *Soslovie* (Estate) Paradigm and Russian Social History," *American Historical Review,* no. 1 (1986), pp. 11–36.

Fuller, William C., Jr. *Civil-Military Conflict in Imperial Russia, 1881–1914.* Princeton, N.J., 1985.

———. *Strategy and Power in Russia, 1600–1914.* New York, 1992.

Galai, Shmuel. *The Liberation Movement in Russia, 1900–1905.* Cambridge, Eng., 1973.

Gan, L. "Ubiistvo Stolypina," *Istoricheskii vestnik,* vol. 135 (1914), pp. 960–97; vol. 136 (1914), pp. 192–215.

Ganelin, R. Sh. "Tvorcheskii put A. Ia. Avrekha," *Istoriia SSSR,* no. 4 (1990), pp. 102–12.

Gassenschmidt, Christoph. *Jewish Liberal Politics in Tsarist Russia, 1900–14.* New York, 1995.

Gaudin, Corinnne. "'No Place to Lay My Head': Marginalization and the Right to Land during the Stolypin Reforms," *Slavic Review,* no. 4 (1998), pp. 747–73.

Geifman, Anna. *Thou Shalt Kill: Revolutionary Terrorism in Russia, 1894–1917.* Princeton, N.J., 1993.

Gerasimenko, G. A. *Borba krestian protiv stolypinskoi agrarnoi politiki.* Saratov, 1985.

———. "Obostrenie borby v derevne v gody stolypinskoi reformy," *Voprosy istorii,* no. 4 (1983), pp. 20–34.

———. "Protivodeistvie krestian stolypinskoi agrarnoi politke," *Istoriia SSSR,* no. 3 (1984), pp. 128–40.

Gershtein, E. E. "Oktiabrskaia politicheskaia stachka 1905 goda v Saratove," *Uchenye zapiski Saratovskii Gosudarstvennyi Universitet.* Vol. 55 (1956), pp. 305–41.

Glagolev, A. I. "Formirovanie ekonomicheskoi kontseptsii P. A. Stolypina (1885–1905)," in Figurovskaia and Stepanskii, eds., *Gosudarstvennaia deiatelnost,* pp. 67–77.

Gokhlerner, V. M. "Iz istorii krestianskogo dvizheniia v Saratovskii gubernii v gody pervoi russkoi revoliutsii (1905–1907 gg.)," *Uchenyi zapiski Saratovskii Gosudarstvennyi Universitet,* vol. 55 (1956), pp. 219–45.

———. "Krestianskoe dvizhenie Saratovskoi gubernii v gody pervoi russkoi revoliutsii," *Istoricheskie zapiski,* vol. 52 (1955), pp. 186–234.

Goriachkin, F. M. *Pervyi russkii fashist: Petr Arkadevich Stolypin.* Harbin, 1928.

Gurliand, I. Ia. [under pseudonym of N. P. Vasilev], *Chto takoe Trudoviki?* St. Petersburg, 1907.

———. *Pravda o Kadetakh.* St. Petersburg, 1907.

Hagen, Manfred. "Der russische 'Bonapartismus' nach 1906," *Jahrbücher für Geschichte Osteuropas*, no. 24 (1976), pp. 369–93.

———. *Die Entfaltung politischer Öffentlichkeit in Russland, 1906–1914*. Wiesbaden, 1982.

———. "*Edinenie* und *obnovlenie*: Traditionale und modernische Züge in Stolypins Staatsnationalismus gegenüber Finland," *Journal of Baltic Studies*, no. 15 (1984), pp. 148–70.

Haimson, Leopold H., ed. *The Politics of Rural Russia, 1905–1917*. Bloomington, Ind., 1979.

———. "The Problem of Social Stability in Urban Russia, 1905–1917," *Slavic Review*, no. 4 (1964), pp. 619–42; no. 1 (1965), pp. 1–22.

Hamburg, G. M. *Politics of the Russian Nobility, 1881–1905*. New Brunswick, N.Y., 1984.

———. "Portrait of an Elite: Russian Marshals of the Nobility, 1861–1917," *Slavic Review*, no. 4 (winter 1981), pp. 585–602.

———. "The Russian Nobility on the Eve of the 1905 Revolution," *Russian Review*, no. 3 (1979), pp. 323–38.

Hans, Nicholas. *History of Russian Educational Policy (1701–1917)*. London, 1931.

Harcave, Sidney. *First Blood: The Russian Revolution of 1905*. New York, 1964.

Harper, Samuel N. "Exceptional Measures in Russia," *Russian Review*, no. 4 (1912), pp. 92–105.

———. *The New Electoral Law for the Russian Duma*. Chicago, 1908.

Harrison, W. "The British Press and the Russian Revolution of 1905–1907," *Oxford Slavonic Papers*, vol. 7 (1974), pp. 74–95.

Healy, Ann E. *The Russian Autocracy in Crisis, 1905–1907*. Hamden, Conn., 1976.

Heilbronner, Hans. "Aehrenthal in Defense of Russian Autocracy," *Jahrbücher für Geschichte Osteuropas*, vol. 17 (1969), pp. 380–96.

———. "Piotr Khristianovich von Schwanebach and the Dissolution of the First Two Dumas," *Canadian Slavonic Papers*, no. 1 (1969), pp. 31–55.

Hennessy, R. *The Agrarian Question in Russia 1905–1907: The Inception of the Stolypin Reform*. Giessen, 1977.

Hildermeier, Manfred. *Die Sozialrevolutionäre Partei Russslands: Agrarsozialismus und Modernisierung im Zarenreich (1900–1914)*. Cologne, 1978.

Hodgson, J. H. "Finland's Position in the Russian Empire, 1905–10," *Journal of Central European Affairs*, vol. 20 (1960), pp. 158–73.

Hosking, Geoffrey A. "P. A. Stolypin and the Octobrists," *Slavonic and East European Review*, vol. 47 (1969), pp. 137–60.

———. *Russia: People and Empire, 1552–1917*. Cambridge, Mass., 1997.

———. *The Russian Constitutional Experiment: Government and Duma, 1907–1914*. Cambridge, Eng., 1973.

Hosking, Geoffrey A., and Roberta Thompson Manning. "What Was the United Nobility?" in Haimson, ed., *The Politics of Rural Russia*, pp. 142–83.

Hutschinson, J. F. "The Octobrists and the Future of Imperial Russia as a

Great Power," *Slavonic and East European Review*, vol. 50 (1972), pp. 220–37.

Ivanov, A. E. "Demokraticheskoe studenchestvo v revoliutsii 1905–1907 gg.," *Istoricheskie zapiski*, no. 107 (1982), pp. 171–225.

Ivanov, Vs. "Stolypin: Ist. ocherk o P. A. Stolypine," *Molodaia Gvardiia*, no. 3 (1990), pp. 43–50.

Izgoev, A. A. "P. A. Stolypin," *Russkaia mysl*, no. 12 (1907), pp. 129–32.

———. *P. A. Stolypin: Ocherk zhizni i deiatelnosti*. Moscow, 1912.

———. "Po povodu ubiistva P. A. Stolypina," *Russkaia mysl*, no. 10 (1911), pp. 1–7.

Johnson, William H. E. *Russia's Educational Heritage*. New Brunswick, 1950.

Kappeler, Andreas. *Russland als Vielvölkerreich: Entstehung. Geschichte. Zerfall*. Munich, 1993.

Karpov, N. I. *Agrarnaia politika Stolypina*. Leningrad, 1925.

Kassow, Samuel D. *Students, Professors, and the State in Tsarist Russia*. Berkeley, Calif., 1989.

Katz, Martin. *Mikhail N. Katkov: A Political Biography, 1818–1887*. The Hague, 1966.

Keep, J. L. H. *Last of the Empires: A History of the Soviet Union, 1945–1991*. Oxford, 1995.

———. *The Rise of Social Democracy in Russia*. Oxford, 1963.

———. "Russian Social Democracy in the First State Duma," *Slavonic and East European Review*, vol. 34 (1955), pp. 180–99.

Khotulev, V. V. *Petr Stolypin: Tragediia Rossii*. Moscow, 1998.

Kiriukhina, E. I. "Vserossiiskii krestianskii soiuz v 1905 g.," *Istoricheskie zapiski*, no. 50 (1955), pp. 95–111.

Klier, John Doyle. *Imperial Russia's Jewish Question, 1855–1881*. Cambridge, Eng., 1995.

Koni, A. F. *Sobranie sochinenii*. Vol. 2. Moscow, 1966.

Korkunov, N. M. *Russkoe gosudarstvennoe pravo*. 2 vols. St. Petersburg, 1983.

Koroleva, N. G. *Pervaia rossiiskaia revoliutsiia i tsarizm: Sovet ministrov Rossii v 1905–1907 gg*. Moscow, 1982.

———. "Sovet ministrov Rossii v 1907–1914 gg.," *Istoricheskie zapiski*, vol. 110 (1984), pp. 114–53.

Korros, Alexandra Shecket. "Activist Politics in a Conservative Institution: The Formation of Factions in the Russian State Council, 1906–1907," *Russian Review*, no. 1 (1993), pp. 1–19.

———. "The Landed Nobility, the State Council, and P. A. Stolypin (1907–1911)," in Haimson, ed., *The Politics of Rural Russia*, pp. 123–41.

———. [Shecket, Alexandra Deborah]. "The Russian Imperial State Council and the Policies of P. A. Stolypin, 1906–1911: Bureaucratic and Soslovie Interests versus Reform." Ph.D. diss., Columbia University, 1975.

Kovalchenko, I. D. "Stolypinskaia reforma (mify i realnost)," *Istoriia SSSR*, no. 2 (1991), pp. 52–72.

Kovalevskii, M. M. "Zemstvo v shesti guberniiakh zapadnogo kraia," *Vestnik Evropy*, vol. 46 (1911), pp. 243–59.

Krasnov, V. "Voskresenie Stolypina," *Grani: Zhurnal literatury, iskusstva, nauki i obshchestvenno-politicheskoi mysli*, no. 41 (1986), pp. 154–85.

Krukones, James H. *To the People: The Russian Government and the Newspaper Sel'skii vestnick ("Village Herald") 1881–1917*. New York and London, 1987.

Kucherov, S. *Courts, Lawyers and Trials under the Last Three Tsars*. New York, 1953.

Kujala, Antti. "The Policy of the Russian Government toward Finland: A Case Study of the Nationalities Question in the Last Years of the Russian Empire," in Conroy, ed., *Emerging Democracy*, pp. 143–97.

———. "Rossiia i Finlandiia v 1907–1914 godakh: Plany vvedeniia voennogo polozheniia," *Otechestvennaia istoriia*, no. 2 (1998), pp. 65–74.

Kusber, Jan. *Krieg und Revolution in Russland: Das Militär im Verhältnis zu Wirtschaft, Autokratie und Gesellschaft*. Stuttgart, 1997.

Lambrozo, Shlomo. "Jewish Self-Defense during the Russian Pogroms of 1903–1906," *Jewish Journal of Sociology*, no. 2 (1981), pp. 123–34.

Laqueur, Walter. *Black Hundred: The Rise of the Extreme Right in Russia*. New York, 1993.

Laverychev, V. Ia. *Tsarizm i rabochii vopros v Rossii, 1861–1917 gg*. Moscow, 1972.

Legras, Jules. "Souvenirs sur P. A. Stolypine," *Vie des Peuples*, vol. 7 (1922), pp. 1003–20.

Lenin, V. I. *Collected Works*. Tr. Abraham Fineberg and Julius Katzer. 46 vols. Moscow, 1977.

———. *Polnoe sobranie sochinenii*. 5th ed. 55 vols. Moscow, 1958–65.

———. *Sochineniia*. 4th ed. 45 vols. Leningrad, 1947.

Leontowitsch, Victor. *Geschichte des Liberalismus in Russland*. Frankfurt, 1957.

Levin, Alfred. "The Fifth Social Democratic Congress and the Duma," *Journal of Modern History*, no. 4 (1939), pp. 484–504.

———. "June 3, 1907: Action and Reaction," in A. Ferguson and A. Levin, eds., *Essays in Russian History: A Collection Dedicated to George Vernadsky*. Hamden, Conn., 1964, pp. 233–73.

———. "More on Social Stability, 1905–1917," *Slavic Review*, no. 1 (1966), pp. 149–54.

———. "P. A. Stolypin: A Political Appraisal," *Journal of Modern History*, no. 3 (1965), pp. 445–63.

———. *The Reactionary Tradition in the Election Campaign to the Third Duma*. Stillwater, Okla., 1962.

———. "Russian Bureaucratic Opinion in the Wake of the 1905 Revolution," *Jahrbücher für Geschichte Osteuropas*, no. 4 (1963), pp. 1–12.

———. "The Russian Voter in the Elections for the Third Duma," *Slavic Review*, no. 4 (1962), pp. 660–77.

———. *The Second Duma: A Study of the Social Democratic Party and the Russian Constitutional Experiment*. New Haven, Conn., 1940.

———. "The Shornikova Affair," *Slavonic and East European Review*, vol. 21 (1943), pp. 1–18.

Lieven, D. C. B. "Bureaucratic Authoritarianism in Late Imperial Russia: The Personality, Career and Opinions of P. N. Durnovo," *Historical Journal*, vol. 26 (1983), pp. 391–402.

———. *Nicholas II: Twilight of the Empire*. New York, 1994.

———. *Russia and the Origins of the First World War*. New York, 1983.

Likhomanov, A. V. "I. Ia. Gurliand i evreiskii vopros v Rossii," *Vestnik Moskovskogo Evreiskogo Universiteta*, no. 4 (1993), pp. 142–53.

Linden, A., ed. *Die Judenpogrome in Russland*. Cologne and Leipzig, 1910.

Löwe, Heinz-Dietrich. *Antisemitismus und reaktionäre Utopie: Russischer Konservatismus im Kampf gegen den Wandel von Staat und Gesellschaft*. Hamburg, 1978.

Lundin, C. L. "Finland," in E. C. Thaden, ed., *Russification in the Baltic Provinces and Finland, 1855–1914*. Princeton, 1981, pp. 357–457.

Luntinen, Pertii. *F. A. Seyn: A Political Biography of a Tsarist Imperialist as Administrator of Finland*. Helsinki, 1985.

———. *The Imperial Russian Army and Navy in Finland, 1808–1918*. Helsinki, 1997.

Lure, Ia. S. *Posle Lva Tolstogo: Istoricheskie vozzreniia Tolstogo i problemy XX veka*. St. Petersburg, 1993.

Lystsov, G. I., ed. *Petr Stolypin: Sbornik*. Moscow, 1997.

Macey, David A. J. *Government and Peasant in Russia, 1881–1906: The Prehistory of the Stolypin Reforms*. DeKalb, Ill., 1987.

———. "The Peasant Commune and the Stolypin Reforms: Peasant Attitudes, 1906–1914," in R. Bartlett, ed., *Land Commune and Peasant Community in Russia*. London, 1990, pp. 219–30.

———. "The Peasantry, the Agrarian Problem, and the Revolution of 1905–1907," in A. W. Cordier, ed., *Columbia Essays in International Affairs*. New York, 1972, pp. 1–35.

———. "Zemelnaia reforma i politicheskie peremeny: Fenomen Stolypina," *Voprosy istorii*, no. 4 (1933), pp. 3–18.

Maevskii, Vl. *Borets za blago Rossii (k stoletiiu so dnia rozhdeniia)*. Madrid, 1962.

Maiskii, B. Iu. "Stolypinshchina i konets Stolypina," *Voprosy istorii*, no. 1 (1966), pp. 134–44; no. 2 (1966), pp. 123–40.

Malinin, G. A. "Saratovskii Sovet Rabochikh Deputatov v 1905 godu," *Uchenye zapiski Saratovskii Gosudarstvennyi Universitet*, vol. 55 (1956), pp. 155–71.

Manning, Roberta T. *The Crisis of the Old Order in Russia: Gentry and Government*. Princeton, N.Y., 1982.

———. "The Zemstvo and Politics, 1864–1914," in Emmons and Vucinich, eds., *The Zemstvo in Russia*, pp. 133–75.

Marshall, Peter. *Demanding the Impossible: A History of Anarchism*. London, 1992.

Martov, L., P. Maslov, and A. Potresov, eds. *Obshchestvennoe dvizhenie v Rossii v nachale XX-go veka*. 4 vols. St. Petersburg, 1909–11.

Maslov, P. *Agrarnyi vopros v Rossii*. 2 vols. St. Petersburg, 1909–14.

McDonald, David MacLaren. *United Government and Foreign Policy in Russia, 1900–1914.* Cambridge, Mass., 1992.

McKean, Robert B. *St. Petersburg between the Revolutions: Workers and Revolutionaries, June 1907–February 1917.* New Haven, Conn., 1990.

Mehlinger, Howard D., and John M. Thompson. *Count Witte and the Tsarist Government in the 1905 Revolution.* Bloomington, Ind., 1972.

Melancon, Michael. "Athens or Babylon? The Birth of the Socialist Revolutionary and Social Democratic Parties and Saratov, 1890–1905," in Wade and Seregny, *Politics and Society,* pp. 73–112.

Menashe, Louis. "Alexander Guchkov and the Origins of the Octobrist Party: The Russian Bourgeoisie in Politics, 1905." Ph.D. diss., New York University, 1966.

Miller, Margaret S. *The Economic Development of Russia, 1905–1914, with Special Reference to Trade, Industry and Finance.* 2d ed. London, 1967 (original ed. 1926).

Mironov, Boris. "The Russian Peasant Commune after the Reforms of the 1860s," *Slavic Review,* no. 3 (1985), pp. 438–67.

Mixter, Timothy R. "Peasant Collective Action in Saratov Province, 1902–1906," in Wade and Seregny, eds., *Politics and Society in Provincial Russia,* pp. 191–232.

Morison, John D. "Political Characteristics of the Student Movement in the Russian Revolution of 1905," in Coquin and Gervais-Francelle, eds., *1905,* pp. 63–75.

Moritsch, A. "Neuere Literatur zur Stolypinschen Agrarreform," *Jahrbücher für Geschichte Osteuropas,* vol. 24 (1976), pp. 230–49.

Morrill, Dan L. "Nicholas II and the Call for the First Hague Conference," *Journal of Modern History,* no. 2 (June 1974), pp. 296–313.

Mosse, W. E. *An Economic History of Russia, 1856–1914.* London, 1992.

———. "Stolypin's Villages," *Slavonic and East European Review,* vol. 43 (1965), pp. 257–74.

Muratov, Kh. I. *Revoliutsionnoe dvizhenie v russkoi armii v 1905–1907 gg.* Moscow, 1955.

Mushin, A. *Dmitrii Bogrov i ubiistvo Stolypina.* Paris, 1914.

Nikolajewsky, Boris. *Azeff the Spy.* Tr. George Reavey. New York, 1934.

Oberländer, Erwin, et al., eds. *Russia Enters the Twentieth Century, 1894–1917.* New York, 1917.

Ostrovskii, I. V. *P. A. Stolypin i ego vremia.* Novosibirsk, 1992.

Owen, Launcelot A. *The Russian Peasant Movement, 1906–1917.* London, 1937.

Pallot, Judith. "Agrarian Modernization on Peasant Farms in the Era of Capitalism," in J. H. Bater and R. A. French, eds., *Studies in Russian Historical Geography,* vol. 2. London, 1983, pp. 423–49.

———. "The Development of Peasant Land Holding from Emancipation to the Revolution," in H. H. Bater and R. A. French, eds., *Studies in Russian Historical Geography,* vol. 1, London, 1983, pp. 84–108.

———. "*Khutora* and *Otruba* in Stolypin's Program of Farm Individualization," *Slavic Review,* no. 2 (1984), pp. 242–56.

Pares, Bernard. *The Fall of the Russian Monarchy.* New York, 1939.

———. "The New Land Settlement in Russia," *Russian Review*, no. 1 (1912), pp. 56–74.

———. "The Peterhof Conference," *Russian Review*, no. 4 (1913), pp. 87–120.

———. *Russia and Reform.* London, 1907.

———. "The Second Duma," *Slavonic Review*, no. 2 (1923–24), pp. 36–55.

Parry, Albert. *Full Steam Ahead! The Story of Peter Demens, Founder of St. Petersburg, Florida.* St. Petersburg, Fla., 1987.

P. A. Stolypin i Istoricheskii Opyt Reform v Rossii: Informatsiia o rabote nauchno-prakticheskoi konferentsii, posviashchennoi 135-letiiu so dnia rozhdeniia P. A. Stolypina. Resheniia konferentsii. Omsk, 1997.

Pavlovsky, G. P. *Agricultural Russia on the Eve of the Revolution.* London, 1930.

Perrie, Maureen. *The Agrarian Policy of the Russian Socialist-Revolutionary Party from Its Origins through the Revolution of 1905–1907.* New York, 1976.

———. "The Russian Peasant Movement of 1905–1907: Its Social Composition and Revolutionary Significance," *Past and Present*, no. 57 (1972), pp. 123–55.

———. "The Social Composition and Structure of the Socialist-Revolutionary Party before 1917," *Soviet Studies*, no. 2 (1972), pp. 223–50.

Pflanze, Otto. *Bismarck and the Development of Germany.* Vol. 3. Princeton, N.J., 1990.

Piatnitskskii, N. V. "P. A. Stolypin i piatidesiateletnie so dnia tragicheskoi gibeli," *Vozrozhdenie*, no. 117 (1961), pp. 52–62.

Pinchuk, Ben-Cion. *The Octobrists in the Third Duma, 1907–1912.* Seattle, Wash., 1974.

Pipes, Richard. *Russia under the Old Regime.* New York, 1974.

———. *The Russian Revolution.* New York, 1990.

———. *Struve: Liberal on the Left, 1870–1905.* Cambridge, Mass., 1970.

———. *Struve: Liberal on the Right, 1905–1944.* Cambridge, Mass., 1980.

Preyer, W. D. *Die russische Agrarreform.* Jena, 1914.

Queen, G. S. "The McCormick Harvesting Machine Company in Russia," *Russian Review*, no. 2 (1964), pp. 164–81.

Raeff, Marc. *Michael Speransky: Statesman of Imperial Russia.* The Hague, 1957.

———. "Patterns of Russian Imperial Policy toward the Nationalities," reprinted in Raeff, *Political Ideas and Institutions in Imperial Russia.* Boulder, Colo., 1994, pp. 126–40.

———. "Some Reflections on Russian Liberalism," *Russian Review*, no. 3 (1959), pp. 218–36.

———, ed. *Russian Intellectual History: An Anthology.* New York, 1966.

Raleigh, Donald J. *Revolution on the Volga: 1917 in Saratov.* Ithaca, N.Y., 1986.

Rawson, Don C. *Russian Rightists and the Revolution of 1905.* Cambridge, Eng., 1995.

Rhyne, George N. "The Constitutional Democratic Party from Its Origins through the First State Duma." Ph.D. diss., Univ. of North Carolina, 1968.

Rieber, Alfred J. *Merchants and Entrepreneurs in Imperial Russia*. Chapel Hill, N.C., 1982.

Riha, Thomas. *A Russian European: Paul Miliukov in Russian Politics*. Notre Dame, Ind., 1969.

Rimlinger, Gaston V. "Autocracy and the Factory Order in Early Russian Industrialization," *Journal of Economic History*, no. 1 (1960), pp. 67–92.

Robbins, Richard G., Jr. *The Tsar's Viceroys: Russian Provincial Governors in the Last Years of the Empire*. Ithaca, N.Y., 1988.

Robinson, Geroid Tanquary. *Rural Russia under the Old Regime: A History of the Landlord-Peasant World and a Prologue to the Peasant Revolution of 1917*. 2d printing. New York, 1949.

Rogger, Hans. *Jewish Policies and Right-Wing Politics in Imperial Russia*. Berkeley, Calif., 1986.

———. *Russia in the Age of Modernisation and Revolution, 1881–1917*. London, 1983.

Roosa. R. A. "Workers' Insurance Legislation and the Role of the Industrialists in the Period of the Third Duma," *Russian Review*, no. 4 (1975), pp. 410–56.

Rosenberg, William G. *Liberals in the Russian Revolution: The Constitutional Democratic Party, 1917–1921*. Princeton, N.J., 1974.

Ruud, Charles A. "A. A. Lopukhin, Police Insubordination and the Rule of Law," *Russian History*, nos. 1–4 (1993), pp. 147–62.

———. *Fighting Words: Imperial Censorship and the Russian Press, 1804–1906*. Toronto, 1982.

Rybas, S., and L. Tarakanova. *Zhizn i smert Petra Stolypina*. Moscow, 1991.

Sanders, Jonathan. "Lessons from the Periphery: Saratov, January 1905," *Slavic Review*, no. 2 (1987), pp. 229–44.

Santoni, Wayne D. "P. N. Durnovo as Minister of Internal Affairs in the Witte Cabinet: A Study in Suppression." Ph.D. diss., University of Kansas, 1968.

Savickij, Nicolas. "P. A. Stolypine," *Monde Slave*, no. 11 (1933), pp. 227–63; no. 12, pp. 360–83.

Schleifman, N. *Undercover Agents in the Russian Revolutionary Movement*. Oxford, 1988.

Schwarz, Solomon M. *The Russian Revolution of 1905: The Workers' Movement and the Formation of Bolshevism and Menshevism*. Tr. Gertrude Vakar. Chicago, 1967.

Sef, S. E. *Burzhuaziia v 1905 godu, po neizdannym arkhivnym materialam*. Moscow and Leningrad, 1926.

Senin, A. S. *Aleksandr Ivanovich Guchkov*. Moscow, 1996.

Serebrennikov, Aleksandr, and Gennadi Sidorovnin. *Stolypin: zhizn i smert*. Saratov, 1991.

Seregny, Scott J. "A Different Type of Peasant Movement: The Peasant Unions in the Russian Revolution of 1905," *Slavic Review*, no. 1 (1988), pp. 51–67.

———. "Politics and the Rural Intelligentsia in Russia: A Biographical Sketch of Stepan Anikin," *Russian History*, no. 7 (1980), pp. 169–200.

———. *Russian Teachers and Peasant Revolution: The Politics of Education*. Bloomington, Ind., 1985.

Seton-Watson, Hugh. *The Decline of Imperial Russia, 1855–1914*. London, 1952.

———. *The Russian Empire, 1801–1917*. Oxford, 1967.

Shanin, Teodor. *The Roots of Otherness: Russia's Turn of the Century*. 2 vols. New Haven, Conn., 1986.

Shestakov, A. *Krestianskaia revoliutsiia 1905–07 gg. v Rossii*. Moscow, 1926.

Shkarovskii, M. V. "Russkie Katoliki v Sankt-Peterburge (Leningrade)," *Minuvshee: Istoricheskii Almanakh*, no. 24 (1998), pp. 439–83.

Shmeruk, Chone. "*Mayufes*: A Window on Polish-Jewish Relations," *Polin: Studies in Polish Jewry*, vol. 10 (1997), pp. 273–86.

Shuster, U. A. *Peterburgskie rabochie v 1905–1907 gg*. Leningrad, 1976.

Sidelnikov, S. M. *Agrarnaia reforma Stolypina*. Moscow, 1973.

———. *Obrazovanie i deiatelnost pervoi gosudarstvennoi dumy*. Moscow, 1962.

Simonova, M. S. "Krestianskoe dvizhenie 1905–1907 gg. v sovetskoi istoriografii," *Istoricheskie zapiski*, no. 95 (1971), pp. 204–53.

Smith, C. J. "The Third Duma: An Analytical Profile," *Russian Review*, no. 2 (1958), pp. 201–10.

Smith, Nathan. "The Constitutional-Democratic Movement in Russia, 1902–1906." Ph.D. diss., University of Illinois, 1958.

Snow, George E. "The Kokovtsov Commission: An Abortive Attempt at Labor Reform in Russia in 1905," *Slavic Review*, no. 4 (1972), pp. 780–96.

Solovev, Iu. B. *Samoderzhavie i dvorianstvo v 1905–1907 gg*. Leningrad, 1981.

———. "Politicheskaia smert P. A. Stolypina," in N. K. Figurovskaia and A. D. Stepanskii, eds., *Gosudarstvennaia deiatelnost*, pp. 137–53.

Solovev, M. E. "Tsarskie provokatory i delo Sotsial-demokraticheskoi fraktsii II gosudarstvennoi dumy," *Voprosy istorii*, no. 8 (1966), pp. 124–29.

Solzhenitsyn, Aleksandr. *August 1914: The Red Wheel: Knot 1*. Tr. H. T. Willetts. New York, 1989.

Sominich, G. E. "Lichnyi fond Petra Arkadevicha Stolypina v TsGIA SSSR," *Sovetskie arkhivy*, no. 1 (1991), pp. 84–92.

Spector, Ivar. *The First Russian Revolution: Its Impact on Asia*. Englewood Cliffs, N.J., 1962.

Spieler, Sile. *Autonomie oder Reglementierung: Die russische Universität am Vorabend des ersten Weltkrieges*. Cologne and Vienna, 1981.

Spiridovich, A. I. *Histoire du terrorisme russe, 1886–1917*. Paris, 1930.

Stanislawski, Michael. *Tsar Nicholas I and the Jews: The Transformation of Jewish Society in Russia, 1825–1855*. Philadelphia, 1983.

Starr, S. F. "Tsarist Government: The Imperial Dimension," in J. R. Azrael, ed., *Soviet Nationality Policies and Practices*. New York, 1978.

Startsev, V. I. *Russkaia burzhuaziia i samoderzhavie v 1905–1907 gg.* Leningrad, 1977.

Steinberg, Arthur K. "The Kholm Question in the Russian Duma Period, 1906–1912: Opinion and Action." Ph.D. diss., Kent State University, 1972.

Stepanov, S. A. *Chernaia Sotnia v Rossii (1905–1914 gg.).* Moscow, 1992.

———. *Zagadki ubiistva Stolypina.* Moscow, 1995.

Stites, Richard. *The Women's Liberation Movement in Russia: Feminism, Nihilism and Bolshevism, 1860–1930.* Princeton, N.J., 1978.

Stockdale, Melissa Kirschke. *Paul Miliukov and the Quest for a Liberal Russia, 1880–1918.* Ithaca, N.Y., 1996.

Stoliarov, I. *Zapiski russkogo krestianina.* Paris, 1986.

Stolypine, Arcady. *De l'Empire a l'exil: Memoires.* Paris, 1996.

———. *P. A. Stolypin.* Paris, 1927. Reprint, Moscow, 1991.

Strakhovsky, Leonid. "Constitutional Aspects of the Imperial Government's Policies toward the National Minorities," *Journal of Modern History*, no. 4 (1941), pp. 462–92.

———. "The Statesmanship of Peter Stolypin: A Reappraisal," *Slavonic and East European Review*, vol. 37 (1959), pp. 348–70.

———. "Stolypin and the Second Duma," *Canadian Slavonic papers*, no. 6 (1964), pp. 13–18.

Struve, P. B. "Otryvki o gosudarstve i natsii," *Russkaia mysl*, no. 5 (1908), pp. 187–93.

———. "Prestuplenie i zhertva," *Russkaia mysl*, no. 10 (1911), pp. 135–44.

———. "Velikaia Rossiia: Iz razmyshlenii o probleme russkogo mogushchestva," *Russkaia mysl*, no. 1 (1908), pp. 143–57.

Suny, Ronald Grigor. *The Baku Commune, 1917–1918: Class and Nationality in the Russian Revolution.* Princeton, N.J., 1972.

Szeftel, Marc. *The Russian Constitution of April 23, 1906: Political Institutions of the Duma Monarchy.* Brussels, 1976.

Taylor, A. J. P. *The Struggle for Mastery in Europe, 1848–1918.* Oxford, 1954.

Thaden, Edward C., ed. *Russification in the Baltic Provinces and Finland, 1855–1914.* Princeton, N.J., 1981.

Timberlake, Charles E., ed. *Essays on Russian Liberalism.* Columbia, Mo., 1972.

Tokmakoff, George. "P. A. Stolypin and the Second Duma," *Slavonic and East European Review*, vol. 50 (1972), pp. 49–62.

———. *P. A. Stolypin and the Third Duma: An Appraisal of Three Major Issues.* Washington, D.C., 1981.

———. "Stolypin's Agrarian Reform: An Appraisal," *Russian Review*, no. 4 (1971), pp. 124–38.

———. "Stolypin's Assassin," *Slavic Review*, no. 2 (1965), pp. 314–21.

Treadgold, Donald W. *The Great Siberian Migration.* Princeton, N.J., 1957.

———. *Lenin and His Rivals: The Struggle for Russia's Future, 1898–1906.* New York, 1955.

———. "Was Stolypin in Favor of the Kulaks?" *American Slavic and East European Review*, no. 1 (1955), pp. 1–15.

Trotsky, Leon. *1905*. Tr. Anya Bostok. New York, 1971.

Troyat, Henri. *Tolstoy*. Tr. Nancy Amphoux. New York, 1967.

Tuck, Robert L. "Paul Miliukov and Negotiations for a Duma Ministry," *American Slavic and East European Review*, no. 1 (1951), pp. 117–29.

Tyrkova-Williams, A. V. "The Cadet Party," *Russian Review*, no. 3 (1963), pp. 173–86.

———. "Russian Liberalism," *Russian Review*, no. 1 (1951), pp. 3–14.

Verner, Andrew M. *The Crisis of Russian Autocracy: Nicholas II and the 1905 Revolution*. Princeton, N.J., 1990.

[Verpakhovskaia, E. V.]. E. V. ed. *Gosudarstvennaia deiatelnost predsedatelia soveta ministrov stats-sekretaria Petra Arkadevicha Stolypina*. 3 vols. St. Petersburg, 1911.

Veselovskii, B. B. *Istoriia zemstva za sorok let*. 4 vols. St. Petersburg, 1909.

———. *Krestianskii vopros i krestianskoe dvizhenie v Rossee (1902–1906 gg.)*. St. Petersburg, 1907.

Vinogradoff, Igor. "A Patriot and His Enemies," *Times Literary Supplement*, Sept. 9, 1983, p. 967.

Volobuev, O. V. "Revoliutsiia 1905–1907 gg. v publitsistike russkikh burzhuaznykh istorikov," *Istoricheskie zapiski*, no. 102 (1978), pp. 278–325.

———. "Sovremennaia istoriografiia revoliutsii 1905–1907 godov," in *Revoliutsiia 1905–1907 godov v Rossii i ee vsemirno-istoricheskoe znachenie* (Moscow, 1976), pp. 82–96.

Von Laue, Theodore H. "Count Witte and the 1905 Revolution," *American Slavic and East European Review*, no. 1 (1958), pp. 25–46.

Vronskaia, Zhanna. "Syn ob otse," *Literaturnaia gazeta*, July 12, 1989, p. 15.

Wade, Rex A., and Scott J. Seregny, eds. *Politics and Society in Provincial Russia: Saratov, 1590–1917*. Columbus, Ohio, 1989.

Waldron, Peter. *Between Two Revolutions: Stolypin and the Politics of Renewal in Russia*. London, 1998.

———. "Religious Reform after 1905: Old Believers and the Orthodox Church," *Oxford Slavonic Papers*, no. 20 (1987), pp. 110–39.

———. "Stolypin and Finland," *Slavonic and East European Review*, no. 1 (1985), pp. 41–55.

Walkin, Jacob. *The Rise of Democracy in Pre-Revolutionary Russia: Political and Social Institutions under the Last Czars*. London, 1963.

Walsh, Warren B. "Political Parties of the Russian Duma," *Journal of Modern History*, no. 2 (1950), pp. 144–50.

Wank, Solomon. "A Case of Aristocratic Anti-Semitism in Austria: Count Aehrenthal and the Jews, 1878–1907," in Leo Baeck Institute, *Year Book* 30 (London, 1985), pp. 435–56.

Warth, Robert D. *Nicholas II: The Life and Reign of Russia's Last Monarch*. Westport, Conn., 1997.

Wcislo, Francis William. *Reforming Rural Russia: State, Local Society, and National Politics, 1855–1914*. Princeton, N.J., 1990.

———. "Soslovie or Class? Bureaucratic Reformers and Provincial Gentry in Conflict, 1906–1907," *Russian Review*, no. 1 (1988), pp. 1–24.

Weber, Max. *Gesammelte Politische Schriften*. Tübingen, 1958.

———. "Russlands Übergang zum Scheinkonstitutionalismus," *Archiv für Sozialwissenschaft und Sozialpolitik*, vol. 23 (1906), pp. 165–401.

———. "Zur Lage der bürgerlichen Demokratie in Russland," *Archiv für Sozialwissenschaft und Sozialpolitik*, vol. 22 (1906), pp. 234–353.

Weeks, Theodore R. *Nation and State in Late Imperial Russia. Nationalism and Russification in the Western Frontier, 1863–1914.* DeKalb, 1996.

Weissman, Neil B. *Reform in Tsarist Russia: The State Bureaucracy and Local Government, 1900–1914.* New Brunswick, N.J., 1981.

———. "Rural Crime in Tsarist Russia: The Question of Hooliganism, 1905–1914," *Slavic Review*, no. 2 (1978), pp. 28–40.

Willetts, Harry T. "The Agrarian Problem," in Erwin Oberländer et al., eds., *Russia Enters the Twentieth Century*, pp. 111–37.

Williams, Beryl J. "The Revolution of 1905 and Russian Foreign Policy," in C. Abramsky, ed., *Essays in Honor of E. H. Carr* (London, 1974), pp. 101–25.

Williams, Harold. *Russia of the Russians.* New York, 1918.

Wolfe, Bertram D. *Three Who Made a Revolution: A Biographical History.* New York, 1948.

Woodcock, George. *Anarchism: A History of the Libertarian Ideas and Movements.* Cleveland, 1962.

Wortman, Richard. "Property Rights, Populism, and Russian Political Culture," in Olga Crisp and Linda Edmondson, eds., *Civil Rights in Imperial Russia* (Oxford, 1989), pp. 13–32.

Yaney, G. L. "The Concept of the Stolypin Land Reform," *Slavic Review*, no. 2 (1964), pp. 273–93.

———. *The Urge to Mobilize: Agrarian Reform in Russia.* Urbana, Ill., 1982.

Zilliacus, Konni. *The Russian Revolutionary Movement.* New York, 1905.

Zimmerman, Judith E. "Between Revolution and Reaction: The Russian Constitutional-Democratic Party, October 1905 to June 1907." Ph.D. diss., Columbia University, 1967.

Zuckerman, Frederic S. *The Tsarist Secret Police in Russian Society, 1880–1917.* New York, 1996.

Zyrianov, P. N. "Petr Arkadevich Stolypin," in A. P. Korelin, ed., *Rossiia na rubezhe vekov: istoricheskie portrety.* Moscow, 1991, pp. 48–78.

———. "Petr Arkadevich Stolypin: Gos. deiatel, 1862–1911," *Voprosy istorii*, no. 6 (1990), pp. 54–75.

———. *Petr Stolypin: Politicheskii portret.* Moscow, 1992.

———. "Problema vybora tselei v Stolypinskom agrarnom zakonodatelstve," in Figurovskaia and Stepanskii, eds., *Gosudarstvennaia deiatelnost*, pp. 99–118.

———. "Tretia duma i vopros o reforme mestnogo suda i volostnogo upravleniia," *Istoriia SSSR*, no. 6 (1969), pp. 45–62.

———. "Zemelno-raspredelitelnaia deiatelnost krestianskoi obshchiny v 1907–1917," *Istoricheskie zapiski*, no. 116 (1988), pp. 103–60.

Index

In this index an "f" after a number indicates a separate reference on the next page, and an "ff" indicates separate references on the next two pages.